THE
ENCYCLOPEDIA OF
Prehistoric
Life

THE
ENCYCLOPEDIA OF
Prehistoric
Life

Edited by Rodney Steel and Anthony P. Harvey

With a Foreword by Dr. W. E. Swinton FRSE.

McGraw-Hill Book Company
New York   St. Louis   San Francisco
Toronto

First Published in 1979

© Mitchell Beazley Publishers Limited 1979
87–89 Shaftesbury Avenue, London W1V 7AD

Typesetting by Tradespools Limited

Printed in England by Hazell Watson & Viney Limited

Project Editor: Lloyd Lindo
Art Editor: John Ridgeway

Library of Congress Cataloging in Publication Data
Main entry under title:

The Encyclopedia of Prehistoric Life.

Includes index,
1. Paleontology. I. Steel, Rodney. II. Harvey, Anthony P.
QE711.2.E5   1979   560   79-14479
ISBN 0-07-060920-9

Contents

On the evolutionary charts, a lighter shading
on part of a line indicates that the evolutionary
pathway is uncertain.

Contributors

Dr D.E.G. Briggs, University of London

Dr H.C.H. Brunton, British Museum (Natural History)

Dr A.J. Charig, British Museum (Natural History)

Dr A.G. Edmund, Royal Ontario Museum

Dr J. Franks, University of Manchester

Dr L.B. Halstead, University of Reading

Mr F.M.P. Howie, British Museum (Natural History)

Dr C.P. Hughes, University of Cambridge

Dr R.P.S. Jefferies, British Museum (Natural History)

Dr P.D. Lane, University of Keele

Mr S.F. Morris, British Museum (Natural History)

Mr C.P. Nuttall, British Museum (Natural History)

Mr E.F. Owen, British Museum (Natural History)

Dr H.G. Owen, British Museum (Natural History)

Dr A.L. Panchen, University of Newcastle-upon-Tyne

Dr R.J.G. Savage, University of Bristol

Dr C.T. Scrutton, University of Newcastle-upon-Tyne

Dr A.T. Thomas, University of Cambridge

Dr D. Tills, British Museum (Natural History)

Mr C.A. Walker, British Museum (Natural History)

Mr S. Ware, British Museum (Natural History)

Dr J.E.P. Whittaker, British Museum (Natural History)

Mr P.J. Whybrow, British Museum (Natural History)

The initials of the contributor appear at the end of each entry in the Encyclopaedia.

Foreword

The Encyclopaedia of Prehistoric Life comes before a world in which the frontiers of knowledge are forever expanding. Within these covers is the story of Planet Earth, with all the changes that have taken place, most of which no man has ever seen occur. This is the wonder of our age, that we can visualize and understand the evolution of Earth and even life itself with a new certainty and by a technology, only recently available, that completely supplants the old individual virtuosity which lasted so long and raised so many questions. We must not forget the allegories of *Genesis* (and Archbishop Ussher's chronology based upon them), or the genius of the medical practitioner Copernicus who doubted their astronomy, or the genius of the medical student, Galileo, who was led by the swaying of a lamp in a cathedral to devise the pendulum for measuring time. Others, equally great in mind, argued over the formation of the Earth's crust, whether it was by sedimentation from floods or by a more uniform, cyclical, process of erosion and deposit, with uplift from subterranean heat and outpourings of lava. Edinburgh, the capital of Scotland, saw the foundation of geology by the medical doctor James Hutton, whose only recorded patient was the Earth. He took its pulse and tried to take its temperature. In the streets of Edinburgh another individual tried to weigh the Earth, using the volcanic mound of Arthur's Seat for his purpose.

Geological time came with the knowledge of radioactivity and isotopes; radioastronomy with the new use of electromagnetic waves; and men in satellites and on the Moon saw the world from afar for the first time.

The Earth is now believed to be 4,600 million years old and life must be nearly as old. The new tectonic theories show how continents have split and moved and how mountains have arisen. Climate, environment, and the ravages of time have moulded a changing world and its ever-changing life. They are part of a unity of Nature, a universal evolutionary process that was not, alas, created only for man.

That man can observe *and question* has only slowly been realized, but the reflections in this volume are those of renowned observers and thinkers of great ability. To read the past in their words is to see the shadows of the future; to realize, as Whitehead, the philosopher, realized, that "Life is an offensive, directed against the repetitious mechanism of the universe" – a universe whose purpose and immensity cannot be wholly grasped by us. The story here unfolded is that of our background; emerging from the rise and fall of animal dynasties. We see their faults and failures. Can we appreciate the evidence? Here is the purpose of the work: to create a reverence for life and to learn to survive in an indifferent immensity of space and time. With the new knowledge and the new technology we can do so, but only if a new unity of purpose is engendered in our society now. We must learn the lessons of prehistoric life quickly, for time, even geological time, is on the wing.

W.T. Swinton.

Toronto, Canada.

Academia Sinica

Academia Sinica

The Chinese Academy of Sciences, established in 1949, after the proclamation of the People's Republic. It merged the National Academy and the Academia Sinica (Nanking) and is responsible, through its branches, research institutes and universities, for much of the scientific research in China. In many respects, it is China's equivalent of the Royal Society (of London) and other Western national academies.

There are two major research institutes: for palaeontology (in Peking) and palaeontology and geology (in Nanking); both have museums which teach and have research collections, and provide exhibits for the public. There are plans to establish a central natural history museum in Peking, which would include palaeontology in its collections and exhibits.   A.P.H.

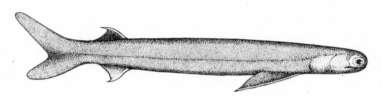

Acanthodians
Acanthodes, *the late-surviving acanthodian, persisted until the Permian and is probably a degenerate member of the group. Length: about 35cm (14in)*

Acanthodians

The earliest known jawed fishes, first appearing in the Silurian and surviving until the Permian. They have become known colloquially as "spiny sharks" because of their superficially shark-like appearance, but were not in fact related to the SHARKS. The body was covered by small stud-like scales, rather than the dermal denticles or placoid SCALES of sharks, and the main lobe of the tail was dorsal. This type of heterocercal TAIL FIN, although also characteristic of living sharks, is the primitive type common to most early fishes.

The most striking acanthodian features were the bony spines along the leading edges of the fins, including the two dorsal fins, the anal fin and the paired lateral fins. The anterior pair of fins were the pectorals and the posterior pair were the pelvics, but in most acanthodians there were also several pairs of accessory fins. In the streamlined jawless fishes, the ANASPIDS, there was a continuous lateral fin, and it is believed that this original fin-fold gradually broke up so that only the most anterior and posterior parts survived to form the pectoral and pelvic fins. The anatomy of the acanthodians represents a halfway stage with the fin-fold broken up into a series of triangular fins, but with the anterior and posterior pairs more fully developed.

Acanthodians have been the centre of a con-

troversy concerning the evolution of JAWS. At one time it was believed that acanthodians represented an intermediate position between the jawless fish and the true fishes, and the name Aphetohyoidea was introduced for fishes in which the anterior (mandibular) gill arch had been transformed into a jaw apparatus, but with the hyoidean arch still part of a functional gill apparatus. Subsequently it was shown that the hyoidean gill had been reduced to a spiracle, and the fact that the hyoid arch played a part in the suspension of the jaw from the braincase of the acanthodians proved that the first gill had also been reduced to a spiracle. The structure is similar to that of the most primitive of the RAY-FIN FISHES, the actinopterygians.

The structure of the scales, with thick outer layers of enameloid and basal bone layers, was also similar to those of early ray-fin fishes, and even the detailed structure of the tail showed similarities. From this evidence it has been concluded that the acanthodians represent the basic stock of all the bony fishes, including both the LOBE-FIN FISHES and the ray-fins.

Most acanthodians had jaws armed with teeth, although the last acanthodian, *Acanthodes* from the Permian, had a long eel-like body and had lost all its dentition. All the acanthodians, however, possessed large eyes, and because these were evidently the major sense organs they must have habitually swum in the surface waters.

The likelihood is that the acanthodians fed on planktonic or nektonic organisms living at or near the surface. Some strained OSTRACODS from the water, but others fed on the armoured jawless fishes, because one specimen of an acanthodian from the Welsh borderland has a CEPHALASPID inside its stomach.   L.B.H.

Agassiz, Jean Louis (1807–73)

One of the foremost naturalists of Victorian times whose studies ranged over zoology, palaeontology and geology. The son of a Swiss pastor, Agassiz was born at Motiers and received his education at Lausanne, Zurich, Heidelberg and Munich. In 1832 he became Professor at the Academy of Neuchâtel and it was from there that his major works on ECHINODERMS and fossil fishes were published.

Already widely travelled in Europe, he went to the USA in 1846 to lecture and in 1847 was appointed Professor of Zoology and Geology at Harvard University. He became influential in science administration in the USA, founding in 1859 the MUSEUM OF COMPARATIVE ZOOLOGY. Agassiz's research was used by Sir Charles LYELL and ironically Charles DARWIN, of whom he was a strong opponent. A great popularizer of science, he also published works on classification and bibliography. In 1915 Agassiz was elected to the American Hall of Fame.   A.P.H.

Acanthodians
Climatius *lived in the Upper Silurian-Lower Devonian. The remains of this so-called "spiny shark" occur in Europe, North America and Spitzbergen. Length: about 75mm (3in)*

Agnathans

Jawless VERTEBRATES, including the oldest known representatives of the phylum Chordata, the OSTRACODERMS.

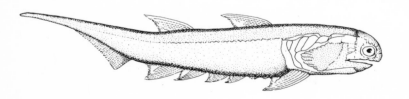

Amblypods

Algae

A diverse group of primitive plants with modern representatives varying from single-celled free-living forms (which colour stagnant water and produce the green discoloration on damp walls and paths) to DIATOMS and the familiar seaweeds seen on rocky shores.

The algae are by far the oldest group of plants recorded as fossils. The earliest known example is the single-celled *Archaeosphaeroides barbertonensis*, a blue-green alga from a Pre-Cambrian flint deposit about 3,200 million years old in South Africa. Filamentous blue-green algae about 1,900 million years old are found in flints in Canada, and by later Cambrian times the green algae had developed highly complex forms; they had central stems with whorls of branches that branched again to build up a solid looking plant body. These forms were frequently encrusted with calcium carbonate.

Not only are the algae the earliest fossil plants but they have also played an important part in rock formation by providing the nucleus around which minerals became precipitated from seas and lakes. The Pre-Cambrian Fig Tree Shales of South Africa contain a black siliceous material from which *Archaeosphaeroides* was described. Chemical analysis of this material shows it to have a high organic content compatible with formation by the action of blue-green algae. The slightly younger Bulawayo Limestone of Rhodesia incorporates structures called stromatolites, which are laminated calcareous bodies thought to be algal in origin.

By the Devonian the algae had evolved to produce the complex stoneworts (*Chara*), whose presence is confirmed by the occurrence of their distinctive spirally ridged oospores.

Fossil limestones and calcareous algae continue to be recorded throughout the whole of geological time. There is, however, a lack of evidence as to how and when the modern seaweeds arose because, with their fleshy structure and lack of protective cuticle (adaptations to an aquatic environment), they are rarely preserved as fossils. J.W.F.

Amber

Fossilized resin that has oozed from the trunks of ancient trees. There are four main types of amber: Baltic, Sicilian, Romanian and Burmese. Baltic amber, formed from the fossilized resin of the conifer *Pinus succinifera*, is the commonest – the specific name *succinifera* refers to the most important constituent of the amber, a hydrocarbon called succinite which is related to the petroleums. This type of amber occurs in a blue-grey clay found in localities on the south shore of the Baltic Sea and is always of a yellowish colour (varying from a whitish- to a brownish-yellow); it may be naturally clear, or opaque due to the presence of millions of small bubbles. The pines that produced it grew during the Cenozoic in areas of northern Europe now largely covered by the Baltic Sea.

Amber often contains the remains of contemporary plants and insects, which provide an invaluable record of Cenozoic fauna and flora.

The most famous amber-producing area was the peninsula of Samland near the town of Kaliningrad (formerly Königsberg). Here the amber was picked up on the beaches or mined. Its production, working and sale has always been strictly controlled, first by land-owners, then by the church and finally by the state. Once collected and mined in great quantities, Samland amber is now scarce and most of the mines are worked out.

Other amber-bearing deposits produce ambers of different chemical composition and colours that are derived from trees other than *Pinus succinifera*. They include red amber from Burma and brown amber from Sicily and Romania. Natural green and blue ambers occur, but they are rare.

Amber has always been a popular material for jewellery and other ornamental objects. Although it was never cheap, it is now becoming increasingly scarce and expensive. Amber is extensively imitated with plastics, to which it is chemically closely related, and the imitations can be difficult to detect. There is also an industry processing amber to produce more desirable effects. By heating amber with oil and then dyeing it, clear coloured amber can be produced; waste amber is heated with amber dust and moulded to make the ambroid extensively used in the manufacture of smokers' requisites. J.W.F.

Amblypods

An order (Amblypoda) of early Cenozoic ungulates (hoofed animals) that were the largest land mammals of their time. They comprise four suborders: the Pantodonta, the Dinocerata, the Xenungulata, and the Pyrotheria.

Pantodonts were abundant in the Palaeocene, *Pantolambda* being a short-limbed Middle and Upper Palaeocene genus that attained the size of a sheep and developed prominent canine teeth. *Titanoides* was a large Late Palaeocene form, with clawed feet and massive canines, that probably lived on roots, and the contemporaneous *Barylambda* was a powerfully built, long-tailed animal about 3 metres (10ft) long.

The bulky *Coryphodon*, with a heavy skull, large canine teeth, short legs and a diminutive tail, became common in the Early Eocene.

Amblypods
The massive Uintatherium *flourished during the North American Middle Eocene. Its name means "Uinta beast" and refers to the Uinta Mountains of Utah, where its remains have been discovered.*
Length: about 3m (10ft)

Ameghino

Procoryphodon was a small, poorly known genus from the Lower Eocene of Asia, a region in which the group persisted through the Late Eocene (*Eudinoceras*) into the Middle Oligocene (*Hypercoryphodon*).

During the Eocene, the Dinocerata were common large ungulates in North America and also occurred in eastern Asia. One of the last surviving members of the group was *Eobasileus*, from the Upper Eocene of the USA. This genus stood about 2.5 metres (8ft) at the shoulder and its long, narrow skull embodied three pairs of horn-like protuberances: a broad anterior pair overhanging the nasal opening, a long cylindrical pair formed from the maxillary bones that also accommodated the roots of the massive upper canine tusks present in male animals, and a club-shaped posterior pair towards the hinder end of the skull roof. A transverse occipital crest across the back of the head combined with ridges extending forward from the two posterior protuberances to form a deep basin (open at the front) on the top of the cranium. The upper incisor teeth had been lost and were presumably replaced by a horny biting pad, but the lower canines were reduced to small incisiform teeth. In males, the lower jaw bore flanges to protect the long upper canines when the mouth was closed, but females had neither tusks nor flanges.

Uintatherium, the Middle Eocene predecessor of *Eobasileus*, was a slightly smaller animal with a shorter, wider skull. The two protuberances on the end of the nose were relatively small, and the upper tusks had not become so well developed as in the later genus. The body was long but exceedingly bulky, and the short limbs were supported by stumpy five-toed feet.

A more primitive stage is represented by the tapir-sized Lower Eocene *Bathyopsis*, which retained prominent lower canines. The skull was broad with scarcely noticeable protuberances and an only slightly concave cranial roof. *Probathyopsis* is an even smaller Late Palaeocene member of the series.

Mongolotherium (Lower Eocene) and *Prodinoceras* (Upper Palaeocene) are from Mongolia, and *Gobiatherium* was a tuskless Asiatic form of the Upper Eocene with a long, low skull lacking any development of protuberances.

The poorly known *Carodnia*, from the Late Palaeocene of South America, may be a distant relative of the uintatheres and is assigned to a special sub-order, the Xenungulata.

Another South American group, the pyrotheres, is also possibly of amblypod descent. *Pyrotherium* itself, from the Lower Oligocene, was as large as a small elephant and had developed tusk-like incisor teeth as well as (apparently) a nasal proboscis, because the nasal openings in the skull have moved back to a position above the eye sockets. *Propyrotherium* was a smaller Upper Eocene predecessor and *Carolozittelia* from the Lower Eocene did not even attain the size of a tapir.   R.S.

Ameghino, Florentino (1854–1911)

Argentine palaeontologist who did much to elucidate the unique fossil mammalian fauna of South America as well as describing some of the first finds of Cretaceous dinosaurs in Argentina. Ameghino, born in Luján, had little formal education and was initially interested in the origin of man in South America. For much of his life he was in financial difficulties, not least due to supporting a two-volume work on the fossil mammals of Argentina in 1880. He travelled to Europe, visiting Denmark, Belgium, Italy and the United Kingdom.

While in Europe he was removed from his teaching post, although he did manage to obtain the Chair of Zoology at Cordoba University in 1884 and in 1886 he joined La Plata Museum, where much of his collection was ultimately to rest. Florentino Ameghino was helped in his field work by his brother Carlos.   A.P.H.

American Museum of Natural History

Founded in New York City in 1869, it covers the whole field of natural history, including anthropology, in all its activities from education to research. The displays are particularly rich in mounted skeletons. Palaeontology is the responsibility of the Department of Invertebrates (where both living and fossil animals are studied) and the Department of Vertebrate Paleontology.

The Museum began in the Arsenal in Central Park and moved to its present building in 1874. Several notable palaeontologists have served on its staff, including Henry Fairfield OSBORN who was the first Curator of Fossil Vertebrates, Bashford Dean (1867–1928) and Charles R. Knight (1874–1953), creator of a series of reconstructions of extinct animals.   A.P.H.

American National Museum of Natural History

An organization within the Smithsonian Institution, Washington DC, which is a complex of major museums, oceanographic and astrophysical institutes, art galleries and zoos. Its origin is due to James Smithson (1765–1829) an English scientist of French birth, who provided funds in his will "to found in Washington under the name of the Smithsonian Institution an

Amblypods
Coryphodon, a common Early Eocene amblypod in Europe, North America and eastern Asia, first appeared in the Upper Palaeocene, and was one of the largest animals of its time. Length: 2.5m (8.2ft)

Ammonites

establishment for the increase and diffusion of knowledge among men."

The displays cover the whole range of palaeontology and the Department of Anthropology is particularly concerned with the history of the American Indian. The Department of Paleobiology, which has one of the largest collections of type specimens in the world, has its main research areas in the study of physical and biological environments, evolution and systematics. The Museum is the base of palaeontologists of the United States Geological Survey.   A.P.H.

Ammonites

Cephalopod MOLLUSCS which occur abundantly in Mesozoic marine rocks. When found in clays, the original mother-of-pearl colouring is often preserved. The univalve shell is internally divided into a series of chambers (camerae) by thin walls (septa), the chambers being linked together by a marginal phosphatic tube (the siphuncle). The initial embryonic chamber of the shell is minute (globular or barrel-shaped) and as growth proceeds the ammonite animal moves forward secreting septa behind it, thus separating off new chambers and extending the siphuncular link.

Most ammonite shells are coiled in a plane spiral, but some are partly coiled and partly straight (*Australiceras*), nearly straight (*Baculites*), or coiled helically (*Turrilites*). The septal walls at their contact with the outer shell produce a complicated pattern (septal suture line). This feature and the rapid evolution of the shell form and ornamentation in ammonite species are used to group them into genera, families and superfamilies.

The Mesozoic ammonites are representatives of the larger group of cephalopods, the subclass Ammonoidea, which first appeared in the Devonian. The early forms typified by the goniatites had died out by the end of the Permian but at that time a small group of prolecanitid ammonoids yielded the numerous Mesozoic members of the group. By the end of the Cretaceous the ammonites had become extinct.

The general structure of the ammonite shell is similar to that of the modern *Nautilus*, the last survivor of the sub-class Nautiloidea, which has a history extending back into the Cambrian. These forms reached the peak of their development within the Palaeozoic. The position and nature of the siphuncle is used to divide the nautiloids into three subclasses: the Endoceratoidea (with marginal siphuncles), the Actinoceratoidea (central and specialized siphuncles), and the Nautiloidea (mainly with central siphuncles). The septal walls where they join the outer shell produce a straight or slightly sinuous simple septal suture line; this feature differentiates the nautiloids from the ammonites and ammonoids, which possess complex septal sutures.

Most Palaeozoic nautiloids have shells that are straight (orthoconic), as in *Orthoceras*, or slightly curved (cyrtoconic), as in *Oonoceras*,

and this characteristic applies to all endoceratids and actinoceratids. But in the Nautiloidea there is every variation between orthoconic and such tightly coiled shells as those of *Tylonautilus* and *Nautilus* itself. With the exception of a few orthoceratid nautiloids in the Triassic rocks, post-Palaeozoic nautiloids are tightly coiled.

Nautiloids were wholly marine and their distribution was worldwide until the mid-Cenozoic. Their numbers then declined to a single genus with four species, and their geographic distribution has today contracted to the seas of the central western Pacific Ocean from Samoa to the Philippines and the Indian Ocean off southern Australia. Modern *Nautilus* is a free-swimming mollusc, the chambers of the shell being filled with air at atmospheric pressure which makes the animal buoyant. It swims by ejecting water through its hyponome and can move rapidly.

The ammonoids evolved from nautiloid stock in the Early Devonian, possibly from the Bactritidae, by developing complex septal sutures and becoming generally coiled. It is

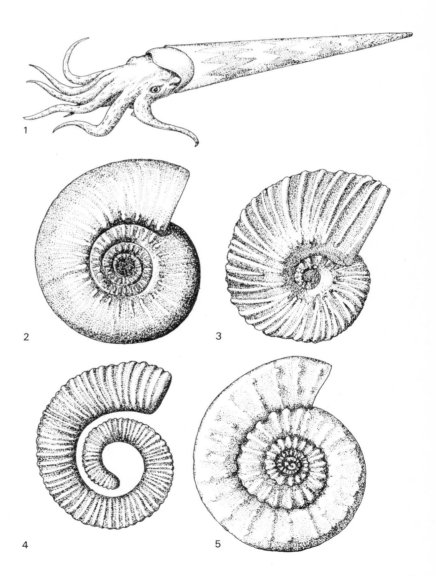

Ammonites
(1) Reconstruction of an Ordovician orthoceratid cephalopod; the shells of these forms were up to 3.8m (12.5ft) long.
(2) The Carboniferous goniatite Gastrioceras *(natural size).*
(3) The Lower Cretaceous ammonite Hoplites *(approx. 3/4 natural size).*
(4) The Lower Cretaceous ammonite Aegocrioceras *(approx. 1/4 natural size).*
(5) The Lower Jurassic (Liassic) ammonite Microderoceras *(approx. 3/4 natural size).*

Amphibians

likely, therefore, that the ammonite animal was comparable to *Nautilus*, although it was almost certainly more highly specialized. Separate sexes occur in *Nautilus* with some slight sexual shell variation, and dimorphism of an apparently sexual nature has been recognized in various ammonites. This dimorphism is not universal, however, and two types have been observed: one in which there is a distinct relationship between large individuals (macromorphs) considered to be female and small individuals (micromorphs) thought to be males, and another (seen in the Cretaceous hoplitid ammonites) where shells of the same general size and ornament pattern have either a narrow whorl section or a broad cross-section.

Most ammonites were probably nektonic (living at the surface of the sea). This is suggested by the occurrence of shells in sediments laid down in areas of foul sea floor in which no benthic (bottom-living) fauna is found. In mid-Cretaceous clays, uncoiled (or heteromorph) ammonites are found associated with benthic animals, but are absent when such a fauna is not present. This suggests that heteromorph ammonites were essentially bottom-dwellers.

The rapid evolution of distinctive shell forms and ornament patterns, the short vertical range of species and genera, and their widespread distribution in marine sediments of many different types make ammonites valuable for the relative dating (zoning) of the Mesozoic. Indeed, ammonoids have proved useful as ZONE FOSSILS since their appearance at the end of the Early Devonian, due to the rapidly increasing complexity of the suture-line pattern.   H.G.O.

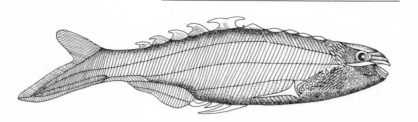

Anaspids
Birkenia, from the Silurian-Devonian of Europe, may have foraged for food in a head-down position, using its sucking mouth to seize small invertebrates.
Length: about 10cm (4in)

Amphibians

The Amphibia are tetrapods, ie VERTEBRATES with legs (sometimes secondarily reduced) rather than fins. REPTILES, BIRDS and MAMMALS either produce an amniote egg (which has a protective shell, an adequate food supply, a "private pond" of liquid, and facilities for storing waste), or give birth to live young (viviparity). Amphibians, on the other hand, produce eggs that have little yolk as food, no amniotic "pond" and no shell, so they must be laid in water. Furthermore young amniotes emerge fully formed, whereas young amphibians usually pass through a tadpole stage during which they complete their development, although some species have developed a form of viviparity and others produce non-amniote terrestrial eggs.

Other distinctive features of living amphibians are probably degenerate rather than primitive. All respire in part through a soft moist, permeable skin; they have simple lungs, and ribs so reduced that they cannot be used to ventilate the lungs. They have a simplified heart and arrangement of associated blood vessels, a skull in which the dermal roofing bones are reduced in number and size, a characteristic ear structure, and teeth which are divided by a region of connective tissue just above the root. Collectively, with related fossil forms, they are now usually known as the Lissamphibia. They include the tail-less FROGS AND TOADS (Anura), the tailed primitive-looking newts and SALAMANDERS (Urodela or Caudata), and the blind, limbless, tail-less, worm-like caecilians (Apoda).

The remaining amphibians, all fossil, were significantly different. Most were well ossified, with a skull covered by a complete roof of dermal bones, strong bony skeletons, and a well-developed rib cage. They used to be known collectively as the Stegocephalia and are included in the Amphibia principally because it is thought that none were amniote, many had a tadpole stage and, like the most primitive tetrapods, they are taken to be related to the most primitive living group of that assemblage.

They probably arose in the early Upper Devonian from pike-like freshwater crossopterygian LOBE-FIN FISHES. Stegocephalians are now divided into two groups, the usually large LABYRINTHODONTS and the small and sometimes degenerate LEPOSPONDYLS. The former survived at least to the end of the Triassic, the latter are known only from the Carboniferous and Lower Permian.   A.L.P.

Anaspids

An order (Anaspida) of extinct jawless fishes (OSTRACODERMS), covered with narrow scales over the trunk and tail and with small plates in the head and gill region. Each gill had a separate opening to the exterior, a third (pineal) eye was situated between the normal eyes, and there was a single nasal opening. In these features the anaspids are clearly related to the CEPHALASPIDS and to the living lampreys.

The anaspids were probably active swimmers feeding on microscopic organisms floating in the water or near the surface.

The first anaspid, *Jamoytius* from the Upper Silurian of Scotland, had simple narrow body scales and paired lateral fins as well as dorsal, caudal and anal fins. The separate gill openings were not compressed into the short oblique line seen in later genera, but were still in the primitive spread condition; the cartilaginous supports of the gill pouches exhibit a lamprey-like arrangement. The circular mouth was bounded by small denticles.

In the same deposits there are the remains of large ARTHROPODS with circular holes in their carapaces which match the circumference of the mouth of *Jamoytius*, suggesting that the parasitic way of life of modern lampreys had early beginnings.   L.B.H.

Angiosperms, *see* FLOWERING PLANTS.

Anthracosaurs

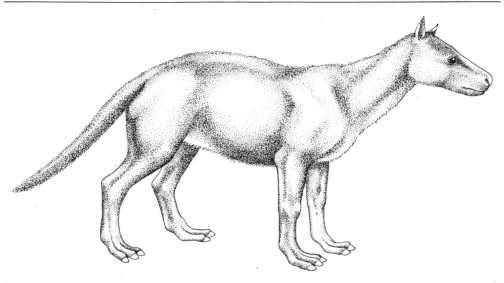

Anning, Mary (1799–1847)

British fossil collector and vendor from Lyme Regis, Dorset. The daughter of a carpenter, who supplemented his income by selling fossils, Mary Anning was introduced to the remains of pre-historic creatures at an early age. Her father died when she was ten years old and from that time she seems to have started the business of selling fossils on her own account, ultimately to become, to quote a contemporary, "the most eminent female fossilist". In order to sell fossils she had first to collect them and it was during her collecting that she made some spectacular finds, including the first articulated ICHTHYOSAUR (1810) and PLESIOSAUR skeletons (1823) and the first British PTEROSAUR (1828). She dealt with many of the famous palaeontologists of the time, including her life-long friend Henry de la Beche (1796–1855), William BUCKLAND and William Conybeare (1787–1857).   A.P.H.

Anoplotheres

An extinct ARTIODACTYL family of tylopod ruminants that flourished in Europe during the Eocene and Oligocene. These short-limbed, heavily proportioned animals with clawed feet attained approximately the size of TAPIRS, but had unusually long tails. The full primitive number of 44 teeth was present, with the upper molars bearing five cusps on the crown, those of the common Late Eocene genus *Anoplotherium*

having bunodont (low-crowned) inner cusps and selenodont (crescentic) outer cusps.

Diplobune, which persisted from the Eocene into the Oligocene, was a specialized form with unusual three-toed feet that retained a powerful second toe. It was more gracefully proportioned than *Anoplotherium*.   R.S.

Antelopes, *see* CATTLE.

Anthracosaurs

The LABYRINTHODONT amphibians are divided into two major groups: the Temnospondyli and Anthracosauria (or Batrachosauria), which are probably not closely related to one another. Like the temnospondyls, the anthracosaurs have labyrinthodont teeth, a consolidated skull roof of dermal bones, and vertebrae in which the centrum is divided into an anterior intercentrum and a posterior pleurocentrum. Unlike temnospondyls, however, the pleurocentrum is the principal ventral element in each vertebra, being a complete and usually massive ring to which the neural arch above is firmly attached. The intercentrum varies from a small concentric wedge to a thin but complete ring.

Central to the group are the large long-bodied embolomeres of the European and American Coal Measures, such as *Eogyrinus* from Northumberland, which was about 4 metres (13

Anoplotheres
Anoplotherium, a common genus from the Upper Eocene and Lower Oligocene of Europe, was 1m (3.3ft) tall at the shoulder.

Anthracosaurs
Eogyrinus was a predominantly aquatic amphibian from the European Coal Measures. Length: about 4m (13ft)

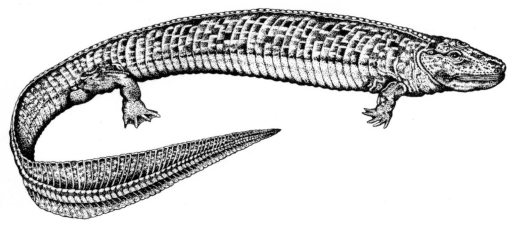

Anthracotheres

ft) long, with a crocodile-like skull, eel-like body and relatively small limbs. These were swamp-living predators probably feeding principally on fish. *Anthracosaurus*, known from Scotland and England (Durham), was similar but probably fed on other tetrapods.

Anthracosaurs of more terrestrial habits, with shorter bodies and stronger limbs, are known from much earlier (Lower Carboniferous) deposits in Scotland and North America. These forms, including *Eoherpeton* and *Proterogyrinus*, probably gave rise to the Coal Measure anthracosaurs, and the Permian seymouriamorphs.

The Seymouriamorpha are included within the Anthracosauria by some authorities, but they are considered a separate group by others. They are named after *Seymouria* from the Lower Permian of Texas, which has a terrestrial, extremely reptile-like skeleton and an aberrant but diagnostically anthracosaur skull. For many years they were regarded as primitive reptiles, but small seymouriamorphs, such as *Discosauriscus* from the European Permian, are known to have had gills when young, and so the whole group must have been amphibians. *Seymouria* was later regarded as a Permian survivor of the presumed Early Carboniferous ancestors of reptiles. The Late Carboniferous *Gephyrostegus*, a terrestrial but non-seymouriamorph anthracosaur with a more normal skull, has also been cast in this role.

All known anthracosaurs, however, like most labyrinthodonts, had a distinctive and irreversible structure of the middle ear and none is likely to have been the ancestor of reptiles.

Thus anthracosaurs have left no known descendants and their distinctive vertebrae, although similar in many respects to those of reptiles and some microsaurs (LEPOSPONDYLS), do not suggest a common ancestry with other labyrinthodonts.   A.L.P.

Anthracotheres

An extinct family (Anthracotheriidae) of primitive pig-like ARTIODACTYLS assigned to the suborder Suina which were numerous in the Old World during the Cenozoic. They first appeared in the Eocene of Asia (eg *Anthracobune* and *Anthracohyus*) and quickly spread to Europe (eg *Haplobunodon*, *Anthracotherium*, *Rhagatherium* and *Lophiobunodon*) before the end of the period.

Subsequently the anthracotheres proliferated to colonize Africa and North America. The group appears to have been declining during the Pliocene, and its last survivor (*Merycopotamus*) occurs in the Pleistocene of Asia and the East Indies.

Bothriodon, from North America, Europe and Africa, was a typical Eocene-Miocene member of the family, attaining a length of about 1.5 metres (5ft) with a long-snouted skull, elongated body, short limbs, four-toed feet (the front foot retained a vestigial first digit), and a full complement of 44 teeth including low-crowned molars.

Later anthracotheres tended to develop grinding teeth of a simple crescentic type with only four cusps (*Merycopotamus* and the Miocene *Arretotherium* from North America), but most had upper molars with a primitive low-crowned five-cusped configuration. It seems likely that the group was amphibious.   R.S.

Apes

Higher PRIMATES with well-developed brains, a semi-erect stance, grasping hands and no tail. They are represented today by the gorilla, the chimpanzee, the orang-utan and the gibbon, all of which are tree-dwellers.

The first evidence of animals directly ancestral to the apes and MAN occurs in the Oligocene. The best record of these early forms comes from the fossil-rich beds of the FAYUM in the Egyptian desert. Two main groups were found, one of which, the Parapithecidae, appears to have no descendants. The other group includes three important fossil apes: *Oligopithecus*, *Propliopithecus* and *Aegyptopithecus*.

Although only one specimen of *Oligopithecus* has so far been found it is of great importance, because it appears to be intermediate between the prosimians and the apes, having some characteristics of both groups. *Oligopithecus* was tree-dwelling, and lived in the forests that existed in the Fayum 35–40 million years ago. *Propliopithecus* appears to be the next stage in the evolutionary line and, although its teeth are more advanced in structure, it still closely resembles *Oligopithecus*. It is sufficiently unspecialized to be regarded as an ancestor of gibbons, apes or MONKEYS. *Aegyptopithecus* could have been the ancestor of all the apes, including man. It was small, with the limbs of a tree-dwelling quadruped, but although it retained the elongated snout of a prosimian its lower jaw was heavy and ape-like. Its large canine teeth and the construction of the crowns of its molar teeth clearly indicate simian affinities.

During the Miocene, adaptive radiations spread apes throughout Africa and into Europe and Asia. These fossil forms of 10–25 million years ago have been given various names but the

Archaeocyathines

most usual is *Dryopithecus*, so called because the fossils often occur with oak leaves. The earliest examples of this group have been found in eastern Africa and were apparently short-limbed tree-dwelling quadrupeds. One of them, *Dendropithecus*, is thought to be ancestral to the gibbons because even at this early date it had developed sharp cutting canines and incisors. One dryopithecine find was named *Proconsul*, suggesting that it was the ancestor of a chimpanzee named Consul in the London Zoo.

After the Middle Miocene these African apes disappeared from the fossil record, but were replaced in Europe and Asia by a further adaptive radiation, which yielded at least five species of *Dryopithecus* that lived in the European and Asiatic forests of 10–14 million years ago. As with the Early Miocene apes, their mode of locomotion was apparently the same as that of modern monkeys, and their diet and social group behaviour were presumably also similar. One of the Middle Miocene apes, *Pliopithecus*, resembled the gibbons, but because its gibbon-like features were less well developed than those of the earlier *Dendropithecus*, it is not thought to be descended directly from the same evolutionary line as modern gibbons.

The origin of the great apes (the gorilla, the chimpanzee and the orang-utan) is less clear, although it has been suggested that two species of *Proconsul* are in the direct line of descent leading to two of them: *Proconsul africanus* to the chimpanzee, and *Proconsul major* to the gorilla. Unfortunately there is much variation within any species and it is often difficult to say whether a fossil is at the extremes of natural variation or whether it constitutes a new species.

Two unusual apes are known from the Middle Miocene. *Oreopithecus* has presented a considerable problem in that it possesses an unusual mixture of ape, monkey and hominid features. This swamp-dwelling ape did not evolve into any later types. *Gigantopithecus* was probably the largest primate that ever lived, and is thought to have left no descendants, unless it was the ancestor of the "Abominable Snowman" of the Himalayas and "Big Foot" of the Rocky Mountains.

During the last phase of the Middle Miocene the climate changed and forests were gradually replaced by savanna. Apes became restricted to these forests, except perhaps those species (including the ancestors of man) that could adapt to the changing environment.   D.T.

Archaeocyathines

A group of marine multicellular animals that flourished in the Lower Cambrian and became extinct in the Middle Cambrian. Their skeletal remains have been found in North America, Australia, Siberia, Sardinia, Morocco and Antarctica. To have attained such a widespread distribution it is probable they developed from a free planktonic growth stage.

Attached to the sea bottom by a strong basal process (holdfast), they built calcareous skeletons of finely granular calcite. The skeleton of *Monocyathus* and similar genera consists of a single wall, whereas more complex genera such as *Ajacicyathus* and *Ethmophyllum* have an additional inner wall with an intervening space (intervallum). The walls are connected through the intervallum by radial tubes (septa), radial rods, perforated transverse plates (tabulae), arched imperforated plates (dissepiments) or radial tubules. Enclosed within the walls is a central cavity varying in depth with the shape of the skeleton. The walls are perforated by numerous pores arranged in longitudinal rows, the pores in adjacent rows being opposite or alternate. These organisms varied from cylindrical to disc-shape, although most grew as slender erect cones or cups. They were predominantly small, ranging from 10–25mm (0.4–1.0in) in diameter and 80–100mm (3.25–4.0in) in height. Disc-like genera such as *Okulitchicyathus* with a maximum diameter of approximately 60cm (2ft) were exceptional. No evidence of soft parts has been recorded but it is presumed that a layer of tissue covered the outer wall and at least part of the central cavity. Archaeocyathines inhabited the sea floor to a depth of 100 metres (328ft) and at 20–30 metres (66–98ft), where they were most prolific, they formed large reefs. Their rapid evolution, which produced more than 450 species, indicates their importance in the benthic (sea-floor) life of the period. Ancestral forms were undoubtedly present in the Pre-Cambrian but they have not been found. In some respects their structure is comparable with CORALS but they have a closer affinity with SPONGES.

Their value as biostratigraphical indices has made possible the division of the Russian Lower Cambrian into four stages based on the time range of certain genera and also the correlation of the beds in the Siberian platform with those in the Altai-Sayan region.   S.W.

Apes
Dryopithecus *apparently arose in Africa during the Lower Miocene.*

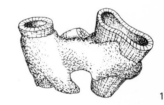

1

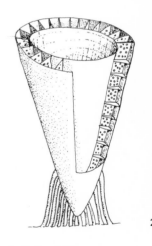

2

Archaeocyathines
(1) *Two specimens of* Coscinocyathus, *an archaeocyathine from the Lower Cambrian of Siberia and Australia.*
(2) *In section, archaeocyathines reveal a structure of internal and external walls joined by horizontal tubulae.*

Archaeopteryx

Archaeopteryx

The oldest known bird, from the Upper Jurassic limestone of Germany. Five skeletons and a single feather have been found, and from these it is possible to produce a fairly accurate restoration. *Archaeopteryx* was about the size of a crow, with well developed feathers on the forelimbs and the tail. Osteologically, however, the skeleton shows a predominance of reptilian features, including the presence of teeth in both the upper and lower jaws, a poorly developed sternum, the retention of fingers in the forelimbs, the occurrence of ventral ribs, and the persistence of a long tail consisting of numerous vertebrae (in later birds this has been reduced to a pygostyle or "parson's nose").

It has been proposed that *Archaeopteryx* was arboreal, with poor powers of flight; it used the fingers of the forelimbs as aids to climbing, and the supposed reversed hallux (first hind-toe) facilitated perching. Alternatively, *Archaeopteryx* might have been cursorial, running after its prey and using the wings as a "fly-swot". Because feathers are fragile, any consistent abrasion caused by climbing or catching prey in this manner would eventually be likely to render them useless for either flying or use as a prey trap. In all likelihood this earliest known bird was a land-dweller which was able to escape would-be predators by gliding from high ground.

The evolutionary history of *Archaeopteryx* is also controversial, although birds undoubtedly developed from ARCHOSAURS. The osteology of this primitive bird so closely resembles that of certain small CARNOSAURS that they might have evolved from this group of DINOSAURS some time during the Early Jurassic. This skeletal similarity may merely be an example of parallel evolution, however, and it is possible that the ancestor of *Archaeopteryx* should be looked for among an unknown early archosaur group that lived during the Triassic.   C.A.W.

Archaeopteryx
Archaeopteryx, *the oldest known bird, is represented by beautifully preserved specimens from the Upper Jurassic (Lithographic stone) of Solenhofen, Bavaria. It was about the size of a crow.*

Archosaurs

The most spectacular of the reptile groups that dominated the Mesozoic. They include the DINOSAURS, PTEROSAURS and CROCODILES.

One of two groups of diapsid REPTILES (the other is the lepidosaurs, comprising LIZARDS and SNAKES), the archosaurs are distinguished principally by a tendency to bipedalism.

In common with the lepidosaurs, they were probably descended from a group of small, primitive Permian diapsids known as the Eosuchia, of which the South African *Youngina*, *Heleosaurus* and their inadequately known relatives from the KARROO SYSTEM represent a likely ancestral group. Alternatively, it is possible that the archosaurs arose directly from captorhinomorph COTYLOSAURS.

The central stem of the archosaurs is represented by the THECODONTIANS, with proterosuchians and PSEUDOSUCHIANS appearing in the Lower Triassic, and aëtosaurs and the superficially crocodile-like PHYTOSAURS developing by the Upper Triassic. The two dinosaurian orders, the SAURISCHIANS and the ORNITHISCHIANS, arose from pseudosuchian stock in the Middle Triassic, and by the Late Triassic crocodiles were becoming well established. The highly specialized pterosaurs were the last major archosaur group to emerge, the earliest representative of these reptiles being present in the Upper Triassic.

Although a varying degree of bipedalism (incipient, actual or relinquished) is widely regarded as the principal characteristic of all these diverse archosaurs, the proterosuchians, aëtosaurs and phytosaurs of the Triassic were sprawling or semi-sprawling quadrupeds, as are the modern crocodiles. The longer-than-normal hindlimbs of all these groups suggest either the secondary assumption of all-fours after a brief initial bipedal career, or perhaps an early aquatic stage in archosaur history after which the later terrestrial forms rotated their elongated hindlimbs (originally acquired for swimming) under the body and abandoned the primitive reptilian sprawling gait in favour of bipedalism.

Some pseudosuchians were apparently fully bipedal, however (eg *Saltoposuchus* and *Scleromochlus*), and this characteristic was retained by the predatory COELUROSAURS, CARNOSAURS and DEINONYCHIDS. The herbivorous SAUROPOD stock was essentially quadrupedal, with an imperfect bipedal early stage represented by the Triassic prosauropods, although they generally retained comparatively long hindlimbs (*Brachiosaurus* and its relatives are exceptions). Few of the plant-eating ornithischians were fully bipedal, and the HORNED DINOSAURS, PLATED DINOSAURS and ARMOURED DINOSAURS were all entirely quadrupedal. Dinosaurs and pterosaurs may well have been WARM-BLOODED, an almost unique feature among reptiles: the MAMMAL-LIKE REPTILES are the only other reptilian group in which this development possibly occurred.

The thecodontians failed to survive beyond the Triassic in competition with their dinosaurian descendants, and only the crocodiles

I Invertebrates

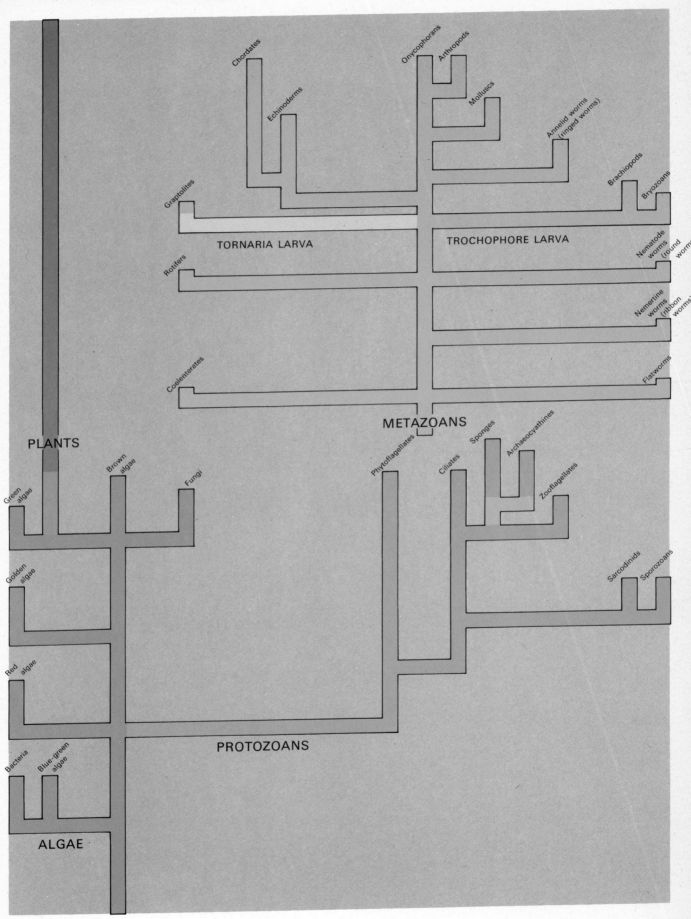

II Vertebrates

III Plants

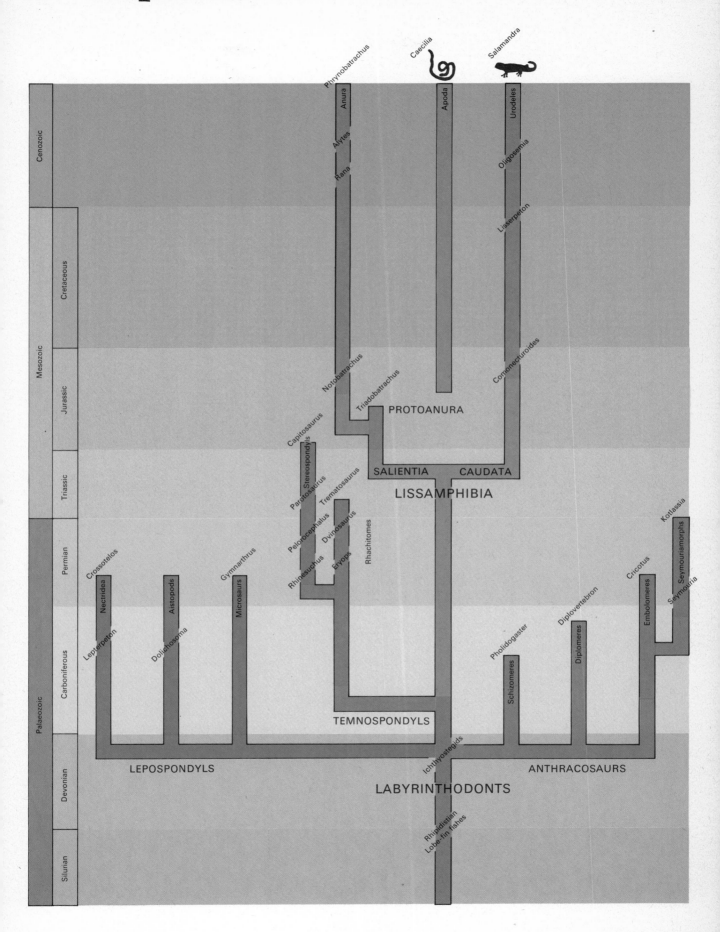

v Fishes

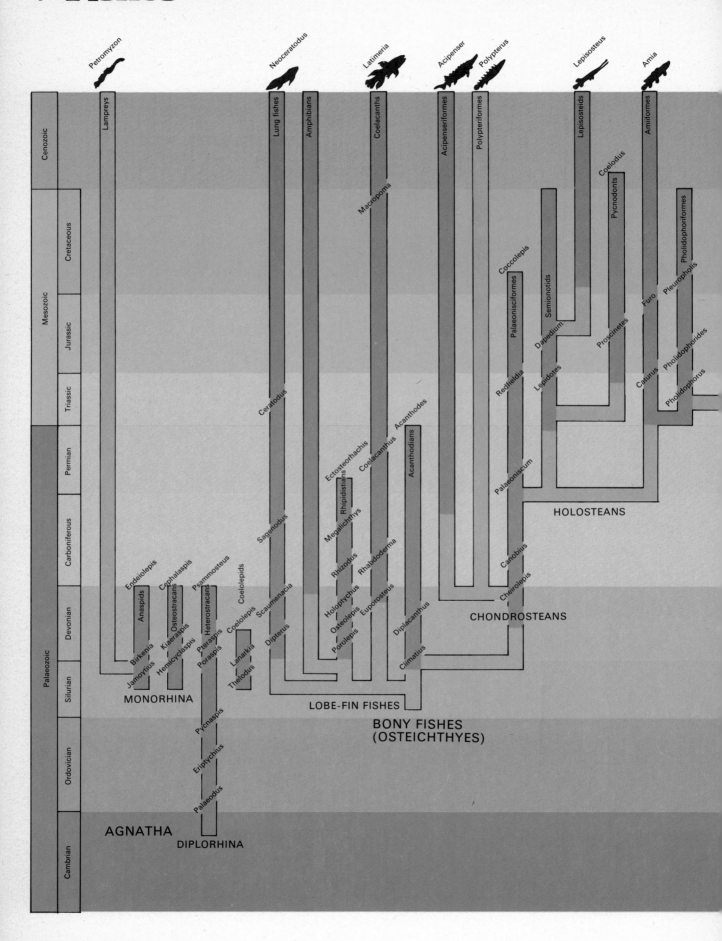

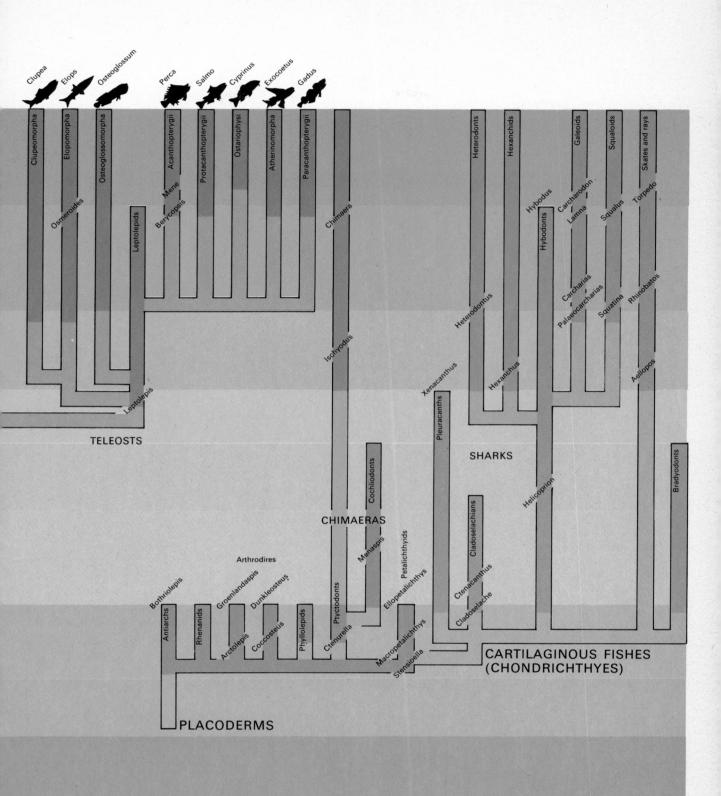

Clupea
Elops
Osteoglossum
Perca
Salmo
Cyprinus
Exocoetus
Gadus

Clupeomorpha
Elopomorpha
Osmeroides
Osteoglossomorpha
Leptolepids
Mene
Acanthopterygii
Berycopsis
Protacanthopterygii
Ostariophysi
Atherinomorpha
Paracanthopterygii
Chimaera
Leptolepis

Ischyodus

Heterodonts
Hexanchids
Hybodus
Galeoids
Squaloids
Skates and rays
Hybodonts
Carcharodon
Lamna
Squalus
Torpedo
Carcharias
Squatina
Rhinobatos
Heterodontus
Palaeocarcharias
Xenacanthus
Hexanchus
Aellopos

TELEOSTS

Pleuracanthus

SHARKS

Cochliodonts

Bradyodonts

Menaspis

CHIMAERAS

Helicoprion

Cladoselachians

Ellopetalichthyids
Petalichthyids

Arthrodires
Cladoselache
Ctenacanthus

Bothriolepis
Groenlandaspis
Dunkleosteus
Ptyctodonts
Ctenacanthus

Rhenanids
Arctolepis
Coccosteus
Phyllolepids
Ctenurella

Antiarchs
Macropetalichthys
Stensioella

CARTILAGINOUS FISHES
(CHONDRICHTHYES)

PLACODERMS

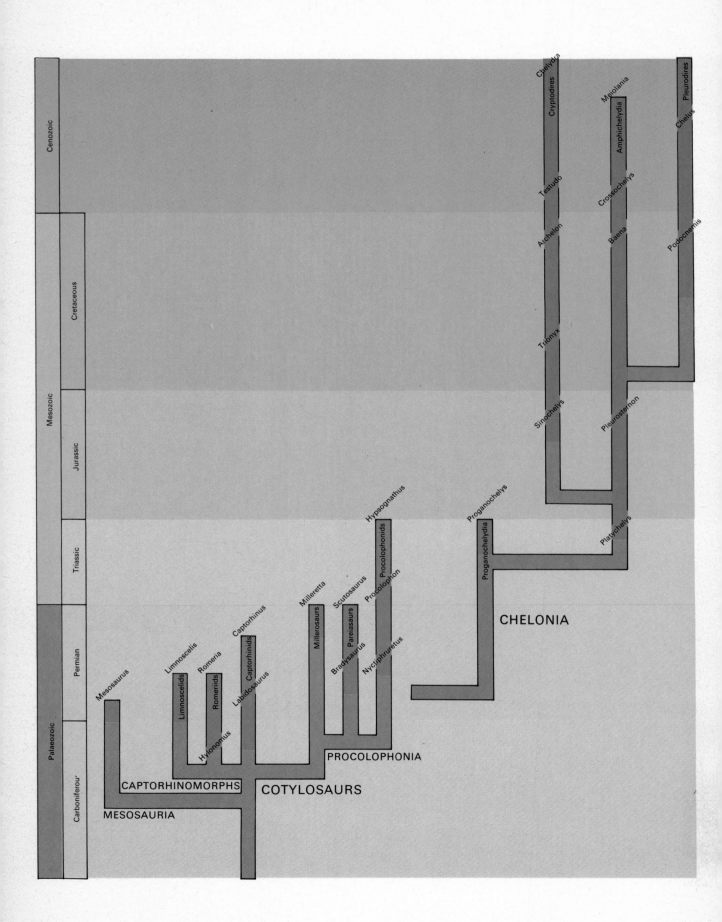

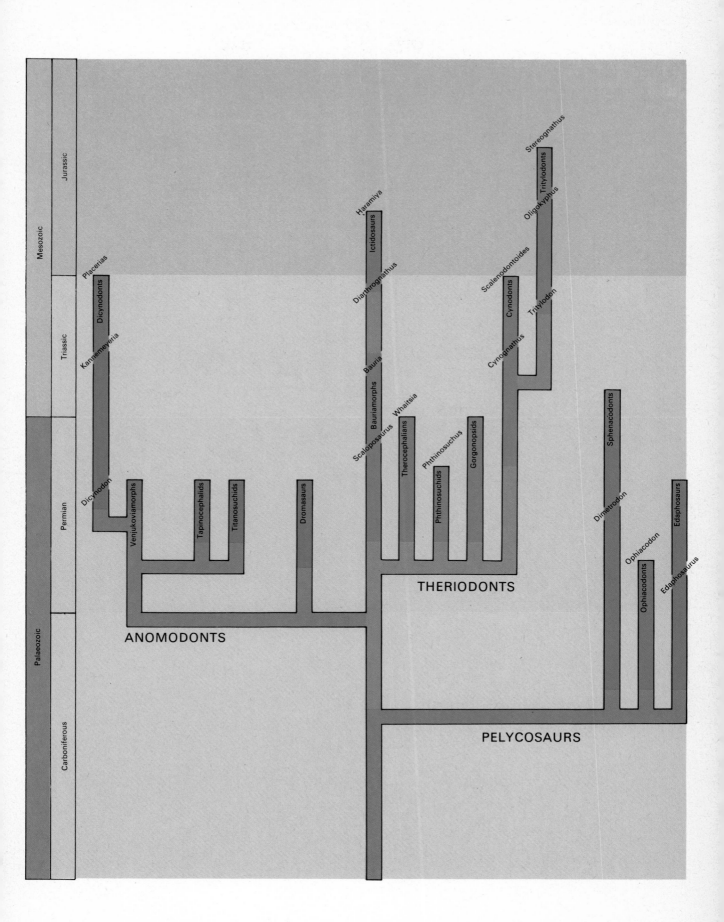

VIII Geological time chart

The span of geological time from the beginning of the Cambrian to the present day is known as the Phanerozoic. Below the Cambrian is the Proterozoic (2,600 million to 570 million years ago) in which evidence of primitive life occurs. The oldest rocks of the Earth were formed in the Archaean.

Present

				Time millions of years ago
Quaternary		Holocene		
	Pleistocene	Upper	Würm glaciation (Wisconsian)	0.1-0.01
		Middle	Riss glaciation (Illinoian)	0.25-0.15
			Mindel glaciation (Kansan)	0.5-0.4
		Lower	Gunz glaciation (Nebraskan)	0.9-0.8
				1.8

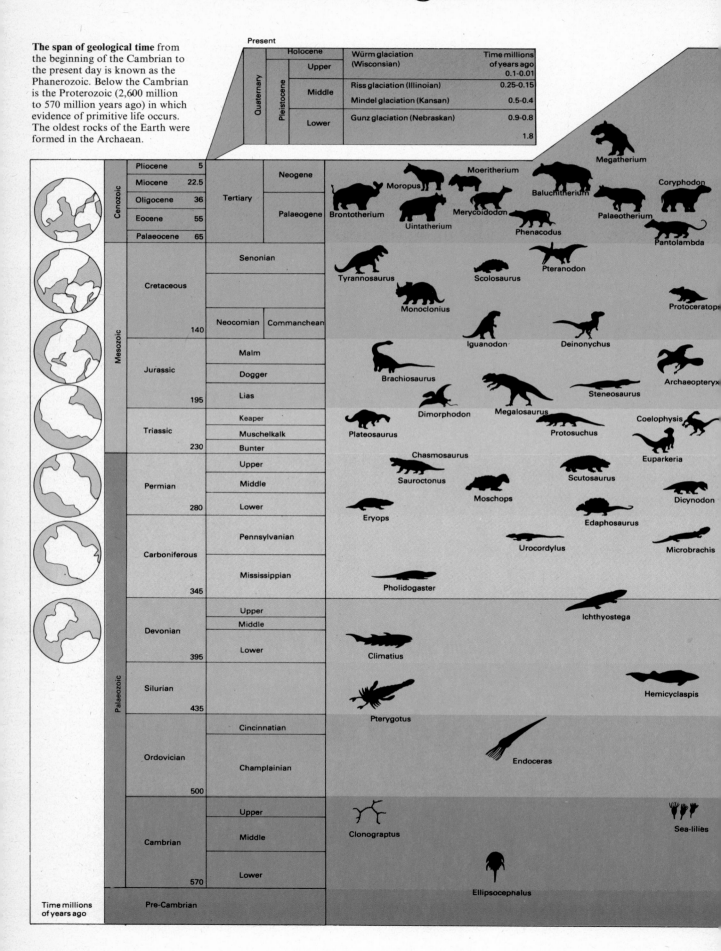

Cenozoic	Pliocene	5	Tertiary	Neogene
	Miocene	22.5		
	Oligocene	36		
	Eocene	55		Palaeogene
	Palaeocene	65		
Mesozoic	Cretaceous		Senonian	
		140	Neocomian	Commanchean
	Jurassic		Malm	
			Dogger	
		195	Lias	
	Triassic		Keaper	
			Muschelkalk	
		230	Bunter	
Palaeozoic	Permian		Upper	
			Middle	
		280	Lower	
	Carboniferous		Pennsylvanian	
			Mississippian	
		345		
	Devonian		Upper	
			Middle	
		395	Lower	
	Silurian			
		435		
	Ordovician		Cincinnatian	
			Champlainian	
		500		
	Cambrian		Upper	
			Middle	
		570	Lower	
	Pre-Cambrian			

Time millions of years ago

Labels: Megatherium, Moeritherium, Coryphodon, Moropus, Baluchitherium, Brontotherium, Merycoidodon, Uintatherium, Phenacodus, Palaeotherium, Pantolambda, Pteranodon, Tyrannosaurus, Scolosaurus, Protoceratops, Monoclonius, Iguanodon, Deinonychus, Brachiosaurus, Steneosaurus, Archaeopteryx, Dimorphodon, Megalosaurus, Coelophysis, Plateosaurus, Protosuchus, Euparkeria, Chasmosaurus, Sauroctonus, Scutosaurus, Moschops, Dicynodon, Eryops, Edaphosaurus, Urocordylus, Microbrachis, Pholidogaster, Ichthyostega, Climatius, Hemicyclaspis, Pterygotus, Endoceras, Clonograptus, Sea-lilies, Ellipsocephalus

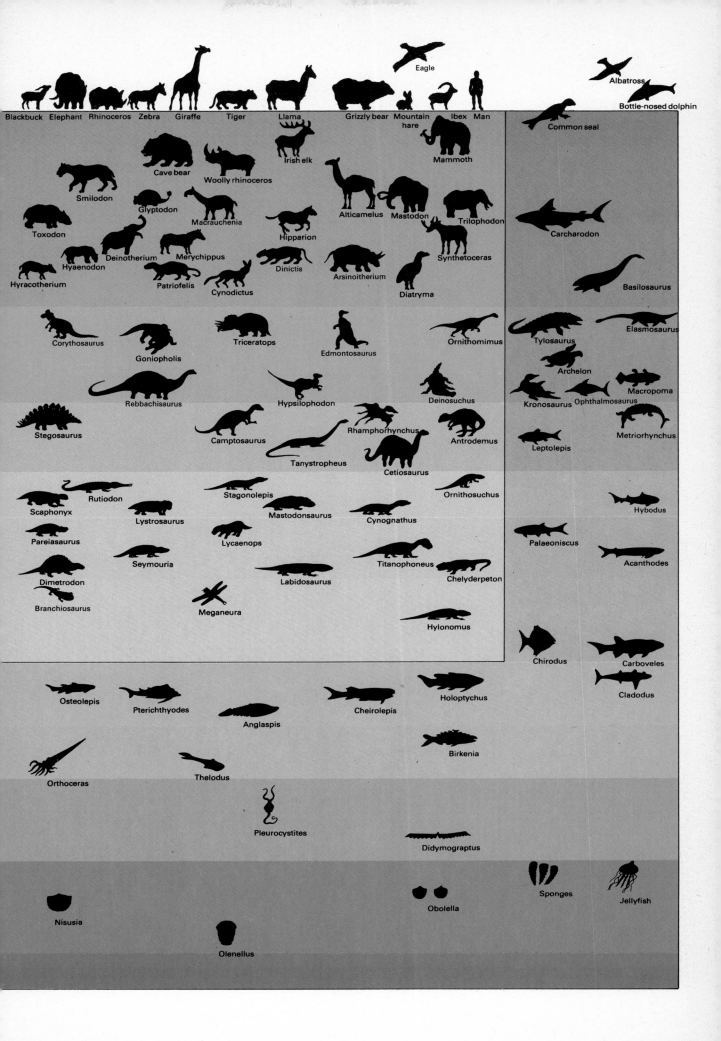

Blackbuck Elephant Rhinoceros Zebra Giraffe Tiger Llama Grizzly bear Mountain Ibex Man
hare

Eagle

Albatross

Bottle-nosed dolphin

Common seal

Irish elk

Mammoth

Cave bear

Woolly rhinoceros

Smilodon

Glyptodon

Macrauchenia

Alticamelus Mastodon

Trilophodon

Toxodon

Carcharodon

Hipparion

Deinotherium Merychippus

Basilosaurus

Hyaenodon

Synthetoceras

Hyracotherium

Patriofelis

Dinictis

Arsinoitherium

Cynodictus

Diatryma

Corythosaurus

Triceratops

Edmontosaurus

Ornithomimus

Tylosaurus

Elasmosaurus

Goniopholis

Archelon

Rebbachisaurus

Hypsilophodon

Deinosuchus

Kronosaurus Ophthalmosaurus

Macropoma

Stegosaurus

Camptosaurus

Rhamphorhynchus

Antrodemus

Metriorhynchus

Tanystropheus

Leptolepis

Cetiosaurus

Rutiodon

Stagonolepis

Ornithosuchus

Hybodus

Scaphonyx

Lystrosaurus

Mastodonsaurus

Cynognathus

Pareiasaurus

Palaeoniscus

Lycaenops

Acanthodes

Seymouria

Titanophoneus

Dimetrodon

Labidosaurus

Chelyderpeton

Branchiosaurus

Meganeura

Hylonomus

Chirodus

Carboveles

Osteolepis

Pterichthyodes

Holoptychus

Cladodus

Anglaspis

Cheirolepis

Birkenia

Orthoceras

Thelodus

Pleurocystites

Didymograptus

Sponges

Jellyfish

Nisusia

Obolella

Olenellus

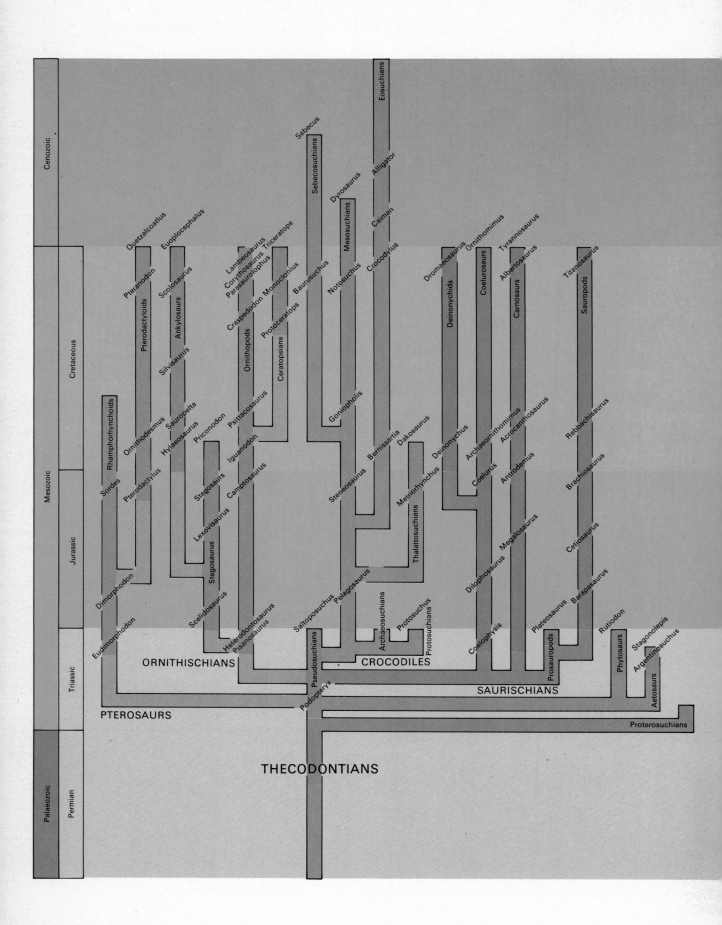

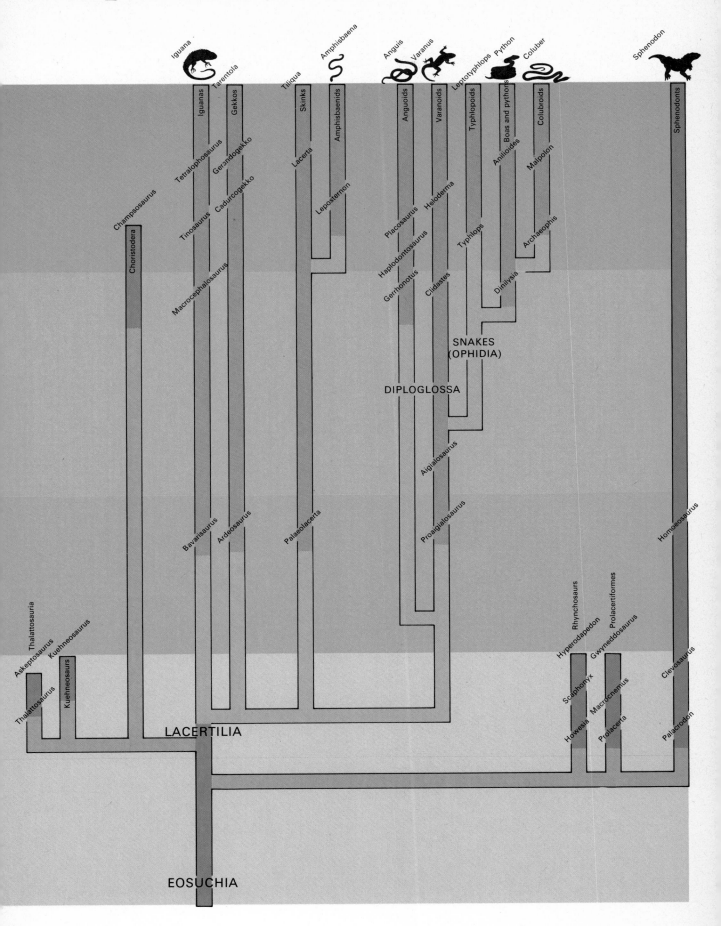

xi Birds

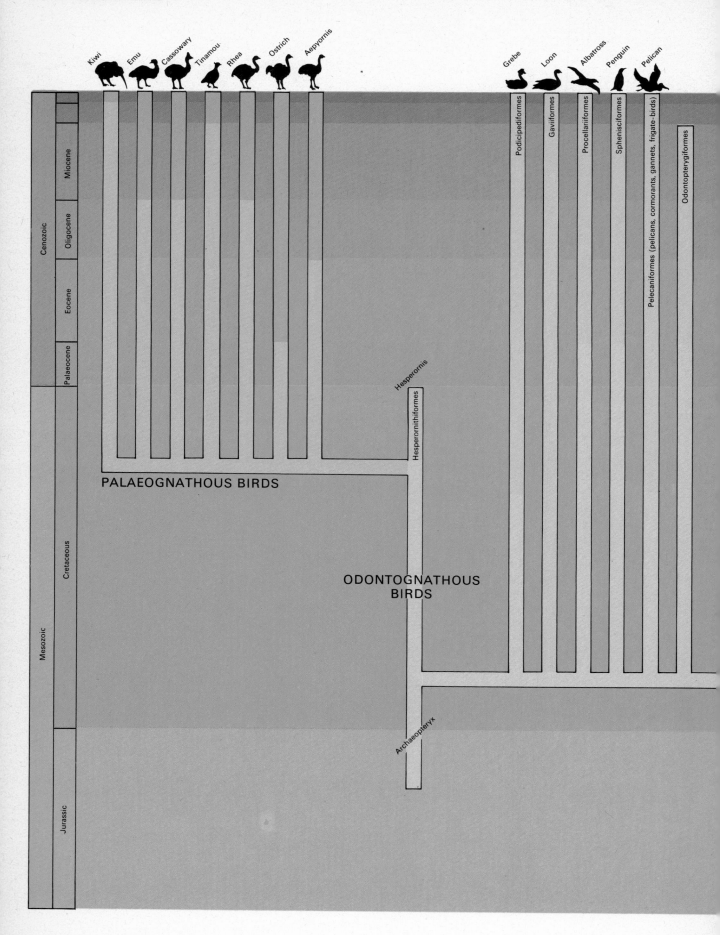

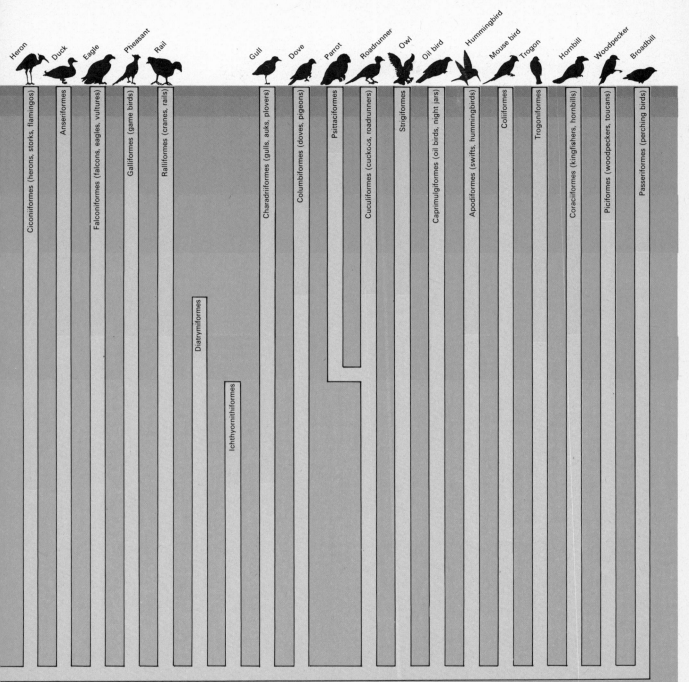

Heron — Ciconiiformes (herons, storks, flamingos)

Duck — Anseriformes

Eagle — Falconiformes (falcons, eagles, vultures)

Pheasant — Galliformes (game birds)

Rail — Ralliformes (cranes, rails)

Diatrymiformes

Ichthyornithiformes

Gull — Charadriiformes (gulls, auks, plovers)

Dove — Columbiformes (doves, pigeons)

Parrot — Psittaciformes

Roadrunner — Cuculiformes (cuckoos, roadrunners)

Owl — Strigiformes

Oil bird — Caprimulgiformes (oil birds, night jars)

Hummingbird — Apodiformes (swifts, hummingbirds)

Mouse bird — Coliiformes

Trogon — Trogoniformes

Hornbill — Coraciiformes (kingfishers, hornbills)

Woodpecker — Piciformes (woodpeckers, toucans)

Broadbill — Passeriformes (perching birds)

NEOGNATHOUS BIRDS

XII Carnivora

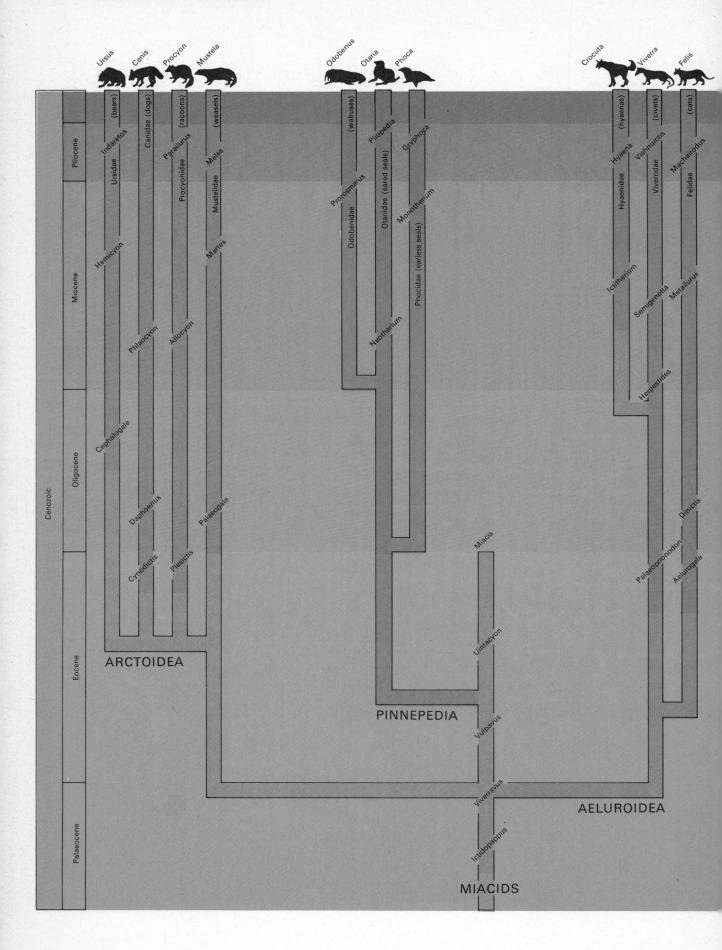

Ursus · Canis · Procyon · Mustela   Odobenus · Otaria · Phoca   Crocuta · Viverra · Felis

(bears) (dogs) (racoons) (weasels)   (walruses) (eared seals)   (hyaenas) (civets) (cats)

Indaretos · Canidae · Parailurus · Meles   Protosmarus · Pliopedia · Gryphoca   Hyaena · Vishnuictis · Machairodus

Ursidae · Procyonidae · Mustelidae   Odobenidae · Otariidae (eared seals) · Monotherium   Hyaenidae · Viverridae · Felidae

Hemicyon · Martes   Phocidae (earless seals)   Ictitherium · Semigenetta · Metailurus

Miocene

Phlaocyon · Allocyon   Neotherium

Cephalogale   Herpestides

Oligocene

Daphoenus · Palaeogale   Dinictis

Cynodictis · Plesictis   Palaeoprionodon · Aelurogale

Pliocene

Cenozoic

Miacis

Uintacyon

ARCTOIDEA

Eocene

PINNEPEDIA

Vulpavus

Viverravus

AELUROIDEA

Palaeocene

Ictidopappus

MIACIDS

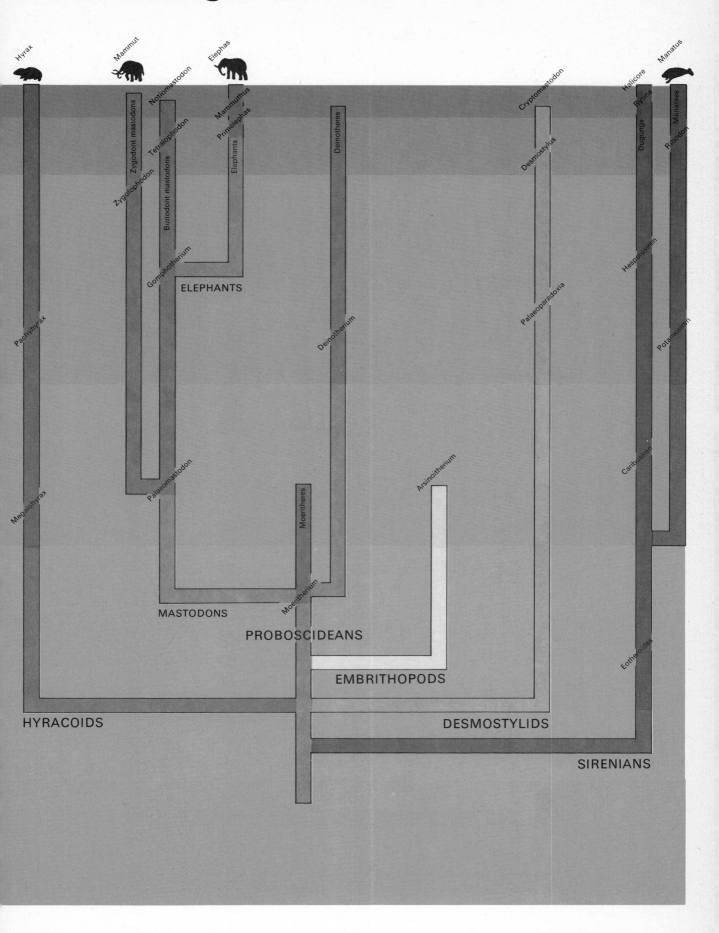

Hyrax
Mammut
Elephas
Manatus

Pachyhyrax
Zygolophodon
Zygodont mastodons
Notiomastodon
Tetralophodon
Bunodont mastodons
Mammuthus
Primelephas
Elephants
Deinotheres
Cryptomastodon
Desmostylus
Halicore
Rytina
Ribodon

Gomphotherium
ELEPHANTS
Deinotherium
Palaeoparadoxia
Hesperosiren
Dugongs

Palaeomastodon
Moeritheres
Arsinoitherium
Caribosiren
Potamosiren

Megalohyrax
Moeritherium
Eotheroides

MASTODONS
PROBOSCIDEANS
EMBRITHOPODS

HYRACOIDS
DESMOSTYLIDS

SIRENIANS

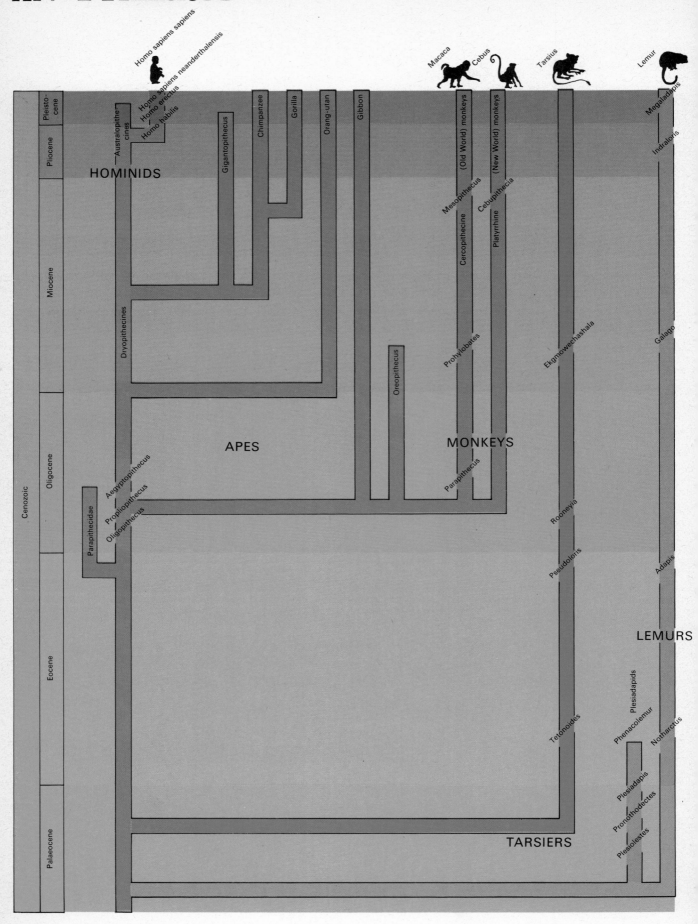

Armoured dinosaurs

made the transition to the Cenozoic – the saurischians, ornithischians and pterosaurs died out at the close of the Cretaceous. R.S.

Argentine Natural Science Museum

The Museo Argentino de Ciencias Naturales "Bernardino Rivadavia" in Buenos Aires founded in 1812. It has collections and research units that cover natural history, including archaeology. The period of the Museum's maximum development was during the directorship of Hermann Burmeister (1807–92). Most of its excellent collection of fossil vertebrates is due to Florentino AMEGHINO, who was director from 1902 and whose brother, Carlos, did much of the field work, especially in Patagonia. Florentino Ameghino was also associated with another famous museum, the Museo de la Plata, in which he worked from 1886–90. He sold part of his collection to the Museum for $16,500. A.P.H.

Armadillos

Members of the mammalian infra-order Loricata, a sub-division of the EDENTATES. They are characterized by great development of dermal armour, which often covers not only the body but also the limbs, tail and head. In life the armour of bony plates is covered by horny skin. The skull has a complete zygomatic arch, in contrast to the condition seen in SLOTHS, and there are five toes on each foot, the front feet usually having well-developed claws.

In the superfamily Dasypodoidea (the true armadillos), the body armour consists of a front and a rear buckler, with several movable bands between. Animals with armadillo characteristics are among the most ancient of edentates, occurring in the Palaeocene of South America, which suggests that they may have been ancestral even to the sloths.

The family Dasypodidae are relatively conservative, with numerous peg-like teeth. Many species still survive in South America and parts of the southern USA; *Priodontes giganteus*, a living South American species, is 1.3 metres (4.3ft) in total length, and weighs up to 100kg (220lb). *Dasypus bellus* from the Late Pleistocene of North America was even larger.

A separate line of giant armadillos, the family Pampatheriidae, developed fewer but larger scutes (dermal plates). The nine teeth in each jaw quadrant were large, with an oval to bilobular section. Pampatheres prospered from the Miocene onwards in South America, and probably invaded the south-eastern USA during the Late Pliocene. They had attained a maximum length of almost 2 metres (6.5ft) on both continents by the time they became extinct about 15,000 years ago.

The superfamily Glyptodontoidea was apparently descended from early armadillos, but developed a solid shield composed of a mosaic of hexagonal plates. There was extensive fusion of the sacral, thoracic and cervical vertebrae under this rigid dome. The flexible tail was well armoured with concentric bony rings, and often

terminated in a bony club. The skull had a deep face and jaws, as well as a complete post-orbital bar – a unique feature among edentates. The teeth, of which there were eight per quadrant, were high, open-rooted and of a characteristic trilobular pattern. Glyptodonts were especially abundant and diverse in the Pleistocene of Argentina, but had a wide range, including the southern USA. A.G.E.

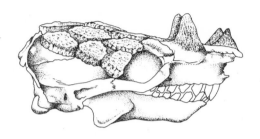

Armoured dinosaurs

An order (Ankylosauria) of ORNITHISCHIANS that developed a massive dermal armour of plates, scutes and spines to protect themselves from the voracious CARNOSAURS. In later forms this armour consolidated into an inflexible carapace. The armoured dinosaurs were fully quadrupedal and first appeared in the Early Cretaceous at about the time that the PLATED DINOSAURS (Stegosauria) were dying out, so it is possible that the ankylosaurs are stegosaur descendants.

There were several primitive armoured dinosaurs in the European Lower Cretaceous that seem to represent an initial stage in the evolution of the group. *Hylaeosaurus* from the English WEALDEN and *Acanthopholis* from the Cambridge Greensand are represented only by extremely incomplete remains, but apparently attained a length of 3–4 metres (10–13ft) with an armour of spines and keeled plates.

These early armoured dinosaurs are included with several persistently conservative Upper Cretaceous genera in the family Acanthopholididae. Among the late surviving members of this assemblage is the Hungarian *Struthiosaurus*, which had a proportionately small, bird-like skull. Its head and body were relatively high and narrow, with a paired series of spines extending down the neck to terminate in two massive shoulder spikes, and another series of posteriorly inclined plates ran along the

Arsinoitherium

tail. Other acanthopholidids include the poorly known *Onychosaurus* (also from Transylvania) and *Rhodanosaurus* from central and southern France. Some scientists include a number of more advanced but still fairly conservative armoured dinosaurs in the same family as these primitive forms, separating only the specialized Late Cretaceous genera as the Ankylosauridae.

More usually, all the heavily built armoured dinosaurs are included in the Nodosauridae, which appear in the Early Cretaceous. These massive forms with large heads, flattened bodies and consolidated armour became the common armoured dinosaurs of the Late Cretaceous.

The lightly armoured *Polacanthus*, about 5 metres (16ft) long, and the poorly known *Polacanthoides* were present in the European Wealden, but the family's development subsequently centred on North America and Asia, with representatives also present in the Indian sub-continent and South America.

In the Lower Cretaceous of the USA there are one or two moderately advanced genera, including the medium-sized *Sauropelta* with a long, narrow skull and a mosaic of flat keeled scutes on the back and flanks, and *Hoplitosaurus* (represented only by fragmentary material). Nodosaurs with the consolidated dermal armour that is characteristic of the family were well established in the early Upper Cretaceous of North America, eg *Hierosaurus* from the marine Niobrara deposits, *Nodosaurus* itself, *Stegopelta*, and *Silvisaurus*, which was about 3 metres (10ft) long and had protective spikes along the body and tail as well as a rigid cuirass over the hips.

There are various large, heavily armoured nodosaurs in the Late Cretaceous Oldman Formation of Canada, including *Dyoplosaurus* (also present in Mongolia), *Euoplocephalus*, *Panoplosaurus* and *Scolosaurus*. In the succeeding Edmonton deposits the ankylosaurs are sparsely represented by the reputedly toothless *Anodontosaurus* and by *Edmontonia*. The Lance deposits, which represent the close of Mesozoic time in North America, have yielded

only a species of *Euoplocephalus* with a greatly flattened skull and trunk, together with *Palaeoscincus* – a genus properly known only from isolated teeth.

Elsewhere, nodosaurs were evidently fairly common in the Upper Cretaceous of Mongolia, where in addition to *Dyoplosaurus* there were *Talarurus*, which had articulating keeled plates protecting the back and tail, and *Pinacosaurus*. Fragmentary ankylosaur material has also been found in greater India, north-western China, and Argentina (*Loricosaurus*, represented by 26 dermal scutes).

Many of these later armoured dinosaurs had developed a formidable club at the end of the tail that consisted of heavy dermal plates or spikes, with ossified tendons to support the immense weight of this massive weapon.   R.S.

Arsinoitherium

A large extinct ungulate (hoofed mammal) from the Lower Oligocene of Egypt that attained a length of 3.3 metres (10.7ft).

The massive skull bore a pair of huge, forward-projecting horns developed on the nasal bones, behind which there was a small pair of prominences rising from the frontal elements. A full complement of teeth was present, the grinders being high-crowned – an unusual specialization at such an early stage of the Cenozoic. The structure of the snout suggests that there may have been movable cropping lips.

Arsinoitherium had a bulky body which was supported on huge limbs with spreading, five-toed feet. Although possibly a distant relative of the elephants, it is assigned to a special order of mammals, the Embrithopoda. The only other known form that may perhaps belong to this assemblage is *Phenacolophus* from the Palaeocene and Lower Eocene of Asia.   R.S.

Arthrodires

An order of Palaeozoic fishes belonging to the extinct PLACODERMS. The arthrodires were the dominant placoderms throughout the Devonian. They ranged in length from 30cm (12in) to 12 metres (39ft) and were the main predators of the time. The head and gill regions were covered by an armour of bony plates arranged in a pattern that is unique to the group and was neither derived from nor ancestral to the pattern found in the bony fishes and the higher vertebrates. The arthrodires represented a separate evolutionary line distinct from the bony fishes and their precursors, the ACANTHODIANS.

The anterior part of the trunk (the thorax) was also encased in a bony armour and this was attached to the head armour by means of a pair of ball-and-socket joints, with a peg on the upper part of the lateral thoracic armour that fitted into a socket on the posterior margin of the head armour. The arthrodires derive their name ("joined-necked fishes") from this feature, which allowed the head to be raised and, at the same time, prevented any rotational movement. A nodding action probably helped in pumping water through the gills. The raising of the skull

Arsinoitherium
The remains of Arsinoitherium *(from the Lower Oligocene of Egypt) were found near the site of a palace built for Queen Arsinoe II (c. 316BC–270BC), after whom the animal was named. It was as large as a rhinoceros.*

Arthropods

Arthrodires
Dunkleosteus *was a giant
Upper Devonian arthrodire.
Length: more than 12m (39ft)*

on the neck joint while lowering the lower jaw would have endowed the arthrodires with an exceedingly large gape for catching prey.

The upper jaws consisted of two pairs of bones, the anterior pair forming a sharp stabbing spike whereas the second pair constituted shearing or slicing blades. The lower jaw was formed from a single pair of bones, the front of which carried a vertical spike with a shearing blade behind. The arthrodires did not possess teeth, and the cutting edges of the jaws were composed entirely of bone.

Arthrodires were bottom-living predators lurking for their prey along the sea bed and over the floors of lakes and rivers. All possessed large, well-developed eyes, and the eyeball shape was confined by a ring of four sclerotic bones. The vertebral column had not developed in that the notochord remained unrestricted, but there were neural arches and haemal arches along the top and under surfaces of the notochord. The arthrodires had the primitive type of heterocercal TAIL FIN and paired pectoral and pelvic fins. The anal fin was often absent, however, and behind the armour the body seems to have been devoid of scales.

The most primitive arthrodires, the arctolepids, had long thoracic armour and are known as Dolichothoraci. This group possessed well-developed pectoral spines projecting towards the rear of the animal, and the amount of movement at the neck joint was small. These pectoral spines acted as stabilizing organs and also protected the leading edges of the pectoral fins, which projected through circular perforations in the thoracic armour.

The pectoral spines became progressively smaller during the evolution of the arthrodires until they served merely to protect the leading edges of the pectoral fins, and at the same time the thoracic armour became greatly shortened. These advanced arthrodires are classified as Brachythoraci.

In the early arthrodires the braincase was heavily ossified, but subsequently there was a gradual reduction of bone. In one advanced group of arthrodires, the ptyctodonts, most of the head armour was reduced and the thoracic armour became merely a thin ring of bone around the shoulder region. The mouth was small but contained strong plates for crushing organisms with a hard protection such as shellfish, crabs and lobsters.

In one ptyctodont, *Rhamphodopsis*, the pelvic region shows a striking dimorphism between the sexes – the males developed special claspers which ensured efficient internal fertilization, as in the living SHARKS and their allies.

In *Ctenurella*, from the Middle Devonian of Germany, the male had well-developed claspers with a short spike of bone just in front of them. This feature together with the long tapering tail and overall proportions are strikingly similar to the living CHIMAERAS. The internal skeleton also exhibits uniquely chimaeran features, such as the peculiar rostral cartilages. L.B.H.

Arthrodires
*Remains of the Lower
Devonian arthrodire* Arctolepis *have been found in Europe,
Spitzbergen and North America.
Length: about 19cm (7.5in)*

Arthropods

Invertebrate animals with jointed legs and an external skeleton that has to be periodically shed as growth proceeds. The three principal constituent phyla comprise the Uniramia (CENTIPEDES AND MILLIPEDES, INSECTS), the Chelicerata (SPIDERS AND SCORPIONS), and the Crustacea (CRABS AND LOBSTERS), with the Trilobita (TRILOBITES) a probable fourth group.

It is likely that the arthropod structure developed, possibly more than once, from a generalized annelid WORM. In the Lower Cambrian such highly developed aquatic animals as the trilobites were already well established, and by the Middle Cambrian numerous types of arthropod had appeared. The invasion of the land by flightless insects and spiders probably occurred at the beginning of the Silurian, although the earliest fossil insect, the springtail *Rhyniella praecursor*, is not found until the Lower Devonian. Flight was acquired during the Carboniferous, and insects later developed in parallel with the evolution of plants.

In the non-marine Devonian are found branchiopods (fairy shrimps, clam shrimps), which lived in fresh or brackish waters. *Cyzicus*

Arthropods
*Beautifully preserved examples
of the Cambrian branchiopod*
Waptia *occur in the Burgess
Shale of British Columbia,
Canada.
Length: about 40mm (1.5in)*

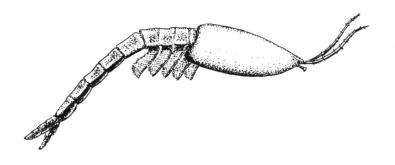

Artiodactyls

ranges from the Lower Devonian to the Recent and becomes sporadically common, especially in beds representing shallow standing water. The branchiopods may have developed from the problematical *Fordilla* that occurs in the Cambrian. OSTRACODS also possibly originated from a *Fordilla*-like animal, but they were already established by the beginning of the Cambrian.

The Chelicerata are largely terrestrial or freshwater animals, so the fossil record of the phylum is sporadic. The earliest chelicerate is the merosome *Palaeomerus* from Sweden; as well as being the oldest xiphosuran (HORSESHOE CRAB) it is also a possible ancestor of the eurypterids (SEA SCORPIONS). The first arachnid, the protoscorpion *Palaeophonus*, occurred in the Lower Silurian and was apparently aquatic. The true scorpions and spiders appeared in the Carboniferous. Five species of mites are present in the Lower Devonian Rhynie Chert, the only other occurrence of fossil mites being in the Oligocene Baltic AMBER.

The Crustacea have their origins in the Cambrian with the Phyllocarida and it is not until the Middle Devonian that the first higher crustaceans (Eumalocostraca) are found. They are *Eocaris* from West Germany and *Devonocaris* from the USA. A hypothetical generalized eumalocostracan termed the

"caridoid facies" is employed in phylogenetic studies and from the caridoid facies it has been inferred that the group was of archaeostracan phyllocarid origin. It is probably from the Eocarida (Devonian to Carboniferous) that the later Decapoda (crabs and lobsters) developed. The earliest recognized decapods are the penaeids of the Permian, but they are rare as fossils because of their thin shells. The thicker-shelled, lobster-like forms appeared in the Triassic and by the end of that period one group, the Pemphicidae, had developed an offshoot in which the abdomen was tucked under the cephalothorax, thus becoming crabs. The earliest true crab is *Eocarcinus praecursor* from the Lower Jurassic of England. Another crustacean group that might be expected to appear frequently in the fossil record is the copepods, but although their biomass in Recent seas would be greater than all the insects, they have only two known fossil occurrences: from the Cretaceous of Brazil and the Miocene of the Mojave Desert of the western USA. · S.F.M.

Artiodactyls

The even-toed ungulates including PIGS, CAMELS, DEER, GIRAFFES and CATTLE. The order Artiodactyla comprises about 500 genera, fossil and living, arranged in 25 families. Only the RODENTS are a larger mammalian order.

Artiodactyls had arisen from CONDYLARTHS by the Early Eocene via the primitive palaeodonts, and their diversity increased through the Cenozoic at the expense of their rivals the PERISSODACTYLS. They have four- or two-hoofed feet, hence their names (paraxonic, even-toed or cloven-hoofed ungulates). Early and non-ruminant artiodactyls, such as pigs, peccaries and hippopotamuses, have short legs and four digits. Advanced types such as antelopes and cattle have long legs and only two digits, the third and fourth carrying all the weight (the lateral digits are extremely reduced or lost). The metapodial bones supporting the two digits fuse to form the cannon bone. In all artiodactyls the astragalus or ankle bone has a double pulley which gives increased forwards and backwards rotation and improves the thrust potential.

The principal feeding problem in herbivores is to break down cellulose (the major constituent of the grass and leaves that they eat) which resists all digestive juices. Mammals rely on bacteria in the gut to accomplish this, and in most herbivores the caecum, a part of the intestine, is the centre of cellulose digestion. In artiodactyls, however, the stomach is enlarged and divided into compartments, enabling food to be rechewed and redigested, a process known as rumination. Ruminant artiodactyls can make efficient use of poor quality vegetation.

Primitive artiodactyls have a complete and unspecialized dentition. During their evolution they tend to reduce and lose the upper incisor teeth, replacing these with a hard pad for cropping. The canine teeth of pigs and hippopotamuses become greatly enlarged, but in most other forms they are reduced and lost. A

Artiodactyls
The forefeet (top row) and hindfeet (bottom row) of representative artiodactyls are shown with the axis of symmetry between the middle toes. They are, left to right, the Pliocene camel Procamelus, *the anthracothere* Bothriodon, *and the palaeomerycid* Blastomeryx.

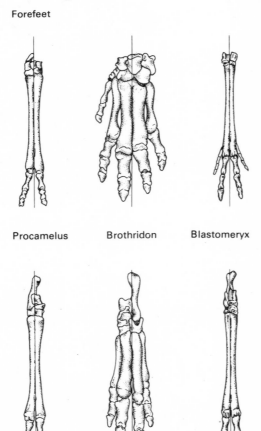

Forefeet

Procamelus   Brothridon   Blastomeryx

Hindfeet

Astrapotheres

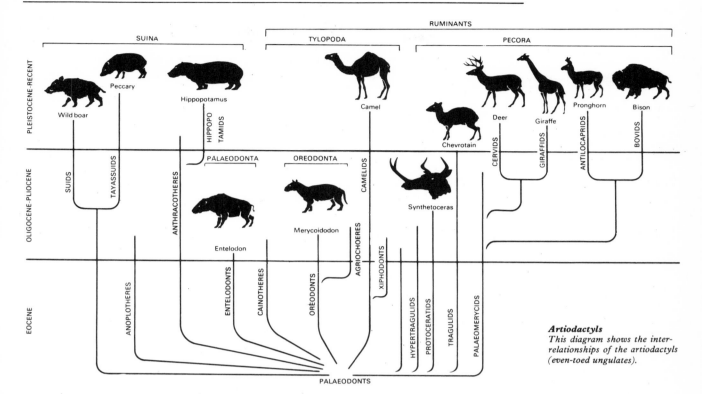

Artiodactyls
This diagram shows the inter-relationships of the artiodactyls (even-toed ungulates).

diastema or gap develops between the cropping incisor teeth and the grinding cheek teeth. Two main types of molar teeth are found: the low-crowned multi-cusped or bunodont teeth of most suines, and the high-crowned crescent-cusped or selenodont teeth of ruminants.

Besides the ancestral palaeodonts in the Eocene and Oligocene of Eurasia and North America, three major divisions are recognized within the artiodactyls.

The suines, with pigs, peccaries, hippopotamuses and the extinct ENTELODONTS and ANTHRACOTHERES, comprise the more primitive, generalized feeders. The tylopods, including camels, the extinct cainotheres (small, slender Eocene and Oligocene forms) and OREODONTS, are mostly browsers feeding on shrubs. The ruminants include deer, giraffes, antelopes and cattle; they are the most specialized and comprise both browsers and grazers.

A distinctive feature of many artiodactyls is the development of bony outgrowths from the forehead or frontal bones. These comprise ossicones in giraffes, antlers in deer and horns in antelopes and cattle.   R.J.G.S.

Astrapotheres

An extinct order (Astrapotheria) of South American ungulates (hoofed mammals). The ill-named *Astrapotherium* (Greek for "lightning beast") first appeared in the Upper Oligocene and was fairly common during the Miocene. It was about 3 metres (10ft) in length and had a long neck to support its short-faced skull. Only two upper and one lower premolar teeth remain (although all the molars are still present), and the upper incisors are entirely absent. The lower incisors, however, project forwards and pre-

sumably functioned against a horny pad situated below the base of a nasal proboscis, and the canines have become projecting tusks resembling those of a hippopotamus. The body is long and slimly proportioned, with the forelimbs apparently terminating in digitigrade, hoofed feet whereas the hindlegs are supported on plantigrade feet in which the second and third digits are much smaller than the first, fourth and fifth.

Astrapotherium was probably semi-aquatic, but its bizarre structure makes it impossible to do more than conjecture on its likely habits. The group did not survive beyond the Miocene. The small *Astrapothericulus*, with poorly developed tusks, was a Lower Miocene form, and *Parastrapotherium* is of Lower Oligocene age. Among Eocene members of the order there is *Astraponotus* (which retained a full complement of premolars) and *Albertogaudrya*. The oldest known genus is *Shecenia* from the Upper Palaeocene.   R.S.

Astrapotheres
Astrapotherium, an extinct South American mammal, existed from the Upper Oligocene to the Lower Miocene. Length: about 2.75m (9ft)

Australian Museum

Australian Museum

Founded in Sydney in 1827, it is concerned with all aspects of natural history except botany. In 1827 Ralph Darling (1775–1858), Governor of New South Wales, received a grant of £200 for the establishment of a museum, although the national museum really dates from 1836 when it was located in a room linked with the Botanic Gardens. It was incorporated by Act of Parliament in 1853. The collections are the oldest and largest in Australia. They include natural history and geological displays. Research and educational activities are also undertaken as major functions. A period of major development for the palaeontological section was during the curatorship of Robert Etheridge Jr. (1847–1920). The Department of Palaeontology is one of 14 scientific departments in the Museum and its exhibition galleries depict the story of life on Earth   A.P.H.

Backbone

Also called vertebral column, one of the principal characteristics of VERTEBRATES. It is generally made up of individual bones, the vertebrae, which articulate with one another.

The backbone is derived from the notochord, a stiff rod of vacuolated cells which is a diagnostic feature of the phylum Chordata, occurring in the life history of all groups in the phylum. The notochord was presumably the first specialized supporting structure that developed in the ancestors of the vertebrates. In primitive fishes, as in the living jawless fishes, the notochord is not restricted, but there are small blocks of cartilage positioned along its length which mark early stages in the development of vertebrae. Among the jawed fishes, both cartilaginous and bony, the notochord becomes severely restricted as the vertebrae develop. The main body of the fish vertebra forms a biconcave spool with the unrestricted notochord between adjacent bones. In the most advanced type of vertebra, such as that found in mammals, the notochord has disappeared and is represented in the adults by the pulpous nucleolus of the intervertebral discs.

The spinal cord runs along the dorsal surface of the notochord and is protected by a bony or cartilaginous neural arch. Dorsal ribs project laterally, separating the main dorsal and ventral muscles of the body. In fishes there is a further set of ventral ribs which surround the body cavity and in the tail join up to form the chevron bones or haemal ribs, so called because they protect the ventral blood vessels of the tail.

The backbone of a fish is subjected to a sideways bending from the action of contracting muscles that throw the body into a series of waves which drive the fish through the water. The arrangement of the swimming muscles ensures that all movement of the backbone is in a lateral direction. In some later bony fishes the notochord was surrounded by a neural arch dorsally and a crescentic bone (the intercentrum) ventrally; in a lateral position between the vertebrae there were two small bones, the true centra. This condition characterized the rhipidistian LOBE-FIN FISHES and led to the structure of the backbone found in the first land vertebrates, the AMPHIBIANS.

In the early amphibian *Ichthyostega*, the vertebral column was essentially that of the lobe-fins, but the neural arches were vertical instead of sloping backwards. At the same time small articulations were developed on the anterior and posterior surfaces of the neural arches, facing upwards anteriorly and downwards posteriorly. These were the zygapophyses and their funcion was to restrict movement of the backbone in a vertical plane while still allowing side-to-side movement.

With the invasion of the land by the vertebrates there were important changes in the backbone. The main part of the vertebra, the intercentrum, gradually underwent reduction at the expense of the true centrum, which became the principal part of the body of the vertebra. This change occurred because the segmental muscles of the body, instead of being attached to a single vertebra, became "resegmented" so that the muscle blocks and the vertebrae were staggered, with the septum between muscle blocks inserted in the middle of a vertebra and not in between them as in fishes.

During the later evolution of the vertebrates, the backbone developed numerous specializations depending on the mode of life of the groups concerned (eg flight in the PTEROSAURS and BIRDS) and there were further specializations among mammals, in which the vertebral column developed clearly demarcated cervical, thoracic, lumbar, sacral and caudal regions.   L.B.H.

Bacteria

Simple, generally ubiquitous, micro-flora. Bacteria may be unicellular and spherical in shape, or consist of an aggregate of filamentous, sometimes branching, clusters of rod-like cells. The individual cells contain no hard parts, may be smaller than one micrometre (39 microinches) in size, and have a primitive structure like certain allied groups of blue-green ALGAE. Chlorophyll is absent.

Bacteria are important constituents of ecosystems. In any food chain they act as a primary agent in the breakdown and chemical alteration of organic matter, and anaerobic bacteria can exist in oxygen-starved environments. Bacteria range from Pre-Cambrian to Recent but their fossil occurrence is often

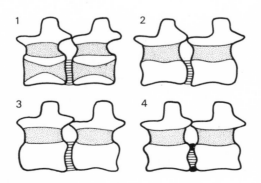

Backbone
In primitive vertebrae (1), the centra (the bodies of the vertebrae) are pierced by a canal for the notochord. Other types of centra include procelous (2), concave at the front, convex at the back; opisthocelous (3), convex at the front, concave at the back; and acelous (4), which has slightly concave faces and an intervertebral disc.

16

inferred rather than real. Anaerobic and iron bacteria are assumed to have been important in the formation of (respectively) euxinic shales and certain iron deposits.

Pre-Cambrian bacteria are of significance in understanding the nature and chronology of the early evolution of life on Earth. Bacteria are procaryotes, ie their cells have no ordered nucleus like that of all higher organisms (eucaryotes). Bacterium-like microbiota present in the Gunflint Iron Formation (1,900 million years old) of Ontario, are among the world's oldest demonstrable fossils. Two of these genera, *Kakabekia* and *Eoastrion*, represent possible budding bacteria, and in addition *Eoastrion* bears a striking morphological similarity to the living manganese-oxidizing bacterium *Metalogenium*, and also to organisms from the 1,600 million-year-old Paradise Creek biota of Queensland. Bacterium-like rods are also known from Early Pre-Cambrian rocks such as the Fig Tree Series in South Africa. Many Recent bacteria are closely similar to fossil forms because the evolution of the group, as with other procaryotes, is slow. J.E.P.W.

Barrande, Joachim (1799–1883)
French pioneer researcher and writer on Palaeozoic stratigraphy and palaeontology. He was born in Sangres, Haute-Loire, and educated in Paris. After his graduation, Barrande was employed by the French Royal Family. After their exile in 1830 he travelled with them, settling finally in Prague, where he lived and worked for the rest of his life. He was an assiduous collector of fossils from the Palaeozoic rocks of central Bohemia and his work is recorded in his 32-volume book *Système Silurien du Centre de la Bohème* (1852–1902; "Silurian System of Central Bohemia"). This book is illustrated with superb drawings and describes more than 4,000 new fossil species; it is still valuable as a reference book.

Although he was a follower of Georges CUVIER, and hence supported the fixity of species principle, the value of his work was that he had undertaken well-organized and detailed collecting. His researches were self-financed and he left funds for the completion of his publication to the Bohemian Museum, which also received his extensive collection. A.P.H.

Bears
Members of the CARNIVORA that descended from the DOG group during the Late Miocene. There are in the Oligocene and Miocene of Europe and North America several beardogs, animals that are either bear-like dogs or dog-like bears. They represent adaptation to omnivorous modes of living and are not on the direct line of ancestry to modern bears. In the Pliocene, however, the genera *Ursavus* and *Agriotherium* come close to true bear ancestry. *Agriotherium* was larger than a Kodiak bear (*Ursus arctos middendorffi*) but retained some dog-like characteristics and although found mostly in Eurasia also occurs in South Africa. It is the only true fossil bear in

Africa, and how it reached the southern tip of the continent remains a mystery.

Modern bears live in North America, the northern parts of South America, Eurasia and until recently in the Atlas Mountains of northern Africa. The Alaskan bear (*Ursus arctos dalli*) is the largest living land carnivore and may weigh 800kg (1,764lb). In the Pleistocene, the cave bear reached about the same size. Dogs and cats stand on their toes, but bears, like man, stand with their heels on the ground. This flat-footedness combined with their heavy build makes bears relatively slow animals, and unlike most carnivores they have short tails. The canine teeth are large, the cheek teeth have lost the normal carnivore specialization for slicing meat and there are instead broad flat multi-cusped molars which resemble those of man and pigs (all three stocks have similarly varied diets comprising meat and vegetables).

Thalarctos, the polar bear, exhibits adaptation to a semi-aquatic life, swimming and fishing in Arctic waters. The genus *Ursus* includes the living brown and black bears of North America and Eurasia; their ancestry can be traced back through the Pleistocene by *Ursus deningeri*, from which in the Late Pleistocene *Ursus arctos*, the brown bear, and *Ursus spelaeus*, the cave bear, were derived. These Late Pleistocene species are abundant and can be distinguished only with difficulty, although the cave bear is usually distinctly larger than the brown bear.

The cave bear is sometimes found in large numbers in cave deposits, and the Drachenhöhle caves in Austria have yielded the remains of about 30,000 individuals. Many of the bones belong to juvenile or old and diseased individuals that failed to survive the winter hibernation. The bears were much hunted by Palaeolithic man and became extinct about the end of Magdalenian times approximately 12,000 years ago.

There is a less detailed record of the Asiatic bears, and their ancestry cannot be traced with certainty. *Tremarctos*, the spectacled bear of northern South America, is distinct from the North American bears and has a few Pleistocene ancestors on the southern continent. *Ailuropoda*, the giant panda of China, is bear-like and probably of the bear family. R.J.G.S.

Bears
Ursus spelaeus, *the massive cave bear of the Pleistocene, was one-third larger than its living relative, the brown bear* (Ursus arctos).
Length: 1.6m (5ft)

Belemnites

Belemnites

The remains of the internal shells of extinct cephalopod MOLLUSCS closely related to modern cuttlefishes that are grouped with them in the subclass Coleoidea. The shell consists of a sub-cylindrical pencil-shaped or flattened rod of prismatic calcite (the guard), made up of concentric growth layers; the back end is pointed whereas the front extremity is gently expanded to ensheathe a chambered phragmocone which is seldom preserved. The chambers (camerae) of the phragmocone are linked by a marginal siphuncle. Sometimes a thin shell-like extension of the guard (pro-ostracum) is preserved. There is evidence that the belemnite animal possessed an ink sac and arms with a series of small phosphatic hooks.

Belemnites are common fossils in marine sediments from the Lower Jurassic to the end of the Cretaceous, but early in the Cenozoic they became extinct. The ancestors of belemnites range back through the Triassic and Permian into the Carboniferous. Belemnites, like AMMONITES, are thought to have originated from a bactritid ancestor, the belemnite structure developing by compression of the length of the chambered phragmocone and the evolution of a rear protective guard.

They are valuable ZONE FOSSILS, particularly in the Cretaceous chalk (*Actinocamax plenus* in the Turonian, *Gonioteuthis quadrata* and *Belemnitella mucronata* in the Senonian). The geographic distribution of various genera during the Jurassic and Cretaceous is latitude controlled (presumably due to mean sea-water temperatures) and geographic boundaries are sharply defined. When the calcite guards have remained chemically unaltered since their burial in the sediment of the sea floor, it is possible to obtain some idea of the sea-water temperature during the growth of the guard by determining the ratio of the oxygen-18 to oxygen-16 isotopes in the calcium carbonate molecules which compose it.

Belemnites apparently formed a major part of the diet of ICHTHYOSAURS. These marine reptiles also took fish, but their fossilized stomachs frequently contain cephalopods.   H.G.O.

Belemnites
The bullet-shaped guard (that part of a belemnite commonly preserved as a fossil) formed the internal skeleton of the pointed rear of the animal.
Approx. 1/3 natural size

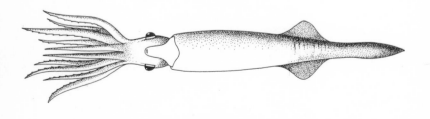

Beringer, Johann (*c*.1667–*c*.1738)

German doctor and lecturer on various topics in natural history, including fossils. Little is known of Beringer but he appears to have spent his whole life at Würzburg, Germany, and was the victim of scheming academic colleagues. He is best remembered for his book *Lithographiæ*

Wirceburgensis (1726) in which he figured a number of "fossils" which had been deliberately planted at his collecting localities. These "Lügensteine" or lying stones as they have become known consisted of shapes in the forms of suns, moons and even Hebrew letters. For many years it was thought that the hoax was no more than a student prank but it was eventually discovered to have been the work of Beringer's academic colleagues who were trying to discredit him. Beringer's credulousness can be accepted, because at that time the true nature of fossils was not clearly understood.   A.P.H.

Biochemistry

In palaeontology, biochemistry is today an established means of studying fossils, but until 1955 it was generally believed that the organic matter of fossils had either completely disappeared, or else been so altered that the biochemistry of fossils could never be examined. In that year, however, fossil bones and shells were digested in acids enabling several amino acids to be extracted and identified. Subsequently research was conducted into the nature of the minute quantities of organic matter in fossils, and the proportions of different amino acids were measured by quantitative analysis.

Such measurements are particularly important because specific proteins can be recognized on amino acid compositional profiles. The fibrous protein collagen, which makes up the organic matrix of teeth and bone, is composed of three polypeptide chains (biochemical molecules) entwined around one another, each comprising a sequence of more than a thousand amino acids. Every third amino acid is glycine and about a quarter of the rest is either proline or hydroxyproline. The amino acid hydroxy-lysine is unique to collagen. The extraction of organic matter with an amino acid compositional profile similar to that of collagen is firm evidence of the survival of protein in the fossil record. Only Pleistocene bones and teeth have given amino acid analyses identical to modern collagen. As earlier material is studied, so the similarities become less evident.

The biochemistry of fossils is beset with problems. The quantity of material available for analysis is invariably minute, the amount of organic matter that can be extracted varying from 1.0–0.00004 per cent by weight. Such small samples are easily contaminated by handling or if left exposed to the elements. Some amino acids (such as cysteine) are characteristic of human finger-prints, and if present they suggest recent contamination. The more usual contamination comes from bacterial proteins that decompose the soft parts of the organism, as well as the organic matrix of the bone or shell being studied, at the time of burial prior to fossilization.

The degree of recent contamination can now be determined by measuring the degree of racemization (change in the proportions of left- and right-handed molecules) of the extracted amino acids. All amino acids except glycine (the simplest) have a right- or left-handed configura-

Birds

tion, and in living organisms only the left (or laevo) form occurs. About 30–40 million years after death the amino acids gradually achieve an equilibrium. If there is more than 50 per cent of laevo forms in fossils older than the Oligocene, it is likely that the sample has been subject to later contamination.

Another problem for palaeobiochemists is the sedimentary environment of the fossils. It is necessary, as a control, to analyse the enclosing sediments to determine the source of the organic matter ostensibly being examined. In some organic-rich deposits such as shales, the amount of some amino acids may be greater than those found in the actual fossils. Similarly, an organic-rich halo around fossils may give some indication of the movement of organic molecules within sediments that are leached out of the fossils. When a fossil is biochemically analysed it is therefore necessary to determine the actual quantity that is preserved, the degree of race-mization and the amino acid content of the enclosing sediment.

With the controls, the differential breakdown of protein in time and under different conditions of burial must be considered. The stability of the protein itself, as well as that of the different amino acids, varies considerably. Hydroxy-proline, which is taken as diagnostic of collagen, is the first to be lost. The study of fossil material reveals new information regarding the stability of particular amino acids. Once all these problems have been satisfactorily resolved, the possibility arises of eventually recognizing evolutionary changes in the collagen molecule. The identification of the sequence of amino acids along the length of a polypeptide chain of collagen was first achieved in 1972, and from such a base even short fragments of fossil protein should be amenable to analysis.

One of the problems of such work is that the extraction of organic matter from fossils involves the breakdown of the material into its component parts, the separate amino acids. Fortunately, techniques which enable the intact protein to be extracted have been developed so that peptide finger-printing can be attempted by breaking down the protein with proteolytic enzymes, which cleave the protein chain at specific loci.

Early peptide analyses of intact fossil collagen produce peptide finger-prints that differ surprisingly from modern collagen. This indicates that changes have occurred in the complete polypeptide chain which are not reflected in the amino acid analyses, nor even in electron microscopy, which shows the characteristic 64 nanometre banding of collagen.

There are other important molecules equally suitable for biochemical studies, in particular carbohydrates such as cellulose and its allies, or even the protein keratin forming the organic matrix of hair and nails, which has been analysed from 40 million-year-old rocks, albeit contaminated by bacterial proteins.

There have been studies on the evolution of proteins through geological history by comparing the amino acid sequences of the same proteins, such as haemoglobin or myoglobins, from one species to another. The differences (which are due to the number of amino acid substitutions) give a measure of changes in the genetic code through time. The only protein which seems to be effectively preserved in the fossil record and is amenable for study is, however, the fibrous protein collagen – hence the concentration on this molecule by palaeobiochemists.　　　　　　　L.B.H.

Birds

Members of the VERTEBRATE class Aves, which are distinguished by the development of feathers, probably from the scales of their reptilian ancestors. The oldest known bird is ARCHAEOPTERYX from the Upper Jurassic. The remains of Cretaceous TOOTHED BIRDS are usually fragmentary and give little indication of their relationship to modern forms. This is unfortunate because by the beginning of the Cenozoic some of the modern orders had evolved, indicating that they must have had their origins in the late Mesozoic.

By the end of the Eocene, half of the approximately 20 recognized orders of living birds were already present. At the same time the Eocene produced its own specialized orders, which were destined to become extinct before the end of the Cenozoic. They included the Odontopterygiformes (long-winged sea birds that had bony tooth-like projections along the

Birds
A comparison of the skeleton of the earliest known bird, Archaeopteryx (left), with the skeleton of a modern bird shows that in living birds the tail vertebrae have become greatly abbreviated and there is a massively developed sternum (breastbone) for the attachment of the flight muscles.

Bivalves

jaws) which occurred in the Lower Eocene of England and the Miocene of New Zealand and North America. Large flightless birds also appeared during the Eocene, with one species, *Diatryma steini*, attaining a height of 2 metres (6.6ft). Apart from its size, the most outstanding feature of *Diatryma* was the large parrot-like bill, which may indicate carnivorous habits, although a bill of this type could also be used for cutting vegetation. A tendency to evolve running forms was also apparent in other orders because *Neocathartes* (a vulture from the Wyoming Eocene) appears to have either scavenged or pursued its prey on foot.

About a quarter of the modern bird families had fossil representatives by the Oligocene, but the most spectacular birds to appear during this period were the New World phororhacids. These cursorial (running) birds were abundant during the Miocene, when *Phororhacos longissimus* reached a height of 2 metres (6.6ft). From the eagle-like bill of this genus there is little doubt that it was a predator, probably feeding upon goat-sized mammals.

In the Miocene the trend towards an increasing proportion of birds with a modern aspect continued, with more than one-third of the forms that were present placed in living genera. The period is best known, however, for its large phororhacids and odontopterygiform sea birds, the latter culminating in *Osteodontornis*, which had an estimated wing span of about 5 metres (16ft) and is the largest known flying bird.

The proportion of modern types continued to increase during the Pliocene until 75 per cent of the avifauna is assignable to living genera, with remains in some instances indistinguishable from those of existing species. Some new forms did evolve, especially among the auks; at least two Californian species of *Mancalla* became flightless with penguin-like flippers.

At the beginning of the Pleistocene, about a quarter of the identifiable birds' remains can be placed in living species; this proportion increased to four-fifths by the end of the period. Many groups, particularly those isolated on islands, produced giant forms, including a giant swan and a vulture from the Mediterranean region, a huge stork from Java, and another comparably large stork from the tar pits of RANCHO LA BREA, which have also yielded the enormous condor-like vulture *Teratornis*, with a wing span of 4.3 metres (14ft).

C.A.W.

Bivalves

Exclusively aquatic MOLLUSCS (pelecypods, lamellibranchs) ranging from the Cambrian to the present day. The shell consists of two laterally compressed valves joined by an elastic, horny ligament along the dorsal margin. Below this there are several hinge-teeth interlocking with corresponding sockets in the other valve.

The valves are held shut by adductor muscles in tension and are opened by the ligament when the adductors are relaxed. The foot protrudes forwards and downwards, and is used for digging and leaping. There is no head or radula. The main function of the gills is to convey suitable food particles, consisting of micro-organisms, to the mouth.

Bivalves are stratigraphically valuable, even though genera may survive for more than 50 million years and species for 10 million years. They are an important source of shell debris for organic limestones, and both oysters and rudists (Hippuritacea) form reef-like accumulations. Most are marine and range from the intertidal zone (the common mussel, *Mytilus*) down to 10,000 metres (32,800ft), but dwell on the continental shelf. They may live just below the surface of the sediment (*Cardium* and *Trigonia*, with short siphons) or they may bury themselves deeply (*Solen* and *Tellina*, with extrudible siphons). Some are rock-borers (*Lithophaga*) and wood-borers (the ship-worm *Teredo*); some stay half-buried (*Pinna*), and others are anchored by byssal threads (*Mytilus*, *Pteria*) or have become sessile and often cemented to the substrate (*Ostrea*, *Spondylus*, *Hippurites*). *Pecten* swims by flapping its valves.

Several groups have invaded fresh water, among them *Archanodon* (from the Devonian OLD RED SANDSTONE), *Carbonicola* (Carboniferous) and *Unio*, the swan-mussel (Triassic – Recent). Interpretation of conditions during the deposition of rocks containing bivalves is therefore often possible, particularly if both valves are still joined, showing that the animal has not been transported elsewhere after death.

The understanding of fossil bivalves and their evolution has been advanced considerably by studies of living animals. Most extinctions within the group are best explained by replacement with more mechanically and biologically efficient forms possessing features such as larger gills and better placed muscles.

Shell features used in classification may also provide clues as to mode of life. These include shape, pattern of hinge-teeth, and the number, size, and position of muscle scars. A pallial sinus and a pronounced posterior gape (as in *Solen* and *Osteomya*) indicate long siphons and an infaunal (buried) habit.

All the major groups were in existence by the end of the Ordovician and can be recognized by their shell structure, the layers of different forms of calcium carbonate crystals occurring in distinctive combinations.

Bivalves
(1) Pterotrigonia *is a cosmopolitan genus of clams that ranged from the Upper Jurassic to the Upper Cretaceous (approx. twice natural size).*
(2) The Ordovician rostroconch Ribeiroidea *(approx. twice natural size).*
(3) Vipricardium, *a genus of cockles that first appeared in the Upper Cretaceous and still exists today (approx. 3/4 natural size).*
(4) Archanodon, *an Upper Devonian–Pennsylvanian bivalve (approx. 1/3 natural size).*

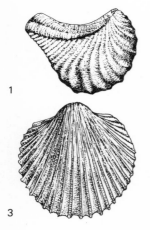

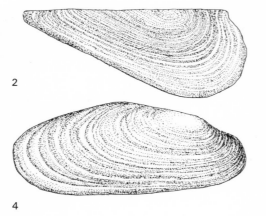

1

2

3

4

Reputedly the earliest known bivalve is *Fordilla troyensis* (Lower Cambrian). Bivalve diversity increased dramatically in the early Cenozoic, and the living fauna is estimated at more than 7,000 species. *Astarte*, from cold northern seas, *Trigonia* (*Neotrigonia*, from Australia), and the rare deep-water *Pholadomya* are survivors of important groups that had a worldwide distribution during the Mesozoic.

C.P.N.

Bone bed

A dense accumulation of fossil organic remains comprising phosphatic nodules, COPROLITES, bones and teeth. Generally the bony material makes up a major proportion of the sediment, hence the name. In a marine environment, the concentration of bones, teeth, fish scales, phosphatic nodules and pebbles is the result of a winnowing action that removes the lighter fraction of the sediment. This occurs at the strand and just offshore as the sea retreats; silt and fine sand are carried away, whereas the coarse debris is left behind and becomes concentrated.

Such a bone bed would, however, be destroyed by the normal processes of erosion with the continued retreat of the sea and its lengthy exposure. The formation of a bone bed in the fossil record depends on a subsequent marine transgression which spreads the debris over a wave-cut platform or into hollows in the uneven surface of the substrate. With the further spread of the sea, the bone bed material would become situated below the level of wave action so that further sedimentation would cover and preserve the deposit.

In Britain the Ludlow Bone Bed marks the base of the Downtonian (Upper Silurian) in the Welsh borderland and comprises coarse sand grains, with the stud-like scales of ACANTHODIANS and the denticles of thelodont agnathans. Similar bone beds with the same fauna occur in the underlying Ludlovian sequence.

The Rhaetic Bone Bed from the European Upper Triassic consists of large fragments of bone, rolled vertebrae, teeth, and limb bones, as well as large coprolites and pebbles. Bone beds that comprise fish teeth and scales characterize certain deposits in the WEALDEN and lower part of the Lower Greensand. In the uppermost Cretaceous of Nigeria there is an extensive bone bed made up of flat fragments from the carapaces of giant turtles and the teeth, scales and vertebrae of sharks and bony fishes.

Other accumulations of bones are also described as bone beds because they consist essentially of bone (eg PIKERMI). Cave deposits often comprise dense accumulations of bones that may be from animals which inhabited the caves and perished there (eg the cave bears of the Pleistocene), or from carcases that were washed down into caves or swallow holes. In the Middle Triassic of Poland there are bone beds in cave- and fissure-infills formed along the coasts of small islands. Pebbles, bones and teeth accumulated on the floors of sea caves and were preserved during the Middle Triassic transgression.

L.B.H.

Boule, Pierre Marcellin (1861–1942)

French palaeontologist who was noted for his studies on human and other mammalian fossils and the geology of French mountains. He was born at Montsalvy, and early in his studies had contact with geologists, anatomists and pre-historians. This blend of subjects in his education is apparent in his later work. In 1903 he became Professor of Palaeontology at the Muséum National d'Histoire Naturelle and Director (1914) of the Institut de Paléontologie Humaine, the first organization devoted to the study of prehistoric man. He set the standard for description in making public the Neanderthal find at La Chapelle-aux-Saints and wrote *Les hommes fossiles*, the first edition of which was published in 1921.

A.P.H.

Brachiopods

A diverse phylum of marine bivalved shellfish with a history extending from the earliest Cambrian to the present day. Usually sessile or attached to objects on the sea bed, brachiopods pass through an embryonic free-swimming stage lasting only a few hours. The soft fleshy parts of their bodies are suspended on a ribbon-like brachidium, or brachial loop, enclosed between two bilaterally symmetrical valves, which are either calcareous or semi-chitinous. The phylum comprises the Inarticulata (with valves held together by strong contractile muscles) and the Articulata (in which the valves are held together by a form of hinge).

The inarticulates are chiefly those genera with chitinophosphatic shells, although there are a few with entirely calcareous valves. The oldest and most primitive members of the phylum are the Lingulida, Acrotretida, Obolellida, Paterinida and Kutorginida. *Lingula* itself has a long, tongue-shaped shell with a strong pedicle or stalk and is the only living brachiopod that inhabits a burrow.

The more diverse Articulata have calcareous shells and can be sub-divided into seven main orders: Orthida, Strophomenida, Pentamerida, Rhynchonellida, Atrypida, Spiriferida and Terebratulida.

Dating from the Lower Cambrian, the Orthida continued to flourish until the Permian. They are characterized by an almost circular outline, a straight hinge-line and a strong ornament of radiating costae (rib-like structures).

The largest order of brachiopods is the Strophomenida, which consists of about 400 genera that range from the Lower Ordovician to the Upper Permian. Characteristically semicircular in outline, they vary from flat-convex to acutely biconvex in lateral profile. Representative genera include *Chonetes*, which has a row of short spines along the hinge-line, and members of the superfamily Productacea, which have long spines covering parts of the ventral valve.

Another order of articulates with an extensive geological range is the Pentamerida, which occurred from the Middle Cambrian to the Upper Permian and have acutely biconvex valves, a short hinge-line, and an incurved umbo (the rear end of the shell). They flourished

Brain

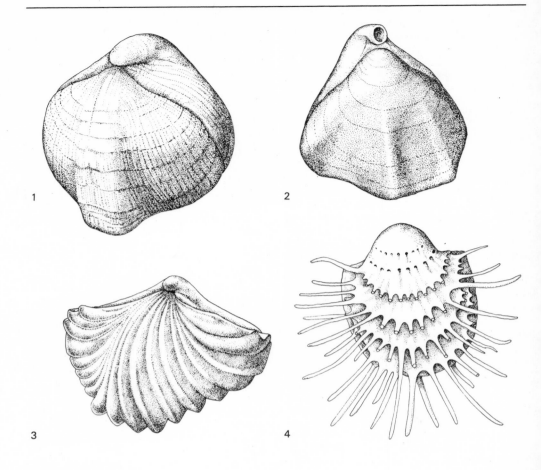

particularly abundant in the Silurian Period.

The Rhynchonellida are usually biconvex, smooth to highly costate, sub-triangular in outline and have a sharp umbo. They are first recorded in the Middle Ordovician and still occur in most oceans today.

The Spiriferida appeared in the Middle Ordovician and became extinct in the Early Jurassic. They are less diverse than most brachiopod orders, having an unmistakable triangular outline with an extensive or elongated hinge-line, strong radiating costae and often a marked median fold in the dorsal valve which is equalled by a sulcus (groove) in the ventral valve.

Possibly the most easily recognizable brachiopods are those represented by the order Terebratulida, from which was derived the now seldom-used term of "lamp shells" – it was thought that they resembled an ancient Roman lamp in lateral profile. This order is well represented in the Lower Devonian and still prospers today, although these conservative forms have changed little in general outline and internal structure during their long history and were probably at their most prolific during the Middle Jurassic. E.F.O.

Brain

In VERTEBRATES, the brain is the swollen anterior end of the hollow spinal cord that is a characteristic feature of the group. In early vertebrates (eg PTERASPIDS), the brain is swollen into three regions. Stimuli pass from the nasal apparatus to the forebrain; from the eyes to the mid-brain; and from the acousticolateralis system (ie hearing and balance) to the hindbrain. The development of extra nervous tissue, especially in the mid-brain and hindbrain, led to the dorsal surface of the tube opening up and the area being covered by vascular tissue, the choroid plexus.

The main association centre of the brain was originally situated in the mid-brain. The forebrain comprised two regions, the anterior (olfactory lobes) and the posterior (with the pineal organ on top and the hypophysis below). In some OSTRACODERMS, the brains are known in great detail because the connective tissues of the interior of the head have been calcified and casts of the brain and cranial nerves can be reconstructed. In the CEPHALASPID brain, there were two large lobes developed in association with the hindbrain – a specialization concerned with the lateral and dorsal sensory fields, which were developments of the acousticolateralis system whereby vibrations are sensed along the body.

Among the fishes, the brain evolved in different directions depending on which sense organs were the more important. For example, the electric fishes developed extra lobes in the hindbrain whereas sharks, with their keen sense of smell, have prominent olfactory lobes.

The major development in the brain came with the move from an aquatic to a terrestrial

Brongniart

environment and was related to the change in emphasis of the different sense organs. The lateral line system for picking up vibrations along the body in the water becomes redundant on land, although an acute sense of hearing is of considerable survival value. Sight remains an important sense, but the sense of smell among the early land vertebrates seems to have been predominant. To recognize substances diluted in air, as opposed to water, requires an enormously augmented sensitivity and, in consequence, there was an increase in the development of the olfactory organs. Even more significant was the shift of association centres to the forebrain. In reptiles, the roof of the mid-brain and the cerebral hemispheres are both equally important as association centres, but with further advances to the birds and mammals, the cerebral hemispheres virtually take over this role. In mammals, the part of the cerebral hemispheres that are concerned with learning develop still further as intelligence increases. This is achieved by a complicated infolding causing more of the outer neopallium to pack into a restricted volume.

With the gradual improvement in gait and posture of land vertebrates, there was a marked improvement in the sense of balance and muscular co-ordination, particularly among members of the group that took to the air. This is reflected in the enormous increase in the cerebellum which, in primitive vertebrates, was only a bundle of nerve fibres at the front margin of the hindbrain. The posterior part of the hindbrain (the brain stem or medulla oblongata) has changed little throughout the history of the vertebrates and controls processes such as respiration, digestion and touch. L.B.H.

Branchiosaurs

Larval or neotenous LABYRINTHODONTS. At the end of the 19th century, a number of small AMPHIBIANS were discovered in Early Permian lake deposits at localities in Germany, Poland, Czechoslovakia and France. These forms were distinguished by: skulls in which some bones were not developed; vertebrae consisting of bilaterally paired, leaf-like neural arches (with little or no development of the vertebral body or centrum); and frequently internal gill bars or even external tadpole-like gills. They were all at first thought to be tadpoles, but one form was known as a growth series in which the larger individuals lost their gills. All these so-called branchiosaurs were therefore placed in a group, the Phyllospondyli (leaf vertebrae), close to but separate from the main assemblage of fossil amphibians, the labyrinthodonts. Subsequently, many small amphibians from Late Carboniferous and Early Permian lake deposits were attributed to the Phyllospondyli.

In 1939, however, A. S. ROMER pointed out that the known tadpoles of labyrinthodonts were indistinguishable from branchiosaurs and that the characteristic skull features of the ANTHRACOSAURS and the temnospondyl labyrinthodonts could be seen in such familiar branchiosaurs as (respectively) Discosauriscus

(see PERMIAN), from the Lower Permian near Prague, and Amphibamus, from the Upper Carboniferous of the USA. Neoteny is well known in living salamanders, some species retaining larval (tadpole) features into the breeding stage. Many branchiosaurs, such as Amphibamus, have subsequently been discovered in the adult condition.

Most described branchiosaurs are now known to metamorphose into small aquatic labyrinthodonts, but members of the genus Branchiosaurus, from the Upper Carboniferous and Lower Permian of Europe (particularly France, Germany and Czechoslovakia) are truly neotenous. This genus always exhibits signs of gill bars (and, when well preserved, external gills), and is comparable to the living axolotl, popular with aquarists, which retains its external gills into the adult stage. A.L.P.

Brea, see RANCHO LA BREA.

British Museum (Natural History)

Founded in London in 1753. The Mineralogy and Geology Departments date from 1857, the latter changing its title in 1956 to the Department of Palaeontology, from which the Department of Anthropology was formed in 1959. In 1881 a new building, the British Museum (Natural History), was opened in South Kensington and in 1963 it became independent of the British Museum.

The Department of Palaeontology is one of five scientific departments in the Museum and its collections now comprise more than seven million specimens. It has two separate but closely interrelated responsibilities: to conserve, curate and enhance the national collections; and to research these collections. In 1977 the Department moved into purpose-built accommodation offering 10,000sq metres (107,640sq ft) of floor area. A.P.H.

Brongniart, Adolphe (1801–76)

French botanist who is often credited as one of the founders of the science of palaeobotany. He was born in Paris, and was the son of a noted geologist, Alexandre Brongniart (1770–1847). He initially studied medicine but became interested in fossil and Recent plants. It was this mixture of studies on the Recent and fossil flora which gave his work such originality. In 1822 he provided the first review of all the fossil plants then known; his other major works are *Prodrome d'une histoire des Végétaux Fossiles* (1828) and *Histoire des Végétaux Fossiles* (1837). Although a supporter of Georges CUVIER's theory of the fixity of species he believed, correctly, that the fossil record of plants showed a gradual development and increasing complexity in succeeding geological eras. He received many honours and in 1838 he was appointed Professor of Botany at the MUSÉUM NATIONAL D'HISTOIRE NATURELLE. In 1852 he was appointed General Inspector of the University of France. A.P.H.

Bronn

Bronn, Heinrich Georg (1800–62)
German palaeontologist and geologist who established the foundations of stratigraphical palaeontology in Germany and wrote several major palaeontological reference works. He was born in Heidelberg, a city with which he was associated all his life. He studied natural science and, after graduating, travelled in Italy and the south of France, returning to Heidelberg as Professor of Natural Science in 1833. His major contributions to palaeontology were *Lethaea Geognostica* (1835–38), which provided a chronological sequence of fossil organisms, and the *Index Palaeontologicus* (1843). Towards the end of his life he was active in preparing the first sections of *Die Klassen und Ordnungen des Thier-reichs, wissenschaftlich dargestellt in Wort und Bild*, which provided a systematic review of living and fossil animals. He contributed to the theory of evolution and translated *The Origin of Species* into German at the request of Charles DARWIN.   A.P.H.

Brontotheres

An extinct group of horned PERISSODACTYLS that attained huge proportions and were numerous in North America and Eurasia during the Eocene and Oligocene. Although they existed for only about 15 million years, about 40 genera of brontotheres have been described, North America apparently being the centre of their evolution. During that time, they increased dramatically in size: *Eotitanops*, from the Early Eocene, stood about 45cm (18in) at the shoulder, whereas *Brontops* from the Early Oligocene was 2.5 metres (8ft) tall and *Brontotherium* stood as tall at the shoulder as an African elephant.

In early brontotheres the legs were short, but as body size increased they lengthened and straightened, developing heavy, elephant-like feet. The hindfoot had three toes, with four digits present on the front foot. Brontothere

Brontotheres
Brontotherium, *an Oligocene brontothere from North America, was 2.5m (8ft) tall at the shoulder.*

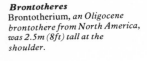

teeth, although impressively large, remained unspecialized throughout the history of their evolution. Incisor and anterior premolar teeth are sometimes reduced in number, and the posterior premolars became molarized. The molars themselves are large, squarish teeth, always low-crowned and with a thick enamel covering. The upper molars are bunolophodont, ie they have a W-pattern formed by the outer cusps, whereas the two inner cusps are low and rounded. The lower molars have two crescents, resembling the teeth of rhinoceroses.

The most characteristic feature of brontotheres, apart from their huge size, is the appearance of paired horns on the top of the nose. Early genera had no horns, but later a pair of smooth bony protuberances appeared at the naso-frontal suture. By the Late Eocene, however, these had evolved into a pair of strong blunt horns.

The horns are true bony outgrowths of the naso-frontal elements and there appears to be no new centre of ossification, nor is there any trace of blood vessels, so they are significantly different from the horns of rhinoceroses. In life the brontothere horn was probably covered with thickened epidermis as in giraffes, rather than with a horny sheath such as is found in CATTLE and antelopes. In the earlier genera, horns (when present) appear to be equally developed in males and females, but later forms have larger horns in the males than in the females.

Brontotheres probably lived like rhinoceroses, browsing on the open plains. In the Eocene and Oligocene there were no grassy prairies and their teeth appear not to have been able to cope with tough vegetation. The horns might have been used for defence against attacks from CREODONT carnivores, but were probably used principally in sparring matches between males. Brontothere origins can be traced back to phenacodont CONDYLARTHS, close to the animals from which the HORSES arose. An adequate explanation for their sudden extinction in the Oligocene after a swift rise to dominance is lacking.   R.J.G.S.

Broom, Robert (1866–1951)

South African palaeontologist and morphologist (born in Paisley, Scotland) who elucidated the origin of mammals and excavated the famous australopithecine sites of South Africa. He acquired an interest in natural history early in life and was initially much concerned with botany and marine biology. He graduated in medicine at Glasgow University and went to Australia (1892) and then to South Africa (1897) where he lived for the rest of his life. He practised medicine (1903–10) and was Professor of Zoology and Geology at Stellenbosch University. From 1934 he was Curator of Palaeontology at the Transvaal Museum. His medical background was particularly valuable in his researches on the MAMMAL-LIKE REPTILES and the origin of mammals. He worked on the classification of the reptiles of the KARROO SYSTEM and was associated with the finds of australopithecines at Sterkfontein, Kromdraai and Swartkrans.   A.P.H.

Burgess shale

Bryozoans

Small sessile polypoid INVERTEBRATES that live in colonies. Each individual, called a zooid, is extremely small, usually less than 1mm (0.04in) long and occupies its own hard calcareous or horny case. Although colonies produced by asexual budding may reach 2 metres (6.6ft) in diameter most living and fossil bryozoans are small. The zooid has a separate mouth and anus adjacent on the oral surface which are connected by a U-shaped alimentary canal. A circular or crescentic lophophore bearing a series of slender, ciliated tentacles surrounds the mouth. In the possession of a lophophore, the Bryozoa are similar to BRACHIOPODS and phoronid WORMS, and these three phyla are thought to be closely related.

Nearly all bryozoans are marine but one small class, the Phylactolaemata, inhabit fresh water; members of this class have no calcified parts and are not known as fossils. Two other large classes have calcified, or partly calcified, zooecial walls and occur abundantly in the fossil record. The Stenolaemata have cylindrical zooecia, as in *Stomatopora*, *Multisparsa* and *Fenestella*, whereas the Gymnolaemata have more box-like zooecia like those of *Flustra*, *Leptocheilopora* and *Myriapora*. Some bryozoans, particularly gymnolaemates, show zooidal polymorphism, with small specialized zooids having a protective function interspersed among normal zooids. Also, occasional zooecia may be expanded wholly (*Multisparsa*) or in part (*Leptocheilopora*) to form an ovicell for brooding the young. Bryozoan colonies show a wide range of growth forms.

The first definite bryozoan is known from the Lower Ordovician and Stenolaemata and Gymnolaemata appear during this period. Stenolaemata rapidly diversified to dominate the Palaeozoic bryozoan fauna, *Fenestella* being a characteristic genus of the later Palaeozoic. Only one order of stenolaemates survived the faunal crisis of the Permo-Triassic to flourish in the Mesozoic and Cenozoic, but this group, the Cyclostomata, includes *Stomatopora* and *Multisparsa* and has some living representatives. Gymnolaemates, represented by one order only, remained insignificant during the Palaeozoic and early Mesozoic, only rising to dominance with the evolution of a second order, the Cheilostomata, in the Cretaceous. The rapid diversification of the cheilostomes, which include *Flustra*, *Leptocheilopora* and *Myriapora*, corresponded to (and was probably responsible for) the decline in the cyclostomes. Cheilostomes are dominant in modern bryozoan faunas.　　　　C.T.S.

Buckland, William (1784–1856)

British geologist and theologian who promoted geology as a science and contributed to Pleistocene palaeontology. He was born in Axminster, Devon, and was the son of a minister of religion; Buckland was himself educated in theology at Oxford. Although an active member of the clergy, becoming Dean of Westminster in 1845, he had a life-long interest in geology, being first Reader in Mineralogy and later

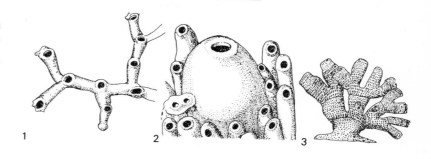

Reader in Geology at Oxford University. His major work was *Reliquiae Diluvianae* (or *observations on the organic remains contained in caves, fissures and diluvial gravel and on other phenomena attesting to the action of a universal deluge*) (1823). A supporter of Georges CUVIER's theory of catastrophes, Buckland was active in the promotion of geology, being President of the Geological Society of London (1824–26 and 1839–41) and President of the British Association for the Advancement of Science (1832). He described the dinosaur *Megalosaurus* in 1824.　　A.P.H.

Buffon, Georges, Comte de (1707–88)

Eminent natural scientist, born in Montbard, France, of noble parents. From an early age he was interested in the natural sciences, especially mathematics. His major work is the *Histoire Naturelle* in 44 volumes, published between 1749 and 1804, which covers the field of natural history. An examination of the contents shows the developments and changes in Buffon's ideas as he fought to establish valid laws for the natural sciences. Buffon's contribution to palaeontology is demonstrated by the *Théorie de la Terre* (1749) and *Epoques de la Nature* (1778) which is important to the theory of evolution. These show clearly that he believed in the succession of fauna and flora in periods which extended farther back than the theologians of the time would accept.　　A.P.H.

Burgess shale

A Middle Cambrian fine siltstone mudstone, light brown or fawn in colour, which outcrops on Mount Stephen in British Columbia, Canada. At one particular horizon in this deposit, numerous exceptionally well-preserved fossils occur, including an enormous variety of ARTHROPODS with all their appendages, gills, walking limbs and antennae remaining intact. Even more dramatic were the numerous soft-bodied marine animals preserved as carbonaceous films (groups of marine WORMS that are living today but are known as fossils only from the Burgess Shale). The modern onychophoran *Peripatus* found in tropical forests had its marine forerunner *Aysheaia* preserved in this deposit. There are also many worms such as *Oesia*, with a large proboscis as well as bristles, which have been preserved completely with even

Bryozoans
(1) Stromatopora *is a genus that first appeared in the Oligocene and is still living today (enlarged).*
(2) Multisparsa *occurs in the Middle Jurassic of France (approx. 20 times natural size).*
(3) The Zoarium of Multisparsa *is depicted here at natural size.*

Cambrian

Upper	Croixian	Shidertinian
		Tuorian
Middle	Albertan	Mayan
		Amgan
		Lenan
Lower	Waucoban	Aldanian

570 million years ago
The Cambrian succession

the intestine and the annelid segmentation. ECHINODERMS were represented by holothurians.

The Burgess Shale gives a glimpse of the tremendous radiation of arthropods and worms that had already occurred by the Middle Cambrian of which there was previously not the slightest hint. Until this discovery there was no way of knowing when many living groups of INVERTEBRATE arose because no fossil record could have been anticipated. In fact special conditions of deposition must have been responsible for the unique type of preservation seen in the Burgess Shale.

It seems probable that the deposit accumulated near the edge of a submarine cliff, with only fine muds drifting down to accumulate on the bottom. Moreover, the water at such depths was devoid of oxygen and there was no scavenging bottom fauna to disturb the remains of any organism that came to rest. Slow bacterial action would have reduced the organic matter to a remanent carbon film.   L.B.H.

Cambrian

The oldest geological period of the PALAEOZOIC Era. Its name is derived from Cambria, the Roman name for Wales, but although originally recognized in northern Wales the rocks of the Cambrian Period are known from all the major continental regions, including Antarctica.

The Cambrian began about 570 million years ago and lasted for about 70 million years. The exact position of the base of the Cambrian system is uncertain, although it appears likely that it will eventually be fixed at a level corresponding to the first major influx of fossils with hard mineralized skeletons. The disposition of the continental areas, epicontinental seas and

the oceans during the Cambrian are not known in detail, but it is probable that the North American and Baltic cratons were separated by an oceanic region (variously termed the Proto-Atlantic, Iapetus Ocean or Caledonide Ocean) just as they are separated today by the Atlantic Ocean. Other Cambrian cratonic areas were centred on the Siberian and south-east Asian (China-Korea) shields, together with GONDWANALAND (composed essentially of Africa, South America, greater India, Australia, Antarctica and probably parts of southern Europe). The positions of these regions on the Earth's surface are speculative, but meagre palaeomagnetic evidence and some general palaeoclimatic information suggest a south magnetic pole in north-western Africa and few (if any) areas of shallow marine deposition north of the tropics, giving an enormous Northern Hemisphere oceanic region.

Little is known of detailed climatic conditions in Cambrian times, but it must have been significantly warmer than that prevailing during the preceding Late PRE-CAMBRIAN glaciation. Widespread occurrences of limestone and evaporite sequences also indicate a warm climate over large areas, and by the beginning of the Cambrian a significant amount of oxygen was present in the atmosphere for the first time.

The most dramatic feature of the life at this time was the relatively sudden appearance early in the period of a great variety of metazoan forms possessing hard mineralized skeletons. It has been suggested that this enormous evolutionary advance was linked to a critical level of atmospheric oxygen being attained.

Compared with the meagre evidence of life (especially of metazoan life) in the Late Pre-Cambrian, the Early Cambrian yields a remarkably diverse fauna. More than 900 species are known: all are marine, and the dominant forms are unquestionably TRILOBITES. The earliest Cambrian (Tommotian) fauna, however, is composed of a variety of small, mainly phosphatic-shelled organisms. Many are of unknown affinity but they include the earliest MOLLUSCS (monoplacophorans and GASTROPODS) and the enigmatic hyolithids.

The Early Cambrian has also yielded the problematical *Fordilla*, and in the Late Cambrian the first cephalopod, *Plectronoceras*, occurs. ARCHAEOCYATHINES were present initially, but became extinct at the end of the Middle Cambrian. Archaeocyathid faunas are especially well developed in the carbonate sequences of North America, Australia and the USSR, but by the succeeding Atdabanian times the trilobites appeared and rapidly became dominant. The phosphatic-shelled, inarticulate BRACHIOPODS are the other major element of Cambrian faunas, with lingulids and obolellids predominating.

All the living phyla that possess hard parts, except the BRYOZOANS, have Cambrian representatives; there is even evidence of early vertebrates (PTERASPIDS). A great variety of "experimental" ECHINODERMS are known, including helicoplacoids and edrioasteroids, some of which became extinct by the end of the

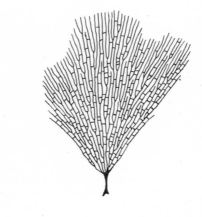

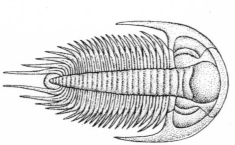

Cambrian
Above: the dendroid graptolite Dictyonema *(showing its attachment process) occurred in the Upper Cambrian. This genus survived until the Lower Carboniferous and had an almost worldwide distribution (natural size).*
Below: Paradoxides *is a trilobite from the Middle Cambrian. Length: 14cm (5.5in)*

Camels

period; many of these early forms do not show the pentameral symmetry characteristic of later types. The earliest known GRAPTOLITES occur in the Middle Cambrian of the USSR and elsewhere, and belong to the sessile Dendroidea; the oldest CORALS also occur in Cambrian rocks.

CONODONTS first appear as rare elements of the microfauna of the Cambrian and consist of simple cone-shaped objects. Other micro-organisms of the period include the earliest FORAMINIFERANS and possibly some OSTRACODS. Acritarchs form the major element of the microflora and are best known from rocks of Late Cambrian age, but other plant life is essentially limited to ALGAE.

The Middle Cambrian fauna from the BURGESS SHALE in the southern Canadian Rockies is uniquely well preserved and contains representatives of most groups of fossils known from other Cambrian faunas as well as numerous forms not known elsewhere, including many soft-bodied organisms. Particularly abundant are the non-trilobite arthropods such as *Marrella*, *Waptia*, *Burgessia* and *Canadaspis*. These have traditionally been placed in the Trilobitoidea, but may represent distinct groups not closely related to each other and generally not attributable to living arthropod assemblages. Of the trilobites present, *Olenoides serratus* is important because it provides detailed information on the appendages of Cambrian trilobites. Much of what is known of Cambrian WORMS and SPONGES has been culled from this fauna: there are priapulid, polychaete and possibly nemertine worms and a variety of sponges, including the glass-sponge *Vauxia*. Also present are monoplacophoran and possible aplacophoran molluscs, rare eocrinoids and early CRINOIDS. COELENTERATES are represented by hydroid and medusoid forms, and a lophophorate (*Odontogriphus*) has been recognized which may be a conodontophorid. Possible protochordates and hemichordates are also known. Many other forms from the Burgess Shale cannot be related to any living phyla and probably represent early metazoan experiments which, like the archaeocyathids of the Early Cambrian, failed to achieve a lasting foothold.

See also the time chart.   C.P.H.

Camels

A superfamily (Cameloidea) of ruminant ARTIODACTYLS, represented today by the dromedary, the bactrian camel, and the South American llamas and vicuñas.

Camels have evolved many unique adaptations to extreme temperatures. In winter they can live for months without water and, when dehydrated, they may lose 25 per cent of their body weight, which can be replaced in about ten minutes. Camels allow their body temperature to rise to 41°C (106°F) before sweating freely, and their blood volume does not change on dehydration. Their urine, furthermore, is concentrated, and their thick fur acts as insulation to prevent heat penetrating or leaving the body; however, by concentrating fat in the hump there is improved heat outflow from the body.

Camels have three-chambered stomachs and they chew the cud. Their upper incisor teeth are reduced to one pair and the molar teeth are crescentic (selenodont), high-crowned for chewing tough vegetation. Their padded feet enable them to traverse soft terrain.

North America was the centre of camel evolution throughout the Cenozoic and they did not invade South America, Eurasia and Africa until Plio-Pleistocene times. *Poëbrotherium* is an Oligocene camel (about the size of a sheep) which still had short legs, hoofs and a complete dentition. In the succeeding Miocene, several separate lineages of camels evolved. There were small, lightly built gazelle-like camels such as *Stenomylus*, giraffe-like camels such as *Oxydactylus* with extremely long necks, and there was *Procamelus* on the main path of camel evolution. *Camelops*, the last camel in North America, survived into post-Pleistocene times and disappeared only a few thousand years ago; it was probably a one-humped camel, but possessed some affinities with the llamas.

Camels
The long-necked Alticamelus, *from the Miocene and Pliocene of North America, was evidently a browsing animal that fed on leaves and branches of trees. Height of head above ground: about 3m (10ft)*

Canadian Nat. Mus.

Camels
Camelops, *from the North American Pleistocene, displayed a mixture of camel-like and llama-like features.*
Height: about 2m (6.6ft) at shoulder

There is no record of camels in South America before the Pleistocene, but they have successfully adapted themselves there to the most rigorous conditions, with vicuñas living on the high Andean plains at 5,750 metres (18,860ft). In the Old World, camels are known in the wild only in Asia but they occur as Pleistocene fossils in Europe and eastern Africa. The camel that is found everywhere in the Sahara is a human introduction.

Two other extinct families of mammals grouped with camels are the OREODONTS and the cainotheres. In the European Oligocene, cainotheres were abundant. They were small and rabbit-like with long hindlegs that would have enabled them to bound along. R.J.G.S.

Canadian National Museum of Natural Sciences

One of the museums in Ottawa forming the National Museums of Canada, which were established by Act of Parliament in 1968. The early history of the national museum is inextricably linked with the Geological Survey (field work and research have always been prominent museum activities). In 1920 the Museum was administratively separated from the Survey, although by that time it had become the Victoria Memorial Museum. In 1927 it became the National Museum of Canada. The work of the Museum is centred on the collections and displays, and it has a grant to conduct research and publish the results. The collections are rich in fossils, and the exhibition galleries include mounted dinosaur skeletons and the reconstruction of an ancient forest. A.P.H.

Carboniferous

The geological period during which most of the world's productive coal deposits were laid down. It includes the MISSISSIPPIAN and PENNSYLVANIAN,

and began about 345 million years ago, lasting for 65 million years. Carboniferous rocks are found on all continents, and in some countries (such as Ireland) they form a high proportion of the surface solid geology.

During Carboniferous times the crustal plates forming the continents were mostly clustered in the Southern Hemisphere, with the Carboniferous equator passing through North America, southern Greenland, Europe and eastwards to the north of Australia. South America, Africa, greater India, Australia and Antarctica were grouped together, with the south pole positioned somewhere near the present site of Buenos Aires. This grouping, known as GONDWANALAND, persisted from the Devonian to the following Permian. The uniform, equable climate of the DEVONIAN became increasingly differentiated so that by the Late Carboniferous a large south polar ice cap had developed, influencing sedimentation and the biology of all five southern continents.

In equatorial and northern regions the Proto-Atlantic and the ocean extending eastwards from southern Europe were closing as a result of drift towards the Mediterranean and north African regions by the North American plus European plate. This continental plate movement led to the contortion, folding and faulting of Upper Palaeozoic rocks in southern and central Europe, eastern North America and northern Africa in a tectonic episode called the Hercynian (or Variscan) orogeny, the main force of which came late in the Carboniferous.

Not only were sedimentary rocks contorted into mountain ranges, the eroded roots of which can be seen across Europe from southern Ireland to Bohemia, but volcanic activity broke out as lava extrusions and the intrusion of granites, such as those of south-western England. Late Palaeozoic rocks involved in the Hercynian orogeny are found across Asia in the mountains bordering the Himalayas and Tibet to the north. Earth movements during the Carboniferous also folded rocks of the Cordilleras in the western USA. Some of the effects of this orogeny have been masked by the more recent Alpine orogeny, affecting similar areas of the world, but starting only about 20 million years ago.

Early in the Carboniferous many land areas, especially those in the Northern Hemisphere, became inundated by warm shallow seas supporting abundant plant life, invertebrates and fishes. The only vertebrates other than fishes were small amphibians which had first left their entirely aquatic environment in the Late Devonian. The seas spread to western Europe and northern Africa, into the western USSR, and extended eastwards to China, the Malay peninsula and the fringes of Australia. Most of South America remained land, but North America (the interior especially) was covered by transgressing and regressing seas. The widespread warmth of the sea is indicated by the similar invertebrates found in widely separated regions, and particularly by the CORALS occurring in Early Carboniferous rocks from Arctic regions to the tropics; today their descendants are limited to tropical waters.

280 million years ago

Upper	Pennsylvanian	Stephanian		Coal Measures
Middle	Pennsylvanian	Westphalian		Coal Measures
Lower	Mississippian	Namurian	Millstone Grit	
Lower	Mississippian	Visean		Avonian (Culm)
Lower	Mississippian	Tournaisian		Avonian (Culm)

345 million years ago
The Carboniferous succession

28

Eventually some of the seas became shallower, such as those of north-western Europe and parts of North America, and received much land-derived sediment. In these areas coastal lakes and lagoons developed which supported forest swamps over sufficiently long periods for the rotting vegetation to collect and turn into peat. Later, deep burial converted the peat into coal. While the coal forests (see FOSSIL FUELS) of the Northern Hemisphere flourished in warm tropical conditions, the southern continents of Gondwanaland were cooling, and by the Late Carboniferous a glaciation was spreading over much of them. The glacial conditions continued into the PERMIAN and resulted in the evolution of a distinctive southern flora and fauna.

An increasingly diverse and impressive vegetation was evolving, and Carboniferous forests contained HORSETAILS more than 15 metres (50ft) tall, and scale-trees (lycopods) from which modern CLUB MOSSES have evolved. Within this vegetation were to be found INSECTS (eg cockroaches) and various arachnids, and by later Carboniferous times winged insects such as dragonflies were feeding on other insects and plants. In addition some pulmonate snails and myriapods had colonized dry land. The humid forests of the Late Carboniferous also sheltered LABYRINTHODONTS, the first vertebrates to crawl on to the land and at that time the highest form of vertebrate evolution. Towards the end of the period primitive REPTILES had evolved; they were the first completely terrestrial vertebrates.

In the pools and streams of the coal forests swam LOBE-FIN FISHES (from which the amphibians had evolved in the Devonian), COELACANTHS and LUNGFISHES. In the Carboniferous seas, SHARKS (looking much like their descendants) were common and PALAEONISCIDS, which led to modern bony fishes, had appeared.

The most abundant and diverse fossils found in rocks originating in the Carboniferous seas are invertebrates, and some Carboniferous limestones are composed almost entirely of the skeletal remains of organisms such as CRINOIDS, CORALS or BRACHIOPODS. Many Carboniferous marine organisms were benthic, ie they lived on or in the sea-floor sediment. Thus the nature of the sea floor was important to support the types of organisms that lived there. Whereas corals, most brachiopods, GASTROPODS and many BIVALVES required hard surfaces on which to live (shelly debris or the fronds of marine algae), other bivalves, some BRYOZOANS and TRILOBITES required or could tolerate entirely soft sediments. In addition to these organisms, SEA URCHINS, blastoids, goniatites (see AMMONITES), OSTRACODS, FORAMINIFERANS and CONODONTS were relatively common Carboniferous fossils.

Of the Foraminifera, the Endothyracea are particularly valuable stratigraphically because of their rapid evolution, especially the archaedicids in the Lower Carboniferous, with the fusulinids becoming important later in the period. Ostracods became diverse and are of stratigraphical significance, but the trilobites waned and finally became extinct in the Permian. Among the molluscs, the bivalves and gastropods were common, but of little value in age determination, other than in the Coal Measures where non-marine bivalves are useful in the correlation of particular coal seams. The cephalopods, however, represented by goniatites, are used widely in Middle and Late Carboniferous stratigraphy.

One of the most characteristic groups of Carboniferous animals is the brachiopods, with the spinose productids evolving into some particularly bizarre forms, especially those living in warm-water reef environments. Their widespread distribution and evolutionary radiation make them useful stratigraphical fossils for most marine sedimentary rocks. Corals are also used extensively for correlations, but because most were confined to tropical seas they are of restricted value.

In many parts of the world the close of the period saw the Carboniferous seas diminishing as tectonic activity raised areas of the older sea floor into mountain chains, heralding the continental conditions that typified some areas during the Permian. Elsewhere, however, such as western North America and the western USSR, marine conditions persisted into the Permian.

See also the time chart.   H.C.H.B.

Carnivora

An order of carnivorous placental mammals that is divided into two suborders: the Fissipedia and the Pinnipedia.

The fissipede assemblage comprises the Arctoidea (DOGS, wolves, BEARS, WEASELS AND STOATS) and the Aeluroidea (CATS, SABRE-TOOTHED CATS, HYAENAS, CIVETS). Both these infra-orders trace their descent to a common origin among the miacids, a group of small, slender, long-tailed Palaeocene-Eocene carnivores that lived in forests and were probably tree-dwelling, because in the forefeet and the hindfeet the first toe was opposable.

Miacis occurs in the Eocene of North America, Europe and Asia. *Viverravus* was comparably widely distributed, and the North American Eocene has yielded the remains of various other genera. *Ictidopappus*, *Simpsonictis* and *Didymictis* were Palaeocene examples of the group, and the family apparently represents the first divergence of the Carnivora from the basic mammalian stock (the INSECTIVORA).

The other suborder of the Carnivora, the Pinnipedia (seals, walruses, sea lions), can be traced back only as far as the Miocene, with one Lower Pliocene genus from western Siberia (*Semantor*) apparently retaining a long tail and limbs still suitable for walking. The pinnipedes may be miacid descendants, or perhaps originated from early primitive fissipedes that adopted a semi-aquatic life.   R.S.

Carnosaurs

Powerful bipedal SAURISCHIAN flesh-eating DINOSAURS, which include the largest terrestrial carnivores that ever lived. They evidently existed in the Late Triassic but, like the

Carnosaurs (cont'd)

COELUROSAURS, were probably upland forms whose carcases rarely became fossilized. In consequence most of the early carnosaurs (Palaeosauriscidae) are known only from fragmentary bones and isolated serrated teeth: for example *Palaeosauriscus* and *Teratosaurus* in Europe, *Staurikosaurus* and *Herrerasaurus* in South America, *Basutodon* in South Africa, and *Zatomus* in North America.

By the Early Jurassic the more advanced Megalosauridae had appeared with high, narrow skulls and massive three-toed feet in which the first digit was either retroverted or absent. The forelimbs were still long, but these reptiles were fully bipedal. The two inner digits of the "hand" were retained (although reduced), and the outer digits were long and slender.

The poorly known Lower Jurassic megalosaurids were of moderate size and lightly built (eg *Sarcosaurus*), but by the Middle Jurassic a few more massive types were in existence, including *Megalosaurus* itself, *Iliosuchus*, and *Proceratosaurus* (with a horn on its snout). Some later megalosaurs attained huge dimensions, with *Antrodemus* (also known as *Allosaurus*) from the North American MORRISON FORMATION apparently growing to about 12 metres (40ft). Most of the Upper Jurassic forms were about 6–10 metres (20–33ft) long, however, and included *Eustreptospondylus* from Europe, *Ceratosaurus* (another horned genus), and the relatively small *Marshosaurus*, 5 metres (16.4ft) long.

Megalosaurids were still present in the Cretaceous, for example, *Erectopus* in Europe, *Carcharodontosaurus* in Africa, *Dryptosaurus* in North America, and the apparently specialized Chinese genus *Chilantaisaurus* with relatively long forelimbs and a hooked claw on the first finger of the "hand". By this time, however, some large carnosaurs had appeared which had the neural spines of the vertebrae along their backs drawn out into grotesque

projections almost 2 metres (6.6ft) long (*Spinosaurus*, *Acrocanthosaurus*). *Deinocheirus* is an obscure Late Cretaceous carnosaur from Mongolia which retained long forelimbs – the humerus was about 1 metre (3.3ft) – with a three-fingered "hand", but the dominant predators at the end of the Mesozoic were the Tyrannosauridae.

These giants were attaining a length of more than 12 metres (40ft) by the end of the Mesozoic and had forelimbs reduced to diminutive proportions with only two functional fingers in the small "hand"; the huge hindfeet were three-toed, with massive claws and a retroverted first digit. *Prodeinodon* was a Lower Cretaceous forerunner from Mongolia, but in the Upper Cretaceous Oldman Formation of North America there were *Daspletosaurus*, about 10 metres (33ft) long, and the heavier *Albertosaurus*. In the succeeding Edmonton beds *Albertosaurus* was still present while *Tarbosaurus* ranged eastern Asia.

The final stage of carnosaur evolution is found in the North American Lance Formation of uppermost Cretaceous age, which has yielded skeletons of *Tyrannosaurus*. This flesh-eater is the largest known land carnivore, with a skull 2 metres (6.6ft) long and 15cm (6in) teeth.

Various fragmentary remains indicate the presence of tyrannosaurids in the Indian subcontinent (*Indosuchus*) and South America (*Genyodectes*), and *Alectrosaurus* is a slenderly proportioned genus from the Iren Dabasu Formation of Mongolia.

The carnosaurs were probably the scavengers of the Mesozoic, but they also killed their prey when necessary, although it is doubtful whether they were capable of running at speed. With their semi-rigid tails extended clear of the ground to balance the weight of the forward inclined body pivoting about the hips, they used the wide track of the hindfeet to swing along with a rolling gait.   R.S.

Carnosaurs
Antrodemus *(and skull), a characteristic carnosaur from the Upper Jurassic Morrison Formation of North America, has also been reported from Tendaguru, Africa, under the alternative names of* Allosaurus *and* Labrosaurus.
Length: about 12m (40ft)

Cattle

Cats

The cat family (Felidae) includes the extinct SABRE-TOOTHED CATS (Machairodontinae) and "false sabre-tooths" (Nimravinae), as well as the Felinae (the living cats) whose fossil history can be traced back only as far as the Pliocene. Virtually all the living cats may be regarded as species of a single genus, *Felis*, the only definite exception being the cheetah (*Acinonyx*), although the lion, tiger, leopard, jaguar and ounce are frequently assigned to *Panthera* on the basis of characteristics that are not always determinable in fossil material.

During the Middle Pleistocene the massive "cave lion", *Felis leo spelaea*, a third larger than any living lion, roamed Europe, and in the Late Pleistocene of North America the "La Brea lion", *Felis atrox*, apparently resembled the living jaguar, but was much larger. A giant cheetah (*Acinonyx pardinensis*) as large as a modern lion occurs in the Lower Pleistocene of Europe, greater India and China, but shows a gradual diminution in size through the Middle Pleistocene until it became extinct.

The leopard (*Felis pardus*) was present in the Middle Pleistocene of Europe, Africa and Asia, with possible Lower Pleistocene ancestors in the Villafranchian (*Felis pardoides*, *Felis palaeosinensis*, *Felis schaubi*), and tigers of enormous size were also present during the Pleistocene of Asia.

Lynxes occur as early as the Lower Pliocene in North America, and the Villafranchian Issoire lynx (*Felis issiodorensis*) is a likely ancestor of all later cats of this group, with the Spanish lynx (*Felis pardina*) present in Europe during the mid-Pleistocene and the northern lynx (*Felis lynx*) appearing in the late Upper Pleistocene.

Other early species of *Felis* include the Tuscany "lion" (*Felis toscana*) from the Villafranchian and the small *Felis lunensis* of the mid-Pleistocene (probably ancestral to the living wild cat, *Felis silvestris*, which is an Upper Pleistocene form); the steppe cat, *Felis manul*, was apparently present in the Upper Pleistocene and has a probable ancestor in the European Middle Pleistocene. The modern puma (*Felis concolor*) occurs at RANCHO LA BREA alongside two closely related extinct species (*Felis bituminosa* and *Felis daggetti*), and the asphalt fauna also includes an extinct subspecies of the lynx (*Felis rufa fischeri*).

The history of *Felis* can be traced back to the Early Pliocene where the genus is represented by several small species no larger than a domestic cat, eg *Felis attica* from PIKERMI, but the origin of the Felinae as a whole is obscure. "False sabre-tooths" were present from the Eocene into the Pliocene and may have been the ancestors of the Felinae if their moderately enlarged upper canine teeth became secondarily reduced. Alternatively the ancestors of modern felines may have lived in obscurity during most of the Cenozoic, unable to compete effectively with the powerful machairodonts and leaving no fossil remains that have been recognized. Perhaps these presumed ancestral cats lived deep in dense forests, where their bones were unlikely to be preserved.   R.S.

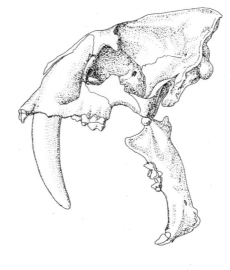

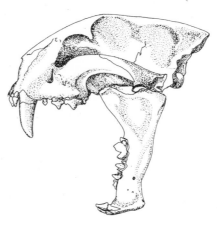

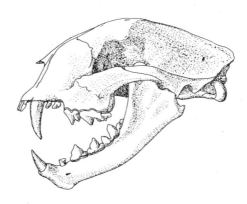

Cats
These skulls (top to bottom) are of the advanced sabre-toothed cat Smilodon *from the Pleistocene of North America, skull length 35cm (14in); the Oligocene felid* Dinictis, *skull length 15cm (6in); the "false sabre-tooth"* Nimravus *from the Upper Oligocene and Lower Miocene of North America (some species of this genus were as large as a lion).*

Cattle

Members of the ARTIODACTYL family Bovidae, a large group with about 50 living genera and many extinct forms. With the antilocaprids they comprise the superfamily Bovoidea whose origins can be traced back to the Miocene, but the group did not begin to spread round the world until the Pliocene, first in the Northern Hemisphere and later into southern Asia and Africa. They never reached South America or Australasia and their presence there is due to

Cattle (cont'd)

human introduction. Bovids have taken over almost all the available grazing niches, with horses and zebras now their only serious competitors. They owe their success largely to an efficient digestive system, with four-chambered stomachs that can digest the cellulose grasses; their high-crowned (hypsodont) teeth with double-crescent (selenodont) crown pattern are resistant to rapid wear by the silica in such plants. Upper incisor teeth are lost and the upper canine teeth are either reduced or absent; the lower incisors crop against a hard pad.

The feet have the typical artiodactyl cloven hoof (two-toed with greatly reduced lateral toes). The cannon bone is fused, which restricts movement to a fore and aft plane but also reduces the risk of sprains on uneven ground. Both males and females usually possess horns – paired bony outgrowths of the skull roof with a horny sheath. In bovids these horns are not shed or replaced and are never branched, although in antilocaprids they are deciduous and branched.

The origin of the bovids is not clear, but there were in the Late Miocene of Europe and Asia some small-sized ruminants with simple horn cores (eg *Palaeoreas*) which appear to be near to an ancestral traguloid stock. The antilocaprids comprise the prongbucks of North America and represent an isolated radiation of bovoids dating from the Miocene on the American continent. They parallel the antelopes of the Old World in their adaptations. The horns of prongbucks grow from a bony core but they branch and are shed annually. In Pleistocene genera the horns were notably complex and the living prongbucks are probably degenerate.

The classification of bovids is complex, with numerous sub-divisions as follows.

Alcelaphines (hartebeests and gnus) although rare as fossils, are extremely numerous today in Africa. They are large animals, with long front legs, sloping hindquarters and long faces, and live in large herds in open savanna.

Antelopines, the gazelles, are small and medium-sized antelopes with long legs which enable them to run fast in the open savanna and desert. *Gazella brevicornis* is recorded from the Late Miocene of PIKERMI, Greece.

Boselaphines are an ancient group extending back into the Early Miocene, with a good fossil record in Eurasia. They are known today only in greater India (nilgai, four-horned antelope).

Bovines comprise buffaloes, bison and cattle, which usually have large, spreading horns. The aurochs (*Bos primigenius*) was a gigantic ox of Pleistocene and post-Pleistocene times, only becoming extinct in 1627. It was hunted and painted on cave walls by Palaeolithic man and is one of the species associated with the ancestry of domestic cattle. In the Pleistocene of Africa the gigantic ox *Pelorovis* had horn cores with a spread exceeding 2 metres (6.6ft).

Caprines are a tribe of medium-sized bovines which often have spirally coiled horns. They comprise ibex, goats and sheep.

Cephalophines, the duikers of Africa, are small antelopes with short horns, frequenting forests and thick scrub.

Hippotragines, plentiful in the Pliocene of Eurasia, are today well represented in Africa by the addax, the oryx and the sable antelope. The horns are usually long and backward curving. These forms prefer savanna or open desert.

Neotragines, the dik-diks, are poorly represented in the fossil record but common in Africa today.

Ovibovines, large cattle with massive, flattened horns, occur in the Pliocene of Asia, the Pleistocene of Eurasia and North America, and are represented today by the musk ox.

Reduncines, medium-sized antelopes, were abundant in the Pleistocene of Asia. In Africa today they include the waterbuck, which have horns only in the males.

Rupicaprines, the chamois and mountain goats, are from mountainous regions of North America and Eurasia.

Saigines, small antelopes with a peculiar, inflated nose, inhabited the tundra of North America and Eurasia during the Pleistocene but are now restricted to the Kirghiz steppes.

Strepsicerotines are represented by many fossil forms. Some, such as *Palaeoreas*, extend back to the Miocene in Eurasia. Living members of the group include the kudu and the eland in Africa. Typically the horns are spirally twisted and paired in a lyre shape.   R.J.G.S.

Cephalaspids

Cave art

The painting and sculpture of men who lived between 25000BC and 10000BC in caves of Europe and Africa.

Decorated caves are the work of advanced PALAEOLITHIC men. Their art form is thought to have been started by peoples of the Gravettian culture, continued by the Solutreans, and brought to its climax by Magdalenian men. This artistic phase ended with the transition from the colder late glacial climate to the present warmer neothermal one. The change had a profound effect on animal and plant life, transforming grassland capable of supporting vast herds of game into thick forests. During the earlier part of the late glacial period, life must have been relatively easy with an abundance of food, and it is the hunter folk of that time who painted the walls of caves.

The Gravettian culture and cave art are associated in particular with the Dordogne region of France. Among the identifying artefacts of this culture, however, are the so-called "Venus figurines" (grotesque caricatures of women, always naked and pregnant), which have now been found widely in central Europe. Archaeological evidence of the Gravettian culture also occurs in Czechoslovakia and the southern USSR, and it appears that this eastern Gravettian culture pre-dates that of France. It seems logical that cave art was an extension of the art forms practised by these early peoples who not only made Venus figurines, but also carved pictures of mammoths and other animals on bone. Models of animals were made either in stone or fire-baked clay, including many species which were later painted as cave figures.

In the cave paintings themselves, animals are represented separately, in herds, or as objects of the hunt with associated human figures. The wealth of detail and the colours used are remarkably accurate, and prehistorians have been able to identify a succession of technical and artistic improvements. The first paintings were only symbolic lines, and no animals appear to be represented until those of the Gravettian culture, whose artists made special emphasis of the back lines of the figures. During the late Solutrean and the early Magdalenian, the drawings of the limbs of animals improved to give a more natural appearance. This style of painting is found in the Lascaux cave with the animals sometimes carved in relief and then painted.

The style of the middle and late Magdalenian is identifiable by more advanced painting methods together with engraving, relief carving, and sculpture. Examples of this style have been found in the caves at Cap Blanc (Dordogne) and Altamira (Spain).

Examples of cave art occur throughout the Mediterranean region, particularly in Italy, and one example is known from the southern Ural Mountains of the USSR. Many countries of Africa, from Tanzania to South Africa's Cape Province, also have painted caves.

It is not known why Palaeolithic man took his rudimentary paints into dark caves and painted by the light of rush lamps. Suggestions include hunting magic and decoration. D.T.

Cenozoic

The last of the eras into which the Earth's history has been divided. It comprises the PALAEOCENE, EOCENE, OLIGOCENE, MIOCENE, PLIOCENE and PLEISTOCENE Periods, and because mammals were the dominant terrestrial animals throughout this time it is frequently referred to as the "age of mammals".

See also NEOGENE, PALAEOGENE, QUATERNARY, TERTIARY and the time chart.

Centipedes and millipedes

Members of the ARTHROPOD superclass Myriapoda, comprising multi-segmented animals with a distinct head and an undifferentiated trunk, in which each segment bears legs. They share a probable common ancestor with the INSECTS through the Symphyla. The first myriapods (archipolypods), from the Upper Silurian (*Archidesmus*) and Lower Devonian (*Kampecaris*) of Scotland, were probably aquatic or semi-aquatic, but later forms are terrestrial. Myriapods became common in the Coal Measures, especially *Euphoberia* and *Acantherpestes* from Mazon Creek (Illinois), England and central Europe where they are found in nodules associated with the coal.

Occurring occasionally at this horizon is a gigantic invertebrate animal, *Arthropleura*, now assigned to the Myriapoda, which probably reached a length of almost 1·8 metres (6ft), although the most complete specimen is only 80cm (2.6ft). *Arthropleura* is the largest known terrestrial arthropod, its size probably being due to uninterrupted growth free from predators. The only likely enemies it might have had would have been some of the amphibians.

Millipedes are essentially herbivorous or possibly omnivorous, living on decaying organic material. *Xylobius* has been found as a cast in the middle of a Coal Measure tree stump. Centipedes are normally carnivorous, employing poison glands and fangs. The earliest true centipede is *Calciphilus* from the Cretaceous of Arizona. After the Carboniferous only a few occurrences of myriapods have been recorded, although several specimens and species are preserved in the Oligocene Baltic AMBER, some of which are assigned to modern genera. S.F.M.

Cephalaspids

An order (Osteostraci) of extinct jawless fishes (OSTRACODERMS) that flourished during the Silurian and Devonian. The head shield of the cephalaspids formed a single unit, with the eyes

	Present	
Quaternary	Holocene	
	Pleistocene	

Pliocene		Neogene
Miocene	Tertiary	
Oligocene		Palaeogene
Eocene		
Palaeocene		

65 million years ago
The Cenozoic succession

Centipedes and millipedes
Upper Carboniferous myriapods from Bohemia:
(above) Acantherpestes gigas *(approx. 1/2 natural size);*
(below) Acantherpestes ornatus *(approx. 3/4 natural size).*

Cephalaspids
Hemicyclaspis *lived in the Lower Devonian.*
Length: 21cm (8.3in)

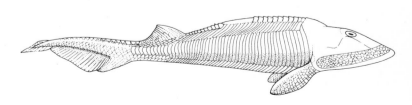

Ceratopsians

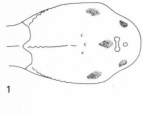

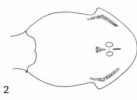

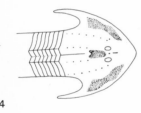

Cephalaspids
Dorsal views show head shield evolution in cephalaspids:
(1) Tremataspis, *with no pectoral "horns" and a large section of the trunk included within the shield;*
(2) Didymaspis, *in which incipient "horns" are developing;*
(3) Kiaeraspis, *with prominent "horns" and most of the trunk exposed behind the shield;*
(4) Thyestes, *in which the "horns" are becoming elongated;*
(5) Cephalaspis, *a typical fully evolved member of the group.*

positioned on the dorsal surface near the midline. Sclerotic bones determined the shape of the eyeball, and between the eyes there was a functional third (pineal) eye, with (immediately in front of it) the single nasal opening – evidence of a close relationship with the living lampreys.

Behind the eyes and close to the lateral margins of the head shield were the dorsal and lateral sensory fields, once thought to be electricity-producing but now recognized as specialized parts of the hearing and balance systems. In life these areas were covered by small movable polygonal plates connected to a system of branching lymph-filled canals, which were extensions from the ear region. Vibrations impinging on the sensory fields would have been transmitted to the ear.

The ventral surface of the head shield incorporates the mouth and up to ten pairs of separate gill openings. The floor of the ventral shield is composed of small plates, which suggest a flexible membrane that may have acted as a pump for feeding as well as respiration. The gills seem to be arranged in a series of pouches as in lampreys (but in contrast to jawed vertebrates), the first complete gill being the hyoidean as in all living vertebrates.

The cephalaspids were specialized for a benthic (bottom-dwelling) mode of life. The ventral surface was flat and the section of the head and trunk was triangular and tapering dorsally. Similarly the anterior profile of the head shield was flat ventrally, the dorsal surface sloping backwards and upwards. This shape ensured that cephalaspids remained close to the bottom; passive movement such as is caused by a current of water would press them to the bottom – a tendency that was counteracted by the development of a heterocercal TAIL FIN which generates lift when acting in conjunction with paired fins.

The tail itself was unique among vertebrates; it possessed a pair of horizontal tail flaps that were extensions of the ventro-lateral ridges extending from the back of the head shield to the tail. There were usually two dorsal fins, as well as paired pectoral flaps that originated from the postero-lateral corners of the head shield and generally had sharp lateral spines (cornua) protecting their leading edges.

The most primitive cephalaspid was *Tremataspis*, in which the anterior half of the trunk as well as the head was encased in armour. The ventral and dorsal surfaces were convex, and the ventral surface sloped upwards anteriorly. There were no paired fins and the tail must have been simple (probably symmetrical); because of the shape of the carapace any motion of the tail driving the animal forward would automatically have provided lift. The main evolution of the cephalaspids involved a reduction of the trunk carapace and the development of pectoral flaps and their protective cornua, together with a heterocercal tail. The profile and cross-section of the body similarly evolved to give the typical triangular section.

A few fragments of bone from the Ordovician have been attributed to a cephalaspid, but the group reached its peak during the Late Silurian and Early Devonian before finally dying out part-way through the Upper Devonian. Specimens of cephalaspids found in Spitzbergen not only had the bony armour preserved, but also exhibited calcified connective tissue in the head region. All the spaces which in life had housed such structures as the brain, nerves and blood vessels were perfectly preserved. By careful dissection as well as reconstruction of serial sections, much of the internal anatomy has been disclosed.   L.B.H.

Ceratopsians, *see* HORNED DINOSAURS.

Chalicotheres

A suborder (Ancylopoda) of PERISSODACTYL mammals, notable for their clawed feet – an exceptional feature in a herbivore. In skeletal and skull characteristics, chalicotheres have features in common with their relatives the HORSES, their heads being of horse-like proportions with long slender nasal bones. The upper incisor teeth are often absent although the lower ones are retained, giving an appearance similar to that seen in bovids. A well developed diastema (space) separates the incisors from the premolar teeth, which are unusual among perissodactyls in not being molarized. The true molars are low-crowned, with a double V-pattern in the lower series, reminiscent of RHINOCEROSES, and in the upper row a bunodont (low and rounded) pattern similar to that of BRONTOTHERES.

The most unusual features are found in the limbs, however. The forelimbs are distinctly longer than the hind, giving sloping rear quarters as in hyaenas. The feet are three-toed, but do not carry hoofs as in almost all other ungulates; instead, they had large fissured phalanges which bore retractile claws like those of CATS so that they were not blunted when the animal walked over stony ground. This combination of sharp retractile claws and a dentition similar to that of a horse suggests an unusual mode of living. Possibly these creatures browsed on tubers dug up with their feet.

Chalicotheres ranged from sheep-size to cart horse proportions. They are found in the Eocene of Eurasia and North America, but were never abundant in the Western Hemisphere after the end of that period, although they persisted there into the Miocene (*Moropus*). In Eurasia they are not uncommon in the Oligocene and Miocene, finally becoming extinct during the Plio-Pleistocene, and from the Early Miocene they were present in eastern Africa, where they lingered into the Pleistocene.   R.J.G.S.

Chalk

Fine-grained limestone of great purity typically consisting almost entirely of organically derived calcium carbonate together with minor amounts of terrigenous (land-derived) muds and silts. Synonymous with the Upper Cretaceous deposit of the same name, chalk is primarily composed of countless microfossils, principally coccoliths (discoid sheaths of minute planktonic ALGAE).

Chimaeras

The tests (hard shells) of FORAMINIFERANS, formerly considered the major component of the matrix of chalk, also occur, but in much less abundance. The macrofauna of chalk includes BRACHIOPODS (such as *Rhynchonella*), SPONGES (*Cephalites*), AMMONITES (*Scaphites*), SEA URCHINS (*Micraster*), BELEMNITES (*Belemnitella*), GASTROPODS (*Bathrotomaria*) and, in particular, BIVALVES such as *Neithea, Chlamys, Spondylus, Pycnodonte* and *Inoceramus*.

Chalk is white, grey or yellowish, with a compact crumbly texture and has typically suffered many biological changes. The harder deposits are characteristically termed rocks (eg Melbourn Rock; Chalk Rock). Nodules of flint and marcasite, often occurring in bands, are not uncommon, and macrofossils are frequently found preserved in the flint itself.

Chalk is widely distributed in the British Isles (Scotland, Ireland, and England from Yorkshire to Dorset) where it forms such notable landscape features as the North and South Downs and the Chilterns. Other European outcrops in France, Denmark, Germany, Sweden and elsewhere are testimony to the widespread transgression of the Chalk sea over what must have been low-lying land. The fine calcareous mud is thought to have accumulated on a firm sea floor in shallow water 50–150 metres (160–490ft) deep adjacent to areas of low relief.　　　　　　　J.E.P.W.

Chimaeras

A small group of fishes with a cartilaginous skeleton that occur today in temperate and cold waters. Known as rat- or rabbit-fish, they attain a length of 60–200cm (24–80in) and have crushing tooth plates for eating shellfish. The tail is reduced to whip-like proportions, and there is a rostrum supported by an internal skeleton of rostral cartilages including paired lateral cartilages. The males possess claspers which assist impregnating the females. In front of the claspers is a pair of short spikes, the tenacula, and the males often have a further clasping organ on the forehead.

The specialized ARTHRODIRE *Ctenurella* had many typical chimaera characteristics (besides similar proportions) including the rostral cartilages, pelvic claspers and tenacula. There

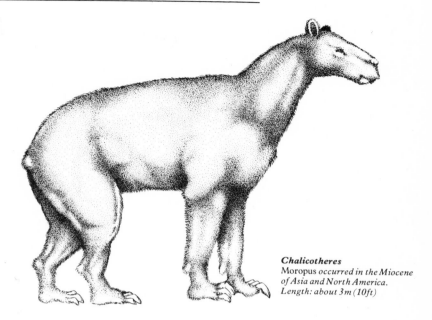

Chalicotheres
Moropus *occurred in the Miocene of Asia and North America. Length: about 3m (10ft)*

seems to be little doubt that the chimaeras are surviving members of a group of PLACODERMS. A partly armoured Permian form (*Menaspis armata*) bore three pairs of head spines and can be linked to some of the later chimaeras which had paired as well as rostral head spines. *Menaspis* is descended from the more heavily armoured Early Carboniferous *Deltoptychius*.

During the Carboniferous there were a group of cartilaginous fishes grouped as bradyodonts (including the cochliodonts), which had paired tooth plates with a characteristic spiral shape, reminiscent of the coil of a snail shell (hence the name cochliodont or "shell tooth"). These fishes are generally linked with the chimaeras because of their tooth structures.

There is still some dispute about the exact ancestors of the chimaeras; one theory favours the ptyctodont arthrodires whereas another prefers such placoderms as the rhenanids which can be regarded as primitive arthrodires. There is general agreement, however, that the chimaeras are direct survivors from a primitive placoderm stock.　　　　　　　L.B.H.

Chimaeras
This female specimen of the chimaera Ischyodus schuebleri *lived in the Upper Jurassic of Europe (approx. 1/10 natural size).*

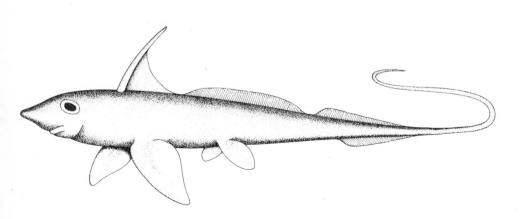

Civets

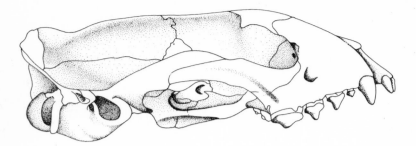

Civets
Herpestides *was a viverrid from the Upper Oligocene of France. The skull (shown here) was 95mm (3.7in) long.*

Civets

With the mongooses, the civets make up the viverrids, the largest living family of the CARNIVORA. There are 36 genera of viverrids, but only a few fossil forms are known. They represent the basal stock of the aeluroid carnivores (CATS and HYAENAS) and are widely distributed in tropical Africa and Asia, although they never managed to invade the Americas. In Spain a genet is the only living European representative of the family. The origins of the viverrids can be traced back to *Herpestides*, a genet-like animal from the Late Oligocene of France; by the Miocene there were also viverrids in Africa and Asia.

The viverrines or civets are mainly Asian and the mongooses mainly African, although each stock has members on both continents. The island of Madagascar has a unique fauna of viverrids that are not closely related to those of either Africa or Asia, and they must have evolved through a long period of isolation. *Cryptoprocta*, the fossa, is cat-like in appearance and is sometimes classified with the cats, but it walks flat-footed.   R.J.G.S.

Classification, *see* TAXONOMY.

Cleveland Museum of Natural History

Founded in Cleveland, Ohio, in 1920, it is concerned with all aspects of natural history including archaeology, ethnology, astronomy, anthropology and medical history. Its founding was due to the initiative and enthusiasm of private individuals, and its first premises were a small room. The collections are wide-ranging but the Museum is particularly fortunate in having in the immediate area exposures of the Cleveland Shales. These Devonian rocks have been extensively collected; they have yielded a rich, excellently preserved fauna including many fishes. In the early years of the Museum's existence many specimens were acquired as a result of building excavations during the period of rapid growth of Cleveland. The collections also contain Pleistocene vertebrates, including the Johnstown mastodon.   A.P.H.

Climates of the past

It seems improbable that the world's present climate is typical of the Earth's earlier climatic evolution. Since the Late Pre-Cambrian there appear to have been several ICE AGES punctuating longer periods when the Earth, free of polar ice caps, had a more equable climate than today's. The major ice ages, which were times of marked seasonal and latitudinal climatic contrasts, occurred in the early Vendian (latest Pre-Cambrian), the Upper Ordovician, the Permo-Carboniferous and the Pleistocene.

Knowledge of the non-glacial climates of the earlier Palaeozoic (Cambrian to Lower Carboniferous) is poor, because one of the most sensitive sources of palaeo-climatic information, the terrestrial flora and fauna, evolved little before the Carboniferous. The evidence that does exist, however, suggests a more uniform climate than today's, with less latitudinal zonation; this is particularly well exemplified by the uniformity of the Lower Carboniferous world flora. Such climatic order contrasts with the marked latitudinal climatic zonation of the Late Carboniferous and Early Permian, when the southern continents were grouped around the South Pole as a single supercontinent (GONDWANALAND), and suffered a prolonged glaciation while warm, humid coal swamps (supporting a luxuriant flora) occupied much of the equatorially situated Northern Hemisphere continents.

The accumulation of coal indicates humid, but not necessarily warm, conditions because modern peat bogs (the first stage in coal formation) occur in cool temperate zones. The nature of the Carboniferous coal's flora and other evidence, such as the associated occurrence of giant insects, suggest a warm climate in this instance. With the continued northwards drift of the continents into the horse latitudes during the Permian, the Carboniferous coal swamps were replaced by deserts and shallow, saline seas, with the deposition of barren wind-eroded sandstones and evaporites. Such conditions persisted into the Triassic in many places, including the British Isles, although the advent of the Mesozoic heralded climatic change.

Throughout the Mesozoic the absence of polar ice caps is thought to have resulted in less climatic zonation. It has been estimated that on an ice-free globe the decrease in mean surface air temperatures from the poles to the equator would be about 22°C (a decrease of 40°F) compared with 42°C (76°F) at present. On such a globe the tropical and sub-tropical zones would be wider than today, with temperate conditions characterizing the polar regions, producing a warmer and more equable climate than at present. Several lines of evidence support this idea, especially during the Jurassic: no tillites ("fossil" boulder clay) or other evidence of glacial action has been recognized; no real zonation can be determined in the Jurassic flora; large reptiles had a wide latitudinal distribution; and hermatypic corals (reef builders) have been recorded as far north as 60° latitude in the Jurassic, although modern reefs are restricted to latitudes lower than 30°, where water temperatures are above 21°C (70°F).

Despite the weak latitudinal zonation, a definite east (humid) to west (more arid) climatic differentiation can be recognized in the Triassic and Jurassic. The humid eastern belts may be the result of monsoonal rains, because at that time two supercontinents, Laurasia and Gondwanaland, bordered the northern and southern sides respectively of an equatorial ocean, the TETHYS, providing the ideal continent–ocean configuration for the production of monsoonal climate.

Although a warm, uniform climate also characterized the early Cenozoic Era, it deteriorated, culminating in the Pleistocene Ice Age, when continental ice sheets spread across much of northern Europe, North America and the poles. Ice covered more than 18.5 million sq km (7.1 million sq miles) of the Northern Hemisphere during its maximum development and in Europe it extended southwards to latitude 49°; the present Greenland ice cap covers only approximately 1.75 million sq km (676,000 sq miles). The prevailing cold, damp conditions promoted the advance of glaciers, and displaced the climatic belts towards the equator. Consequently the "Westerlies" produced pluvial (rainy) phases in the northern parts of the modern deserts, as elevated shoreline terraces such as those around Lake Bonneville in the USA testify.

The influence of the glaciers diminished progressively towards the equator, the maximum decrease in temperature being 8–13°C (a decrease of 14–23°F) in the temperate zones but less than 4°C (7°F) in the tropics. During interglacial phases the climate improved, reverting to conditions probably similar to today's, and the areas of "temperate" tundra were gradually recolonized by mixed oak forests.

Studies have related climatic changes to variations in the Earth's rotation rate, suggesting an association between spin minima and ice ages, and between spin maxima and climatic optima (equable climate).   C.T.S.

Club mosses

A group of plants (Lycopsida) with both fossil and living representatives. There are five living genera, *Lycopodium* and *Selaginella* being common. Modern lycopods are small whereas many of the fossil forms were large trees, eg *Lepidodendron*. The group has exhibited a remarkable uniformity from its earliest appearance through to the present day.

Club mosses exist in two forms: a gametophyte with a single set of chromosomes, and the larger dominant sporophyte, differentiated into a shoot (having stems and leaves) and a root system. The leaf arrangement is basically spiral with the leaves overlapping one another. Whereas the leaves of the modern genera tend to be small and even scale-like, some fossil lycopods had leaves of large size.

The oldest known plant with definite lycopod characteristics is *Baragwanathia* from the Early Devonian of Australia. It was a dichotomously branched plant with spirally arranged leaves completely clothing its branches. *Asteroxylon*, found beautifully preserved in the Rhynie Chert, is another early lycopod; it was about 50cm (20in) tall and the main axis was unequally branched, the side branches being dichotomous. The internal anatomy of *Asteroxylon* was essentially the same as that of a modern lycopod.

In the Carboniferous Period the lycopods developed many giant forms, the best known of which were the lepidodendrons and the sigillarias. These trees were about 30 metres (100ft) tall and dominated the Carboniferous scene. Their fossil remains yielded most of the present coal seams. *Lepidodendron* had an extensive dichotomously branched root system, from which arose a large straight trunk that was unbranched for a considerable height. The crown of the tree was produced by dichotomous branching and must have had an umbrella-like shape with a rigid symmetry. The branches were covered with spirally arranged linear to lanceolate leaves which when shed left a characteristic pattern used in identification. At the ends of the branches, elaborate cone-like structures (strobili) were borne from which the seed-like megaspores were produced.   J.W.F.

Coal forests, *see* FOSSIL FUELS.

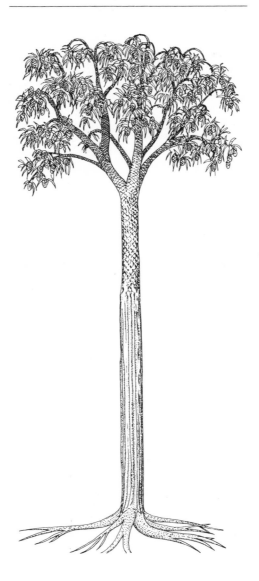

Club mosses
The giant Carboniferous lycopod ("scale tree") Lepidodendron *occurred in the Coal Measures of Europe and North America. The branching roots are known as* Stigmaria.
Height: about 30m (100ft)

Coelacanths

Coelacanths

A suborder of LOBE-FIN FISHES that are well known from freshwater Devonian rocks, but subsequently occur only in marine deposits during the Mesozoic. They were believed to have died out at the end of the Cretaceous, but in 1938 a living specimen (*Latimeria*) was caught off the coast of South Africa. Curiously this fish had been known to the local people for at least several decades previously because they used the scales, with their ornamentation of small denticles, as a substitute for sandpaper when repairing bicycle tyre punctures.

Perhaps the most striking feature of the coelacanths is that they have hardly changed since the Devonian. They have muscular pectoral and pelvic fins of the characteristic lobe-like configuration, and there are two dorsal fins (the posterior one located opposite the anal fin) which are also lobe-shaped. In the living *Latimeria* they work in concert to scull the fish through the water. The tail is symmetrical, with a long narrow axial lobe, together with almost equal upper and lower caudal fins (this type of three-lobed fin is termed diphycercal). An unusual feature of the coelacanths is the calcified air bladder, although it is difficult to imagine a functional reason for this development. The braincase is ossified in two parts, as in rhipidistians.

One of the features recognized from the fossils is that not only were coelacanths fertilized internally, but the embryos attained their full development within the mother. This has now been confirmed in the living *Latimeria*. Coelacanths are important because they represent a structural stage in the evolution of fishes corresponding to the point when the first steps on to the land were taken. The only important change that has occurred since the Devonian is that the skeleton is now less completely ossified, otherwise the group has remained structurally almost unaltered.

An assemblage of fishes that may be related to the coelacanths were the struniiformes, which have a mixture of characteristics that make it difficult to assign them to any other well-known group. A superficial examination suggests that they are PALAEONISCIDS because they have very large eyes, a broad head and a blunt snout. The fins seem to be more like those of RAY-FIN FISHES. Unlike the palaeoniscids, however, they have two dorsal fins, and the TAIL FIN is not heterocercal but diphycercal, with the long narrow axial lobe characteristic of the coelacanths and juvenile rhipidistians. A transverse suture in the braincase further indicates a relationship with the coelacanths and rhipidistians, but the pattern of skull roofing bones (although removing them from any possible relationship to the palaeoniscids) does not clearly associate them with any of the lobe-fins. Their nearest relatives seem to be the coelacanths and for the present they may be tentatively classified with them.   L.B.H.

Coelenterates

Invertebrate animals in which the body wall is constructed from only two layers of cells (ectoderm and endoderm). The coelenterates are usually regarded as comprising two phyla, the Cnidaria and the Ctenophora. Cnidarians have a good geological record but the Ctenophora (sea gooseberries) are soft-bodied and unknown as fossils. The first authenticated cnidarians occur in the Late Pre-Cambrian and are among the oldest known fossil animals.

The earliest cnidarians were mainly jellyfishes (also known as medusae) – one of two basic body forms found in the phylum, the other being the polyp. The two cell layers of the body wall are separated by a median structureless substance, the mesogloea, which in jellyfishes may be thick to form the main mass of the bell. The mouth, in the centre of the upper surface of the usually sessile polyp and in the centre of the lower (subumbrella) cavity of the normally free-swimming medusa, is surrounded by tentacles bearing groups of special stinging cells called nematocysts used in capturing prey. The cnidarians show little cellular specialization and are primitive metazoans, only slightly more advanced than SPONGES.

There are three main classes of cnidarians: Scyphozoa, Hydrozoa and Anthozoa. In the Scyphozoa, the jellyfish form is dominant, although these are usually budded off a special small polypoid form called a scyphistoma. Hardly any Scyphozoa have hard parts, and therefore the fossil record is poor. Even so, *Kimberella quadrata*, known as impressions from an Australian Late Pre-Cambrian sandstone, is interpreted as a scyphozoan medusa,

Coelacanths
The living coelacanth Latimeria *has been caught in the Indian Ocean near the Comoro islands, off Madagascar.*
Length: about 1.5m (5ft)

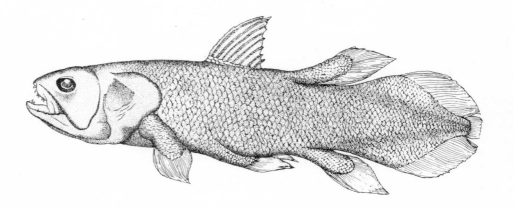

Coelurosaurs

and apparently looked similar to the living sea wasps. Other Late Pre-Cambrian jellyfishes are also thought to be scyphozoans and there are, in addition, scattered records throughout the Phanerozoic.

A rare tubular fossil from the Cambrian and Ordovician called *Byronia* may be the outer chitinous covering of a scyphistoma, and other chitinophosphatic fossils (conularids) that occur from the Cambrian to the Trias are also possibly related to the Scyphozoa. No direct evidence for the tentacles reconstructed in *Archaeoconularia fecunda* is known, however, and although conularids may be cnidarians, perhaps forming a separate class, their relationships are uncertain.

The Hydrozoa is represented by both polypoid and medusoid forms. When these occur in the same animal, the polyp is a juvenile which buds off medusae that reproduce sexually; the resulting planuloid larva settles on the sea floor and grows into a polyp. By budding asexually the polyps then form a colony, and complex floating polyp colonies called chondrophores are the earliest known hydroids. *Eoporpita medusa* is one of several Late Pre-Cambrian forms, whereas *Archaeonectris benderi* occurs on the Ordovician-Silurian boundary, and *Plectodiscus cortlandensis* comes from the Upper Devonian. In these colonies, the polyps are specialized in their functions with a central gastrozooid (feeding), inner circles of gonozooids (reproductive), and marginal tentacles. A chambered float, sometimes with a sail, forms the upper surface of the colony.

Sessile benthic hydroid colonies are common in shallow seas today (eg *Obelia geniculata*), but have a poor fossil record; *Desmohydra flexuosa* from the Ordovician is one of the earliest known. *Protulophila gestroi*, from the Mesozoic and Cenozoic, is only preserved because the serpulid worms on which it grew incorporated the colony into their calcareous tubes. Some colonial hydroids that secreted a massive calcareous skeleton appeared late in the Mesozoic, with millepores (common on living coral reefs) and stylasterines making their debut in the Upper Cretaceous.

Another calcareous hydrozoan, *Hydractinia*, which usually encrusts gastropod shells, first definitely appeared in the Cenozoic (some Mesozoic fossils may belong to this genus), but the Stromatoporata (Ordovician–Eocene) and the Chaetetida (Cambrian–Miocene), once thought to be hydrozoans, are now classified with sponges. Hydrozoan medusae, which are generally smaller than scyphozoan medusae and lack their four-pouched gut, are extremely rare as fossils; only a few doubtful examples are known.

In the Anthozoa (which include the CORALS) the medusoid form is absent. Solitary polypoid anthozoans without a skeleton, the anemones, are extremely scarce as fossils, although they were probably common in the past, and trace fossils such as *Bergaueria* from the Cambrian and Ordovician may be the cavities formed in sediment by burrowing anemones similar to *Cerianthus lloydi*. There are two other major groups of anthozoans represented in the fossil

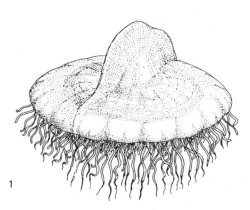

Coelenterates
(1) Plectodiscus *was an Upper Devonian siphonophore (hydrozoan); approx. 2/5 natural size.*
(2) Archaeoconularia *occurred from the Lower Ordovician to the Silurian of Europe and North America; approx. 1/2 natural size.*

record, the octocorals, which may have horny or calcified skeletal parts that are often spicular, and the true corals with fully developed calcareous skeletons. The true corals have a well-documented geological history beginning in the Cambrian, but octocorals (sea fans, sea pens) are rare as fossils. Some Pre-Cambrian organisms such as *Glaessnerina longa* are considered to be possible sea pens although the resemblance may be superficial, and the earliest convincing sea fan is *Pragnellia arborescens* from the Ordovician.   C.T.S.

Coelurosaurs

Bipedal archosaurian reptiles that were in some ways the most conservative of all the DINOSAURS grouped as SAURISCHIANS. Throughout their long history they retained the lightly built proportions of their ancestors, the PSEUDOSUCHIANS, and from their first appearance in the Triassic to their final extinction at the end of the Cretaceous they adhered remarkably closely to the same basic structural type.

The typical Triassic coelurosaurs are included in the family Podokesauridae which occurs in Europe, North America, Asia and southern Africa. When these small bipeds first appeared in the Middle Triassic they had already developed forelimbs that possessed at least a measure of grasping ability, together with hindlimbs modified to generate speed (a short femur, a long shank and bird-like feet). Many of them are known only from a few fragmentary bones, because they were probably animals of the dry uplands where conditons rarely favoured the preservation of corpses. Nevertheless *Coelophysis*, about 3 metres (10ft) long, is represented by numerous complete skeletons found in New Mexico that are apparently the remains of a group of animals overwhelmed by a sudden Upper Triassic sandstorm. Two of these specimens contain the remains of smaller individuals within their body cavities – apparently *Coelophysis* practised cannibalism. Some podokesaurids were of diminutive size, *Saltopus* from Scotland measuring only 60cm (24in).

The Procompsognathidae are a second Triassic family that contains two genera

Cold-blooded animals

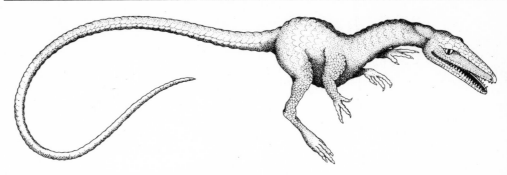

Coelurosaurs
*Syntarsus, a small, lightly built
dinosaur from the Upper Triassic
of southern Africa, is known only
from incomplete remains.
Estimated weight: 30kg (66lb)*

(*Procompsognathus* and *Halticosaurus*). These
animals had very long, flexible necks and
remarkably small forelimbs retaining five digits
in the "hand".

The Coeluridae of the Jurassic and Cretaceous are also generally represented only by
fragmentary material, but usually had an astragalus (ankle bone) with a prominent ascending
process – a modification of the ankle joint that
facilitated efficient running. They were of
almost worldwide distribution, and ranged in
size from the small *Compsognathus* of the
European Upper Jurassic, only about 50cm
(20in) long, to *Coelurus* of the North American
MORRISON FORMATION which measured 2 metres
(6.6ft). The Early Jurassic *Dilophosaurus*, from
Arizona, had a remarkable skull bearing a pair
of longitudinal crests and *Elaphrosaurus*, from
TENDAGURU, must have been similar to *Coelurus*;
the Morrison genus *Hallopus* may have been a
hopping animal, because it had a calcaneal
"heel", and *Microvenator* was a small Early
Cretaceous member of the family.

In the Lower Cretaceous the Ornithomimidae
made their appearance. These highly specialized
toothless coelurosaurs up to 4 metres (13ft) long
were superbly adapted for running at high
speeds on their long-shanked hindlimbs.
Analysis suggests that 80km an hour (50mph)
might have been possible if, as seems likely, they
were WARM-BLOODED. Their small skulls had
proportionately huge eye sockets, and there was
a secondary palate.

Two specimens of one ornithomimid,
Oviraptor from the GOBI DESERT, have been
found associated with the primitive HORNED
DINOSAUR *Protoceratops*. One skeleton was on
top of a nest of *Protoceratops* eggs, and the other

animal was apparently locked in combat with an
adult *Protoceratops* when both were smothered
by a desert storm. Probably the ornithomimids
lived on the eggs of other dinosaurs, which
would explain their toothlessness, evident agility
(for raiding forays), secondary palate (so that
they could breathe while sucking the contents of
an egg), and three-fingered "hand" which had
limited grasping power but could have been used
as a rake to search for clutches of eggs. Other
less probable suggestions include a diet of fruit,
molluscs or insects.

Archaeornithomimus is a very early
ornithomimid from the Lower Cretaceous of
North America and Mongolia. The Upper
Cretaceous Oldman Formation of Canada has
yielded the remains of *Struthiomimus*, with
Dromiceiomimus the dominant member of the
family in the succeeding Edmonton, and
Ornithomimus itself characteristic of the Lance
deposits at the summit of the North American
Cretaceous. *Gallimimus* is an exclusively Asiatic
genus from Mongolia with a long, flattened
snout, and fragmentary material apparently
indicates the presence of the family in Europe
and the Indian sub-continent.   R.S.

Cold-blooded animals

The living lower VERTEBRATES (fishes,
amphibians and reptiles, also called ectotherms)
depend on the temperature of their surroundings to maintain optimum body heat. The heat
produced by metabolic activity in the body cells
of an ectotherm is only about a quarter of that
generated in the cells of WARM-BLOODED ANIMALS
(endotherms) – birds and mammals. Metabolic
activity alone is therefore insufficient to sustain

Coelurosaurs
*Coelurus, a North American
coelurosaur, occurred in the
Upper Jurassic Morrison
Formation and has also been
reported from the Lower
Cretaceous of Maryland.
Length: 2m (6.6ft)*

Collecting

the body temperature of a resting cold-blooded animal.

The sea provides an environment that, even at high latitudes, is sufficiently warm to support fish life, but the range of amphibians and reptiles that live in northern and southern temperate zones is severely limited by winter temperatures. Both groups are today essentially tropical or sub-tropical in distribution, although small forms that hibernate can survive colder winter seasons. Crocodiles, for example, have an optimum body temperature of about 35°C (95°F), which they maintain by retreating at night into rivers and lakes, where they are insulated from the cool night air. In the morning they emerge to bask on sandbanks, and frequently re-enter the water to shelter from the mid-day heat.

Lizards similarly alternate between basking in the sun and seeking refuge in the shade. They can move quickly for limited periods, but spend perhaps 90 per cent of their time resting to conserve energy. Rapid movement requires a high metabolic rate for the oxidation of the carbohydrates and fats that provides energy, but the sluggish ectothermic physiology of living reptiles can maintain only a low metabolic rate. Their lungs are less convoluted internally than those of endotherms and so cannot extract as much oxygen from the air they breathe. Their hearts have only a single ventricle, in which oxygenated and de-oxygenated blood tend to mix, instead of remaining separated in two different ventricles (as in the hearts of birds and mammals).

It is probable that the DINOSAURS and PTEROSAURS, together with some at least of their ancestors (the PSEUDOSUCHIANS), were warm-blooded; the MAMMAL-LIKE REPTILES also may have been endotherms. The occurrence of other groups of fossil reptiles in latitudes that are now unfavourably cold for the survival of large ectotherms is evidence of a more equable world climate in past ages, and helps to substantiate the theory of CONTINENTAL DRIFT.   R.S.

Collecting

The scientific importance of a fossil depends to a large extent on information recorded when it was collected. A collector should have a field notebook to record the name of the collected specimen (eg ammonite), the locality where it was found, and the geological name of the rock or bed from which it came. The same information should be written on a label and placed with the fossil in a linen or polythene bag. Fossils from differing rock types (eg limestone or sandstone), separate localities, and different stratigraphic horizons should be placed in individual bags and not muddled together. Drawings of the rock sequence should also be made in the notebook.

Additonal items for the collecting kit are a good survey map of the area so that grid references of the locality can be plotted; a 10 times magnifying hand lens; pencils; a pen containing waterproof ink; and a metric steel rule. First aid items for minor cuts and abrasions should not be forgotten.

The choice of collecting tools depends on the type of rock that the fossils are preserved in. A geological hammer is essential. Chisels made of good quality steel, a heavier 1kg (2lb) hammer, trowels, knives, spades, picks and sieves may all be required if the fossils are encased in hard limestone or soft clay. Generally, little cleaning of the fossil should be attempted in the field because this is more easily accomplished at home or in the laboratory. Adhesives and hardening solutions must be used with great care or not at all; hardened rock, dirt and dust will have to be removed later. Only water- or solvent-based synthetic adhesives should be applied – never epoxy

Condylarths

Condylarths
Phenacodus *was a characteristic condylarth from the Upper Palaeocene and Lower Eocene of North America and the Lower and Middle Eocene of Europe. Length: about 1.7m (5.5ft)*

resins. If the fossil breaks during excavation, mark the joins and place all the pieces, with the label, in a bag for later assembly.

The most usual finds are fossil shells, fragments of plants and vertebrate remains. If a really large fossil such as a complete ichthyosaur or a slab containing the remains of a crinoid colony is found, then (unless professional help is available) the slab or skeleton must be encased in a protective cocoon. This involves placing damp tissue paper over the area to be removed followed by several layers of hessian soaked in plaster of Paris mixed in water. For added strength, wood battens are attached to the block, which is then carefully undercut. More hessian and plaster is then applied to the exposed rock. Eventually the whole slab containing the fossil can be turned over and further strengthened ready for transport. This procedure demands skill and patience and, because every specimen creates different collecting problems, new techniques such as the use of expanding polyurethane foam are continually being explored.

Collecting fossils can be dangerous. The sedimentary rocks containing them have been exposed by weathering or by the action of man, and therefore loose or decayed rocks can easily fall during excavation and injure the collector. Disused quarries, mines, cuttings and tip heaps are all hazardous areas. Sea cliffs are especially dangerous: winter storms may expose more fossils but they also weaken the cliff face. If a cliff fall does start, run into the sea – and always watch for the high tide.

A good collector asks permission from the landowner to collect fossils on his property and never damages the locality so that future collectors cannot find fossils. Various regulations, such as the obligatory wearing of a protective helmet, may govern collecting from working

quarries, road cuts and mines. Always ask permission first and obtain further information from geological societies.   P.J.W.

Condylarths

An extinct mammalian order (Condylarthra) that includes the earliest herbivorous mammals and the ancestors of all later herbivores. Condylarths first occurred in the Late Cretaceous, became abundant in the early Cenozoic, and died out in the Miocene. They occurred on all continents except Australasia and Antarctica.

Condylarths are so primitive that it is difficult to identify characteristic features. They are small, quadrupedal, five-toed (with hoofs), and usually have a complete dentition. Their most distinctive feature is the cheek teeth, which are squarish, have four primary cusps and are capable of grinding vegetation. In other features, however, they resemble primitive carnivores (both groups share a common ancestry).

Seven stocks of condylarths are recognized. The arctocyonids are the most primitive (*Protungulatum* from the Late Cretaceous of North America is the basal member) and the other six stocks can be derived from the arctocyonids.

The mesonychids were carnivore-like in appearance, but lacked the specialized carnassial teeth of the true carnivores. They probably had life habits similar to those of pigs, which are omnivores and sometimes eat flesh as well as vegetable material. Some mesonychids became as large as bears, for example, *Andrewsarchus* from the Late Eocene of Mongolia. It is believed that WHALES possibly arose from mesonychid ancestors.

The phenacodontids are ancestral to HORSES and other odd-toed ungulates, and *Phenacodus* itself from the Palaeocene of North America is almost indistinguishable from the earliest horses. Some members of this group were small, whereas others were as large as ponies. As well as being the forerunners of PERISSODACTYLS, the phenacodontids are the probable ancestors of hyracoids, proboscideans (ELEPHANTS), desmostylians, sirenians (*see* DUGONG) and tubulidentates. The aardvark is the nearest living mammal to the extinct condylarths. Phenacodontids are known from the early Cenozoic of North America, Europe and Asia.

In the early Cenozoic of South America there were the didolodontids. They were medium-sized herbivores, and ancestors of the South American ungulate stocks: the ASTRAPOTHERES, pyrotheres, LITOPTERNS and NOTOUNGULATES. The Late Palaeocene and Early Eocene deposits of North America contain meniscotheres, which had cheek teeth that developed true crescentic (selenodont) characteristics, later a feature of ARTIODACTYLS. Finally, the periptychids were a short-lived North American group that had specialized, fluted teeth.

Condylarths were evidently successful early herbivores, radiating rapidly into a wide variety of ecological niches, from which their successors became established in all the major regions and habitats of the world.   R.J.G.S.

Condylarths
In Meniscotherium, *from the Upper Palaeocene and Lower Eocene of North America, the teeth had crescentic crown patterns of a remarkably advanced type for so early a mammal. It was about the size of a fox terrier.*

Conodonts

Conifers

Woody branching plants whose reproductive organs are grouped into the familiar cones that give the group its name.

The earliest conifers date from the Carboniferous, but even at this early stage in their history they had become separated into two distinct geographical groups by the TETHYS Sea. The northern group (including *Lebachia*, *Ernestiodendron* and *Walchia*) are referred to as the "walchias". They were regularly branched trees, clothed with spirally arranged leaves that were needle- or scale-like on the ultimate branches; those on the main stems had bifid tips.

In general appearance, walchias probably looked much like the modern Norfolk Island pine (*Araucaria heterophylla*). The male and female cones were borne on the same plant; the male cones occurred singly at the tips of ultimate branches, and the female cones were either similarly located, or grew on the penultimate branches. The female cones had bracts with secondary fertile shoots, but the male cones were of a simpler type (basically a single shoot bearing a spiral arrangement of microsporophylls). This type of male cone has remained essentially unchanged through to the modern conifers. Throughout the Permian and Mesozoic the reduction and fusion of the fertile appendages continued, producing cones that increasingly resembled the familiar pine cones of today.

Modern conifers are grouped into about 500 species belonging to more than 50 genera, arranged in six families: the Pinaceae, Taxodiaceae, Cupressaceae, Podocarpaceae, Cephalotacaceae, and Araucariaceae. Coniferous forests cover vast areas of the Earth's surface, and the group includes the tallest known trees, one specimen of *Sequoia* being more than 112 metres (367ft) tall. The oldest living trees are specimens of *Pinus aristata*, more than 4,000 years old, growing in the mountains of California.

Many modern species and genera of conifers have a markedly disjunct distribution. This is usually considered to be an indication of great antiquity, and each of the six modern families has a fossil record dating back to the Mesozoic. The famous dawn redwood, *Metasequoia glyptostroboides*, was long thought to be extinct; its fossil leaves occur at various localities throughout the world. Eventually a single group of trees was discovered in a temple garden in China. Seeds were distributed and successfully grown, and now most botanic gardens have an example of this LIVING FOSSIL.   J.W.F.

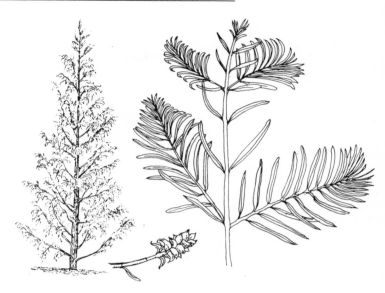

Conifers
The dawn redwood, Metasequoia, was thought to be extinct until some examples were discovered growing in China. The living species, Metasequoia glyptostroboides, grows to a height of 35m (115ft).

GASTROPODS, Cephalopoda, Annelida (WORMS), Chordata (*see* VERTEBRATES) and as unclassified or unknown animals.

Each conodont is formed by the acertion of thin layers, either above a single central pulp cavity or along numerous growth axes. Based on external form, three general morphological types can be distinguished: simple fang-like distacodontids, plate-like conodonts, and compound blade-like or bar-like conodonts. Several types of individual conodont elements, when grouped in bilateral left and right fashion, reconstruct a natural assemblage (conodont apparatus). Each such association is believed to be a functional entity of the conodont animal.

It is reasonable to assume that the conodont animal must have been soft-bodied and bilaterally symmetrical but its suggested identification in the fossil record, based on discoveries in the carboniferous of Montana and the Cambrian BURGESS SHALE of British Columbia, remains unconfirmed. The Canadian animal had been interpreted as a lophophorate in which conodont-like, tooth-shaped elements anchored a food-gathering system of tentacles around the mouth. The conodonts occurring within the Montana fossils were reconstructed either as part of a free-swimming animal ancestral to the vertebrates, or as conodont eaters (not the conodont animal itself).   J.E.P.W.

Conodonts

Dark-brown or greyish-black, tooth-like marine microfossils, about 0.5–3.0mm (less than 0.1in) long, composed primarily of calcium phosphate. They have a worldwide distribution and occur from the Late Pre-Cambrian to the Triassic (faunas reported from the Jurassic and Cretaceous may be derived). Conodonts were discovered in the middle of the 19th century, but their zoological affinities remain uncertain. They have been variously referred to as

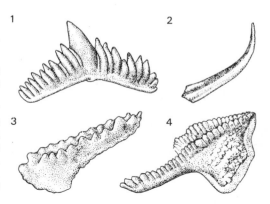

Conodonts
(1) Ozarkodina ranged from the Middle Ordovician to the Upper Triassic (approx. 30 times natural size);
(2) Paltodus occurs from the Lower Ordovician to the Lower Mississippian (approx. 20 times natural size);
(3) Icriodus is a Devonian genus (approx. 25 times natural size);
(4) Gnathodus is present in the Carboniferous (approx. 25 times natural size).

Continental drift

Continental drift

A hypothesis first proposed in 1915 and again in 1922 by the German geographer Alfred Wegener (1880–1930). He suggested that a supercontinent, which he called Pangäa (PANGAEA), existed in the Carboniferous and was subsequently broken up by a process of continental displacement (his original term).

The complementary outlines of Africa and Europe on one side of the Atlantic Ocean, and South and North America on the other side, was noted as long ago as the 16th century. Suggestions that these continental areas once fitted together with the elimination of the Atlantic Ocean were made in the 19th century, and by the early part of the 20th century scientists had begun to recognize the significance of the long mountain chain which runs the length of the central Atlantic Ocean. This chain has a configuration reflecting the outline of the continental margins that border the Atlantic Ocean to east and west. It was thought that the crust of the Atlantic Ocean might have been formed in this central area, and progressively displaced the continents away from it.

The hypothesis of continental displacement

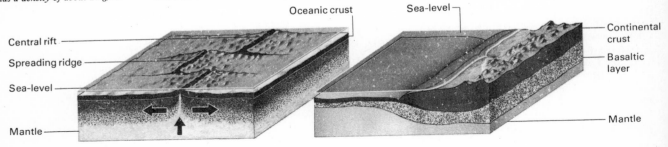

Continental drift
The patterns of palaeomagnetism represent reversals of the Earth's magnetic polarity. They form matching sequences on each side of an oceanic ridge from which ocean-floor spreading has occurred.

was largely rejected by geophysicists, who knew of no mechanism by which such large-scale displacements of continental crust could have occurred. In 1937, however, the South African worker A. L. du Toit (1878–1948) combined the concept of continental displacement with the recognition of palaeogeographic faunal and floral provinces. He showed that the concept of GONDWANALAND in the Southern Hemisphere, separated from Laurasia in the Northern Hemisphere by the TETHYS Sea, was much more logical if the continents were fitted together without the Atlantic and Indian Oceans.

A few geologists, notably Arthur Holmes (1890–1965), speculated on a possible convection current within the Earth's mantle which would permit continental drift, but in the absence of detailed information on the history of the ocean basins no conclusions could be reached. In 1958 analysis of the evidence for global tectonic processes and continental drift showed that a better fit of the continents could

Continental drift
Left: During ocean-floor spreading, the central rift is frequently interrupted by a transform fault – one in which the movement is parallel to the direction of the fault.
Right: This section of the Earth's crust shows part of the upper mantle (density 3.4g/cc), the basaltic layer, and the overlying oceanic crust (sima) which has an average density of 3.0g/cc. The continental crust (sial) has a density of about 2.7g/cc.

be obtained if the Earth was smaller in size (although not in mass) at the time of Pangaea.

Two main lines of research subsequently provided fruitful results. The first concerns the magnetic properties of rocks. All rocks that contain magnetic minerals, such as iron-bearing compounds, preserve a record of the direction of the Earth's magnetic field at the time the rocks were consolidated. Such rocks range from continental red beds consolidated into ferruginous (rust-coloured) sandstone, to basaltic lava which hardened on cooling after eruption from a volcano or after injection into the oceanic crust. When measured, the fossil magnetic orientation (remanent palaeomagnetism) is often found to be different from today's orientation.

Measurements of remanent palaeomagnetism in rocks of progressively different ages, collected from a limited geographic area, showed that the Earth's magnetic pole has changed its position through geological time. Thus the concept of polar wandering developed, and it was found that the polar wander curves of, say, South America, Africa and greater India coincide with each other only if these continents had once been joined together as part of Gondwanaland in the Triassic and Jurassic, and had then separated by continental displacement. It was also discovered that periodic reversals of the Earth's magnetic field had occurred, in which a compass needle would have pointed towards what is now the south magnetic pole.

The second line of research concerned the age and manner of formation of the Earth's oceanic crust. Holmes thought that a system of convection currents in the Earth's mantle, which underlies both the light, low-density continental regions and the heavier, higher density oceanic areas, could be the cause of the continents moving apart. The idea was taken a step further when it was realized that the worldwide system of mid-oceanic ridges were the source of the oceanic crust. These ridges are structures marked by tensional earthquakes and high heat flow. The concept of sea-floor spreading suggested that new oceanic crust welled up as lava at the ridges to form dikes running parallel to the ridge, and the crust so formed was progressively pushed away from the ridge as new crust was injected. If the continental margins displaced from each other by the generation of oceanic crust were of the Atlantic type, without volcanic activity, a full record of the sea-floor spreading history could be obtained.

In margins flanking the central and northern Pacific Ocean, the seismic record indicates that old ocean floor is being thrust down beneath continental (or even oceanic) crust. This concept

Oceanic crust

Sea-level

Central rift

Spreading ridge

Sea-level

Mantle

Continental crust

Basaltic layer

Mantle

Continental drift (cont'd)

is supported by earlier magnetic measurements across the ocean floor, which revealed alternate strips of north and south magnetically oriented crust, running parallel to the mid-ocean ridge. Evidently this sequence of magnetically normal (north-oriented) and anomalously reversed (south-oriented) oceanic crustal strips reflects the already known reversals in the Earth's magnetic field; the new crust was generated almost continuously, but took on the Earth's magnetic field orientation as it was at the time that the lava consolidated. Moreover, the sequence of magnetic strips is found to be symmetrical on each side of the generating ridge. The study of palaeomagnetism and sea-floor (more correctly ocean-floor) spreading has shown that continental displacement did occur.

Ocean-floor spreading data is at variance with the continental drift theory if the Earth has remained the same size (and therefore kept the same surface area) during the last 200 million years, but the data does support the concept of an expanding Earth. Apart from the ocean-floor spreading evidence, the distribution of the land-living dicynodont reptiles during the Triassic is anomalous if a wide Tethyan Sea existed separating greater India in Gondwanaland from China in Laurasia. Fitting together the continents to form Pangaea on an Earth with its present diameter demands the presence of such an ocean, which is in reality a geometric artefact, but the increased surface curvature of a smaller Earth at the time of Pangaea allows Laurasia and Gondwanaland to fit together.

The evidence indicates that 200 million years ago, a large Pacific Ocean already existed. In the mid-Jurassic, the southern part of the North Atlantic Ocean was initiated by the development of a spreading axis between the north-west African margin and the East Coast embayment of the USA. Subsequent ocean-floor spreading, which penetrated progressively northwards, split North America and Greenland away from north-western Africa and Europe, the ocean ridge finally extending into the Arctic region to form the two basins of the Arctic Ocean. The South Atlantic Ocean first developed at the southern end of the joint South American–South African margins in the earliest Cretaceous, later than the initiation of the North Atlantic Ocean. The spreading ridge of the South Atlantic Ocean also extended northwards, splitting Africa and South America away from each other as the ocean widened. These two basins of the Atlantic Ocean became one in the Upper Cretaceous.

The Indian Ocean started to develop at the end of the Jurassic, while Australia and Antarctica together split away from greater India and Africa. Within the Upper Cretaceous the spreading direction changed, with Australia and Antarctica moving southwards relative to greater India and Africa. Greater India was displaced northwards, crumpling up against the southern margin of Laurasia to form the thick pile of sialic rocks under Tibet. Later, in the Cenozoic, a new spreading ridge developed between Australia and Antarctica, separating them from each other by the generation of

Continental drift

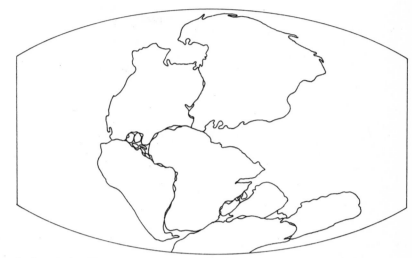

At the end of the Triassic, *the land masses were joined as the supercontinent Pangaea.*

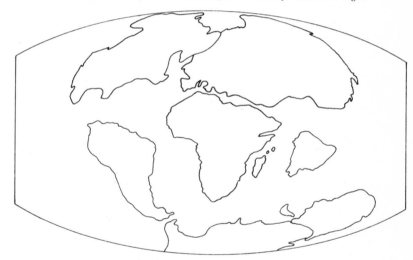

By the end of the Cretaceous, *greater India had separated from Africa.*

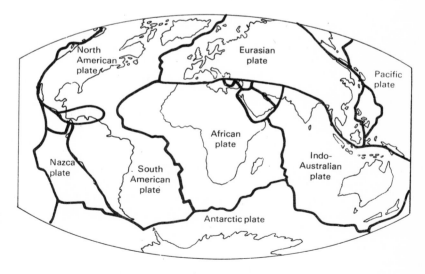

The modern world, *showing the tectonic plates.*

45

Cope

oceanic crust. It then moved progressively north-westwards through the older Indian Ocean crust to separate Arabia from Africa, with the formation of the Gulf of Aden and the Red Sea from the Miocene onwards. This phase also produced the East African Rift Valley system and the Himalayan ranges.

The spreading patterns in the Pacific Ocean show that much of the older pre-Jurassic oceanic crust has been subducted at the continental margins in response to subsequent spreading in the Pacific Ocean and the displacement of North America westwards by the development of the Atlantic Ocean. The pattern of subduction in the North Pacific Ocean appears, superficially, to support the concept of an Earth of constant dimensions. In the South Pacific Ocean, however, there is a vast area of oceanic crust generated from the Late Cretaceous to the present day which is not compensated for by subduction. The insertion of this crustal area and the contemporary areas of the southern ocean ringing Antarctica (parts of the Indian and South Atlantic Oceans) can be reconciled only with an expanding Earth.   H.G.O.

Cope, Edward Drinker (1840–97)

American naturalist who described vertebrate fossils that were discovered during the opening up of the western USA, and became a fierce opponent of Professor Othniel MARSH. Cope was born in Philadelphia, where he later studied. In 1863 he visited Europe, and from 1865 devoted all his research effort to the study of vertebrate fossils. He was a member of several expeditions that described many new types of fishes and reptiles. His most notable contributions were on the Permian reptiles of Texas and the Tertiary vertebrates of the Rocky Mountains. He also attempted a correlation of European and North American vertebrae faunas. He was not a supporter of Charles DARWIN, preferring to ally himself with the theories of Jean-Baptiste LAMARCK.   A.P.H.

Coprolites

The fossilized excrement of animals; the word is derived from the Greek *kopros* (dung) and *lithos* (stone). William BUCKLAND, when working on the Lias of Dorset in the early 19th century, was the first to coin the term and to determine successfully the nature of coprolites.

Although variously defined, it is generally accepted that coprolites include all sizes and chemical compositions of fossil excrement, including small faecal pellets, which are often difficult to distinguish from inorganic pellets or from eggs. The recognition of true coprolites is aided by their structural patterns (spiral or annular markings), contents (undigested food fragments), and associated fossil remains. Sizes vary from less than 5mm (0.2in) in diameter for faecal pellets, to more than 5cm (2in) for the larger coprolites. There are innumerable external forms: cigar-, lens-, kidney-, discoidal- and cone-shaped, or round, oval, cylindrical and spiral, depending on the type of animal and the method of deposition and subsequent preservation. Most of the coprolites analysed are composed chiefly of calcium phosphate, with minor amounts of unaltered organic matter.

Coprolites have been recorded from Ordovician to Recent deposits and a few rare specimens have been used as stratigraphical guide fossils (eg *Favreina* in the Portlandian of Haute-Savoie, France). Some marine (coprogenic) sediments are known to contain a high proportion of faecal pellets. Characteristically, however, animal excrement is easily fragmented and destroyed and has little chance of being fossilized. As with TRACE FOSSILS, a group in which coprolites are sometimes included, Linnean nomenclature is used for their classification, even though the animals responsible typically remain unidentified.   J.E.P.W.

Corals

Invertebrate animals, classified with the COELENTERATES as anthozoan cnidarians which secrete a hard calcium carbonate skeleton.

There are three main orders of corals. The Rugosa and Tabulata are essentially confined to the Palaeozoic, whereas the Scleractinia first appeared in the Middle Triassic and are widely distributed today.

In the Scleractinia, the skeleton or corallum is secreted by the basal calcioblast layer of the coral polyp. In some Scleractinia, the polyp and corallum are solitary, but alternatively the polyps may bud asexually to form a colony, each polyp secreting its own corallite to form a compound corallum (eg in *Cladocora caespitosa*). Radiating vertical partitions (septa) in the corollite correspond to the interspaces between soft fleshy partitions (mesenteries) in the gastric cavity of the polyp. These mesenteries appear during the growth of the polyp in a characteristic pattern of multiples of six, which is reflected in the pattern of septal insertion in the corallite.

Rugose corals also have well-developed septa, but the pattern of septal insertion is different, and new septa occur at only four points in the corallite. Rugose corals may also be either solitary or colonial, but all tabulate corals are colonial. Septa are suppressed in tabulates, being either absent or largely spinose rather than solid plates; each corallite, however, is prominently partitioned by transverse plates called tabulae, which give the group its name.

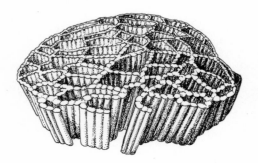

Corals
Halysites *was a common Ordovician and Silurian coral (slightly reduced).*

Cotylosaurs

The first known corals appear in the Cambrian, but they are extremely rare until the Ordovician, when tabulate and rugose corals became widespread. The tabulate corals diversified slightly earlier than the Rugosa, with forms such as *Halysites* and *Favosites* occurring prominently in limestones and calcareous shales of the later Ordovician and the Silurian. After mid-Silurian times, tabulate corals declined steadily until their extinction at the end of the Permian. The rugose corals evolved rapidly in the Early Silurian and had become the dominant group by the middle of that period, retaining an extensive diversity of form until their extinction in the uppermost Permian or earliest Triassic. Solitary forms such as *Chonophyllum* and *Dalmanophyllum* occur in a range of calcareous environments, but colonial rugosans such as *Phillipsastrea* tend to be confined to purer limestones where, with tabulate corals, they may contribute to reefs.

Scleractinian corals probably evolved from a group of naked anemones rather than from the rugose corals. They diversified steadily throughout the Mesozoic and Cenozoic and are at their peak of development today. The scleractinians are more successful than the Rugosa as colonial corals and have evolved complex forms, such as the brain coral (*Platygyra lamellina*). In colder and deeper waters they construct banks.　　　C.T.S.

Cordaitales

Extinct plants which included the tall slender trees that formed great forests in the Upper Carboniferous. The straight unbranched main trunks rose to a height of about 30 metres (100ft) with a crown of branches at their summits. The strap- or paddle-shaped leaves, a metre (3.3ft) or more long, were borne spirally on these branches. Several divisions into subgenera have been suggested, based on the shape of the leaves, but generic identifications are related to details of internal stem anatomy. The arrangement of veins on the leaves bears some resemblance to that of the GINKGOS, whereas the wood of the main stem is remarkably like that of the modern araucarias.

The roots of the cordaitales are placed in the form-genus *Amyelon*; they closely resemble those of modern CONIFERS and, like them, commonly contained (or were associated with) mycorrhizal fungi. The reproductive organs are usually known as *Cordaianthus*, although *Cordaitanthus* is the correct name. The male and female cones are essentially similar in structure and consist of a main axis with bracts, which have short, secondary fertile shoots in their axils.

Several genera of flattened seeds (eg *Cardiocarpus*) are presumed to belong to this group because they are frequently associated with the leaves and other remains of cordaitales. Occasionally, seeds are found with a well-preserved reproductive system (prothallus and archegonia) and pollen grains frequently occur in the chamber of the seed. Like the internal stem anatomy, the pollen grains have a similar structure to the modern araucarias.　　　J.W.F.

Cotylosaurs

The "stem reptiles" which appear in the Early Carboniferous (having descended from undetermined amphibian ancestors) and constitute the ancestral stock of the entire Reptilia. The cotylosaur skull is basically of the anapsid type (*see* REPTILES), with no temporal openings, and the amphibian otic notch has closed up while the reptilian eardrum moved downwards to a position in the side of the cheek just above the jaw articulation.

The earliest cotylosaurs, and hence also the earliest reptiles, were members of the sub-order Captorhinomorpha. The oldest known genus is *Hylonomus*, a small reptile about 1 metre (3.3ft) long with short, sprawling limbs, an abbreviated neck and a long tail. Its remains have been found in the fossilized stumps of Lower Pennsylvanian coal forest trees in Nova Scotia. Along with several other primitive captorhinomorphs of Pennsylvanian or Lower Permian age (eg *Protorothyris*, *Romeria*, *Cephalerpeton*, *Melanothyris* and *Solenodonsaurus*), *Hylonomus* is referred to the Romeriidae. In this family the head tapers to a short, pointed snout; the skull roof is imperfectly bound to the cheek region (where the otic notch had been eliminated); and the teeth possess simple cone-like crowns, with incipient development of caniniform elements and enlarged "incisors".

In the Lower and Middle Permian Captorhinidae, the skull table and cheek region were firmly united and the dentition was becoming specialized, with multiple rows of marginal teeth and considerably enlarged "incisiforms". *Captorhinus* itself is a typical member of this

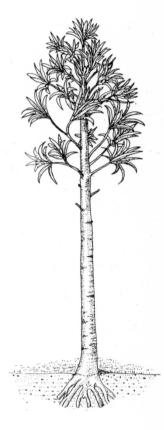

Cordaitales
In the Upper Carboniferous the cordaitales formed extensive forests, with their trunks rising to a height of about 30m (100ft).

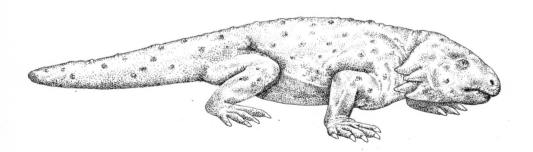

Cotylosaurs
Hypsognathus *was a late-surviving procolophonid from the Upper Triassic of New Jersey. Length: about 33cm (13in).*

Crabs and lobsters

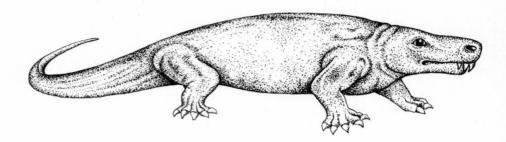

family, and attained a length of about 25cm (10in); *Labidosaurus* was larger, measuring 70cm (28in).

Although a persistently primitive family restricted to the Lower Permian, the sluggish, marsh-dwelling Limnoscelidae nonetheless attained a considerable size, growing to about 1.5 metres (5ft) long. *Limnoscelis* was a massively built sprawling reptile, with short stubby legs, broadly proportioned feet and a low, wide skull. The slender-limbed *Bolosaurus*, an incompletely known genus from the Lower Permian of Texas, had a small lateral temporal opening low in the cheek region but appears to be an aberrant captorhinomorph cotylosaur rather than a synapsid. *Eunotosaurus*, with its remarkably expanded ribs, is also probably a captorhinomorph rather than an ancestral chelonian, as has been suggested.

The suborder Procolophonia includes a variety of small cotylosaurs in which the jaws are shortened and a typical reptilian otic notch is being excavated at the back of the cheek area. There are three constituent superfamilies: the Procolophonoidea, the Pareiasauroidea and the Millerosauroidea.

Procolophonids were superficially lizard-like forms that persisted into the Triassic. Primitive procolophonids are assigned to the Nyctiphruretidae and include *Nyctiphruretus* itself, with a skull about 2.5cm (1in) long, from the Middle Permian of the USSR, *Barasaurus* from the Upper Permian of Madagascar, and *Owenetta* from the Upper Permian of South Africa. More advanced members of the group (Procolophonidae) were widespread in the Early Trias, occurring in Europe (*Koiloskiosaurus*), eastern Asia (*Neoprocolophon*) and South Africa (*Myocephalus* and *Procolophon*). They ranged through the mid-Triassic (*Candelaria* from South America) into the Upper Triassic, where *Hypsognathus* from New Jersey was a highly specialized, spiky-skulled form with a broad, flattened body.

The pareiasaurs were massively built herbivorous cotylosaurs that were common in the Middle and Upper Permian and may have originated from early nyctiphruretid procolophonids. Primitive members of the group were conspicuous in the Middle Permian of the USSR (Rhipaeosauridae), with the more specialized Pareiasauridae subsequently proliferating in Europe (*Scutosaurus*, 2.5 metres (8ft) long), South Africa (*Bradysaurus*, *Embrithosaurus*) and eastern Asia (*Shihtienfenia*), with the small *Elginia* present in Scotland. *Anthodon* and

Pareiasaurus occur in Africa and eastern Europe.

The milleretids, from the Middle and Upper Permian of South Africa, show the development of a lateral temporal opening. This feature is absent in *Millerettops* and *Millerettoides*, incipient in *Milleretta*, and well established in *Millerosaurus*. These small reptiles have no obvious affinities with the synapsids (which are probably of romeriid captorhinomorph origin), but could possibly be diapsid ancestors if a second (upper) temporal opening subsequently formed.

R.S.

Crabs and lobsters

Ten-legged CRUSTACEANS in which the head and thorax are united under a rigid carapace. The cephalothorax contains 13 segments, although one segment may be free outside the carapace, and each segment bears a pair of appendages. In front of the mouth there are two pairs of antennae; behind the mouth are six pairs of appendages for feeding, followed by five pairs of walking appendages, some of which may be grasping (chelate). Typically the appendages are biramous, consisting of an inner branch (endopodite) and an outer branch (exopodite); both branches are jointed and arise from the segmented protopodite. The foremost edge of the carapace is frequently extended into a median spine or rostrum, and its top surface is strongly grooved (representing the sites of internal organs and the location of muscle attachments). The under surface of the carapace is closed by segmental plates (sternites) between the bases of the walking legs.

The abdomen consists of seven segments, which are free in lobsters but may be partly fused in crabs. The first six segments have small appendages (pleopods) which are primitively for swimming, but the front segments may become modified for a reproductive function. The seventh and rearmost abdominal segment is the telson.

The first known true lobster was *Protoclytiopsis* from the Permo-Triassic of Siberia, but various lobster-like genera are also found at about the same time. During the Jurassic the lobsters flourished (eg *Eryma*), but one of the lobster-like groups, the Pemphicidae, began to tuck its extended abdomen under the cephalothorax, and in the Lower Jurassic a true crab, *Eocarcinus*, occurs. Throughout the Jurassic and Cretaceous, lobsters and crabs were competitors for the inshore area. By the Upper

Creodonts

Cretaceous many of today's families of crabs had become established and they slowly assumed domination of the inshore area, so that by the Cenozoic their ascendancy was nearly complete and the lobsters retreated to deeper water.

The development of an air-breathing apparatus by crabs finally established their supremacy, although it is not until the Miocene that the first freshwater or river crabs, Potamonidae, are found as fossils.

The last two groups of crabs to appear are the Cancridea (which contains the common edible crab *Cancer pagurus*) and the Oxyrhyncha (abundant in tropical and sub-tropical seas). They are both present in the fossil record from the Eocene onwards.

See also HORSESHOE CRABS.   S.F.M.

Creodonts

The most powerful carnivorous mammals of the early Cenozoic until the CARNIVORA became the dominant mammalian predators, during the Oligocene. The order (Creodonta) comprises two suborders: the Deltatheridia (already present in the Late Cretaceous) and the Hyaenodontia, which reached their peak in the Eocene and Oligocene and comprise the Hyaenodontidae and the Oxyaenidae.

The later hyaenodontids probably bore a superficial resemblance to hyaenas, as their name implies, but early representatives of this group were slenderly built forms, with elongated skulls and short limbs supported on plantigrade, five-toed feet. *Limnocyon*, from the Middle and Upper Eocene of North America, is probably still close to the common ancestry of both the Hyaenodontidae and the Oxyaenidae, but *Tritemnodon* (an older North American Eocene genus) is a typical early hyaenodontid in which the molar teeth display only incipient development of the shearing carnassials that appear in later genera. *Sinopa* was a Lower and Middle Eocene form that had the outer cusps of the upper molars prominently enlarged, and in *Pterodon* (which appears in the Upper Eocene) three pairs of carnassials can be distinguished: the fourth upper premolar opposing the first lower molar, the first upper molar cutting against the second lower molar, and the second upper molar meeting the third lower molar.

Hyaenodon itself first appeared in the European Eocene and subsequently became the common North American Oligocene member of the family, as well as extending its range into Africa (where it survived until the Miocene) and Mongolia. It was long-bodied and had a massive skull, powerful jaws, a short neck, strong loins, and relatively elongated limbs. The smaller American species of *Hyaenodon* are assigned to the long-tailed subgenus *Protohyaenodon*, and the larger, short-tailed New World forms are assigned to the subgenus *Neohyaenodon*.

Hemipsalodon, from the Lower Oligocene, is the largest known North American creodont, but the Hyaenodontidae became extinct in the Western Hemisphere at the end of the Oligocene. In the Old World, *Pterodon* persisted through the Oligocene into the African Miocene

(where *Metapterodon* and *Leakitherium* are present) and *Dissopsalis* apparently survived into the Late Miocene on the Indian subcontinent, as well as being part of the east African fauna. The giant *Megistotherium*, with a skull 66.5cm (26in) long, was another creodont with a wide geographical range, occurring in the Lower Miocene of Libya and Pakistan (Bugti Hills).

The geological longevity of the Hyaenodontidae was probably due, at least in part, to their well-developed brains, but it seems they were unable to compete effectively with the large felids that appeared during the Oligocene.

The Oxyaenidae are a smaller group than the hyaenodontids with a much more restricted geological range. The heavily built *Patriofelis* from the Middle Eocene of North America was one of the last survivors of the group. This short-bodied creodont had a long, thick tail and stoutly proportioned limbs with spreading five-toed feet. The skull was massively constructed with short powerful jaws, and the dentition had been considerably reduced. Only three premolars remained in each jaw, and the sole surviving upper molar (the first) was a sectorial cutting against the second lower molar (the third lower molar had been lost). A smaller pair of carnassials was formed by the fourth upper premolar and the first lower molar.

Sarkastodon was a large relative of *Patriofelis* from the Upper Eocene of Mongolia that has massive canine teeth but is known only from a single imperfect skull and lower jaw.

The ancestor of *Patriofelis* is probably the Upper Palaeocene and Lower Eocene *Oxyaena*,

Creodonts
Patriofelis, *the characteristic oxyaenid creodont of the North American Eocene, was about the size of a bear.*

Creodonts
Hyaenodon *first appeared in the Upper Eocene and persisted until the Miocene. It ranged in size from the dimensions of a small coyote to large species as big as a wolf.*

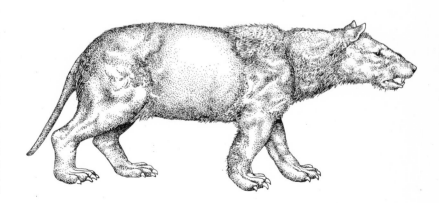

a form in which only the last molars of the upper and lower jaws have been lost.

Palaeonictis occurred in the Early Eocene of North America and Europe and had teeth of a more primitive type than those of *Oxyaena*, the first upper molar and second lower molar being only incipiently developed as carnassials.

The ancestors of the creodonts may have been the Deltatheridia, a suborder of small Late Cretaceous and early Cenozoic animals that are often regarded as insectivores.

Deltatheridium itself, from the Mongolian Upper Cretaceous, had a skull only 4.5cm (1.8in) long, but possessed proportionately large canines and upper molars with sharply V-shaped crowns resembling those found in early creodonts. It has been suggested, however, that this problematical small genus may be a marsupial (*see* CRETACEOUS). R.S.

Cretaceous
Tyrannosaurus, *the largest known terrestrial carnivore, lived in North America during the closing stage of the Cretaceous.*
Length: about 12m (40ft)

65 million years ago

Upper	Maestrichtian	Senonian	Lance
			Edmonton
	Campanian		Oldman
	Santonian		
	Coniacian		
	Turonian		
	Cenomanian		
Lower	Albian		
	Aptian		
	Barremian		
	Neocomian		

140 million years ago
The Cretaceous succession

Cretaceous

The closing period of the Mesozoic Era commencing about 140 million years ago and lasting for 75 million years. The Cretaceous is named after the CHALK (Latin *Creta*) that was laid down in Europe, parts of North America and in western Australia at this time. Some of the deposits exceed 300 metres (984ft) in thickness, and accumulated at a rate of about 30cm (1ft) every 30,000 years.

Early in the Cretaceous, the South Atlantic Ocean began to open up as ocean-floor spreading drove South America and Africa apart, while in the Northern Hemisphere the Labrador Sea appeared and rifting occurred between Greenland and northern Europe about a fulcrum located near the New Siberian islands. The resulting compression and uplift in Siberia led to the birth of the Verkhoyansk Mountains. By the middle of the period, greater India had separated from the east coast of Africa and started its northwards migration, while closure of the eastern end of the future Mediterranean Sea was beginning.

Initially the mild, equable climate of the preceding JURASSIC Period seems to have continued; there was the vast WEALDEN delta in north-western Europe, iguanodont dinosaurs occurred as far north as Spitzbergen, and the reef belt was located at about 45°N, having retreated slightly from its TRIASSIC northern limit of 55°N. Although coal-forming swamps flourished in North America, there was an arid zone in eastern Asia, and the southern USA and southern Europe were still dry. The desert belts, however, had almost settled in their present positions.

During the Middle Cretaceous, extensive greensands accumulated in shallow water, and bluish muds were deposited in deeper seas.

The last 30 million years of the period witnessed widespread incursion of the ocean over subsiding land areas. Rivers flowed sluggishly across the worn-down continents and carried little sediment to the sea. In these conditions the characteristic Cretaceous chalk deposits were laid down while the broken-up remains of coccoliths (ALGAE) – the principal source of the calcium carbonate in chalk – gradually settled through the placid water, accompanied by small fragments of MOLLUSC shells and the calcareous shells of FORAMINIFERANS.

An arm of the sea extended northwards across North America from the Gulf of Mexico into the Canadian North-West Territories, to the west of which the Laramide orogeny was throwing up the Rocky Mountains. The temperature of the water that covered southern Alberta at that time was about 25°C (77°F), and the sea that had flooded Denmark was then about 22°C (72°F),

Cretaceous (cont'd)

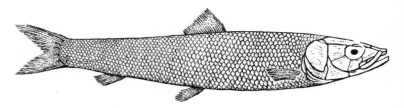

after at one stage in the period falling as low as 16°C (61°F).

Invertebrate life in the seas included abundant BIVALVES (among them the remarkable coral-like rudists, which built reefs along the margins of the TETHYS) and AMMONITES, initially with coiled shells but later becoming partly uncoiled (*Scaphites*) or straight (*Baculites*) before dying out at the end of the period. BELEMNITES were also declining, while BRACHIOPODS consisted principally of terebratulids and rhynchonellids.

The bed of the chalk sea was populated by SEA URCHINS (cidarids, *Echinocorys*, *Micraster*), STARFISHES and CRINOIDS (free-swimming and stalked). SPONGES were numerous, contributing their siliceous skeletons to form the flint that occurs in chalk, and BRYOZOANS included the first cheilostomes. Reef CORALS were not widespread, but there were many solitary types (eg *Parasmilia*), and lobsters had become common.

Modern teleost fishes were much in evidence during the Upper Cretaceous. Forms that are related to salmon and herrings occurred in abundance, together with early members of the tarpon group (*Osmeroides*) and several large fishes such as *Xiphactinus* which probably include the ancestors of the living freshwater osteoglossids. A few palaeoniscoids lingered on for a while, and many of the deep-bodied pycnodont. holosteans survived beyond the end of the period into the Cenozoic, but the flourishing holostean stocks of the Early Cretaceous suffered an abrupt decline when teleosts began to proliferate in the latter part of the period.

COELACANTHS (eg *Macropoma*) flourished briefly for the last time before disappearing into total obscurity, but modern SHARKS were already appearing (*Carcharias*, sand sharks; *Isurus* and *Lamna*, the mackerel sharks and porbeagles), while skates, RAYS and sawfishes were all present in the Cretaceous seas virtually as they are today.

Amphibian life during the Cretaceous was represented only by existing groups (frogs, salamanders), but the reptiles were the lords of creation. COELUROSAURS continued their highly successful career, with two off-shoots from this line appearing in the Lower Cretaceous – the predatory DEINONYCHIDS and the toothless ornithomimids. Early Cretaceous CARNOSAURS included giant forms with greatly elongated dorsal neural spines (*Acrocanthosaurus*, *Spinosaurus*), and by the end of the period the giant tyrannosaurids had spread from their probable evolutionary centre in Mongolia into North America, South America (*Genyodectes*) and greater India (*Indosuchus*).

SAUROPODS had become rare in eastern Asia and North America. Apparently they were unable to compete with the DUCK-BILLED DINOSAURS, which occurred abundantly in these regions, and withdrew to South America, greater India and Transylvania.

PLATED DINOSAURS barely survived the transition from the Jurassic, but ARMOURED DINOSAURS flourished throughout the period, with massive nodosaurs becoming common, and HORNED DINOSAURS arose in Mongolia from psittacosaurid

ORNITHOPODS to reach their peak in North America when the Mesozoic Era began to wane. A few iguanodonts persisted (eg *Craspedodon*), and the smaller type of ornithopod was represented by the Wealden *Hypsilophodon* and the later *Parksosaurus* and *Thescelosaurus*. The curious pachycephalosaurids, with dome-like skulls, occur from the Wealden to the Lance.

PTEROSAURS lost their tails and teeth but grew to enormous sizes, eg *Quetzalcoatlus* with a wing span of 10 metres (33ft). CROCODILES included eusuchians (crocodiles, alligators, thoracosaurines) as well as some surviving mesosuchians (dyrosaurs, pholidosaurs, goniopholids, notosuchids), early sebecids, and a few thalattosuchians.

LIZARDS were becoming common, and giant predatory lepidosaurs had moved into the seas to adopt a fully aquatic mode of life (MOSASAURS). The PLESIOSAURS evolved long-necked elasmosaurid types, alongside which the short-necked pliosaurs continued to prosper, but the ICHTHYOSAURS began to decline early in the period and had become extinct well before its close. TURTLES

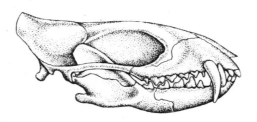

were represented by both pleurodires (among them *Podocnemis*, still living in South America today) and cryptodires (including the huge marine *Archelon*).

Birds had progressed a long way since the Upper Jurassic ARCHAEOPTERYX. Some at least still retained teeth (eg the flightless diver *Hesperornis*, see TOOTHED BIRDS), but the small *Ichthyornis* was undoubtedly capable of efficient flight. Both forms occur in the Niobrara chalk, and *Hesperornis* apparently migrated north to breed at the northern end of the American inland sea, because substantial quantities of juvenile *Hesperornis* remains occur in the North-West Territories (at Banks Island, Eglinton Island, and along the Anderson and Horton Rivers).

Cretaceous mammals included many multituberculates and, in the early part of the period, symmetrodonts, but the pantotheres had become

Cretaceous
Osmeroides *was an Upper Cretaceous fish of the tarpon group. Length: 75cm (2.5ft)*

Cretaceous
Deltatheridium *was a small placental mammal from the Upper Cretaceous of Mongolia. It is often regarded as an insectivore but may have been a member of the creodont group. Skull length: 4.5cm (1.8in)*

Crinoids

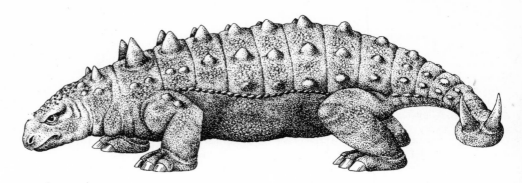

Cretaceous
Scolosaurus lived in the Upper Oldman Formation of Alberta, Canada. No fossil remains of the skull have been found.
Length: more than 5m (16ft)

extinct after giving rise to true therian mammals, including MARSUPIALS not far removed from the living opossums and placentals of the insectivore type. As the Cretaceous drew to a close, there is evidence of a cooler, seasonal type of climate, which apparently led to the EXTINCTION of the dinosaurs and brought the Mesozoic age of reptiles to an end.

See also the time chart. R.S.

Crinoids

A group of ECHINODERMS with a head bearing a crown of arms (usually five). Most fossil crinoids lived attached to the sea floor by a stalk, and their superficially flower-like appearance led to the popular name "sea lilies" by which they are widely known. Surviving crinoids are mostly free-swimming, but pass through an immature stalked stage. In the Palaeozoic, crinoids were abundant but during the Mesozoic the various groups of free-living echinoderms (eg STARFISHES and SEA URCHINS) tended to supplant them, and since the beginning of the Cenozoic the crinoids seem to have been less successful.

Pentacrinites, from the Jurassic of Britain and Germany, is a representative crinoid. It seems to have lived attached to floating driftwood and complete colonies are often found. The stem, which can be many metres long, is made up of calcite ossicles in the shape of a five-pointed star. Occasional ossicles have five

long, jointed, grasping appendages (cirri), and the cup of the head is made up of five large triangular radial plates (to which the arms are attached) and five small basal plates between and beneath the radials, with a hidden whorl of so-called infrabasals. The cup was roofed over by a tegmen incorporating the mouth in its centre and the anus situated in one of the inter-ambulacra. Each arm of *Pentacrinites* divides several times and each portion of the arm is fringed on both sides by short straight twigs called pinnules. When the arms were fully extended they would have made a delicate, fine-meshed network, like a spider's web. The upper surface of the arm had a branch of the water vascular system extending to the end of every twig, and on either side of the radial water vessel there would have been groups of tube-feet.

Modern relatives of *Pentacrinites* live in gentle currents, attached to rocks by the end of the stem. The head of the crinoid trails downstream of the attachment and orients itself so that the arm network is practically vertical, with the mouth and water vascular system on the downstream face. Microscopic animals carried by the current bump into the extended tube-feet, mucus is shot out, and the animals are caught. No doubt *Pentacrinites* lived in much the same way.

The crinoids are divided into four subclasses. *Pentacrinites* represents the subclass Articulata, which includes all post-Palaeozoic crinoids.

Cretaceous
The horned dinosaur Styracosaurus lived in the Upper Cretaceous of North America.
Length: about 6m (20ft)

Crocodiles

Other articulates, placed in the order Comatulida (feather stars), have lost the stem and grasp rocks on the sea floor by a crown of cirri fixed directly to the theca.

Among Palaeozoic crinoids, the subclass Inadunata (eg *Botryocrinus*) is like the articulates, except that special plates are incorporated below the anus into the cup. Inadunates usually have the anus on the end of a tall anal tube. The other two sub-classes are the Flexibilia (eg *Forbesiocrinus*) and the Camerata (eg *Actinocrinus*), both of which have the bases of the arms involved in the cup to a large extent. In camerates the cup so produced is rigid, whereas in flexibles it is (as the name implies) flexible.

The Middle Cambrian *Echmatocrinus* is the earliest and probably the most primitive crinoid known. It was a small attached form with no clear distinction between theca and stem.   R.P.S.J.

Crocodiles

The only surviving ARCHOSAURS. There are several probable crocodiles in the Upper Triassic of southern Africa and China, but all are poorly known and separable only with difficulty from the ancestral PSEUDOSUCHIAN stock. *Protosuchus* from the Upper Triassic of Arizona is an undoubted crocodilian. It was a small reptile, 1 metre (3.3ft) long, and had a short, flattened skull that was beginning to develop a crocodile-like snout. *Protosuchus* was fully quadrupedal, but the hindlimbs were considerably longer than the forelimbs.

The Mesosuchia were the typical crocodiles of the Jurassic and Cretaceous. They had started to evolve a secondary palate that enabled them to breathe while holding prey in the jaws, although at this stage only the premaxillary, maxillary and palatine bones took part in its formation. The most generalized mesosuchians were the goniopholids, which had broad snouts that were only moderately elongated. *Goniopholis* itself had a skull up to 70cm (28in) long and ranged from the Upper Jurassic to the Upper Cretaceous, occurring in Europe, North America and South America.

A series of small, lightly built crocodiles from the Upper Jurassic are assigned to the Atoposauridae, and the short-snouted Upper Cretaceous *Paralligator* from Asia is allocated to a separate family; *Hsisosuchus* from the Upper Jurassic of China and *Gobiosuchus* from the Mongolian Late Cretaceous are similarly isolated forms. Several small short-snouted genera that occur in the Upper Cretaceous of South America are grouped together in the Notosuchidae, *Libycosuchus* from North African deposits of approximately the same date being either a relative or a parallel development.

The best known of all the mesosuchian families are the Teleosauridae – long-snouted forms that lived on fish and superficially resembled the living gavial. *Pelagosaurus* is a conservative genus which occurred in the European Lower Jurassic, but *Machimosaurus* was a more massively built Middle and Upper

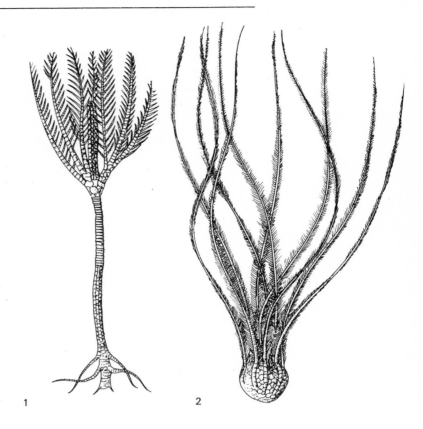

Crinoids
(1) Botryocrinus *was a stalked crinoid from the Silurian (approx. 1/2 natural size).*
(2) Uintacrinus *was a free-swimming Cretaceous crinoid from the Niobrara Chalk of Kansas (approx. 1/4 natural size).*

Jurassic form occurring in Europe, and *Steneosaurus* and *Teleosaurus* became common in the same region during the Late Jurassic. The Pholidosauridae was another long-snouted group; it achieved widest distribution in the Cretaceous after the teleosaurs had become extinct.

A final mesosuchian survival is represented by the Lower Cretaceous–Middle Eocene Congosauridae, which had long slender skulls up to 2 metres (6.6ft) long. They were restricted to Africa (*Dyrosaurus* and *Phosphatosaurus*) and may be pholidosaur descendants.

The purely aquatic crocodiles that lived from the Middle Jurassic into the Lower Cretaceous are known as the Thalattosuchia. *Metriorhynchus*, with its limbs converted into paddles and a fish-like reversed heterocercal TAIL FIN, was essentially an Oxfordian European form, but it also occurs in South America. *Geosaurus* was a more advanced Late Jurassic genus with a long, thin snout. The short-skulled *Dakosaurus* attained a length of 4 metres (13ft) and persisted into the Lower Cretaceous.

During the Late Cretaceous and early Cenozoic one group of crocodiles (the Sebecosuchia) evolved deep skulls with laterally directed eye sockets. They were probably essentially terrestrial forms (*Sebecus*, *Baurusuchus*).

Modern crocodiles (Eusuchia) have the pterygoid bones incorporated in their secondary palate. Early examples of this suborder include *Hylaeochampsa* and *Bernissartia* from the European Wealden and the aberrant Upper Cretaceous *Stomatosuchus* from Egypt with a broad, flat skull about 2 metres (6.6ft) long.

Crustaceans

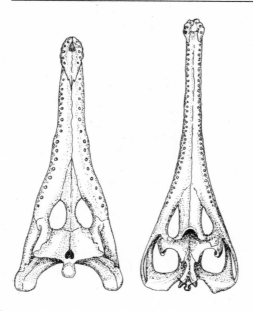

Crocodiles
*Ventral views of crocodilian
skulls.
Left:* Tomistoma *is a eusuchian
with a secondary palate and the
internal nasal opening at the
back of the palatal surface.
Right:* Steneosaurus, *a
mesosuchian, had no secondary
palate and the internal nasal
opening was situated farther
forwards.*

The Crocodilidae itself was present in the Early Cretaceous, represented by *Deinosuchus* which grew to 16 metres (52ft) long during the Upper Cretaceous and *Crocodylus* appearing in the early Cenozoic.

Alligators and caimans date from the Palaeocene. Large forms occurred in the mid-Cenozoic of South America, and *Diplocynodon* was a common Old World genus until the mid-Pliocene. The Thoracosaurinae (*Tomistoma* and its allies) can be traced back to the Late Cretaceous, and *Rhamphosuchus* from the Siwalik series attained a length of about 18 metres (60ft). Gavials are of slightly later origin but appear in the Eocene or Early Oligocene; *Ikanogavialis* is perhaps an aberrant Pliocene relative. *Pristichampsus* is a heavily armoured form that has dinosaur-like teeth and occurs in the Eocene of Europe and North America; it is assigned to a separate family.

The Nettosuchidae consists only of *Mourasuchus*, a large, flat-skulled South American crocodile of Upper Miocene-Pliocene age that was probably totally aquatic. R.S.

Crustaceans

A class of arthropods that includes decapods, ostracods, branchiopods, copepods and cirripedes. The origin of the Crustacea lies with an unidentified coelomate that was segmented metamerically (ie along the primary axis of the body into similar parts). The earliest fossil thought to be a crustacean is the Pre-Cambrian *Parvancorina* from the Ediacara fauna of South Australia, which may have affinities with the branchiopod order Notostraca.

The most abundant forms today (the copepods, euphausiids, isopods and amphipods) have poor fossil records, but ostracods occur abundantly and are invaluable as stratigraphical markers and environmental indicators. The earliest ostracods (from the Cambrian) are marine, but in the Silurian some brackish-water forms appear, and in the Carboniferous there are freshwater examples of the group. It is probable that the most ancient Cambrian forms (the Leperdittidae, eg *Fordilla*) include ancestors of the true ostracods and the bivalved branchiopods (Conchostraca). The first conchostracans are found in Lower Devonian marine sediments, and they quickly became essentially freshwater forms that are locally abundant in the non-marine upper Palaeozoic and Mesozoic.

Another crustacean group that is well represented in the fossil record is the Phyllocarida. It now comprises only four living genera, but probably includes the ancestral stock from which all the higher Crustacea evolved, as well as the cirripedes (barnacles), which have a long geological history and are now widespread. S.F.M.

Cushman, Joseph (1881–1949)

American palaeontologist who established the use of foraminiferans as stratigraphical indices. He was born in Bridgewater, Massachusetts, and attended Harvard University, where he became interested in botany and marine biology. While at the Woods Hole Oceanographic Institute, and later at the United States Geographical Survey (which he joined in 1912), he conducted research on the foraminiferans.

His work was particularly important for the oil exploration industry (then in its infancy) and Cushman soon became an independent consultant. The Cushman Foundation for Foraminiferal Research was established in 1923 and Cushman himself devoted the rest of his life to the study of these protozoans, making more than 550 contributions to the scientific literature, including the classic *Foraminifera, their classification and economic use.* A.P.H.

Cuvier, Georges (1769–1832)

French anatomist and palaeontologist who founded the discipline of vertebrate palaeontology. He was born in Montbéliard (then in Würtemburg), educated in Stuttgart, and quickly rose to fame. He was Professor of Anatomy at the Muséum National d'Histoire Naturelle (1795), Professor of Natural History at the College of France (1800) and Professor of Anatomy at the Botanic Garden (1802). He received many honours and was a Councillor of State (1814), Peer of France (1831) and Minister of the Interior (1832). He had a talent for assimilating and analysing facts but was not an outstanding original theorist.

Cuvier used his skill as a comparative anatomist to untangle some of the problems of studying vertebrate fossils. He was famous for his reconstructions of fossil animals from fragmentary remains, and he was one of the first to make use of the muscle scars on bones while reconstructing an animal's musculature. His classic study *Récherches sur les Ossemens Fossiles de Quadrupèds* was first published in 1812. He propounded the theory of a series of catastrophes that caused the extinction of entire faunas. A.P.H.

Cycads

Cycadeoids

A group of plants that have no modern representatives, but which flourished throughout most of the Mesozoic until they became extinct at the end of the Cretaceous.

Of all the groups of fossil gymnosperms, the cycadeoids have aroused the greatest interest, despite the small number of known species. This is partly because the most familiar genus, *Cycadeoidea*, had reproductive organs that superficially resembled the flowers of angiosperms (FLOWERING PLANTS), ie an elongated central receptacle bearing petal-like bracts, accompanied by whorls of ovules and microsporangia. This arrangement appeared sufficiently like the angiosperm flower to suggest a scheme of angiosperm evolution in which the cycadeoids figured prominently, but it was soon realized that the resemblances are only superficial.

Another theory invoked a link with the living CYCADS, and it is true that the foliage of many cycadeoids and cycads cannot be distinguished on the basis of gross morphology alone. The abundance of these large fronds led to the Mesozoic being referred to as the age of cycads, but cuticle studies immediately separate the two types.

There are two principal groups of cycadeoids. The first includes two families (the Williamsoniaceae and the Wielandiaceae), which comprise plants with slender trunks 2–3 metres (6.6–9.8ft) tall. These plants were often unequally branched and bore a crown of fronds, which were shed as growth progressed to leave a sheath of persistent leaf bases. The second type of cycadeoids fall within one family, the Cycadeoideaceae. They were generally less than 1 metre (3.3ft) tall, and almost 1 metre across, often appearing almost globular. Occasionally branching occurred and produced a cluster of trunks, and flower buds can be seen among the persistent leaf bases, often in great profusion.   J.W.F.

Cycadeoids
A typical example of one of the taller Jurassic cycadeoids, Williamsonia *stood about 3m (10ft) tall.*

Cycads

Woody plants, most of which have unbranched stems. The leaves are large and pinnate, and the reproductive organs are borne in cones. They are often confused with palms. Cycads are ancient and exhibit several "primitive" characteristics. They first appeared in deposits of the Late Triassic and are the only section of the Cycadopsida to have living representatives.

The earliest cycad was *Palaeocycas integer* from the Triassic rocks of Sweden. It had seed-bearing structures and large simple non-pinnate leaves, but reconstructions of this plant are extremely speculative because there are no known examples demonstrating the attachments of its parts.

The most intensively studied fossil cycads are those from the rich flora of the Jurassic rocks on the Yorkshire coast of England. *Beania* from these deposits is a good example of a fossil cycad. The generic name is associated with seed-bearing structures of peltate form (like a nasturtium leaf) arranged into loose cones.

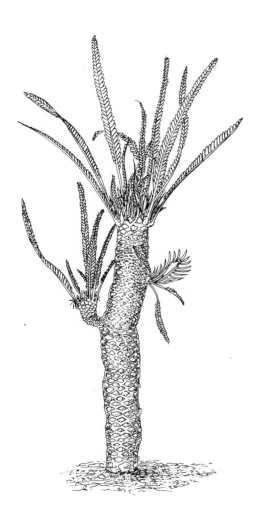

Cycadeoids
Bennettitalean cycadeoids were abundant plants during the Mesozoic.
Height: about 2m (6.6ft)

Detailed investigations of the seeds borne on these structures revealed pollen grains identical with those obtained from the male cones of the genus *Androstrobus*. These cones were smaller and more compact than the female cones, although the spore-bearing organs were of a similar peltate form.

Associated with this reproductive material is a leaf, *Nillsonia compta*, about 40cm (16in) long. The frequent association of these remains and the close resemblance of their cuticles make it highly probable that these three genera represent one complete plant. The bases of the *Nillsonia* leaves are broad, so it seems likely that the stem was a stout structure. This Jurassic cycad was thus a plant with a thick trunk sheathed in leaf bases, and bearing a crown of large leaves, the female cones probably being pendulous.

Modern cycads are represented by nine genera and more than sixty species. They are small remnants of a group that has been in existence for about 200 million years, and formerly was of worldwide distribution, but now occurs naturally only in Central America, South Africa, eastern Asia and Australasia. J.W.F

Dart, Raymond Arthur (1893–)

Australian anatomist who described the first australopithecine fossil. Dart was born in Brisbane, Australia, trained in medicine, and received his degree from the University of Sydney. After the first world war he became senior demonstrator in anatomy at University College, London, and went to South Africa (1923), where he became Professor of Anatomy at Witwatersrand University.

In 1924 the now famous fossil skull of a six-year-old child was unearthed at Taung, Botswana, and sent to Dart for examination. He painstakingly removed the matrix and immediately recognized the significance of the specimen, placing it in the family of man in spite of its ape-like characteristics. He named the find *Australopithecus africanus* (southern ape of Africa) and in 1925 described it to a hostile audience of scientists and non-scientists. Subsequently, other finds of australopithecines have been made in Africa, and Dart's initial ideas have been vindicated. A.P.H.

Darwin, Charles Robert (1809–82)

British naturalist and founder of the modern theory of EVOLUTION. He was born in Shrewsbury, England, and educated in theology at Edinburgh and Cambridge universities, where his interest in natural history was greatly stimulated.

A decisive event in his life was his appointment as naturalist to the survey ship HMS *Beagle* on a voyage (1831–36) to Atlantic Ocean islands, South America and the islands of the Pacific and Australasia. At the time of HMS *Beagle's* departure, the history of the Earth was generally viewed as a series of catastrophies, and the immutability of animal and plant species was still widely accepted. Darwin, however, had access to the first volume of Charles LYELL'S *Principles of Geology* (1830), and by his own acute observation and interpretation he gained a considerable amount of evidence to support Lyell's theories.

As a result of the voyage of HMS *Beagle*, Darwin published several books: *Journal of researches into the Geology and Natural History of the various countries visited by HMS Beagle* (1839); *The structure and distribution of coral reefs* (1842); *Geological observations of the volcanic islands* (1844); and *Geological observations in South America* (1846).

From his observations during the voyage, Darwin conceived his theory for change in species, and he applied himself to this theory on his return to England. In 1858 when he was preparing his results, he learned of the work of Alfred Russell Wallace (1823–1913) on the same theme. Their joint paper was presented to the Linnean Society of London in 1858, followed by Darwin's epoch-making book *On the Origin of Species by Means of Natural Selection* (1859), in which he established evolution by NATURAL SELECTION. Themes within this book were developed later in: *The variation of animals and plants under domestication* (1868), *The descent of Man* (1871) and *The expression of the emotions in man and animals* (1872). A.P.H.

Dating the past

Assessment of the age of rocks either in relative terms, on the basis of their fossil content, or as an absolute value by analysing the decay of radioactive isotopes that occur in some minerals.

At the simplest level, the fossil content of sedimentary rocks gives an indication of relative age – rocks containing TRILOBITES (which became extinct in the Permian) are clearly older than those yielding DINOSAURS (which do not appear until the Triassic). Such events in the evolution of life can be placed on an absolute time scale only by dating rocks associated with them, using radioisotope methods. Thus the trilobites appear in the fossil record at the same time as many other groups with mineralized skeletons – nearly 600 million years ago, at the beginning of the Cambrian. The fact that fossils could be used as an indication of relative age was appreciated by early stratigraphers, but an accurate indication of the length of time involved had to await the development of radioisotope methods. Charles Walcott (1850–1927), one of America's most distinguished early palaeontologists, wrote only in 1911 that the fossils of the Middle Cambrian BURGESS SHALE were "buried in mud 15–20 million years ago"–a gross underestimate.

Dating with fossils offers two main advantages to the stratigrapher. Field identification often gives an on-the-spot indication of the age of the strata concerned, and even where dating depends on microfossils their extraction or preparation in thin section is considerably simpler and cheaper than using radioisotope methods. Furthermore, fossils as yet permit a much finer sub-division of the stratigraphic column than methods utilizing radioactive decay; there are, for example, more than 30 divisions (biozones) of the Silurian Period based on

GRAPTOLITES. Ages indicated by radioactive dating, on the other hand, are generally cited with an error of between 2 and 5 per cent of the value obtained, due to uncertainties in the analytical technique; thus dates in the Silurian incorporate a possible inaccuracy of ± 8 to 20 million years.

Some fossil groups are more suitable than others for use in correlation and in subdividing the stratigraphic column. A common shortcoming is restricted distribution, due to environmental or geographical factors. For example, the first comprehensive attempt to devise a method based on fossils for correlating the Lower Carboniferous (Dinantian) rocks of Britain was made in 1905, using CORALS and BRACHIOPODS to define a succession of zones in the Avon Gorge. The occurrence of these particular ZONE FOSSILS depends, however, on certain ecological factors, and they tend to be confined to specific rock types. A similar scheme was worked out a few years later for northern England, which was separated from the Avon Gorge in the Lower Carboniferous by an east–west trending land mass known as St. George's Land, but all the zones used (except one) were differently named and based on different diagnostic corals and brachiopods. This emphasizes the localized use of such groups for correlation in the Dinantian.

Fossils such as the graptoloids in the Ordovician and Silurian, and the AMMONITES in the Mesozoic (which are widely used for relative dating and correlation) have several attributes in common. They tend to be abundant and (being planktonic) are widely distributed, allowing correlation of outcrops separated by large distances. Their presence depends less on environmental factors than does the occurrence of animals that live on the sea bottom. Ideally, a zonal scheme is based on rapidly evolving lineages, with each fossil group replacing another in quick succession and usually displaying trends in morphological change that are easily observed, such as the elaboration of thecal form in many monograptid lines.

Radioisotope dating is essential to compare the relative time scale based on palaeontological evidence to a scale measured in years, and is also important for clarifying the stratigraphy of the Pre-Cambrian, where fossils are largely absent. Radioisotope methods date the formation of new minerals and have only a limited application to sedimentary rocks. They are usually used to date the recrystallization of minerals due to metamorphism and the formation of igneous rocks. For example, the ages of igneous rocks can be compared with those of the biozones of sedimentary strata.

Most radioisotope dating is based on the accumulation of daughter atoms produced by a radioactive parent atom. Decay occurs at a constant rate and is expressed as a decay constant, which indicates the proportion of existing radioactive atoms that will decay in a unit of time. The time taken for half the radioactive parent atoms to decay is called the half-life, and is unique for each isotope. Most radioisotope age determinations use a few isotopes which combine several essential properties, including a stable decay constant. These are potassium-argon (K40–A40, half-life 11,900 million years), rubidium-strontium (Rb87–Sr87, half-life about 50,000 million years, which makes it suitable for dating Pre-Cambrian rocks) and uranium-lead (U238–Pb206, half-life 4,500 million years; U235–Pb207, half-life 713 million years).

Ages may also be determined on the basis of tracks produced in minerals by the spontaneous fission of the most common isotope of uranium (U-238). Fission track dating involves comparing the density of such tracks with a measure of the uranium present, and can be used to date rocks as old as 1,000 million years. D.E.G.B.

---

da Vinci, Leonardo, *see* LEONARDO DA VINCI.

Deer

The dominant browsing forest ruminants (cervids) of the northern temperate regions since the late Cenozoic. The most characteristic feature of the group is their antlers: bony outgrowths of the skull roof (normally present only on males) that are shed and regrown annually, and impose a considerable strain on the animal's metabolism.

The origins of cervids can be traced back to the early Cenozoic. In Late Eocene and Early Oligocene deposits of Eurasia are found gelocids, small herbivores with four toes on each foot (although the lateral toes are reduced) and skulls without any trace of antlers. From these stocks the dremotheres of the later Oligocene were derived: cervids with two-toed feet, low-crowned browsing teeth and stout upper canine tusks, but no antlers. Dremotheres appear to include the ancestors of deer, giraffes and the North American blastomerycids – a group that reached the Western Hemisphere from Asia in the Early Miocene and survived into the Pliocene. *Blastomeryx* was a small browsing herbivore without antlers but possessing long canine tusks, which were probably used more in sparring than in food gathering.

The protoceratids were another North American stock of deer-like herbivores that are common in Oligocene and Miocene deposits. Although they have a separate ancestry from the cervoids, the males developed branching bony outgrowths not only from the back of the skull, but also on the nasal region.

The true cervids can be traced back to the Miocene in Eurasia but do not appear to have reached the Americas until the Pleistocene. Deer have never penetrated Africa, although a few are known from the Atlas Mountains.

The muntjacs are survivors of the primitive group, and their ancestry can be traced back to the Miocene of Asia through forms such as *Stephanocemas*. This was a medium-sized deer with stout canine tusks and a forest of tines borne on two long bony pedicles. The living muntjacs are small deer that retain prominent tusks and have long bony pedicles from which the single-tined antlers (carried only on males and shed annually) are developed.

Deinonychids

Deer
The so-called "Irish elk" was a giant deer (Megaceros) from the European Pleistocene with antlers spanning about 3m (10ft).

Cervines are well known throughout Europe and North America and include such species as red deer, wapiti and fallow deer. They are large forest browsers, with massive branching antlers in the male.

Megaceros is a gigantic extinct Pleistocene deer. It is sometimes misnamed the Irish elk, but it is really related to the fallow deer and also occurred across temperate Europe and Asia as far as China. *Megaceros* had antlers similar in form to those of fallow deer, but their spread reached more than 3 metres (10ft) and weighed about 50kg (110lb). These deer survived the ICE AGES and did not finally become extinct until about 500BC.

The best known representatives of the Odocoileinae are the elk and the reindeer, both of which inhabit cold wet tundra forests in North America and Eurasia. The elk (or moose, as it is called in North America) has large palmate antlers, and the reindeer is characterized by long antlers that are carried by both males and females.   R.J.G.S.

Deinonychids

A group of carnivorous SAURISCHIAN dinosaurs that appeared in the Cretaceous and are notable for their relatively sophisticated level of specialization. They were apparently bipedal hunting animals capable of sustained intensive activity and endowed with brains that had attained a level of intelligence comparable to that of birds.

Usually assigned to their own infra-order (the Deinonychia) they were probably derived from a COELUROSAUR such as *Coelurus*, and could evidently move extremely quickly on their hindlimbs. In advanced forms the tail was a rigid structure supported by rod-like bony processes growing forwards from each vertebra; in life it was apparently stretched out stiffly backwards to balance the weight of the forward-inclined body.

The forelimbs of deinonychids were long for a carnivorous dinosaur, attaining more than half the length of the hindlimbs. Each had a three-fingered "hand", in which one digit was partly

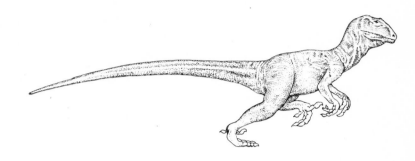

opposable – an indication that it could grasp. The hindlimbs had the shank (tibia) longer than the femur, as in all mechanically efficient running bipeds. There was a highly specialized hindfoot, in which the two outer toes were greatly reduced so that the animal's weight was borne only by the third and fourth digits. The second digit was slightly divergent and modified to carry a huge curved claw, which was drawn upwards clear of the ground when the animal was walking or running but became a formidable weapon for slashing at prey that had been seized in the jaws (which were armed with serrated teeth), or gripped by the forelimbs.

The brain had cerebral hemispheres of considerable size by reptilian standards, which suggests that the deinonychids probably possessed complex behaviour patterns. The olfactory bulbs were prominently developed and the eye sockets were large, so deinonychids may have had exceptionally acute senses of smell and sight for hunting agile prey at night. A COLD-BLOODED reptile would not be able to maintain for more than a few minutes the high level of activity apparently achieved by the deino-nychids, and it seems likely that these very specialized dinosaurs were WARM-BLOODED.

Deinonychus itself was about 3 metres (9.8ft) long, and comes from the Lower Cretaceous of Montana and Wyoming. *Dromaeosaurus* (of which *Chirostenotes* may be a synonym), from the Upper Cretaceous of Alberta, and *Velociraptor*, a Late Cretaceous Mongolian genus, are similar carnivores of smaller size. These three forms may well have preyed on small ORNITHOPODS, because the remains of *Deinonychus* are frequently associated with the bones of a moderate-sized member of this ornithischian group. They probably hunted in packs, judging from the presence of more than one *Deinonychus* skeleton at a single site.

Saurornithoides (Upper Cretaceous of Mongolia and the USA) and *Stenonychosaurus* (Upper Cretaceous of Canada) were more lightly built than the *Deinonychus* group, and possibly represent a separate subfamily in which the tail may not have developed any stiffening rods. Their evident agility probably enabled them to prey on nocturnal mammals.   R.S.

---

de Lamarck, Jean-Baptiste, *see* LAMARCK.

Deshayes, Gérard Paul (1797–1875)
French conchologist whose comparative studies of fossil shells established the divisions of the Tertiary. He was born at Nancy, France, and studied medicine at Strasburg and Paris. He did not go into practice but became a private tutor, which left him time to pursue his conchological and geological interests.

Between 1824 and 1837 Deshayes published one of his most important works, *Description des Coquilles fossiles des environs de Paris.* Having studied and compared hundreds of living and fossil specimens, Deshayes proposed a three-part division of the Tertiary. This was based on the proportion of "living" species to

fossil forms, and was extensively used by Charles LYELL in volume three of his *Principles of Geology* (1833) in establishing the Eocene, Miocene and Pliocene Periods. Forced to sell his collections in 1868, Deshayes became Professor of Conchology at the MUSÉUM NATIONAL D'HISTOIRE NATURELLE, Paris, in 1869.   A.P.H.

Devonian
The oldest of the three geological periods comprising the upper PALAEOZOIC Era. The Devonian began about 395 million years ago and lasted for 50 million years. The name is derived from the county of Devonshire in south-western England, where rocks of this age are extensively developed. The Devonian system comprises seven stages, which are (in order of decreasing age) the Gedinnian, Siegenian and Emsian (Lower Devonian); the Eifelian and Givetian (Middle Devonian); and the Frasnian and Famennian (Upper Devonian).

Devonian rocks are widely distributed, and occur on all of the present continental land masses. A full range of sedimentary rock types is known, including significant areas of non-marine deposits. In Europe, the continental sediments are known as the OLD RED SANDSTONE, after the dominant rock type, and considerable difficulty has been experienced in correlating them with the standard marine Devonian beds. The distribution of the continents was different from that of today, and the "Old Red Continent" covered a large area of north-western Europe, Greenland and North America, forming a single huge land mass.

Devonian life represented the continuance of evolutionary trends inherited from the Silurian after being established in the Ordovician. Some significant changes in the invertebrates occurred, however, and vertebrates and plants showed spectacular evolutionary advances.

Freshwater and marine fishes showed a tremendous proliferation of different forms, many of them possessing heavy dermal armour which has left a good fossil record. The jawless agnathans were represented by a variety of groups, such as the PTERASPIDS and CEPHAL-ASPIDS, but almost all became extinct in the Upper Devonian, leaving only the living lampreys and hagfishes as possible descendants. The first major radiation of the true fishes was a Devonian event, with ACANTHODIANS and, in

Deinonychids
The agile dinosaur Deinonychus *lived in the Lower Cretaceous of the* USA.
Length: about 3m (10ft)

345 million years ago

	Stage	Series
Upper	Famennian	Chautauquan
	Frasnian	Senecan
Middle	Givetian	Erian
	Eifelian	
Lower	Emsian	Ulsterian
	Siegenian	
	Gedinnian	Cayugan

395 million years ago
The Devonian succession

Devonian (cont'd)

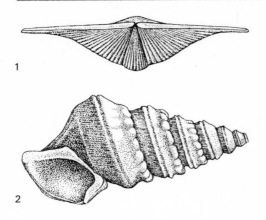

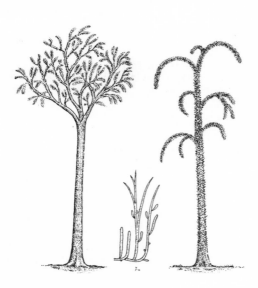

Devonian
(1) The brachiopod
Cyrtospirifer *ranged from the Middle Devonian to the Lower Carboniferous (approx. 1/2 natural size).*
(2) Murchisonia *was a Devonian to Lower Carboniferous gastropod (approx. natural size).*

Devonian
Left: In the Upper Devonian the club moss Cyclostigma *grew to tree-like dimensions.*
Centre: The psilophyte Rhynia, *from the Middle Old Red Sandstone of Scotland, was only about 18cm (7in) tall.*
Right: By Middle Devonian times there were already tree-like club mosses (Protolepidodendron *).*

particular, PLACODERMS characterizing the period. The first representatives of the Chondrichthyes, which includes the living SHARKS and RAYS, occur during the Devonian. The bony fishes (Osteichthyes), which had been represented by only a single suborder in the Silurian, underwent a remarkable radiation in the Devonian with the advent of actinopterygians (RAY-FIN FISHES), crossopterygians (LOBE-FIN FISHES) and dipnoans (LUNG-FISHES). The crossopterygians were particularly diverse and included the rhipidistian fishes, which gave rise to the first LABYRINTHODONT amphibians in the Late Devonian.

Land (vascular) plants also show remarkable diversification in the Devonian, and the forerunners of all the major elements of the well-known CARBONIFEROUS flora appeared during the period. Evidence comes from both plant macrofossils and from palynology (the study of fossil spores), although there are difficulties in relating the two. The first forests occurred in the Middle Devonian.

Among the invertebrates, a rich fauna of BRACHIOPODS, CORALS, stromatoporoids, TRILOBITES, MOLLUSCS, BRYOZOANS, and ECHINODERMS flourished in the shallow seas. SPONGES were locally abundant. In-shore, sandy and silty rocks are characterized by brachiopods (particularly

the "long-eared" spiriferids), with BIVALVES, burrowing organisms and a few specially adapted corals. Offshore, in water free from detritus, carbonate banks could develop, sometimes with reef edges constructed of stromatoporoids, corals and a rich associated fauna including brachiopods, trilobites, bryozoans and CRINOIDS. In deeper offshore environments, muds accumulated that are characterized by the remains of goniatite cephalopods (*see* AMMONITES), small planktonic styliolinids, and OSTRACODS.

The major invertebrate faunal change in the Devonian was the evolution from the nautiloids of the cephalopod molluscs known as goniatites (with their coiled, chambered shell), corresponding closely with the extinction of the planktonic GRAPTOLITES. The last monograptid occurred in the Emsian, whereas the first goniatite appeared in the immediately preceding Siegenian, after which these cephalopods diversified rapidly and maintained a high evolutionary rate throughout the period. Among benthic (bottom-dwelling) molluscs, bivalves and GASTROPODS increased in variety, and scaphopods appeared for the first time. Of the other invertebrate groups, the brachiopods show great diversity, with the evolution during the Devonian of the terebratulids and productids.

Rugose corals reached a peak with many new genera, and the tabulate corals continued their decline in variety although remaining common in carbonate environments. The stromatoporoids flourished briefly for the last time before becoming virtually extinct at the end of the Devonian, and TRILOBITES had a brief resurgence with phaeopids the most common group, although only proetid forms survived the period. The giant eurypterid arthropods (SEA SCORPIONS) of the fluviatile and brackish-water environments reached their peak, and crinoids were particularly abundant. Other echinoderm groups, including blastoids, cystoids (which disappeared by the end of the Middle Devonian), holothurians, ophiuroids (brittle stars) and asteroids (STARFISHES), were also present. The enigmatic CONODONTS were most diverse during the Upper Devonian.

The goniatites and the conodonts are the most important fossils for dating marine Devonian rocks, although other organisms have to be used when these forms are absent. Plant spores and fishes are used to date non-marine sequences. Correlation of continental with marine rocks relies on fish remains swept down into the marine environment, and the inter-tonguing of marine and non-marine fossiliferous sediments.

Faunal provinces were not strongly marked in the Devonian, although they were more pronounced than in the Silurian. Northern and southern high-latitude provinces of limited diversity continued from the Silurian and were most marked in the Lower Devonian. In addition, corals and brachiopods clearly differentiated an East American realm, including northern South America, from an "Old World" realm comprising the rest of the equatorial area during the Lower and Middle

Devonian. This East American realm was an epicontinental sea isolated by areas to the north, west and east which were generally emergent throughout this period.

See also the time chart.   C.T.S.

Diatoms

Members of the brown ALGAE (Phaeophyta) whose cells are enclosed in siliceous shells, like a box with an overlapping lid. They are either unicellular or colonial, but never form structured plant bodies.

The peculiar construction of the silicified cell membrane leads to a large variation in size within a single population which is not related to the age of the individuals. The silica shells bear complex markings which are constant for genera and species and enable identifications of these small plants to be made.

Diatoms are common in fresh water and salt water, usually reaching a peak of abundance in spring, when they form a large constituent of algal blooms in fresh water and of coloured tides in coastal regions. They are important geologically because the hydrated silica of their shells is usually insoluble and persists after the death of the diatom. Deposits of these shells form diatomaceous earth, diatomite or kieselguhr. Extensive deposits of diatomaceous earth occur in many geological periods, some (such as those at Dolgellau in northern Wales and Blin in Czechoslovakia) being of great thickness.

Diatomaceous earth has several commercial uses. Once employed extensively as a constituent of dynamite, it is now used for insulating materials and as a filtering, packing, and fine-polishing medium (Tripoli powder). The nature, arrangement and regularity of the markings on the shells of diatoms made them useful for testing microscope lenses.   J.W.F.

Dinosaur National Monument

A quarry near Vernal, Utah, discovered in 1909 by Earl Douglass (1862–1931), where the 4.5 metres (14.8ft) thick strata of the MORRISON FORMATION has been tilted by Earth movements into an almost vertical position. The later deposits which had buried this Upper Jurassic rock were cut away by palaeontologists to reveal a wealth of dinosaur bones, and in the 1950s a permanent building was erected so that visitors could see the fossils preserved in the 9 metres (30ft) high wall of the quarry. There are two spectators' galleries, the upper one providing a view of the higher section of the 59 metres (194ft) long exposure, and explanatory exhibits provide background information.

The original 32-hectare (80-acre) site (since substantially extended) was designated the Dinosaur National Monument by President Woodrow Wilson in 1915, and until the spring of 1923 the excavations there were under the auspices of the Carnegie Museum, for which Douglass worked. In 1923 the American National Museum spent a season there, but little subsequent work was undertaken at the quarry

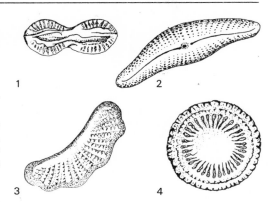

1   2   3   4

until the National Park Service began construction of the present display building in 1953, completing the work in 1958.

Palaeontologists are continuing to work on the quarry face, developing the material to relief the bones and in the process frequently discovering new and valuable material. The fauna represented at the Dinosaur National Monument includes the CARNOSAURS *Antrodemus* (alternatively known as *Allosaurus*) and *Ceratosaurus*, the SAUROPODS *Camarasaurus*, *Diplodocus* and *Atlantosaurus*; the PLATED DINOSAUR *Stegosaurus*; the small ornithopod *Laosaurus*; and the large bipedal ornithischian *Camptosaurus*.

During the Upper Jurassic the site was apparently a shallow part of a large river, perhaps the location of a sandbar. Some of the animals whose remains are preserved may have become bogged down while attempting to ford the river at this point, but most of the skeletons are probably from carcases swept down the watercourse into the shallows. The long necks and tails of the sauropods seem to have trailed out in the current and are preserved in extended positions, aligned with the assumed direction in which the river flows.   R.S.

Dinosaurs

The name Dinosauria, meaning "terrible lizards", was proposed by Sir Richard OWEN in 1841 during an address to the British Association for the Advancement of Science, at Plymouth.

The ORNITHOPOD *Iguanodon*, the CARNOSAUR *Megalosaurus* and the ARMOURED DINOSAUR *Hylaeosaurus* had all been described within the preceding 20 years, and since they could not be satisfactorily fitted into any known group of reptiles, Owen erected for them a "distinct tribe or suborder", the Dinosauria.

More land-living Mesozoic reptiles of large size soon came to light, particularly in North America where Edward COPE and Othniel MARSH engaged in a fierce scientific rivalry that led to rapid exploitation of the fossil-rich MORRISON FORMATION. The term Dinosauria was retained to embrace all of these newly discovered Jurassic giants until the English palaeontologist H. G. Seeley (1839–1909) recognized that two different groups of extinct reptiles, the "lizard-

Diatoms
(1) Diploneis, *from the Pliocene, was about 33 micrometres (1.3 × 10⁻³in) long.*
(2) Cymbella, *from the Pliocene to the Recent, was about 34 micrometres (1.34 × 10⁻³in) long.*
(3) Eunotia, *from the Pliocene, was about 34 micrometres (1.26 × 10⁻³in) in diameter.*

Disease

Dinosaurs
Above: the triradiate pelvis of an ornithischian (Thescelosaurus) has a pubic bone (black shading) that extends backwards and downwards parallel to the shaft of the ischium in a bird-like fashion, only a pre-pubic process continuing to project forwards. Below: in saurischians (Antrodemus) the pubis (black shading) is conventionally orientated, projecting forwards and downwards to form a triradiate pelvis.

hipped" SAURISCHIANS and the "bird-hipped" ORNITHISCHIANS, were being placed within a single assemblage. He announced his conclusions in 1887 and formally proposed the names Saurischia and Ornithischia for his two new orders.

Thereafter "dinosaur" became merely a convenient collective term to describe members of both the Saurischia (COELUROSAURS, DEINONYCHIDS, carnosaurs and SAUROPODS), which had a triradiate reptilian type of pelvic girdle, and the Ornithischia (ornithopods, armoured dinosaurs, PLATED DINOSAURS, DUCK-BILLED DINOSAURS and HORNED DINOSAURS) in which the pelvis was bird-like with the posterior process of the pubis directed backwards parallel to the shaft of the ischium.

Although both groups were ARCHOSAURS descended from thecodontians and tended to attain large size, they appear to be no more closely related to each other than CROCODILES are to PTEROSAURS — archosaur groups which also trace their ancestry back to the thecodontians.

With increasing evidence of WARM-BLOODED (endothermic) physiology in ornithischians and saurischians, the term Dinosauria was resurrected in the mid-1970s to embrace both of these reptile groups and their probable descendants, the birds, together with their ancestors, the PSEUDOSUCHIANS. The class Dinosauria, it was suggested, might be placed in a superclass Endosauropsida that included pterosaurs, because these flying reptiles were also almost certainly endothermic and may even have developed a hairy covering to conserve body heat.　　　　　　　　　　　　R.S.

Disease, *see* PALAEOPATHOLOGY.

Dogs

Members of the family Canidae. These medium-sized representatives of the CARNIVORA include wolves, foxes, jackals and coyotes. Canids lack the extreme specialization of the CATS and HYAENAS, and can live on varied diets, thus occupying a large range of habitats.

The family now occurs on all continents, although in Australasia and Antarctica they owe their introduction to man. They can withstand climates ranging from arctic cold to tropical heat and can outwalk almost any other animal. Their digitigrade feet carry the weight on the toes, which effectively still further increases the length of the already elongated limbs. There are four clawed digits on each foot, and a vestigial dew claw on the forefoot.

Although primarily flesh eaters with a strong carnassial dentition, the canids tend to be catholic in their tastes and eat a wide range of vegetable and animal food, which they crush with their broad, flat molar teeth. Canids are highly intelligent, have keen vision and hearing, and a well-developed sense of smell.

The earliest true dogs (eg *Hesperocyon*) appear in the North American Oligocene. They were small, like a fennec or desert fox, and retained a number of characteristics indicating

their miacid ancestry. Distinguishing features included an ossified auditory bulla, a long face, and a well-developed shearing blade on the carnassial teeth. This basal stock continued into the Miocene through *Enhydrocyon*, a large hyaena-like dog, but several groups of advanced dogs had meanwhile evolved from the ancestral *Hesperocyon* stem.

The borophagines thrived in the Miocene and the Pliocene in North America, with a few surviving into the Pleistocene. They were relatively short-faced dogs, their foreheads having a swollen appearance like some domestic breeds. The neck and limbs were short, the jaws massive, and there were robust canine teeth and large rear premolars (closely resembling those of hyaenas). These dogs probably specialized in bone crushing, filling the hyaenoid niche in America.

The amphicyonids were a successful stock with resemblances to both dogs and bears. They are found in Holarctic regions from the Early Oligocene through into the Pliocene, and during the Miocene were living in Africa. Amphicyonids were similar to cursorial canids and ambulatory ursids in dental and postcranial anatomy, *Daphoenodon* from the North American Miocene being a typical genus with wolf-like proportions.

All the living canids can be considered to belong to the subfamily Caninae. Although traceable back only to the Pliocene, they have been immensely successful during the past five million years and have radiated to almost all parts of the world. The small arctic fox *Alopex* is found in arctic regions of the Northern Hemisphere; southwards in temperate regions are other foxes of the genus *Vulpes*. Still farther south in the Sahara Desert is the small desert fox *Fennecus*, and *Otocyon* (the bat-eared fox) inhabits near-desert areas in eastern and southern Africa. The hunting dog *Lycaon* occurs throughout much of Africa south of the Sahara and hunts in packs, usually of 6 to 20 dogs.

Canids reached South America in the Pleistocene and rapidly radiated across the continent, evolving many species in an area where they had little competition because the only native carnivores were the few surviving borhyaenid MARSUPIALS. *Speothos*, the bush dog, is a small stocky genus with short legs and a short tail, first described from fossils collected in a Brazilian cave. *Chrysocyon* is the maned wolf from the pampas, which resembles a fox but has extremely long legs.

The genus *Canis* includes the wolves, the coyote, jackals, the dingo and domestic dogs. There are two living species of wolf, one inhabiting northern parts of North America and Eurasia and the other restricted to the southern USA. Equalling them in size was the dire wolf, *Canis dirus*, from the Pleistocene tar pits of RANCHO LA BREA, where the remains of more than 2,000 individuals have been recovered.

The coyote, *Canis latrans*, ranges widely from Alaska to Central America and feeds mainly on rodents. The jackals inhabit Africa, with one species extending into Asia, and are the medium-sized canine predators filling the niche occupied

Domestication

by wolves in the extreme northerly latitudes.

Australia is the home of the dingo, *Canis dingo*, a wild species which was probably introduced into Australia by man. The domestic dog, *Canis familiaris*, was one of the first mammals to be domesticated. Domestic dogs occur at Starr Carr in Yorkshire (7500BC), and were present in Iran at about the same time. They appear to have been derived from wolves, but are unknown in Palaeolithic levels, so their origins may date from the Mesolithic of Asia in about 10000BC.   R.J.G.S.

Domestication

In the early stages of modern man's development, the need to obtain food by hunting, fishing and gathering fruits severely restricted human progress. In the 10,000 years that followed the commencement of farming, *Homo sapiens* established permanent settlements, began to accumulate historical records, and developed a section of the population whose activities were not directly related to obtaining food. In turn these social advances led to the forming of villages, towns, city states and nations.

Farming was a gradual transition begun by the peoples of the advanced PALAEOLITHIC and MESOLITHIC, and was not solely confined to the NEOLITHIC, despite frequent allusions to the "Neolithic revolution". The cultivation of crops undoubtedly arose from the gathering of plant seeds. It seems reasonable to assume that some tribes would know of areas within their territory where seeds of grasses could be found at certain seasons. This collecting of seeds would regulate the tribe's movements, so that they could be in that area at the time of harvest. Such areas occurred in south-eastern Asia, where natural stands of two-seeded Einkorn grass were collected by Mesolithic peoples. It is not known why they first considered settling near this valuable food source, but it may have been done to protect their group from other nomads.

Dogs
(1) Cynodictis, *a primitive member of the dog family, first appeared in the Late Eocene and was fairly common in the Lower Oligocene. It was about the size of a fox.*
(2) Daphoenodon, *the Lower Miocene "bear-dog" from North America, was the largest canid of its time.*
Length: about 1.5m (5ft)
(3) The dire wolf, Canis dirus, *which is the same size as modern wolves, is common in the asphalt deposits of Rancho La Brea.*

d'Orbigny

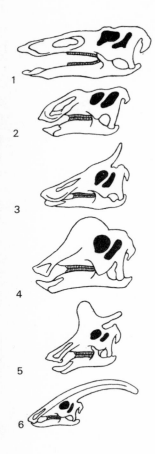

Duck-billed dinosaurs
*Above: skulls showing
crest development*
(1) Anatosaurus;
(2) Kritosaurus;
(3) Saurolophus;
(4) Cheneosaurus;
(5) Lambeosaurus;
(6) Parasaurolophus.
*Below: the uncrested
hadrosaurine* Anatosaurus *was
about 10m (33ft) long.*

Once man had settled, he probably began to notice that some of the seeds were larger and better than others, and would have started a deliberate policy of selecting the best seed and sowing it in the next season. As a result the quality of the grain steadily improved. The archaeological evidence in south-eastern Asia indicates that man was cultivating three grasses as cereals about 11,000–9,000 years ago: two-rowed barley and Emmer and Einkorn wheat. He probably first collected the seeds by hand-picking, and later used flint sickles made by setting flint blades in horn; examples of such tools have been found, with the flints polished by constant use. This area of wild cereals stretched from Jordan and Israel through Anatolia into northern Iraq and western Iran, and it is here that the remains of the first permanent human settlements are found, together with carbonized seeds of the cereals cultivated. These cereals are still so closely related to our modern varieties that they can be easily crossed. In addition to cereals, peas and capers were grown. From this primary area the knowledge of farming techniques spread into Europe and Asia during the next 3,000–4,000 years.

During the early stages of farming, hunting was still important, but gradually the keeping of livestock replaced this activity. Apart from the dog, apparently kept as a pet 10,000 years ago, the first animals to be domesticated were the goat (8500BC), sheep (7500BC), pig (7000BC) and cattle (6500BC).

South-eastern Asia was not the only centre in which cultivation developed. In China the people developed their own cultures, the first peasant cultivations being located in the Yellow River basin. From this point of origin, the idea of agriculture progressed northwards and southwards through the deciduous tree zone and then, in the north, into the coniferous tree belt. During this movement cattle, sheep and the horse were domesticated and in southern China and south-eastern Asia rice was added to the cultivated plants.

Agriculture was also a separate development in the New World, but because the Old World cereal plants were not available, farming in the Americas was usually based on maize (corn), with the main areas located in Mexico and Peru. In the absence of maize, some New World communities achieved a form of settled agriculture based on tubers, squashes and beans. The New World development was late (5000BC), and did not include much of North America.

African agriculture was also late in developing, and evidence indicates that the first African farmers did not become established until 3000BC. In Australia, the aborigines never did succeed in evolving any form of settled agriculture.   D.T.

d'Orbigny, Alcide, *see* ORBIGNY.

Dubois, Eugène (1858–1940)

Dutch anatomist and palaeontologist (born in Eijsden, The Netherlands) who discovered JAVA MAN (*Homo erectus erectus*). Dubois attended medical school and became a lecturer at the University of Amsterdam. He always had an interest in natural history and from an early age collected fossils. He was inspired by the work of Charles DARWIN and Alfred Russell Wallace (1823–1913), both of whom believed that man's ancestors lived in the tropics. He was particularly taken by Wallace's description of an orang-utan. Unable to raise funds for an expedition to find the "missing link", he enlisted in the Dutch East Indian Army and left for Sumatra, transferring to Java in 1890.

Practically all his time in Java was occupied with palaeontological research, and he had modest support from the Dutch government. His famous discovery on the banks of the Solo River was described in 1893 as *Pithecanthropus erectus*. When he returned to The Netherlands in 1895 he learnt that his find was the centre of scientific controversy. Throughout his life Dubois maintained that what he had found was the "missing link" between man and the apes. It is now accepted that his discovery is the earliest undisputed record of the genus *Homo*.   A.P.H.

Duck-billed dinosaurs

Members of the ORNITHISCHIAN family Hadrosauridae, which constitute the final stage of ORNITHOPOD evolution. The duck-billed dinosaurs did not appear until the Upper Cretaceous and were probably semi-aquatic. Their hindlimbs were long and powerful, however, with three-toed feet, and the hadrosaurs were essentially bipeds. The relatively long forelimbs had a four-fingered "hand", with hoof-like ungual phalanges at the end of the second, third and fourth digits that indicate regular reversion to quadrupedal habits, perhaps while feeding. The deep, laterally compressed tail appears to have been adapted for swimming, and the flattened, duck-like muzzle strongly suggests a diet of water plants, but the teeth formed complex grinding batteries of up to 60 vertical

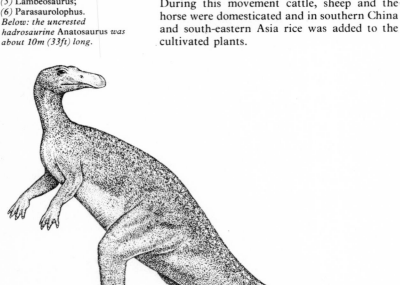

Duck-billed dinosaurs (cont'd)

rows that made a tessellated pavement suitable for crushing hard, abrasive food, and the fossilized stomach contents of one hadrosaur contained deciduous twigs and conifer needles, from which it must be assumed that these animals foraged in the Late Cretaceous forests.

An early hadrosaur is probably represented by a single tooth from the Cambridge Greensand of England (*Trachodon cantabrigiensis*), but in North America, where the duck-bills eventually became particularly abundant, the oldest genus is *Claosaurus* from the Niobrara Chalk. This slender form with a long tail is assigned to the subfamily Hadrosaurinae, together with other fairly conservative duck-bills that had not developed the elaborate skull crests characteristic of more specialized members of the family. *Edmontosaurus*, from Alberta, is a typical hadrosaurine, attaining a length of up to 10 metres (33ft); *Anatosaurus* from the Late Cretaceous of Wyoming and Montana is similar. *Kritosaurus*, ranging from Canada to New Mexico, has a slightly modified skull with arched nasal bones, as did *Lophorhothon* from Alabama and *Aralosaurus* from Kazakstan. Other Old World forms included *Tanius* from China, *Mandschurosaurus* from Mongolia and Indochina, and the small and primitive *Orthomerus* from Europe.

The Saurolophinae represent a slightly more specialized stage in hadrosaur evolution, *Prosaurolphus* (from Alberta) and *Saurolophus* (from Canada and eastern Asia) having developed an incipient backward-projecting crest still formed principally from the nasals. *Brachylophosaurus* combines this rudimentary type of crest with arched nasal bones and is usually classified as a saurolophine, together with the Chinese *Tsintaosaurus*, which has a tube-like nasal process projecting almost vertically upwards.

Two intermediate genera that have crests of moderate size are grouped in the Cheneosaurinae, but both *Cheneosaurus* itself (from Canada) and *Procheneosaurus*, 4.5 metres (14.8ft) long, from North America and eastern Asia, are relatively small.

The most advanced hadrosaurs are the Lambeosaurinae, in which the crest (formed from the premaxillae as well as the nasals) acquires a substantial size. *Hypacrosaurus*, 9 metres (29.5ft) long, and *Corythosaurus*, 10 metres (33ft), have a helmet-shaped crest through which the nasal passage forms a loop. *Parasaurolophus* has a parallel-sided extension of the nasals curving backwards and enclosing two pairs of tubes; *Lambeosaurus*, possibly up to 16 metres (52.5ft) long, developed a crest rising at an angle of 90 degrees or more from the facial profile. All of these genera are exclusively North American.

The purpose of the hadrosaur crest is unknown. It is difficult to imagine how it could have facilitated respiration when the animal was in the water, as is sometimes suggested, but it may have enhanced the sense of smell, fulfilled a species- and sex-recognition function (with associated soft tissue), or acted as a resonator. The arched nasal bones of *Kritosaurus* might have been used as a butting weapon.   R.S.

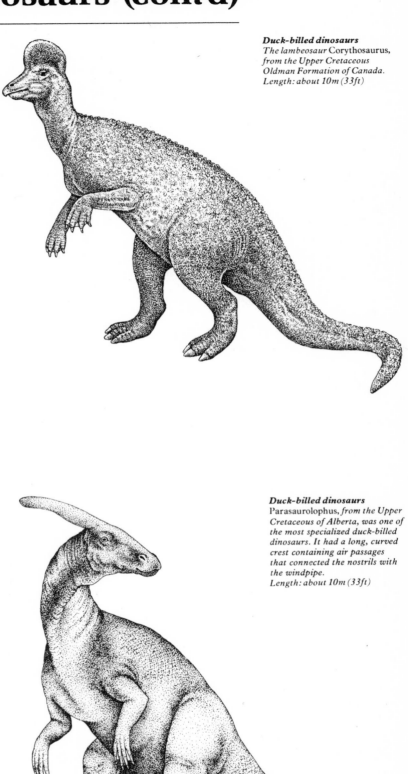

Duck-billed dinosaurs
The lambeosaur Corythosaurus, from the Upper Cretaceous Oldman Formation of Canada. Length: about 10m (33ft)

Duck-billed dinosaurs
Parasaurolophus, from the Upper Cretaceous of Alberta, was one of the most specialized duck-billed dinosaurs. It had a long, curved crest containing air passages that connected the nostrils with the windpipe.
Length: about 10m (33ft)

Dugongs

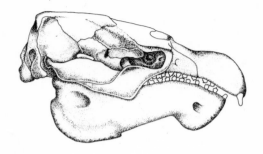

Dugongs

Included with the manatees in the mammalian order Sirenia ("sea cows"). Dugongs live off the shores of eastern Africa and Australia, feeding on sea grasses, whereas manatees occur in rivers flowing to the Atlantic Ocean in North America, South America and western Africa, and feed on surface vegetation.

Protosiren was a primitive Egyptian form of Eocene age, and *Prorastomus*, a comparably conservative genus, lived at the same time in Jamaica. *Eotheroides*, common in the Egyptian Eocene, still retained vestigial hindlimbs, but appears to have been evolving towards the dugongs, which subsequently became particularly abundant in the Mediterranean region during the Oligocene (*Halitherium*), Miocene (*Halianassa*) and Pliocene (*Felsinotherium*).

The fossil history of the manatees is poorly known, and the sirenians as a whole may possibly share a common ancestry with the ELEPHANTS. *Desmostylus*, *Paleoparadoxia* and several related aquatic genera from the mid-Cenozoic of the northern Pacific Ocean may share a common ancestry with the sea cows and the elephants, but retained fully developed forelimbs and hindlimbs, and are customarily assigned to a separate order, the Desmostylia.   R.J.G.S.

Ear

In fishes, the ear region is concerned with balance and the detection of vibrations in the water. The latter function is performed by the lateral line system, comprising a series of small nerve organs in the head region and running the length of the body. When the VERTEBRATES emerged on land, such a system could no longer operate and a new mechanism for detecting faint vibrations in the air, ie sound waves, developed. The spiracle became closed off by a membrane, the tympanum or eardrum, and the upper part of the hyoidean GILL support, the hyomandibular bone (immediately behind the spiracle), ceased to participate in the suspension of the JAWS from the skull. Instead this bone took on the new function of conducting sound. Vibrations impinging on the tympanum are transmitted via the oval window (fenestra ovalis) to the fluid-filled region of the inner ear. This sound-conducting bone is known as the stapes (stirrup) or columella and is found in amphibians, reptiles and birds.

In MAMMALS, the ear is different: there are three sound-conducting bones. During the evolution of the paramammals (MAMMAL-LIKE REPTILES), the tooth-bearing bone of the lower jaw, the dentary, increased in size at the expense of the posterior bones. The development of the jaw-closing muscle into two components, the masseter and temporalis, resulted in a reduction of force on the bones that made up the joint (the quadrate in the upper jaw and the articular in the lower jaw) and they gradually became reduced in size. Immediately below the articular, forming the angle of the jaw, was the angular bone. During embryonic development, the ear apparatus was relatively enormous compared with the developing bones. Hence the tympanic membrane, situated close to the angle of the jaw, came in contact with the angular bone which developed around it to form its circular boundary. In this way the angular bone of the reptile became the tympanic bone of the mammal.

The articular bone, as well as articulating with the quadrate of the upper jaw, had a projection (the manubrium) which was associated with the angular. This projection would have made contact with the eardrum. Vibrations impinging on the eardrum could then be transmitted, not simply via the stapes to the inner ear, but also via a second route from the articular to the quadrate and then again via the stapes to the inner ear. The complete connection was possible because there was a bony link between the stapes and the quadrate.

The significance of this transmission of sound waves across three bones instead of one was that at each stage the vibrations were amplified, and the ability to pick up faint sounds therefore gave the animal a more acute sense of hearing. The stapes was freed from the eardrum, which now had only the malleus (hammer or articular) attached to it, and sound travelled along the incus (anvil or quadrate) to the stapes and the inner ear. Mammals have an acute sense of hearing which is aided by the pinnae (external ears), which collect sound.   L.B.H.

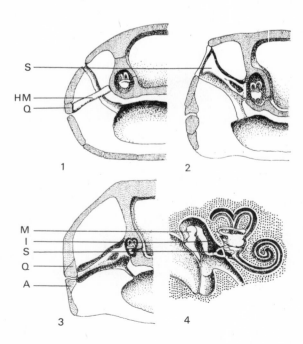

Echinoderms

Echinoderms

A phylum of invertebrate animals (Echinodermata) that includes SEA URCHINS, STARFISHES, CRINOIDS and sea cucumbers. Typically, these forms have a well-developed radial symmetry, usually based on the number five. There is a system of internal tubes (the water vascular system) that consists of a tubular ring round the oesophagus, from which radial tubes (usually five) originate. Numerous flexible finger-like tube-feet are attached to the radial tubes and provide the means of walking, respiration and capturing food. An internal tube, the stone canal, extends from the ring to an opening in the surface which may be a single pore (hydropore) or a sieve-like plate (madreporite). The skeleton comprises plates of calcium carbonate, each of which is microscopically a three-dimensional meshwork in the living animal and has the molecular structure of a single crystal of the mineral calcite.

Echinoderms are known as fossils from the Lower Cambrian to the Recent. All are marine and there is fossil evidence that they are closely related to the VERTEBRATES.

The holothurians, or sea cucumbers, are sausage-shaped, with mouth and anus at opposite ends as in regular sea urchins. Around the mouth there is a bush of modified tube-feet with which the animal catches food particles, and the five ambulacra extend from the mouth region to near the anus. The skeleton of holothurians is usually composed of up to 20 million small platelets and spicules, with a stout calcareous ring round the oesophagus. Holothuroid spicules often occur as microfossils and can be used in STRATIGRAPHY.

Several other echinoid groups are exclusively fossil and have no living representatives. The helicoplacoids, from the Lower Cambrian of North America, were spindle-shaped flexible animals with mouth and arms at opposite ends and no trace of pentameral symmetry. There is a single ambulacrum, forked and extending round the body in a spiral. Eocrinoids (Lower Cambrian to Ordovician) and cystoids (Ordovician to Silurian) are ill-characterized groups. Together with the blastoids they should probably be placed in an assemblage called the Blastozoa, whose members possess a peculiar type of slender arm known as a brachiole. A typical brachiole is unbranched and was made up of two series of floor plates, with a groove for the water vessel, and two series of cover plates lapping over the groove.

Blastoids are blastozoans of Silurian to Permian age with bud-shaped thecae (spore cases) and a clearly distinct stem. They have five-rayed symmetry and complicated respiratory organs known as hydropores inside the theca. Cystoids are characterized by varying kinds of specialized respiratory structures and often have well-defined pentameral symmetry, especially in the water vascular system, but distinct stems are not always present. One group of cystoids, the Glyptocystitida, have respiratory organs known as pore rhombs which may have developed into the hydrospores of blastoids, suggesting a close relationship between the two

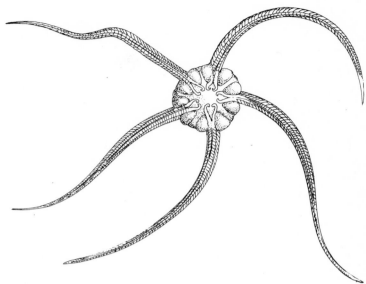

groups. The remaining blastozoan assemblage, the eocrinoids, are primitive forms which lack specialized respiratory structures.

The edrioasteroids were primitive disc-shaped echinoderms ranging from the Lower Cambrian to the Ordovician. They were usually attached by the lower surface of the disc, the upper surface having a central mouth with a five-rayed ambulacral system, anus, genital pore and hydropore. They may represent the group from which echinoids (sea urchins), holothuroids and asterozoans (starfishes) arose.

Paracrinoids were a small group of lower Palaeozoic echinoderms with branched, uniserial arms (not brachioles) and no signs of five-rayed symmetry. The carpoid echinoderms (Cambrian to Devonian), also known as heterosteleans, homolozoans and calcichordates, are curious asymmetrical forms with a typically echinoderm skeleton but no trace of radial symmetry.

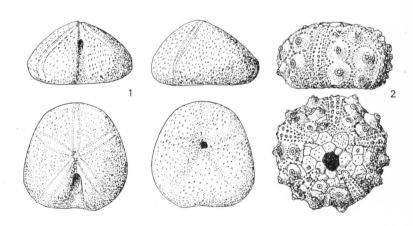

1

2

Cothurnocystis is a primitive calcichordate from the Ordovician of Scotland and France and the Middle Cambrian of the USA which consists basically of a head and a tail. The head is boot-shaped and flattened and lay with one surface on the sea bed; it had a frame of marginal plates around the edge, a flexible roof and floor, and a

Echinoderms
(1) Four views of Nucleolites, *Middle Jurassic to Upper Cretaceous (approx. natural size); (2) Acrosalenia, a Jurassic to Lower Cretaceous echinoderm that is believed to trace back to the Upper Triassic (approx. natural size)*

Ecology

series of gill slits in the roof of the head on the left side (it is noteworthy that the larva of the living primitive chordate *Amphioxus* also has left gill slits only). The mouth was near the front end of the head, whereas the anus and genital pore were joined together and lay just to the left of the front end of the tail (which was therefore, as in all chordates, post-anal). The tail could wag from side to side and would have had notochord and muscles inside it, and the brain was situated where the head and tail joined. *Cothurnocystis* probably pulled itself backwards across the sea floor, gripping the mud with the end of its tail.

A more advanced calcichordate is *Mitrocystella* from the Ordovician of France and Czechoslovakia. It also has a head and a tail but, seen from outside, the head is almost symmetrical and contained right gill slits as well as left ones. With complicated nerves and a brain, *Mitrocystella* could be described as a vertebrate, despite its calcite skeleton.   R.P.S.J.

Ecology

The study of the complex relationship between organisms and environment: functional morphology, mode of life, habitat, relations to other organisms etc. It includes consideration of individual groups as well as the interrelationship between communities of organisms and their surroundings.

Research on the ecology of modern environments is based essentially on direct observation. Palaeoecology depends largely on the interpretation of fragmentary evidence preserved in the fossil record, but it does provide an opportunity to study the evolution of communities through time. Results are at least partly speculative because the soft tissue of animals is rarely preserved, and the hard parts only selectively so. It is unusual for the evidence to even approach a complete picture of life at any point in geological time. Organisms are frequently transported and preserved in a different environment to that in which they lived. The evidence is often merely a collection of organic fragments of uncertain relationship to the containing sediment. – a death assemblage. Levels of abundance within communities are also generally distorted. ARTHROPODS, for example, tend to be over-represented by the numerous moults they shed during growth. It is only in exceptional circumstances, for example the Middle Cambrian BURGESS SHALE of British Columbia, that the soft-bodied members are preserved and communities are potentially complete. Even in this example, however, some information is lost because the fossils have suffered a degree of transport and do not occur exactly *in situ*. The results of palaeoecological studies can never be exact but a statistical approach (often using a computer) is used in handling large amounts of data and is widely applicable to palaeoecological problems.

The study of the palaeoecology of a community relies in the first instance on an interpretation of the modes of life of the individuals which make it up. This can be approached in several ways. First, a comparison can be made with living forms. For example, a study of the relationship between the shape of the skeleton and the depth of burrowing in species of the modern heart-urchin *Spatangus* allows a distinction to be drawn on comparative grounds between deep- and shallow-burrowing forms of the Cretaceous ECHINODERM *Micraster*. Again, the soft parts of GRAPTOLITES are unknown but the skeleton of this extinct group is similar to that in some related modern colonial forms, the pterobranchiates (particularly the genus *Rhabdopleura*). The graptolite zooid is therefore reconstructed looking similar to *Rhabdopleura*, bearing two tentacled arms which are used in feeding. The individual zooids of the colony are likewise assumed to have been connected by flexible extensions of a common stalk, the stolon.

Next, much can be deduced from morphological considerations, such as a study of the mineralized parts of a fossil. The zig-zag valve margins of rhynchonellid BRACHIOPODS, for example, probably bestowed several advantages. The area of aperture allowing intake of water (for feeding and respiration) was enlarged without a corresponding increase in the separation of the valve edges. This prevented the intake of unwanted large particles while at the same time lengthening the sensitive mantle edge tissue, which follows the margin of the valves, and enhancing the animal's ability to sense the environment.

The occurrence of a fossil also provides palaeoecological evidence. Graptoloids are often found preserved in pyrites in a black shale with few associated fossils and no evidence of burrowing. The lithology and the nature of preservation suggest deposition in deep water, and the absence of bottom-dwelling organisms indicates a lack of oxygen. This is consistent with the interpretation of the graptoloids as planktonic.

Traces of activity often provide the only evidence of the nature of the soft tissues of a fossil organism; these vary from locomotion, feeding and resting trails produced by marine invertebrates to the footprints of dinosaurs. Unfortunately the conditions favouring the preservation of organisms and the TRACE FOSSILS produced by them are different and the two are rarely found in association.

Considerable attention has been focused on the ecology of the DINOSAURS and it has been suggested that their success may have been due to the fact that they were WARM-BLOODED, like mammals, rather than COLD-BLOODED reptiles. This conclusion is based on various lines of evidence, one of which involves calculating predator–prey ratios in fossil communities. A cold-blooded predator (a crocodile for instance) requires much less food, because of its low energy output, than does a warm-blooded one of similar weight. Hence a given prey population can support fewer warm-blooded than cold-blooded predators. The predatory–prey ratios in dinosaur communities are from 1 to 3 per cent, similar to those in later mammal communities, and much lower than the ratio for cold-blooded reptiles.   D.E.G.B.

Economic palaeontology

The use of palaeontology as a means of locating and exploiting the economically valuable constituents in sedimentary rocks.

Palaeontology is essential to the exploration of minerals such as coal, oil, gas and limestone. Its application begins with the preliminary stages of geological mapping or the drilling of trial boreholes, through to the extraction phases. Furthermore, most of the world's currently available fuel resources are themselves composed of fossil plant and animal remains (*see* FOSSIL FUELS).

In geological surveys throughout the world, field geologists work with palaeontologists to produce geological maps and locate deposits of economic importance. Macrofossils are rarely as valuable as microfossils in producing accurate age determinations and for reconstructing the conditions under which the many different types of rocks were laid down. Nevertheless, throughout much of the Palaeozoic only macrofossils are available, and GRAPTOLITES, TRILOBITES and some BRACHIOPODS are employed for dating and correlation. In the Mesozoic, AMMONITES remain of great importance when they can be collected with care, but are used in reconnaissance mapping only when there is adequate time for detailed collecting or when borehole cores are all that is available to the palaeontologist. MOLLUSCS generally have long age-ranges, but are useful palaeo-environmental and palaeogeographical indicators, particularly in the Cenozoic.

Since the 1920s, however, microfossils – originally FORAMINIFERANS and OSTRACODS, and subsequently the organic-walled groups (dinoflagellates, spores and pollen) – have been extensively employed in biostratigraphy and the correlation of sediments. Almost all the world's oil occurs in sediments of Mesozoic or younger age, and the small size, common occurrence and ease of extraction of microfossils make them particularly useful when only small samples or pieces of borehole chippings are available for analysis.

Oil company micropalaeontologists form part of a team which includes stratigraphers, structural geologists, geophysicists and petroleum engineers, who work together to produce a picture of the sub-surface geological structures and of the environmental conditions under which deposition occurred. The necessity to obtain fast and accurate age determination is often crucial when expensive drilling operations are in progress.

Specialist micropalaeontological consulting companies have developed to augment the services provided by the oil companies' own laboratories. The most sought-after specialists are in the fields of palynology (spores and pollen), other organic-walled microfossils (mainly dinoflagellates and acritarchs), coccoliths, foraminiferans and ostracods. Hydro-geological and mining companies, in addition to oil and gas companies and geological surveys, also employ palaeontologists for operations where palaeontological control is essential.

In the laboratory the sedimentary samples from borehole cuttings, or from small amounts of rock collected in the field, are broken down using either chemical or simple physical means, and then washed through sieves. Identification of the separated and concentrated microfossil content is carried out under a powerful microscope, with the aid of specialized catalogues published for this purpose. Usually each company has its own reference catalogue and comparative collection of microfossils. When the rocks are too hard for disaggregation (eg limestone), thin sections that are transparent to light are cut and viewed under the microscope by transmitted light. Examination of most larger foraminiferans and calcareous ALGAE is carried out in this way. It is usual in applied palaeontology, where speed is paramount, for unorthodox names and combinations of letters and numbers to be used rather than the normal binomial (Linnaean) taxonomy. Age determinations based on assemblages is also a common method employed. Standard zonations exist for planktonic foraminiferans and for coccoliths and dinoflagellates, and these are applicable for most of the Cretaceous through to the Recent, worldwide.

Oil, gas and coal are the most important forms of fossil fuels. Oil deposits originate from the decay of minute marine life – various organic-walled microfossils and planktonic foraminiferans and radiolarians which secrete droplets of oil within their skeletons. This is subsequently concentrated and trapped in a permeable lithology surrounded by an envelope of impermeable layers of rock. Natural gas is a less dense by-product of oil formation, and occurs in similar sub-surface geological conditions. Coal is a vast accumulation of decaying plant matter which has been fossilized and subjected to temperature, pressure and chemical changes.

Fossil animals not only help to date rocks but may also be rock builders themselves. Many Permian, Cretaceous and Eocene limestones, for example, are composed primarily of giant foraminiferans, and some familiar building stones (eg Portland freestone) are made up of the fossilized remains of animals that once lived in the shallow seas where these carbonate rocks were deposited.   J.E.P.W.

Edentates

An order (Edentata) that originally accommodated several genera of toothless ant-eating mammals, most of which are unrelated to the majority of the fossil animals currently included in the group. The Edentata is divided into the suborder Xenarthra and the poorly known ancestral suborder Palaeanodonta. There are three major groups of xenarthrans, comprising the Loricata (or Cingulata, ARMADILLOS and Glyptodonts), the Pilosa (tree SLOTHS and the extinct ground sloths), and the Vermilingua (ant-eaters).

All living and most fossil xenarthrans have extra articulations on the posterior trunk vertebrae (hence the name Xenarthra), and the cervical vertebrae vary in number from six to nine. The ischium articulates with (or is fused

Eggs

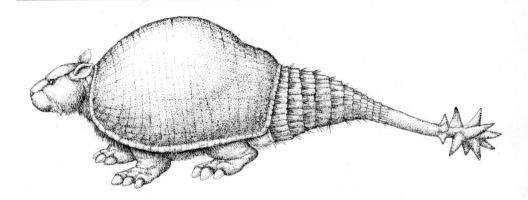

Edentates
The glyptodont Doedicurus *was a specialized South American edentate that lived in the Pleistocene.*
Length: about 4m (13ft)

to) the proximal caudal vertebrae to form a peculiarly elongated sacrum, and the limb bones are customarily short and massive. Claws are often well developed, especially on the manus (forefoot). The premaxilla is usually greatly reduced, with the front dentition absent. The cheek teeth are few, simple, lacking enamel, and open-rooted. The brain is not considered to be highly evolved.

Xenarthrans are essentially herbivores, but some may be omnivorous or carrion feeders. Living forms, and presumably their antecedents, are slow moving but capable of rapid bursts of speed if threatened. No known xenarthran appears to have been adapted to a carnivorous life style.

Most of the history of the Xenarthra occurred

Edentates
The giant ground sloth Megatherium *first appeared in the Late Pliocene and was common in North and South America during the Pleistocene.*
Length: about 6m (20ft)

in South America while that continent was isolated during the Cenozoic. Protected from more progressive North American mammals, the xenarthrans evolved numerous successful lines which formed a significant proportion of the terrestrial megafauna. Their ancestry seems to lie in North America, where Palaeocene and Eocene fossils of palaeanodonts have many characteristics common to the earliest South American xenarthrans. Presumably forms similar to *Metacheiromys* reached South America before the severance of the Panamanian land bridge, but most known North American palaeanodonts are too late in time to be true ancestors of the Xenarthra. A.G.E.

Eggs

Fossilized eggs may occur either as petrified shells (not necessarily calcareous) or as outline impressions within the mother's body cavity.

The oldest known REPTILE egg is from the Permian of Texas, and a small but well-preserved egg has been found in the Upper Triassic of Patagonia associated with small DINOSAUR skeletons. The Upper Cretaceous of Provence is well known for abundant shell fragments and occasional whole eggs, roughly ovoid in shape and with a long axis measuring up to 25cm (9.8in), attributable to the SAUROPOD *Hypselosaurus*. The GOBI DESERT of Mongolia has yielded numerous finds of smaller elongated eggs about 20cm (8in) long that were associated with skeletons of the primitive Late Cretaceous HORNED DINOSAUR *Protoceratops*; these occur in nests which originally included several dozen eggs arranged in concentric circles.

Dinosaur egg-shells are highly porous and consist of an outer prismatic zone and an inner mammillary zone, the exterior surface being ornamented with wrinkles, bumps or ridges. No matter how big the parent, the size of the egg was probably limited by the fact that a large egg needs a disproportionately thick shell, which would hinder gaseous exchange between the developing embryo and the atmosphere and might be too difficult for the hatchling to break through.

The eggs of moas (eg *Dinornis*) and the so-called elephant birds (*Aepyornis*) are common. The largest known egg, laid by an elephant bird, is 34.3cm (13.5in) long, with a maximum girth around its middle of 76.8cm (30.2in) and a capacity of 11 litres (2.4 gallons). A.J.C.

Ehrenberg, Christian (1795–1876)

German naturalist and founder of MICROPALAEONTOLOGY. He was born in Delitzsch, Leipzig, Germany, and initially studied theology at Leipzig and medicine at the University of Berlin. During the 1820s he was a member of two scientific expeditions: the first to Egypt, Libya and the shores of the Red Sea, and the second under Alexander von Humboldt (1769–1859) to the USSR. As a result of the first expedition Ehrenberg published a classic account on the CORALS of the Red Sea, and suggested that they were not "the builders of new islands, but only the preservers of islands

Elephants

already existing". His other major contributions to geology and palaeontology were through his researches on microfossils which are summarized in his *Mikrogeologie* (1854). This pioneering work revealed the beauty of RADIOLARIAN skeletons and the true nature of CHALK and some other limestones.   A.P.H.

Elephants

Members of the mammalian order Proboscidea, which also includes MAMMOTHS and MASTODONS. The major trend in the evolution of proboscideans has been increase in weight. An African elephant weighs about 6.5 tonnes, and some Pleistocene elephants reached 8 tonnes. *Moeritherium* from the Eocene of Egypt, the earliest known ancestral form, weighed only about 200kg (441lb), which indicates an increase of 33 times within about 50 million years. Volume increases as the cube of a quantity whereas surface area increases only as the square, so while the volume has also increased 33 times the surface area has increased only 11 times; thus the large elephants suffer cooling problems which they solve by having large ears that add little to their volume but greatly increase the surface area.

The earliest elephants were like pigs or pigmy hippopotamuses, and if they had simply increased their weight without altering their limbs they would have been unable to move. To retain mobility it became essential to lengthen the legs, to increase their diameter and to straighten them out so that the load was borne along the bones (graviportal limbs). With up to 2 tonnes load on each limb, they could not be maintained in an S-curve like a dog's hindleg. Between *Moeritherium* and *Elephas*, the forelimb length has increased 3.5 times and the diameter of the humerus has increased 28 times. Elephants have grown so large that they cannot gallop, but with their long legs they have a tremendous stride and comfortably achieve reasonable speeds.

The energy that a mammal expends is roughly proportional to its volume, but the amount of food that it can process is proportional to the surface area of its dentition. As has been demonstrated, the increase in surface areas lags far behind volumetric increases, and whereas *Moeritherium* had a battery of six cheek teeth in each side of its jaw in adult life, the elephant has only one tooth in each side of its jaw, which is replaced five times, making six teeth in a lifetime. *Moeritherium* probably lived for about 15 years compared to an elephant's 75 years, so although the surface area of the cheek dentition of elephants is only about three times that of moeritheres, elephants live five times as long and have five replacements of their teeth.

This threefold increase in area would nevertheless not suffice to masticate food for a 33 times volumetric increase. The life of a tooth also depends on its height or thickness, and moerithere teeth are shallow whereas elephant teeth are deep and achieve a 100 times volumetric increase. This enabled them to feed on tough grasses, and therefore to survive.

Elephants
Stegodon, from the Pliocene and Early Pleistocene of Asia, was a primitive true elephant that stood about 3m (10ft) tall at the shoulder.

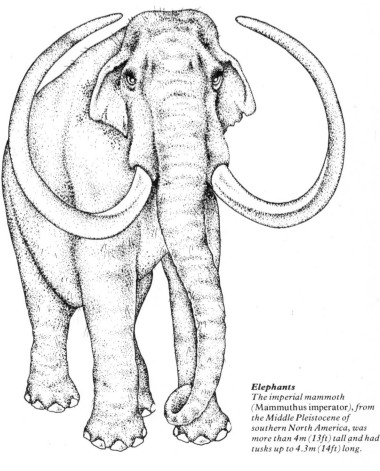

Elephants
The imperial mammoth (Mammuthus imperator), from the Middle Pleistocene of southern North America, was more than 4m (13ft) tall and had tusks up to 4.3m (14ft) long.

Enteledonts

Elephants
Above: Palaeoloxodon, *a massive forest elephant from the Pleistocene was more than 4m (13ft) at the shoulder.*
Below: Archidiskodon meridionalis, *the primitive southern mammoth from the Lower and Middle Pleistocene of Europe, was about 4m (13ft) at the shoulder.*

It is characteristic for proboscideans to enlarge a pair of front incisor teeth as tusks. In early forms these were used in food gathering, although in later genera this is secondary to their use in social behaviour and in maintaining dominance. Individual large tusks may weigh 50kg (110lb), and a pair of these, plus four large cheek teeth and the rest of the skull, can add up to a head weight in excess of half a tonne. It

would be impossible to carry this weight on the end of a long neck like a giraffe's, and with its necessarily long legs, the elephant would have had difficulty in drinking if it did not possess a trunk, the feature which gives the order its name, Proboscidea.

Africa was the centre of proboscidian evolution until about 25 million years ago, when elephants crossed first into Europe and Asia, and later into America. By the Pleistocene elephants had reached most parts of the world, extending into South America and reaching islands in south-eastern Asia, although not quite making the step into Australia.

The dominant proboscideans during the Miocene were mastodons, but mammoths replaced them in the Pleistocene. Mammoths spread around the tundra regions; the imperial mammoth grew to more than 4 metres (13ft) tall at the shoulder. Mastodons evolved from the small pig-like moeritheres and palaeomastodons of the African Eocene and Oligocene. The stegodons were an offshoot of the mastodon lineage, and an interesting side-line of proboscidean evolution produced *Deinotherium*, an elephant-like mammal with a pair of down-turned tusks in the lower jaws. *Deinotherium* appeared in the African Miocene, migrated to Europe and Asia, and finally died out during the Pleistocene in Africa.   R.J.G.S.

Enteledonts

Extinct suine ARTIODACTYLS, often called "giant pigs". They were certainly large (*Dinohyus* was bison-sized), but were not true pigs, although sharing a common ancestry with pigs through the early palaeodonts.

Enteledonts occurred mainly in the Oligocene: *Entelodon* was common in Europe and *Archaeotherium* in North America. They had long legs and only two toes on each foot. Their incisor teeth were prominent and pointed, and the canine teeth were heavy and exhibited wear facets, suggesting that the diet of these animals included tubers. The molar teeth were simple, four-cusped and bunodont. Enteledont skulls were long, some more than 1 metre (3.3ft), and developed distinctive excrescences. The zygomatic arch had a deep flange behind the orbit, flared out laterally and downwards, and the mandible was heavy with pairs of tuberosities below the symphysis at the front extremity.

These unusual bony developments appear to have been for the attachment of jaw muscles and, with the wear facets on the molar teeth, suggest a unique method of masticating food; it may have been possible for enteledonts to close the front part of their jaws and at the same time grind food with their back teeth. Muscles attached to the mandibular tuberosities would have kept the front end of the jaws firmly closed, and interlocking of the canine teeth would have further restricted movement. The zygomatic flange muscles could then have contracted alternately on left and right sides to produce a sideways grinding action with the cheek teeth.   R.J.G.S.

Eocene

Eocene

The second geological period of the Cenozoic Era, beginning 55 million years ago and lasting for 16 million years. The name is of Greek derivation and means *dawn* (of) *recent* life.

Sediments of Eocene age are much better represented and its fauna better known than those of the preceding PALAEOCENE. During the period there was considerable tectonic activity: ocean floors were spreading and continents altering their shapes and positions. The North Atlantic Ocean had by the end of the Eocene broken through between Greenland and Scandinavia to link up with the Arctic Ocean, thus severing the land connection between North America and Europe. Similarly, the land connection was broken between South America and Antarctica, allowing much freer circulation of cool Antarctic waters. This fragmentation resulted from activity along the mid-oceanic ridges, and was accompanied by outpourings of lava, as in Greenland and Scotland; similar extensive lava extrusions are known from South America and greater India.

In many parts of the world sea-levels rose considerably in the mid-Eocene, and marine transgressions, which at their peak may even have divided Africa between Libya and Nigeria, can be traced around the TETHYS Sea. Again, in Australia, Eocene seas extended north of the Great Australian Bight across the Nullarbor Plain, while the Obrik Sea linked the Arctic Ocean with the Tethys Sea across central Siberia via the Turgai Straits.

The climates of the Eocene appear to have been less stongly differentiated than today, and the tropics extended from Britain to Malaysia, with temperate conditions northwards. This assessment of climatic conditions is largely based on knowledge of the flora. For example, the Early Eocene clays on the Isle of Sheppey in the London basin have yielded more than 300 species of flora, almost all of which are angiosperms (FLOWERING PLANTS); a quarter of the 100 genera are still living. Most of these plants belong to families that are almost exclusively tropical in distribution, and have their closest equivalents today in Malaysia, eg Nipa palms, myrtles, flaxes and lianes. Farther north, on Mull in Scotland and in Greenland, earlier floras include more temperate plants, with GINKGO, vines, oaks, plane trees and *Metasequoia*. Late Eocene floras from the Isle of Wight have Chinese affinities, suggesting cooler conditions than in the Early Eocene, with such plants as pines, pondweeds, roses and borages.

In the oceans, large amounts of organic silica (DIATOMS and RADIOLARIANS) were deposited, and on the continental shelves carbonate-rich environments predominated. The most characteristic and useful FORAMINIFERANS were the gigantic nummulites, some up to 2cm (0.8in) across. Nummulitic limestones were used to build the pyramids in Egypt, and in Europe the Eocene and Oligocene are often known as the Nummulitique. Hexacorals, BIVALVES and GASTROPODS abound in the shelly fauna. *Nautilus* thrived, along with the last of the BELEMNITES and early cuttlefishes, and crabs began to take on a modern appearance.

Fishes were also like living forms, with many modern families represented in the well-preserved fauna of MONTE BOLCA in Italy and the Green River succession in Wyoming. For the first time there were marine mammals – the earliest WHALES and sirenians (*see* DUGONGS). Already whales such as *Basilosaurus* had reached lengths of 16 metres (52.5ft).

On land, many orders of INSECTS are known, having acquired great importance for the

Evolution

Eocene
*Archaeomeryx, a chevrotain-like artiodactyl that occurred in the Upper Eocene of Mongolia, may be close to the common ancestry of all the deer and bovids.
Height: about 30cm (1ft) at the shoulder*

Eocene
*Archaeomeryx, a chevrotain-like artiodactyl that occurred in the Upper Eocene of Mongolia, may be close to the common ancestry of all the deer and bovids.
Height: about 30cm (1ft) at the shoulder*

pollination of the flowering plants. Crocodiles, chelonians and lizards were the dominant reptiles. Birds included ducks, geese, bitterns, herons, owls and hawks, and the gigantic flightless *Diatryma* reached a height of 2 metres (6.6ft).

The most marked feature of the Eocene mammal fauna is the radiation of many new forms to fill the ecological niches left vacant since the disappearance of the DINOSAURS. This dispersal was, however, largely composed of archaic types which died out during the Oligocene. In the Early Eocene there was still considerable similarity between faunas on different continents, emphasizing the continuation of intercontinental connections, with North America and Europe, for example, forming a single zoogeographic realm. These links broke down during the Middle Eocene, and Late Eocene faunas show much more provinciality.

During the Eocene the multituberculates were steadily replaced by RODENTS, which soon became the dominant small mammal stock. In the holarctic region the MARSUPIALS survived in North America and Europe, but they never reached Asia and it was only in South America that they competed successfully with placentals. The INSECTIVORA were numerous, many being arboreal (tree-dwelling), and from their kin arose the bats, which by the Eocene were true fliers. The contemporary PRIMATES varied. They

included forest-dwelling animals that resemble the LEMURS and TARSIER of today. The CONDYLARTHS, so prolific during the Palaeocene, were giving way to their successors, a vast array of herbivorous stocks. AMBLYPODS such as *Coryphodon* were plentiful, and in North America and Asia there were rhinoceros-like uintatheres. The PERISSODACTYLS were more diverse and abundant than ARTIODACTYLS. *Hyracotherium* and other horses were common in North America and Europe, although they never reached Asia, where their place was taken by tapiroids, and RHINOCEROSES (*Amynodon*) browsed the leafy vegetation. Among the artiodactyls, ANTHRACOTHERES were filling a pig-like ecological niche in Eurasia.

Africa had a distinct fauna, still little known except from Egypt, where there were early ELEPHANTS (*Moeritherium, Barytherium*). In South America the condylarths had evolved in isolation to yield numerous herbivorous stocks, with medium- to large-sized NOTOUNGULATES, ASTRAPOTHERES and elephant-like pyrotheres. These evolved alongside EDENTATES and marsupials. No Eocene mammal fauna is known from Australia.   R.J.G.S.

Evolution

The modern theory of evolution dates from the publication of Charles DARWIN's *On the Origin of Species* in 1859. Darwin's work was based on careful experimentation and on observations, many of which were made during his voyage around the world in the survey ship HMS *Beagle* (1831–36). He worked during a period of considerable scientific advance. The acceptance of Linnaeus' scheme for the classification of plants and animals led to a surge of activity in their description, which persisted into the first half of the 19th century. William SMITH and particularly Charles LYELL (the author of *The Principles of Geology*, 1830–33, and later editions) had demonstrated that there is evidence of change in the nature of the fossils preserved in successive strata through geological time, and this was observed first-hand by Darwin who found the remains of large Cenozoic mammals in Patagonia.

Darwin was influenced by the ideas expressed by Malthus in his *Essay on Population* (1798) in which he argued that population increase would be enormous if all the offspring survived; because this does not happen, factors such as food supply, availability of living space and predation must act to keep the population in check. Darwin noted that geographical isolation on the various Galapagos islands resulted in the differentiation of species of giant tortoise. He also observed several different finches on the islands, distinguished by the structure of their bills, which varied according to the food source they exploited. Darwin's major achievement was in synthesizing this wealth of information and ideas into a unified theory.

NATURAL SELECTION, the basis of his theory, is still acknowledged as one of the most important factors involved in evolution. Not all the individuals produced by reproduction in a pop-

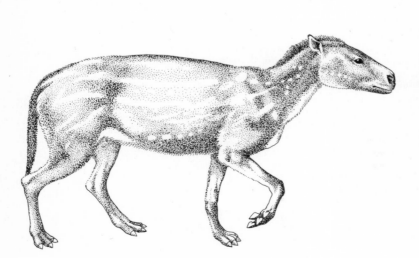

Eocene
The primitive perissodactyl Hyrachyus, from the Eocene of North America, is usually regarded as an early member of the rhinoceros evolutionary line. Species ranged in size from some as large as a modern tapir to others no bigger than a fox.

ulation survive to breed – some are more proficient than others at catching food or avoiding predators, at mating and rearing their offspring. Thus it is the most successful which contribute to the next generation, and they are selected by a natural process of "survival of the fittest". A comparable scheme is operated artificially by stock breeders who use only a champion bull to sire a herd, assuring the continuity of the most desirable attributes of a breed.

The main shortcoming of Darwin's theory was the apparent lack of a mechanism for the transfer of the characteristics of one generation to the next. It was difficult to explain why an advantageous characteristic would not be lost by mixing with the normal characteristics in the rest of the population. Equally Darwin could not positively refute Jean-Baptiste LAMARCK'S earlier notion (1809) that attributes acquired by animals during their lifetime could be passed on to their offspring (the inheritance of acquired characteristics). A bizarre and hackneyed example is provided by the giraffe. Lamarck's theory suggests that generations of giraffes acquired longer necks by stretching to reach tender young shoots on trees. Darwin's theory argues that the giraffes with the longer necks have simply been selected as they were better equipped for life in their environment, possibly due to their ability to exploit a food source denied to other browsers, and also perhaps to other factors such as a facility for spotting predators at greater distances due to their extra height.

The laws of inheritance were discovered in 1866 by Gregor Mendel (1822–84) from experiments with garden peas, but they remained largely unknown until they were rediscovered in 1900. Mendel showed that the characteristics of the parents are inherited by an offspring as pairs of "factors", one from each parent, which do not merge or blend. The paired factors separate during the formation of the sex cells, and are transmitted singly by the gametes (the sperm or ova). These "factors" are now identified as genes; the genetic make-up of an organism is carried by the chromosomes and is known as the genotype.

When a gene occurs in biochemically different forms these are referred to as alleles, which may be dominant or recessive. The dominant form is usually expressed, recessive alleles appearing only when they are inherited from both parents (the occurence of the disease sickle-cell anaemia in man, which occurs in parts of Africa, is genetically determined in this way). Mendel's theory of inheritance was based on many carefully controlled breeding experiments with peas, observing the fate of characteristics such as colour and smoothness of the seeds, and analysing the results by statistical methods. Later it became possible to observe the chromosomes in the nuclei of cells during the process of cell division and replication, and their behaviour is precisely what would be expected on the basis of Mendel's theory. In normal cell division (mitosis) the chromosomes of the daughter cells correspond in number to those of

the parent; in the production of sex cells (meiosis) the number is halved.

The synthetic theory of evolution which was formulated in the late 1930s combined Darwin's theory of natural selection with the Mendelian theory of inheritance, and incorporates discoveries in the field of population genetics. Evolution depends on genetic variation within populations as a basis for natural selection. The rate of evolutionary change depends on the degree of genetic variation. Gradual change in the types and frequencies of alleles in the genotype of a population results in "mutations" which may be "selected" if they prove beneficial.

The biochemical basis for evolution was discovered in the 1950s through research in molecular genetics. The genetic material which makes up the chromosomes includes the nucleic acids DNA (deoxyribonucleic acid) and RNA (ribonucleic acid). These molecules are usually replicated exactly during cell division, but occasionally a different sequence of nucleotides (the compounds making up the DNA molecule) is produced, such a change constituting a mutation. These mutations lead to an alteration of the genes within the chromosomes and may thus affect the biochemical processes within the organism. The result may alter the animal's "fitness" for better or worse, or not at all.

The fossil record provides the only evidence for evolution through time. Evidence for the relationship of organisms to their environment (ECOLOGY) may also permit an assessment of the kind of selection pressures which operated. Modern species are defined by reproductive isolation, in that species do not actually or potentially interbreed. Fossil species cannot be defined in this way; the only basis for the identification of genetic changes is morphology.

Evolution appears to occur on two levels. Anagenetic changes involve a pronounced increase in structural complexity or adaptive potential, and generally lead to "biological improvement" (giving rise to families as opposed to genera or species). Cladogenetic changes are

Evolution (cont'd)

smaller and involve the evolution of new species or genera. Species tend to evolve in areas on the margins of the range of the ancestral population. It is assumed that they become isolated and that natural selection under different environmental pressures yields a new species. If this new species then re-invades the area occupied by the ancestral population and replaces it, a morphological gap will separate them in the fossil record.

The notion that the environment plays an important role in natural selection and therefore in the evolution of new species has long been accepted. It has now been suggested that this was not a gradual process as assumed in traditional evolutionary terms, but that evolution occurred as a series of leaps in isolated areas separated by periods of little change. This has come to be known as the concept of "punctuated equilibria". Unfortunately it is not possible to verify this model satisfactorily – the postulated isolated populations where rapid changes take place are localized in distribution and rarely preserved. Anagenetic evolution commonly occurs during the colonization of new and relatively unoccupied habitats. Expansion into a new area allows a burst of evolutionary activity to exploit a number of different habitats and modes of life in the absence of effective competition. Such an adaptive radiation occurred in the Lower Cambrian when several major groups with mineralized hard-parts appeared. A second example is the radiation of the mammals in the Cenozoic, following the demise of the DINOSAURS.

A study of the fossil record provides additional illustrations of "patterns" of evolution. For example, parallel evolution occurs when two separate groups evolve along similar lines in response to the same environmental pressures. An example is provided by the ARTHROPODS which have acquired the arthropodan type of organization (chitinous exoskeleton, serially segmented body, jointed legs) from at least two independent ancestors. The TRILOBITES, CRUSTACEANS and chelicerates form one or more lineages whereas the Uniramia (including CENTIPEDES AND MILLIPEDES and INSECTS) constitute a separate evolutionary series.

In another concept, similar morphologies were thought to evolve in some groups at several points in time from the same parent stock. Further investigation of two of the classic groups has revealed that this model is an oversimplification. Many Jurassic and Cretaceous AMMONITES are no longer thought to have originated as repeated offshoots from a conservative stock. Similarly, the oyster *Gryphaea* has been shown to have a continuous history, and did not arise independently on several occasions during the Jurassic, becoming extinct each time.

When unrelated groups evolve similar morphologies, usually in response to the same functional requirements, convergent evolution occurs. Dolphins (mammals), ICHTHYOSAURS (reptiles) and SHARKS all evolved a streamlined fish-like body for swimming; likewise bats, birds and flies have all acquired wings. Many less

striking examples occur in the invertebrates, within the fossil ammonites and BRACHIOPODS for example.

More often than not selection acts at different rates on different characteristics. Thus a mosaic of forms may evolve (mosaic evolution) from a common ancestor, as in the early monograptids of the Silurian. An individual group likewise commonly acquires the characteristics that distinguish it from an ancestral form gradually, rather than simultaneously. Thus in the evolution of human beings from early ape-like ancestors, an erect gait precedes the development of a large brain.

The attainment of sexual maturity at a larval stage (neoteny) and the retention of some larval characteristics in the adult (paedomorphosis) are important processes in evolution. The chordates may have arisen from a sessile invertebrate by evolving the ability to reproduce in the free-swimming "tadpole" larval stage. It is possible that the small pelagic or planktonic anostoid trilobites arose from larger bottom-dwelling forms by the same process.

There are several examples of organisms occurring today which the fossil record shows to have first appeared many millions of years ago. Celebrated examples of LIVING FOSSILS are the brachiopod *Lingula*, which has survived for more than 400 million years with little morphological change; the COELACANTH *Latimeria* which resembles fishes from the upper Palaeozoic; and the reptile *Sphenodon*, which is similar to Triassic forms about 200 million years old. Such longevity is presumably due to extremely slow rates of evolution in a stable environment, and is generally achieved only by forms that show a low degree of specialization.

One of the unique contributions of palaeontology to evolutionary studies is in providing an indication of evolutionary rates. A time scale in years can be superimposed on the fossil record using radioisotope dating (*see* DATING THE PAST). Rates are assessed on the basis of morphological change, which may be reflected in diversification and radiation into new species. Appearances and disappearances in the record, corresponding to origins and extinctions, give an indication of the rate of turnover. A comparison between the BIVALVE molluscs and mammals, for example, shows a much higher rate in the latter; mammal species last for about 1 million years, whereas bivalve species persist for about 7 million years. There is more intense competition between mammal species for resources, and they therefore become more specialized in their modes of life. The variation in evolutionary rates may reflect a consequently higher susceptibility to environmental change.

The CONTINENTAL DRIFT theory of plate tectonics has been invoked to explain fluctuations in the diversity of life through geological time. When the continents are widely separated, the world climate is stabilized by the influence of the oceans, and food sources are increased. The high diversity resulting is enhanced by land and ocean barriers, which lead to separate radiations in different areas. Such a diversification occurred with the break-up of the continents and the opening of the Atlantic Ocean in the Cretaceous. Alternatively, when the continents combine into large masses such as the Permian supercontinent PANGAEA, climate and resource levels become unstable and the available habitats are reduced, leading eventually to EXTINCTIONS. D.E.G.B.

Extinction

The regular dying-out of species, genera, families and larger groups, and their replacement by more advanced forms is essential for the normal process of EVOLUTION. Without such extinctions there could be no progression from simpler, primitive forms to more advanced, sophisticated types.

Sometimes, however, whole orders of animals and plants have disappeared abruptly from the fossil record after occupying a position of numerical dominance for many millions of years, and these sudden incidents of mass extinction cannot readily be explained by the normal course of evolution. One of the first major animal groups to disappear after a substantial period of prosperity were the TRILOBITES, which had been among the most successful early Palaeozoic life forms. By the Carboniferous, however, their numbers were thinning, and none of them survived beyond the end of the Permian.

The boundary between the Permian and the Triassic, which also marks the transition from the Palaeozoic to the Mesozoic, witnessed the extinction of several previously prominent marine invertebrate groups, notably the massive productid BRACHIOPODS, the fusulinid FORAMINIFERANS, and many AMMONITE families. After a renewed burst of vigour early in the Triassic, the ammonites were again decimated towards the end of the period, all the old groups dying out to be replaced by new families.

Possibly the most spectacular episode of mass extinction occurred 65 million years ago at the close of the Mesozoic, when the giant reptiles that had dominated the Earth for more than 150 million years suddenly perished, leaving an almost empty world into which the mammals and birds were able to proliferate.

The DINOSAURS, PTEROSAURS, PLESIOSAURS, ICHTHYOSAURS and MOSASAURS were by no means a degenerate, spent force at the time of their demise. CARNOSAURS of immense size were present in the last stage of the Cretaceous, DUCK-BILLED DINOSAURS, HORNED DINOSAURS and ARMOURED DINOSAURS attained their full development only in the Late Cretaceous, mosasaurs and plesiosaurs flourished in the seas until late in the Mesozoic, attaining enormous dimensions, and a pterosaur with a 10-metre (33ft) wing-span soared in the warm Cretaceous thermals.

Only the ichthyosaurs were evidently fading in the Early Cretaceous, although there is evidence that SAUROPODS were being supplanted by duck-billed dinosaurs spreading from a probable eastern Asiatic centre of origin westwards into Europe and via the Bering region into North America. In the Western Hemisphere the sauropods were apparently pushed southwards by the invaders and survived in relative abundance only in South America, which the duck-bills evidently did not reach in large numbers.

This sudden series of widespread extinctions at the end of the Cretaceous has become known as "the great dying". Racial senescence has been suggested as one possible cause. Just as individuals grow old, lose their teeth, and develop warty skin excrescences, so, it has been argued, do whole groups gradually age. Some dinosaurs (eg ornithomimids and possibly one ankylosaur) had become toothless by the Late Cretaceous, and many proliferated bony nodules on their skulls and bodies. Alternatively, it has been pointed out that the pituitary body below the brain was disproportionately large in most dinosaurs, and this hypertrophy may be a symptom of physiological disorder. The pituitary is a ductless gland whose secretions not only control growth but also influence other ductless glands that are concerned with the regulation of such vital functions as metabolism and reproduction. Any imbalance in the hormonal secretions of the pituitary could therefore result in giantism, spinescence, or impaired reproductive ability.

The appearance of deciduous FLOWERING PLANTS in the mid-Cretaceous would undoubtedly have affected the diet of herbivorous dinosaurs, but they seem to have adapted to it well enough by the latter part of the period. There is also a theory that this new vegetation photosynthesized additional oxygen, which enriched the atmosphere and raised the metabolic rate of the dinosaurs until they literally burned themselves out.

Selenium poisoning caused by the eating of plants which had absorbed this element from decaying selenium-rich rocks has been suggested. Mammals were assumed to be intelligent enough to avoid contaminated herbage, and as a further extension of this idea there is the proposal that poisonous alkaloids in the new flowering plants could not be detected by the dinosaurs' insensitive taste buds, and led to death in convulsions (suggested by the contorted positions of some fossil skeletons) and thinning dinosaur egg shells (also supported by fossil evidence) in a manner paralleled today by the eggs of pesticide-affected birds of prey.

Cosmic catastrophies invoked to account for "the great dying" include a supernova among the Sun's nearby neighbours in the galaxy that inundated this planet with mutation-inducing cosmic radiation, and the collision of a comet with the Earth.

It is noteworthy, however, that the extinctions of the Cretaceous period coincided with the break-up of the huge supercontinent PANGAEA due to CONTINENTAL DRIFT. Such a massive redistribution of the land masses would have led to submergence in some areas and mountain-building in others (the Rocky Mountains date from this time). Furthermore, the climate itself would be affected as the stabilizing effect of a single vast continent was lost, tending to become more variable, and as the Cretaceous waned the temperature gradient from the equator to the

Extinction (cont'd)

poles began to widen. By the dawn of the Cenozoic, seasonal conditions were becoming established with the appearance of an increasingly severe winter.

Reptiles as large as the dinosaurs could not hibernate to avoid an inclement season and, despite their probable development of WARM-BLOODED physiology this sort of climatic change (precipitated at least in part by continental drift), seems the most probable reason for their extinction. With their familiar environments being gradually destroyed as Pangaea broke up, they were unable to migrate to more favourable regions and found themselves too large and too specialized to survive.

Even so, their disappearance would not have been abrupt. In the Upper Cretaceous there was an interior sea running northwards across what is now Alberta, and the dinosaurs lived on a coastal flood-plain along its western margin, with rivers flowing eastwards from the newly risen Rockies. About 10 million years before the close of the period there were FERNS, redwoods, GINKGOS and sycamores 640km (400 miles) from the Cretaceous north pole (located in the Chukchee Sea north of the Bering Strait). Hadrosaurs, tyrannosaurs and ornithomimids lived in northern Alberta, and the site of Banks Island and Eglinton Island was then a breeding colony of the sea bird *Hesperornis*, with mosasaurs and plesiosaurs hunting the inshore waters.

About 8 million years later, in Hell Creek times, *Triceratops*, *Anatosaurus*, *Tyrannosaurus* and other dinosaurs still flourished amid 37-metre (120ft) metasequoias in Montana, enjoying a warm-temperate or sub-tropical climate. By this time, however, the climatic belts had already shifted another 10° towards the equator, the interior sea was withdrawing southwards, and the coniferous forests to the north of it were moving down.

With the ameliorating influence of the sea gone, the climate acquired a more seasonal, continental aspect. The fossils of the uppermost 30 metres (100ft) of the Hell Creek beds, which would have taken between 1 and 2 million years to accumulate, show a progressive change to coniferous forest, with the dinosaurs becoming increasingly rare until they disappeared altogether.

Farther south, in New Mexico, dinosaurs persisted for about another half a million years after the Montana community perished, but eventually the shift towards the equator of the climatic belts reached them too. The small mammals, which had been unable to compete with the giant reptiles throughout the Mesozoic, inherited the Cenozoic world by default. A sudden ICE AGE or an extended period of worldwide drought is not supported by geological evidence. The probability is that an increasingly seasonal climate killed off the dinosaurs during a period of about 10 million years – brief by geological standards, but by no means sudden.

Why some marine groups failed to survive is still difficult to explain. The thalattosuchian CROCODILES are consistently associated with holostean fishes (eg *Hypsocormus*), which were being replaced by the more progressive teleosts, so possibly the sea crocodiles became extinct because their principal prey disappeared. Some large Late Cretaceous pterosaurs were apparently carrion feeders, and if the dinosaurs died out they would have had no carcasses to feed on. For the passing of the plesiosaurs and the mosasaurs there is no plausible explanatory theory, and two other abundant groups of marine animals to disappear suddenly from the Mesozoic oceans were the ammonites and the rudist BIVALVES – again, without obvious cause.

The seasonal climatic conditions that were established early in the Cenozoic became gradually more pronounced until the Pleistocene ice age occurred. By the end of the Cenozoic there were many large mammals in existence that were seemingly well adapted to their environments. Even the advance of the glaciers is not an adequate cause for the sudden extinction of MASTODONS, glyptodonts, ground SLOTHS, SABRE-TOOTHED CATS and giant bison; there was no reason for these animals not to migrate towards the equator where the climate remained warm, and in any event cold-adapted animals such as the woolly RHINOCEROS, the MAMMOTH and the cave BEAR also died out. There is also the unsolved mystery of the disappearance of all the North American HORSES and CAMELS – forms which flourished there when re-introduced by man.

Disease and parasites might have played a part in the Pleistocene extinctions. During the warm inter-glacial episodes, populations cut off from each other for thousands of years by the glaciers might have regained contact – eg, the Old World-Alaskan fauna and the North American fauna – as the ice withdrew temporarily northwards. If disease and parasites carried by one population (which was resistant to them) were introduced into another population with no such resistance, extensive epidemics might well result. It is difficult, however, to reconcile the extinction of about 200 genera of mammals during the Late Pleistocene with disease alone, or with a combination of disease and adverse climate. Many of the now-extinct large Pleistocene animals seem to have survived the ice age and were still in existence as recently as 50,000 years ago, when warmer inter-glacial conditions were becoming re-established.

A significant factor may have been the spread of sapient MAN from (possibly) an African centre of origin about 40,000 years ago, when several big African forms suddenly became extinct (*Pelorovis*; the giant pig *Afrochoerus nicoli*; a huge hippopotamus, *Hippopotamus gorgops*; and a massive baboon, *Simopithecus*). Man's arrival in North America via Alaska about 12,000–15,000 years ago seems to correlate with the dying out of large mammals there about 11,000 years ago. In South America, radiocarbon analysis of ground sloth dung found in caves gives an age of 10,000 years, which also correlates well with the appearance of man on the continent.

Australia and New Zealand supported huge numbers of giant flightless birds (moas) as well as unusually large MARSUPIALS (*Diprotodon*, *Nototherium*, and the giant kangaroo *Palorchestes*). The arrival of man between 8,000 and 13,000 years ago seems to correlate with the disappearance of these forms, and moas are known to have been hunted by man (as was *Aepyornis* on Madagascar).

The disappearance of the extraordinary South American Cenozoic mammal fauna can be adequately explained by the influx of more sophisticated ungulates and predators from North America when the isthmus of Panama was re-established in the Late Pliocene. Elsewhere there seems to be a close correlation between the appearance of man and the extinction of large Late Pleistocene mammals and flightless birds, together with the predators that preyed on them.

An alternative theory which could account for some mammalian extinctions earlier in the Cenozoic is a worldwide reduction in sea-level, due perhaps to Earth movements or glaciation. This would lead to a fall in the ground water table and hence to drought, initiating environmental changes that might precipitate extinctions. Such episodes may have occurred at the Eocene–Oligocene boundary, when there was a transition in North America and central Asia from forest to woodland, and also at the end of the Miocene when prairie conditions began to spread with a concomitant wave of mammalian extinctions.   R.S.

Fayum

An isolated depression, measuring about 80km (50 miles) from east to west and 56km (35 miles) from north to south, located in the Western Desert to the south-west of Cairo, Egypt.

During the Pleistocene, this depression formed Lake Moeris, which filled when the River Nile (then flowing about 18 metres (59ft) higher than it does today) apparently breached the gravelly ridge between the Fayum and the river valley. The fauna at that time included ELEPHANTS, hippopotamuses, wild DOGS, and hartebeests, together with CROCODILES and chelonians (TURTLES AND TORTOISES).

In the early Palaeolithic, the water of Lake Moeris was 37 metres (120ft) above sea-level, but the depression gradually emptied until, about 10,000 years ago, it was nearly 5 metres (16ft) below sea-level. A brief rise took place in the early Neolithic, before the lake finally shrank to form the existing Birkat Qārūn.

The older vertebrate-bearing beds of the Fayum date back to the Upper Eocene and the Lower Oligocene. They are of great evolutionary significance because the first known proboscideans (elephants) occur in the lower (Qasr-el-Sagha) series (*Moeritherium*, *Barytherium*), together with an early DUGONG (*Eotheroides*), ancient whales (*Prozeuglodon*, *Eocetus*, *Basilosaurus*), a huge "elephant bird" (*Eremopezus*), and an extremely large python (*Gigantophis*).

Moeritherium is still found in the Lower Oligocene (Gebel Qatrani) deposits, but here it is accompanied by *Palaeomastodon*; ARSIN-OITHERIUM; some of the earliest known APES; the conies *Sagatherium*, *Geniohyus* and *Megalohyrax*; an ANTHRACOTHERE (*Rhagatherium*); CREODONTS (*Hyaenodon* and *Pterodon*); a CONDYLARTH (*Apterodon*); and a number of crocodiles and chelonians.

The remains of fishes associated with the Eocene-Oligocene mammals of the Fayum include SHARKS (for example *Carcharodon* and *Carcharias*), sawfishes, the eagle-ray *Myliobatis*, and siluroid RAY-FIN FISHES (*Fajumia*, *Socnopaea*).   R.S.

Fayum
Moeritherium, *the ancestral proboscidean from the Upper Eocene and Lower Oligocene of the Fayum, was about the size of a tapir.*

Ferns

An extensive group of plants that have a long geological history and form an important part of the modern flora. As might be expected in an assemblage as large and diverse as this, the exact limit of what may be considered a fern is uncertain, but the group may reasonably be held to include the primitive fern ancestors (Primofilicales) and the true ferns, with the exception of the TREE-FERNS. All the true ferns have a uniform early development, with a spore that germinates to produce a flat plate of cells (prothallus), from which the dominant sporophyte generation is produced.

The Primofilicales appeared in the Middle Devonian and survived until the end of the Palaeozoic. As their name suggests, they may be the ancestors of the modern ferns. There are two main lines: the Cladoxylales and the Coenopteridales. The Cladoxylales show features similar to the psilophytes and the coenopterids. The best-studied member of the group, *Pseudosporochnus*, was originally considered to be a psilophyte. Most of these forms possessed a main stem, from which branches developed that divided dichotomously. These branches bore leaves that were again dichotomously divided, sometimes more than once, to produce fan-like structures. On other

Field Museum

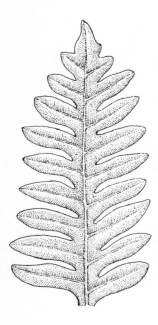

Ferns
The fern frond Alethopteris *was abundant in Britain during the Upper Carboniferous (natural size).*

branches the leaves were replaced by fertile appendages, which were also fan-shaped, each bearing a small terminal sporangium.

The Coenopteridales constitute a large and varied group of ferns with a wide range of growth forms, including creeping stems, erect trunks, and epiphytes (which grow on other plants). Coenopterids, such as *Austroclepsis* from the Lower Carboniferous of Australia must have looked superficially like the modern tree-ferns, except that within the mass of roots forming the trunks there were several stems instead of just one. The fronds of these ferns differed from those of modern ferns in being three- rather than two-dimensional, presumably giving them the appearance of a leafy branch system. In many species the fertile fronds follow closely the arrangement of the leafy ones, but in *Tedelia* from the Upper Carboniferous of North America there is a development of a fertile frond with expanded branches (pinnae) bearing sporangia, which more closely approaches the modern arrangement of reproductive structures.

The remainder of the ferns belong to families of which there are still living representatives. The Carboniferous was once frequently referred to as the age of ferns because of the abundance of large fern-like fronds, but it is now known that many of these belonged to seed-bearing gymnosperms. Specimens that are not fertile cannot with certainty be placed in either group, but others (such as *Asterotheca*) which bear sori of thick-walled sporangia on their pinnules, certainly are ferns and are placed in the Marattiales.

The last group of ferns is the Filicales, which include most of the modern ferns. The first of these appeared in the Carboniferous and by the Mesozoic they were widespread. The two most primitive families are the Schizeaceae and the Gleicheniaceae.   J.W.F.

Field Museum of Natural History
Founded in Chicago in 1893 by Marshall Field, this museum has had a number of names during its history, including the Columbia Museum of Chicago, the Field Columbian Museum, and the Chicago Natural History Museum.

The emphasis of the collections is on the Cenozoic mammals of North and South America, Mesozoic and Cenozoic reptiles and amphibians of North America, and the vertebrates of the KARROO and Australia. The collection of Devonian fishes is also extensive, and the museum has the only significant North American collection of NOTHOSAURS. The exhibition galleries are devoted to vertebrate palaeontology and zoology.   A.P.H.

Fischer von Waldheim, Gotthelf
(1771–1853)
German palaeontologist (born in Waldheim) who helped to establish the study of palaeontology in the USSR. He studied mineralogy at Freiberg, and medicine at Leipzig. He was appointed Professor of Natural History at the Mayence Central School, Paris, but an administrative muddle prevented him from taking up the post, and in 1804 he accepted the position of Professor and Director of the Moscow Museum of Natural History. In 1805 he founded the Moscow Society of Naturalists.

After the Moscow fire of 1812 Fischer had the daunting task of rebuilding the collections. It is from this period of his life that his increasing interest in geology and palaeontology stems. He made about 150 original contributions to the literature, including the *Oryctographie du Gouvernement de Moscou* (1830–37) and *Récherches sur les ossemens fossiles de la Russie* (1836–39).   A.P.H.

Fishes
Cold-blooded, gill-breathing, aquatic VERTE-BRATES possessing JAWS and both paired and median fins. Normally they are streamlined in shape and propel themselves through the water by side-to-side movements of the trunk and tail. In the more primitive types, or those with elongated bodies, the contractions of the trunk and tail muscles throw the body into a series of waves that pass back down the length of the body and drive the fish through the water. During normal swimming there are 54 waves per minute in the dogfish, whereas in a mackerel there are 170 per minute. In the faster swimming fishes the TAIL FIN is larger, but the body is less flexible and comparatively shorter. This reduces the amount of lateral movement in the body, but gives a substantial lateral sweep to the tail fin, which exerts up to 40 per cent of the forward thrust.

Among the more primitive fishes, the major muscular part of the tail was in the upper lobe, and the effect of a sideways movement was to raise the tail and automatically depress the head. This action was counteracted by the hydrofoil-shaped pectoral fins, which generated lift in a similar way to the action of the aerofoil-shaped wing of a bird or aeroplane. With the subsequent development of hydrostatic organs, such as air bladders, the need to generate lift became less important and the tails became symmetrical.

Living fishes can be divided into two major groups: cartilaginous (the Chondrichthyes) and bony (the Osteichthyes). The skeleton of a cartilaginous fish is composed of cartilage or gristle, and the body is covered in small tooth-like placoid scales. There are two major divisions of the Chondrichthyes: the SHARKS and RAYS, and the rat- or rabbit-fishes (CHIMAERAS). These two groups are placed in two separate classes, even though it is recognized that they have had a common ancestor in the distant past. A major group of extinct fishes, the PLACODERMS (which were heavily armoured) are now known to have been related to the living cartilaginous fishes, in particular the chimaeras. It is believed that there was a gradual loss of armour during their evolution.

The bony fishes also fall into two major groups, distinguished by the nature of their paired fins. The most highly evolved of modern fishes, the teleosts, belong to the RAY-FIN FISHES,

Flight

in which the internal skeletal supports of the fins are short and there are long dermal fin rays, which fan out, enclosed in a membrane. In the living bichir *Polypterus* from Africa, the most primitive of living ray-fin fishes, the paired fins possess a fleshy base. Nevertheless, the internal structure of the fins shows it to be a ray-fin and not a member of the second major group, the LOBE-FIN FISHES, in which the paired fins have a variable central bony axis that may support a fringe of fin rays.

The LOBE-FIN FISHES are divided into two groups: the crossopterygians, which include the rhipidistians (the ancestors of the land vertebrates and the COELACANTHS), and the LUNGFISHES or dipnoans, which are confined to fresh water in Africa, South America and Australia.

All the bony fishes appear to be related distantly to the ACANTHODIANS or "spiny sharks", but in spite of this they are best regarded as a separate class. Just as the land-living vertebrates are divided into several separate classes, so also are the fishes. At present, seven classes are recognized: the acanthodians, actinopterygians (ray-fin fishes), crossopterygians and dipnoans (both grouped as lobe-fin fishes), placoderms, selachians (sharks and rays), and holocephalans (chimaeras).   L.B.H.

Flight

Four different animal types have acquired the power of true flight. The earliest fliers were the INSECTS, which reached gigantic proportions during the Carboniferous – one dragonfly-like species had an estimated wing span of 70cm (28in). These large insects are thought to have occupied the same ecological niche as do the modern woodland birds.

The first vertebrates to take to the air were the PTEROSAURS. The oldest known example of these flying reptiles comes from the Triassic rocks of Europe but, along with their relatives, the DINOSAURS, they died out at the end of the Cretaceous. There is no obvious reason for such a successful group to have become extinct. Towards the end of their career, the pterosaurs evolved the largest known flying animal, *Quetzalcoatlus*, which had an estimated wing span of 10 metres (33ft) – three times greater than that of *Osteodontornis* or *Teratornis*, the largest flying birds so far discovered.

The third group to achieve flight was the birds, which are without doubt the most successful of all flying animals. They appear to have evolved sometime during the Jurassic from the COELUROSAURS, a group of lightly built, bipedal, flesh-eating dinosaurs. The first identifiable bird remains were found in Germany and named ARCHAEOPTERYX but there is some doubt as to whether *Archaeopteryx* was capable of powered flight. It lacks the keel to the sternum which is necessary for the attachment of the major flight muscles in birds, so it is possible that birds did not attain the power of flight until the Cretaceous.

The last group of animals to become fliers were the mammals. Bats are thought to have

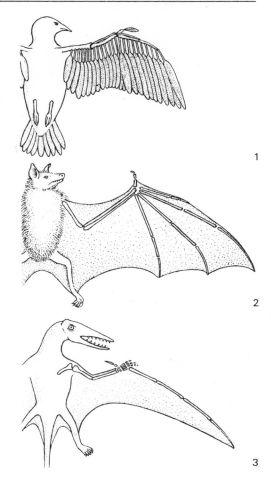

Flight
Three vertebrate solutions to the conquest of the air.
(1) Birds have flight feathers (modified scales) on the fore-limbs. The second "finger" is the longest of the three surviving digits, the fourth and fifth having disappeared.
(2) Bats retain all the fingers of the "hand", employing the second, third, fourth and fifth to support a flying membrane.
(3) Pterosaurs used a greatly elongated fourth "finger" only to carry the flying membrane, although the first, second and third digits were still present. The fifth digit is absent, but there is a projecting "pteroid" bone that may have supported an accessory membrane that extended from the neck.

evolved from tree-dwelling INSECTIVORA sometime before the Early Eocene about 50 million years ago.

Many other vertebrates are said to fly, but they are really gliders. Flying fishes, flying frogs, flying snakes and lizards, flying opossums, flying squirrels and flying lemurs are all gliders of varying efficiency. Flying fishes project themselves into the air by powerful swimming strokes of the tail, and then glide on the enlarged pectoral fins. Other animals have developed membranes that enable them to land safely after launching themselves into the air; a species of tree frog uses its enlarged webbed feet for this purpose, and various lizards and mammals have developed lateral membranes between the forelimbs and hindlimbs. One of the most bizarre methods of descent is that of the Indian parachute snake, which when disturbed throws itself off a branch and falls, keeping its ribs expanded and belly drawn in, forming a primitive parachute that enables the snake to make a reasonably soft landing.

For true powered flight, however, a different type of structure is required. First, an extension of the forearm skeleton is necessary which may involve the individual fingers, as in the pterosaurs (digit four) and birds (digit two), or the complete hand, as in the bats. The elongation of particular parts of the forelimbs produces a larger area to which feathers or membranes

Flint implements

can be attached. The development of the musculature in that region, coupled with lightening and strengthening of the bones and enlargement of pectoral girdle elements, enables the membraned or feathered wing to be raised and lowered to impart lift and forward motion. The lightening and strengthening process is well demonstrated by the bird skeleton, in which the bony tissue has been reduced to the absolute minimum. The bones of birds, like those of pterosaurs, are hollow, but have great mechanical strength. Some of the larger bones, which in most animals are filled with marrow, are in birds occupied by membranous sacs filled with air. Thus the bones are pneumatic, and because the air sacs are outgrowths of the breathing apparatus, the bird has reserves of air which are essential for flight.   C.A.W.

Flint implements

Although the chimpanzee occasionally uses a stick, either as a threat or to fish for termites, hominids have been the only primates to use tools in a continuously purposeful manner. Many animals have sharp cutting claws or teeth, but man lacks these attributes, and if he wants to skin an animal or to dig for edible roots he must use some form of tool. This link between man and tools is considered one of his most important characteristics ("man the toolmaker"). During much of hominid history such tools have been made of stone – most frequently of flint.

Four "tool kits" are known for the Pleistocene and one for the Holocene. The Pleistocene had chopper-core cultures, Acheulean hand-axe cultures, Mousterian cultures and the "blade and burin" culture of the upper PALAEOLITHIC. The Holocene culture comprised the microlith industries of the MESOLITHIC peoples. Occasionally these industries are referred to as modes, and are then numbered from one (chopper-core tools) to five (microlith technologies).

The chopper-core cultures are the oldest known stone tools and have been found at OLDUVAI (the Oldowan culture) associated with the remains of early hominids dating from 1.75 million years ago. To produce these tools, their makers struck flakes from one end of a pebble to leave a sharp edge, which could then be used for cutting skins and meat or for shaping wood, although they quickly became blunt. Animal kills have been found surrounded with many

such tools. Chopper-core tools have a wide distribution; they are found throughout Africa and occur widely in Asia (eg, with the remains of PEKING MAN dating from 400,000 years ago). In Asia chopper tools remained in use up to the Late Pleistocene, but in Europe, where they are found in England and France (the Clactonian culture), they were replaced by other technologies.

The Acheulean hand-axe could be called the first standardized all-purpose tool. It was a pear-shaped stone tool with two edges, a point and a base. The base could be used for hammering, the point for digging, and the edges for cutting. Experiments have shown that it is extremely efficient for skinning animals and it was a logical development of the chopper tool, with both faces worked to give the characteristic appearance. Some examples have been found with the point replaced by a cutting edge (cleavers). Acheulean hand-axes are named after the site in France at which they were originally found, although the earliest types come from Africa, with a progression from chopper-cores to hand-axes clearly evident at Olduvai and sites in Morocco. The method of production changed from simply striking with stones to the more controlled technique of working the core with wood or bone. Hand-axes are widely distributed and often occur with bones of *Homo erectus*; they are present throughout Africa, Europe and greater India. In England, hand-axes have been found with the remains of Swanscombe man, who is thought to have been an advanced *Homo erectus*.

Mousterian cultures show a different industrial evolution from that of the hand-axes and seem to have developed from the chopper-core industry of Clacton. The classical Mousterian tools comprise a thick flint flake which is shaped by secondary flaking into a side-scraper, knife, or triangular point (probably bound to wood and used as a spear). Where the Mousterian culture came into contact with the Acheulean, small hand-axes are also found, but these are not present in what was then the heavily forested areas of central France. Mousterian tools are most commonly discovered with the remains of NEANDERTHAL MAN and have the same distribution.

The Upper Palaeolithic blade industries developed on the foundation of a completely new technology. Flints were carefully selected, and successive long thin blades were struck from the

Flint implements
Palaeolithic tools include:
(1) Acheulian lava hand axe;
(2) and (3) Mousterian side scraper (racloir);
(4) Levalloisian pointed flake-tool;
(5) Solutrean piercer or "hand-drill".

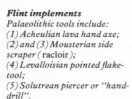

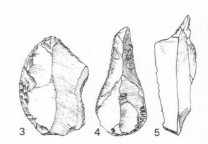

prepared core. These blades were then used as blanks, which by careful chipping could be made into a series of different tools, for example scrapers, awls and knives. This Aurignacian industry is the first one that can be associated with true men (*Homo sapiens*) and dates from about 34,000 years ago. In Europe, it coincides with the spread of sapient man about 32,000 years ago and is found above the layers containing the Neanderthal Mousterian artefacts. A succession of modifications to the original type of blade industry can be traced in the form of the blade tool. Leaf-shaped points were used by the Szetetian culture about 27,000 years ago in Czechoslovakia and Hungary, narrow knife blades were introduced by the Gravettian culture of Europe and Asia 25,000 years ago, and the Solutrean technology excelled in making long thin spear points, often measuring more than 18cm (7in) – a technique that developed in Hungary and spread to France about 19,000 to 15,000 years ago. The identifying tool of the Magdalenian peoples of about 15,000 years ago was the burin, which was probably used for working bone and antler into hooks, spears with barbed points, etc, as well as for decorating cave walls and bone artefacts. The Magdalenian peoples were the final inheritors of the CAVE ART tradition started by the Gravettian culture.

With the climatic change to warmer conditions about 12,000 years ago, trees once more covered much of northern Europe. Wood came into use for the manufacture of tools and weapons, and these were made more effective by the addition of small flint flakes (microliths) as cutting edges and as tips for arrows and spears.

The Americas and Australasia were settled by man much later than were Europe, Asia and Africa, and these outlying regions have their own cultures, which bear a significant resemblance to the classic sequence of Old World stone tool industries.   D.T.

Flowering plants

The largest and most diverse group in the plant kingdom, collectively known as angiosperms. As land PLANTS, they predominate over all other groups not only in numbers of species – more than a quarter of a million – but also in numbers of individuals. Most habitats have vegetation cover dominated by flowering plants.

A major feature leading to this pre-eminence is the evolutionary adaptability of the group. Flowering plants are found high in the mountains, in tropical conditions, and in deserts. The only habitat not successfully colonized by them is salt water. They range from minute forms such as duckweeds to the giant Australian eucalypts, some of which reach 100 metres (330ft) in height. A typical angiosperm is a green photosynthetic plant, but the group has also evolved numerous other forms. Saprophytes and parasites, which lack chlorophyll, abound in tropical regions and also have temperate representatives (for example broomrapes, Orobanchaceae, and mistletoe, *Viscum*). Others have become adapted to growing on larger plants (epiphytes) and several carnivorous

groups have sticky surfaces, fall traps and devices involving movement to catch the "prey".

The key to this diversity and success is the development of the flower itself. As a means of reproduction it is unsurpassed in the plant kingdom for efficiency under a wide range of conditions. The angiosperm flower is generally a much more complicated structure than the gymnosperm cone or the sporangial arrangements of the FERNS, but the sexual operation is greatly simplified. The necessary preliminaries to fertilization occur in the quickest and simplest way and with a high success rate.

The true ancestors of the flowering plants are still largely unknown. Charles DARWIN called their origin "the abominable mystery of evolution" and in some ways the quotation is still apt. Certainly none of the many fossils that have been proposed as the missing link in flowering plant evolution has proved to be an acceptable ancestor.

Remains of angiosperms occur in the Lower Cretaceous, and although these fossils are mostly leaves, probable flowering plant pollen grains occur even earlier.   J.W.F.

Folklore of fossils

Man's relationship with fossils stretches back to the STONE AGE. K.P. Oakley (1911–   ), the distinguished British palaeontologist and anthropologist, has thus summarized the entry of fossils into folklore thus: "One may infer that to Palaeolithic men fossils were among the various *objets trouvés* which were valued as conferring prestige or good luck by reason of uniqueness, aesthetic appeal or through symbolizing a virtue or desired attribute.

"Although in the earliest phases of culture certain fossils were perhaps just regarded as 'lucky', in more advanced phases they would be thought to contain magical power, and then, as animism gave place to belief in gods and ghosts, the fossils became a fetish, or habitat of a god; finally, when the religion decayed or was replaced by another the fetish was no longer an object of specific belief, but degenerated in folk memory to become once again merely an object conferring 'good luck'."

Vertebrate and invertebrate fossils have been used in adornment and have become embodied in folklore. Of the vertebrates, fossil sharks' teeth, which are common in some localities, have been used for necklaces and credited with offering protection against rheumatic pains and warding off the evil eye. Toadstones, believed to be stones that formed on the head of a toad, are in reality fish teeth, often of *Lepidotes*. Unlike the pointed and sharp sharks' teeth, they are found as stud-like masses.

The unearthing of large mammal bones was often regarded as evidence of the former existence of giants, particularly when masses of such bones were found together. For example, in the Ukraine, where mammoth bones were used to form the framework of prehistoric huts, the discoverers thought that they had uncovered a graveyard of giants. There are also links, especially in medieval times, with St Christo-

Footprints

pher, who was considered to be a giant. Several churches displayed bones, usually of mammoth, believing them to be remains of the saint.

China has long been the source of stories about "dragons' bones" and "dragons' teeth". For hundreds of years fossils have been mined and sold to chemists. Many of the teeth used are derived from an early form of horse, *Hipparion*. When the crushed fossil is sold, the purchaser believes that he will be aided by his patron dragon. A medicinal value has also been claimed for the pulverized fossils.

The seeking out and purchasing by scientists of the "dragons' teeth" and a determined search for the source of supply resulted indirectly in the discovery of PEKING MAN. *Gigantopithecus*, probably the largest ape that ever lived, was described initially on the basis of teeth purchased from a druggist by Professor Gustav von KOENIGSWALD.

Invertebrate fossils are generally more available than vertebrate fossils and therefore are more commonly featured in folklore. Some of the more spectacular and commonly occurring fossils are AMMONITES. These coiled molluscs were originally compared with the horns of a ram. Sacred to the Greeks, rams were linked with the god Jupiter-Ammon, hence the name Ammon's horns and eventually "ammonites". To many, they bore a striking resemblance to a coiled snake: hence their popular name, snakestones. BELEMNITES are often known as devil's fingers or thunderbolts and were used to cure ailments in horses and man.

Mollusca (in particular gastropods) have been strung together into bracelets and necklaces for adornment since Palaeolithic times. Even in the Stone Age, there seems to have been a considerable trade in fossil shells.

An example of sympathetic magic is the use of *Gryphaea* (a bivalve genus including a form in which the left valve has become strongly incurved) as a cure for rheumatism. The devil's toe-nail is the popular name of this fossil.

Brachiopods, sponges, crinoids and worm tubes all have a place in folklore: Echinoderms are still placed on larder shelves because it is believed that they will preserve dairy produce.

A.P.H.

Footprints

Fossil footprints are a record of the activity of an animal during its lifetime, in contrast to most fossils which are produced only after the death of the organism concerned.

Many extinct animals are known only from footprints. Among the most familiar are the Triassic trackways, named *Cheirotherium* ("beast hand"), which occur in both western Europe and eastern North America. One digit projected sideways and was at first thought to be a thumb, but because it pointed laterally the early workers assumed the animal crossed its legs every time it took a step. Later, it was realized that this digit was actually the fifth finger. The animal evidently held its body off the ground and had a narrow trackway, the hindlimbs being much heavier and longer than the front ones. From the length of the stride, it was possible to determine the distance between the shoulder and hip girdles as well as the length of the limbs (*Cheirotherium* was reconstructed on the basis of footprints alone).

Eventually, fossil skeletons of an animal conforming to this description were discovered in the Triassic of Switzerland and named *Ticinosuchus*. These remains not only fitted the footprints but also confirmed in all respects the restorations previously proposed for *Cheirotherium*.

Footprints have been especially helpful as evidence of the way DINOSAURS lived, and the most northerly known occurrence of these reptiles are some *Iguanodon* footprints from Spitzbergen. Although skeletons can be reconstructed to give an idea of stance and gait, only the evidence of footprints determine exactly how a dinosaur stood and walked. A trackway found in the Jurassic rocks of southern England shows two parallel rows of three-toed prints that were initially interpreted as a carnivorous bipedal dinosaur walking slowly. Subsequent excavation revealed that the two lines of prints diverged, and that there was an adjacent single track which proved that the feet were placed one in front of the other with the limbs positioned more or less beneath the body. A study of the trackways of such dinosaurs shows that they are sinuous and that the animals were slightly pigeon-toed. The giant CARNOSAURS must have waddled like geese or ducks and taken short strides – they were evidently not adapted for swift running.

Once the maker of the trackways has been identified, the height of the limbs can be calculated, and from this information it is possible to estimate the speed at which the animal was moving. This does not indicate the maximum speed possible but only the rate at which the particular animal that left its footprints was travelling. The lightly built ostrich-dinosaurs (eg *Ornithomimus*), credited with a speed of 80km/h (50mph) were, on the evidence of footprints, capable of only 20km/h (12mph). In contrast, the giant quadrupedal SAUROPODS, which it has been suggested could have run at 50km/h (31mph) seem, from their footprints, not to have moved faster than 4km/h (2.5mph), and studies on the strength of bone

Footprints
(1) Fore and hind footprints of Matthewichnus, *an Upper Carboniferous amphibian from North America;*
(2) footprints of Orchesteropus, *an Upper Carboniferous amphibian from Argentina;*
(3) fore and hind footprints of Parabaropus, *an eryopoid labyrinthodont from the Lower Permian of Arizona.*

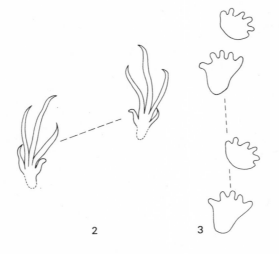

1
2
3

Foraminiferans

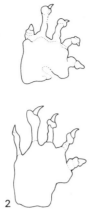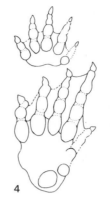

1   2   3   4   5

determine their maximum possible speed as 20km/h (12mph).

The trackways of sauropods showing numerous individuals walking along parallel tracks with the smaller individuals in the centre has led to the suggestion that sauropods lived in structured herds. One of the curious features of sauropod tracks is the rare occurrence of tail drag marks. There are two interpretations of this: either the tail was held high up, or else the animals lived in shallow water and the tails were floating. One sauropod track consists of the forefeet only, but when a change of direction is made, the print of a single hindfoot suddenly appears on the outer bend of the turn. This set of footprints can only mean that the individual was floating and pawing itself along the bottom with its forefeet, bringing a hindfoot down to get a grip on the substrate as it swung its body round to change direction.

Fossil footprints have conclusively proved that some PTEROSAURS were capable of walking on level ground, the edges of the wings being dragged along as the animal walked unsteadily across the moist sand. In the marine NOTHOSAURS of the Triassic, the fingers and toes are elongated and seem to approach a paddle-like condition; it is only footprints that prove these reptiles possessed webbed feet.

In many European Pleistocene caves there are large bear footprints on the floors associated with vertical and horizontal scratch marks on the walls and polished areas, where the bears must have rubbed themselves. All these features suggest that the animals spent much time there, but because there is no sign of food it is concluded that the bears hibernated in these particular caves. The presence of bear bones shows that many must have died while asleep.

Fossil footprints of birds are rare, although there is a famous set of duck-like prints which are webbed and show occasional dabble marks. The three-toed dinosaur footprints which occur so abundantly in the Triassic rocks of the Connecticut valley were thought by their discoverer E. B. Hitchcock (1793–1864) to have been left by extinct birds, and he vividly described vast flocks of huge imaginary "birds" walking along the Triassic river shores.   L.B.H.

Foraminiferans

Single-celled members of the animal kingdom (PROTOZOANS) belonging to the order Foraminiferida. They live in all depths of brackish and marine water and secrete a shell or test, usually either of calcium carbonate or of fine sand grains cemented together with calcium carbonate. The shell is variable in shape, and ranges in size from a fraction of a millimetre to several centimetres or more, although most species are about 0.5–1.0mm (0.02–0.04in) in diameter. They have a long geological history, from the Cambrian to the present day, and there are some even earlier forms of crude sac-like configuration that might belong to the group.

In life the foraminiferal shell contains cytoplasm, which is extruded through apertures, and in some genera through perforations as well. This extruded cytoplasm (pseudopodia) catches food and can be used for locomotion.

There are two main types of foraminiferans: planktonic (free-floating) and benthic (living on sediment or seaweed). Benthic species may grow to large sizes.

Some planktonic foraminiferans are covered

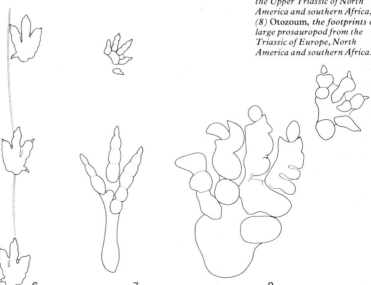

6   7   8

85

Fossil fuels

in life with spines, but these break off on death and the shell then sinks to the ocean floor to contribute to foraminiferal oozes. These deposits are sometimes known as *Globigerina* oozes, after one of the most common genera they contain. The planktonic mode of life was taken up by foraminiferans early in the Mesozoic, but did not become successful until the Cretaceous. Planktonic foraminiferans are of paramount importance for dating rocks and as ZONE FOSSILS: they have evolved rapidly, occur in all but the shallowest marine sediments in large numbers, and have a wide geographical range. A fine-scale zonal scheme, using these microscopic animals, has almost worldwide application from the Upper Cretaceous to the Pleistocene.

Benthic foraminiferans, however, are more useful as indicators of past environments. Many living species are restricted to particular sediment types and water depths, and by using this information on analogous fossil representatives it is possible to reconstruct the conditions under which a particular rock was originally deposited. Benthic foraminiferans first grew to large sizes, more than 1cm (0.41in) at the end of the Carboniferous, and in the Tethyan belt these fusuline foraminiferans have proved to be valuable zonal fossils from the Upper Carboniferous to the latest Permian. They were also the first foraminiferans to be important rock builders. Other larger foraminiferans are important for dating the shallow water carbonates that were deposited over wide areas in the Cretaceous (eg *Orbitolina*) and at various times within the lower Cenozoic (eg *Lepidocyclina*, *Discocyclina*,

Miogypsina, *Nummulites* and the alveolines, which include the living genus *Borelis*).   J.E.P.W.

Fossil fuels

Fuels composed of or derived from the organic remains of past eras. They comprise coals, which originate wholly from plants, and petroleum, produced by the decay of marine organisms.

Coal lies towards the end of a sequence beginning with PEAT and ending at anthracite. The position of any fuel in this sequence can be determined by the extent of its decomposition, the degree of fossilization undergone by components, and the carbon content. Peat is about 50–60 per cent carbon; lignite (brown coal) is about 70 per cent carbon; bituminous coals are 75–85 per cent carbon; and anthracite may be almost 100 per cent carbon.

Coal occurs in seams separated by layers of other rocks. Underlying the coal seam, there is often a seat earth which is the original soil, whereas the overlying deposit is a marine or freshwater band which has sealed in the seam. Coal is formed from massive accumulations of land plants that died and decomposed in an oxygen-deficient system, yielding a peat-like deposit rich in carbon. Deposits of this sort that build up in deltas and lagoons become sealed in and compressed by further deposition, and the build-up of a coalfield with its numerous seams is due to the constant repetition of this process.

Most coals began as peat-like deposits. Lignites have a higher percentage of carbon than peat but still retain some moisture and recognizable plant structures. Bituminous coals include those used domestically as well as some from which gas, steam and coke are produced. Anthracite burns slowly with little flame and almost no smoke to produce great heat per unit weight compared with other coals. It is the product of great compression and is usually found at the deepest parts of a coalfield.

In the Northern Hemisphere, the most extensive coal deposits are of Carboniferous age; in the Southern Hemisphere, most of the coal comes from the Permian. There are a few occurrences of coal in the Jurassic, but most of the later coals are lignites.

Petroleum is the other major fossil fuel. It includes an enormous group of substances, all of which are hydrocarbons, ranging from the gaseous methane (natural gas), through various grades of liquid oils, including petrol (gasolene), paraffin (kerosene) and mineral oil, to solid asphalt. The minerals of the petroleum group occur in oil shales or in liquid or gaseous form trapped in reservoir rocks. Oils have generally migrated to the places where they are found and offer few clues as to their source. Petroleums originate from the decomposition of small marine organisms (plants and animals) over a long period of time. When the muds of the sea bottom became compacted into rock, the petroleums were either trapped *in situ* to form oil shales or were squeezed out with the water and gases into surrounding porous rocks. The oil separated from the water and rose to the top, being less dense, and the gases accumulated

Fossil fuels
The succession of strata in which coal seams (black bands) develop: peat (light tone) is found near the surface, whereas lignite occurs at moderate depths, about 1,000m (3,280ft); bituminous coal lies relatively deep, at about 3,000m (9,800ft), and anthracite is the oldest and hence normally the deepest coal deposit, 6,000m (19,700ft). Folding and the erosion of overlying rocks may result in coal lying near the surface today, but compression at great depth is necessary at some stage for its formation.

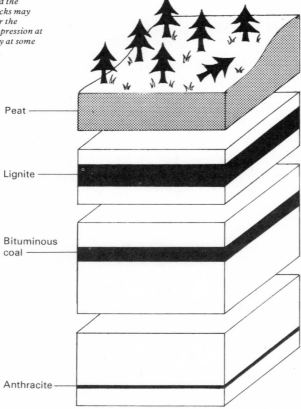

Peat

Lignite

Bituminous coal

Anthracite

above them. A combination of porous reservoir rocks and impermeable capping rock is required before an oilfield can form.   J.W.F.

Fossilization

The process by which traces of the activities of once living organisms (TRACE FOSSILS) or the actual remains of plants and animals are preserved as fossils in rock. The word fossil is derived from the Latin *fossilis* (*fodere*, "to dig"), meaning "something dug up". A fossil is the remains of ancient life, but it is not practical to define a minimum age limit for fossils. Nevertheless, about 10,000 years before the present is often taken as an arbitrary dividing line between what is fossil and what is Recent.

There are many factors that govern whether or not a dead organism is eventually fossilized; the presence and nature of its hard parts and its environment are particularly significant and only rarely are soft parts preserved. The processes at work are selective. Some groups stand little chance of possible representation in the fossil record, so there must be many ancient forms of life, especially plants and entirely soft-bodied animals, of which the palaeontologist has no knowledge.

Whether an organism is preserved after death also depends on the action of biological, mechanical and chemical agents. Predators and scavengers, winds, waves and currents, and chemical solutions – sometimes acting even after fossilization has occurred – all combine to rob a sedimentary sequence of part, or even all, of its potentially fossilizable material. The total number of known fossil species of animals and plants (*c.*250,000), essentially spanning the last 600 million years of the Earth's history, is only about 5 per cent of the estimated total species (more than 4 million) living today. It would appear that many new fossil groups await discovery.

Areas of sediment deposition are more favourable to preservation, and therefore fossilization, than are areas where erosion is predominant. In this respect, terrestrial flora and fauna are at a disadvantage compared with their marine counterparts. On the land, burial by sediment is generally much slower (if it occurs at all), bacteriological decay and decomposition generally tends to be more rapid, and the chances of pre-burial destruction by the elements and by scavengers is high.

The hard parts of vertebrates (bones and teeth) are composed mainly of calcium phosphate, a relatively insoluble substance. The skeletal minerals of the major invertebrate groups in the fossil record vary between phyla. Usually the hard parts of BRACHIOPODS, COELENTERATES, ECHINODERMS, MOLLUSCS and some SPONGES and Protozoa (FORAMINIFERANS) are chiefly composed of calcium carbonate crystals (calcite or aragonite) in an organic matrix. Other sponges and protozoan skeletons (RADIOLARIANS) are formed from silica. ARTHROPODS and GRAPTOLITES are two important fossil groups in which organic substances (chitin and scleroprotein, respectively) form the chief skeletal material. Cellulose and lignin are the main structural elements in plants.

The organic and the mineral parts of these skeletal elements are subject to changes during fossilization. Sometimes the mineral constituents remain largely unaffected, but the organic substances decay. More normally, however, the rapid decay of the soft tissues is followed by changes affecting all the skeletal substances. Sometimes loss by solution of the entire hard parts occurs, due to the action of percolating ground water, leaving only the *in situ* fossilized impression of the skeleton or shell in the form of external or internal moulds.

There are some well documented examples in which atypical preservation conditions have resulted in the rare fossilization of the organic matter of hard parts, and in some instances even the soft tissues. They include the famous insect remains of the Oligocene AMBER deposits from the southern Baltic, the extinct Siberian woolly MAMMOTHS found frozen complete with stomach contents preserved, the numerous fossil vertebrate finds from peat bogs (eg in Ireland), and the sites of former tar pools such as those in Poland and at RANCHO LA BREA. Rapid entombment combined with conditions that inhibit bacteriological decay are key factors for such fossilization.

Plants, together with those animals with mainly organic hard parts (eg graptolites) are often preserved as carbonaceous films on bedding planes. This type of fossilization (carbonization) involves the gradual expulsion of volatiles, and an increase in carbon content. The impressions of some soft-bodied creatures, such as worms, may be recorded in this way.

The fossilization process whereby the mineral substance of the hard parts is changed into stone (petrification) results from either impregnation of extremely small voids left by the loss of the organic matrix, or by the more complete replacement of the original skeletal mineral by a substitute mineral. Percolating ground water containing minerals in solution is the agent of chemical change, which transforms the hard parts into heavier, more robust objects while retaining their shape and surface detail. The most common occurrence is to find the original calcareous hard parts augmented by calcite impregnation. When aragonite formed the original skeletal mineral, fossilization also involves its recrystallization to the more stable calcite, a process that often entails complete obliteration of the shell remains. Compounds of iron (pyrites, haematite and limonite) are other important replacement agents, as is silica.

See also ZONE FOSSILS.   J.E.P.W.

Frogs and toads

The superorder of AMPHIBIANS known as the Salientia. Their origin, evolutionary history and relationships are uncertain. The skeleton of frogs is specialized for jumping, with long hindlegs and a hip girdle in which the sockets for the two thigh bones are close together. The whole girdle is sprung with long processes that extend forwards for articulation with the

Gastroliths

vertebral column. Frogs also have short, stout forelimbs, a strong shoulder girdle to take the impact of landing, an abbreviated vertebral column with reduced or absent ribs, and no tail (except in the tadpole stage).

The earliest fossil which shows clear frog-like features is a skeleton from the Early Triassic of Madagascar known as *Triadobatrachus*. Whereas the limbs remain primitive, the skull is frog-like; the number of vertebrae has been reduced to 14 (compared with about 24 in primitive amphibians and 9 or 10 in modern frogs and toads), the ribs are short, and the tail is reduced to six short vertebrae. Study of the skeleton suggests that the distinctive hindlimbs of frogs originally evolved not for jumping but for swimming with simultaneous strokes of both hindlegs.

The earliest true frogs (Anura) appeared in the Jurassic. *Vieraella* comes from the Lower Jurassic and *Notobatrachus* from the Middle Jurassic, both of Patagonia, with *Eodiscoglossus* occurring at the Jurassic–Cretaceous boundary in Spain. *Notobatrachus* and *Eodiscoglossus* are attributable to the primitive living families Ascaphidae and Discoglossidae respectively, and *Vieraella* could be ancestral to both families. With the exception of one extinct family (Palaeobatrachidae, Cretaceous to Pliocene of Europe) all other well-preserved fossil frogs can also be attributed to living families, with the Pipidae first appearing in the Lower Cretaceous of Israel. A.I.P.

Frogs and toads
The early frog Triadobatrachus *lived in the Lower Triassic of Madagascar.*
Length: 10cm (4in)

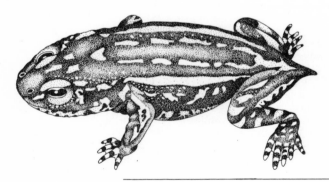

Gastroliths

Rounded pebbles ("stomach stones") that are found within the rib cages of some fossil reptiles. In some instances, eg in the aquatic PLESIOSAURS, they were perhaps ingested to control buoyancy; gastroliths are also known in SAUROPOD dinosaurs, which may have been largely water-dwellers.

Exotic pebbles occur in many deposits, but their occurrence cannot be explained by normal sedimentary transport. Hence in the WEALDEN marls there are found rounded, highly polished pebbles which were transported there from distant sources and are identified as DINOSAUR gastroliths. In the same deposits there are footprints and, occasionally, dinosaur bones, so that it is not unreasonable to accept this interpretation.

The grit in the crop or gizzard of a bird helps to break up food for digestion. Crocodiles have a gizzard-like muscular stomach containing pebbly gastroliths. The function of these stones has been studied in modern crocodiles by X-ray cinematography, which showed that the stones are used to pound food until it is broken down into small pieces. The large size and polished nature of "fossil" gastroliths suggests that the stomachs of some dinosaurs must have functioned in a similar way to those of modern crocodiles. L.B.H.

Gastropods

The MOLLUSCS of the class Gastropoda. They have snail-like soft parts with a foot used for creeping or burrowing, and a distinct head with tentacles and eyes. A rasping organ (radula) is used in feeding, and internal organs show bilateral asymmetry.

The shell is usually coiled in a right-handed helical spiral and lacks the septa characteristic of CEPHALOPODS. Some have cap-shaped shells (*Patella*, limpet), and various modifications occur in certain groups that are unimportant as fossils, such as pelagic Pteropoda. The shell is internal or totally absent in slugs and sea slugs.

Although gastropods originated in the sea (the small spirally shelled *Aldanella* and *Helcionella* range down to the basal Cambrian) and have a marine depth distribution similar to that of BIVALVES, they have also successfully invaded brackish and fresh water – the only molluscs to have adapted to a terrestrial existence.

Several different gastropod lineages have exploited non-marine environments. The Patellidae (from the Jurassic onwards) and the winkles or Littorinidae (Cenozoic) remain exposed for long periods, and the terrestrial Pomatiasidae (also Cenozoic) are close relatives of winkles. *Viviparus* (the pond-snail) formed limestone bands in the Purbeckian (Upper Jurassic or Lower Cretaceous) of southern England, and the closely related Cyclophoridae are terrestrial. Most land snails, however, belong to the subclass Pulmonata in which the mantle cavity acts as a lung, typical molluscan gills being absent.

Moisture conservation is an important factor for terrestrial snails, which are most prolific in humid tropical areas. One of the earliest known, *Maturipupa* (Carboniferous), probably evolved in the almost ideal conditions of luxuriant swampy Coal Measure forests. Pulmonates were uncommon before the Cenozoic; they include *Helix*, *Achatina* (on land), *Planorbis*, *Lymnaea* and the extinct *Filholia* (in fresh water). Primitive brackish-water Ellobiidae date from the Mesozoic. Land snails are invaluable as indicators of past climate and vegetation, particularly in relation to Pleistocene glaciations.

Many gastropods are herbivores but at least three extremely successful carnivorous stocks evolved during the Mesozoic. Except for the Naticacea, they have a siphonal notch or canal, also found in herbivores such as the Aporrhaidae,

Geography of the past

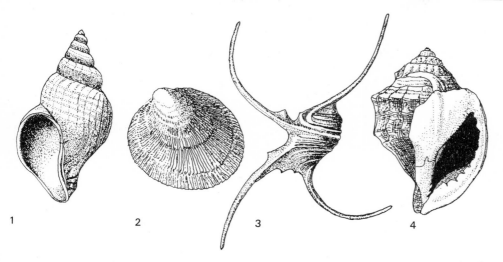

1   2   3   4

worldwide in the Mesozoic but now confined to the North Atlantic Ocean. Tonnacea (*Cassis*, *Galeodea*) attack echinoderms but the prey of Buccinacea ("whelks", *Clavilithes*, *Neptunea*) and Volutacea (*Athleta*) includes other molluscs, marine worms and arthropods. In Conacea, the radula is modified into a poisonous harpoon; small forms (Turridae) usually eat worms, but some large species (*Conus*) take fishes.

Muricacea (*Pterynotus*) and Naticacea (*Sigatica*) bore round holes through the shells of molluscs, the muricacean holes being jagged whereas naticacean drillings are neatly bevelled. Such borings are uncommon before the Late Cretaceous but become abundant throughout the Cenozoic.

As in bivalves, gastropod diversity increased markedly with the beginning of the Cenozoic. Of the estimated 37,000 living species, 17,000 are pulmonates; most of the remainder are marine.   C.P.N.

Geography of the past

The physical geography of the past (palaeogeography) can be deduced by several geological and geophysical means. The extent of seas formerly covering continental crustal regions (epicontinental seas) at a given time can be determined by mapping the sediments, at outcrop and underground, which contain fossilized remains of the marine fauna known to have lived in the seas at that time. The margins of the sea can be detected by the distribution of coarse ill-graded sediments, which show bedding structures normally associated today with shallow-water, near-shore sediments. Such sediments might even contain brackish-water fossils, indicating the former proximity of a river mouth. Rarely, the remains of cliff lines with associated boulder and pebble beach beds may be preserved.

Sediments laid down in salt marsh, freshwater deltaic or even lake environments can also be identified by comparison with those seen today, peculiarities of their composition, microstructures and bedding being closely similar in this type of sediment throughout the geological column. Although often unrelated,

the floral and faunal contents nonetheless show morphologically similar forms because they occupied similar ecological niches. Occasionally, fossil soils have been found with plant remains, including fungal mycelia.

The extent of the oceanic areas during the last 200 million years can be determined by mapping the distribution of oceanic crust of an age range indicated by the magnetic anomaly patterns (*see* CONTINENTAL DRIFT) present in this crust. Deep-sea boreholes give information about water depths, temperature, chemistry and the physical environment of the sea bed at a specified time.

Oceanic areas existed during the Palaeozoic beyond 200 million years ago, particularly in the area of the Pacific Ocean. Nothing of this ancient crust has survived to modern times to indicate its original configuration, but it can be deduced from a variety of geological and geophysical observations.

The development of the ocean basins seen today has produced major changes in the Earth's physical geography and the distributions of land and marine fauna and flora. In the early Mesozoic, most of the modern continental areas were grouped together in a supercontinent called PANGAEA. From the mid-Jurassic onwards, this enormous land mass underwent a progressive break-up due to CONTINENTAL DRIFT.

The bulk of the ancient sediments that contain the fossil evidence of past changes in geography were laid down in the oceans and epicontinental seas – only comparatively rarely are continental deposits preserved, and most of these are sea-marginal in nature, such as swamp, deltaic and sand-dune sediments, or the infill of large tectonically controlled intermontane lake basins (eg the Cretaceous of the GOBI DESERT).

The scattered and chance nature of terrestrial deposits is one of the major reasons for our poor knowledge of the spread and development of land faunas and floras when compared with marine faunas. Areas undergoing marked tectonic and associated volcanic activity, such as the East African Rift Valley, have produced important sediment sequences laid down in terrestrial and lake environments, some fortuitously preserved by lava flows. Knowledge of early hominid development from the Miocene

Geological time

onwards has largely come from such sequences in eastern Africa.

The development of an animal or plant, its evolutionary pattern and its final extinction may be due largely to changes in the physical and geographic environment. For example, the special development of Australian marsupials was almost certainly due to the opening of seaways between Australia and continental regions to the north and south. Marsupials also occur today in South America, possibly indicating a common origin in the Late Cretaceous while South America and Australia were still both connected to Antarctica, and climatic conditions were sufficiently clement to allow migration between the two continents.   H.G.O.

Geological time, *see* individual periods.

Gills
Respiratory structures that occur in aquatic vertebrates and invertebrates. They absorb oxygen from the water and release carbon dioxide.

The living protochordates, such as the seasquirts and *Amphioxus*, have a perforated pharynx in the form of a "basket" of longitudinal and transverse gill bars – a structure comparable to that which the ancestors of the vertebrates must have possessed. Water passes over and through this mesh, and oxygen is extracted from the water while carbon dioxide is released into it. In the midline along the ventral part of the basket is the endostyle, producing mucus that is carried up the gill bars; this mucus traps small particles of food which are gradually transported to the intestine. In the living jawless vertebrates, the pharynx is divided into an upper region through which food passes, and a lower one which is concerned solely with respiration.

In the CEPHALASPIDS, the ANASPIDS and their living relatives the lampreys, the skeleton of the gill supports forms a simple basket and the individual gills are small pouches in which the gill filaments face inwards. Each gill pouch opens separately to the exterior. This type of gill can be derived from the pre-vertebrate condition, but it is completely distinct from that which characterizes the jawless PTERASPIDS and all the jawed fishes.

Among the jawed vertebrates the water flows over gill filaments to the exterior. The gill arches, which support the gill filaments, are internal and the filaments spread outwards, whereas in pouched gills the gill filaments are partly enclosed by the gill skeleton. In the jawed fishes there are also stiff gill rakers on the inner surfaces of the arches that prevent particles getting into the delicate gill filaments.

Septal gills, found in SHARKS, have the gill filaments carried on a fleshy septum, with one set on the anterior surface and one on the posterior.

The bony fishes have opercular gills. Instead of the delicate gill filaments of one gill arch being separated by a fleshy septum they are free, with a bony operculum on the outside.

Among the LUNGFISHES and in the most primitive living member of the RAY-FIN FISHES (*Polypterus*), as well as in larval amphibians, there are external gills. These are developed from the skin of the gill region but are not directly related to the gill system.   L.B.H.

Gilmore, Charles Whitney (1874–1945)
American museum curator and researcher on fossil reptiles. He was born in Pavilion, New York, and graduated from the University of Wyoming in 1901. He worked for a short while at the Carnegie Museum and then at the United States National Museum (NATIONAL MUSEUM OF NATURAL HISTORY).

The museum already had the collection made for the United States Geological Survey by

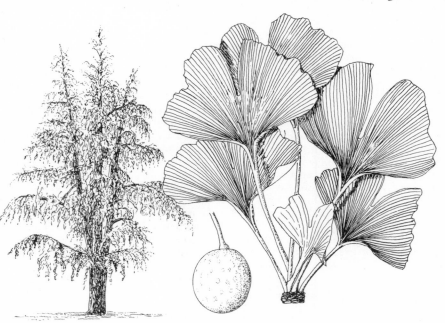

Ginkgo
A ginkgo tree, with its fruit and foliage; living ginkgos grow to a height of about 30m (100ft).

Glossopteris flora

Othniel MARSH, and Gilmore himself led fifteen expeditions, mainly to the western USA, to enlarge the collections. Most of the fine collection of mounted specimens in the museum were erected under his care.

His main research interests were in reptiles, including the DINOSAURS, LIZARDS, TURTLES, SNAKES and fossil FOOTPRINTS; his first paper was published in 1902. He was noted for his keen observations, thoroughness, and extensive knowledge of reptilian osteology. A.P.H.

Ginkgo

The only living representative (*Ginkgo biloba*) of a group of gymnosperm plants that was once worldwide in distribution. The appearance of the leaves of the modern species are virtually identical to those found in rocks of Triassic age (about 200 million years old).

As well as *Ginkgo* itself there are fifteen other genera, grouped in the Ginkgoales. Their leaves are generally fan- or strap-shaped and often deeply divided into the characteristic dichotomous ginkgo shape.

Ginkgo trees grow to a height of about 30 metres (100ft), and are either male or female. The seeds of the living ginkgo are borne on short stalks in the axils of the leaves and when mature have a fleshy integument. The male organs are catkin-like and are also borne in the leaf axils. J.W.F.

Giraffes

The giraffoid ARTIODACTYL ungulates which were widespread in Eurasia and Africa during the Cenozoic before the rise of the grazing herbivores. Characteristically they have long legs, long necks, large eyes and large ears. Both of the surviving genera, *Giraffa* itself and the okapi (*Okapia*), are two-toed with fused cannon bones.

Giraffoids are browsers – giraffes in savanna and okapis in forest – and their cheek teeth are medium- to high-cusped with rugose enamel. A notable feature of the more advanced members of the group is the presence of ossicones ("horns") on the head. There are usually three of these bony outgrowths, although there are only two in the okapi and sometimes five in the giraffes (other variations occur in fossil species). Ossicones occur in males and females, and are never shed or replaced. They are permanently covered with skin, and thus differ from the antlers of deer and the horns of cattle.

Three families comprise the superfamily Giraffoidea: the Palaeomerycidae, the Sivatheriidae and the Giraffidae.

Palaeomerycids are confined to the Miocene of Europe and Africa. They are close to the ancestry of giraffes and deer and are sometimes classified as cervids. The ossicones, present in some of them, have a long proximal stalk terminating in a whorl of short tines. The teeth of palaeomerycids are low-cusped, selenodont and lightly wrinkled.

The sivatheres are large giraffoids from the

Giraffes
Sivatherium, *from the Pleistocene of southern Asia and Africa, represents an extinct side-branch of the giraffe line of evolution. Height: 2.2m (7ft) at the shoulder*

Plio-Pleistocene of Eurasia and Africa. Their body proportions are deer-like, with long legs but short necks. *Sivatherium* carried large and palmate branched ossicones on the fronto-parietal bones, resembling the antlers of fallow deer. Sivatheres survived into post-Pleistocene times, and there is a Sumerian figurine depicting one, as well as rock paintings in the Sahara Desert indicating that they were known to Palaeolithic man.

The giraffids proper have two divisions: the palaeotragines and the giraffines. The palaeotragines are a medium-sized primitive stock known as far back as the Miocene in Eurasia and Africa, with the okapi as their sole survivor. Their limbs and neck are moderately elongated, the teeth low-cusped and selenodont, and they carry a single pair of short ossicones.

The giraffines, represented today by a single species of *Giraffa* with several sub-species in different parts of Africa, can be traced back to the African Miocene. They are large and have high-cusped, selenodont teeth and short, unbranched ossicones. R.J.G.S.

Glossopteris flora

The characteristic flora of GONDWANALAND during Permo-Carboniferous times. In the Early Carboniferous the floras of the Northern and Southern Hemispheres were comparable, but by the end of the Carboniferous a completely different flora was developing in the Southern Hemisphere. The remains of this flora are now found in rocks of Late Carboniferous and Permian age in Antarctica, Australasia, South Africa, South America and greater India – continents which at that time formed Gondwanaland – and is known as the *Glossopteris* flora from the widespread occurrence of the characteristic leaf form *Glossopteris*. As the Latin name implies, these

Gobi Desert

leaves were tongue-shaped. They range in length from a few centimetres (1–2in) to several decimetres (about 12in) and their veins form a regular reticulum, giving the leaf an extremely distinctive appearance.

In common with many fossil plant groups, the remains of the *Glossopteris* flora, although abundant and well preserved, are fragmentary. This means that the parts of one plant may be described under a series of form genera, and reconstruction of a whole plant with any degree of certainty is virtually impossible.

A peculiar type of axis (*Vertebraria*) is found in association with *Glossopteris*-type leaves. It was at one time thought that these were stems from which the leaves had been shed, but it now seems probable that they represent rhizomes. The more delicate stems to which the leaves are sometimes found attached probably arose from these *Vertebraria* rhizomes.

Associated with glossopterid leaves and axes are numerous small seeds and microsporangia, so that for a long time it was assumed that *Glossopteris* was gymnospermous in character. Subsequently, about six genera and nineteen species of fructification were described, but none of this material was in the form of petrifactions, so nothing is known of the internal structure of the organs.

The sporangia found alongside leaves of *Glossopteris* type in Africa were borne terminally on slender branched axes and contained pollen grains with two air sacs. Similar pollen grains were found in the micropyles of the ovules, so it seems certain that the same species was involved, and that these organs belonged to a plant with a *Glossopteris*-type leaf.

The significance of this group of plants which developed in the isolation of Gondwanaland is not clearly understood, but they cannot be put forward as the ancestors of angiosperms (FLOWERING PLANTS).   J.W.F.

Glossopteris
Fronds of Glossopteris, *possibly a tree-fern (approx. 1/6 natural size).*

Gobi Desert

An arid region in Mongolia bounded by the Altai and Hangayn Mountains to the north, the eastern Tien Shan to the west, and the mountain ranges of China to the south and east. Palaeontologically, it is notable for outcrops of fossil-bearing continental rocks of Cretaceous and Cenozoic age.

The fossil-bearing deposits were discovered in 1922 by a large expedition from the AMERICAN MUSEUM OF NATURAL HISTORY (New York City), led by Roy Chapman Andrews. Further expeditions were mounted by this museum in 1923 and 1925, followed in the 1940s and 1960s by Soviet-Mongolian and Polish-Mongolian expeditions.

The Upper Cretaceous deposits occur mainly within large post-Oligocene tectonic depressions. Exclusively red beds, their varied lithology indicates conditions of deposition that range from aeolian (dune sands) to fluviatile. Three formations are recognized: the Djadokhta is considered to be of upper Santonian or lower Campanian age, the Barun Goyot is regarded as middle Campanian, and the Nemegt is believed to range from the upper Campanian into the lower Maestrichtian. No physical contact between the first two has yet been discovered, but faunal comparisons suggest that any time gap was short.

The Gobi Desert may well have been a centre of vertebrate evolution and dispersal during the Late Cretaceous, when the faunas were dominated by DINOSAURS and MESOZOIC MAMMALS, although there are also remains of TURTLES, LIZARDS, CROCODILES and a BIRD. The invertebrates include abundant OSTRACODS, phyllopods and BIVALVES, some GASTROPODS and a diplopod. The flora consists of many different charophytes and fossilized wood of the Araucariaceae. Also present are fossil reptile EGGS, sometimes arranged in "nests", that were first discovered at the Flaming Cliffs of Shabarakh Usu, a locality now officially named Bayn Dzak; they are generally attributed to the small primitive HORNED DINOSAUR *Protoceratops*.

The dinosaurs include representatives of most of the families occurring in the Upper Cretaceous of western North America. The fauna nevertheless differs significantly from that of North America in the extreme rarity or absence of horned dinosaurs, hypsilophodontids (small ORNITHOPODS) and nodosaurids (advanced ARMOURED DINOSAURS), in the scarcity of DUCK-BILLED DINOSAURS, and in the occurrence of such remarkable but little-known forms as the presumed CARNOSAURS *Deinocheirus* and *Therizinosaurus*. The mammals include several multituberculates (among them the North American genus *Catopsalis*) and primitive placentals; marsupials, however, are absent.

Lower Cretaceous deposits with vertebrate remains, including fishes and dinosaurs, have also been found in the Gobi Desert.

The Cenozoic strata are of Palaeocene, Eocene, Oligocene, Miocene and Pliocene age. The most interesting of their mammal faunas occurs in the Gashato Formation of the Late Palaeocene, the earliest Cenozoic vertebrate fauna known from Asia. It includes (*inter alia*) multituberculates, deltatheridiids, zalambdalestids, mesonychids, barylambdids, NOTOUNGULATES and uintatheres (AMBLYPODS).   A.J.C.

Gondwanaland

A land mass that formed part of PANGAEA, the late Palaeozoic-early Mesozoic supercontinent. Pangaea shows that in the Southern Hemisphere, South America, Africa, Arabia, Madagascar, greater India, Australia, New Zealand and Antarctica were joined together and partly separated from Laurasia to the north by the TETHYS Sea. In the Carboniferous and Permian, there are strong floral and faunal similarities within the sediment sequences of each of these continental areas, and before the concept of CONTINENTAL DRIFT was proposed these Southern Hemisphere continents were grouped into Gondwanaland and Antarctis. With the discovery of more fossil and geological matches, the name Gondwanaland was extended to the entire group of southern continents.

Grasses

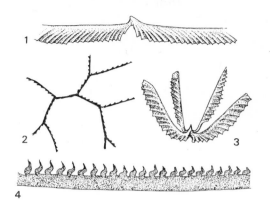

The geological matches and the common distribution of land faunal and floral elements formed an important indication that continental drift had occurred since the Triassic. When Gondwanaland is reconstructed for the late Palaeozoic, sediments such as tillites (fossil boulder clay accumulated under glacial conditions in the region of the South Pole) and the direction of ice striations become grouped together, instead of being widely separated and discordant. Moreover, it is possible to trace the migration of the polar ice cap southwards from the Lower Carboniferous to the Permian.

The name Gondwana (land of the Gonds) stems from a locality in greater India at which freshwater plant-bearing deltaic sediments of Lower Carboniferous to Permian age are found resting directly upon old Pre-Cambrian gneiss. The flora includes two genera, *Glossopteris* and *Gangamopteris*, which occur in beds of the same age throughout Gondwanaland (*see also* GLOSSOPTERIS FLORA). Additional evidence for a unified southern continent of Gondwanaland during the Permian and the Triassic is provided by the distribution of the Permian reptile MESOSAURUS and the occurrence of land-living herbivorous dicynodont reptiles (*Lystrosaurus, Kanneymeyeria*) in the Lower Triassic of South Africa, South America, greater India and Antarctica, indicating a common land area over which these terrestrial animals could migrate. It is perhaps significant in the reconstructions of Gondwanaland made on a smaller diameter Earth that this dicynodont fauna is also known from China, which on a constant-dimension reconstruction is separated from greater India by a wide Tethyan sea.

The distribution of monotreme, marsupial and placental mammals seen in the modern continents reflects the manner in which Gondwanaland disintegrated in response to ocean-floor spreading during the Mesozoic and Cenozoic.

See also GEOGRAPHY OF THE PAST.   H.G.O.

Graptolites

Small colonial marine organisms that flourished widely early in the Palaeozoic, but became extinct in the Carboniferous. They left no living descendants and their relationships have always been uncertain, although it is now reliably assumed that they have pterobranch affinities.

Dendroid graptolites ranged from the Middle Cambrian to the Carboniferous, and were almost all sessile forms living attached to the sea floor by a root-like base. Colonies varied in appearance from shrub-shaped organisms (*Ptilograptus, Dendrograptus*) to conical forms (*Callograptus*). The branches (stipes) comprised paired series of autothecae and bithecae (probably female and male zooids), and thread-like connections between adjacent stipes occurred in some genera (*Dictyonema*). The colony grew from a stolon enclosed within a continuous sclerotized tube (stolotheca), the cortical tissue which surrounds the thecae forming the outer wall of the stipe.

The true graptolites (Graptoloidea) were apparently planktonic, attaching themselves to floating seaweed by means of a slender thread (the nema or virgula) that developed from the apex of the sicula; some forms evolved buoyancy organs that enabled them to float freely. Graptoloid colonies consist only of autothecae and appear not to have possessed a stolon. Growth in both dendroid and graptoloid groups was initiated from a conical embryonic cell (the sicula).

Graptoloid forms appear to be simplified developments of dendroid graptolites adapted to a pelagic environment, and the early multi-branched genera such as *Clonograptus*, *Anisograptus* and *Bryograptus* seem to indicate a close relationship with the contemporary *Dictyonema*. The Lower Ordovician *Tetragraptus* generally had only four branches, whereas *Didymograptus* was a two-branched genus. By the Lower Silurian, reduction had led to single-branched graptoloids (*Monograptus*), but the group became extinct in the Early Devonian.

The true graptolites are widely used as ZONE FOSSILS in the Ordovician and Silurian; their rapid rate of evolution and extensive geographical distribution make them ideal for this purpose. They are the commonest fossils in black shales, in which benthic (sea-bed) fossils are rare, this type of deposit having been laid down in water that had poor bottom circulation. Such sea-bed conditions would have been unfavourable to life, with no scavengers and only a relatively slow rate of decomposition. R.S.

Grasses

One of the largest and most economically valuable families of FLOWERING PLANTS. Grouped collectively in the Gramineae, they can be divided into about 600 genera with 10,000 species, and belong to the monocotyledons. The flower of a grass, known as a spikelet, is essentially the same as that of other flowering plants, with a stigma, style and ovary, stamens, and protective perianth segments that are the equivalent of petals.

Grasses are extremely important to man, forming major components of his agricultural systems. Crops of wheat, oats, barley, maize, millet, sorghum and rice form the staple diet of most of the world's population. As a feed-stock

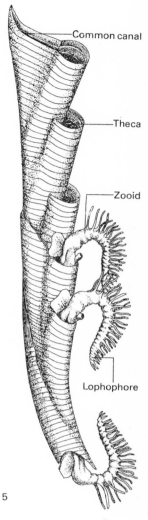

Graptolites
(1) Didymograptus *occurred in the Lower and Middle Ordovician (approx. twice natural size).*
(2) Clonograptus *was from the Lower Ordovician (slightly reduced).*
(3) Tetragraptus *occurred worldwide in the Lower Ordovician (approx. twice natural size).*
(4) Monograptus *was a Silurian genus (approx. twice natural size).*
(5) The detailed structure of a graptolite (greatly enlarged).

Common canal

Theca

Zooid

Lophophore

5

Guano

for secondary food production, adequate grassland is essential for almost all domesticated animals.

The fossil record of the grasses is particularly poor. There are few recorded grass fossils, even from the Cenozoic, and their pollen grains do not appear regularly in deposits before the Pleistocene. It is perhaps significant that their present abundance mirrors closely the rise in importance of man as a factor in the development and dispersal of these plants.   J.W.F.

Guano

A soft, friable phosphate rock formed by the gradual accumulation of the excrement of animals, particularly by large colonies of sea birds. Bat droppings in caves are a less extensive source of this primary phosphate deposit. Fresh guano consists chiefly of carbonates, nitrates and phosphates. Guano can show indications of bedding, is earthy in texture, and has commercial uses as a source of fertilizer.

Guano is particularly soluble and, because of the special nature of its origin, significant quantities are formed only in dry oceanic regions, such as the islands of the West Indies, off the western coast of South America, and off the eastern coast of Australia. After deposition, diagenetic processes lead to the depletion of various soluble and volatile substances and to the concentration of calcium triphosphate. In slightly less arid areas, leaching results in the formation of a less soluble phosphatic residue, together with possible replacement of rocks (such as limestones) by phosphate-rich solutions.   J.E.P.W.

Gymnosperms

Plants that form their seeds from ovules that are not enclosed in an ovary. They include CONIFERS, CYCADEOIDS, CYCADS and PTERIDOSPERMS.

Hadrosaurs, see DUCK-BILLED DINOSAURS.

Hall, James (1811–98)

American geologist and palaeontologist who was a chief founder of the "American school" of palaeontology. Hall was born in Hingham, Massachusetts, and became interested in natural history, although in his early years he was self-taught. In 1836 Hall joined the infant State Geological Survey of New York City, an organization with which he retained contact until his death. He later became State Geologist and Director of the Museum of Natural History in Albany (the precursor of the New York State Museum).

During times of financial restraint Hall sold his own collection to raise funds to continue his work. His major contributions to palaeontology are embodied in the palaeontology volumes of the New York State Natural History Survey, and are mainly concerned with Palaeozoic invertebrates. Hall was also active in the promotion of science; he was a charter member of the

National Academy of Sciences (1863), and the first President of the Geological Society of America (1889).   A.P.H.

Hares, see RABBITS AND HARES.

Hawkins, Benjamin (1807–89)

British sculptor and creator of life-size restorations of prehistoric animals. He was born in London, and studied sculpture under William Behnes. In 1851 he was appointed Assistant Superintendent of the Great Exhibition at Crystal Palace. The idea for a display of restorations of prehistoric animals at the Exhibition was that of Richard OWEN, who engaged Hawkins as the sculptor. Owen provided anatomical advice to make the models, which included a dicynodont, a labyrinthodont, *Plesiosaurus*, *Ichthyosaurus*, *Teleosaurus*, *Hylaeosaurus*, *Megalosaurus*, *Iguanodon*, *Mosasaurus* and pterodactyls. More recent palaeontological research has shown many of the reconstructions to be inaccurate.

Hawkins became a popularizer of palaeontology, and in 1868 he went to New York City, where as a result of the popularity of the Crystal Palace "animals" he was contracted to create similar models for Central Park. Before they could be completed, however, local politics intervened and the moulds and casts were broken up and buried.   A.P.H.

Histology

The study of various body tissues (in fossils, confined to hard tissues such as bones, teeth and shells).

The outer surface of the bony armour of the earliest vertebrates, the PTERASPIDS or heterostracans, is ornamented with either ridges or tubercles. When microscopic sections are examined it can be seen that fine tubules with terminal tufts and delicate lateral branches radiate from a central pulp cavity towards the surface. This tissue is identical in structure to the dentine of vertebrate TEETH, but in these early vertebrates, which were without either teeth or jaws, it provided the main covering of the body and functioned in a similar manner to skin, with the fine tubules acting as routeways of sensation enabling the animal to monitor changes in osmotic gradient in the water.

The formation of dentine, which is a mesodermal tissue, must initially be beneath the soft tissue of the epidermis, but it is evident from fine abrasion of the ornament that during life such skin was present only around the bases of the tubercles or ridges. If the animals suffered a break in the armour, either by accident or because of an attack by a predator, this network of skin spread over the fracture or wound and initiated the formation of new dentine, which sealed off the damaged parts. Where the armour was subjected to irritation, either physical or chemical, this skin network formed a blister covering the ornamentation and again induced the formation of new dentine tissue, covering the old surface. Among the early vertebrates, the new generation of dentine units always developed on top of the old, and in many instances the underlying tubercles were eroded away to accommodate the developing new ones.

This system of replacement appears to be the exact opposite of teeth, in which the new generations erupt from below. (It would be impossible to have a functional dentition if new teeth had to form on top of the old.) Although the patterns of tubercle and tooth replacement appear to be diametrically opposite from one another, during the early stages of development the germs of the second teeth originate above those of the first generation teeth, and it is only by subsequent differential growth that they come to take up their positions, with the new located below the old. The entire system of tooth replacement found throughout the backboned animals can be traced back to healing and regenerative mechanisms in the armour of the first vertebrates.

Among the large mud-grubbing heterostracans such as *Psammosteus*, the parts of the armour in contact with the substrate were subjected to continual wear, and a different type of healing mechanism developed. The skin between the tubercles induced the formation of dentine-forming cells, which invaded the spaces of the underlying bony tissue, laying down a type of dentine containing only a few tubules in place of the soft tissues. As the outer surface of the armour was worn down, dentine was deposited within the spongy tissue to keep pace with the rate of wear. This infilling dentine is termed pleromic dentine, and has been recognized among some of the early jawed fishes. An analogous process occurs when tooth tissue is rapidly destroyed by dental decay or by the dentist's drill. Such wear stimulates the dentine-forming cells to produce a secondary dentine to compensate for the loss of tissue.

In the jawed fishes, teeth evolved from dentine tubercles and the initial dentine that formed was highly mineralized and without tubules, so that it had a glassy appearance. This same type of dentine was also developed on the scales of many fishes. In older descriptions, this hyper-mineralized dentine was named enamel. Although it resembles enamel, it differs fundamentally from true enamel in its development, and for this reason the name enameloid, meaning enamel-like, was introduced. True enamel is produced by epidermal cells and is characteristic of the terrestrial vertebrates (the amphibians, reptiles and mammals). The size of the calcium phosphate crystallites, which form long ribbons, and the organic matrix upon which mineralization takes place are completely different in the two tissues. From the formation of the initial dentine shell of a tooth, further dentine is laid down within the space defined by this first layer, whereas the enamel-forming cells move in the opposite direction away from their starting point, so that the surface area of enamel must of necessity be greater than that of the dentine it covers.

The vertebrate tissues discussed so far have been those which were situated at the outer surface of the animal in the form of armour and teeth. The inner part of the armour of the pteraspids, beneath the superficial dentine layer, was made up of a three-dimensional scaffolding forming a spongy meshwork. Below this was a compact laminated layer incorporating a few vertical canals that connected the spaces in the spongy material with the internal tissues of the animal. This laminated tissue was given the non-committal name aspidin. It shows no sign of typical bone-cell spaces, so as an acellular bone it was probably the precursor of true cellular bone. Within the mineralized tissue there appear to be spindle-shaped spaces. These have been identified as primitive bone cells, but another interpretation is that they represent the former positions of bundles of the fibrous protein collagen, which is known to make up the organic matrix of both dentine and bone.

Some structures do in fact represent the former position of bundles of collagen which anchored the armour in the skin (Sharpey's fibres), but examination under a scanning electron microscope has established that the supposedly spindle-shaped spaces are artefacts, formed during the process of fossilization. Further studies of aspidin have nonetheless confirmed that it was a possible antecedent of bone. The organization of the organic matrix was originally the same as dentine, but in the more advanced pteraspids it became identical to modern bone. Similarly, aspidin was capable of remodelling, a feature it shared with bone but not with dentine.

The CEPHALASPIDS, ACANTHODIANS, PLACODERMS, bony fishes and all higher vertebrates possessed bone which included bone cells, although some of the most advanced of the modern RAY-FIN FISHES have developed acellular bone.

In section, most bones have a spongy texture, but as more bone is laid down the spaces become smaller and the bone is then said to be compact. The limb bones of terrestrial vertebrates are hollow cylinders with a compact outer cortex and a middle spongy medulla. Large forms such as the DINOSAURS and ungulate (hoofed) mammals developed a special kind of compact bone, known as laminar or "wire-netting" bone, which comprised concentric layers of thin bone with zones containing a fine network of blood vessels. This type of bone has an efficient blood supply and is stronger than the typical Haversian bone of the higher vertebrates, which is made up of closely packed cylinders of bone. Haversian bone has, however, one supreme advantage, even though it is not as strong or as well supplied by blood as laminar bone: it is capable of remodelling. This means that Haversian bone can respond to changes by either laying down extra bone or resorbing bone from areas where it is no longer required. Haversian bone is thus highly adaptable. If part of the laminar blood supply is blocked, the surrounding bone dies and is then removed by bone-destroying cells. These drill out a cylindrical tunnel that forms the lining for an Haversian system, which will further disrupt the laminar blood supply and cause further Haversian

Holocene

systems to form. Thus a chain reaction results in the entire bone becoming Haversian. The details of this process can be followed in sections of dinosaur bones.

In early vertebrates, bone was confined to the outer armour, and the internal skeleton consisted of cartilage or gristle. The Early Ordovician heterostracans, such as *Eriptychius*, possessed an internal skeleton in which the cartilage had become calcified, forming mineralized globules. In the SHARKS and their allies, which have retained a cartilaginous internal skeleton, the vertebrae are mineralized in varying patterns; some have a primitive globular arrangement, but others have radial or concentric alternating zones of calcified and uncalcified cartilage.

Birds and reptiles lay shelled EGGS, and the microstructure of their eggshells enables the evolution of different types of eggs to be traced. In some of the shells of dinosaur eggs, for example, it is possible to recognize diseases that are due to hormone deficiencies and stress which would never have been suspected had it not been for the histological studies of their shells. L.B.H.

Holocene
The period of geological time that has elapsed since the end of the last PLEISTOCENE glaciation, ie the Wisconsin glaciation in North America and the Würm glaciation in Europe (*see* ICE AGES).

The Holocene thus normally includes the Recent, which corresponds to the present and is usually held to constitute post-Pleistocene time. Sometimes, however, the Recent is extended back to the last glaciation as a sub-division of the Pleistocene, so that it becomes identical to the Holocene.

See also the time chart. R.S.

Hooke, Robert (1635–1703)
British physicist, mathematician and Curator of Experiments at the Royal Society of London. Hooke was born in Freshwater, Isle of Wight, and received his early education at home. He went to Westminster School in 1648 and later attended Oxford, where he served as research assistant to Robert Boyle (1627–91).

He had broad interests and his contributions to geology and palaeontology were of high and advanced standards. He was the first to use a compound microscope, and also to describe the structure of fossil wood. Hooke's main palaeontological ideas were published posthumously in the *Discourse on Earthquakes* (1705), much of which was written between 1686 and 1689, but which also had parts dating from 1668. The work describes the possible chronological uses of fossils, variation and progression of species, and fossils as indicators of climatic change; it also illustrated the suture lines of AMMONITES. A.P.H.

Horned dinosaurs
An order (Ceratopsia) of ORNITHISCHIAN dinosaurs that became a conspicuous and highly successful element in the reptile faunas of the North American Late Cretaceous.

Horned dinosaurs apparently originated in eastern Asia from a partly bipedal ORNITHOPOD similar to *Psittacosaurus*. The earliest ceratopsians were small reptiles, about 3 metres (9.8ft) long, that had reverted to all fours.

Protoceratops is the best known of these primitive horned dinosaurs, and its remains have been found in abundance in the early Upper Cretaceous of Mongolia, including nests of eggs and immature skeletons that demonstrate the changing proportions of the skull and skeleton as growth proceeded towards maturity. In *Protoceratops*, the back of the beaked skull had already begun to expand to form a crest, which was larger in males than in females. The crest probably served principally as an attachment area for powerful muscles moving the head and bringing to bear the incipient horns that were developing above the eyes and on the snout – probably more for use in combat between rival males than as a protection against predators.

Two other small protoceratopsians occur in Asia: *Bagaceratops* and the lightly built *Microceratops*. These conservative forms also continued to survive in North America alongside their larger descendants until late in the Cretaceous. *Leptoceratops*, from the upper Edmonton Formation, lacked horns entirely, and *Montanoceratops* retained clawed toes.

Horned dinosaurs
Triceratops *was the commonest dinosaur in North America at the end of the Cretaceous. Length: about 8m (26ft)*

Horned dinosaurs (cont'd)

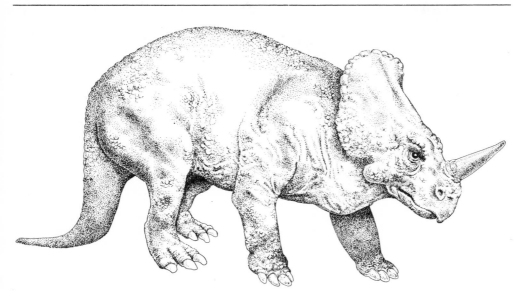

The massive advanced ceratopsians with hoofed feet and prominent facial horns appear to form two groups. In one the crest represents less than half the total length of the skull, whereas in the other it is greatly extended backwards, so that in *Torosaurus* the head measures 2.6 metres (8.5ft) long – the largest known skull of any land animal.

In both groups, the nose horn seems initially to have been longer than the brow horns. The short-crested *Monoclonius* from the Oldman Formation had a prominent nasal horn, as did the contemporaneous *Styracosaurus*, in which the back edge of the crest had developed a series of long horn-like projections. Towards the close of the Cretaceous, *Triceratops* brought the short-crested line to an end and evidently enjoyed a brief period of relative abundance, as indicated by the number of skulls that occur in the Lance Formation. More than a dozen species have been described, the largest (*Triceratops horridus*) having a skull 2.5 metres (8.2ft) long. *Pachyrhinosaurus* was apparently an aberrant member of the group with no horns at all.

The long-crested group also display varying development of horns. Those with a long nasal horn had short brow horns (most species of *Chasmosaurus*), whereas progressive forms displaying well-developed brow horns had a nasal horn of reduced size (*Anchiceratops. Pentaceratops* and *Arrhinoceratops*). The final member of the series, *Torosaurus*, occurs above *Triceratops* in the Lance Formation and appears to have survived until the end of the Cretaceous.

Advanced ceratopsians are almost unknown from outside North America, although a bone from the edge of a crest has been found in Mongolia, the end of a humerus was reported from the Kysyl-Kum Desert of western Asia, and *Notoceratops* is based upon a jaw fragment of doubtful identity from Argentina. The presence of *Monoclonius* as far south as Coahuila, in Mexico, has been confirmed.

It is likely that the crest of the later ceratopsians served to protect their necks as well as giving powerful muscles the necessary leverage to lift the massive skull. Possibly animals in combat would pivot about their widely braced forelegs to keep facing their adversary, although disputes between contending males were probably little more than pushing matches.   R.S.

Horned dinosaurs
Monoclonius *was a relatively small horned dinosaur measuring about 5m (16.5ft) in length.*

Horned dinosaurs
The primitive horned dinosaur, Protoceratops, *occurred in the early Upper Cretaceous of the Gobi Desert.*
Length: about 2m (6.6ft)

Horses

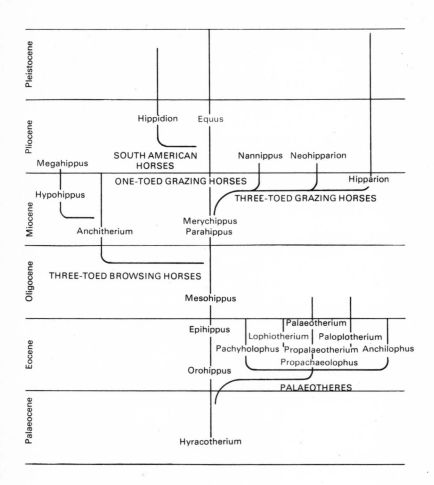

Horses

The most numerous of living PERISSODACTYLS, horses have a history extending back 60 million years.

Some isolated molar teeth from the Upper Palaeocene of Baja California belong to *Hyracotherium*, the small primitive horse that ranged across North America and into north-western Europe during the Lower Eocene. Measuring only 25–50cm (about 10–20in) tall at the shoulder, this animal had four-toed forefeet and three-toed hindfeet. The tooth crowns were low, indicating a diet of soft vegetation, and it had a short neck, an arched back with little flexibility between the lumbar vertebrae, and a long, stout tail. The toes ended in small hoofs, although the weight was largely supported by a pad, and *Hyracotherium* probably already trotted, cantered and galloped like a horse (*see* PERISSODACTYLS).

In the Old World, the *Hyracotherium* line led to *Pachynolophus*, *Anchilophus* and the PALAEOTHERES, but in North America its immediate descendant was the whippet-sized Middle Eocene *Orohippus*. In the Upper Eocene *Epihippus* the middle toe in each foot was beginning to enlarge, leading to the Lower and Middle Oligocene *Mesohippus*, which had functionally three-toed forefeet and averaged about 61cm (2ft) tall (*see* PERISSODACTYLS).

By the latter part of the Oligocene, horse evolution was centred exclusively in North America, where *Miohippus* persisted into the Lower Miocene. The appearance of *Parahippus* coincided with the early spread of grasses, and to cope with this abrasive food, horses began to develop high-crowned (hypsodont) teeth. To make way for the roots of the high-crowned teeth the face was becoming longer, and *Parahippus* also walked principally on its middle toes only, although the side toes were still present.

Another line of equine evolution that probably originated from *Miohippus* retained low-crowned teeth and browsing habits. The Miocene *Anchitherium* occurs in North America and the Old World, and its descendants *Hypohippus* and *Megahippus* persisted into the Lower Pliocene before this conservative group of functionally three-toed horses died out.

The progressive hypsodont horses continued through the prolific *Merychippus*, from the North American Middle and Upper Miocene and Lower Pliocene, which stood up to 1 metre (3.3ft) tall at the shoulder. The grinding teeth of this form are longer than those of *Parahippus* and always bear cement on the crowns, but the primitive foot-pad had finally been lost. The subgenus *Merychippus* (*Merychippus*) led to a series of persistently three-toed hypsodont horses that were common in the Pliocene (*Hipparion*, *Neohipparion* and *Nannippus*), while the *Merychippus* (*Protohippus*) line yielded *Pliohippus* and eventually *Equus* itself.

Hipparion probably first appeared in North America during the Middle Miocene and then crossed into Asia across the Bering Strait. In Africa, *Hipparion* persisted into the Pleistocene, but elsewhere it seems to have been unable to compete with *Equus* and died out by the end of the Pliocene. *Neohipparion* was a slenderly built North American Lower and Middle Pliocene relative, and the diminutive gazelle-like *Nannippus* had unusually long-crowned teeth.

The first one-toed horse was *Pliohippus*, from the North American Lower and Middle

Horsetails

Pliocene, in which the lateral toes were eventually reduced to mere splint bones beside the cannons. From the subgenus *Pliohippus* (*Astrohippus*), the modern horse (*Equus*) arose at the end of the Pliocene.

During the Pliocene, the two American continents were re-united and equids crossed into the neotropical region, where they developed into a series of specialized small- to medium-sized Pleistocene forms with large heads, short feet and long, slender nasal bones. *Hippidion* was the largest of these, *Onohippidion* had stoutly proportioned limbs, and *Parahipparion* was probably a mountain-dweller.

North America supported a wide variety of horses during the Pleistocene, from *Equus tau* (the size of a Shetland pony) to the huge *Equus giganteus*. Before the end of the period they had all died out, for no obvious reason, and subsequent horse evolution took place in the Old World, where the Upper Pliocene *Equus stenonis* is typical of the heavily built European animals that continued into the Pleistocene and attained a height of about 1.5 metres (5ft).

The origin of domestic breeds (*Equus caballus*) is largely unknown, but during the Pleistocene zebras apparently spread throughout southern and south-eastern Africa, onagers (*Equus hemionus*) ranged from Palestine through central Asia to greater India and China, and asses (*Equus asinus*) occupied northern and easternAfrica.   R.S.

Horseshoe crabs

With their fossil relatives, the horseshoe crabs (including the king crab) are assigned to the class Merostomata. They are chelicerate ARTHROPODS (those with biting claws) in which the body is composed of two separate parts. The anterior region is the cephalothorax or prosoma, and the posterior portion the abdomen or opisthosoma. The median part of the prosoma is indicated by two sub-parallel grooves and incorporates two lateral eyes. Ventrally there are five pairs of appendages which terminate as pincers, the proximal end of each appendage acting as a masticator. The abdomen consists of six or seven fused segments (although some of the earlier merostomes had many more free segments) and six pairs of appendages. In addition there is a long styliform spine or telson.

The merostomes are nearly extinct, only five species in three genera surviving to the present day. Their history is long, starting with *Palaeomerus* from the Lower Cambrian of the USA. These genera are eurypterid-like, and *Palaeomerus* may possibly be the ancestor of the SEA SCORPIONS. By Coal Measure times, merostomes had acquired a horseshoe crab shape (*Belinurus*, *Euproops* and *Paleolimulus*). There are sporadic occurrences of true horseshoe crabs in the Mesozoic, especially in the Solenhofen LITHOGRAPHIC STONE of Upper Jurassic age, but the modern genus *Tachypleus* is not encountered until the Miocene of central Europe. The other two Recent genera (*Carcinoscorpinus* and the king crab *Limulus*) have no fossil record.

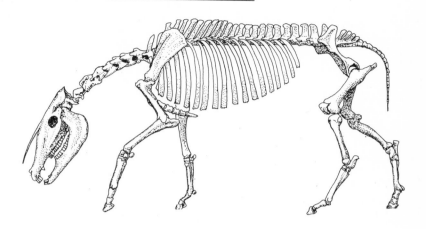

Study of the development of the Recent *Limulus polyphemus* shows that it goes through three recapitulative stages before it reaches the adult. These stages are known as the trilobite stage, the synziphosuran stage, and the *Euproops* stage. The appearance of the TRILOBITE stage was partly the reason for the assumption that trilobites and horseshoe crabs were closely related.   S.F.M.

Horsetails

The common name of the plant genus *Equisetum*, which contains a few species that are remarkable for their uniformity. During the Carboniferous the horsetails were an important plant group and showed a marked trend towards gigantism (eg *Calamites*).

Horses
The South American Pleistocene horse Hippidion *became extinct in the Middle Pleistocene when modern horses (* Equus *) arrived from North America.*
Height: about 1.5m (5ft) at the shoulder

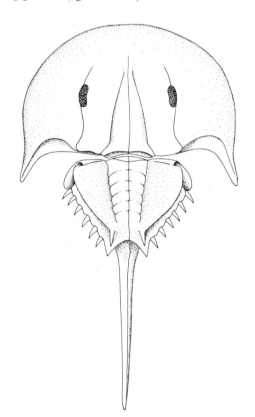

Horseshoe crabs
Paleolimulus was a Permian horseshoe crab from Kansas (approx. twice natural size).

Hyaenas

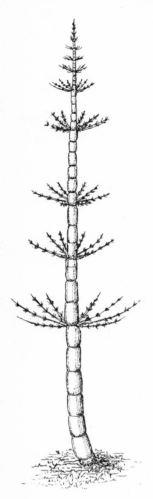

Horsetails
Calamites, *a Carboniferous horsetail, was abundant in the Coal Forests of Europe and North America. Some members of this group grew up to 30m (100ft) tall.*

Hyaenas
One of the earliest hyaenas, Percrocuta, *from the Miocene of Africa and Asia, closely resembled the living spotted hyaena* (Crocuta).

The remains of horsetails tend to be fragmented, and it is therefore difficult to be precise about the size of the large calamites, but some specimens must have been about 30 metres (100ft) tall. These plants had hollow trunks with internal diameters of up to 30cm (12in). There were whorls of from four to sixty leaves, and the marked tendency to fusion of the leaves into sheaths shown by modern equisetums did not occur.

In some species the cones formed singly at the nodes, whereas in others they occur as terminal groups or are borne on special branches. The cones of the calamites are characteristic and are placed in two form-genera, *Calamostachys* and *Palaeostachya*. In both, there are whorls of cross-shaped or peltate (like a nasturtium leaf) sporangiophores alternating with whorls of bracts.

The structure of these cones confirms the relationship between horsetails and the Hyeniales and Sphenophyllales. Sphenophyllums, which are common Coal Measure fossils, have broader wedge-shaped (and often lobed) leaves. The stems tend to be thin, and they are thought to have been of a scrambling rather than an erect habit.

After the end of the Carboniferous the large calamite forms rapidly became extinct. Smaller, more modern-looking horsetails (*Equisitites*) persisted throughout the Mesozoic and were the direct ancestors of the modern genus *Equisetum*. J.W.F.

Hyaenas

Scavengers of large size with robust premolar teeth that enable them to crush bones and extract the marrow. Their stomachs can partly digest bone fragments.

There are three modern genera, *Crocuta* (the spotted hyaena), *Hyaena* (the striped hyaena), and the peculiar ant-eating aardwolf, *Proteles*. In addition there are about eight extinct genera, found in the later Cenozoic of Eurasia and Africa.

Hyaenas are extremely powerful animals, with forelimbs that are longer than the hindlimbs, a short tail, and exceptionally heavy jaw musculature. As carnivores they are surpassed in size only by the largest cats and bears; they hunt in packs and can bring down prey many times their own size. Living hyaenas are found mainly in Africa (some live in Asia), but as fossils they are widely distributed thoughout Eurasia and Africa.

The group evolved from viverrid (CIVET) progenitors in the Early Miocene, *Herpestides* being close to the ancestry of both the viverrids and the hyaenas. The first true hyaenas are *Percrocuta* from the Miocene of Asia and Africa, and *Miohyaena* (*Progenetta*) from the Miocene of Europe. Both these genera have robust premolar teeth capable of crushing bone, and the carnassial blades of their molars are enlarged and elongated in hyaena fashion.

In the Pliocene there was an extensive radiation of hyaenas, about twelve species being present. The *Ictitherium* group included the ancestors of the living *Hyaena*, and the *Lycyaena* group included the forebears of *Crocuta*. Hyaenas were abundant and diverse during the Pleistocene, and in Africa often filled niches later occupied by some of the larger cats. The present limited range of species and distribution is a post-Pleistocene phenomenon.

The cave hyaena, *Crocuta spelaea*, was abundant in Britain and Europe during the ice age and is closely related to the spotted hyaena. At Tornewton cave in Devon more than 20,000 teeth of this form have been found.

The aberrant *Proteles* has no direct fossil ancestry and its inclusion within the hyaenids has been questioned. R.J.G.S.

Hyatt, Alpheus (1838–1902)

American geologist and palaeontologist (born in Washington, DC) who researched ammonite systematics, and was one of the leaders in the splitting of ammonite genera and species towards the end of the 19th century. Hyatt was a graduate of Harvard University, and later became Professor of Zoology and Palaeontology at the Massachusetts Institute of Technology, and also Professor of Biology at Boston University.

Hyatt worked initially on the Liassic ammonites and suggested many new genera; he also defined diagnostic features more narrowly than had been previously accepted. By studying the primary chambers, he was able to establish the essential differences in embryonic development between the Nautilidae and the Ammonitidae. Hyatt supported the new theories of Jean-Baptiste LAMARCK, although he was in agreement with the role of NATURAL SELECTION in removing the "unfit". A.P.H.

Ice ages

On at least three occasions during the Earth's history abnormally cold climates have led to the establishment of polar ice caps and, eventually, extensive glaciation in high latitudes.

There is some indication of continental glaciation about 2,000 million years ago (the Huronian tillites), but the first ice age for which there is comprehensive geological evidence dates from before the beginning of the Cambrian. A second glacial episode occurred in the Ordovician, followed by another during the transition from the Carboniferous to the Permian, with the last such interlude occurring during the Pleistocene.

The presence of polar ice caps on the Earth is probably unusual; for much of the Palaeozoic, the whole of the Mesozoic, and the early Cenozoic, they were absent. In the Pre-Cambrian rocks of Russia, Scandinavia, Greenland, Spitzbergen, Africa, China and Australia, however, there are extensive tillites – the consolidated remains of glacial moraines. These tillites immediately antedate the first appearance of TRILOBITES and apparently indicate widespread glaciation at about the beginning of the Palaeozoic, the so-called Eo-Cambrian ice age.

Subsequently, the climate during the Cambrian became much warmer, and generally remained so until the Carboniferous, apart from an interval of icy conditions in the Ordovician. By the Carboniferous, however, GONDWANALAND had become subject to widespread glaciation that continued into the Permian and constitutes the Permo-Carboniferous ice age.

In South America and South Africa, this glaciation began as early as the Lower Carboniferous, although it did not occur in greater India, Australia and Antarctica until the Late Carboniferous or the Lower Permian. Evidently the southern continents were gradually moving, as a whole, across the Earth's south polar cap, with the result that the area of glaciation travelled over the united land mass and affected different regions at different times. There seem to have been periodic regressions of the ice, and in these milder intervals the GLOSSOPTERIS FLORA is the most characteristic Gondwanaland vegetation.

By the Middle Permian, the Gondwanaland ice sheets, which once covered about 10,350,000sq km (4 million sq miles), were in retreat and by the dawn of the Mesozoic the Earth had entered a warm period in its history during which evidence of glaciation is almost totally absent. Not until the late Cenozoic did extensive polar ice caps return, as the Earth's climate gradually cooled and became more seasonal in character, with glaciers appearing on high mountain chains.

Towards the end of the Pliocene the climate turned substantially colder as ice age conditions were initiated. Glaciers in the Northern Hemisphere eventually spread over Europe from several centres (Scandinavia, the British Isles, the Barents Sea, and the Alps) and across North America from the Laurentian ice centre in the Hudson Bay area and the Cordilleran ice complex (centred on British Columbia). About 44 million sq km (17 million sq miles) of the Earth's surface were eventually ice-bound, and sea-levels fell by 90–120 metres (295–394ft) due to the amount of water locked up in land ice,

resulting in the appearance of land bridges across the English Channel and the Bering Strait which cold-adapted animals used as migration routes.

Five principal glacial episodes have been distinguished in Europe: the first is the Donau, followed by the Gunz, the Mindel, the Riss and the Würm (the names are derived from Bavarian rivers). Between each glaciation there was an interglacial when milder conditions returned and the ice retreated, with some slight regression of the cold also occurring during the glacial episodes themselves (interstadials). Measurement of oxygen isotopes in oceanic sediment suggests that a greater number of cold spells may have occurred than the five conventionally recognized.

In Britain the ice at one time reached as far south as the River Thames, and from the 3,000 metres (9,842ft) thick Scandinavian ice centre the ice pushed 2,000km (1,240 miles) into central and eastern Europe to the northern edge of the Carpathians and the basins of the Dnieper and the Don, as well as extending eastwards across the Yenesei to cover western Siberia. Huge glaciers, up to 360km (224 miles) long, flowed down from the Alps where the snow line was 1,200 metres (3,940ft) lower than it is today.

In North America the Nebraskan glaciation coincides with the European Gunz glaciation, the Kansan with the Mindel, the Illinoian with the Riss, and the Wisconsin with the Würm. At the height of the Wisconsin glaciation, the Catskill and Adirondack Mountains were under an ice sheet more than 1,000 metres (3,280ft) thick, and during an earlier glaciation the ice reached almost as far south as St Louis.

There were only small glaciers in Africa, where the northern glacials are apparently represented by pluvial intervals of heavy rainfall, although the last glacial maximum 18,000 years ago seems to have been accompanied by extensive desert conditions. Ice sheets of limited extent occurred in Australia, but larger areas became glaciated in Tasmania and in New Zealand's South Island, and an ice sheet originating in the Andes Mountains spread over the Patagonian plains and eventually reached the Atlantic Ocean in the southern extremity of Argentina.

The Würm glaciers began to retreat 15,000 years ago, and the present time probably represents an interglacial, with temporary minor re-advances of the glaciers occurring in the 16th–19th centuries after a period (5000BC–3000BC) when temperatures in Europe were 2–3°C higher than today. About 4,000 years ago, the hardwood forests in Scandinavia began to dwindle, and a new glaciation is now apparently slowly gaining ground.

Each interglacial seems to have been slightly less warm than the one that preceded it, but temperate animals and plants (straight-tusked ELEPHANT, hippopotamus, red fox, roe deer, macaque and broad-leaf trees) were able to return to high latitudes. During glacial intervals the woolly MAMMOTH, woolly RHINOCEROS, steppe rhinoceros (*Elasmotherium*), saiga antelope,

Ichthyosaurs

cave BEAR and musk ox frequented the tundra along the edges of the ice sheets, where only birch trees and conifers maintained a precarious existence, while around the northern shores of the Mediterranean there were pine forests. At each interglacial there was a reduction in the number of warm-climate trees (eg sweet gum, swamp cypress and tulip tree) that re-colonized northern temperate latitudes, until, during the present interglacial, none have returned.

Suggested causes of ice ages include the presence of high mountains on the continents during mountain-building episodes, combined with the reflection of sunlight (and hence heat) from a small primary polar ice cap (self-induced cooling), and the eruption of volcanic ash into the atmosphere cutting off some of the Sun's heat.

A complex possible solution to the problem involves computing variations in the orbit of the Earth round the Sun in correlation with the inclination of its axis and the precession of the equinoxes. From these calculations, solar radiation curves have been extrapolated which indicate periods when the Earth received a reduced insolation appear to coincide with from the Sun, due to the simultaneous occurrence of axial tilt, orbital eccentricity, and a winter perihelion. These theoretical periods of reduced insolation appear to coincide with known intervals when the summers were cool and likely to foster the accumulation of ice.

Mountain-building has undoubtedly been associated with ice ages during the Permo-Carboniferous transition and the Pleistocene. As mountains were pushed up, there was regression of the sea, exposing a greater area of land – which is a less efficient absorber of heat than water.

When the new mountain peaks were thrust upwards towards a lowering snow line, they acquired permanent ice caps, and if ranges are orientated north–south they lead to increased precipitation in the form of snow when the prevailing winds are deflected upwards along their rising contours. Alternate thawing and freezing of the snow on the peaks leads first to the formation of névé and then, after compaction by the weight of later snowfalls, to ice and ultimately glaciers.

In the Northern Hemisphere, cool summers (usually associated with mild winters) reduce the amount of inland ice that melts and hence facilitate the build-up of glacial conditions as self-induced cooling begins. Conversely hot summers (and the associated cold winters) are not conducive to the initiation of an ice age.　R.S.

Ichthyosaurs

A subclass (Ichthyopterygia) of marine reptiles. Complete skeletons of ichthyosaurs (fish-lizards) were first discovered by Mary ANNING on the south coast of England at the beginning of the 19th century, although isolated vertebrae had been described as early as 1712. The ichthyosaurs represented the most complete adaptation of the reptiles to an aquatic mode of life. They were highly streamlined, with the limbs modified into paddles and the main propulsive force for swimming generated by the tail.

From specimens found in southern Germany, in which skin impressions were preserved, it was apparent that the tail skeleton bent downwards to form the lower border of a large symmetrical tail fin. The effect of a side-to-side movement by such a fin would have been to lower the tail and raise the front part of the body, whereas the shape of the head would have tended to direct it downwards. The head and tail thus balanced one another so that, using also slight adjustments of the pectoral fins, the ichthyosaurs were capable of accurately controlling their position in the water. The preservation of skin impressions also revealed that there was a large triangular fin in the middle of the back, although in the skeleton there was no hint of its existence. Similarly, the paddles had a hydrofoil-shaped cross-section with a tapering trailing edge exactly as in the wing of a penguin. This suggested that the pectoral fins must have functioned in a similar way in the water to the wings of a bird in the air. By adjusting the angle of the fins relative to the direction of travel, an ichthyosaur would have been able to generate lift.

In some specimens the actual pigment cells of the skin can be studied, and from these it has been possible to determine the colour of the skin, which on the dorsal side was a brown tortoiseshell colour. These are the only fossil reptiles in which the skin colour can be portrayed with any real confidence.

From the streamlined shape and the long jaws

Ichthyosaurs
The evolution of ichthyosaurs.
(1) The Middle Triassic
Cymbospondylus.
(2) The Jurassic Ichthyosaurus.
(3) The Jurassic-Cretaceous
Ophthalmosaurus. *These aquatic reptiles acquired a progressively more streamlined shape, with the tail fin becoming an increasingly efficient propulsive organ and the hindlimbs diminishing in relative size.*

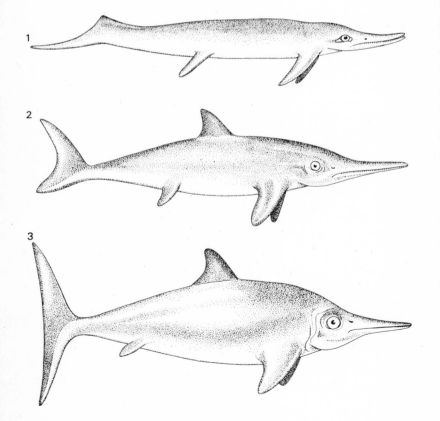

Ichthyostegids

with numerous teeth, it can be safely inferred that the ichthyosaurs were active hunters. Further evidence of their diet occurs in the form of COPROLITES: it is usually impossible to determine what animal produced these, but there are a few instances where fossil droppings are still preserved within the animal and contain scales and spines from the fast-swimming, surface-dwelling ray-fin fish *Pholidophorus*. Much of the diet must have comprised fish of this type. When complete skeletons are examined carefully, about a third of them have a blackened area in the stomach region, and this seems to be from the ink of cephalopods. Also present are myriads of curved chitinous hooks 1–2mm (0.04–0.08in) long, which come from the tentacles of cephalopods. One young ichthyosaur 1.5 metres (4.9ft) long had about 478,000 hooks in its stomach, which must have represented about 1,590 cephalopods. None of these hooks appears in coprolites, but instead accumulated in the stomach to be subsequently spewed out through the mouth (sperm whales, which also feed on cephalopods, regurgitate the indigestible hooks in the same way).

Some ichthyosaurs became virtually toothless, and this suggests that they must have fed exclusively on cephalopods. The typical Early Triassic ichthyosaurs (Mixosauridae, Shastasauridae) seem to have been mainly fish-eaters, with one short-lived side-branch (the Omphalosauridae) that evolved blunt, rounded teeth at the back of the jaws for crushing shellfish. The later Jurassic and Cretaceous genera seem to have become better adapted for feeding on cephalopods.

There were two main groups of post-Triassic ichthyosaurs, which are distinguished by the structure of their paddles. In one family (the Stenopterygiidae) there were long, narrow paddles with extra joints or phalanges on the fingers, a condition known as hyperphalangy. The second family (the Ichthyosauridae) had shorter and broader paddles with extra fingers (up to nine in some instances) in each paddle, a condition termed hyperdactyly. The individual bones of the paddles were set in cartilaginous and fibrous tissue, so that apart from movement at the shoulder and to a small degree at the elbow, the entire limb acted as a rigid structure.

The adaptations of the ichthyosaurs for an ocean-going way of life were such that it seemed unlikely they could have gone on to land to lay eggs, like conventional reptiles. Several specimens from southern Germany contain perfect skeletons of young individuals. Had they been taken as food, they would have become broken up, and in a few instances the young are preserved on the point of actually being born, thus proving that the ichthyosaurs gave birth to live young and hence were not obliged to leave the water in order to reproduce. L.B.H.

Ichthyostegids

A group of early fossil AMPHIBIANS, known principally from a geological horizon in East Greenland which is usually regarded as uppermost Devonian but may possibly be basal Carboniferous. For many years the eastern Greenland ichthyostegids were the earliest known amphibians, but in 1972 amphibian tracks were discovered in Victoria, Australia, at an horizon lower in the Devonian, and in 1977 a primitive amphibian jaw (*Metaxygnathus*) was described from New South Wales, again from a pre-ichthyostegid horizon.

Like the LABYRINTHODONTS and all other land vertebrates, the ichthyostegids are almost certainly descended from Devonian crossopterygian LOBE-FIN FISHES, and in some ways have evolved little from the ancestral form. In other respects, however, ichthyostegids are aberrant forms and it is unlikely that they have any known descendants.

The group is based on *Ichthyostega*, represented by numerous but disarticulated fossil specimens. Because of this, and because all the material has not been systematically described, it is not certain how many species are represented or whether they should all be referred to *Ichthyostega*. Two other genera, probably not closely related, have been named from skulls only: they are *Ichthyostegopsis* and *Acanthostega*.

The primitive, fish-like characteristics of *Ichthyostega* include a skull that retains traces of the movable joint between the front and back parts of the braincase, seen in its fish ancestors, and the last remnant of the fish bony gill cover or operculum. Also, the tail had a dorsal fin supported by bony rays of fish type, and the vertebrae were frail hoops surrounding a persistent notochord (the fluid-filled compression member present in primitive and embryonic vertebrae and retained in the crossopterygians). The notochord extended forwards in the skull to the back of the anterior braincase region, so that there was no bone-to-bone articulation of the skull on the spine.

Ichthyostega was certainly capable of locomotion on land, however, using stout if primitive

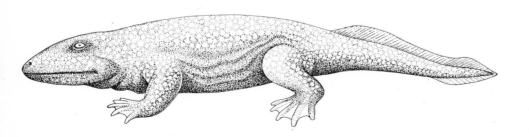

Ichthyostegids
Ichthyostega *from the Late Devonian of Greenland is one of the oldest known amphibians. Length: about 1m (3.3ft)*

Insectivora

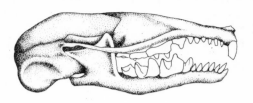

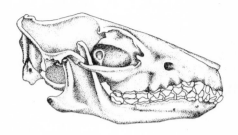

Insectivora
Above: the skull of the Oligocene-Miocene mole Proscalops *was about 2.5cm (1in) long.*
Below: the skull of Anagale, *a primitive member of the tree-shrew group from the Lower Oligocene of Mongolia, was about 7cm (2.8in) long.*

limbs, of which the forelimbs seem to have been permanently bent into a primitive walking position; massive ribs, compensating for feeble vertebrae, gave a strong but rigid trunk.   A.L.P.

Insectivora

The most primitive living placental mammals, including hedgehogs, moles and shrews. This order can be traced back into the Cretaceous and is of great importance because it incorporates the direct ancestors of bats, carnivores, primates and rodents, as well as the indirect ancestors of almost all other placental mammals.

Most insectivores are small and their diet, although basically of insects, ranges widely from small animals (both vertebrate and invertebrate), to berries, fruit and tubers. Their senses of smell and hearing are normally well developed, although sight is often weak; some shrews can echo-locate (using sound waves). Insectivores are frequently spiny. Some have a poison gland, most are nocturnal, many burrow, and a few are aquatic.

The order is a complex group and not easy to classify. It contains many divergent and ancient stocks, and when only the teeth are preserved, fossils can often be puzzling. Basically there is a two-fold division of the Insectivora into Menotyphla and Lipotyphla.

The Menotyphla (or Proteutheria) are the most primitive, and to this suborder belong most of the early Cenozoic forms, together with the living tree-shrews. Menotyphla possess a caecum and have a complex arterial system that supplies blood to the brain. They comprise seven or eight extinct families and the living Tupaiidae. The pappotherids, represented by *Pappotherium* from the Middle Cretaceous of Texas, can be included here, although known only from a few cheek teeth. They represent not only the earliest insectivores, but the earliest recognizable placental mammals. In the Late Cretaceous there were zalambdalestids present in Mongolia: *Zalambdalestes* itself retained many primitive characteristics, but had an aberrant anterior dentition with enlarged canine teeth and reduced premolar teeth. Close to these were the

lepticids, which survived into the Late Oligocene and appear to have included the ancestors of both primates and rodents.

Deltatheriids were more carnivore-like and ranged from the Late Cretaceous into the Oligocene in North America and Asia, including among their stock the ancestors of carnivores and ungulates. Apataemyits were rodent-like insectivores from the Eocene and Oligocene of North America and Europe. The strange pantolestids were fairly large and possibly aquatic insectivores known from the early Cenozoic of North America, Eurasia and possibly Africa. The surviving tupaiids or tree shrews from south-eastern Asia are arboreal primate-like insectivores, with a poor fossil record.

The Lipotyphla comprise most of the late Cenozoic forms and all living taxa other than tree shrews. They lack a caecum and have a simplified arterial blood supply to the brain. The erinaceids (hedgehogs) can be traced back to the Late Eocene of Eurasia, the continents on which they are mostly found today; *Deinogalerix* from the Miocene of Italy was a gigantic hedgehog the size of a badger. The soricids or shrews share a common ancestry with the hedgehogs, whereas the talpids (moles) can be traced back only as far as the Oligocene in Europe and North America. Most talpids are burrowers, and they occur frequently as well-preserved fossils, eg *Proscalops* from the Miocene of the USA.   R.J.G.S.

Insects

Members of the ARTHROPODA, usually small to minute, in which the body can be divided into three distinct regions: head, thorax and abdomen. In most insects, after the larval stages, the number of segments for each region is fixed, ie six in the head, three in the thorax and twelve in the abdomen, but many primitive flightless insects do not conform to this pattern. The head contains one pair of antennae, one pair of compound eyes and three pairs of ocelli; the underside of the head bears three pairs of appendages modified from walking limbs for chewing and sucking.

The three thoracic segments each carry a pair of jointed legs with a claw-like termination. Wings are usually borne by the second and third segments; they are outgrowths of the body strengthened by a series of veins that are the relics of the insect respiratory system, a function that has now been taken over by the spiracles and tracheae. The abdomen carries the genital appendages towards its posterior end. Metamorphosis is now common in most insect groups, but it evolved only as a result of intense competition, a few cockroach nymphs such as *Rochdalia* being known from the Carboniferous.

Insects appear as fossils in Devonian rocks, and the advanced state of their development suggests that they must have evolved at least in the Silurian, having developed from a lobopod ancestor similar to the Onychophora (the *Peripatus* group). The earliest recorded fossil insect is *Rhyniella praecursor* from a Lower Devonian fossil peat bog, the Rhynie Chert in Scotland. This insect is a spring-tail, ie flightless, and it is only in the Middle Carboniferous that flying forms are found. At first the wings probably made only a simple vertical flapping movement and were unfolded when at rest like the wings of modern dragonflies.

Later, in the Upper Carboniferous, more advanced wings were developed which could be folded back when at rest, while the jugal field of the wings became more highly developed to increase the lifting area. During this period the only predators that threatened insects were primitive terrestrial vertebrates and other members of the arthropod assemblage, so that many insects reached an enormous size, eg *Meganeura*, which had a wing span of 70cm (28in). As the competition grew, so insect structure became more sophisticated, with the evolution of a complex metamorphism.

Further development occurred in parallel with the evolution of the land plants. During the Mesozoic most of the modern orders of insects are represented, but a huge proliferation of insects followed the appearance of the FLOWERING PLANTS in the Middle Cretaceous, with pollinating insects such as butterflies and bees evidently becoming common. Some Cenozoic insect localities reveal an abundance of specimens and forms, the best known being MONTE BOLCA (Italy), Estonia (for Baltic AMBER), Aix-en-Provence (France), Florissant (Colorado) and Oeningen (Switzerland).

Most insect fossils found are isolated wings, which are the only parts strong and flexible

Primitive single-celled flagellates are at the base of the invertebrate evolutionary series. Subsequently, the SPONGES seem to have been a separate side-branch from choanoflagellate origins that led to no higher forms. The main path of invertebrate evolution traces up through COELENTERATES, flat-worms, nemertine worms, nematodes and rotifers to a dichotomous branching, where groups with a trochophore larva (displaying a ring of hairs around the body just anterior to the mouth) led to BRYOZOANS and BRACHIOPODS in one direction and MOLLUSCS, annelids (WORMS) and ARTHROPODS in another, whereas the ECHINODERMS, with a tornaria larva that has a ring of hairs surrounding the mouth, share a common ancestry with the chordates.

See also colour plate on invertebrates. R.S.

Java man

An early ancestor of man discovered in Java in 1891 after a deliberate search by the Dutch anatomist Eugène DUBOIS. Charles DARWIN suggested in 1871 that the remains of man's ancestors would probably be found in Africa, the home of two of the great apes, the gorilla and the chimpanzee. Others suggested a search in the East Indies, the home of the orang-utan.

Dubois discovered the top of a skull at Trinil on the banks of the Solo River, and later unearthed a tooth and a femur near the site of his original find. The skull had a capacity of only 860cm³ (53in³), whereas that of modern man is

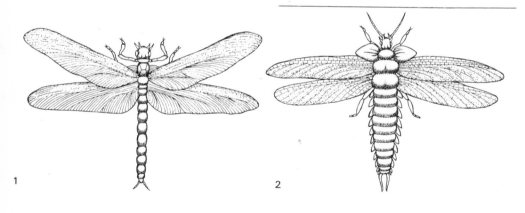

1

2

Insects
(1) The giant Carboniferous dragonfly Meganeura *had a wing span of 70cm (28in).*
(2) Stenodyctia *was a primitive and generalized type of Carboniferous insect.*

enough to be preserved, although beetle wing cases also occur frequently. The wings of fossil insects can be compared to those of modern forms by their vein patterns, which are characteristic in each of the different orders.

Insects are a successful group, more than a million species having been identified. It has been estimated that there may be as many as 4 or 5 million species existing today, and it can reasonably be assumed that at least as many species must have lived in the past. S.F.M.

Invertebrates

Animals that lack the notochord and BACKBONE characteristic of chordates (which include VERTEBRATES).

about 1,300cm³ (79in³). Additional primitive features were the large ridges above the eyes and the sagittal crest running down the centre of the skull. This hominid was called *Pithecanthropus erectus* by Dubois, but his find was not accepted as a hominid during his lifetime.

Only in 1936 was the true merit of his work realized, when Gustav von KOENIGSWALD found a mandible of *Pithecanthropus erectus* at Sangiran in Java, and the following year the skull of a juvenile (which was better preserved than Dubois' Trinil specimen) was recovered at nearby Modjokerto. After the second world war more cranial finds were made but the femur found by Dubois is still the only post-cranial bone of Java man so far discovered.

The Java hominids range from 2 million years

Jaws

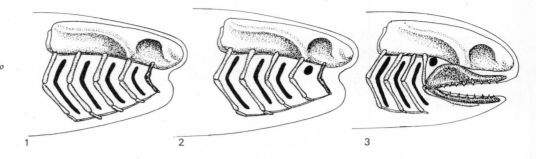

Jaws
*The evolution of the vertebrate
jaw mechanism:
(1) a primitive aquatic vertebrate
at the stage of the Agnatha with
no jaws and the mouth opening into
a pharynx from which the gill slits
(black) between the gill arches
communicate with the outside;
(2) the next stage of evolution in
which the foremost gill slit
becomes reduced in size to acquire
the function and configuration of
a spiracle;
(3) finally the front gill arch is
modified to form jaws. The upper
section of the front gill arch has
become the upper jaw, braced to
the braincase behind the spiracle
by the upper part (the
hyomandibular) of the succeeding
(hyoidean) gill arch; the lower
element of the front gill arch
forms the lower jaw and
incorporates the lower portion of
the hyoid arch.*

to about 750 thousand years old. The material indicates that during this period Java man underwent considerable evolutionary change, with the jaw and teeth assuming a more modern form and the brain increasing in size to 1,000cm³ (61in³).

Java man was about the same size as modern man and is so close to the living hominids that he has been re-classified as *Homo erectus erectus*.

See also MAN.   D.T.

Jaws

Hinged structures that evolved from the upper and lower halves of the GILL supports in FISHES.

Primitively, vertebrate jaws comprised a dorsal component (which may be made up of three separate bones) hinged to a lower portion (consisting of two elements). The first gill support is the mandibular arch situated in front of the hyoidean gill, behind which is the hyoidean arch. This condition is found in jawless vertebrates, such as the PTERASPIDS from which the jawed fishes have evolved.

One of the first stages in the development of jaws is found among a group of pteraspids from the Devonian of Siberia called amphiaspids, in which the hyoidean gill is reduced to a spiracle, a specialization that allows water to be drawn from the dorsal surface over the gills and prevents them getting clogged with mud. It was originally believed that the spiracle formed as a consequence of jaw development, but it now appears that the spiracle already existed in jawless vertebrates. The reduction of the hyoidean gill allowed the first (mandibular) arch to expand so that it came into contact with the hyoid arch. The two arches then united, and the upper part of the hyoid arch (the hyomandibular) joined the skull, to which the upper jaws also became attached. This condition is found in the ACANTHODIANS and is known as amphistyly.

In SHARKS the jaw apparatus is suspended from the skull by the hyomandibular alone; this type of jaw suspension is known as hyostyly. Where the hyoid is free and only the upper jaw is attached, the jaws are said to show autostyly, for example in CHIMAERAS. In advanced land vertebrates, the hyomandibular no longer functions as part of the jaw suspension but becomes instead a sound-conducting bone (*see* EAR).

Among the RAY-FIN FISHES, a gradual change can be followed in the development of the jaws. One of the bones that formed the main part of the upper jaw became smaller and the hinge of the jaw became loose so that it could slide forwards. The jaw joint was no longer fixed, and the jaws could therefore open as wide as 180 degrees. Such an extension of the jaws would have created a "vacuum", and nearby small fishes would have been sucked into the mouth.

The land vertebrates showed a different development of the jaws. The tooth-bearing bone of the lower jaw increased in size at the expense of all the other bones, and the bones of the jaw joint became incorporated into the middle ear of the mammals where they look on the new function of sound conducting. Hence the hyomandibular has changed from being a gill support to becoming part of the jaw suspension, and finally acquired an auditory function.   L.B.H.

Jellyfishes

One of the two forms in which COELENTERATES occur; the other is the polyp. Jellyfishes are rare as fossils but under favourable conditions impressions of their soft bodies are sometimes preserved. Some Pre-Cambrian fossils are apparently jellyfishes.

Jurassic

The second of the three MESOZOIC periods beginning 195 million years ago and lasting for 50 million years. It is named after the Jura

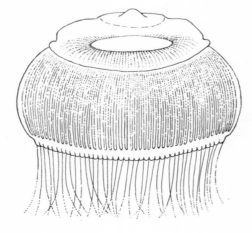

Jellyfishes
*Brachnia, a Pre-Cambrian
medusoid from Australia, is
reconstructed here to show it in a
moderately contracted state
(approx. 2/3 natural size).*

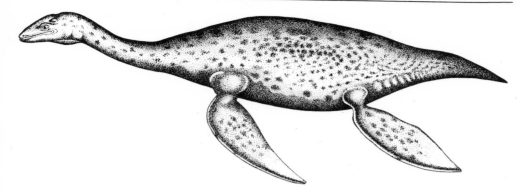

Mountains on the borders of France and Switzerland, where rocks of this age are particularly well represented.

During the Jurassic, further widening of the newly formed oceanic basins occurred as CONTINENTAL DRIFT continued to break up the old Palaeozoic supercontinent of PANGAEA, with the North Atlantic Ocean beginning to open between north-western Africa and eastern North America. The southern continent, GONDWANALAND, was also beginning to fragment as rifting was initiated between south-western Africa and the conjoined Antarctic–Australian land masses, although greater India remained temporarily pressed against the eastern margin of Africa.

The ancient Palaeozoic mountain chains, already weathering down in the TRIASSIC, were worn away still further in the Jurassic, and amounted to little more than low ranges of hills. In a predominantly mild, sub-tropical climate, with no evidence of polar ice caps, luxuriant vegetation flourished across swampy, low-lying plains with lakes and meandering rivers. Deserts had diminished in size, and the rainfall was evidently sufficiently heavy to support the growth of thick forests containing FERNS, towering CONIFERS, an astonishing abundance of CYCADEOIDS, CYCADS, many TREE FERNS, and the ubiquitous maidenhair trees (GINKGO, *Baiera*). Although growth rings in some fossilized Jurassic tree trunks indicate a locally seasonal climate, conditions were on the whole remarkably equable; Jurassic floras throughout the world demonstrate a notable uniformity of character, even if the constituent species are not always closely related. Insect life in the forest groves included the first flies, saw-flies, early butterflies (*Palaeontina*), grasshoppers, ter-mites, beetles and dragonflies; there were also many spiders and centipedes, and the ponds and lakes supported enormous numbers of freshwater snails (*Viviparus*), whose fossilized shells form beds of limestone such as the Purbeck Marble.

In the seas invertebrate life was dominated by the proliferation of AMMONITES, which were undergoing rapid evolution and are so numerous as fossils that they are employed as Jurassic ZONE FOSSILS. Some genera were sea-floor crawlers; others swam near the surface. Another cephalopod group that flourished in the warm seas of the period were the BELEMNITES, which included some forms with internal ink sacs – presumably related to squids.

BRACHIOPODS had started to decline, although the smooth-shelled terebratulids and the ribbed rhynchonellids occurred abundantly in Jurassic seas. They were being gradually supplanted by BIVALVES, however, with trigonias and oysters (*Gryphaea*) becoming especially numerous. In shallow waters, the hexacorals that had made their debut during the Triassic were now important reef-builders (along with hydrozoans), and calcareous SPONGES and CRINOIDS (both stalked and free-swimming) were common. In clearer water, SEA URCHINS and brittle stars established thriving communities, and the first CRABS made their appearance. Various lobster-like crustaceans (*Eryon*) were also present, their remains being beautifully preserved in the famous LITHOGRAPHIC STONE of Solenhofen alongside an ancient HORSESHOE CRAB which was not significantly different from its living descendants.

Fish life was dominated by the holosteans, which first appeared during the Triassic. In these RAY-FIN FISHES the maxillary bone of the

140 million years ago		
Upper	Malm	Portlandian
		Kimmeridgian
		Oxfordian
Middle	Dogger	Callovian
		Bathonian
		Bajocian
Lower	Lias	Adlenian
		Toarcian
		Pliensbachian
		Sinemurian
		Hettangian

195 million years ago
The Jurassic succession

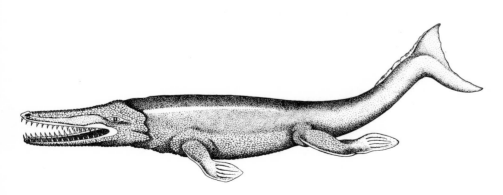

Karroo system

upper jaw was undergoing reduction and the tail structure approached the homocercal condition. The relatively primitive semionotids, which still retained a heavy layer of ganoine on their scales, were common and have a surviving relative in the garpike (*Lipisosteus*). The pycnodonts were deep-bodied forms. *Aspidorhynchus* and *Belonostomus* superficially resembled the modern gars (although not closely related to them); the amiiformes have left the freshwater bow-fin as a living descendant, and the pholidophoriformes were apparently transitional to the teleosts, which first appeared in the Late Jurassic (*Leptolepis* and its allies). Surviving relics of more archaic fish groups include a few palaeoniscoids, some sub-holosteans, and an early sturgeon (*Chondrosteus*). Coelacanths were still common (*Holophagus*), and sharks included not only numerous hybodonts but also some primitive modern types (*Heterodontus*, the Port Jackson shark, and *Hexanchus*, the six-gilled shark), and *Aellopos* was an Upper Jurassic banjofish.

On land, the reptiles reigned unchallenged, with the DINOSAURS attaining enormous size. Prosauropods died out, leaving the true SAUROPODS as their successors. Early members of this assemblage (*Cetiosaurus*, *Rhoetosaurus*) are present in the Lower Jurassic, and by the end of the period such relatively specialized genera as the elongated *Diplodocus* and the massive *Brachiosaurus* had appeared. The adaptable COELUROSAURS remained common, ranging in size from the small *Compsognathus* to *Coelurus*, about 2 metres (6.6ft) long. The giant carnivores were well established from the Lias onwards: *Megalosaurus* was widespread in the Middle and Upper Jurassic, *Antrodemus* attained a length of 10 metres (33ft) or more in the MORRISON FORMATION, and one or two types developed horned snouts (*Ceratosaurus*, *Proceratosaurus*).

ORNITHISCHIAN evolution still principally centred upon the ORNITHOPODS, with the large *Camptosaurus* present in the Morrison Formation alongside some diminutive cursorial bipeds (*Othnielia*, *Nanosaurus*) that have a probable relative in the TENDAGURU deposits (*Dysalotosaurus*). An early ornithischian specialization is represented by the PLATED DINOSAURS, which arose from a Liassic ancestor (*Scelidosaurus*) and subsequently developed through *Dacentrurus* and *Lexovisaurus* to the Late Jurassic *Stegosaurus* and *Kentrosaurus*.

There were no surviving thecodontians from the Triassic, but two other ARCHOSAUR groups are well represented. The PTEROSAURS, already firmly established in the Lias (*Dimorphodon*), had become common by the Upper Jurassic (*Rhamphorhynchus*, *Pterodactylus*), and meso-suchian CROCODILES included the goniopholids of rivers and lake shores, the long-snouted semi-aquatic steneosaurs, and the marine thalattosuchians with paddle-like limbs and a lobed tail fin (*Metriorhynchus*).

PLESIOSAURS and ICHTHYOSAURS were common in the seas. Short-necked, long-headed plesiosaurs (*Pliosaurus* and its allies) achieved enormous dimensions — the skull of *Kronosaurus* must have been 3 metres (10ft) long.

Some of the more conservatively proportioned genera (for example *Thaumatosaurus*) seemed to be evolving longer than normal necks with proportionately small skulls.

Ichthyosaur evolution had been rapid, and in addition to the common Jurassic forms (*Ichthyosaurus* and the elegantly streamlined *Opththalmosaurus*, with a deep tail fin) there was a series of predominantly Liassic forms with a reduced number of digits in the pectoral fins (Stenopterygiidae), one member of this group (*Eurhinosaurus*) having a lower jaw that was much shorter than the upper jaw.

The MAMMAL-LIKE REPTILES became extinct, and their descendants, the MESOZOIC MAMMALS, were still furtive, diminutive creatures (*Docodon*, the triconodonts, the symmetrodonts, pantotheres, *Plagiaulax* and its relations). The first BIRDS, still reptile-like, appeared in the Upper Jurassic (*Archaeopteryx*) but amphibians have disappeared almost entirely from the fossil record. Lepidosaurian reptiles are represented by RHYNCHOCEPHALIANS (*Homoeosaurus*), some probable early iguanas (*Bavarisaurus*, *Euposaurus*), and a few primitive types that may be allied to the geckoes (*Ardeosaurus*, *Broilisaurus*).   R.S.

Karroo system

A sequence of rock units, up to about 9,000 metres (29,530ft) thick, developed in southern Africa and ranging in age from Late Carboniferous to Early Jurassic. Its outcrops extend northwards from Cape Province as far as Zaire and Tanzania, but in the main Karroo basin itself they form a series of concentric ovals with the youngest (volcanic) beds in the middle, centred on Lesotho.

The sediments were laid down in a shallow basin as a succession of glacial deposits, sandstones, shales and mudstones, chiefly of continental origin, with abundant sills and dykes of dolerite and other igneous rocks. The lowest part of the Karroo contains strong evidence of intense glaciation, but the mean temperature seems to have risen gradually so that in the later Permian and the Triassic the climate was evidently much warmer.

Although the richest faunas occur in the Beaufort and Stormberg Series, the Upper Dwyka has yielded the small semi-aquatic reptile *Mesosaurus*, the fish *Palaeoniscus*, crustaceans, invertebrate tracks and tree trunks. One locality in the Upper Ecca has yielded a primitive dicynodont (*Eodicynodon*), and from elsewhere in the Ecca have come the terrestrial reptiles *Eccasaurus* and *Archaeosuchus*, fish scales, conchostracan and BIVALVE shells, the tracks of both invertebrates and small vertebrates, and plant remains.

The oval outcrop of the Beaufort Series, occupying an area of about 600,000 sq kilometres (231,680 sq miles), together with the outcrop of the Stormberg Series which it surrounds, constitute the richest known source of Permian and Triassic reptiles, including MAMMAL-LIKE REPTILES, COTYLOSAURS, PELYCOSAURS, millerosaurs, eosuchians, pro-

Laboratory techniques

lacertilians, sphenodontids, rhynchosaurs, THECODONTIANS, and araeoscelidians. Non-reptilian fossils include amphibians, freshwater fishes, ARTHROPODS (among them crustaceans, millipede-like forms and INSECTS), freshwater bivalves, and plants (*Glossopteris* leaves and silicified wood).

The Molteno Beds at the base of the Stormberg Series are remarkable for their complete lack of animal remains except for those of the holostean fish *Semionotus*. They contain, however, an abundant and well-preserved flora. The Red Beds and the Cave Sandstone have yielded excellent reptile faunas, but these contrast markedly with the Beaufort fauna in their progressive aspect. The evolution of the mammal-like reptiles culminated in the appearance of the first true mammals, among them the small *Megazostrodon* from the Red Beds. Also present in the Stormberg Series were ornithischian DINOSAURS (eg *Heterodontosaurus* and *Fabrosaurus*), PSEUDOSUCHIANS, early CROCODILES, prosauropods, theropods, advanced cynodonts (including tritylodontids), fossil FOOTPRINTS, fishes and insects.   A.J.C.

Kenya National Museum

Until 1964 the museum was known as the Coryndon Memorial Museum, after Sir R. Coryndon. It was founded by the East Africa and Uganda Natural History Society in 1909.

The palaeontological collections and research were originally the responsibility of the Coryndon Centre for Prehistory and Palaeontology, which was founded in 1962 when responsibility for the prehistoric sites at Olorgesailie and Kariandusi passed to the National Museum. At its foundation Dr Louis LEAKEY retired from the Museum and became Honorary Director of the Centre. In 1972 the Centre lost its autonomy and became the Department of palaeontology of the Museum.   A.P.H.

Koenigswald, Gustav von (1902–   )

German geologist and palaeoanthropologist (born in Berlin) who discovered the remains of prehistoric man in Java. Koenigswald had an interest in fossils from childhood and collected from such classic sites as Mauer and Steinheim. He studied geology and palaeontology at Berlin, Tubingen, Cologne and Munich.

In 1930 he became palaeontologist to the Geological Survey in Java, and reported on the hominid fossils from Ngandong (discovered 1931–32).   A.P.H.

Laboratory techniques

Mechanical and chemical processes for treating fossils after excavation. The usual treatments include the removal of matrix (termed development), consolidation (hardening), repair and restoration of friable material by the use of synthetic resins, concentration of bulk matrices for microfossils by sieving, and preparation of thin sections.

The art of fossil preparation has advanced considerably since the early days when stone masons laboriously chipped rock from dinosaur bones. Modern preparators have at their disposal a wide range of tools: mechanical methods include the use of dental burs, electric vibro-pens, chisels and saws powered by compressed air, ultra-sonic tanks and probes, and air abrasives (miniature sand blasters). Minute details of bone or shell structure can be revealed, and virtually no rock type is intractable.

The application of chemical methods in fossil preparation commenced during the 19th century when silicified invertebrate specimens were acid-etched from limestone. During the 1940s the use of dilute aqueous solutions of acetic and formic acids revolutionized the preparation of vertebrate specimens. These acids readily dissolve limestone, but do not generally attack fossil bone.

Acid development involves immersing the limestone block containing the bones in dilute acetic acid (5–10 per cent) for about a day; the limestone is etched to a depth of a few millimetres and bone exposed. The next stage is a lengthy washing in fresh water (about four times as long as the period spent in acid) followed by oven or air drying. Before the block is re-immersed in acid the exposed bone is cleaned and strengthened by the application of a dilute solution of acid-resistant polybutylmethacrylate resin in an organic solvent. Successive cycles of such treatment enable complete removal of matrix from bone.

Other acids used in chemical preparation include thioglycollic acid for the removal of iron-rich matrices; hydrofluoric acid for the extraction of carbonized plant fossils from siliceous rock; and brominated nitric acid for the removal of pyrite. The softening and breaking down of clays and shales can sometimes be accomplished by soaking in solutions of Calgon (sodium hexametaphosphate) or by immersion in hydrogen peroxide, and this treatment is often required before samples of such material can be sieved. Dilute solutions of caustic soda have been used to remove carbonaceous shale from vertebrate specimens, as have solutions of sodium hypochlorite.

The consolidation and repair of specimens is carried out using various synthetic resins. Specific resins and solvents are used, depending upon the porosity of the material to be treated. Sub-fossil bones, teeth and some types of fossil wood can be readily hardened by immersion in dilute solutions of polyvinyl acetate emulsion in water. Slow drying after immersion and subsequent storage in conditions that do not become too dry help to minimize the chance of splitting and warping. Mineralized bone and many invertebrate fossils require little, if any, consolidation; where necessary, dilute solutions of resin such as Alvar, Butvar, Perspex or polystyrene in organic solvents may be used.

Perhaps the most difficult problem for the palaeontological conservator is the preservation of pyritic fossils. Pyrites (iron disulphide) is extremely susceptible to oxidation in humid air. The products of oxidation include sulphuric acid, and total loss of specimens can result. To

La Brea

prevent this happening, pyritic fossils are stored and exhibited in dry conditions. Where specimens have started to deteriorate, the only effective treatment is the neutralization of acid by ammonia gas and consolidation of damaged areas by the application of resins such as Bedacryl. The use of resins on pyritic fossils will not, however, prevent their deterioration in humid storage areas.

Numerous techniques for casting fossils are in use, perhaps the most widely employed being moulding in silicone rubber and casting in light-weight reinforced polyester or epoxy resins. Such casts are easier to use in exhibitions of, for example, mounted fossil mammal skeletons or dinosaurs than are either the original bones or plaster casts of them.   F.M.P.H.

La Brea, *see* RANCHO LA BREA.

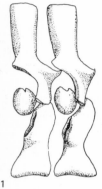

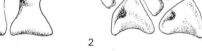

Labyrinthodonts
The vertebrae of labyrinthodonts:
(1) Ichthyostega, *a primitive form, but already displaying typical temnospondyl structure with a large intercentrum;*
(2) Eryops, *a progressive rhachitomous genus with reduced pleurocentra;*
(3) the advanced stereospondyl Mastodonsaurus *with pleurocentra absent altogether.*

Labyrinthodonts

A group of fossil AMPHIBIANS that ranged in geological time from the Devonian until the end of the Triassic and may have persisted into the Jurassic, although all are now extinct.

The name of the group refers to the structure of the teeth. Seen in microscopic section, the dentine gives the labyrinthodont tooth its distinctive appearance: wavy radial lines of primary dentine extending inwards into the pulp cavity. This type of tooth is shared with the LOBE-FIN FISHES, which almost certainly included the ancestors of labyrinthodonts.

Although classified as Amphibia, the labyrinthodonts are different from living FROGS AND TOADS, SALAMANDERS, and caecilians. Some were large animals, ranging up to about 4 metres

(13ft) in length. The skull was massive, and the outer (dermal) layer of bones formed a complete covering, not only for the bony braincase, but also for the jaw-closing muscles. This dermal roof was perforated only for the external nostrils, the eyes, and the small median pineal eye. The surface of the skull was ornamented with a raised pattern of bumps and ridges, typically giving a honeycomb appearance. The legs of labyrinthodonts, like those of the early primitive reptiles, were held with the upper arm and thigh practically parallel to the ground (on land, at least). The relative size of the legs and the length of the trunk varied greatly, although almost all of these animals possessed a long tail. Labyrinthodonts differed from the living amphibians in having well-developed bony ribs. Bony scales are preserved with some of them and it is uncertain whether they could breathe in part through the skin as do living amphibians.

The features that characterize the labyrinthodonts are all inherited from their fish (or early tetrapod) ancestors, and they are probably not a natural group. Most belong to the order Temnospondyli, which may not be related to the primitive and aberrant ICHTHYOSTEGIDS or to the apparently reptile-like ANTHRACOSAURS (groups customarily included in the subclass Labyrinthodontia). Temnospondyls are characterized by vertebrae in which the centrum (body) was divided, as in most labyrinthodonts, into an anterior intercentrum and a posterior pleurocentrum. In early temnospondyls, the intercentrum is a crescentic wedge with its apex dorsal in side view, whereas the pleurocentrum consists of an inverted wedge, usually divided into two bilateral blocks. During temnospondyl evolution, however, the intercentrum came to dominate, the pleurocentrum disappeared, and in some late temnospondyls the intercentrum is a thick disc.

Correlated with this development, a series of trends led from stout-limbed terrestrial forms in the Early Permian, such as *Eryops* and *Cacops*, to large but flattened and feeble-limbed forms in the Triassic, such as "*Capitosaurus*" (correctly *Parotosaurus*) and *Buettneria*. An odd group in the Triassic were the broad-skulled plagiosaurs which seem to have swum by vertical undulations of the body. Fresh water seems to have been the last refuge of the labyrinthodonts from competition with advanced bony fishes. It is now clear, however, that not all temnospondyls followed the terrestrial (*Eryops*) to aquatic (capitosaur) evolutionary line. Most large tem-

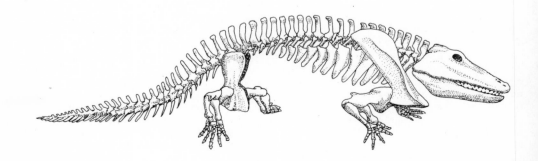

Labyrinthodonts
The Lower Permian rhachitome
Eryops *was about 1.5m (5ft) long.*

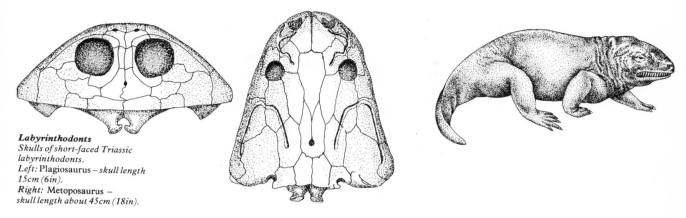

Labyrinthodonts
Skulls of short-faced Triassic
labyrinthodonts.
Left: Plagiosaurus – skull length
15cm (6in).
Right: Metoposaurus –
skull length about 45cm (18in).

Labyrinthodonts
Seymouria, *from the Lower
Permian of Texas, was once
regarded as a primitive reptile but
is apparently an anthracosaurian
labyrinthodont.
Length: about 60cm (2ft)*

nospondyls were swamp-dwelling predators throughout the history of the group.

There is general agreement about the ancestry of labyrinthodonts from freshwater crossopterygian lobe-fin fishes in the Devonian. It has also been held that all living tetrapods (including man) had labyrinthodont ancestors, but although labyrinthodonts may have yielded at least some of the living Lissamphibia it is improbable that they were the forerunners of reptiles, birds and mammals.   A.L.P.

Lake Rudolf

A lake, also called Lake Turkana, that lies in northern Kenya and was formerly a much larger body of water than it is today. The old lake bed has produced a confusing array of fossils, many of which still require explanation. Hominid material has been found by Louis LEAKEY'S son Richard, the first specimens to be excavated probably belonging to *Australopithecus boisei*. The skulls included some specimens with and others without the classical male sagittal crest, so enabling the sexes to be distinguished for the first time. As at OLDUVAI, these fossils occur together with stone tools, so the search began at Lake Rudolf for a *Homo habilis* type of hominid.

In 1972 a skull was found that had been broken into a large number of pieces. When carefully reassembled, it appeared to be more modern than *Homo habilis*, with a cranial capacity of 770cm³ (50in³) – well into the range of later *Homo erectus* specimens. This skull, number 1470, is classified as *Homo*, but no species name has been given to it. It is also thought that 1470 may be older than any of the Olduvai hominids. Other fossil bones subsequently obtained have been divided between *Australopithecus boisei* and 1470. The thigh bones of the 1470 type are particularly interesting because they closely resemble those of modern man, implying that 1470 walked with an upright posture.

Since these finds, the picture at Lake Rudolf has become more complicated by the discovery of material that resembles *Australopithecus africanus* from South Africa and other remains that resemble *Homo habilis* from Olduvai.

When deposits half a million years older than those already excavated were examined, remains of *Australopithecus boisei* were found together with bones from a hominid virtually indistinguishable from true man. Hand axe tools also occur at this level. The East Rudolf finds are particularly important because of the co-existence of so many hominids during the same period and the presence of such an apparently advanced form as 1470 at so early a date.   D.T.

Lake Turkana, *see* LAKE RUDOLF.

Lamarck, Jean-Baptiste de (1744–1829)

French palaeontologist (born in Bazentin-de-Pitit) who is regarded as the founder of modern invertebrate palaeontology. Lamarck trained in medical science but always retained an interest in all the natural sciences. Little is known of his life; he was initially a military man but wounds caused him to seek a new career. His interest turned to botany and in 1778 he issued the *Flore Française*. Late in life he studied the invertebrate animals and the fossils of the Paris Basin which resulted in his publication (1815–22) of the classic *Histoire naturelle des animaux sans vertèbres*. His palaeontological work was greatly enhanced by his knowledge of the living invertebrates.

Lamarck is also remembered for his theories on evolution, in which he maintained that acquired characteristics could be passed on to descendants and become permanent in a species. Although his theoretical work has not been so enduring, he did understand the great length of time required for evolution to have taken place, and anticipated the later supporters of uniformitarianism.   A.P.H.

Leakey, Louis Seymour (1903–72)

British palaeontologist (born in Kenya) who devoted his life to the understanding of man's evolutionary history. Leakey was educated at Cambridge University, but never lost his love of Africa; between 1926 and 1935 he was involved with four scientific expeditions to the continent.

Leakey's first contact with OLDUVAI Gorge, with which his name is now inseparably associated, was in 1931. He was always supported by his wife Mary, and in later years by his son Richard. In July 1959 the family's long search for fossils of prehistoric man (which con-

Leidy

tinued through the 1950s and 1960s) was rewarded when Mary Leakey found a skull of *Zinjanthropus* (now *Australopithecus*) *boisei*. Since then the finds by the Leakey family, not only in the Olduvai Gorge but throughout eastern Africa, have become world famous, changing entirely the picture of man's evolution.

For many years Leakey was associated, as Honorary Director, with the Coryndon Museum Centre for Prehistory and Palaeontology (now part of the KENYA NATIONAL MUSEUM), but his work as a collector is undoubtedly his most significant contribution to palaeontology.   A.P.H.

Leidy, Joseph (1823–91)
American anatomist (born in Philadelphia) who founded vertebrate palaeontology in the USA. Leidy graduated from the University of Pennsylvania, but was unsuccessful in his venture into private medical practice. His interest in natural history and his ability in drawing earned him his appointment as Professor of Anatomy at the University of Pennsylvania. He produced masterly descriptions of fossil vertebrates, mainly from the western USA.

Much of Leidy's research was on fossil reptiles and mammals, and he was the first to describe the North American dinosaurs. Among his many contributions to the scientific literature is "Extinct mammalian fauna of Dakota and Nebraska", issued in the *Journal of the Academy of Natural Sciences of Philadelphia* (1869), an organization to which he had been elected in 1849. With the increasing rivalry between Othniel MARSH and Edward COPE, Leidy found it difficult to obtain new specimens and so in later life he turned his attention to research in other fields.   A.P.H.

Lemurs
The skull of the North American Eocene lemur Notharctus *(approx. 5/6 natural size).*

Lemurs
The lemurs and the lorises are the most primitive of the living PRIMATES. Lemurs are small arboreal animals of nocturnal habit that now occur only in Madagascar. They have long limbs and fox-like faces. The brain is relatively primitive, the eyes are laterally orientated, and the lower incisor teeth and canine teeth are directed forwards for use in grooming (the upper incisors are small or absent). Living representatives of the group subsist mainly on fruit and insects. *Megaladapis* was a gigantic tail-less lemur, the size of a chimpanzee, which lived in Madagascar during the Pleistocene and has only recently become extinct. Lemurs owe their survival today to their isolation on an island free from competition with the higher primates.

Lorises are found in southern Asia and tropical Africa (but not Madagascar) and have many characteristics in common with lemurs. They are mostly small, arboreal and nocturnal. Like lemurs, they feed on fruit and insects, but usually have short tails, abbreviated faces and eyes placed more forward in the skull so as to give stereoscopic vision. Their brains are larger and more advanced than those of lemurs.

In tracing the ancestry of lemurs and lorises, it is necessary to study the origins of the primates. The classification of these early forms is extremely complex. Usually only teeth are found and there are few skulls and fewer skeletons. Although many species are known from the early Cenozoic, most of these appear to be side-lines to the main path of evolution leading towards the higher primates, and middle Cenozoic fossils are sparse.

Purgatorius from the Late Cretaceous of Wyoming is the earliest recognized primate. In Palaeocene deposits, mainly from North America, there are several specialized and aberrant forms, eg *Carpolestes* (which had enlarged and serrated premolar teeth) and the squirrel-like *Plesiadapis*. Eocene species come closer to the ancestry of living lemurs, and *Notharctus* from North America was extremely lemur-like: it had an elongated face, a long tail, grasping hands, normal upper incisors, tusklike canines, and a full cheek dentition. It was evidently an arboreal animal of tropical forests, like its present-day relatives in Madagascar.   R.J.G.S.

Leonardo da Vinci (1452–1519)
Scientist, engineer, artist and genius of the Italian Renaissance. Leonardo was born in Vinci, and initially worked as an engineer constructing canals in northern Italy. Like William SMITH more than three hundred years later in England, he undoubtedly gained much of his first-hand knowledge of fossils and strata during such work.

He did not agree with the popular conceptions on the origin of fossils, and argued against the universal deluge. His notebooks, in which his ideas were written in his familiar mirror-hand, were probably little used by his contemporaries. He recognized fossils as the remains of creatures once living that were often to be found in place as in life and could be used to determine changes in the relations of land and sea. He also understood the process of FOSSILIZATION, and explained the derivation of casts and impressions.   A.P.H.

Lepospondyls
Small extinct AMPHIBIANS of the subclass Lepospondyli that possess simple teeth and a skull from which a number of the primitive bones have disappeared (although the roof is usually consolidated); occasionally there is also some degeneration of the skeleton. The name

Limbs

Lepospondyli refers to a supposed common characteristic of the vertebrae, in which the centrum below the neural arch is not compound, as in LABYRINTHODONTS, but consists of a simple spool. The group occurred principally in the Upper Carboniferous and Lower Permian.

Three orders of lepospondyls are recognized, but there is no strong reason to believe that they are closely related to one another. The first is the Aistopoda, which are small but long-bodied and snake-like, with more than a hundred vertebrae, a reduced skull and no trace of limbs. They appear early in the amphibian fossil record, in the Lower Carboniferous Oil Shale Group of Scotland, and subsequently occur in the Coal Measures of Europe and North America. It is possible that aistopods are not true members of the Amphibia.

The second group, the Nectridea, are known first from the British Coal Measures as relatively short-bodied newt-like forms, with well-developed limbs and distinctive vertebrae possessing fan-like neural arches that bear extra articulatory processes. One family, represented by *Batrachiderpeton* from Northumberland and elsewhere, had small horns at the back of the skull. Large related forms such as *Diplocaulus* from the American Permian developed grotesquely widened skulls that spanned 30cm (11.8in).

The last and most important order of lepospondyls is the Microsauria. The earliest microsaurs come from the Scottish Lower Carboniferous, but many species are known from the Coal Measures. It used to be thought that aquatic long-bodied forms such as *Microbrachis* from the late Coal Measures near Prague were typical, but it is now known that most microsaurs were sturdy terrestrial animals with reptile-like skeletons, eg *Cardiocephalus* and *Pantylus* from the Lower Permian of the southwestern USA.

All microsaurs have a superficially reptile-like skull, but with a detailed bone pattern which could not have evolved into (or been derived from) that of reptiles. Their immediate origin is unknown but it has been suggested that they could have been ancestral to the living worm-like caecilians. Their vertebrae are now known to have been compound and to have paralleled closely those of reptiles and anthracosaur labyrinthodonts. A.L.P.

Lhwyd (Lhuyd), Edward (1660–1709)
British palaeontologist (born in Cardiganshire) who wrote the first book devoted to British fossils. He studied at Oxford University and became assistant to Robert Plot (1640–96), the first Keeper of the Ashmolean Museum, Oxford, and author of *The Natural History of Oxfordshire* (1677). From 1687 he worked full-time at the Museum and succeeded Plot as Keeper in 1691.

Lhwyd collected many fossils from the rocks around Oxford, and his collection is still in the Ashmolean. In a letter to John Ray (1628–1705) in 1699, he considered fossils to originate from "moist seed-bearing vapours" that had their source in the sea and then penetrated the rocks. His *Lithophylacii Britannici Ichnographia*, devoted to the description and illustration of British fossils, was issued in 1699. A.P.H.

Limbs
The appendages of tetrapods (AMPHIBIANS, REPTILES and MAMMALS) and BIRDS, which have evolved from the pectoral and pelvic fins of LOBE-FIN FISHES.

In the Devonian period, the crossopterygian lobe-fins were apparently denizens of freshwater pools that tended to dry up during seasonal droughts. RAY-FIN FISHES have a structure of parallel rays (as their name implies) to support the blade of the pectoral and pelvic fins, but the lobe-fins had instead a series of median or axial bony elements to which subsidiary bones were articulated laterally and distally. The bones in this type of archipterygial fin that was developed by Devonian crossopterygians correspond remarkably well to those of primitive tetrapod limbs. They comprise a single proximal element that articulates with the shoulder or pelvic girdle (representing the humerus or femur of land animals), a pair of bones making up a median segment (the equivalent of the forearm and lower leg bones), and an irregular development of bones that are the counterparts of a tetrapod's hand or foot bones.

Early crossopterygians are believed to have had functional lungs, and during dry seasons some of them probably started to drag themselves out of their fast-dwindling pools to seek refuge in a larger pool a short distance away. Their archipterygial fins would have provided sufficient support for limited terrestrial locomotion, and because the adaptive value of this facility enhanced an individual's chances of survival in drought conditions, NATURAL SELECTION would favour lobe-fins with increasingly limb-like fins.

At the amphibian stage, tetrapod limbs still sprawled straight outwards from the body, articulating at elbow and knee to bring the foot to the ground in an inefficient position with its long axis orientated at almost 90 degrees to the longitudinal axis of the animal's body.

In a few progressive LABYRINTHODONTS that must have spent little time in the water, the humerus had begun to rotate backwards to lie parallel with the body, and the femur was undergoing a corresponding forward rotation. This made it much easier for the limbs to lift the animal up off its belly. By the Permian, some of the early reptiles (eg PELYCOSAURS, MAMMAL-LIKE REPTILES and pareiasaurian COTYLOSAURS) were evidently capable of walking fairly efficiently with their weight supported by limbs that had started to evolve towards a vertical position, the articulatory surfaces of the joints being modified accordingly.

By the end of the Triassic, the reptiles were proliferating into a diverse variety of specialized forms that filled a wide range of ecological niches. Many PSEUDOSUCHIANS were bipedal and their descendants, the DINOSAURS, continued this trend. Early COELUROSAURS and CARNOSAURS

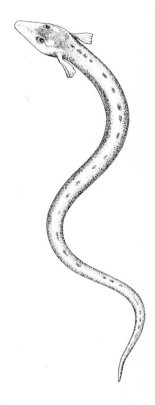

Lepospondyls
Dolichosoma *was a limbless aistopod from the Lower Pennsylvanian of Europe. Length: about 1m (3.3ft)*

113

Limbs (cont'd)

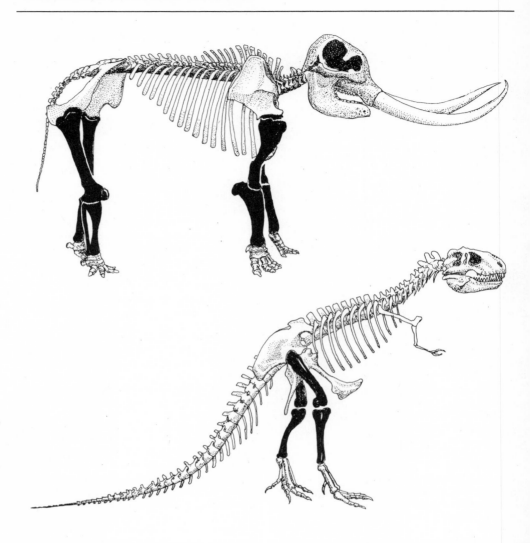

Limbs
*Large, heavy land animals such as the mastodon (*Mammut americanus*) evolved columnar graviportal limbs to bear their weight. Typically this structure incorporates a long humerus and femur, a relatively short shank retaining a well-developed ulna and fibula, and short, broad feet. In a biped such as the giant carnivorous dinosaur* Tyrannosaurus *(below), the limb structure is adapted for rapid movement. The shank of the leg exceeds the femur in length to provide optimum mechanical efficiency for a long stride, the metatarsal bones are elongated, and the feet have extended flexible toes. The forelimbs of this particular reptile have been extremely reduced in size.*

developed elongated hindlimbs with functionally tridactyl feet, the forelimbs were shortened and the "hand" acquired some degree of grasping capability. These agile predators had typically efficient hindlimb proportions for cursorial animals, with the shank significantly longer than the femur to provide optimum speed. As an additional refinement, the metatarsals were elongated and functionally joined to the distal tarsals, and the astragalus and calcaneum capped the lower ends of the tibia and fibula respectively to form a rolling hinge (metotarsal) joint. SAUROPODS rapidly increased in bulk and by the Jurassic had already acquired graviportal limbs in which the bones articulated almost vertically to provide a strong weight-bearing column.

Some reptiles returned to the vertebrates' early home, the sea, and turned their limbs into paddles by drastically abbreviating the long bones. PLESIOSAURS and marine CROCODILES (metriorhynchids) retained the original five digits, but the more fully aquatic ICHTHYOSAURS went further and acquired additional phalangeal bones, sometimes exhibiting hyperdactyl.

When PTEROSAURS took to the air during the Triassic, the fourth digit of the manus ("hand")

became greatly elongated to support a flying membrane. By the Late Jurassic, however, birds had appeared, and their wing structure was based on an elaboration of the humerus, forearm bones and metacarpals, the fingers being reduced. The avian hindlimb embodies a unified tibiotarsus which articulates with a tarsometatarsus —a further refinement of the structure seen in bipedal dinosaurs.

The earliest mammals had inherited from their reptilian ancestors relatively unspecialized limbs with five-toed feet, but adaptations for specific ecological niches soon appeared. Only a few mammals have become bipeds (eg man and kangaroos) and the land-dwelling carnivores remained relatively conservative in their limb proportions. The graviportal limb reappeared in large ungulates, however, and among the hoofed mammals that relied on speed to escape their enemies there was a progressive reduction of the toes to only one (PERISSODACTYLS) or two (ARTIODACTYLS) on each foot, with the tarsal elements developing into cannon bones. The hindfeet of the oldest known HORSES had already reached a three-toed stage, however, although digital reduction either began later or proceeded more slowly in the front feet, which were still four-toed in the Palaeocene.

Litopterns

Unconventional limb specializations are found in fossorial mammals (eg moles, with legs modified for digging), flying mammals (bats, with the bones of four fingers supporting the flight membrane), and aquatic mammals (eg seals and whales, with limbs converted into flippers).

In PRIMATES, the primitive count of five digits is retained in hand and foot, together with conservatively proportioned limbs articulating freely with the shoulder and pelvic girdles — adaptations for an arboreal life that have provided man with his potential for manual dexterity.

R.S.

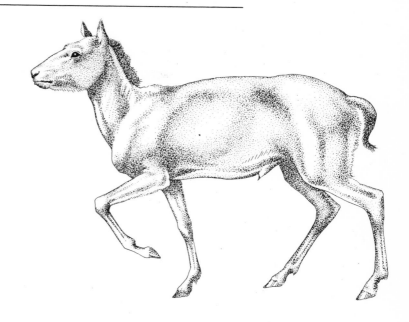

Lithographic stone

The fine-grained limestone, used for the traditional lithographic printing process, that frequently contains exceptionally well-preserved fossils. It is compact, dense, hard, homogeneous and clayey, with a conchoidal, foliated and thick slaty fracture; the constituent particles are of uniform size and smaller than those in clay. It is impermeable and usually pale creamy yellow or greyish in colour, occasionally pale or dark blue.

In a palaeontological context, lithographic limestone customarily refers to stone quarried at Solnhofen (Bavaria) and elsewhere along the Altmuhl River. Its age is Kimmeridgian (Late Jurassic), and near Solnhofen itself it is 20–60 metres (66–197ft) thick.

Lithographic stone of a sort has also been quarried in France (and adjacent parts of Italy), England (the White Lias of Bath, Somerset), Spain, Greece, the USSR (as far east as the Urals), the Middle East, Algeria, North America, New Caledonia and New Zealand.

The Solnhofen limestone is renowned for its fossils, which include ARCHAEOPTERYX, PTEROSAURS, the little DINOSAUR *Compsognathus*, a sphenodontid (*Homoeosaurus*), about 150 species of fishes, and numerous species of INSECTS, as well as HORSESHOE CRABS, OSTRACODS and larger crustaceans, oysters, AMMONITES, BELEMNITES and squids, pelagic CRINOIDS (mainly *Saccocoma pectinata*, the only really common macrofossil), jellyfishes, FORAMINIFERANS, RADIOLARIANS, coccoliths and ALGAE.

It used to be thought that the Solnhofen limestone represented coastal mudflats that were inundated by the sea only intermittently. It is now more generally accepted that the sediments were permanently submerged, with carbonate mud being deposited in the warm, shallow, and often stagnant lagoons behind the offshore reefs of SPONGES and CORALS.

A.J.C.

Litopterns

An order of extinct ungulate mammals which flourished in South America during the Cenozoic. The Litopterna possessed hoofed feet, with the axis of symmetry passing through the middle toe (as in PERISSODACTYLS), and customarily retained a complete set of cheek teeth (four premolars and three molars on each side) in both upper and lower jaws.

The last surviving members of the group were representatives of the Macraucheniidae, which persisted into the Pleistocene. *Macrauchenia* itself was the most advanced genus of this family. It stood as high as a camel, and was of similar proportions, although it had three-toed feet and a long-snouted skull in which the nasal openings were located almost above the eye sockets. Either this extraordinary long-legged, long-necked creature had a trunk-like proboscis or it must have been a swamp-dweller, living mostly in the water. A full complement of 44 teeth were present and the grinders were high-crowned. Reference of these forms to the Perissodactyla is precluded by the distinctive structure of the ankle and heel joints found in *Macrauchenia* and all other litopterns: the calcaneum has a conspicuous facet for the fibula, and the astragalus is excluded from the cuboid (with which it articulates in CONDYLARTHS and NOTOUNGULATES) but possesses a convex head that fits into the navicular.

An Early Pliocene forerunner of *Macrauchenia* was the much smaller *Scalibrinithe-*

Living fossils

rium, with relatively low-crowned teeth, and the nasal opening less posteriorly displaced. In the Miocene, *Theosodon* was little larger than a guanaco and had extremely low-crowned teeth, a short face, and an anteriorly located nasal opening. The neck was long in relation to the short trunk, and the limbs were of slender proportions.

Cramauchenia from the Upper Oligocene was smaller still, and had an almost conventionally constructed nasal opening, its Lower Oligocene predecessor apparently being *Coniopterium*. *Ernestohaeckelia* and *Ruetimeyeria* are from the Eocene and *Victorlemoinea* can be traced back to the Late Palaeocene.

A second major family of litopterns, the Proterotheriidae, paralleled the horses in the development of one-toed feet, only vestigial traces of the lateral toes eventually remaining – a degree of specialization that even modern horses have not attained.

These pseudo-horses seem to have died out by the end of the Pliocene, but they were numerous in the Miocene. Despite their advanced limb structure, the later proterotheres still had short, deep skulls and low-crowned teeth, two of the incisors in both jaws and the upper canines having been lost. The small *Thoatherium* was fully monodactyl, but *Diadiaphorus* – about 1.2 metres (4ft) long – still had three toes on each foot. Digital reduction was not accompanied by any real compensatory adjustment in the articulations of the carpals and tarsals, such as occurred in horses (adaptive reduction), and the non-functional lateral digits retained their original carpal and tarsal connections (inadaptive reduction). *Thoatherium*, for example, still had an articulation between the calcaneum and the fibula in the hindlimb, and the astragalus was in contact with the navicular.

Proterotherium was a notably slender Lower Miocene to Lower Pliocene genus, whereas *Licaphrium* was more sturdily proportioned; all these genera except *Thoatherium* developed tusk-like incisors. In the Upper Oligocene, *Prolicaphrium* and *Prothoatherium* appear to have been ancestral to the correspondingly named Miocene forms, but the earliest members of the family are not well known. *Ricardolydekkeria* of the Upper Palaeocene is one of the most ancient of these South American pseudo-horses.

The Adianthidae are poorly represented Oligocene and Lower Miocene litopterns. *Adianthus* had chisel-shaped incisors and canines, with high-crowned molars.   R.S.

Living fossils

Animals and plants that have survived virtually unchanged since the remote past. One of the most celebrated living fossils is *Latimeria*, the only COELACANTH fish that is known to have survived to the present day. Coelacanths occur extensively in Mesozoic rocks and then disappear from the fossil record at the end of the Cretaceous. The remarkable discovery of a Recent genus of coelacanth living off the coasts of South Africa and Madagascar provided an invaluable opportunity to examine closely the anatomy of an animal group formerly known only as fossils. Living fossils provide information for answering questions about the phylogeny of allied groups and their morphology is characteristically the result of little or no evolutionary change, often over long periods of geological time. Further illustrations of this conservative pattern of evolution can be found among vertebrates, invertebrates and plants.

In New Zealand today the superficially lizard-like tuatara (*Sphenodon punctatus*), which was close to extinction in recent historical times, is now protected by law. Undoubtedly an exceptional survivor, it is the sole living member of the RHYNCHOCEPHALIANS, a group of diapsid REPTILES that were widespread and highly diverse in the Triassic, but thereafter declined in importance and numbers. *Sphenodon* shows close morphological similarity with its Triassic and Jurassic relatives (eg *Homoeosaurus*) and its lineage has obviously been little modified since the early Mesozoic.

Perhaps no other invertebrate can be more aptly described as a living fossil than *Neopilina galatheae*, a MOLLUSC immediately identifiable with the primitive, limpet-like class Monoplacophora. Before its discovery in 1952 by the Danish Galathea Expedition, in the deep ocean off the Pacific coast of Mexico, the known stratigraphical range of the Monoplacophora was Cambrian to Devonian. Knowledge of the soft parts of this monoplacophoran, a group significant in terms of the origin of the Mollusca in general, has suggested possible ancestors of, among others, the GASTROPODS.

Araucaria (monkey-puzzle tree) and GINKGO (maidenhair tree) demonstrate the characteristics of a living fossil. Ginkgoales have distinctive wedge-shaped leaves, and during the Mesozoic they had a worldwide distribution. At the present time, however, only one species of *Ginkgo* remains (*Ginkgo biloba*), and its natural occurrence is restricted to parts of China and Japan. The leaves of many fossil ginkgos are indistinguishable from those of the single living descendant.   J.E.P.W.

Lizards

A suborder (Lacertilia) of REPTILES that belong to the diapsid order Squamata, which also includes SNAKES.

Lizards are the most numerous living reptiles. Their skull structure clearly distinguishes them from other modern reptiles, because although the upper temporal opening remains complete, the lower opening has lost its ventral margin

Lizards
Heloderma, a genus represented by the living gila monster, occurred as far back as the Oligocene.
Length: about 56cm (22in)

Lobe-fin fishes

and is open below. With the loss of the quadratojugal bone, the quadrate bone is freely movable on the reduced squamosal (a paired membrane bone), providing the jaws with enhanced flexibility. Other important lacertilian characteristics are the nature of the tooth attachment (normally fused to either the inner sides or the edges of the jaws), the absence of palatal teeth, the generally persistent pineal eye, and, usually, the procoelous articulation of the vertebrae (*see* BACKBONE).

The first lacertilians apparently evolved as small insectivores and most of them have remained like that ever since, although a few have adapted to a variety of other ecological niches. Fossil lacertilians essentially similar to the modern forms have existed since the Late Triassic, the younginiform family Paliguanidae being a possible ancestral group. The earliest forms regarded definitely as lizards are of Late Triassic age and were already specialized – the terrestrial Fulengidae of China, divergent from the main line of lizard evolution, and the gliding Kuehneosauridae of western England and New Jersey. The kuehneosaurids, like the modern *Draco*, supported flying membranes on extended ribs.

Most major groups of modern lizards became differentiated in the Jurassic and Cretaceous. Also present in the Cretaceous, however, were two semi-aquatic families related to the living monitors: the aigialosaurs, from which the MOSASAURS are descended, and the dolichosaurs. Snakes are also of lacertilian origin, and probably arose sometime during the Cretaceous. The largest known terrestrial lizard was *Megalania*, perhaps 7 metres (23ft) long, from the Australian Pleistocene. The largest modern form is *Varanus komodoensis*, about 4 metres (13ft) long, from Indonesia.   A.J.C.

Lobe-fin fishes

Members of a subclass (Choanichthyes, or Sarcopterygii) of fishes. In one group (the ripidistrians) there are internal nostrils (choanae) present. The lobe-fin fishes, like the RAY-FIN FISHES, apparently arose from ACANTHODIAN ancestors.

The Choanichthyes includes the LUNGFISHES (dipnoans) and the crossopterygians. The SCALES are of cosmoid type, and early choanate fishes had fleshy paired fins together with one anal and two dorsal fins. The TAIL FIN was generally heterocercal, with the main axis located in the dorsal lobe. Examination of the detailed pattern of the skull roofing bones suggests that they were produced by the fusion of smaller elements.

The crossopterygians comprise the rhipidistrians and the COELACANTHS. The rhipidistrians are the only lobe-fin fishes that have not survived to the present day. In spite of this, they are especially important because it is from this group that the terrestrial vertebrates came.

Coelacanths and rhipidistians have a pattern of skull roofing bones that can be matched with those of the terrestrial vertebrates, although the identity of homologous bones is obscured by the practice of early anatomists, who gave the bones

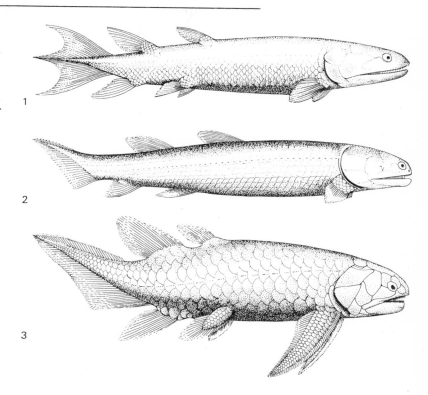

of fish skulls the same names as the bones of tetrapod skulls when they appeared in similar relative positions on the head. Hence the pair of bones between the orbits were identified as "frontals" in fishes whereas they are now known to be homologous to the parietals of tetrapods. This confusion has arisen because the proportions of the skull have altered as the relative importance of the different sense organs changed, and even within the rhipidistians it is possible to trace the gradual shortening of the posterior part of the skull and an increase in the length of the snout region.

The identifications of the particular group of lobe-fin fishes which actually evolved into the amphibians depends on a study of minor anatomical details. All tetrapods possess an internal, third nostril, the choana, whereas fishes have an incurrent and excurrent duct to each nasal capsule. The "internal" nostril of lungfishes is not a true choana but only the fish excurrent duct, and coelacanths also do not possess a choana.

When the details of the snout region are examined in further detail, it is seen that the two main groups of rhipidistians, represented by *Osteolepis* and *Holoptychus*, show striking similarities to two groups of modern amphibians. Osteolepids resemble frogs and early LABYRINTHODONTS, and holoptychids have affinities with urodeles (SALAMANDERS and newts). This has led to the suggestion that two separate lineages crossed the threshold of the amphibian grade of organization.

The very early amphibian *Ichthyostega*, from the Upper Devonian of eastern Greenland, was also derived from the rhipidistians, but seems to have been on a separate lineage which died out without yielding any later forms.   L.B.H.

Lobe-fin fishes
(1) The Upper Devonian rhipidistian Eusthenopteron *was about 60cm (2ft) long.*
(2) Osteolepis, *a common denizen of Middle Devonian freshwater ponds and streams, was about 23cm (9in) long.*
(3) Holoptychus, *from the Late Devonian and Early Mississippian, had paired fins resembling the appendages of lungfishes. It measured up to 75cm (2.5ft) in length.*

Lobsters

Lobsters, *see* CRABS AND LOBSTERS.

Los Angeles County Museum of Natural History

Founded in 1910, and now known as the Natural History Museum of Los Angeles County. The discovery of the important deposits at RANCHO LA BREA did much to spur the development of the Museum, which now administers a centre at La Brea where visitors can see palaeontologists excavating and preparing fossils.

The Los Angeles Museum houses the largest collection of Late Pleistocene fossils in the world, together with extensive collections of Cenozoic marine vertebrates (sharks, bony fishes and mammals) and birds. The emphasis of the collections is on the Cretaceous and Cenozoic vertebrates of the western USA and Mexico. The exhibition area, which includes the Hildergarde Howard Cenozoic Hall opened in 1977, illustrates the evolution of the vertebrates. A.P.H.

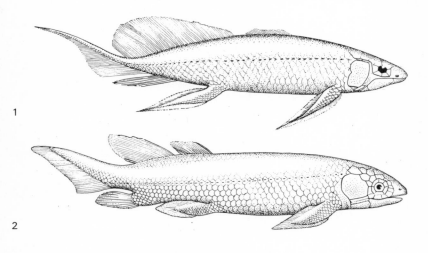

1

2

Lungfishes
(1) The progressive genus Scaumenacia, *from the Upper Devonian, had median fins concentrated towards the rear of the body.*
Length: 15cm (6in)
(2) In Dipterus, *from the Devonian, the median fins are still comparable to those of lobe-fin fishes.*
Length: 36cm (14in)

Lungfishes

An order (Dipnoi) of the subclass Choanichthyes (choanate fishes), which also includes the LOBE-FIN FISHES and COELACANTHS. They are the only living fishes that possess functional lungs, a feature that has been retained from the Devonian.

The overall appearance of an early lungfish is best seen in the Middle Devonian *Dipterus*. There were two dorsal fins and fleshy pectoral and pelvic fins. The TAIL FIN was heterocercal and there was a prominent anal fin. The first lungfishes were similar to most of the other contemporary lobe-fin fishes, but by the end of the Devonian they were beginning to evolve modern features. The Upper Devonian *Scaumenacia* illustrates a half-way stage in which the anterior dorsal fin had almost disappeared, whereas the posterior one had expanded and migrated backwards towards the tail; the extension of the body in the upper lobe of the tail was slender, and the anal fin approached the lower lobe of the tail fin.

In the modern lungfishes, the upper lobe of

the tail fin is formed from the posterior dorsal fin, and the anal fin contributes to the lower lobe to produce a diphycercal type of tail. During subsequent evolution, the pectoral and pelvic fins were reduced to simple whip-like projections (the living *Protopterus*) and appear to function in a similar manner to the limbs of the higher vertebrates.

The lungfishes were once thought to be possible ancestors of the amphibians, because the nasal capsules opened within the cavity of the mouth, and this was interpreted as an internal nostril of the terrestrial vertebrate type. It is now recognized that this is only the excurrent fish nostril that has migrated into the mouth and is not a true choana or third nostril.

The other feature that makes it difficult to relate the lungfishes to other vertebrates is the pattern of skull roofing bones. These cannot be identified with those of any other group of fishes, and their pattern seems to have been derived from a mosaic of small plates in a different manner to that of the other bony fishes.

Lungfishes have a specialized dentition that generally comprises large ridged tooth-plates with the cusps arranged in a fan-like pattern. These crushing plates are for dealing with shellfish, which they seem to have preyed on since early in their history.

Unlike some of the other lobe-fin fishes, lungfishes never developed the capability of crawling on land when their ponds or rivers began to dry up. Instead they bury themselves in mucus-lined burrows and sleep throughout the dry season, a process known as aestivation. Fossil lungfish burrows have been recognized in Carboniferous rocks and, in a few instances, have been found to contain lungfish remains. L.B.H.

Lungs

Structures that allow terrestrial VERTEBRATES to extract oxygen directly from the air and simultaneously excrete carbon dioxide. They are characteristic of amphibians, reptiles, birds and mammals. In the birds, extensions of the lungs even invade the bones, and similar pneumatic bone was also evolved independently in the PTEROSAURS.

Lungs first evolved among the fishes, during the Devonian Period. The tropical rivers that they inhabited were subject to a seasonal drying up, but even before this stage of dessication was reached the oxygen in the water would have become exhausted so that the fishes died of asphyxiation. By this time in the Earth's history, however, there was a substantial plant cover and an oxygenated atmosphere, so the fishes that stood the best chance of survival were those that developed some mechanism for exploiting the oxygen in the atmosphere during the seasonal dearth of dissolved oxygen in the water.

Most of the later Devonian fishes evolved some form of accessory breathing organs or lungs: the PLACODERM *Bothriolepis*, for example, developed a pair of rounded pouches from the floor of the gill region. The living bichir *Polypterus* from Africa, which is a surviving

Mammal-like reptiles

member of the PALAEONISCIDS (the most primitive of RAY-FIN FISHES), also has a pair of lungs, which are ventrally situated and derived from the last pair of gills. A similar condition occurs in the African and South American LUNGFISHES (*Protopterus* and *Lipidosiren*) and among rhipidistians (LOBE-FIN FISHES), the ancestors of the amphibians. Consequently the lungs always develop on the ventral side and the entrance to the lungs is invariably beneath the oesophagus. In the Australian lungfish (*Neoceratodus*), the lung originates on the ventral surface by a duct, but the main functional part lies above the alimentary canal.

Among the ray-fin fishes, the lung becomes transformed into the air bladder and loses its respiratory function, acting simply as a buoyancy organ. In the more primitive forms it is still linked by a tube to the gill region, but in advanced types its connection is completely severed and it lies along the dorsal surface of the alimentary canal.   L.B.H.

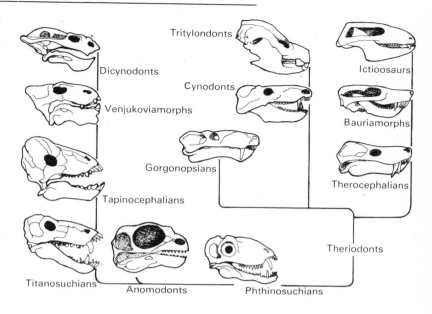

Lyell, Sir Charles (1797–1875)

British geologist and author of the *Principles of Geology* (1830–33), perhaps the most important and influential geological text ever published. Lyell was born in Kinnordy, Scotland, and attended Oxford University, where he met William BUCKLAND. After graduating in 1819 he studied law, but after his father's death in 1827 he devoted all his time and energy to geology. The publication of the three volumes of the *Principles of Geology* brought Lyell fame, and the importance of the work can be judged by the need for twelve editions up until 1875. The key to the book's concept is given in its sub-title *An attempt to explain the former changes of the Earth's surface by reference to causes now in operation.* Lyell travelled widely throughout his life and made numerous important contributions to geology.   A.P.H.

Mammal-like reptiles

The synapsids (paramammals), which were the dominant reptilian stocks of the Permo-Triassic. They became extinct early in the Mesozoic, having been supplanted by ARCHOSAURS, but left their own descendants in the mammals, which were eventually to succeed the dinosaurs as the dominant land vertebrates in the Cenozoic.

The mammal-like reptiles ranged in size from the dimensions of a small lizard to the bulk of a rhinoceros, comprised both herbivorous and carnivorous stocks, and evolved many features which are paralleled among the mammals. Nevertheless, they remained essentially conservative; there are no bipedal, flying or truly aquatic forms.

The most diagnostic feature of the mammal-like reptiles is the presence of a single paired opening in the skull roof for the attachment of jaw muscles. Another characteristic was their experimentation with temperature control. Mammals and birds are physiologically able to maintain their body temperature at a constant and optimal level regardless of the ambient air

temperature (*see* WARM-BLOODED ANIMALS), whereas reptiles are referred to as COLD-BLOODED.

The earliest mammal-like reptiles were the PELYCOSAURS, which had been replaced as the dominant synapsids in the Middle Permian by the Therapsida, comprising three main groups: dinocephalians, dicynodonts and theriodonts. The dinocephalians are the most primitive, and many were large, heavy, slow-moving herbivorous animals with chisel-edged cropping teeth, such as *Moschops* from the Permian of South Africa. The name "Dinocephalia" means "big-headed", and their skulls were large relative to their body size, often with thickened bones.

The dicynodonts were more active animals, varied considerably in size, and were all herbivores. Among their most characteristic features are the loss of cheek teeth, so that they had jaws like turtles. Another feature, seen for example in *Dicynodon* itself, was the presence in many (although not all) individuals of a pair of tusks in the upper jaw, suggesting sexual dimorphism similar to that seen in some living

Mammal-like reptiles
The evolution of the mammal-like reptiles.

Mammal-like reptiles
Moschops was a Middle Permian tapinocephalid from South Africa.
Length: 2m (6.6ft)

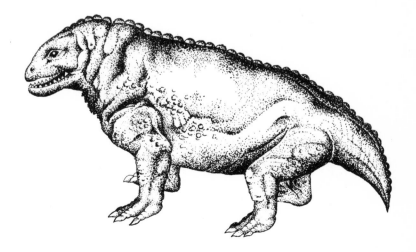

Mammal-like reptiles
The Early Triassic dicynodont
Lystrosaurus *(probably semi-aquatic) has been found in Africa,
Asia, South America and
Antarctica.
Length: about 1m (3.3ft)*

mammals. *Lystrosaurus*, a dicynodont with limbs that appear to have been adapted for swimming, has been found in South America, South Africa, India and Antarctica. These regions are now separated by wide oceans but in the Triassic, when the southern continent of GONDWANALAND was still largely intact, the genus was obviously widespread; subsequent CONTINENTAL DRIFT has isolated its remains on four continental fragments.

The theriodonts were the most mammal-like of reptiles – the name means "mammal-toothed". Their dentition consisted of incisor, canine and cheek teeth (like those of mammals), and many features of their skeletons were also similar to mammals. They are numerous and varied, six major stocks being recognized.

The gorgonopsians, with forms such as *Lycaenops* from the Late Permian of South Africa, were carnivorous lizard-like animals, with primitive features of pelycosaur origin. The dentition, however, had differentiated, making the animal an efficient predator. Therocephalians, again a Permian group, paralleled the gorgonopsians in many ways and include carnivorous animals such as *Lycosuchus*.

The cynodonts replaced the gorgonopsians as the dominant carnivorous stock in the Early Triassic, with various fox-like types, eg *Cynognathus*; they probably played a role similar to that of jackals today. Also belonging to the cynodonts were forms such as *Thrinaxodon*, which is in many ways extremely close to mammalian ancestry, and it was from this stock that the mammals probably arose. So

many cynodont features are mammalian that it is simpler to note the remaining repitilian characteristics. The mandible still comprised several small bones apart from the large dentary; the middle ear had only one ossicle; and the vertebral column could not be twisted (from which it may be concluded that these animals were unable to lie on their sides and suckle their young – an almost exclusively mammalian characteristic).

Bauriamorphs parallel the cynodonts in many ways. Whereas the skull and dentition of this group are mammal-like, the mandible is less advanced towards the mammalian condition and the stock appears to have become extinct during the Early Triassic, although it may be ancestral to the Ictidosauria, a small Late Triassic stock from South Africa of which *Diarthrognathus* is the best known genus. The name of this form is derived from the double jaw articulation: it possesses both reptilian (quadrate-articular) and mammalian (squamosal-dentary) articulation of the skull and mandible, and therefore marks a transitional stage from reptile to mammal in that important feature.

The tritylodonts were an aberrant side-line of rodent-like theriodonts that persisted long after all the other members of the group had become extinct, and were only ousted in mid-Jurassic times by the mammalian multituberculates. *Oligokyphus* from the Early Jurassic of England was similar to a vole, and as it could twist its back, it may have curled up to keep warm and even suckled its young.

Many theriodonts probably had some degree

Mammal-like reptiles
Cynognathus, *an advanced
theriodont from the Lower and
Middle Triassic of southern
Africa, was about the size of a
large dog.*

of temperature control, and some may have developed a hairy skin but they lacked a mammalian-type hearing apparatus and, with the possible exception of *Oligokyphus*, appear to have lacked the mammary glands which are so diagnostic of mammals. During the Triassic, however, some of these theriodonts must have made the transition into true mammals of diminutive size.   R.J.G.S.

Mammals

The fur-bearing, WARM-BLOODED vertebrates which suckle their young after birth. Most young mammals are born alive, placental mammals (Eutheria) retaining the shell-less egg within the uterus, where the embryo is nourished by a placenta until birth. MONOTREMES still lay eggs, however, and MARSUPIALS give birth to extremely immature young which undergo further development in a pouch.

The MESOZOIC MAMMALS can be traced back to the Early Triassic, and the pantotheres of the Jurassic are probable ancestors of the marsupials and the placentals, both of which appear in the Late Cretaceous.

The most conservative placentals are the INSECTIVORA, and from them probably arose, directly or indirectly, all the more advanced eutherian groups. Primitive PRIMATES such as LEMURS and TARSIERS are present in the Eocene, and miacids were early (Palaeocene–Eocene) representatives of the CARNIVORA.

Ancestral hoofed mammals (CONDYLARTHS) quickly yielded the ARTIODACTYLS and the PERISSO-DACTYLS, together with the LITOPTERNS, ASTRA-POTHERES and NOTOUGULATES which became characteristic of the South American Cenozoic. RODENTS and EDENTATES appeared during the Upper Palaeocene along with *Eurymlus*, the first known member of the Lagomorpha (RABBITS AND HARES).

One group of large, hoofed mammals that flourished in the Eocene (the AMBLYPODS) evidently diverged from the condylarth stock well back in the Palaeocene, and the ELEPHANTS and sirenians (eg DUGONGS), together with ARSINOITHERIUM, also seem to be the culmination of an ancient indpendent lineage. WHALES are apparently descended from the primitive early carnivore stock, but CREODONTS seem to be a sterile mammalian side-branch, possibly originating from *Deltatheridium* and its Upper Cretaceous relatives.

The Upper Cretaceous, Palaeocene and Eocene witnessed the rapid diversification of the basal placental stock into the various major groups of mammals that flourished in the late Cenozoic. Most mammalian orders are now in decline as a result of the spectacular success of the primates, through MAN.   R.S.

Mammoths

Extinct ELEPHANTS, descended in common with *Loxodonta* (the African elephant) and *Elephas* (the Indian elephant) from Pliocene MASTODONS.

Mastodons were primarily browsers, but elephantids evolved cheek teeth capable of grazing on abrasive grasses. The number of molar teeth functional at any one time is reduced to one, and there are five replacements during an animal's lifetime. Each tooth has a large surface area and is also extremely high, which results in an enormous volume; the crown has many transverse ridges of thin, wrinkled enamel and the space between the ridges is filled with hard-wearing cementum. There are no mandibular tusks, but the upper tusks are often large and curved.

Primelephas from the Pliocene of Kenya is the earliest elephantid, and its dentition displays transitional characteristics from a gomphothere mastodon ancestor. The line of *Loxodonta* is the least specialized series of elephantids, and fossil remains of this genus are restricted to the continent of Africa. Fossil species of the *Elephas* line are known from Africa, Europe and Asia. For example, the gigantic Upnor elephant *Palaeoloxodon*, which was 4 metres (13ft) tall at the shoulder, occurred in England and a dwarf species was present in Malta. The molar teeth are intermediate between those of *Loxodonta* and *Mammuthus*.

The peak of elephantid evolution was achieved in *Mammuthus*, a genus with Pliocene representatives in Africa, but best known from tundra-adapted species in the Pleistocene of the arctic regions of Eurasia and North America. The Pliocene forms had widely spaced ridges on their cheek teeth, but in later species these became densely packed.

Mammuthus primigenius is the classical mammoth with long fur. Its bones and teeth occur in abundance in Late PLEISTOCENE deposits, and in the tundra regions where permafrost conditions persist, occasional complete frozen carcases have been found. Mammoths were hunted by Palaeolithic man, and the last survivors died out 12,000 years ago.   R.J.G.S.

Man

A PRIMATE that has a common evolutionary heritage with the anthropoid APES, including the chimpanzee and the gorilla. The primate stock probably arose from a small mammal that lived about 70 million years ago and evolved initially into tree-dwelling animals similar to the modern prosimians.

These early primates had one great advantage: they were relatively unspecialized and so could occupy a wide range of environmental niches. Most primates do, nonetheless, share certain characteristics notably the possession of five-fingered hands and feet, nails instead

Mammal-like reptiles
The gorgonopsian Lycaenops *from the Upper Permian of South Africa grew to about 1m (3.3ft) in length.*

Man (cont'd)

1

2

3

4

5

6

Man
The evolution of modern man.
(1) Australopithecus africanus.
(2) Australopithecus robustus.
(3) Homo haibilis.
(4) Homo erectus.
(5) Neanderthal man (Homo sapiens neanderthalensis).
(6) Cro-Magnon man (Homo sapiens sapiens).

One of the dryopithecine apes, *Ramapithecus*, is considered to be a probable hominid ancestor. Its remains have been found in the Middle Miocene deposits of China, Hungary, Kenya, the USSR and Turkey. *Ramapithecus* is still predominantly ape-like but has some human features. The teeth in particular show changes, with the canines and incisors reduced in size and the molars possessing steep sides and flat crowns. These could be adaptations to a changing diet, with the dental modifications suggesting a change to "small object" feeding. One theory of human evolution is based on the hypothesis that *Ramapithecus* and its descendants, the early hominids, were living in an inhospitable environment and adapted to it by eating grass seeds. This would account for the reduction in the canines and incisors and for the large flat molars, ideal for grinding hard seeds.

A diet of this nature would mean that the seeds had be to picked by manual grazing in a sitting posture, leading to enhanced manual dexterity in co-ordination with the eyes, both factors which could have led to an increase in brain size. This theory, however, offers no explanation for the origin of bipedalism, and the suggestion that standing upright was a habit acquired to look out for predators in high grass is not acceptable to most anthropologists.

The next advance in hominid evolution occurred in Africa, where the australopithecines arose about 5 million years ago. These "southern apes" lived until 1 million years ago and some of them may have become the ancestors of man. Others, however, were relatively specialized and eventually became extinct without leading to any later forms.

Raymond DART, the discoverer of the first australopithecine, in 1924, encouraged considerable difficulty in having his "new" hominid accepted. At that time PILTDOWN MAN had still not been exposed as fraudulent and its key feature of a human-sized brain combined with an ape-like jaw was thought to be the evolutionary model for man's development. Dart's australopithecines, with their ape-like skulls and light jaws, therefore came to be considered not as hominids but as fossil apes that were not closely related to man. Further work in South Africa and the discovery of more material led to the eventual acceptance of australopithecine, in 1924, encountered conman was finally exposed as a hoax.

The Taung skull, of a child about six years old, was named *Australopithecus africanus*. Finds of adult australopithecines were subsequently made at several South African sites, including Sterkfontein, Makapan, Kromdraai and Swartkrans. Analysis of the material showed that two types were present: one resembled the Taung material and was called the gracile form; the other was more heavily built and much more robust. Some authorities considered that they were representatives of two separate species, but others believed them to be males and females of a single species exhibiting marked sexual dimorphism. The "two species" theory is now accepted and the gracile form retains the name of *Australopithecus africanus*,

of claws, and the development of sensitive finger pads. The snout is reduced, the eyes have moved to the front of the face, and the brain size has increased, with elaboration of the optical centres.

About 35-40 million years ago, animals that were the ancestors of both apes and man had evolved. One of these, *Aegyptopithecus* from the FAYUM in the Egyptian desert, was still a small, tree-dwelling quadruped with a heavy, ape-like jaw and teeth closely resembling those of the modern apes.

During the Miocene, ape-like creatures (dryopithecines) were very successful and several different forms spread throughout Africa and into Europe and Asia. One of these dryopithecines, *Dendropithecus*, is thought to be a direct ancestor of the gibbon.

The climate changed during the Late Miocene and the forests were replaced by grasslands. Most of the ape species seem to have been unable to adapt to this change and became restricted to the shrinking forests. Those that could leave the arboreal existence and live in their new environment probably included the ancestors of man.

with the robust type identified as *Australopithecus robustus*.

Australopithecus africanus had essentially human teeth with canines slightly bigger than those of modern man. His brain was small, with a capacity of approximately 400–450cm³ (24–27in³) – the same as a chimpanzee but only a third that of modern man. From the limited quantity of limb bones available and from the characteristics of the skull, it seems that he was capable of walking upright and would have stood about 1.25 metres (4ft) tall. He is estimated to have weighed about 30kg (66lb), about half the weight of modern man.

Australopithecus robustus was much larger, approximately the same height and weight as modern man, and walked upright, but his proportionally large skull and jaw exhibited significant differences. The teeth are often worn down by eating what is thought to have been a predominantly vegetarian diet: further evidence of this is seen in the large bony prominence on top of the skull (the sagittal crest), which also occurs in gorillas for attachment of the powerful muscles used in chewing. It is thought to have performed a similar function in *Australopithecus robustus*.

These differences between the two australopithecines led to the suggestion that *Australopithecus robustus* was a peaceful vegetarian, whereas *Australopithecus africanus* included meat in his diet (one of the reasons for regarding this species as a probable ancestor of man). It is also suggested that the "killer instinct" in man is deeply embedded in his consciousness, and is responsible for the "dark side" of his nature. Excavations farther north in Africa have now led to the alternative theory that neither of these hominids was man's ancestor and that they represent evolutionary side-lines.

Excavating at OLDUVAI among the remains of the Oldowan chopper-core industry, Louis LEAKEY and his family found the skull of a hominid that appeared to be an extreme form of *Australopithecus robustus*. It was named *Zinjanthropus* but has since been re-identified as *Australopithecus boisei*. The discovery of *Australopithecus boisei* in association with artefacts from the Oldowan culture suggested that he was their manufacturer about 1.75 million years ago, but further excavations at the same level revealed the bones of a more modern-looking hominid, *Homo habilis* ("handy man"). It is now thought that he was the originator of the Oldowan culture and may even have preyed on *Australopithecus robustus*. His remains indicate that he had a brain size of 650cm³ (40in³), stood 1.2 metres (4ft) tall and could walk upright.

Excavations at OMO, Afar and LAKE RUDOLF have extended knowledge of early hominids but at the same time confused the picture. Remains of *Australopithecus africanus* and *Australopithecus robustus* were found in relative abundance, but the most striking discovery was a skull (identified only as 1470) from Lake Rudolf with a cranial capacity of 770cm³ (50in³) that is older than the Olduvai forms. Post-

cranial bones thought to belong to the 1470 type are like those of modern man. From all this evidence it seems that several different species of hominid co-existed in Africa about 2 million years ago, but it is uncertain which became the ancestor of modern man, although the best candidate would appear to be the 1470 hominid.

The next evolutionary step is represented by *Homo erectus*, with a cranial capacity of about 850cm³ (52in³). The original find was made in Indonesia (JAVA MAN), but other specimens have been discovered throughout the world and include PEKING MAN. *Homo erectus* appears to have evolved in Africa, where material from Olduvai has been dated at 1 million years old, and then spread into Europe and Asia.

The evidence of this form in Europe includes the lower jaw found at Heidelberg, which is believed to be a specimen of *Homo erectus*, and it is also thought that *Homo erectus* used a chopper-core industry before evolving the Acheulean hand-axe technology. About 250,000 years ago a people that used hand-axes lived in England on the banks of the River Thames at Swanscombe. The remains of one of these individuals has been classified by some authorities as an advanced *Homo erectus*, although others regard it as probably the earliest example of *Homo sapiens*. Another skull of about the same date has been found at Steinheim, near Stuttgart, and this is also thought to be a late *Homo erectus* of early *Homo sapiens*, with a cranial capacity of just under 1,200cm³ (73in³). Many other specimens have been found, particularly in Europe, which show features intermediate between *Homo erectus* and *Homo sapiens neanderthalensis* (NEANDERTHAL MAN), with dates ranging from 120,000 to 70,000 years ago.

Neanderthal man occurred in Europe from 70,000 to 35,000 years ago. At the beginning of this interval the climate of the world changed and the last ICE AGE commenced. Neanderthal man managed to survive and hunted the herds of game, using caves for shelter and wearing clothing. Fire must also have played a part in his survival under these harsh conditions. The remains of Neanderthal man are found together with his Mousterian culture artefacts (*see* FLINT IMPLEMENTS).

About 30,000 years ago a new type of man recognizable as *Homo sapiens sapiens* appeared in Europe. Known as Cro-Magnon man after a site in France, his industry differs from that of Neanderthal man in that he used a blade technology. These people are the immediate ancestors of modern man. It is interesting to speculate whether they evolved from the Neanderthals or were immigrants from outside Europe – perhaps descendants of peoples from the Middle East and Ethiopia, where relatively modern-type skulls have been found that date from about 120,000 years ago. Whatever their origins, the Cro-Magnons founded the advanced PALAEOLITHIC societies which led to the MESOLITHIC and NEOLITHIC cultures and the introduction of farming economies which required the establishment of settled communities.   D.T.

123

Mantell

Mantell, Gideon Algernon (1790–1852)

British geologist and palaeontologist who described the second DINOSAUR (*Iguanodon*) to be named, and contributed to the description of the geology of south-eastern England, in particular the rocks of the Cretaceous system. He was born in Lewes, Sussex, and practised medicine, but was always an ardent fossilist. He made an extensive collection of fossils, which Charles LYELL referred to in 1833 as "a monument of original research and talent".

Mantell's main claim to fame was due to the discovery, by his wife, of the tooth of a fossil reptile in the Tilgate Forest, Sussex. He recognized similarities with the teeth of a living lizard (*Iguana*), and in 1825 named the newly discovered reptile *Iguanodon*. It was reconstructed life-size, but incorrectly, by Benjamin HAWKINS for the Crystal Palace exhibition. During his work on the Cretaceous rocks, Mantell introduced the term WEALDEN Formation. He also wrote several popular works.   A.P.H.

Marsh, Othniel Charles (1831–99)

American palaeontologist and describer of countless fossils, mainly from the central and western parts of the USA. He was born in Lockport, New York, educated at Yale University and then travelled to Europe. He became Professor of Palaeontology at Yale University (1866), and director of the Geological and Palaeontological Department of the Museum, which had been founded by his uncle, the wealthy philanthropist George Peabody (1795–1869).

Marsh was deeply committed to collecting and was much involved with the expeditions to the western USA which uncovered many vertebrate fossils from the Jurassic and Cretaceous rocks of Wyoming and Colorado. He often used his own money to finance the expeditions and was a bitter opponent of Edward COPE. From 1882 he was also vertebrate palaeontologist to the United States Geological Survey.   A.P.H.

Marsupials

The pouched mammals whose young are born prematurely and continue development in the mother's pouch. This characteristic differentiates the marsupials from the egg-laying MONOTREMES and also from the placental mammals.

Living marsupials are found in Australasia and South America, and there are fossil records of the stock in North America and western Europe, but none are known from either Asia or Africa. Characteristics in the bones and teeth differentiate marsupials from placentals. Marsupial teeth are not replaced, save sometimes for one premolar, whereas placental mammals have a milk dentition which is replaced in youth with a permanent set. Further, marsupials have more incisor and molar teeth than are usually found in placentals.

The earliest records of marsupials go back to the Middle Cretaceous, and in the Cenozoic they radiated into a wide range of ecological niches, developing insectivorous, herbivorous and carnivorous stocks which have parallels among the placentals, as well as evolving the unique kangaroos.

In North and South America, the Cretaceous marsupials were all basically insectivorous forms (not unlike the living opossums) and it was from these that all later types evolved. Rodents arrived in South America only in the Oligocene and placental carnivores first appeared there in the Pliocene, so during much of the Cenozoic marsupials filled these niches, evolving a wide variety of species. The caenolestids were rodent-like forms, and their radiation included jerboa-like species. Among the carnivorous marsupials, *Borhyaena* was hyaena-like, *Lycopsis* dog-like, and *Thylacosmilus* had great sabre-like canine teeth, paralleling the SABRE-TOOTHED CATS.

The fossil marsupial record in Australia is rich in the Pliocene and Pleistocene, but poor earlier. The oldest known Australian marsupials are from the Oligocene of Tasmania, and

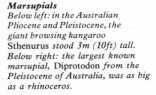

Marsupials
Below left: in the Australian Pliocene and Pleistocene, the giant browsing kangaroo Sthenurus *stood 3m (10ft) tall. Below right: the largest known marsupial,* Diprotodon *from the Pleistocene of Australia, was as big as a rhinoceros.*

124

Mastodons

include a primitive phalanger. Most Australian fossil marsupials can be fitted into living families, but their origins are unknown. Of the eight families of Australian marsupials, six are living and two (the thylacoleonids and the diprotodontids) became extinct in the Pleistocene. *Thylacoleo* was a large, lion-like marsupial with peculiar tusks and enormous carnassials (slicing cheek teeth), suggesting it was carnivorous, but the rest of the skeleton was like that of a phalanger, so its mode of life remains a mystery. *Diprotodon* was an enormous rhinoceros-like creature, again with large incisor tusks but possessing a cheek dentition similar to that of a kangaroo and certainly adapted for feeding on vegetation. Among the fossil species belonging to living families are gigantic kangaroos such as *Sthenurus*, which probably reached 3 metres (10ft) tall. This is probably as large as a bipedal hopping mammal can grow, because this means of progression becomes increasingly inefficient when the weight of the animal exceeds about 100kg (220lb).

The disjunct distribution in time and space of the marsupials is of great interest zoogeographically, and CONTINENTAL DRIFT has helped to explain the patterns. The marsupials probably originated in South America during the Cretaceous and soon radiated to North America. From there in the Early Eocene some migrated via Canada and Greenland into western Europe, before the opening of the North Atlantic Ocean. These stocks never radiated into a wide variety of niches and became extinct by the end of the Miocene. In South America they were more successful, because they faced little competition from placentals. It was from there that they travelled via Antarctica into Australia, probably in the Palaeocene or Eocene, at a time when an almost complete land bridge still existed between these continents.   R.J.G.S.

Mastodons

Proboscideans that were the dominant large herbivorous mammals of the Miocene. Some persisted into the Plio-Pleistocene and even into the Holocene, but from the Pliocene onwards they were rapidly displaced by ELEPHANTS.

Palaeomastodon occurs in the Early Oligocene of Egypt, but there is a long gap before the next proboscidean fossil is found, in the Early Miocene of Africa. By then two distinct mastodon lineages had become established: the bunodonts and the zygodonts. Both lineages spread from Africa during the Miocene Period, first to Eurasia and then (into North America via Beringia.

In zygodont mastodons the lower tusks are reduced or lost, the mandibular symphysis retreats and the lower jaw becomes similar to that of elephants. The molar teeth retain three yoke-like lophs (transverse ridges) with simple patterns and little or no cementum. *Zygolophodon* is present in the Eurasian Miocene and eventually migrated to North America.

Mammut is the generic name of the large Pleistocene zygodont mastodon. It was

descended from *Zygolophodon*, which is recorded from Eurasia and North America. The American mastodon (*Mammut americanus*) reached a shoulder height of about 3 metres (10ft), slightly less than a large African elephant and much less than the large mammoths of the time. It was adapted to tundra conditions with a protective coat of shaggy brown hair, and became extinct only within the last 10,000 years. Stegodons are a side-branch of zygodonts, well known in the Pleistocene of greater India. They had long spirally curved upper tusks, vestigial lower tusks, and complexly ridged molar teeth which approach the pattern seen in elephant molars. The stegodons were once considered to be ancestral to true elephants, but fossil discoveries in Africa indicate that elephants arose from bunodont gomphotheres, and that the stegodons merely paralleled the early elephantids in many characteristics.

The bunodont mastodons were more numerous and more diverse than the zygodonts. They tended to retain and enlarge the lower tusks, often as flattened shovel-like implements (*Platybelodon*). The molar teeth in early species of *Gomphotherium* had three lophs, but later forms developed four lophs, with complex

Marsupials
The sabre-toothed marsupial carnivore Thylacosmilus *from the Pliocene of South America was as large as a jaguar.*

Mastodons
Gomphotherium *(also known as* Trilophodon *and* Tetrabelodon *) was the typical Miocene bunodont mastodon, although its origin may be traceable to the Late Oligocene and survivors of the genus apparently persisted into the Lower Pleistocene.*
Height: up to 3m (10ft) at the shoulder

Mesolithic

mastodons eventually crossed Central America to reach South America in the Lower Pleistocene, *Notiomastodon* and *Cuvieronius* occurring as far south as Argentina.

During the Pliocene the bunodonts evolved four- and even five-lophed genera such as *Tetralophodon* and *Pentalophodon*, and in these the lower tusks were reduced and lost. In Africa members of these stocks yielded true elephants, and *Primelephas gomphotheroides* from 5 million-year-old deposits in Kenya is the most primitive known elephant, still retaining several gomophothere features. R.J.G.S.

Mesolithic

The Middle Stone Age of the HOLOCENE, in which the stone tool technology of early man (*see* FLINT IMPLEMENTS) attained its most advanced stage of development with the appearance of microliths.

The Mesolithic separates the advanced PALAEOLITHIC hunters from the agriculturists of the NEOLITHIC. During this interval human life was altered by climatic change. The ICE AGE glaciers finally retreated and conditions similar to those of today transformed the European tundra into dense forest. The herds of game were gone and large animals occurred only beside lakes and rivers or in occasional forest clearings.

The best known Mesolithic culture is the Maglemosian of a people who hunted along the edges of the forests, lakes and rivers of northern Europe, living on deer, elk, wildfowl, fish and water-plants. Their tools were thin flakes of flint (microliths) used as tips or barbs for hunting, as burins for working bone and antler, and as scrapers for preparing hides and skins. They also used the bow and arrow, their arrows either having microlith tips or flat flints. For fishing they used nets and unbarbed fish hooks carved from bone.

The only evidence of domesticated animals is the remains of dogs found at a few sites in England and Denmark. Mesolithic hunter-fisher-gatherers were expert engravers and worked teeth, bone, pebbles, and (in the Baltic region) AMBER. These engravings were occasionally of animals or men, but more often comprised abstract patterns of barbed or criss-cross lines, chevrons and hatching. D.T.

Mesosaurus

A small aquatic reptile whose remains are found only in the Lower Permian rocks of southern Africa and Brazil.

Measuring about 71cm (28in), *Mesosaurus* had an elongated, slender snout with numerous fine, sharp teeth that varied in size and were implanted in sockets. This type of dentition is usually found in fish-eating forms. The extremities evolved into broad paddles, the hind pair being substantially larger than the front pair. The tail was long, and a single temporal opening was present low down in the cheek — indicating affinities with the PELYCOSAURS, although no other aspect of mesosaur structure supports assignment to that group. ICHTHYOSAUR

Mastodons
Above: Palaeomastodon, *from the Lower Oligocene of Egypt, was about 2.3m (7.5ft) tall.*
Centre: Stegomastodon *survived into the Pleistocene in South America; about 2.7m (9ft) tall.*
Below: Mammut Americanus, *a contemporary of early man in North America, was about 3m (10ft) tall.*

patterns and often a deposit of cementum on the grinding surface to reduce the rate of wear on the relatively low crowns. *Gomphotherium* had well-developed lower tusks and spread in the Early Miocene, or even as early as the Upper Oligocene, into Eurasia, where its remains are common from Portugal to Japan. A branch of flat-tusked gomphotheres reached North America in due course and bunodont

Mesozoic mammals

relationship seems equally unlikely, because these Mesozoic forms had fore paddles that exceeded the hind paddles in size.

Mesosaurus cannot with certainty be referred to any established group of reptiles, but its distribution is evidence to support the concept of CONTINENTAL DRIFT. It occurs in only two places, on opposite sides of the South Atlantic Ocean, and because it was apparently a freshwater form that would have been physically ill-equipped to cross an open ocean, the conclusion must be that Africa and South America were formerly joined together.   R.S.

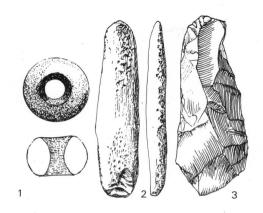

Mesolithic artefacts
(1) Sarsen-stone "mace-head", with a section (below) to show the hour-glass perforation.
(2) Limpet hammer (two views).
(3) Core axe with transversely sharpened cutting edge (tranchet).

1   2   3

Mesozoic

The era of "middle life" in the history of the Earth, comprising the TRIASSIC, JURASSIC and CRETACEOUS Periods. The Mesozoic Era is frequently referred to as the "age of reptiles" because, during its 165 million years, reptiles (*see* DINOSAURS) were not only the dominant terrestrial animals but also invaded the sea (PLESIOSAURS, ICHTHYOSAURS, MOSASAURS) and acquired the power of flight (PTEROSAURS).

See also the time chart.   R.S.

Mesozoic mammals

The earliest known MAMMALS, which first occur in the Late Triassic of Britain (*Morganucodon*), South Africa (*Megazostrodon*) and China (*Sinoconodon*). All of these forms were similar and shrew-like. Their cheek teeth have a central cusp flanked by small front and rear cusps, an arrangement that allowed the cusps to overlap when the jaws closed and so efficiently tear food. Their mandibles articulated in a mammalian fashion (ie hinging between the squamosal and dentary bones), and so there would have been three middle ear ossicles and not one as in REPTILES.

Two major evolutionary streams can be traced from Late Triassic mammals: one stock yielded triconodonts, docodonts and multituberculates, the other yielded symmetrodonts and pantotheres.

Triconodonts occur in the Middle and Upper

Jurassic of Europe (*Triconodon*) and North America (*Priacodon*). Although most were small insectivorous types, others grew as large as cats and were probably carnivores. Their cheek teeth had three cusps arranged in an anterior-posterior row, hence the name.

Docodonts are limited to the Middle and Upper Jurassic of Europe and North America. Their upper cheek teeth had a peculiar dumb-bell shape and their relationship to other stocks is uncertain.

Multituberculates were the most successful of these early groups. They are found in Eurasia and North America, in strata ranging from the Late Jurassic through to the Early Eocene, and had adapted to a vegetarian diet, paralleling RODENTS with their gnawing incisor teeth and

Mesosaurus
Mesosaurus, *from the Lower Permian of southern Africa and South America, was the first reptile to become secondarily adapted for an aquatic life. Length: about 40cm (16in)*

Mesozoic mammals
Megazostrodon, *from the Upper Triassic of southern Africa, was one of the most primitive mammals. Length: about 10cm (4in)*

Micropalaeontology

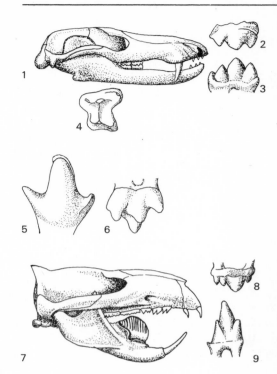

Mesozoic mammals
(1) The skull of the Upper Triassic triconodont, Sinoconodon, *from eastern Asia; skull length 4cm (1.5in).*
(2) A right upper molar (external view) of the North American Upper Jurassic triconodont Priacodon.
(3) A left lower molar (external view), also of Priacodon.
(4) The crown of a right upper molar (anterior to left, external margin above) of Docodon, *from the Upper Jurassic of Europe.*
(5) A left lower molar (external view) from Dryolestes, *a North American Upper Jurassic pantothere.*
(6) A right upper molar (external view) from Melanodon, *a North American Upper Jurassic pantothere.*
(7) The skull of Ptilodus, *a multituberculate from the Palaeocene of North America; skull length about 5cm (2in).*
(8) A right upper molar (external view) of Eurylambda, *a symmetrodont from the Upper Jurassic of North America.*
(9) A left lower molar (external view) of Spalacotherium, *a European Upper Jurassic symmetrodont.*

Micropalaeontology
Foraminiferans (shown here) are microscopic single-celled marine animals.
(1) Climacammina, *Lower Carboniferous to Permian (approx. 25 times natural size).*
(2) Endothyranopsis, *Lower Carboniferous (approx. 20 times natural size).*
(3) Marginulina, *Triassic to Recent (approx. 25 times natural size).*
(4) Nummulites, *Palaeocene to Recent (approx. 20 times natural size).*

complex multicusped cheek teeth. Multituberculates filled the niche left by the tritylodonts (*see* MAMMAL-LIKE REPTILES) and they had no competitors for their mode of life until the rodents appeared during the Palaeocene.

These three stocks – triconodonts, docodonts and multituberculates – are often grouped together as quasimammals. Their basicranial characteristics and the structure of the inner ear differ from the patterns seen in all other mammals except the MONOTREMES, which appear to be their only living descendants.

The symmetrodonts are known from the Jurassic of North America (eg *Eurylambda*), Europe (eg *Spalacotherium*) and possibly from the Early Cretaceous of Asia. Some were the size of small carnivores, and their upper cheek teeth

had three cusps arranged in a symmetrical triangle. They appear, however, to have been a small group, never numerous or diverse.

From the evolutionary viewpoint, it is the pantotheres that were the most important of all Mesozoic mammals, because they are the ancestors of the MARSUPIALS and placentals, ie all living mammals other than monotremes. In pantotheres the upper cheek teeth are triangular but asymmetrical, and in the lower teeth the triangle of cusps has behind it a heel or talonid that serves to receive the impact of the internal cusp at the apex of the triangle on the upper teeth, thus adding a crushing function to the slicing action of the reversed triangles. The earliest pantotheres appear in the Middle Jurassic (eg *Amphitherium*).

Most of the pantotheres occur in Upper Jurassic strata in Europe and North America (eg *Melanodon* and *Dryolestes*), with one isolated occurrence in eastern Africa. During the Early Cretaceous, little is known of the group and by the Middle Cretaceous they were being replaced by their descendants, marsupials and placentals.

Marsupials have a shelf on the outer border of their cheek teeth and possess four molar teeth. Placentals lack the shelf and have only three molar teeth. During the Late Cretaceous the marsupials rapidly became the dominant mammalian stock, with placentals catching up only at the close of the Mesozoic. Cretaceous marsupials are known from North and South America, from whence they migrated in the early Cenozoic into Europe and Australia. By the close of the Cretaceous, however, it was the placentals that were poised in the Northern Hemisphere to take over the niches left by the disappearance of the DINOSAURS and other reptilian stocks.   R.J.G.S.

Micropalaeontology

The study of extremely small fossils, usually involving specific microfossil groups, which can normally be examined only with the aid of a microscope. This field could, however, also embrace the smaller forms and growth stages of typical macrofossils such as GRAPTOLITES, GASTROPODS and BRACHIOPODS, and some members of recognized microfossil groups, such as FORAMINIFERANS, attain macrofossil proportions.

When present, microfossils generally occur in large numbers. This factor, combined with their small size and particular patterns of occurrence and evolution, led to the widespread use of microfossils as palaeofacies and palaeoenvironmental indicators, and as important tools in biostratigraphical correlation. They are of particular significance in the geological search for supplies of energy, where usually only a fragment of a borehole core is needed to date the stratigraphical succession with the aid of micropalaeontology.

Since the scanning electron microscope became available in the 1960s, morphological and taxonomic studies of microfossils have undergone a revolution, with consequent substantially increased biostratigraphical refinements. With magnifications exceeding 50,000, it is difficult to over-estimate the impact of this single innovation upon micropalaeontological studies.

Microfossils show a wide variety of zoological affinities and chemical compositions, ranging down to the Pre-Cambrian and including some of the earliest known life forms. Foraminiferans (calcareous protozoans occurring from the Cambrian to the Recent) were formerly the focus of much of the early micropalaeontological study, and even today they remain the most widely studied of all microfossil groups. The other noteworthy fossil Protozoa are the siliceous-shelled RADIOLARIANS (Cambrian–Recent). OSTRACODS, calcareous bivalved crustaceans, also range from Cambrian to Recent, and are an important constitutent of most microfossil assemblages. CONODONTS (Late Pre-Cambrian or Cambrian–Triassic), tooth-like microfossils made of calcium phosphate, have proven to be of great value in the dating and correlation of Palaeozoic rocks, but their true nature is still in doubt.

Organically walled microfossils include acritarchs (of uncertain affinity, Cambrian–Recent), the dinoflagellates (unicellular phyto-plankton, possibly present in the Silurian and subsequently ranging from the Triassic to the Recent), and Chitinozoa (problematical fossils, occurring from the Ordovician to the Devon-ian). Other phytoplankton of importance are coccoliths (tiny calcareous "scales" of plank-tonic ALGAE, Jurassic–Recent), and the siliceous DIATOMS (Jurassic – Recent). The use of these organically walled fossils, together with pollen analysis, has tended to eclipse the more traditionally employed groups (foraminiferans and ostracods) in some fields of applied palaeontology, and has established palynology as a major field of study.   J.E.P.W.

Millipedes, *see* CENTIPEDES AND MILLIPEDES.

Miocene

The longest geological period of the Cenozoic Era, beginning 22.5 million years ago and lasting for 17.5 million years. The Miocene (meaning *less recent*, ie with fewer modern types of animals than the succeeding PLIOCENE) wit-nessed enormous changes in the geography of the world and its life forms.

The oceans were actively spreading and CONTINENTAL DRIFT raised great mountain chains in the Alpine orogeny. Africa moved northwards against Europe, constricting the TETHYS Sea to a narrow seaway and elevating the Atlas Moun-tains, the Alps and the Carpathians. Greater India collided with Asia and forced up the Him-alayas while the Americas were moving west-wards against the Pacific plates, pushing up the Rockies and the Andes. A major ice cap covered Antarctica in the Late Miocene, resulting in lowered sea-levels around the world. The Tethys (or Mediterranean) dried up and thick evaporite deposits of anhydrite, gypsum and rock salt formed, so that land mammals were able to cross

Miocene
The protoceratid Syndyoceras *from the Lower Miocene of North America was about the size of a small deer.*

between Africa and Eurasia. By the end of the Miocene the Atlantic Ocean had broken through the Strait of Gibraltar, but did not succeed in linking up again with the Indian Ocean. South America and Australia remained isolated throughout, although towards the end of the Miocene some mammals may have been able to island-hop across the Caribbean Sea. The Great Rift Valley began to form along the African continent, accompanied by extensive outpour-ings of lava.

Miocene vegetation shows marked zonation and seasonality. In the northern temperate belt of America, hardwood deciduous and conifer forests clothed the landscape with oaks, hickory, plane, sycamore, elm, GINKGO, *Metasequoia* and *Taxodium*, and similar forests thrived across Europe. In the southern parts of North America there were semi-arid oak woodlands with figs and euphorbias. East Africa had woodland savanna with riparian gallery forests. There were probably few, if any, treeless prairies, but grasslands became extensive in the wooded savanna regions.

In the seas, calcareous microfaunas and floras were abundant, with planktonic globigerinas and large benthic (bottom-dwelling) miogyp-sinid FORAMINIFERANS. BRYOZOANS, CORALS, GASTROPODS and SEA URCHINS were all plentiful. SHARKS such as *Carcharodon* reached lengths of 20 metres (65.6ft). SIRENIANS (DUGONGS) were numerous and diverse in tropical waters, and odontocete and mysticete WHALES proliferated. Freshwater faunas included many INSECTS, the gigantic salamander *Andrias* – 1 metre (3.3ft) long – from Germany, and even a whale from an African lake.

More than one-third of known Miocene birds are referable to extant genera, with PENGUINS 1.5

Mississippian

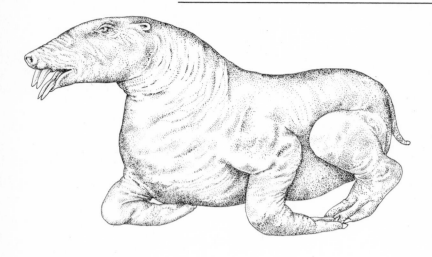

dog-like amphicyonids (*Daphoenodon*) and by SABRE-TOOTHED CATS.

Eurasia portrays a similar picture of faunal diversity, eg PIKERMI and the SIWALIKS, although some of the stocks are different. Eurasia lacked camels and oreodonts, but PIGS and ANTHRACOTHERES were prominent among the browsers, and the first DEER and GIRAFFES arose in this region. The CARNIVORA included viverrids and the first HYAENAS.

The African fauna is particularly well known from the extensive volcanoclastic sediments of the Rift Valley in Kenya. There were anthracotheres, pigs, giraffes, early ruminants, rhinoceroses, chalicotheres, gomphotherine proboscideans and deinotheres. Creodonts persisted alongside viverrids, amphicyonids and CATS. PRIMATES were numerous and diverse.

In South America the EDENTATES were now abundant, although still only small to medium-sized, and included ARMADILLOS, glyptodonts and anteaters. There were fewer NOTOUNGULATES and the LITOPTERNS evolved a horse-like stock (eg *Thoatherium*). Primates in the form of cebid MONKEYS appeared, probably from Africa because the order was extinct in North America. In Australia the MARSUPIALS had diversified in the absence of other competition, although the fauna is poorly known.

Inter-continental migrations are the second outstanding feature of Miocene faunas. With the drying up of the Tethys, mammals could move freely between Africa and Eurasia. Proboscideans, which until the Miocene had been exclusively African, migrated into Europe and Asia in the early part of the period and later entered North America. Deinotheres also reached Eurasia but never colonized America. Other groups that probably left Africa during the Miocene were cercopithecids, pongids, tubulidentates and hyracoids. Stocks that appear to have arrived in Africa from Eurasia included lagomorphs, cricetid rodents, viverrids, felids, suids, tragulids, giraffids and bovids.

Waves of mammals migrated from America into Asia and across into Europe. In the Early Miocene these included the anchitherine horses, and in the Late Miocene the three-toed horse *Hipparion* followed the Bering land bridge route westwards. *Hipparion* gives a valuable datum for correlation, since it appeared in Eurasia and Africa about 11 million years ago, and its success in spreading round the world testifies to the extent of the grassland habitats.

See also the time chart.   R.J.G.S.

metres (4.9ft) tall frequenting southern continents, and the flightless, predatory phororhacids of Patagonia standing up to 2 metres (6.6ft) tall.

Miocene mammal faunas had an essentially modern appearance. Many of the archaic early Cenozoic families had disappeared and half the living families were already present. Mammal diversity reached its peak during the Miocene, with abundant faunas known from all the continents except Antarctica. The two most striking characteristics of these faunas are the rise of numerous grazing stocks and the intercontinental migrations.

On each continent there were both browsing and grazing mammals. In North America the variety of mammals was similar to that of the modern African savanna: among the browsers and mixed feeding ungulates there were anchitherine horses, CHALICOTHERES, peccaries, protoceratids, giraffe-like camels (*Oxydactylus*), and mammutid proboscideans (*see* MASTODONS). Alongside these were many agile, relatively long-legged running types with high-crowned teeth, such as horses (*Merychippus*); dicerotherine, teleocerotine and other RHINOCEROSES; OREODONTS; pronghorns; prolabine CAMELS; and gomphotherine proboscideans. Evolution among the small mammals, the RODENTS and lagomorphs (RABBITS AND HARES), also included lineages which took advantage of the spread of grasslands and at the same time acquired burrowing habits (geomyoid or pocket gophers) – the only way to shelter from predators on open plains. The herbivores were hunted by large,

Mississippian

A division of the PALAEOZOIC Era corresponding to the Lower CARBONIFEROUS of European classifications.

The Mississippian began 345 million years ago and lasted for 35 million years. The period takes its name from the marine limestones laid down at this time in the Mississippi Valley (at St Louis, Burlington, Keokuk etc) by a shallow sea that covered most of the USA.

These deposits contain rich invertebrate faunas with an abundance of CRINOIDS,

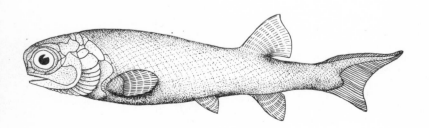

Monkeys

numerous CORALS, BRYOZOANS, MOLLUSCS and ARTHROPODS, and also some fish remains, mostly in the form of isolated teeth or spines.

North American amphibians of Mississippian age include *Proterorhinus* and *Greererpeton* from Greer, West Virginia, and an anthracosaur from Horton Bluff, Nova Scotia, where amphibian FOOTPRINTS also occur.

See also the timechart.   R.S.

Molluscs

A phylum of soft-bodied INVERTEBRATES that usually have a mantle cavity containing gills. In addition to cephalopods (eg AMMONITES and BELEMNITES), GASTROPODS and BIVALVES, the group includes the Polyplacophora (chitons or coat-of-mail shells), which are apparently primitive and first occur in the Late Cambrian, and the limpet-shaped Monoplacophora that appear at the base of the Cambrian.

The planispiral Bellerophontacea, extinct since the Lower Triassic, are now regarded as monoplacophorans and probably yielded the Cephalopoda in the Late Cambrian.

The Rostroconcha occur in the Early Cambrian and are thought to be monoplacophoran descendants. Their shells resemble those of bivalves, although the two halves are joined dorsally, often resulting in a saddle-shaped appearance, and they may have been bivalve ancestors. The last surviving rostroconchs (Conocardiacea) died out in the Late Permian.

Some poorly preserved tubes found in the Ordovician might be early scaphopods (tusk shells) and definite members of this group are known from the Devonian onwards, although they are rare until the Cenozoic.   C.P.N.

Monkeys

The most abundant and widely distributed of living PRIMATES. Monkeys differ considerably from the LEMURS and lorises and have close affinities with APES and hominids. They have large eyes that give good binocular vision, and short faces; the brain is large compared with the lemuroid stocks from which they arose.

There are two main streams of monkey evolution: the New World monkeys, or platyrrhines, and the Old World monkeys, or catarrhines. Platyrrhine monkeys are restricted to Central and South America and are less advanced than the catarrhines. The name platyrrhine refers to their flat noses, with the nostrils well separated. They are diurnal and small to medium-sized; almost all have long tails.

Two platyrrhine families are distinguished. The callithricids (marmosets) are small squirrel-like monkeys with bushy tails. They lack an opposable thumb and their hindlegs are longer

than the forelegs, but they can run and hop nimbly through forest trees. The earliest fossil marmosets occur in Oligocene deposits in South America.

The second family of this group is the Cebidae. Like all New World monkeys, they have three premolar teeth, but unlike all other primates they have prehensile tails. They include spider monkeys and the howler monkey *Alouatta*.

Few fossil cebids are known, the earliest occurring in Miocene strata in Columbia. Primates must have reached South America by island-hopping, either from North America or from Africa.

The catarrhines include the Old World monkeys of Eurasia and Africa, together with the apes and man. Some catarrhine monkeys are arboreal, whereas others are terrestrial and walk on all fours on the soles of their feet. Many are wholly vegetarian and have broad cheek teeth for efficient chewing, but not more than two premolar teeth are ever present. Their nostrils are close together, they have opposable thumbs for grasping, and their brains are proportionally larger than those of platyrrhines. In some genera the face is short; in others it is elongated.

The family Cercopithecidae has two sub-families. The cercopithecines include several widely divergent types, such as the macaques of Asia, *Cercopithecus* itself and the baboons. The colobines or langurs live mainly in Asia.

The fossil record of cercopithecoids goes back to the Early Oligocene, when *Parapithecus*, a lemur-like genus close to the ancestry of all later Old World monkeys, was present in the FAYUM deposits. *Mesopithecus*, from Late Miocene strata in Greece and Asia Minor, had macaque-like limbs (suggesting both terrestrial and arboreal habitats) and a largish brain; it is probably close to the ancestral langur.   R.J.G.S.

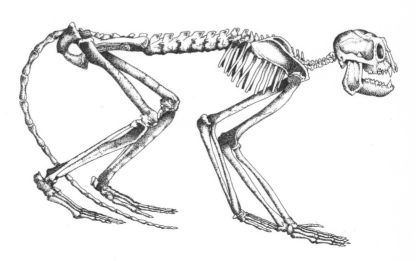

Monotremes

Monotremes

The duckbill platypus (*Ornithorhynchus*) and the spiny anteaters (*Tachyglossus* and *Echidna*) of Australasia, which are the most primitive modern mammals and constitute the living members of the order Monotremata. They lay eggs and have skeletal characteristics that reflect their reptilian ancestry, but also possess some mammalian characteristics, including an ability to suckle their young. The living monotremes are specialized, surviving in niches from which the marsupials have not been able to oust them.

The platypus has a way of life that combines behaviour patterns seen in otters, beavers and ducks; it has otter-like webbed feet, a beaver-like tail, and a duck-like beak.

The echidnas (*Echidna* in Australia and *Tachyglossus* in New Guinea) are hedgehog-like and specialized for feeding on insects (mostly ants and termites), using their elongated toothless jaws and long tongues.

There is almost no fossil record of monotremes. Some teeth from the Middle Miocene of Australia are the only known remains of ancestors. The characteristics of the ear and the features of platypus teeth suggest that the monotremes are an ancient stock, possibly related to multituberculates (*see* MESOZOIC MAMMALS) and the haramiyids (ictidosaurs, *see* MAMMAL-LIKE REPTILES), and certainly originating early in mammalian history, probably in the Jurassic.   R.J.G.S.

Monte Bolca

A fossiliferous locality near Verona in northern Italy, noted for its finely preserved fishes. The remains of more than 150 different kinds of fishes have been found in the hard Monte Bolca limestone, which is of Middle Eocene (Lutetian) age. The deposit was apparently laid down in the quiet water of an estuary or lagoon, and the fishes are mostly comparable to coastal types now found off sub-tropical shores in the Indo-Pacific region.

Several late surviving holostean pycnodonts are the only major extinct group represented at Monte Bolca. Other forms include about 15 species of SHARKS and RAYS (eg members of the genera *Alopiopsis*, *Mesiteia* and *Dasyatis*), and a wide variety of RAY-FIN FISHES, among them herrings (*Clupea*), eels (*Anguilla*), pipe fishes (*Urosphen*), sea bream (*Sparnodus*), horse mackerel (*Exellia*), sea perch (*Cyclopoma*),

snappers (*Lutjanus*), bat fish (*Platax*), soldier-fishes (*Holocentrus*) and spearfish (*Blochius*). Trigger-fishes, puffers, gobies, anglers, mackerel, wrasse, coral fishes and butterfly fishes have also been found in the Monte Bolca limestone deposits.

Examples of palms and other plants are also present, together with crocodile remains ("*Crocodilus*" *bolcensis*, *Megadontosuchus arduini*) and abundant fossil insects.   R.S.

Morrison formation

A thin band of shales, siltstones, sandstones, limestones and coarse conglomerates that varies from 30 to 275 metres (100 to 900ft) in thickness, and stretches across the western USA from Montana southwards through Utah and Colorado to New Mexico. This Upper Jurassic deposit is named after the town of Morrison in Colorado, where Oxford-graduate schoolteacher Arthur Lakes discovered a DINOSAUR vertebra embedded in the rock during March 1877.

Lakes ascertained that the deposit was rich in dinosaur bones and sent more than a ton of specimens to Othniel MARSH. Getting no quick reply, Lakes sent further bones to Edward COPE. Hearing of this development, Marsh promptly sent his collector Benjamin Mudge to negotiate an exclusive agreement with Lakes, and the newly located quarry quickly yielded the first known remains of both *Atlantosaurus* and *Stegosaurus*.

In the summer of 1877 Cope opened a further Morrison quarry at Canyon City, Colorado, that had been discovered by O. W. Lucas (another schoolteacher prospector), while Marsh moved on to Como Bluff, Wyoming, where two railwaymen, William E. Carlin and Bill Reed, had discovered what they believed to be a giant sloth – it was in fact a specimen of *Atlantosaurus*. The site proved to be a rich vein of dinosaur remains, and Carlin and Reed became full-time excavators for Marsh, working through the winter of 1877–78 despite bitter cold and heavy snow.

In 1898 an AMERICAN MUSEUM OF NATURAL HISTORY expedition led by Jacob Wortman (1856–1926) stumbled on the Bone Cabin Quarry, Wyoming, where bones of Upper Jurassic dinosaurs lay exposed on the surface and had been used by a shepherd to construct a cabin (hence the name). The Morrison beds near Vernal, Utah, that were excavated by Earl

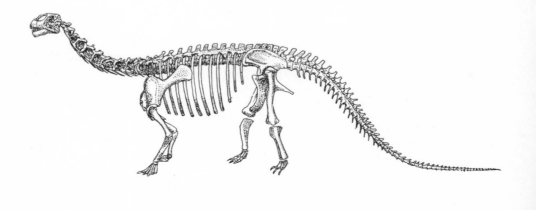

Morrison formation
Camarasaurus *was a sauropod dinosaur.*
Length: about 10m (33ft)

Mosses

Douglass (1862–1931) later became the DINO-SAUR NATIONAL MONUMENT, where today visitors can see a section of quarry face in which bones are embedded.

The Morrison dinosaur fauna comprises various SAUROPODS (*Atlantosaurus, Diplodocus, Camarasaurus*), *Stegosaurus*, COELUROSAURS (*Coelurus*), CARNOSAURS (*Antrodemus, Ceratosaurus, Marshosaurus*), and ORNITHOPODS (*Laosaurus, Dryosaurus, Camptosaurus*), as well as a few CROCODILES (*Hoplosuchus, Goniopholis*); the remains of MESOZOIC MAMMALS also occur (triconodonts, multituberculates, pantotheres, symmetrodonts).

The environment in which the Morrison beds were laid down appears to have been a swampy lowland with meandering rivers that deposited mud and silt over their flood plains at high water, and occasional lakes where fine clays accumulated. An almost exact correlation in time exists between the Morrison beds and the TENDAGURU deposits of East Africa. R.S.

Mosasaurs

A family of fossil LIZARDS, found only in Upper Cretaceous rocks. They differ from all other true lizards in their gigantic size, attaining a length of 5–10 metres (16–33ft), and in their complete adaptation to life in the sea.

The head is long, the neck short, and the body and tail are elongated and slender; the tail is flattened from side to side and served as the main organ of propulsion. The limbs are modified into steering paddles, with extremely short main bones and five widely spaced digits, sometimes incorporating a few extra phalanges and presumably webbed. The skull is like that of a varanid (monitor) lizard, with a well-developed joint along the length of the lower jaw between the angular and splenial bones. The teeth differ from those of other lizards in that they are contained in sockets.

It is likely that mosasaurs subsisted largely on fish (there was an abundance of primitive teleosts in the Late Cretaceous), and that they were replacing the ICHTHYOSAURS – then slowly declining – as large marine predators, but they would still have been competing with the contemporary PLESIOSAURS. Cephalopods evidently formed an important part of the mosasaurs' diet, because there are records of AMMONITE shells bearing what appear to be mosasaur teeth-marks. One genus, *Globidens*, possessed teeth with unusual sphaeroidal crowns suitable for crushing BIVALVES.

Mosasaurs were widely distributed, having been found in every continent except Antarctica and Australia (although they were present in New Zealand). They are particularly abundant in the Niobrara Chalk of Kansas, and in north-western Europe they occur in The Netherlands and in the English Chalk. The best known genera are *Mosasaurus, Platecarpus, Tylosaurus, Clidastes, Liodon* and *Taniwhasaurus*.

The origin of the mosasaurs apparently lay among the aigialosaurs, small semi-aquatic relatives of the monitors, which are found lower down in the Cretaceous and which, in turn, had evolved from *Proaigialosaurus* of the Upper Jurassic. All the mosasaurs became extinct at the end of the Cretaceous, leaving no descendants.

The first recorded specimen of a mosasaur was a pair of enormous jaws more than a metre (3.3ft) long, furnished with gigantic teeth, which was found in 1770 in the subterranean caverns quarried in the chalk of Maastricht (south-eastern Holland). Hewn out by the quarrymen and bought by a local collector, a Dr Hoffmann, the jaws were claimed by the owner of the estate beneath which the caverns lay. The landowner in question, Canon Godin, took the dispute to court and won possession of the fossil, which he kept in his château. So famous did this specimen become that when a French Republican army was approaching Maastricht in 1795 the commander, General Pichegru (1761–1804), deliberately refrained from attacking the château. Later, when Maastricht had fallen, Pichegru ordered his troops to seize the fossil for the Republic.

Although Canon Godin had removed his specimen elsewhere during the night, his efforts to save it were thwarted by General Pichegru's offer of a reward of 600 bottles of wine to anyone finding it. A party of soldiers discovered it within hours and it was taken to Paris, later to be studied by Georges CUVIER. Many years afterwards, William Conybeare (1787–1857) named it *Mosasaurus*, the "Meuse lizard", after the region in which it had been found. A.J.C.

Mosses

Small green plants (bryophytes) belonging to the class Bryopsida. The fossil history of the mosses is patchy and unsatisfactory, but two early species of the group occur in the Carboniferous and have been assigned to the genus *Muscites*. The only other record of mosses in the Palaeozoic is some well-preserved material from the Permian of Angaraland, in the USSR, which includes examples of the Sphagnidae and the Bryidae.

These early ancestors of *Sphagnum* from Russia complete a sequence that continues

Mosasaurs
The skull of the mosasaur Clidastes *was about 52cm (20in) long.*

Mosasaurs
Mosasaurs are common in the Upper Cretaceous Niobrara Chalk of Kansas. Tylosaurus *is one of the best known animals of the group.*
Length: up to 8m (26ft)

through the Mesozoic, where *Sphagnum* itself (and its spores) occur in the Jurassic and Cretaceous. These fossil types show the development of the typical *Sphagnum* leaf with its network of two types of cell.

The other group of Permian mosses, which possess affinities with the modern *Bryum* type, exhibit features which, nonetheless, clearly separate them from modern forms. Fossil mosses from the late Cenozoic can generally be referred to modern genera and species.   J.W.F.

Muséum National d'Histoire Naturelle
The French National Museum of Natural History, founded in 1635 in Paris. The establishment of the Jardin Royal des Plantes Médicinales was the first stage in the long history of the Museum. In 1718 there was a major administrative change, with the separation of the functions of the Premier Médecin du Roi and the Surintendant du Jardin. The great naturalist, Georges BUFFON was in charge of Jardin du Roi from 1739 to 1788. In 1793 the Museum d'Histoire Naturelle was established, with an administration consisting initially of twelve professors. Among palaeontologists elected to this office were Jean-Baptiste LAMARCK, Adolphe-Theodore BRONGNIART, Georges CUVIER and Alcide d'ORBIGNY.

The palaeontological collections were greatly expanded by Buffon, and the Museum has since been the major centre for French palaeontology. It does research on all aspects of the subject and provides exhibition galleries for the public. The Musée de l'Homme also forms part of the Museum.   A.P.H.

Museum of Comparative Zoology
A major collection of vertebrate fossils administered by Harvard University. It originated from the collections of fossils brought to North America by Jean AGASSIZ in 1846 and the then existing specimens in the College. The Museum acquired its first building in 1850 and a grant (since 1858) from the University. In 1858, a gift of $50,000 was received from Mr Francis C. Gray on the condition that the name Museum of Comparative Zoology was adopted.

The Museum's early development owes much to the labours of its first two directors, Jean Agassiz and his son Alexander (1835–1910). The Museum came under the direct control of the University in 1876. The collections are now particularly strong in fossil vertebrates, including fishes from Europe and North America, and South American Triassic amphibians and reptiles.   A.P.H.

Národní Museum
The national museum of Czechoslovakia, founded in 1818 in Prague. The collections are particularly noted for the wealth of 19th century specimens, including many type specimens.

The STERNBERG collection was an important early acquisition, and during the directorship of Dr A. Fric (1832–1913) the collection of

Joachim BARRANDE went to the Museum. The first Keeper of the Barrande collection, O. P. Novák (1851–92), became well known for his research on TRILOBITES.   A.P.H.

Natural selection
A concept that was first publicly proposed as the principle of evolution during a lecture by Charles DARWIN and Alfred Russell Wallace (1823–1913) to the Linnean Society of London in 1858. Following the work of Thomas Malthus (1766–1834) on human population growth, Darwin indicated that organisms produce sufficient offspring to cause an enormous population increase if they all survived. Populations do not usually behave in this way, however, but tend to remain constant in size. Under conditions of potential rapid population increase there is competition within and between species for food, mates, space and other necessities of limited supply. Because of natural variation in populations, some individuals will be more likely to reproduce and contribute to the next generation. If advantageous variations are inheritable, then the composition of the population will change with time: the successful variants and their descendants will survive.

Darwin's main problem in putting forward his theory was his ignorance of the mechanism of inheritance. Like most of his contemporaries, he believed that inheritance involved blending parental characteristics in the offspring. If this were so, the amount of variation in a population would decline rapidly and natural selection would have to operate with extreme rapidity in order to be effective. In 1866 Gregor Mendel (1822–84) had shown that blending inheritance does not occur, but his work was overlooked for almost 40 years. In fact inheritance permits and enormous store of transmittable information upon which natural selection can act.

Probably the most famous example of natural selection in action concerns industrial melanism in the peppered moth, *Biston betularia*. Prior to the mid-19th century, this insect was always white with black speckles. In about 1850, a black variety was caught in Manchester and now such melanic forms often constitute 95 per cent or more of urban populations. *Biston betularia* rests in exposed positions, commonly on tree trunks, and relies on its camouflage for protection from bird predation. In unpolluted environments, trees are lichen covered and the speckled form is at an advantage, but where lichen has been killed by pollution and tree trunks are blackened, melanic forms are favoured. Spread of melanic forms has also occurred in some rural areas, because melanic larvae have physiological advantages over those of non-melanic moths. In this example, the selective advantage of the physiological changes is sufficient to outweigh the selective disadvantages of being conspicuous.   A.T.T.

Naturhistorisches Museum
Founded in 1876 in Vienna as the Naturhistoriches Hofmuseum although the original

Neogene

collections were purchased in 1748 by Emperor Franz Stephan Lothringen (*r* 1745–65) from a private collector. This foundation collection consisted of 30,000 specimens in the disciplines of mineralogy, palaeontology and zoology.

The study of palaeontology in the Museum is divided between the Department of Geology and Palaeontology, and the Department of Botany and Palaeobotany. The collections are particularly rich in 19th-century specimens. The exhibition galleries contain several mounted skeletons, including a moa and various mammals from Austrian ice-age sites. A.P.H.

Natur-Museum und Forschungsinstitut Senckenberg

Founded in 1817 in Frankfurt, the Museum first opened to the public in 1821. Among the founding members of the original society was Johann Christian Senckenberg (1707–72), a doctor and philanthropist; Wolfgang von Goethe (1749–1832) contributed financially to the establishment of the Museum.

The initial collections were enhanced by the specimens collected by Eduard Rüppell (1794–1884) during his African expeditions. The Museum contributed extensively to the establishment of palaeontology in Germany and founded, in 1939, the first micro-palaeontological laboratory in the country.

The exhibition galleries cover all aspects of palaeonotology and are particularly noted for their displays of vertebrates, which include ICHTHYOSAURS, PLESIOSAURS and a mummified hadrosaur. A.P.H.

Nautiloids, *see* AMMONITES.

Neanderthal man

An extinct hominid (*Homo sapiens neanderthalensis*) present in Europe during the last glaciation of the Pleistocene ice age. The first remains of Neanderthal man to be discovered were found in a cave in the Neander Valley, Germany, during 1856. Subsequent finds made it clear that this was a new and advanced form of early MAN.

In physical appearance, Neanderthal man was shorter and stouter than modern man, with limb bones within the present average for length, although possessing larger joints. The head was the most characteristic feature, with heavy ridges over the eyes, a much reduced chin and a bun-like projection at the back of the skull. The brain was on average larger than that of modern man; some specimens reached 1,600cm³ (98in³).

The Mousterian stone culture (*see* FLINT IMPLEMENTS) is almost always associated with Neanderthal finds. In this type of flint industry, flakes of flint have been carefully struck from a core and used as scrapers and knives, and may even have been bound to wooden handles.

The remains of Neanderthal man are mainly found in Europe, which he occupied during the last glaciation (beginning about 75,000 years

Neanderthal man
The average male Neanderthaler was almost 1.7m (5.5ft) tall.

ago). To survive these severe conditions he must have been extremely competent at adapting his way of living and culture to meet the environmental challenge. He also showed a concern for the dead, burying them with grave goods and flowers, which would tend to indicate a belief in an after-life.

Since the original discovery, finds have been made in the British Isles, Czechoslovakia, Israel, Italy, the USSR and Spain. The Israeli specimens are particularly interesting because they show features of Neanderthal and modern man, leading to speculation about the exact position of the Neanderthals in the evolutionary scale.

One theory is that this hominid was a distinct species that diverged from the main line of human evolution 250,000 years ago and eventually became extinct. Alternatively, the specimens found may represent the ranges of normal variation of man at that time, and these types contributed to modern man. The most likely explanation is that the Neanderthal type finally interbred with new groups of *Homo* who arrived in Europe from the east.

One interesting development concerns the calculated position of the pharynx in Neanderthals, which indicates that they were unable to produce the full range of human sounds. D.T.

Neogene

A sub-division of the CENOZOIC Era comprising the MIOCENE and PLIOCENE Periods. The term is now only infrequently used.

See also the time chart.

Neolithic

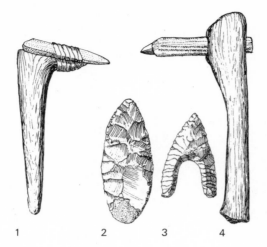

Neolithic artefacts
(1) Hoe or adze, with polished stone head.
(2) and (3) Arrowheads made by pressure flaking.
(4) Stone adze blade with antler sleeve, mounted in wooden handle.

1   2   3   4

Neolithic

The New Stone Age, sometimes called the period of the "agricultural revolution", although the term implies rapid change which, on present evidence, did not occur.

While the MESOLITHIC people of Europe and Asia were still hunters, fishers and gatherers, their contemporaries in south-western Asia were slowly beginning to cultivate and domesticate the local plants and animals (*see* DOMESTICATION). This transition seems to have occurred from 9000BC to 7000BC. The technology was still based on that of the Mesolithic, with flint microliths adapted to the new way of life. Similar cultivation and domestication of plants and animals occurred at other centres in the world – one has been recognized in China dating from about 5000BC, and another in Mexico from about 1500BC.

It seems that south-western Asia well deserves its name "fertile crescent", because the ancestors of modern cereals grew there, and the stock which later became domesticated sheep and goats were roaming wild in the area.

This new extension into agriculture forced man to adopt a settled way of life to protect his crops and animals. Now that he had a permanent home, he no longer had to migrate from cave to cave in search of game, or to carry his home, in the shape of a hide tent, with him. He could instead build houses – first of wood, and then later of sun-baked bricks (evidence for both types of structures has been found).

The grain he produced had to be stored for use either as food or for seed for the next sowing. Pottery therefore developed to provide adequate containers. The first pots were hand-made and undecorated; firing was probably accomplished in an ordinary hearth. As techniques improved, ovens were used to fire the pots, and decorations of lines and chevrons appeared. Later still, better pots were made on the potter's wheel, with intricate decorations obtained by the use of coloured clays (slips).

Trade also became important between groups of people. In south-western Asia, one of the most sought-after materials was obsidian, which occurs naturally in Anatolia. The occurrence of this jet-black material has been used by archaeologists to trace trade routes in south-western Asia and the Mediterranean.

The technique of agriculture spread outwards into Europe and Asia, but the process was slow and it has been estimated, for instance, that it took 3,000 years to spread from Greece to Denmark.   D.T.

Nopsca, Baron Franz (1877–1933)

Palaeontologist (born in Hatzog, Romania) who described Cretaceous dinosaurs and researched on their relationships, classification and evolution. While still a student, he described his first dinosaur, *Limnosaurus*, the remains of which had been discovered on his estate. The Cretaceous rocks of his homeland, Transylvania, are rich in dinosaur fossils, and Nopsca published several scientific papers on the various finds, travelling widely to examine comparative material and spending some time in Great Britain. His writing turned from descriptive papers to more general classifications.

After the first world war, Nopsca's fortunes altered; his estate became split between Hungary and Romania. For a while he was President of the Hungarian Geological Survey, but continual quarrelling forced him to resign. Nopsca committed suicide after killing his secretary.   A.P.H.

Nothosaurs

An extinct suborder (Nothosauria) of euryapsid REPTILES forming a sub-division of the order Sauropterygia.

They were one of the first groups of reptiles to return to the sea, and show the beginnings of several features that heralded the more extreme specializations of the later PLESIOSAURS. The neck was more elongated than in most contemporary reptiles, and the snout was long, with numerous sharp-pointed teeth eminently suitable for trapping fish. The bones of the shoulder girdle were powerfully constructed and the forelimbs had become longer and more massive than the hindlimbs – a condition in marked contrast to that of less specialized reptiles.

The limbs demonstrate the first stages in the development of paddles: the epipodials (radius–ulna and tibia–fibula) were shortened, the phalanges had increased in number and length, and the feet were webbed. It is clear that the limbs could function as organs of propulsion through the water. The tail remained long, as in reptiles generally, but bore a fin along most of its length on its upper surface, suggesting that the major propulsive force was provided by side-to-side movement of the tail.

The nothosaurs lived along the shores of the TETHYS Sea. They are known from England, The Netherlands, Germany and Switzerland, to China and Japan, as well as on the northern shores of GONDWANALAND in Tunisia, Jordan and Israel, with a single record in greater India. Sea cave deposits from south-western Poland contain enormous quantities of nothosaur bones together with fish remains, and the impression is that nothosaurs were the dominant animals

Notoungulates

Nothosaurs
Nothosaurus *was a common member of this Triassic group from which the plesiosaurs arose. Length: about 3m (10ft)*

inhabiting the sea shores. They do not seem to have been ocean-going forms, like the ICHTHYOSAURS or their own descendants, the plesiosaurs, but were evidently land-based, living as both scavengers and fishers.

One remarkable specimen from Switzerland is surrounded by seven other small individuals, which were initially interpreted as newly-born young, inferring that the nothosaurs gave birth to live young in the same way as the ichthyosaurs. A detailed study of these remains shows that the larger animal and the small forms belong to different genera: the small nothosaurs may have been scavenging on the corpse of the large individual only to be themselves overcome in the glutinous black mud.

By the end of the Triassic the nothosaurs had already yielded the plesiosaurs, so that although they themselves became extinct their descendants nevertheless continued to flourish throughout the rest of the Mesozoic.   L.B.H.

Notoungulates

An extinct order of hoofed mammals that flourished in South America thoughout the Cenozoic. The Notoungulata is a diverse assemblage, including the massive toxodonts (with the clawed homalodotheres), the rodent-like typotheres, the hegetotheres which paralleled rabbits and hares in appearance, and the primitive early forms (Notioprogonia). All these types display a uniquely specialized auditory region with a hollow, inflated bulla that communicates with a second chamber inside the squamosal bone. An additional common characteristic is the high zygomatic arch, and the upper molar teeth tend to develop accessory cusps in the central valley of the crown. On the lower molars, primitive genera have an entoconid occupying an isolated position inside the curve of the rear crescentic ridge.

During the Pleistocene, the commonest large ungulate in South America was apparently *Toxodon*, a massively built animal about 3 metres (10ft) long with a heavy skull, deep body, three-toed hoofed feet, and a short tail.

Toxodon first appeared during the Pliocene, where it co-existed with the related *Trigodon*, which had a horn projecting from its forehead.

Notoungulates
The massive Pleistocene *Toxodon (left) was as large as a rhinoceros, but the Eocene* Thomashuxleya *(right) was only about 1.5m (5ft) long.*

Ocean deposits

Notoungulates
Homalodotherium, *a clawed notoungulate, occurred in the South American Miocene. Length: about 2m (6.6ft)*

Notoungulates
Pachyrukhos *was common in the Miocene of South America (about the size of a rabbit).*

The line of toxodont evolution continues back through the Miocene *Nesodon*, with its second upper incisor teeth converted into tusks, to the Oligocene *Proadinotherium* and finally *Oldfieldthomasia* of the Lower Eocene.

Related to the toxodonts are two poorly known families: the Oligocene Leontiniidae and the Notohippidae. *Colpodon*, from the Upper Oligocene, was the last surviving leontiniid. These medium-sized, heavily built ungulates had been particularly common in the Lower Oligocene (*Scarrittia* and the tusked *Leontinia*). The Notohippidae have molar teeth superficially like those of horses, but the appearance of these obscure notoungulates is uncertain.

The Homalodotheriidae did not survive beyond the Lower Pliocene (*Chasicotherium*) and were probably root-eaters, with long forelimbs, clawed front feet, and plantigrade hind feet. The Miocene *Homalodotherium* was about 2 metres (6.6ft) long and had a massive skull with the nasal opening farther back than normal, suggesting the presence of a tapir-like

snout in life. The Early Oligocene genus, *Asmodeus*, was a large form, generally similar to *Homalodotherium*, but the diverse Palaeocene–Eocene members of the group are much more generalized notoungulates assigned to the Isotemnidae. They include *Thomashuxleya*, about 1.5 metres (5ft) long, which lacks the disproportionately elongated forelimbs of more advanced types, and *Periphragnis* with short, hoofed feet.

The Typotheria includes two families of relatively small notoungulates. *Typotherium* itself was a Pliocene–Pleistocene genus which included one species as large as a black bear. It had a deep skull with a narrow, tapering snout; the first incisor teeth in the upper and lower jaws grew throughout the animal's life, and the rootless molar teeth were high crowned. There were no canine teeth, and two of the upper and three of the lower premolars had been lost.

Pseudotypotherium was a Pliocene genus, with *Eutypotherium* taking the line back through the Miocene to *Trachytherus* of the Lower Oligocene, which still retained all its premolars.

A less specialized family of typotheres, the Interatheriidae, did not survive into the Pleistocene. *Protypotherium*, the Pliocene representative of this group, had a full complement of 44 teeth, only the high-crowned cheek teeth being rootless. The short-limbed *Interatherium*, with a long tail, a short broad head and enlarged upper and lower first incisors, is a Miocene animal, and the Oligocene form was *Cochilius*. *Guilielmoscottia* occurs in the Eocene, with *Transpithecus* and *Notopithecus* present as early as the Palaeocene.

Various small, rabbit-like forms with elongated hindlegs, short tails and open-rooted chisel-pointed incisors are grouped in the Hegetotheroidea. *Pachyrukhos* ranged from the Late Oligocene to the Upper Pliocene, but did not grow as large as the abundant Miocene genus *Hegetotherium*, which first appeared in the Upper Oligocene. *Eohegetotherium* and *Eopachyrukhos* are from the Eocene, and a number of primitive genera dating back to the Palaeocene are assembled in the Archaeohyracidae.

Some of the oldest and most archaic notoungulates are included in the Notioprogonia, among them the common Eocene genus *Notostylops* and the Palaeocene–Eocene *Henricosbornia*. Two members of this order, *Arctostylops* from the Lower Eocene of North America and *Palaeostylops* from the Upper Palaeocene of Mongolia, are the only notoungulates so far discovered outside South America.   R.S.

Ocean deposits

Many deeper parts of the oceans are floored with extensive finely textured deposits termed oozes, composed principally of organic remains derived from phytoplankton (eg DIATOMS) and zooplankton (eg RADIOLARIANS, FORAMINIFERANS). Such deposits which today are characteristically accumulating slowly and far from

Old Red Sandstone

land, normally contain little terrigenous material.

The type of ooze varies according to the type of the micro-organisms. Some are entirely siliceous (radiolarian and diatomaceous oozes), others are predominantly calcareous (foraminiferal, coccolith, and pteropod oozes), or else show a mixed composition. Siliceous plankton is far less soluble than the calcareous type, whose tests (shells) are dissolved below a depth of about 4–6km (2.5–3.7 miles). Siliceous deposits occur at depths down to 8km (5 miles), where they are generally succeeded, laterally and vertically, by red clays (brown in colour and the most common type of non-biogenic sediment). In other areas, notably the central and eastern Pacific Ocean, the deep-sea floor is covered with manganese nodules which are precipitated from solutions in the sea water and surface sediment layer.

The planktonic foraminiferal genus *Globigerina* gives its name to the commonest type of calcareous ooze, which covers much of the Indian, Pacific and particularly the Atlantic basins. *Globigerina*-ooze extends northwards to the Arctic Circle and is especially abundant in the tropics. In addition to planktonic foraminiferans and subordinate siliceous remains, *Globigerina*-ooze sometimes contains local concentrations of small, pelagic pteropod and heteropod molluscs, particularly on the shallower flanks of the ocean ridges. Pteropod oozes first received scientific attention from the *Challenger* Expedition (1872–76), which discovered them in the Atlantic Ocean. Another local variety of calcareous ooze is chiefly composed of the hard parts of coccolithophorid ALGAE (coccoliths). Sedimentation rates for these calcareous oozes has been estimated to be about 1–3cm (0.4–1.2in) per 1,000 years – an extremely slow but never-ending rain of planktonic "fall-out".

Of the siliceous oozes, those formed largely from radiolarians are the most extensive. Radiolarians sometimes form more than 75 per cent of these deposits, with foraminiferans, siliceous diatoms and SPONGE spicules as additional minor components. At times, however, as in the diatomaceous oozes of the Bering Sea and the Antarctic, radiolarians are not the dominant microfossils.

It is doubtful whether all fossil deposits of siliceous and calcareous oozes are of deep-water origin. The classic Cenozoic radiolarian oozes of Barbados do appear to be true abyssal deposits, since uplifted, but many of the fossil radiolarian cherts (eg in the Ordovician of Scotland, or the Mesozoic Alpine cherts) were probably formed in only moderately deep seas which were receiving limited amounts of land-derived detritus.
J.E.P.W.

Old Red Sandstone

A fossiliferous deposit of DEVONIAN age that extends from eastern North America through the Canadian Arctic to Spitzbergen, Greenland and western Europe.

During the early days of geology in Britain, it was recognized that separating the marine Silurian deposits and the Carboniferous limestone there was a thick sequence of rocks that were mainly sandstones. Similar sandy deposits were also recognized above the coal-bearing strata. The older suite of sandstones were named the Old Red Sandstone, to distinguish them from the later New Red Sandstone.

At first the Old Red Sandstone was thought to be unfossiliferous, but it was not long before several strange-looking armoured fishes were recovered from it (*see* OSTRACODERMS). Many of the original discoveries were made by a stonemason, Hugh Miller (1802–56), who admonished his fellow workmen to improve themselves by the study of nature rather than indulging in the radical politics of the day. In 1841 Hugh Miller's classic book *The Old Red Sandstone, or New Walks in an Old Field* was published, and has since become a classic of English geological literature.

Although the Devonian system was erected in 1839 for the geological period between the Silurian and the Carboniferous, the term Old Red Sandstone has remained in constant use for the continental rocks of the Devonian as distinct from their marine equivalents.

Sediments many thousands of metres thick were deposited when the huge mountain chains of Caledonia eroded away. The collision of two continental masses previously separated by the protoatlantic or Iapetus Ocean had originally forced up these lofty ranges, and the new continent that resulted from this event is known as the Old Red Continent, to distinguish it from

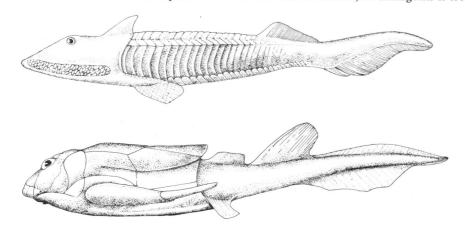

Old Red Sandstone
(1) Cephalaspis, *an ostracoderm from the Lower Old Red Sandstone, was about 30cm (1ft) long.*
(2) The placoderm Bothryolepis, *a Middle and Upper Old Red Sandstone fish, was about 38cm (15in) long.*

Olduvai

other contemporary continental masses such as Angaraland or the Tungussian Realm, which were separated from the Old Red Continent by the Uralian Ocean. The Old Red Continent was situated in equatorial and tropical latitudes, and the rivers that flowed through the land were colonized by jawless as well as jawed fishes which had previously inhabited the seas.

Some of the major evolutionary events in vertebrate history have been documented from remains discovered in the Old Red Sandstone of western Europe, eastern North America, Spitzbergen, Greenland and the Canadian Arctic around the margins of the Old Red Continent. The remains of fossil fishes are used throughout this province to correlate the different sequences of strata from one area to another. Perhaps of greater significance is the fact that it is possible to trace series of migrations from one region to another and also to identify evolutionary centres that were the source areas from which waves of migration spread to other, more distant regions. The evolution of the horse in North America and the periodic waves of migration over to Eurasia has its exact parallel among many groups of fishes found in the Old Red Sandstone.   L.B.H.

Olduvai

A gorge in Tanzania where Pleistocene deposits containing the remains of early MAN have been discovered.

The suggestion by Charles DARWIN that Africa was the evolutionary home of man has proved to be an extremely accurate forecast. Australopithecines occur in southern Africa, and spectacular finds have been made in eastern Africa in the region of the Rift Valley, Lake Victoria, LAKE RUDOLF and the OMO BASIN. One of the most famous sites in this region is Olduvai in northern Tanzania, where a gorge has been cut by Recent rivers through a fossil lake and volcanic deposits. The six identified beds cover a period of about 2 million years ranging from Early to Late Pleistocene. The fossil lake on the edge of the Serengeti plain existed for most of this time and had a rich animal life surrounding it, including man's hominid ancestors.

The first scientist to visit Olduvai was a German lepidopterist in 1911. It soon became clear that the area was rich in fossil animal bones and primitive stone tools that were sufficiently unique to be given a name of their own, the Oldowan culture.

Olduvai has become synonymous with the LEAKEY family, who started excavations in 1931. Regular excavations since then disclosed hominid occupation sites and living floors that contain animal bones and stone tools. Places have been found where animals were killed and butchered, with the stone tools used and the skeletons of the animals.

In 1959 the Leakeys found the skull of a hominid, which they called *Zinjanthropus boisei* (Zinj being the ancient name for eastern Africa and Boise the name of the financial backer of the excavation). The skull, which occurred with Oldowan pebble tools, was massive (much larger than the specimens of *Australopithecus robustus* from South Africa) and had a large sagittal crest. At the time, the most startling thing about *Zinjanthropus*, or "dear boy" as the Leakeys called him, was his date. Using the then new technique of potassium-argon dating, he was found to be in the region of 1.8 million years old.

It is now generally accepted that *Zinjanthropus* is an australopithecine, and he has been re-identified as *Australopithecus boisei*. Because he was found with an associated tool industry it was assumed that he manufactured these implements, and it was suggested that he was the descendant of *Australopithecus africanus*. This idea was dispelled quickly by the finding of a new hominid at the same level as *Australopithecus boisei*. Parts of a jaw, skull, collarbone, lower leg, foot and hand were discovered, representing two individuals. The skull indicated a cranial capacity of 650cm^3 (40in^3) – much larger than that of *Australopithecus boisei*. The other fragments demonstrated that he had a powerful grip, stood about 1.2 metres (4ft) tall and walked with an upright posture. This hominid is now thought to have been the user of the Oldowan stone tools and because of this the Leakeys called him *Homo habilis* ("handy man"). He is believed to have co-existed with *Australopithecus boisei* and may even have eaten him.   D.T.

Oligocene

The last geological period of the PALAEOGENE (a sub-division of the CENOZOIC), beginning 39 million years ago and lasting for 16.5 million years. The name is derived from two Greek words meaning "few recent" (forms of life).

The Oligocene is in many ways a transitionary epoch between the earlier and later parts of the Cenozoic. Compared with the succeeding MIOCENE there were few geographic changes, but those that did occur were of great importance. Australasia finally separated from Antarctica, permitting ocean to encircle Antarctica, and this had a marked cooling effect on other oceans, so that cool planktonic fauna and flora invading equatorial latitudes. North and South America, which had been isolated in the Middle Eocene, still remained separate, and ice formed at sea-level in Antarctica; world temperatures dropped in the oceans and on the land.

The nummulites which had been so numerous in the Eocene began to decline and by the Late Oligocene their place had been taken by large miogypsinid FORAMINIFERANS. CORALS, GASTROPODS, BIVALVES, SEA URCHINS, crabs and barnacles were all prominent in marine faunas. WHALES are known from Europe to New Zealand; they comprised the last of the archaeocetes and the first of the odontocetes (peg-toothed whales).

On land, the changing climates are reflected in the flora: areas that had tropical vegetation during the Eocene now supported plants of a more temperate type. At Bembridge on the Isle of Wight the flora includes pines, reeds, walnut, poppies and honeysuckle, although the water was still warm enough for medium-sized

Oligocene (cont'd)

crocodiles to thrive. Another feature of the landscapes was the diminishing extent of forested regions. Their place was taken by woodland savanna in which grasses were becoming prominent, as in the Florissant flora from Colorado. Mammals consequently began to evolve from browsers on leafy vegetation to forms with high-cusped teeth adapted for grazing.

Insects probably expanded too, although the fossil record is sparse. Most living orders are known to have been present, and a notable addition is the appearance of social ants and termites – soon to become the special food of large, anteating mammals. Insectivorous mammals were precluded from growing much larger than a mouse while their food had to be caught as individual insects, but as soon as insects evolved a social structure and lived in colonies, only a small expenditure of energy was necessary to secure a large food supply and the insectivorous mammals could grow large. This happened independently at least five times, ie the MONOTREME *Echidna* and the MARSUPIAL *Myrmecobius* in Australia, the EDENTATE myrmecophagids of South America, the tubulidentate aardvarks of Africa and the pholidote pangolins of Africa and Asia.

Oligocene mammal faunas are reasonably well known in Eurasia and the Americas, less so in Africa and hardly at all in Australia. In general, they display a transition from the Late Eocene peak of the archaic radiation, with the decline of many old stocks and the appearance of new groups, which became the dominant forms of the succeeding Miocene. Among those to disappear were multituberculates, primitive INSECTIVORA, most CONDYLARTHS, early PRIMATES, uintatheres, many CREODONTS, primitive tapiroids and other early PERISSODACTYLS and ARTIODACTYLS. Rising to prominence were the first true muroid RODENTS, DOGS, mustelids, cats, RHINOCEROSES, PIGS, and PECCARIES. There was some interchange between Europe and Asia although the Turgai Strait still persisted, at least in Early Oligocene times. European and North American mammals are markedly distinct, and the American fauna has its closest affinities with that of eastern Asia.

Among the carnivores, the most significant feature of the Oligocene is the decline of the creodonts, which totally disappeared from America, although they continued in the Old World until the Miocene. In the Oligocene, however, *Hyaenodon* was still an important large predatory carnivore and the emerging dogs (eg *Hesperocyon*), WEASELS AND STOATS, and cats were beginning to compete successfully. Rodents made major advances, with the appearance of the first muroids and caviomorphs. Muroids are best known today as the ubiquitous voles, rats and mice, and the caviomorphs of South America include agoutis and guinea pigs.

Perissodactyls were still a numerous and diverse order. Rhinocerotoids abounded, with the running hyracodontid *Hyracodon* in America, and amphibious amynodonts such as *Caducotherium* in Europe and *Metamynodon* in America. True rhinocerotids were represented

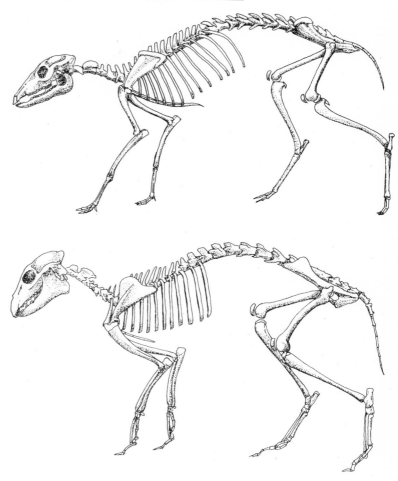

by *Caenopus* in America, *Aceratherium* in Europe and the gigantic *Baluchitherium* in Asia. Horses flourished in North America, but in Europe the PALAEOTHERES were in decline. True tapirs (*Protapirus*) also appeared in the European Oligocene and gigantic BRONTOTHERES roamed North America and Asia. Many of these perissodactyls had evolved lophodont or ridged teeth with moderately high cusps, which would have made them efficient browsers on leafy vegetation, and probably also enabled them to cope with limited amounts of grass.

Artiodactyls were less diverse than perissodactyls during the Oligocene, although in some areas they were beginning to expand rapidly. The ANTHRACOTHERES, with low-crowned (bunodont) teeth, were abundant and diverse in Asia, plentiful in Europe and present in North America and Africa. Pigs and peccaries appeared in the European Oligocene and later migrated to other continents. Small rabbit-like cainotheres were common in Europe, and early ruminants made their debut. CAMELS were another artiodactyl stock which began to become established (*Poëbrotherium*), but the dominant American artiodactyls of the Oligocene were the OREODONTS (*Merycoidodon*).

South America remained in isolation and the evolution of its native fauna continued. The Deseadan fauna of Patagonia contains numerous carnivorous marsupials, some the size of a bear, and early ground SLOTHS and

Oligocene
Above: the primitive pecoran artiodactyl Leptomeryx *appeared in the Lower Oligocene; about 60cm (2ft) long.*
Below: the early ruminant Cainotherium *first appeared in the Middle Oligocene of Europe; about 30cm (1ft) long.*

141

Omo basin

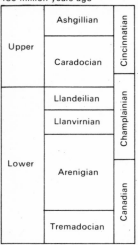

435 million years ago

Upper	Ashgillian	Cincinnatian
	Caradocian	
Lower	Llandeilian	Champlainian
	Llanvirnian	
	Arenigian	Canadian
	Tremadocian	

500 million years ago

The Ordovician succession

ARMADILLOS made their appearance. Among the exotic ungulates were small LITOPTERNS, numerous NOTOUNGULATES, large ASTRAPOTHERES and gigantic elephant-like pyrotheres. From Australia the only known Oligocene mammal is a phalanger (*Wynyardia*) from Tasmania, belated evidence of the probable Eocene arrival of marsupials on the continent.

Our knowledge of African Oligocene mammals is based solely on the FAYUM fauna from Egypt, where MASTODONS (*Palaeomastodon*) lived alongside hyracoids, rodents, creodonts, anthracotheres and primates; *Aegyptopithecus* was possibly a common ancestor of both apes and man.

See also the time chart.   R.J.G.S.

Omo basin

The site of Cenozoic deposits containing fossil vertebrates of Miocene–Pleistocene age. The Omo River rises in south-western Ethiopia, in the highlands of Kaffa province, and then flows southwards for 644km (400 miles) until it empties into the northern end of LAKE RUDOLF.

At the top of the Omo series are deposits of Upper Pleistocene age (Kibish formation) laid down during the retreat of Lake Rudolf. These deposits have yielded three incomplete crania of *Homo sapiens*, as well as remains of reedbucks, a buffalo possibly ancestral to the living *Syncerus caffer*, RHINOCEROSES (*Diceros*) and ELEPHANTS (a primitive form of *Elephas loxodonta* and an advanced type of *Elephas recki*).

The Lower Pleistocene beds of the area contain the remains of the early hominid *Australopithecus*, proboscideans (*Deinotherium*, *Archidiskodon*), rhinoceroses (*Diceros*), a three-toed HORSE (*Stylohipparion*, probably a subgenus of *Hipparion*), zebras (*Equus zebra*), an extinct species of hippopotamus, swine (*Omochoerus*, *Metridiochoerus*, *Phacochoerus*), giraffids (*Sivatherium* and an extinct species of the living genus *Giraffa*), MONKEYS (*Dinopithecus*), numerous antelopes (*Gazella*, *Antidorcas*, *Alcelaphus*, *Oryx*, *Strepsiceros* etc), a CAMEL (*Camelus*) about the size of a modern bactrian camel, a SABRE-TOOTHED CAT (*Homotherium*), crocodiles, chelonians, and a few fishes (eg *Polypterus*, *Potamotrygon*, *Tilapia*).

Some of these forms still exist in Africa today, but at a lower level in the Omo basin there is a Burdigalian (Miocene) fauna of much older character that includes MASTODON, the rhinoceros *Aceratherium*, the ANTHRACOTHERE *Brachyodus*, a coney (*Pliohyrax*), a tragulid (*Dorcatherium*), primitive deer, and swine (*Bunolistriodon*). These earlier beds clearly show evidence of repeated volcanic episodes. R.S.

Ontario Museum,
See ROYAL ONTARIO MUSEUM.

Orbigny, Alcide Charles d' (1802–57)
French naturalist (born in Couëzon, France) who established the value of invertebrate fossils to stratigraphy. He travelled to South America (1826–34) and collected a wide range of natural history specimens which were important for his formulation of ideas of zoological provinces.

In 1853 he became Professor of Palaeontology at the Muséum d'Histoire Naturelle, in Paris, a post which was specially created for him. His palaeontological researches, concentrating mainly on the Mesozoic fauna, were wide ranging and included work on FORAMINIFERANS and the compilation of such encyclopaedic works as the *Paléontologie Française*, which was continued after his death.   A.P.H.

Ordovician
The second oldest geological period of the PALAEOZOIC Era. It began about 500 million years ago, lasted for 65 million years, and was the last of the geological systems to be named, having been segregated from the overlying SILURIAN by Charles Lapworth (1842–1920) in 1879. It is named after the Ordovices, a Celtic tribe that lived in the area of Wales where rocks of this period were first identified.

Thick sequences of Ordovician sediments, in places exceeding 7,000 metres (22,970ft), are known from all the major continental regions except Antarctica. No internationally agreed position for the Cambro–Ordovician boundary exists, and the Tremadoc is sometimes consigned to the top of the CAMBRIAN; it may with equal justification be included in the Ordovician, however, and seems to have been a time when major continental regions, surrounded by epicontinental seas, were based on north-eastern USSR, North America and GONDWANALAND (composed essentially of Africa, parts of southern Europe, South America, greater India, Australia and Antarctica with the Baltic Shield also closely associated).

Slightly later in the Ordovician, during Arenig-Llanvirn times, the Baltic region formed a distinct mass separated from Gondwanaland by a mid-European ocean, and the north-eastern USSR block had closed on North America. Gondwanaland appears to have been sited with the south magnetic pole in what is now north-western Africa, the North America–north-eastern USSR block was equatorial, and the Baltic region occupied a position south of the equator. During the Ordovician, movements of the various regions tended to reduce the amount of continentality. The Iapetus Ocean between the Baltic and North American units reduced considerably in width before the Baltic and Gondwanaland blocks came together. This general closing up of isolated cratonic areas during the later part of the Ordovician is reflected in a distinct reduction in the degree of provincialism shown by the major invertebrate faunas, culminating in the essentially cosmopolitan fauna of Ashgill times.

The Ordovician climate was initially warm, as is shown by the existence of Bahamian-type tropical limestones and evaporites in many sequences. Towards the end of the period, during the Ashgill, glacial conditions existed with a south polar ice-cap centred on a point in north-western Africa. Evidence for this glacia-

Oreodonts

tion is provided by the spectacular glaciated pavements in the Anti-Atlas Mountains of Morocco. Glacial deposits are also known from Normandy, Nova Scotia, South Africa and South America, and the glacial climate is further reflected in a drastic lowering of the overall diversity in invertebrate faunas.

The Early Ordovician faunas show a major evolutionary burst, during which most Palaeozoic groups representing the major invertebrate phyla were established from relatively few Cambrian lineages. This diversification occurred remarkably quickly, and it is therefore difficult, indeed often impossible, to identify the direct ancestors of many of the Early Ordovican groups. As in the Cambrian, most known animals are marine.

The TRILOBITES form an important element in Ordovician faunas, as they did in the preceding period, being characterized by groups such as the trinucleids, calymenids, asaphids and cheirurids. Non-trilobite ARTHROPODS are chiefly represented by OSTRACODS, but other forms, notably the phyllocarids, appear sporadically. Articulate BRACHIOPODS occur in profusion, particularly in shallow-water marine deposits, with orthids and strophomenids especially abundant: representatives of the pentamerids and rhynchonellids were also present. The inarticulate brachiopods occur everywhere in Ordovician rocks, although their overall diversity is relatively low, with acrotretids and lingulids the main groups present. GRAPTOLITES form the third major element of the fauna, and consist mainly of the planktonic graptoloids, although during the Tremadoc the dendroid *Dictyonema* was notably prevalent. In the Early Ordovician (Arenig), the genera present tend to be multi-stalked with such forms as *Zygograptus* and *Tetragraptus*. The Llanvirn is typified by the "tuning-fork pendant" *Didymograptus*, and biserial forms dominated the later part of the Ordovican.

The pelecypods showed remarkable radiation during the Early Ordovician, with all the major groups becoming established. Nautiloids (*see* AMMONITES) also diversified rapidly from Late Cambrian origins, reaching their peak during the Ordovician, where they represent a significant part of many limestone faunas. GASTROPODS form a minor, and as yet poorly understood, element of Ordovician faunas along with other minor molluscan groups including the rostroconchs.

CORALS, although occurring as rarities in the Cambrian, became more abundant; rugose streptalasmids and colonial tabulates were also present, especially towards the end of the period. Knowledge of Ordovician ECHINODERMS is not extensive, but most groups, including the cystoids, CRINOIDS and early echinoids, became established; their disarticulated plates are relatively common in many limestone sequences. SPONGES were present throughout the Ordovician, isolated spicules of the hexactinellids being particularly abundant. The colonial BRYOZOANS made their first appearance, and although they were the last major invertebrate phylum to appear they evolved quickly and

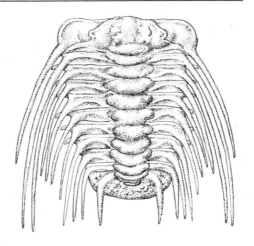

Ordovician
Selenopeltis *was an Ordovician trilobite (approx. 1 1/4 natural size).*

reached the peak of their diversity before the end of the period.

ALGAE of various types abounded in the Ordovician seas, but only those secreting a calcareous skeleton are preserved.

CONODONTS became important elements in many limestone sequences and other elements of the microfauna and microflora include FORAMINIFERANS, acritarchs and chitinozoans. Also present in micropalaeontologic preparations are dermal plates and spines of early vertebrates, presumably jawless fishes.

Thus by the end of the Ordovician only the insects, higher vertebrates and the vascular plants remain unrepresented. Although most groups present have some biostratigraphical use, the graptolites, brachiopods and trilobites are the most important.

See also the time chart.   C.P.H.

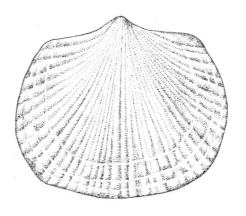

Ordovician
Onniella *was a characteristic Middle and Upper Ordovician brachiopod (approx. 5 times natural size).*

Oreodonts

An extinct family (Merycoidodontidae) of ruminant ARTIODACTYLS that are known only from North America. They were heavily built, superficially pig-like in proportions, and usually had short limbs, four-toed feet, and an elongated body with the relatively large skull supported by a short neck. They first appeared in the Early Oligocene, and quickly became so numerous that the deposits in which their remains occur are known as the "Oreodon beds".

Origin of life

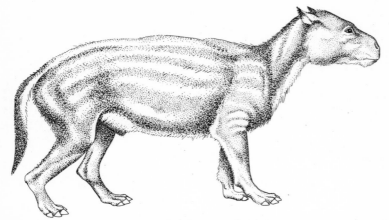

Oreodonts
The common Oligocene oreodont Merycoidodon *was about the size of a sheep.*

A full series of cheek teeth was retained, but there was no diastema and the lower canine teeth had become incisiform in most genera, their function having been taken over by enlarged first premolars that opposed chisel-like upper canines. The relationship of the oreodonts to the ruminants is evident from the nature of their cheek teeth, which had four-cusped selenodont (crescentic) crowns.

The last survivors of the family are to be found in the Pliocene, where *Ustatochoerus* persisted until the middle of the period, and represents the culmination of an evolutionary line (the Ticholeptinae) that developed moderately high-crowned teeth and were evidently grazing animals. The predecessor of this genus in the Miocene appears to be *Ticholeptus* itself, which links the *Ustatochoerus* series with the Merychyinae – a Miocene subfamily that also possessed hypsodont (high crowned) grinders.

The oreodonts attained their greatest diversity in the Miocene, and several subfamilies prospered during this period. Of the Merycochoerinae, *Merycochoerus* and *Brachyrus* were short-faced animals that apparently had an elongated flexible snout in life and were semi-aquatic, with the eye sockets and the ear openings located high in the skull. The Desmatochoerinae included *Megoreodon*, with a skull up to 35cm (14in) long, *Desmatochoerus* itself, and *Pseudodesmatochoerus*, with their Oligocene forerunners *Subdesmatochoerus* and *Prodesmatochoerus*. Among the Promerycochoerinae there were *Promerycochoerus*, *Mesoreodon* and *Promesoreodon*; Eporeodontinae and the Phenacocoelinae (an assemblage that includes several genera with conspicuous facial pits in front of the eye sockets) also had Miocene representatives.

Cyclopidius was a small Miocene form with a short, deep skull and hypsodont molar teeth. The ear openings and the huge eye sockets were placed high up, the premolar, canine and incisor teeth were reduced, and it had a short tail. This seemingly aquatic line traces back through the Late Oligocene–Lower Miocene *Leptauchenia*, with *Sespia* and *Megasespia* constituting a divergent Miocene branch of the same subfamily (the Leptaucheniinae), and *Pithecistes* probably representing the central stem.

The immensely abundant oreodonts of the Oligocene include the common *Merycoidodon*, which may occupy a central position in the evolutionary history of the family. A typical species of this genus was slightly smaller than a peccary, with a short skull incorporating a pit in front of the eye socket, five-toed forefeet that retained a vestigial first digit, and a long tail. *Genetochoerus* was a small Oligocene contemporary of *Merycoidodon* that is assigned to the same subfamily (Merycoidodontinae), possible Miocene survivors of this group including *Epigenetochoerus* and *Pseudogenetochoerus*.

The Oreonetinae (containing two small genera, *Oreonetes* and *Limnenetes*) and the Miniochoerinae (including *Miniochoerus*, *Platyochoerus*, *Stenopsochoerus* and *Parastenopsochoerus*) are restricted to the Oligocene.

Apparently related to the oreodonts were the Agriochoeridae, a family that ranged from the Eocene to the Miocene in North America. They had clawed feet, a long tail, a diastema in the tooth row, five-cusped upper molar teeth, and a molariform (or partially molariform) fourth premolar tooth. *Agriochoerus* itself is present in the Miocene and the Oligocene, its probable ancestor being *Protoreodon* from the Upper Eocene, which is close to the common stem of agriochoerids and oreodonts. R.S.

Origin of life

The subject of various theories of the physical and chemical changes on the primitive Earth that led to the development of life. In general, any organic structure that can reproduce, convert food into materials for its own use and react to external stimuli is considered to be alive.

Living organisms are extremely complex – even the most lowly. Atoms are organized into organic molecules, which are in turn arranged in regular configurations to form organelles, and organelles join to form a viable structure (a cell). The simplest possible form of life is a single cell. Cells in turn are further organized into tissues, and from tissues all higher life forms are constructed.

The oldest fossils, bacterium-like PRE-CAMBRIAN organisms from near Barberton, South Africa, are about 3,200 million years old. Although these ancient fossils have no direct bearing on how life evolved (even bacteria are complex organisms), their importance lies in demonstrating that life originated prior to that date, but just how long before is an unanswerable question. The origin of life at this early stage in the history of the Earth means that it arose under conditions that were very different from those of today.

Although the evidence is not unequivocal, it appears that the early atmosphere of the Earth (before 3,200 million years ago) was made up first of gases that originated in the Earth's interior and escaped by volcanic action, and then of gases that were a primary constituent of the atmosphere. These gases could not escape the Earth's gravitational field, so they formed an atmosphere.

The gases are hydrogen (H_2), water vapour (H_2O), carbon dioxide (CO_2), nitrogen (N_2), ammonia (NH_3), methane (CH_4), sulphur (S_2) and the halogen gases (fluorine, chlorine and bromine). Several of these, notably ammonia and methane, occur in the atmospheres of the planets Jupiter, Saturn and Uranus. Free oxygen must have been almost absent because it could only be secondarily produced from carbon dioxide and water, and would have readily oxidized (and itself been reduced by) other gases in the atmosphere. Probably, therefore, life originated in a reducing (and not an oxidizing) environment.

The oceans at this early time would also have been different from modern oceans. The condensed water vapour would have contained few products of terrestrial weathering, and must obviously have lacked an organic content, but there would have been dissolved acidic gases such as carbon dioxide and sulphur dioxide, implying some level of acidity.

A further special factor is associated with the extremely low level (or total lack) of oxygen in the primitive atmosphere. Much of the radiation arriving at the Earth today is absorbed by oxygen and ozone (O_3) in the atmosphere, so that only a small proportion reaches the surface of the planet. In the primitive atmosphere which was oxygen- and ozone-free, or nearly so, such absorption would not have occurred, so that the level of ultra-violet radiation reaching the Earth's surface would have been much higher.

From such theoretical considerations, hypotheses were put forward in the 1920s suggesting that in these primitive conditions the energy from ultra-violet radiation or lightning may have created organic molecules of large size, either in the ocean or in the hot crust of the Earth. Such molecules are the basic building bricks of life – amino acids. Having formed, these amino acids may have aggregated, probably in the primitive oceans, into units of increasing size. From this primaeval "soup", the aggregates may have gained increasingly life-like characters by random associations of different molecules, this process culminating in the production of the genetic material which controls life and reproduction.

During the 1950s, the physical constraints of these hypotheses were experimentally tested. Water vapour, ammonia and methane were mixed in a chamber and subjected to electric sparks. After circulating the fluids in these conditions for several hours, a brownish liquid resulted which on analysis contained amino acids – those building bricks of life which it had been deduced might be formed in such a way. To further the suggestion that a volcanic environment is ideal for a biological synthesis, a mixture of ammonia, methane and water vapour was passed through a heated tube at 1,000°C (1,832°F); it also produced amino acids.

Experimentation has thus shown that the first step towards life could have been taken in what was, by today's standards, a peculiar chemical environment, but by perfectly simple processes. Research is now concentrated on the next step, the aggregation of amino acids into proteins and DNA-like materials. Results indicate that this is also chemically feasible.

It therefore seems that life originated on or near the surface of the primitive Earth, in acidic, reducing conditions which were further affected by ultra-violet, electric or heat radiation. No special event for the origin of life is indicated by the theory or its experimental reconstruction. Presumably such conditions existed on Earth for a vast period, and primaeval "soups" may have developed on several occasions. In one of these "soups" life arose, and its development and evolution began.

The theory that life originated elsewhere in the solar system or farther afield and was transported to Earth on meteorites is unnecessary in a consideration of the origin of life on Earth. It is unlikely that even the most simple life form could have survived the cosmic journey in suspended animation, due to the exposure to radiation over what must have been vast periods of time, and the high temperatures experienced on entry into an atmosphere, even if only arriving from our nearest celestial neighbour. Furthermore, there is as yet no evidence of life existing elsewhere in our own solar system, despite an extensive search.   P.D.L.

Ornithischians

An extinct order of ARCHOSAURS, and one of the two groups of Mesozoic reptiles that are commonly described as DINOSAURS.

The Ornithischia ("bird-hipped") have a pelvis resembling that found in birds. The ilium and ischium are of orthodox reptilian construction, but the body of the pubis is rotated backwards and extended into a long process paralleling the shaft of the ischium. Anteriorly, the pubis has developed a new forward-projecting process (prepubis) that lies along and under the belly.

The earliest known ornithischians appeared in the Middle Triassic (*Pisanosaurus*), and by the Upper Triassic two distinct families are present: the Fabrosauridae and the Heterodontosauridae. Both were essentially bipedal, and the ORNITHOPODS, which represent the central stem of the order throughout the Jurassic and Cretaceous, retained this posture, although some large iguanodonts and the DUCK-BILLED DINOSAURS (Hadrosauridae) appear to have occasionally reverted to a quadrupedal stance, for example when feeding.

The PLATED DINOSAURS (suborder Stegosauria) were an Early Jurassic off-shoot of the ornithopod assemblage. In the Cretaceous, the ARMOURED DINOSAURS (suborder Ankylosauria) and, slightly later in time, the HORNED DINOSAURS (suborder Ceratopsia) appeared, the former possibly descendants of the stegosaurs and the latter derived from psittacosaurid ornithopods.   R.S.

Ornithopods

The central stem of the ORNITHISCHIAN group of DINOSAURS is represented by the essentially bipedal Ornithopoda, which first appeared in the Middle Triassic.

The Heterodontosauridae ranged from the

Ornithopods (cont'd)

Ornithopods
Iguanodon *was one of the largest animals of the Lower Cretaceous Wealden fauna.*
Length: up to 8m (26ft)

saurus). A single poorly known genus, *Pisanosaurus*, has been reported from the Middle Triassic of Argentina.

The Fabrosauridae contains only *Fabrosaurus*, an Upper Triassic South African genus. It attained a length of about 1 metre (3.3ft), and had short forelimbs, no cheek pouches, and cheek teeth with narrow, pointed crowns.

A line of persistently conservative ornithopods that extends from the Late Triassic until the end of the Cretaceous is grouped as the Hypsilophodontidae. None of these reptiles attained more than moderate dimensions and some were small. The long forelimbs suggest occasional reversion to quadrupedal habits. The front of the upper jaw still contained premaxillary teeth, and the cheek dentition comprised only a single row of laterally compressed grinders. Caniniform teeth do not occur, but cheek pouches were universally present.

A possible Upper Triassic representative of this family was present in China (*Tatisaurus*), but it is known only from the left ramus of a lower jaw. In the Upper Jurassic, the hypsilophodonts include *Dysalotosaurus* from TENDAGURU; *Echinodon* from southern England, and *Laosaurus* (or *Dryosaurus*) from the MORRISON FORMATION.

In the Lower Cretaceous, *Hypsilophodon* is the typical genus of the family, occurring in the European Wealden and also in North America. Attaining a length of up to 2.25 metres (7.4ft), this form had elongated hindlimbs with the shank longer than the femur, an obvious specialization for fast running. The stiff tail, supported by ossified tendons, suggests that it was extended backwards to balance the forward-inclined trunk when *Hypsilophodon* moved quickly. The forelimbs were short, with a five-fingered "hand" that may have had a partly opposable fifth digit.

The last survivors of the Hypsilophodontidae were *Parksosaurus* and *Thescelosaurus*, heavily built ornithopods of moderate size from the Late Cretaceous of North America.

In the Late Jurassic, a more specialized family of ornithopods made its appearance, the Iguanodontidae. Some of these reptiles attained a large size, and had functionally three-toed feet; the "hand" had hoof-like unguals at the

Middle to the Upper Triassic and comprises small ornithopods with a differentiated dentition: the front teeth in the upper jaw are of a carnivorous type, and there is a battery of specialized cheek teeth. Many heterodontosaurid skulls have canine-like teeth, and it is believed that they were probably males.

Abrictosaurus is a primitive heterodontosaurid from South Africa. Other members of the family from the same region include *Heterodontosaurus* itself, which is an advanced form with the teeth inset from the jaw margin (an indication that it had developed cheek pouches to retain food in the buccal cavity while it was being chewed), and *Lycorhinus* (intermediate between *Abrictosaurus* and *Heterodonto-*

Ornithopods
The ornithopod Hypsilophodon, *a cursorial dinosaur, occurred in the Lower Cretaceous.*
Length: up to 2.3m (7.5ft)

Ostracoderms

end of the second, third and fourth digits, indicating frequent reversion to quadrupedalism. A single tooth row was retained, but the premaxillary dentition had been lost.

Camptosaurus, attaining a length of up to 7 metres (23ft), is a generalized early member of this family from the Upper Jurassic of North America and Europe. It apparently persisted into the Lower Cretaceous, where the commonest iguanodont was *Iguanodon* itself – 8 metres (26ft) long, with the first finger of the "hand" projecting like a spur. *Tenotosaurus* was an Early Cretaceous genus from North America, and *Probactrosaurus* is from the Mongolian Lower Cretaceous. The last representatives of the family included *Craspedodon* (known only from specialized teeth occurring in the Santonian of Belgium) and *Rhabdodon*, a relict survivor, about 4 metres (13ft) long, which was present in Europe until the close of the Mesozoic.

The last stage of ornithopod evolution is represented by the DUCK-BILLED DINOSAURS, but there are also two other Cretaceous ornithischian families that are customarily included in the Ornithopoda. The Psittacosauridae are small dinosaurs about 1.5 metres (5ft) long, with beak-like snouts, which occur in the Lower Cretaceous of eastern Asia (*Psittacosaurus*, *Protiguanodon*) and Europe (*Stenopelix*). They appear to have been reverting to quadrupedalism and were probably the ancestors of the HORNED DINOSAURS.

The Pachycephalosauridae seem to have retained a bipedal posture, but are remarkable for their domed skulls bearing a grotesque ornamentation of spikes and rugosities. A characteristically thickened skull cap from the WEALDEN of the Isle of Wight appears to be from an early representative of the family (*Yaverlandia*), with *Stegoceras* occurring in the Upper Cretaceous of Canada and China, and the relatively large *Pachycephalosaurus* restricted to the Late Cretaceous (Lance Formation) of the USA.   R.S.

Osborn, Henry Fairfield (1857–1935)
American vertebrate palaeontologist, expedition leader and President of the AMERICAN MUSEUM OF NATURAL HISTORY. He was born in Fairfield, Connecticut, and attended Princeton University. While a student, he organized his first expeditions to Colorado and Wyoming to collect fossils. He visited England and received tuition from T. H. Huxley (1825–95), evolutionist and comparative anatomist, and Francis Balfour (1851–82), embryologist. Osborn returned to Princeton University, and moved in 1891 to the American Museum of Natural History. There he first became curator of the new Department of Vertebrate Palaeontology and, in 1908, President of the Board of Trustees.

His ability as an administrator was of considerable benefit to the Museum. He organized several major expeditions, including those to central Asia, to collect fossils, and contributed more than 600 scientific papers.   A.P.H.

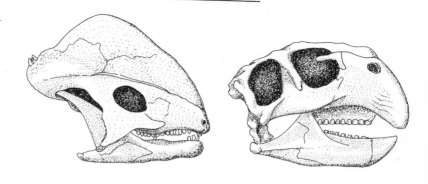

Ostracoderms
The exclusively fossil jawless vertebrates, which are characterized by the possession of bony armour, hence the collective name ostracoderms, meaning "shelled skins". The jawless vertebrates (Agnatha) are traditionally divided into two contrasting groups: those still living, and those represented only by fossil forms. The living agnathans include the parasitic lampreys and the scavenging hags, which are classified as cyclostomes ("round mouths") or marsupibranchs ("pouched gills"). They have single nostrils, lack paired fins, and are without scales. Fossil examples of this assemblage are rare, but the primitive lamprey *Mayomyzon* occurs in Upper Carboniferous rocks in North America.

The ostracoderms unite two fundamentally distinct groups that have little in common, beyond the fact that neither possessed jaws and both had a bony covering. The first group, the subclass Diplorhina ("two nostrils") with paired olfactory capsules, includes primarily the PTERASPIDS (order Heterostraci). The armour of these fishes comprised a primitive bone-like tissue, termed aspidin, which does not contain bone cell spaces and is surmounted by a superficial ornamentation of dentine tubercles or ridges. The early forms fall into two categories, one in which the armour is made up of a mosaic of small plates (tesserae) and one in which there are only four major plates (a dorsal, a ventral and paired lateral plates covering the branchial region).

In all the pteraspids there is a common opening for the gills. In some of the more advanced forms, such as *Pteraspis* itself, there is a well-defined pattern of plates and some evidence that the large plates result from the fusion of smaller elements. The pteraspids which flourished during the Middle and Upper Devonian belong to a group known as the psammosteids, an early member of which was the Lower Devonian *Drepanaspis*. This has a pattern of plates comparable to that of *Pteraspis*, although the median and lateral plates are separated by a zone of small polygonal tesserae – apparently surviving remnants from the primitive tessellated forms of the Ordovician.

A second major group included in the Diplorhina are the thelodonts (order Coelolepida). They are covered by small scales of dentine that are identical, microscopically,

Ornithopods
Left: the skull of the Upper Cretaceous pachycephalosaurid Stegoceras *was about 19cm (7.5in) long.* Psittacosaurus, *from the Upper Cretaceous of eastern Asia, was close to the ancestry of the horned dinosaurs and had a skull (right) that was about 15cm (6in) long.*

Ostracods

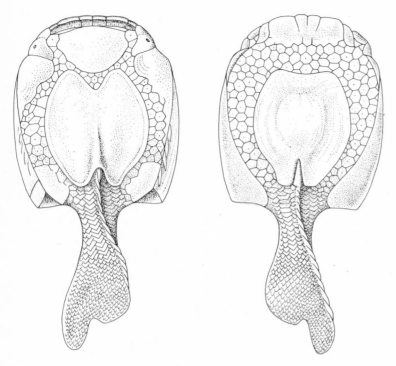

Ostracoderms
The Lower Devonian heterostracan Drepanaspis *is shown here in dorsal (left) and ventral views.*
Length: about 30cm (1ft)

Ostracoderms
(1) Jamoytius, *from the Middle Silurian of Scotland, was a primitive early anaspid about 27cm (10.5in) long.*
(2) Thelodus *was a coelolepid that ranged from the Middle Silurian through to the Lower Devonian, about 18cm (7in) long.*

and blood vessels to be investigated. The cephalaspids had paired pectoral flaps, and the tail fin possessed horizontal flaps (an unusual development among vertebrates). One of their more striking features was the development of lateral and dorsal sensory fields, a specialization of the acousticolateralis system for monitoring vibrations in the water.

The ANASPIDS, which are much more fish-like in shape, can be linked with the cephalaspids by the presence of a single nostril and the individual openings of the gill pouches. The anaspids are significant because it seems that their early members probably included the ancestors of the living lampreys.

In the galeaspids, a group of ostracoderms from the Devonian of China, the head and gill region are encased in bony armour that was superficially similar to that of certain Siberian pteraspids (the amphiaspids), but these Chinese forms must nonetheless be included in the Monorhina because they have only a single nostril on the dorsal surface of the carapace. They cannot be included within the cephalaspids proper (the group with which they show the closest affinity) because they do not possess the characteristic sensory fields.   L.B.H.

to . the ornamentation of heterostracans. Unfortunately, little is known about the internal anatomy of this group. The postero-lateral corners of the head region seem to be drawn out and acted as lateral stabilizers, and in some genera there may have been a series of separate gill openings as well as anteriorly placed eyes. The thelodonts are classified with the heterostracans because the hollow scales of both are similar in microscopic structure, but *Lepidaspis* seems to be a probable linking form between the two orders. Its overall shape is reminiscent of a thelodont, but each crenulated dentine ridge is fused onto an underlying bony plate – a condition that seems to be intermediate between a thelodont and a tessellated heterostracan.

The second group of ostracoderms are those united in the subclass Monorhina: they have only a single nasal organ and a single nostril. The most familiar of these fishes are the CEPHALASPIDS. The armour is made of bone exhibiting normal bone cell spaces, with the ornamentation of tubercles likewise made of bone, but incorporating cell processes drawn out to give a dentine-like structure termed mesodentine. The ossification of the head region has allowed details of the brain, cranial nerves

Ostracods

Microscopic CRUSTACEANS, each consisting of a hinged bivalved shell (carapace) which in life contains the head, thorax, appendages and other soft parts of the animal. Ostracods first appeared in the Cambrian, are common throughout the fossil record and remain one of the most widespread forms of aquatic life today. The phylogenetic origins of these ARTHROPODS is uncertain.

Most species have calcareous shells. Notable exceptions include the Cambrian–Ordovician Archaeocopida (a problematical order with a shell that has a high chitin content and is only slightly calcified) and members of the Myodocopida, some of which may entirely lack calcification. Externally, adult shells are either smooth or variously ornamented, and on average are about 1mm (0.04in) long. The thick-shelled Leperditicopida (eg *Leperditia*) of the Palaeozoic are, however, typically four to five times larger than most other ostracods, and the free-swimming marine Myodocopida include macroscopic forms up to 2–3cm (1in or more) in diameter.

The Ostracoda are successful colonizers of all types of aquatic environments. In the fossil record they are known from marine, brackish and freshwater sediments, an ecological range often unmatched by other coeval microfossil groups. Marine ostracods (eg most Cytheracea) are characteristically benthic (bottom-dwelling), exhibit considerable morphological diversity and occur (fossil and Recent) in shore-line to deep ocean habitats. Most pelagic Ostracóda belong to the specialized Myodocopida (Ordovician–Recent). Others, typically the smooth or poorly ornamented cypridacean and darwinulacean Podocopida, are important indicators of various non-marine

Palaeocene

aquatic environments and are extensively used as palaeo-ecological tools, especially in studies of Mesozoic and Cenozoic faunas.

Pre-adult growth includes several larval stages, and therefore any one species may show a variety of fossilized shell morphologies. In many ostracods, sexual dimorphism further augments shell polymorphism. Dimorphism can be simple, involving merely a posterior inflation in the female (Kloedenellacea), or it may be complex and prominent, as developed in various ways in the important group of Palaeozoic straight-hinged, lobate ostracods, the Palaeocopa (eg *Beyrichia*, *Primitiopsis*, *Eurychilina*). The dimorphic feature in female palaeocopes is often pouch-like and possibly functioned as an egg receptacle and a temporary home for the brood.

The biostratigraphical worth of ostracods is highlighted by their relative abundance and by their often short stratigraphical range, combined with a distribution that frequently embraces many types of sediment (clays, shales, limestones, sandstones). Differentiation of fossil types is based on details of internal features (muscle scars, hinge, inner lamella) and external characteristics (shape, outline, ornamentation) of the carapace. Rarely, freak conditions of fossilization preserves the soft parts of the animal (*Pattersoncypris* from the Cretaceous of Brazil).

Ostracods are of great importance in the correlation of all post-Cambrian systems, and at many stratigraphical levels they constitute the most significant zonal microfossils.   J.E.P.W.

Otoliths

Calcareous deposits located in the fluid-filled sacs of the ear that enable a fish to orientate itself vertically and horizontally, as well as providing it with a sense of movement (acceleration and deceleration).

The inner ear of fishes comprises three semicircular canals (an anterior, a horizontal and a posterior), which are developed from the dorsal utriculus. The ventral part of the ear is the sacculus, and from this there is a small projection, the lagena, which in mammals is developed into the coiled cochlea. In each of these fluid-filled sacs are the large calcareous otoliths, situated adjacent to patches of sensitive cells so that with any movement of the head the otolith slides over the cells. In this way the fish is able to recognize its position relative to the vertical and horizontal. The physical nature of otoliths has led to the suggestion that they may also act as depth indicators.

In fishes there are three types of otolith. The largest (known as the sagitta) is the one from the sacculus, and this generally shows well-marked growth rings from which it is possible to determine the age of the individual fish concerned. Smaller otoliths occur in the utriculus, lapillus, and ventral lagena (the asteriscus). Most species of fishes have characteristic otoliths, and can be identified from isolated examples discovered in a sediment where few identifiable fish bones occur. Many major groups of the advanced RAY-FIN FISHES are first known in the fossil record on the

basis of their otoliths. For example, the oldest bony remains of the herring group come from Cretaceous rocks, whereas their otoliths are known from the much earlier Jurassic; the armoured cowfish, the siluroids, are known from Cenozoic rocks, but their otoliths have been found in the Cretaceous; and the salmon family is first recorded from the Cenozoic but salmon otoliths have been recovered from as far back as the Jurassic. The geological record of many groups of fishes has been considerably extended by the study of otoliths.

Some fishes possess, in addition to otoliths, a series of tiny bones or ossicles associated with the ear region and with hearing. These are the Weberian ossicles, which connect the air bladder to the ear region and act as sound-conducting bones that transmit vibrations from the air bladder to the ear apparatus. There are four bones, the claustrum being the most anterior, followed by the scaphium, the intercalarium and the large tripos. These ossicles are modified parts of the vertebrae.   L.B.H.

Owen, Sir Richard (1804–92)

British anatomist, palaeontologist and first Director of the British Museum (Natural History). He was born in Lancaster, and studied medicine and surgery at Edinburgh University and St Bartholomew's Hospital, London. In 1827 he became Assistant Conservator at the Hunterian Museum of the Royal College of Surgeons, and in 1836 became the first Hunterian Professor of Comparative Anatomy and Physiology there. Leaving the College in 1856 to become Superintendent of the Natural History Departments of the British Museum, he became the first Director of the British Museum (Natural History) on the removal of the natural history collections from Bloomsbury to the new site at South Kensington in 1881.

Owen's distinguished research on fossil vertebrates included establishing the group Dinosauria in 1841, describing the giant birds of New Zealand and recognizing the true nature of ARCHAEOPTERYX, as well as the description of fossil mammals from Great Britain, Australia, South America and Asia. He wrote the first English book on general palaeontology, and was actively involved with both the Great Exhibition and the display of models of prehistoric animals at the Crystal Palace, for which he employed Benjamin HAWKINS. Owen was a friend of the Royal Family, and Queen Victoria granted him a residence in Richmond Park; he received numerous scientific awards.   A.P.H.

Palaeocene

The first geological period of the CENOZOIC Era. It began 65 million years ago and lasted for 10 million years.

Movements of the continental plates (CONTINENTAL DRIFT) during the CRETACEOUS had elevated mountain ranges such as the Rockies and opened up the Atlantic rift, allowing the seas to move northwards to about 50° latitude. About the beginning of the Palaeocene,

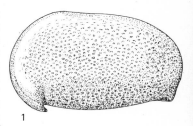
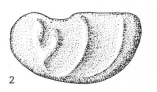

Ostracods
(1) Cypridea *occurred from the Middle Jurassic to the Lower Cretaceous (approx. 25 times natural size).*
(2) Tallinnella *was from the Ordovician (approx. 14 times natural size).*

Otoliths
(1) The shaded areas of the fluid-filled ear sacs (greatly enlarged) of Aplodinotus, *the freshwater drum, represent the positions of otoliths.*
(2) Two views of an otolith from the Lower Eocene belonging to Albula, *the living bonefish, are shown here natural size.*

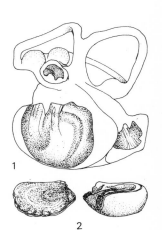

Palaeocene (cont'd)

Palaeocene
Champsosaurus, *an aquatic, fish-eating reptile, inhabited fresh water. It was common in North America and Europe during the Upper Cretaceous, Palaeocene and Eocene, but its ancestry is unknown. Although a diapsid, it is not a crocodile.*
Length: about 1.5m (5ft)

however, the seas retreated from many of the areas they had occupied in the Late Cretaceous. Seas that covered the whole of Great Britain, depositing CHALK, withdrew southwards, and the waters that separated North America into western and eastern halves also fell back; marine incursions dividing the Sahara and Australia also retreated, and similar oceanic withdrawals occurred in many other areas.

The extents of the continental land areas were dramatically enlarged, and this in turn had major effects on climates, flora and fauna. There is some evidence of a worldwide drop in temperature at about the Mesozoic–Cenozoic boundary, but the fall was not sufficient to initiate glaciation and the tropical and temporal belts soon expanded again.

Palaeocene sediments and faunas are less well known than those of any other Cenozoic period, and the large reptiles that dominated the Mesozoic are conspicuous by their absence. DINOSAURS, PLESIOSAURS, ICHTHYOSAURS, PTEROSAURS and MOSASAURS had all become extinct, as had the Cretaceous TOOTHED BIRDS.

Deposits of Palaeocene age are found mostly along the margins of the continents, either close to the coastal zones or, more often, on the continental shelf. For example, Palaeocene sediments are recorded in most Mediterranean countries, where they accumulated in the seas of the Tethyan trough. The only known extensive areas of Palaeocene continental sediments occur in North America and central Asia.

A major floral change occurred during the mid-Cretaceous, when the FLOWERING PLANTS began to dominate the land flora. Towards the end of the Cretaceous, forested areas contracted and were replaced by savanna-type habitats; in the earliest Cenozoic, however, these were not grass-dominated and many may have remained steppe or semi-desert. In the Northern Hemisphere, the Mesozoic conifer stands of *Sequoia* and *Taxodium* were largely replaced by pines, but in the Southern Hemisphere the araucarias and podocarps continued to prosper.

The Palaeocene seas contained several survivors from the Mesozoic. BELEMNITES, for example, so abundant during the Cretaceous, still occurred (although rarely) in the Palaeocene and finally became extinct during the Eocene. New stocks, however, had arisen, with GASTROPODS and BIVALVES replacing AMMONITES as the dominant molluscs. They included siphonostome gastropods (especially Cypraeidae, Fusinidae, Volutidae and Conidae), and among the bivalves *Chama*, *Crassatella* and the Veneridae became important, with the total or near extinction of Trigoniidae, rudists and *Inoceramus*. Among the SEA URCHINS, the familiar Cretaceous genera *Holectypus*, *Conulus*, *Cardiaster* and *Holaster* had disappeared, to be replaced by clypeasteroids and brissids. The FORAMINIFERANS of the Palaeocene were different stocks from those that abounded during the Cretaceous, with the rise of the Globigerinidae and the planktonic foraminiferans, which are so important in the correlation of the Cenozoic marine sequences.

SHARKS are the most abundant fishes preserved in Palaeocene strata, and they include *Odontaspis*, *Lamna*, *Myliobatis* and the gigantic *Carcharodon*. Bony fishes are also represented in some faunas, with ganoid genera (*Amia* and *Lepidosteus*), the sturgeon *Acipenser*, the eel *Albula* and the wrasse *Phyllodus*. Among Palaeocene birds there were large flightless forms such as *Diatryma*.

Palaeocene mammals are comprehensively represented only in North America, Europe and central Asia, although a few isolated specimens are known from South America and Africa. The best known European faunas of the period occur in the Paris basin; they comprise 40 per cent CONDYLARTHS (with *Arctocyon* and *Pleuraspidotherium* the most abundant genera), 25 per cent primates (notably *Plesiadapis*), and

Palaeocene
The multituberculate mammal Ptilodus *and its relatives were common in the Palaeocene forests of Europe and North America.*
Length: about 30cm (12in) from the nose to the base of the tail.

Palaeoniscids

the rest made up of CREODONTS, multi-tuberculates and INSECTIVORA. The Palaeocene mammals of Walback in eastern Germany comprise 50 per cent condylarths (with *Arctocyon* common), 40 per cent insectivores (especially *Adapisorex*), and the rest primates and creodonts; there are no multituberculates.

The Late Palaeocene mammal fauna of Mongolia comprises Cretaceous survivors (multituberculates and insectivores) and immigrants (condylarths, AMBLYPODS, pantodonts and NOTOUNGULATES). In the intermontane basins of the Rocky Mountains, Palaeocene mammals are found from Alberta to Texas. They accumulated in deposits with ferns, palms, conifers, dicotyledons, insects, molluscs, fishes, amphibians, crocodiles and lizards, all of which are indicative of warm to sub-tropical climates. The mammals belong to 14 orders and more than 100 genera, condylarths accounting for 30–40 per cent, insectivores 15–20 per cent, multituberculates 10–20 per cent, primates 10 per cent, creodonts 5–10 per cent, and marsupials, rodents, carnivores and pantodonts making up the balance.

Two generalizations emerge from a study of Palaeocene faunas. The first is that, following the extinction of the dinosaurs, the mammals expanded rapidly to fill the vacant ecological niches. In this radiation, the older Cretaceous stocks, the marsupials and non-therian mammals, waned while the therian (placental) mammals quickly diversified into carnivorous and herbivorous forms. The other generalization is that considerable similarity exists, even at generic level, in the faunas on land masses that are today separate continents isolated by vast oceans. North America and Europe shared 70 per cent of their mammalian genera in common; there was also a significant correspondence between the faunas of central Asia and North America, and even in South America and Africa similarities are found. All this points to extensive land connections, a product of low sea-levels and the immaturity of the rifting that later isolated continental blocks.

See also the time chart.   R.J.G.S.

Palaeogene

A sub-division of the CENOZOIC comprising the PALAEOCENE, EOCENE and OLIGOCENE Periods. The term is now only infrequently used.
See also the time chart.

Palaeolithic

The Old Stone Age of the Pleistocene, during which man evolved a series of stone tool cultures (*see* FLINT IMPLEMENTS) beginning with chopper cores and continuing through the Acheulian and Mousterian cultures to the "blade and burin" culture of the upper Palaeolithic.

The importance of stone implements is that, together with the few remains of man himself and of the animals he killed, they constitute significant evidence of the way early man lived, and of the technological advances he was making. By examining the progressive technology used in the manufacture of stone tools and weapons, archaeologists have classified the Palaeolithic into lower, middle and upper divisions.

The Palaeolithic lasted nearly 2 million years, during which man grew no crops and kept no animals. His whole economy was based on hunting animals and gathering edible plants. Man is the only surviving primate who has meat as a major part of his diet. This distinctive characteristic was acquired early in human evolution: *Homo habilis* caught birds, fishes and small game, and, on the evidence of the animal remains found with PEKING MAN, it seems that *Homo erectus* was also a successful hunter, despite his primitive technology.

These activities led to some important developments in the way human society evolved. To be able to hunt such large animals as the elephant needed co-operation, probably within an extended family group. The co-ordination of such activity would require accurate communication, and this is probably how human speech developed. Furthermore, because man's activities were divided between hunting game and collecting plant food, a division of labour occurred. The men assumed the duties of hunters and the women took over the collection of edible fruits, roots, nuts and berries. This would have accentuated the sexual dimorphism already present in man.

One of the most successful of the middle Palaeolithic peoples was NEANDERTHAL MAN, whose Mousterian artefacts have been found from Atlantic Europe to mid-Asia. In Neanderthal man's culture, there is evidence for the first time of religious thought and the idea of an after-life. Instead of leaving the dead where they lay, he appears to have buried them in graves in which were placed plants and animals as grave goods.

Advanced Palaeolithic peoples were probably little different from ourselves; they painted the caves of France (*see* CAVE ART) and left carved stone and bone artefacts executed with considerable skill and beauty.   D.T.

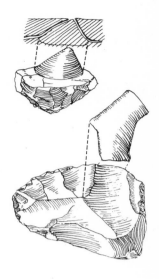

Palaeolithic
Above: a cone of percussion can be formed when flakes are struck from a flint. The presence of a well-defined cone of percussion is a characteristic of man-made stone implements.
Below: flint hand-axes were fashioned by striking to remove flakes.

Palaeoniscids

The first bony fishes (Osteichthyes) to originate from the ancestral ACANTHODIANS. They are members of the chondrostean group of RAY-FIN FISHES.

A few palaeoniscid SCALES are known from Silurian rocks, and well-preserved specimens occur from the Lower Devonian to the Cretaceous. These fishes were chiefly active predators; evidence of their diet is afforded by the occasional specimen that contains the remains of an acanthodian taken as prey.

In contrast to the LOBE-FIN FISHES, the palaeoniscids had only a single dorsal fin. Their TAIL FINS were heterocercal, and the scales were thick and heavy, comprising a basal bony or isopedin layer, a middle layer of dentine or cosmine, and a glassy outer layer of enameloid (ganoine), from which they are popularly known as ganoid fishes. The braincase is basically similar to that of acanthodians, and both groups had an amphistylic jaw suspension in which the

Palaeontology

upper jaw is directly attached to the braincase with the hyomandibular functioning as a support. The first gill, the hyoid, had been transformed into a spiracle.

The early palaeoniscids inhabited fresh water. Most were elongated or fusiform, with broad-based fleshy fins. The living bichir *Polypterus* is a surviving example of this stage, with an armour of ganoid scales and fleshy pectoral fins, but its dorsal fin consists of a series of small triangular fins and the tail is almost symmetrical. *Polypterus* is unusual among the ray-fin fishes in retaining a pair of ventral lungs.

During the early evolution of the palaeoniscids, a considerable radiation occurred. Numerous conventional palaeoniscids appeared, but others such as *Chirodus* were deep-bodied. The dorsal fin of *Chirodus* was elongated so that it ran along the back from the highest mid-point to the base of the tail, and the individual scales were elongated dorsoventrally. A contrasting specialization is found in *Tarrasius*, in which the dorsal and anal fins became continuous with the tail fin, and the pelvic fins were completely lost; the pectoral fins, however, remained fleshy, as in *Polypterus*.

One of the more advanced palaeoniscids was *Dorypterus*, a deep-bodied form that lacked scales and had the front part of the dorsal fin drawn out until it was almost as long as the entire body.   L.B.H.

Palaeoniscids
Cheirolepis *was a primitive Middle and Upper Devonian palaeoniscid (approx. 1/2 natural size).*

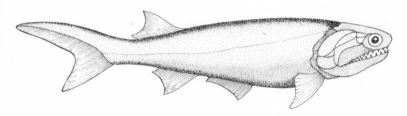

Palaeontology
The study of the past life of geological ages as revealed by fossils. The word "palaeontology" is derived from the Greek words meaning "the study of ancient beings". Fossils are the preserved remains of organisms and their activity during life, the word "fossil" meaning "anything dug up from the earth".

Palaeontology stands between the biological and the geological sciences. It consists of several defined facets, which are allied to the various branches of the subject. Linked to the biological sciences are the study of fossil plants (palaeobotany), fossil animals (palaeozoology) and MICROPALAEONTOLOGY (the study of fossil organisms with the aid of a microscope). Palynology (research on spores, pollen, dinoflagellates, acritarchs and chitinozoans) is usually regarded as distinct from micropalaeontology. Palaeobiology is a collective term for palaeozoology and palaeobotany that has come into increasing use because of renewed interest in evolutionary and biological palaeontology. Other aspects of palaeontology more closely linked with the geological sciences

are biostratigraphy and palaeoecology. Biostratigraphy (often used synonymously with stratigraphic palaeontology) is the study of the fossil content of strata, usually with correlation as its aim; palaeoecology is the study of ancient organisms and their environments.

Man has long speculated on the origin and nature of fossils. During the Stone Age, fossils were collected and used for adornment, and later became part of myth and FOLKLORE. The great Greek and Roman scholars, including Theophrastus (368BC–284BC), Strabo (54BC–AD24) and the elder Pliny (AD23–79), all pronounced on the nature of fossils with widely differing theories. During mediaeval times, it was generally accepted that fossils were formed within the Earth by a "plastic force" or "formative virtue". Such views, and others like them, were still held in the 17th century; Edward LHWYD considered fossils were formed from "moist seed-bearing vapours". Throughout the early period in the history of palaeontology, there were men of vision who began not only to explain the true nature of fossils, but also to indicate their significance. Among them were LEONARDO DA VINCI, Robert HOOKE and Niels Stensen (1638–87).

The increasing interest in the study of strata in the 18th century quickly dispelled the lingering theories of the inorganic origin of fossils, and by the commencement of the 19th century the true nature of fossils was recognized. It was also becoming clearer that they could be used in establishing a time-scale, and for correlating strata. Fossils, at least those of the invertebrates, became linked to the interpretation of strata and hence their study was readily incorporated into the science of geology. Palaeontology was set to become the handmaiden of stratigraphy, a position it continues to hold for many researchers. The splitting of palaeontological research between the geological and biological communities has frequently been lamented in histories of the subject.

The domination of palaeontology by the geological sciences began to be seriously challenged in the 20th century, more particularly since the second world war. Such dominance was most noticeable in invertebrate palaeontology because, since the beginning of scientific palaeontology, palaeobotany and vertebrate palaeontology have attracted researchers from the botanical and zoological sciences respectively, a fact that stems from the comparative work of Adolphe-Theodore BRONGNIART and Georges CUVIER.

Palaeontology was established as a distinct discipline during the early 19th century, and in 1825, the word "palaeontologie" was introduced by H. M. D. de Blainville (1778–1850) in his *Manuel de Malacologie*. "Palaeontology" gradually replaced the older terms such as oryctology, petrefakologie and petrefaktenkunde.

The development of palaeontology in Britain owes much to the work of James Parkinson (1755–1824) and his *Organic remains of a former world* (1804–11), a popular work which was directed at the general reader. This was the

Palaeopathology

first of a series of books by various authors which laid, chiefly through the medium of illustrations, the foundations of the science of palaeontology. The continuing detailing and modification of stratigraphic horizons required more detailed fossil identification manuals. This led to the establishment of palaeontography.

The outstanding example of the era was the work of the SOWERBY family with their *Mineral Conchology* (1812–46), which can still claim to be of value to the palaeontologist, largely because of its minutely accurate coloured illustrations. The inability of their book to cope with the increasing amount of material available for publication led to the establishment of the Palaeontographical Society (1847), and its monographs are published to the present day.

Until the mid-19th century, palaeontology consisted mainly of the collection and description of fossils, with the broader systematic aspects still dominated by Cuvier's invariability of species. This was to change with the publication (1859) of Charles DARWIN's *On the Origin of Species by means of Natural Selection* which, among its other attributes, aroused great interest in palaeontology and the concepts of evolution.

The second half of the 19th century was also a time of great exploration and discovery. Many major collecting expeditions were mounted to the interior and western areas of the USA by such men as Othniel MARSH and Edward COPE. Such expeditions provided a wealth of vertebrate material for study, and did much to establish vertebrate palaeontology in North America. Such was the interest generated in the subject that a Society of (American) Vertebrate Palaeontologists was formed. It was also a period of the compilation of textbooks that attempted to survey the whole of palaeontology – the most notable among them being Karl ZITTEL's *Handbuch der Palaeontologie*, which served as a model for most of the other 19th-century compilations.

The first forty years of the 20th century witnessed great changes in the general emphasis of palaeontology, due mainly to the involvement of the large commercial companies in prospecting for oil. This became the era of the micro-palaeontologist. The palaeontological community was relatively slow to develop, and for many years lacked any professional soceites of its own, relying on the geological organizations to provide a focal point for meetings and publications. The first palaeontological society was the Palaeontographical Society, which has already been mentioned.

In the USA, the Paleontological Society was founded in 1908, and was itself an outgrowth from the Society of (American) Vertebrate Paleontologists. Reflecting the increasing economic importance of palaeontology in the 20th century, the Society of Economic Palaeontologists and Mineralogists was established in 1926. Several other countries now have societies devoted exclusively to palaeontology, eg Argentina, Australia, West Germany, India, Italy, Japan, USSR, Switzerland and Great Britain.

The general development and evolution of the universities during the 19th century provided palaeontologists with a much needed academic environment, although palaeontological posts were usually within departments of geology. The development of the geological surveys also assisted in the professional development of palaeontology.

Collections of fossils often have long and varied histories. Although several museums had major collections of fossils before the turn of the 18th century, most of the early "cabinets of fossils" were either the property of individuals (eg *see* Gideon MANTELL) or belonged to the learned societies. The gradual development of museums, especially the national museums, was of major importance to the establishment and maintenance of fossil collections.

See also AMERICAN MUSEUM OF NATURAL HISTORY, AMERICAN NATIONAL MUSEUM OF NATURAL HISTORY, ARGENTINE NATURAL SCIENCE MUSEUM, AUSTRALIAN MUSEUM, BRITISH MUSEUM (NATURAL HISTORY), CANADIAN NATIONAL MUSEUM OF NATURAL SCIENCES, CLEVELAND MUSEUM OF NATURAL HISTORY, FIELD MUSEUM OF NATURAL HISTORY, KENYAN NATIONAL MUSEUM, MUSÉUM NATIONAL D'HISTOIRE NATURELLE, MUSEUM OF COMPARATIVE ZOOLOGY, NÁRODNÍ MUSEUM, NATURHISTORISCHES MUSEUM, NATUR-MUSEUM UND FORSCHUNGSINSTITUT, PEABODY MUSEUM OF NATURAL HISTORY, ROYAL ONTARIO MUSEUM and SOUTH AFRICAN MUSEUM.   A.P.H.

Palaeopathology

The study of disease in fossil material is rarely possible unless the disease process has directly affected the skeleton. The usual malformations seen are due to trauma, which in some instances were clearly the cause of death. Numerous baboon skulls from Pleistocene cave deposits in South Africa have a characteristic double fracture which could have been caused by a blow from a blunt instrument wielded by a right-handed adversary. The long bones of antelopes with their double condyle are most likely to have been used as such a weapon, and the wielder was undoubtedly the hominid *Australopithecus*. Some australopithecines appear to have suffered a similar fate. Perhaps the most poignant fossil is of an australopithecine child with fractures that could only have been made as the child was carried off with its head held firmly in the jaws of a leopard. A different occurrence is seen in a skull of the Oligocene sabre-toothed cat *Nimravus* which had been stabbed in the head by another North American sabre-tooth, *Eusmilus*. The canine tooth penetrated the frontal sinuses but, in spite of the damage, the wound had subsequently healed.

A wound of unknown origin is preserved in the femur of *Homo erectus erectus* (JAVA MAN). Near the head of the femur is an irregular bony outgrowth that has been interpreted as a bone cancer. This exostosis is probably better interpreted as having been produced by the ossification of a blood clot or haematoma formed from a wound which caused a large amount of internal bleeding in the thigh. Fractures of

Palaeotheres

230 million years ago

Permian
Carboniferous
Devonian
Silurian
Ordovician
Cambrian

570 million years ago

The Palaeozoic succession

bones, such as those which occur in the tails of SAUROPOD dinosaurs, can be readily identified from the bony callus uniting the broken parts.

When wounds and fractures become infected with bacteria, the periosteum (a thick membrane covering the bone) may become inflamed (periostitis). An example of this is known from a DUCK-BILLED DINOSAUR in which the abscess that developed would have contained several litres of pus; there must have been a suppurating sore during the latter part of the animal's life. A few sauropod tails show examples of osteomyelitis, in which the infection has invaded the cavity of the bone itself. These secondary infections are rare in fossil material.

One of the clearest examples of infection is seen in the teeth of *Homo rhodesiensis* (Rhodesia man). The cheek teeth show large cavities caused by dental caries, and the bone had been eroded around the roots of the teeth as a consequence of dental abscesses. One massive abscess on the side of the head excavated a large circular hole in the skull and is likely to have severed a major blood vessel within the braincase, bringing about the death of the individual.

The most common bone disease seen in fossils is osteoarthritis, a degenerative disease which affects joints and erodes the joint surfaces. As a reaction, there is a proliferation of bone around the margin of the affected part which shows itself in a characteristic lipping, termed osteophytosis. In time this lipping may result in the complete fusion, or ankylosis, of two adjacent bones.

The first complete neanderthal skeleton to be found was that of an old man who had lost most of his teeth and whose neck and backbone were severely distorted by disease. As a consequence, a shambling ape-like posture and gait was incorrectly attributed to NEANDERTHAL MAN, and the mistake was not corrected for almost half a century.

See also EXTINCTION.   L.B.H.

Palaeotheres

Early representatives of the HORSE group that were extremely common in the Eocene and

Oligocene of Europe, where they are characteristic of lower Cenozoic vertebrate faunas.

Hyracotherium, the oldest known and most primitive member of the horse lineage, occurred in North America and Europe. In the Western Hemisphere its descendants retained lightly built proportions, but in Europe early horse evolution followed a different course with the development of large, heavily built animals that retained low-crowned teeth, three- or four-toed forefeet and three-toed hindfeet. They had reduced nasal bones that may indicate the presence of a flexible, tapir-like snout.

The Old World line of descent from *Hyracotherium* seems to have passed initially through the Lower Eocene *Propachynolophus* (with slightly higher-crowned cheek teeth than the ancestral genus), but then apparently separated into two or more divergent branches. *Anchilophus* (Middle and Upper Eocene) remained small and slenderly proportioned, and *Pachynolophus* (also Middle and Upper Eocene) seems to have been an open-country dweller; *Propalaeotherium* became the largest of all known Eocene equids with a skull exceeding 25cm (10in) in length and a geographical range that extended to China.

The typical swamp and forest palaeotheres of the Late Eocene (*Palaeotherium* itself and *Lophiotherium*) probably originated from a point close to *Propalaeotherium*, but by the dawn of the Oligocene the early Cenozoic forests were giving place to grassland. *Palaeotherium* survived into the Lower Oligocene, as did another Eocene genus, *Paloplotherium* (*Plagiolophus*), which was a more specialized form with higher-crowned teeth, only three toes in the forefeet, and enlarged middle toes. Thereafter, the palaeotheres becomes extinct.   R.S.

Palaeozoic

The era of "ancient life" in the history of the Earth. It comprises the CAMBRIAN, ORDOVICIAN and SILURIAN Periods (the Lower Palaeozoic), followed by the DEVONIAN, CARBONIFEROUS (MISSISSIPPIAN and PENNSYLVANIAN) and PERMIAN (the Upper Palaeozoic).

See also the time chart.   R.S.

Pangaea

A single supercontinent that can be re-created if the continental regions now bordering the Atlantic and Indian Oceans are fitted together by eliminating the intervening oceanic crust. It was named by Alfred Wegener (1880–1930), the pioneer protagonist of CONTINENTAL DRIFT. If it is assumed that the Earth possessed its modern dimensions throughout much of geological time, Pangaea can be divided into a northern region called Laurasia and a southern region called GONDWANALAND. These two halves of the continental crust were almost separated by an equatorial sea – the TETHYS – which widened eastwards from Europe towards a Pacific Ocean much larger than its modern counterpart. The Alpine–Himalayan mountain chains are thought to represent the ancient crust and sedi-

Palaeotheres
Palaeotherium, from the Upper Eocene and Lower Oligocene of Europe, stood about 75cm (30in) at the shoulder.

Peking man

ments of the Tethyan Sea which have been thrusted and folded by the developments of the modern Indian and South Atlantic Oceans as the Tethys shrank in size.

Some geologists believe there is evidence that the Earth has gradually grown larger during geological time. Using ocean-floor spreading patterns, they can reconstruct a supercontinent that fits together more completely, and is not divided by a Tethyan Sea. A major wrench fault and fold belt along the general line of the Alpine–Himalayan mountain chains was occupied by a comparatively small, Mediterranean-like Tethys. Major differences between the fauna and flora of Laurasia and those of Gondwanaland have been recognized, but these anomalies can be better accounted for by the "expanding Earth" model.

Wegener thought that Pangaea was of Carboniferous age, and that the supercontinent broke up by continental displacement (continental drift) after that time. Palaeomagnetic and geological-match evidence from the continents and the dating of the oceanic crust show that Pangaea existed through to the Early Jurassic and did not break up before the Middle Jurassic.

See also GEOGRAPHY OF THE PAST.   H.G.O.

Peabody Museum of Natural History
Founded in 1866 by George Peabody (1795–1869) and administered by Yale University. Peabody also founded, at Harvard University, the Museum of Archaeology and Ethnology, and financed his nephew, Othniel MARSH, in his expeditions to collect fossil vertebrates.

The collections of the Museum date back to the early 19th century. The emphasis, in the vertebrate field, is now on Mesozoic and Eocene mammals, and dinosaurs of the western USA. The collections also house material from the FAYUM (Egypt) and the SIWALIKS of greater India. The exhibition galleries are arranged systematically, and include Recent as well as fossil specimens. The Hall of Mammalian Evolution was opened in 1976.   A.P.H.

Peat
The partly fossilized remains of plant communities preserved in the place in which they were growing. The contents of peat are therefore always relevant to the area in which it is found.

There are several types of peat deposit, which vary according to the nature of the landscape and the climate at the place of development. Upland or blanket peats are formed mainly from the remains of the moss *Sphagnum*, and are a response to climatic conditions. In wet uplands and in some lowland areas of poor drainage, great thicknesses of *Sphagnum* peats have developed in geologically short periods of time. *Sphagnum* peats also develop in valleys where the run-off is acidic and the drainage obstructed. In these conditions a raised bog may develop, frequently with central depths of 10 metres (33ft). Sedge peats develop in valleys and

around the edges of lakes, their main components being various members of the Cyperaceae.

The degree of preservation of the plant remains in peat bogs varies considerably, and in some peats almost no structure remains. Most peats, however, contain great numbers of pollen grains and therefore preserve a record of the surrounding area's development.   J.W.F.

Peking man
An extinct subspecies of *Homo erectus* (*Homo erectus pekinensis*) from Choukoutien, 60km (37 miles) south-west of Peking.

The first evidence of early MAN in eastern Asia came from the shops of Chinese druggists, who ground fossils to powder for medicinal purposes. In 1903 some of these fossils were recognized as belonging to either an ape or a hominid.

Following the final recognition of JAVA MAN as a hominid, excavations began at Choukoutien ("Dragon Bone Hill") in 1921, but it was not until 1926 that two hominid teeth were discovered, followed by the finding of a molar tooth a year later. On the evidence of these teeth, Davidson Black (1884–1934), from the medical school of Peking, described a new hominid, *Sinanthropus pekinensis*.

The deposits of the Choukoutien caves were rich in hominid material, and skulls, limb bones and jaws from approximately 40 individuals were obtained. Associated with these remains were FLINT IMPLEMENTS, many animal bones, and evidence of the first use of fire by man.

Animal bones were found more frequently than could be explained by casual accumulation and on this evidence it is thought that Peking man was a hunter. His diet appears to have included deer, elephants and rhinoceroses, probably supplemented by fruits and berries. The finding of broken and charred human bones possibly indicates cannibalism. Fire was undoubtedly of great importance for warmth (Peking man represents the first occurrence of hominids outside the tropics) and for keeping large predators away.

Peking man was present at Choukoutien about 0.5 million–0.75 million years ago, making him a contemporary of later Java man, whom he resembled in many ways, although possessing a larger brain.   D.T.

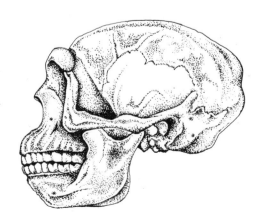

Peking man
The skull of an adult female of Homo erectus pekinensis.

Pelycosaurs

Pelycosaurs
The herbivorous pelycosaur
Edaphosaurus *first appeared in
the Upper Pennsylvanian and
became common in the Lower
Permian.*
Length: about 3.3m (11ft)

Pelycosaurs
(1) Casea *was an herbivorous
pelycosaur about 1.2m (4ft) long.
(2)* Dimetrodon, *a common Lower
Permian carnivorous pelycosaur,
was 3.3m (11ft) long.*

Pelycosaurs

An order (Pelycosauria) of synapsid REPTILES that became the dominant land animals of the Lower Permian. They were one of the earliest groups of reptiles to diverge from the central COTYLOSAUR stem, and represent the first step in the eventual evolution of mammals from reptiles.

There are three suborders of pelycosaurs: the conservative Ophiacodontia, the carnivorous Sphenacodontia, and the herbivorous Edaphosauria. The ophiacodonts were still sprawling, short-legged reptiles, with hindlimbs noticeably longer than the forelimbs *Clepsydrops* is an early (Upper Pennsylvanian) genus and by the Lower Permian this line of pelycosaur evolution was represented by the still primitive *Varanosaurus*, which measured about 1 metre (3.3ft) in length.

Varanosaurus probably lived on PALAEONISCID fishes and co-existed in the Texas Red Beds with its morphological successor, *Ophiacodon*, a large reptile up to 3.75 metres (12ft) in length

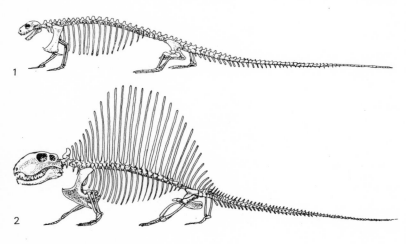

with a high, narrow skull and an elongated snout. A specialized group of ophiacodonts, the Eothyrididae, includes the short-faced *Eothyris* with two pairs of large caniniform teeth, and several other poorly known forms.

The most formidable terrestrial predators of the Early Permian, however, were the sphenacodonts. *Varanops* was a small North American form about 1 metre (3.3ft) long, that represents an early stage in the evolution of this group. Its skull remains low, there is no real elongation of the face, and the tooth row is almost straight.

The more advanced Sphenacodontidae had evolved high, long-snouted skulls in which the upper tooth row was interrupted by a marked "step" at the point where the two pairs of massive caniniform elements were implanted. The front teeth were becoming more incisiform in character, and the teeth were fewer as well as closer together. At the angle of the lower jaw there was a characteristic notch, and the limbs were more slender than those of ophiacodonts.

Haptodus is a conservative form, occurring in the Upper Pennsylvanian of Kansas and the Lower Permian of Europe, that still had only small canine teeth, but in *Sphenacodon* from New Mexico a partly differentiated carnivorous dentition is evident and the vertebral neural spines were tending to become elongated. *Dimetrodon* represents the culmination of sphenacodontid development, and it is common in the Red Beds of Texas and Oklahoma, measuring up to 3.5 metres (11.5ft) with massive caniniform teeth and enormously elongated neural spines. Presumably the spines were joined together in life by a membrane, and probably served as a temperature regulator. *Ctenosaurus* from the Bunter (Lower Triassic) of Germany may be a later survivor of this family.

Morphologically primitive herbivorous pelycosaurs are included in the Nitosauridae. These animals measured up to about 3.3 metres (11ft) and had pointed, recurved teeth. *Nitosaurus* itself is from New Mexico, whereas *Mycterosaurus* is a Texas form.

Edaphosaurus is the characteristic North American Lower Permian herbivorous pelycosaur, having first appeared in the Upper Pennsylvanian. It had a short, low skull with an essentially straight tooth row: there is no "step" in the canine region, and the dentition is composed of blunt teeth that vary little in size and are supplemented by a pair of palatal tooth batteries. The greatly elongated neural spines of the "sail" all bears distinctive crossbars.

A second family of advanced plant-eating pelycosaurs was the Caseidae. *Casea* itself, from Texas, measured about 1.2 metres (4ft) long and had a diminutive skull with enormous external nostrils in a projecting nasal rostrum. *Cotylorhynchus* is a similar but larger form measuring 3.75 metres (12ft) that survived into the Middle Permian, along with other caseids.

The Pelycosauria are presumably descended through some unknown common ancestor from captorhinomorph cotylosaurs. The origin of the MAMMAL-LIKE REPTILES is almost certainly to be found among the sphenacodonts.   R.S.

Pennsylvanian

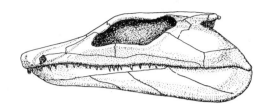

Penguins

Flightless, semi-aquatic birds of the order Sphenisciformes which have been restricted throughout their history to the Southern Hemisphere. Fossil members of the group have been found in Australia, New Zealand, South America, Seymour Island (close to Antarctica), and southern Africa. Their geological history shows that they are one of the oldest known groups of birds, with remains occurring as far back as the Upper Eocene. Their origin, however, remains obscure. Even the earliest forms had already acquired their modern structure and habit, differing only in size and possibly in having a greater ecological range.

Some authorities claim that penguins are the descendants of flightless terrestrial birds that had taken to an aquatic environment; others believe they originated from marine flying forms, which may have belonged to the order Procellariiformes (albatrosses and petrels). These supposed flying ancestors are thought to have used their wings for swimming and because of an increase in size (which is generally believed to be advantageous for an aquatic mode of life) to have become less efficient fliers. Eventually a point was reached when it was more important for them to continue the development of flipper-like wings that improved their aquatic performance than to maintain any power of flight.

Much of the interest in fossil penguins has been centred on their large size. Unfortunately this has been exaggerated, and it is improbable that any species even approximated to the height of an average European man. The largest known forms are *Pachydyptes* and *Anthropornis*, which are said to have been, respectively, 1.6 metres (5.3ft) and 1.5 metres (4.9ft) in height, compared with the living Emperor penguin (*Aptenodytes forsteri*), which is about 90cm (3ft) tall.   C.A.W.

Pennsylvanian

An American division of the PALAEOZOIC Era corresponding to the Upper CARBONIFEROUS of European classifications. It began 310 million years ago and lasted for 30 million years. The period derives its name from the coal measures of Pennsylvania, which were formed at this time from the decaying plants of swampy forests and include sediments laid down in shallow bodies of fresh or brackish water.

Early in the Pennsylvanian, a great part of North America lay in a basin demarcated to the east and south (as far west as Texas) by mountain ranges, with Canada emergent to the north. A shallow sea in which FORAMINIFERANS abounded invaded the central basin and, while the shorelines alternately advanced and receded, the coal forests proliferated in the moist lowlands with a fauna that included amphibians, reptiles and many species of insects, including giant dragonflies.

The oldest Pennsylvanian deposits in North America, such as those at Pottsville, are barren of fossil remains, but at Joggins and North Sydney, Nova Scotia, there are the remains of Lower Pennsylvanian forests with the trunks of the trees (mostly *Sigillaria*) preserved in an upright position, just as they grew in life. When they died, the interior of the trunks decayed and became filled with mud and sand which occasionally preserved the bodies of small amphibians (eg *Dendrerpeton* and *Calligenethlon*) and early reptiles (eg *Hylonomus* and possibly a pelycosaur) that apparently lived in these old tree stumps.

The skeletons of Middle Pennsylvanian amphibians occur in concretionary nodules at Mazon Creek, Illinois (larval or immature individuals identified as *Micrerpeton*, *Mazonerpeton*) together with a probable early reptile (*Cephalerpeton*), and also in the cannel coal of Linton, Ohio (*Stegops*, *Leptophractus*, *Saurerpeton* and *Macrerpeton*).

The closing stage of the Pennsylvanian is represented by various exposures in Pennsylvania, West Virginia and Ohio (the Dunkard fauna, with the pelycosaur *Edaphosaurus*), and also by the Danville bone pocket in Illinois on the Vermillion River. The Danville site is now exhausted, but it yielded the remains of a pelycosaur (*Clepsydrops*), various amphibians (*Cricotus*, *Diplocaulus*, *Lysorophus* and a diadectid) and some fishes. The Danville material evidently accumulated in a stream or pond, and all the fossils are of water-dwelling forms.

Coal forest conditions gave place to a more arid climate at the end of the Pennsylvanian, with the deposition of red shales and sandstones in Texas at the beginning of the succeeding PERMIAN Period.

See also the time chart.   R.S.

Pennsylvanian
The skull of the labyrinthodont Megalocephalus, *a Lower and Middle Pennsylvanian loxommid, was 30.5cm (12in) long. The orbit in these amphibians was enlarged and may have accommodated a facial gland as well as the eye.*

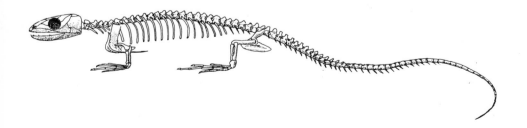

Pennsylvanian
The remains of the oldest known reptile, Hylonomus, *found inside a fossil tree stump of the Lower Pennsylvanian Coal Measures in Nova Scotia.*
Length: about 1m (3.3ft)

Perissodactyls

Upper	Thuringian	Lower Beaufort (Karroo system)
Middle	Saxonian	
Lower	Autunian	Clear Fork (Texas)
		Wichita (Texas)

280 million years ago
The Permian succession

Perissodactyls
Above: Hyracotherium, *from the Palaeocene and Lower Eocene, is also known as* Eohippus *(the drawn horse). It was no taller than 50cm (20in) at the shoulder.*
Below: Mesohippus, *from the Lower and Middle Oligocene of North America, was about 60cm (2ft) at the shoulder.*

Perissodactyls

A mammalian order of ungulates (including the HORSES, RHINOCEROSES and TAPIRS) in which the foot's axis of symmetry passes through the middle (third) toe.

The hindfeet of perissodactyls had already become three-toed as early as the Eocene, the first and fifth digits having been lost, but initially the forefeet were four-toed, with a small functional fifth digit still retained. This condition is still found in tapirs, but by the end of the Oligocene all other perissodactyls had acquired three-toed forefeet.

In the later, more advanced, members of the group the dentition underwent considerable specialization; the cheek teeth tended to become high-crowned and the premolar teeth acquired the size and shape of the molars.

The horses include the PALAEOTHERES of the Old World Eocene and Oligocene, and may conveniently be grouped with the extinct BRONTOTHERES in a suborder Hippomorpha. The tapirs and rhinoceroses constitute the suborder Ceratomorpha, and the CHALICOTHERES are segregated as the Ancylopoda. The Perissodactyla trace their origins back through the Eocene, where the lines of descent gradually converge, and it becomes increasingly difficult to distinguish between an ancestral horse (*Hyracotherium*), an early rhinoceros such as *Hyrachyus*, and some of the primitive contemporaneous tapiroid forms (lophiodonts). The order is ultimately presumed to be of condylarth origin.   R.S.

Permian

The last geological period of the PALAEOZOIC Era, named after the province of Perm in the Ural Mountains, where rocks of this age are extensively developed. The Permian began 280 million years ago and lasted for 50 million years.

The ancient supercontinent of PANGAEA was still in existence, but the equable climatic conditions that had fostered the widespread growth of coal forests during the preceding CARBONIFEROUS Period came to an end. Mountain ranges of great height were thrust up (the ancestral Alps and Rockies, the Appalachians, the Urals), volcanic activity was extensive, and the climate became diverse. Alternating wet and dry conditions in Europe and North America gradually gave way to permanent desiccation as a continental type of climate, influenced by the Appalachian and Variscan fold movements, was established.

By the end of the Permian, the seaway down eastern North America that had been such a conspicuous feature of the continent throughout the Palaeozoic finally disappeared, while the mid-continental sea which occupied the Great Plains region became progressively more saline as evaporation exceeded precipitation until it, too, ceased to exist and only a vast desert marked its former bed.

An Asiatic arid belt extended east from the Urals to the upper reaches of the Yangtse River, and ice caps on the high plateaux of southern continents spread over the lowlands as glaciers in what has become known as the Permo-Carboniferous ICE AGE. The presence of bitterly cold conditions in South America, southern Africa, the Indian sub-continent and over the whole of Australia indicate that these continents and Antarctica were at this time joined together as GONDWANALAND. Later in the period, the glaciers of the Southern Hemisphere retreated and swampy conditions prevailed in some parts of Gondwanaland, with partial deserts appearing elsewhere.

Shallow marine water, especially along the shores of the Tethys Sea, supported rich invertebrate faunas with such an abundance of globular and spindle-shaped FORAMINIFERANS (fusulinids) that some limestones of the period are composed entirely of their shells. BRYOZOANS became sufficiently numerous to build reefs, and BRACHIOPODS remained common, reaching their greatest size in the massive spiny productids and also evolving the remarkable *Richthofenia*, which closely resembled a cup-coral in appearance.

BIVALVES were common (eg *Eurydesma* of the Southern Hemisphere) and AMMONITES evolved rapidly in the open sea with goniatites persisting until the end of the period. BELEMNITES made their first appearance, but the close of Permian time brought to an end the history of several formerly prominent groups, including the TRILOBITES, the rugose corals, and fenestellid bryozoans. Neither the fusulinids nor the productids survived into the succeeding Triassic.

Fish life in the seas apparently suffered widespread extinctions towards the end of the Carboniferous, although a few primitive SHARKS

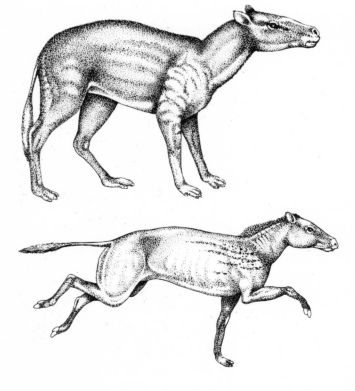

Permian (cont'd)

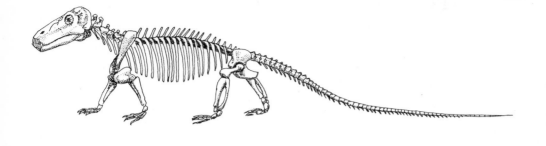

Permian
Titanophoneus, *a primitive dinocephalian reptile, lived in the Middle Permian of the* USSR. *Length: 2m (6.6ft)*

still survived (eg *Ctenacanthus* and *Janassa*).

In fresh water, PALAEONISCIDS became abundant, with holosteans appearing before the end of the period and some actinopterygians beginning to colonize saline water. COELACANTHS and LUNGFISHES continued to thrive, but rhipidistian LOBE-FIN FISHES died out early in the Permian (*Ectosteorhachis* is one of their final representatives), as did the last ACANTHODIAN (*Acanthodes*). Pleuracanth sharks began to decline after the Lower Permian, but survived into the Late Triassic in Australia.

On land, the formerly abundant scale-trees, lycopods and giant HORSETAILS dwindled in both size and numbers as the climate deteriorated, but FERNS, TREE-FERNS and seed ferns remained common in northern continents, while the GLOSSOPTERIS FLORA occurred along the margins of the Gondwana ice sheets. Modern orders of INSECTS were emerging, including bugs, cicadas and beetles, and among vertebrates the amphibians remained successful during the Early Permian. Rhachitome LABYRINTHODONTS were represented initially by forms such as the massive *Edops*, with a skull 45cm (18in) long, but this early group quickly gave place to more advanced types such as *Eryops*, 1.5 metres (5ft) in length, in North America and *Actinodon* in Europe.

Other lines of labyrinthodont evolution that prospered during the Permian include the small dissorophids (eg *Cacops*) which evolved back armour and were well adapted to a predominantly terrestrial life, the degenerate fish-eating trimerorhachids with flattened, short-snouted skulls, and the long-nosed archegosaurids that may have been trematosaur forerunners. By the end of the period, *Rhinesuchus* and its allies were initiating the neo-rhachitomous type of labyrinthodont that eventually led to the characteristic stereospondyls of the Triassic. There are also Late Permian forms suggestive of plagiosaur ancestry (eg *Peltobatrachus* from eastern Africa) and an early stage in brachyopid evolution (*Trucheosaurus*, from Australia).

Embolomeres (eg *Archeria*) were common in the Early Permian, but subsequently declined rapidly, as did the related seymouriamorphs (represented by *Diadectes* and *Seymouria* itself, among other genera, in the Lower Permian). The last ANTHRACOSAURS (eg the degenerate *Kotlassia* from the USSR) perished before the end of the period, as did the few surviving LEPOSPONDYLS.

Terrestrial Permian faunas were dominated by REPTILES, however. Although the primitive COTYLOSAURS (pareiasaurs, procolophonids and, in the early part of the period, the captorhinomorphs) were successful, there was an early flowering of synapsids in the arid "red beds" of North America and their Old World equivalents, where PELYCOSAURS achieved a pre-eminent position. Subsequently, the richly fossiliferous KARROO SYSTEM of southern Africa and the corresponding beds elsewhere in the world demonstrate the astonishing abundance of MAMMAL-LIKE REPTILES in the Late Permian.

The massive dinocephalians are numerous in

Permian
The amphibian Diplocaulus *was a degenerate Upper Pennsylvanian to Lower Permian pond-dweller from North America.*
Length: about 60cm (2ft)

Middle Permian deposits, but by the Upper Permian the dicynodonts had become the commonest tetrapods of their time. Predators included gorgonopsids, which appeared in the Middle Permian and were successful in the latter part of the period, and therocephalians (the dominant mid-Permian carnivores, but represented principally by *Whaitsia* and its allies in later beds). Towards the close of the period, some early cynodonts made their first appearance.

Other reptile groups, which subsequently proliferated in the TRIASSIC to become the dominant MESOZOIC vertebrates, are only sparsely represented from Permian deposits. Early diapsids, however, included *Youngina* and similar South African genera, and there were some primitive euryapsids (eg *Araeoscelis* and *Protorosaurus*) which showed little indication of the aquatic specializations evolved by their NOTHOSAUR and PLESIOSAUR successors.

See also the time chart.   R.S.

Permian
Discosauriscus *was a seymouriamorph from the Lower and Middle Permian of Europe (approx. natural size).*

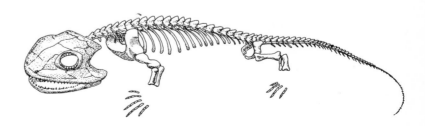

Petrified forests

Petrified forests

Areas of fossil trees where fossilization has occurred *in situ*. As the name suggests, they are literally forests that have been turned into stone. The two principal agents of petrifaction are silica and calcium carbonate, and preservation may either retain great detail or merely result in the replacement of the plant tissue by mineral material in a crystalline form.

Preservation by petrifaction occurs only when two conditions are fulfilled: a retarded rate of decay, and a supply of mineral-rich water.

Wood consists essentially of small spaces and tubes held together by a small amount of solid material. Even the individual cells are cavities surrounded by thin walls, and in life the wood is filled with liquids. After death the tissue begins to decay. The rate of decay is determined by temperature, moisture and the supply of oxygen. If oxygen is not available, for example, the micro-organisms that cause decay are excluded and the wood lasts for a long time. If a forest is buried by rising water or by volcanic activity, the first prerequisite for petrifaction is satisfied.

The second important requirement is the supply of mineral-rich water. When this is also present, the mineral-rich water soaks into the wood and the mineral crystallizes out of the solution.

The exact mechanism that leads to the replacement of the plant tissue by the mineral is not fully understood. In ideal conditions this replacement preserves even the finest structures perfectly, so that the smallest details can be studied. Sometimes the structure is lost and only the mineral is visible. If the wood has partially decayed, free crystals may develop so that the centre resembles a geode, with amethyst or other gem crystals in a siliceous petrifaction or calcite crystals in a calcareous one.

Interest in petrified forests dates from the mid-19th century when Fossil Grove in Victoria Park, Glasgow, a Carboniferous petrified forest, was discovered and excavated. In America, the town of Adamana became the headquarters for tours of Chalcedony Park, the famous Triassic petrified forest. In 1906 the ara was made the USA's second national monument, and it became a national park in 1962. J.W.F.

Phytosaurs

An extinct suborder (Phytosauria) of THECODONTIAN reptiles that are found only in Upper Triassic rocks. The alleged occurrence of a phytosaur in the Lower Triassic of Germany may reasonably be discounted: the unique specimen, *Mesorhinosuchus* (sometimes wrongly referred to as *Mesorhinus*) is of doubtful provenance, might not have been a phytosaur

at all, and was destroyed during the second world war.

The suborder comprises amphibious carnivores which closely paralleled the crocodilians in their size, structure and mode of life, but were evidently not closely related to them. Phytosaurs were heavily armoured, with a solid covering of bony plates on the back and some on the belly; the limbs, although short, showed the disparity usual in ARCHOSAURS, with the hindlimbs longer than the forelimbs. The phytosaurs differed from the crocodilians mainly in the position of the external nasal openings, which were not at the end of the long snout but situated instead in a bony crater on top of the skull, between and just in front of the eyes (so that the animal could breathe when the rest of the head was submerged below water). The elongation of the deep and narrow snout is therefore produced by the lengthening of the premaxillae, not of the nasal bones as in crocodiles. The teeth were sharp (probably for seizing fish), the pelvis was primitive, and the ankle-joint was apparently crurotarsal (*see* THECODONTIANS).

The phytosaurs must have evolved from some unknown pseudosuchian of Middle to Upper Triassic age, and they seem to have left no descendants. Their geographical range is almost entirely restricted to the modern Northern Hemisphere – chiefly the USA, Germany and greater India, although a number of Phytosaur teeth and scutes have been obtained from Madagascar. A.J.C.

Pigs

Suine ARTIODACTYLS, which include the peccaries and hippopotamuses. All have low-crowned (bunodont) teeth, short legs and four hoofed toes on each foot. The stomach usually has three compartments and their diet varies from purely vegetarian, as in hippopotamuses, to omnivorous, as in most pigs.

The true pigs or suids are restricted to the Old World, and can be traced back to the Early Oligocene. Their canine teeth are often large, retain open roots and continue to grow throughout life; the cheek teeth are multicusped and similar to two other omnivore stocks, BEARS and MAN. The last molar tooth tends to become greatly elongated.

Peccaries, known today from North and South America, fill the niches occupied by pigs in the Old World. Their canines do not become enlarged, the molar patterns remain simple, and they have a primitive cannon bone. Peccary ancestors are known from the Eurasian Oligocene and Miocene, and specimens have also been found in Pliocene deposits in South Africa. *Catagonus* is a well-known genus from the Pleistocene of South America that was thought to be extinct until living populations were found in Paraguay.

Hippopotamuses are the only aquatic artiodactyls, and also the largest members of the order. Their origin is obscure, but they may have evolved from either ANTHRACOTHERES or peccaries. Characteristic trefoil hippopotamus molar teeth first appear in Middle Miocene

Phytosaurs
Rutiodon, *from the Upper Triassic of North America and Europe, was about 3m (10ft) long.*

Placoderms

deposits of eastern Africa, and the group subsequently evolved and radiated within Africa during the late Cenozoic, migrating to Eurasia in the Pleistocene. Specimens have been found in Britain as far north as Durham.   R.J.G.S.

Pikermi

A locality near Athens where mid-Pliocene BONE BEDS containing the remains of huge numbers of mammals have accumulated at three different levels in a red marl matrix that also incorporates pebble beds and occasional layers of yellowish sand.

The individual bone beds are not much more than 30cm (1ft) thick, and within them the bones are jumbled together in a largely disarticulated state.

Isolated long bones are particularly abundant, and fully articulated feet and limbs are fairly common, indicating that many of the carcases were buried before decomposition was far advanced. Sometimes a largely complete spinal column occurs (although usually without its ribs) and occasionally the bodies of whole groups of either horses or antelopes are found clustered together.

The mammals recovered from Pikermi include numerous horses (*Hipparion*) and rhinoceroses (*Diceros, Dicerorhinus*), together with giraffids (*Helladotherium, Samotherium, Palaeotragus*), antelopes (*Tragoreas, Tragocerus, Gazella, Palaeoeas, Palaeoryx*), and occasionally specimens of *Deinotherium* and *Mastodon, Mesopithecus* skulls, the shells of tortoises, a hyaena (*Ictitherium*), a canid (*Simocyon*), the SABRE-TOOTHED CAT *Metailurus*, a large porcupine, a skunk-like form (*Promephitis*), and a marten (*Mustela*) have also been found. There are no traces of plants, and no bones of small rodents, insectivores or bats. The bodies of these animals were probably swept by flood water into a lake, where they sank and became buried. The fauna has affinities with Africa rather than Europe and represents the classic Eurasian *Hipparion* fauna of Pontian age. Similar bone beds occur on the nearby island of Samos.   R.S.

Piltdown man

A supposed "dawn man" ("*Eoanthropus*"), described from remains obtained at Piltdown in East Sussex, England.

In 1912, a lawyer and amateur archaeologist named Charles Dawson (1864–1916) took to Sir Arthur Smith WOODWARD, of the British Museum (Natural History), some fragments of a skull he said he had found in a gravel pit at Piltdown. During a series of subsequent excavations undertaken by Dawson, Woodward and the French palaeontologist Pierre Teilhard de Chardin (1881–1955), further fragments of the skull were found together with a lower jaw.

The finds indicated to Woodward that the skull of "*Eoanthropus*" had a similar brain size to modern MAN, whereas the teeth and jaw were essentially ape-like. This discovery was used to suggest that the Taung skull, found by

Raymond DART in South Africa (which had a humanoid jaw and dentition but a small brain), was an APE and not in the evolutionary line leading to man.

Although more samples similar to those discovered by Dart were being excavated, no further Piltdown-like specimens were found and doubts about the authenticity of "*Eoanthropus*" increased. In 1953, the fluoride dating technique showed that "*Eoanthropus*" was fraudulent. The skull fragments were those of a modern man, and the lower jaw was from an ape and had been deliberately modified.

Shortly before his death, J. A. Douglas (1884–1978), Professor of Geology at Oxford University from 1937 to 1950, recorded on tape his conclusion that W. J. Sollas (1849–1963), who held the Chair of Geology at Oxford University before Douglas, was the probable perpetrator of the hoax.   D.T.

Placoderms

An extinct class of early jawed fishes with a bony covering that protected the head and flanks. They first appeared in the SILURIAN, and were exceedingly abundant in the succeeding DEVONIAN.

The most numerous placoderms were the ARTHRODIRES, which constituted the major predators of the Devonian. This order acquired its name (meaning "jointed necked") because of the manner in which the head armour (bearing jaws with large shearing blades) articulated, by ball-and-socket joints, with the shoulder armour. The arthrodires seem to have been the basic placoderm stock, and from a careful study of the pattern of the bony plates that make up the dermal armour it is generally possible to see how the other groups could have been derived from them.

One group of arthrodires, called ptyctodonts, showed a striking reduction of the armour, but most of the main plates can still be identified. This suborder evolved pelvic claspers in the males and in one genus, *Ctenurella*, several specializations were developed that link the group with the living CHIMAERAS. This evidence suggests that the placoderms included the ancestors of the cartilaginous fishes (SHARKS and RAYS).

The other groups of placoderms diverged sufficiently from the basic arthrodire pattern to be classified as separate orders. The small, flattened *Phyllolepis* had the shoulder or thoracic armour reduced to a single dorsal and a pair of lateral plates, with short lateral spines. The head armour comprised a greatly expanded central dorsal plate, which developed at the expense of the other plates and had a surrounding rim of

Placoderms
The petalichthyid Lunaspis *lived in the Lower Devonian. Length: 27cm (10.5in)*

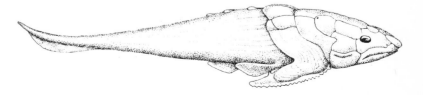

Placodonts

small platelets. At first this genus was thought to be a pteraspid OSTRACODERM, but eventually came to be recognized as a relative of the arthrodires. There is no evidence to indicate the position of the eyes and mouth, and it is difficult to guess at its mode of life, but *Phyllolepis* may have fed on microscopic food particles or been a sediment feeder, filling the ecological niche of the ostracoderms that had already died out by the Upper Devonian.

A further group of flattened placoderms, the petalichthyids (eg *Lunaspis*), have scimitar-like, laterally projecting spines. In spite of the different proportions of the body, the individual bones of the armour can be matched with the basic arthrodire pattern, except at the front of the head where there is a mosaic of minute plates. The eyes are dorsally placed and the body is covered in scales, with three median ridge-scales along the dorsal surface.

Among the placoderms there is one group, the rhenanids, which developed specializations that exactly parallel the skates and rays. They were flattened fishes with the pectoral fin enlarged to form a huge semi-circular projection which extended part way down the trunk to meet the pelvic fins. The thoracic armour was reduced to a narrow zone of bones, and the head was covered by a mosaic of small tesserae or tubercles. A few isolated bones set in this mosaic can be identified with those of the arthrodire pattern. The similarity of such genera as *Gemuendina* to the skates suggests that they might be possible ancestors, but the generally held view is that the rhenanids represent a striking example of convergent evolution.

Perhaps the most bizarre of the placoderms were the antiarchs. In this group the thoracic armour was increased, so that it covered the front half of the body, whereas the plates protecting the head were greatly reduced. The small, weak mouth was ventrally located, with the eyes and nostrils centrally placed on the top of the head. These fishes were bottom-dwelling sediment-feeders and apparently became astonishingly successful, especially during the Upper Devonian, when they filled the ecological niche left vacant by the extinction of the jawless ostracoderms. Antiarch remains have even been found in the Arctic and Antarctic.

In early members of the Antiarchi the body and tail were covered in scales, but later forms were naked. One of the most unusual aspects of the group was the structure of the pectoral fins, which were completely encased in armour and articulated at the shoulder by means of an unusual ball-and-socket joint. A goblet-like bony projection from the thoracic armour was enclosed by the upper part of the limb, and there was a single joint about half way down. In contrast to the normal vertebrate condition, all the nerves and muscles of the limbs were encased in the skeleton, paralleling the condition found in arthropods.   L.B.H.

Placodonts

An order (Placodontia) of marine REPTILES belonging to the subclass Euryapsida. They are known only from Triassic rocks laid down around the shores of the ancient TETHYS Sea in Germany, Switzerland, Palestine and Tunisia. They had short, stout bodies encased in a bony armour, with paddle-like limbs, the fingers and toes remaining separate although joined by a web of skin. The ribs were strongly angled to give the body a box-like shape and there were strong gastralia (abdominal ribs). In the more primitive forms, a mosaic of small bones was fused to the skeleton but in the last of the placodonts, *Henodus*, a complete bony carapace had been evolved. This "false turtle" closely resembled the true turtles in basic structure, even to the extent of having lost all its teeth.

The typical placodonts such as *Placodus* had a battery of huge flat crushing teeth, comparable to those of RAYS and skates. *Placodus* had three pairs of incisor-like teeth at the front of the jaws for pulling up shellfish from the sea floor, with six flat trapezoidal crushing plates towards the back of the mouth for cracking them open. In the more advanced *Placochelys*, the limbs had become paddles and the pointed tip of the snout was without teeth, forming a bony forceps-like beak for plucking shellfish off the sea bed. There were two massive oval-shaped crushing plates, as well as several smaller rounded ones.

During the Triassic, the reptiles invaded the seas and began to fill different ecological niches. The placodonts became specialized shellfish eaters and were particularly successful during the Middle Triassic, but towards the end of the period the RAY-FIN FISHES developed powerful crushing jaws and, together with skates and rays, moved in to occupy this particular niche. The placodonts in consequence rapidly went into decline. Their final representative, *Henodus*, seems to have paralleled the modern turtles, but even this was of little avail because the true turtles supervened.   L.B.H.

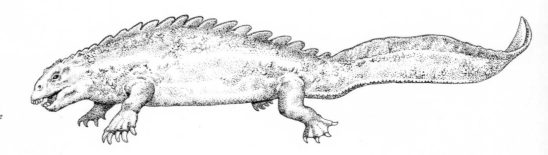

Placodonts
Placodus, *from the Lower and Middle Triassic of Europe, was a conservative representative of the aquatic placodonts.*
Length: about 2m (6.6ft)

Plated dinosaurs

Plants

Green-coloured living organisms that have roots, shoots and leaves but do not move about. The fungi and the parasitic plants (which are not green) and the ALGAE (which may not be differentiated) are accommodated without difficulty into this general concept.

To the botanist who is concerned with evolution within the plant kingdom, the distinction between plant and animal may be blurred and indistinct. Viruses and BACTERIA are not green and do not photosynthesize; the chemical nature of fungi has much in common with that of the animal world; and in the unicellular algae and protozoans, there are continuous variations from the undoubtedly plant-like to the obviously animal-like.

Evolution in plants has not been a steady progression from one form to another, but occurred in a series of bursts of activity in a few groups. Often a period of activity was followed by the extinction of all or part of such a group. Whereas the pattern of evolutionary activity within specific groups can often be readily followed, the transition from one major group to another is a more obscure process that apparently tended to coincide with periods when the environment was undergoing radical changes.

The various stages of plant evolution do not necessarily accord precisely with geological divisions. The earliest plants were algae, first recorded from rocks 3,200 million years old. Together with some fungi and bacteria, they provided the oxygen and organic food for the evolving animals, this initial stage occupying the first 2,500 million years of evolutionary time. The algae continued their evolution in watery environments, where to this day they are still important. Some members of this group, however, must have carried within them the potential for terrestrial survival and differentiation, because the next stage of development in the plant kingdom begins with the appearance of the first land plants at or slightly before the commencement of the Devonian, and includes their rapid diversification throughout the Devonian, Carboniferous and the Early Permian. During this stage, the appearance of the PSILOPHYTES, CLUB MOSSES, calamites, true FERNS, seed ferns and other early gymnosperms occurred. It is noteworthy that in this phase of plant evolution, several groups (notably the calamites and the lepidodendrons) developed gigantic forms which geologically have only a short time spread and

were extinct by the Middle Permian, leaving only small modern survivors.

The rise of the gymnosperms occurred in the Late Permian and these plants continued to flourish throughout the Mesozoic. The fossil gymnosperms were a diverse assemblage derived from Carboniferous forms and included the GLOSSOPTERIS FLORA types, CYCADS, CYCADEOIDS, and GINKGOS, as well as more readily recognizable ancestors of modern CONIFERS. The cycadeoids developed flower-like structures that bore some resemblance to the angiosperm flower, but this group was too sophisticated to be ancestral to the FLOWERING PLANTS.

The last stage of plant evolution began in the Cretaceous, and is marked by the development of flowering plants, which had assumed a dominant role in the world's flora by the beginning of the Cenozoic.   J.W.F.

Plated dinosaurs

An order (Stegosauria) of ORNITHISCHIANS, the first of the DINOSAURS to develop plates and spines for protection. The group takes its name from the Upper Jurassic genus *Stegosaurus* which occurred in the North American MORRISON FORMATION, and attained a length of up to 9 metres (30ft). Although quadrupedal, its hindlimbs were substantially longer than the forelimbs, the head was small, and along the back there were two alternating rows of bony plates that continued down the tail and terminated in two pairs of massive spikes. The largest plates in the dorsal series occurred in the hip region, where the huge sacral vertebrae were excavated to accommodate an enlargement of the spinal cord which presumably served as a subsidiary nerve centre (a similar nerve centre, of smaller size, was present in the shoulders). *Stegosaurus* is usually reconstructed with the dorsal plates in a vertical position, but it has been suggested that they might instead have lain flat. Their protective value could not have been great, and because they received a copious blood supply it is possible that their primary function was temperature regulation.

During the Upper Jurassic, a plated dinosaur was also present at TENDAGURU in eastern Africa, where *Kentrosaurus* attained a length of 5 metres (16.4ft). It had small dorsal plates along the neck and front of the body only, but carried eight pairs of elongated spines down the back and tail. In the European Late Jurassic, the imperfectly known *Dacentrurus* had forelimbs

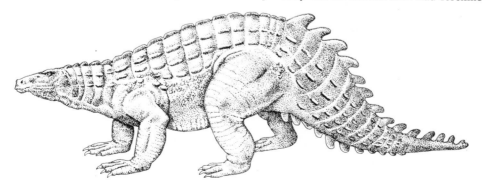

Plated dinosaurs
Scelidosaurus, *from the Lower Jurassic of southern England, was probably an early plated dinosaur.*
Length: about 4m (13ft)

Pleistocene

Plated dinosaurs
Stegosaurus *was the characteristic plated dinosaur of the North American Morrison Formation. This Upper Jurassic reptile attained a length of about 9m (30ft).*

that were longer than usual in an advanced stegosaur, and its armour apparently consisted exclusively of spines. Both these Old World genera were probably descended from *Lexovisaurus*, which occurred in the early Upper Jurassic of England and France. This form had plates and spines, as well as relatively massive forelimbs. The only known plated dinosaur from the mid-Jurassic is *Chialingosaurus* from China, a slenderly built stegosaur with proportionately long front legs and small, plate-like spines.

In the basal Lower Jurassic of England, there is a small and primitive ornithischian named *Scelidosaurus*, which attained about 4 metres (13ft) in length and may have been still partly bipedal, with the toes ending in claws instead of the hoofs of the Late Jurassic stegosaurs. This form had numerous rows of small keeled plates along its back, with additional lateral accessory rows. These features suggest that it may be the earliest known plated dinosaur, representing a stage in the evolution of the group that is still close to the essentially bipedal ORNITHOPODS.

A few stegosaurs have been reported from the Early Cretaceous but the material is, in every instance, fragmentary and identification is exceedingly doubtful. It is possible, however, that the plated dinosaurs may have been the ancestors of the ARMOURED DINOSAURS that became common in the Late Cretaceous. R.S.

Pleistocene

The concluding period of the CENOZOIC Era. The name is of Greek derivation and means "most recent", the period having begun about 1.8 million years ago and ended about 10,000 years ago.

The Pleistocene is dominated by ICE AGES, when extensive ice sheets built up in Antarctica and around the Arctic regions. The ice spread towards the equator until much of North America and Eurasia were covered, with glaciers forming in mountainous regions. Sea-levels were lowered around the world by about 100 metres (330ft) during glacial maxima, due to the large volume of water locked up in the ice sheets. Ocean currents and air circulation were in consequence greatly altered, while the vegetation belts were deflected towards the equator.

There were no major shifts in the position of the continents during the Pleistocene, but minor changes occurred. The Rift Valley fault system of Africa, extending from Rhodesia northwards into the Red Sea and Asia Minor, was active during the period, and associated with it were extensive volcanic outpourings in eastern Africa and Ethiopia. With the melting of the ice caps, sea-levels rose again, but partly compensating for this was the elevation of the land masses as the weight of the ice was removed; areas of Scandinavia and northern Canada are still rising, as is the Himalayan mountain chain. In front of the ice sheets, strong winds carried fine-grained dust great distances and deposited it as thick loess across the Sahara Desert, southern USSR and China. Glaciers caused erosion features such as U-shaped valleys, roches moutonnées and striated platforms, as well as being responsible for the accumulation of boulder clays and moraines.

Evidence for the alternation of cold and warm periods comes from a study of the fauna, and from an analysis of the isotopic composition of marine FORAMINIFERANS. Two isotopes of oxygen, O-16 and O-18, occur in a constant ratio in the oceans. When the temperature drops and water freezes, the lighter O-16 isotope freezes more readily, thus enriching the oceans in the heavier O-18. Hence animals that incorporate oxygen in their skeletons (eg foraminiferans) contain a higher proportion of O-18 in cold waters. By sampling ocean cores, which record the history of sedimentation, it is possible to construct temperature graphs.

The last ice sheets disappeared about 10,000 years ago, and the climate steadily improved to reach a warm peak about 5,000 years ago; since then it has gradually declined towards another ice age.

The marine and freshwater faunas of the Pleistocene resemble the living fauna in composition, although their distribution latitudinally has varied. The profusion of Pleistocene mammal remains is sometimes overwhelming. The Dragon Cave in Austria, for example, has yielded the remains of about 50,000 cave BEARS, and large quantities of mammal bones have been recovered from RANCHO LA BREA. Occasionally, complete MAMMOTH and RHINOCEROS carcases have been preserved in crevasses, deep frozen for more than 10,000 years.

Few living species of mammals date back to the earliest Pleistocene, although most existing families can be traced to the Miocene. The Pleistocene was an epoch of widespread extinction, including the disappearance of many gigantic forms – in part possibly due to the appearance of MAN. On some islands, however, dwarf faunas appeared, eg diminutive hippopotamuses and elephants in Malta. A feature of mammals in middle latitudes was the alternation of warm and cold faunas, reflecting successive glacial and interglacial phases.

The Northern Hemisphere had an Holarctic fauna during the Pleistocene, with lowered sea-levels that enabled many species to range across North America and Eurasia (eg mammoth, musk ox, reindeer, bison, HORSE and bear), although the Old World woolly rhinoceroses never crossed the Bering region. The North American Pleistocene faunas are rich and varied. Most of the elements comprise descendants of Pliocene forms, with squirrels, ground-squirrels, beavers, DOGS, bears, WEASELS, horses, peccaries, DEER and pronghorns. All these stocks have descendants living on the continent today, although horses became locally extinct at the end of the Pleistocene and were later re-introduced by man. TAPIRS and CAMELS were also present in the North American Pleistocene, although tapirs now range no farther north than Central America, and llamas (which are related to camels) occur in

Pleistocene
The woolly mammoth (Mammuthus primigenius) was protected by thick fur from the bitter cold of the ice age.
Height: about 3.7m (12ft) at the shoulder

Pleistocene (cont'd)

Pleistocene
The woolly rhinoceros
(Coelodonta antiquitatis).
Height: about 2m (6.6ft)

South America. SABRE-TOOTHED CATS and MASTODONS also roamed North America at this time but left no survivors. There were also a few new arrivals: glyptodonts and ground SLOTHS entered from South America, and the mammoth crossed from Asia along with several bovids (bison, saiga, musk ox and sheep).

Europe had a similarly varied Pleistocene mammal fauna. Many of the Late Pleistocene species survive today, either farther north if they are cold forms like reindeer, musk ox, bear, arctic fox, glutton, lynx, lemmings and voles, or farther south for more temperate animals such as MONKEYS, HYAENAS, CIVETS and hippopotamuses. Others, such as the cave lion, cave bear, giant deer, aurochs, mammoth and woolly rhinoceros, have become extinct – all large creatures, most of which were hunted by early man. There were several species of rhinoceroses and mammoths in the European Pleistocene. *Mammuthus primigenius* (woolly mammoth) and *Coelodonta antiquitatis* (woolly rhinoceros) frequented cold tundra; *Palaeoloxodon antiquus* (straight-tusked elephant) and *Dicerorhinus kirchbergensis* (Merck's rhinoceros) were inhabitants of warm climes. Stone implements bear witness to the presence of man in Europe in the Early Pleistocene, and by the Middle Pleistocene there are hominid bone remains from Heidelberg and Swanscombe. Later, NEANDERTHAL MAN inhabited the Mediterranean area in large numbers before radiating to other parts of Europe.

The history of mammal faunas in the Pleistocene of Asia is well documented in the USSR, China and greater India. Many European species probably originated in Asia, having migrated westwards, eg mammoths and rhinoceroses. The best known sequences are those from the SIWALIKS, but Middle Pleistocene deposits in China and Indonesia have yielded remains of PEKING MAN and JAVA MAN, with evidence of later Pleistocene man occurring at many other sites.

The tropical African faunas of today bears a close resemblance to those of the Pleistocene, although in earlier times it was much more widespread. In South Africa, caves in the Transvaal have yielded good mammal assemblages, famous for their inclusion of early hominids, notably australopithecines. Louis LEAKEY and his family have discovered prodigious quantities of Pleistocene mammals at OLDUVAI in Tanzania, LAKE RUDOLF in northern Kenya, and other sites; similar faunas have also been found in the Afar region of Ethiopia. The sediments in all these locations are waterlain, usually in lakes and rivers, and include much volcanic material which can be dated using radioisotopes. In several sites the sequences go back about 3.5 million years. The most abundant mammals were elephants, PIGS, bovids, and hippopotamuses, but monkeys, dogs, civets, CATS, hyaenas, horses, CHALICOTHERES, rhinoceroses and GIRAFFES were also present. Some of the pigs and bovids reached gigantic proportions: the bovid *Pelorovis* had a horn-core span of more than 2 metres (6.6ft), and the pig *Afrochoerus* was as big as a rhinoceros. Australopithecines abound, along with forms much closer to the ancestry of modern man, and there are sequences of tools used by early hominids.

The Australian Pleistocene mammal fauna is almost wholly MARSUPIAL and best known from sites in South Australia, with scattered localities also occurring in many other parts of the continent. It has not been possible to sub-divide the fauna into Early and Late Pleistocene, but three groups of marsupials can be recognized. First, there are species still living in the area today, ie wallabies and bandicoots. Second, there are species that now have a restricted distribution, such as the koala and *Sarcophilus* (the Tasmanian devil). Third come the extinct species, comprising a number of giant forms such as *Sthenurus* (a large kangaroo) and *Diprotodon* (the largest known marsupial), together with *Thylacinus* (the marsupial wolf) and *Thylacoleo* (the marsupial lion). New Zealand had no mammals, but giant RATITES such as the moa were present.

The pampas of Argentina has yielded rich

Plesiosaurs

Pleistocene mammal faunas, but the invasion of the continent by North American stocks had a devastating effect on the native forms, many of which were replaced in their ecological habitats by descendants of the invaders. Among the immigrants were horses, tapirs, deer, camels (*Lama*), peccaries, racoons, weasels, dogs, sabre-toothed cats and gomphotheres. Numerous endemic South American families and orders remained abundant and diversified during the Pleistocene, but did not survive into Recent times. They include toxodont and typothere NOTOUNGULATES, LITOPTERNS, ground sloths, glyptodonts and carnivorous marsupial borhyaenids. Others that survived have been greatly reduced in numbers – marsupials, rodent-like caenolestids, tree sloths, ARMADILLOS and anteaters. Cebid monkeys and caviomorph rodents are among the stocks that continue to prosper relatively undiminished, although the capybara is the only surviving giant rodent.

See also the time chart.   R.J.G.S.

Plesiosaurs

An extinct suborder (Plesiosauria) of aquatic euryapsid REPTILES forming a sub-division of the order Sauropterygia.

The plesiosaurs were ocean-going reptiles that flourished from the end of the Triassic up to the end of the Cretaceous. They had a barrel-shaped body, a short tail and paddle-like limbs for swimming. There are two sorts of plesiosaur: a long-necked type with a small head, and the short-necked plesiosaurs (pliosaurs) with a large head.

The long-necked plesiosaurs had numerous needle-sharp teeth which were eminently suitable for trapping fish. The forelimbs were larger than the hind ones, as with the nothosaurs, but the tail, while still retaining a dorsal fin, had been greatly reduced. One of the gradual changes that occurred was a shortening of the propodials (the humerus and femur). This meant that the muscles attached to the shoulder and hip girdles, which moved the paddles, also became shorter. A limb of this type was specialized for speed of movement but could not generate a powerful swimming stroke. Other gradual changes occurred in the shoulder girdle, with the scapula developing into a wide flat plate that extended in front of the shoulder joint, enabling the muscles that moved the limbs to pull just as strongly from the front as from the back. The long-necked plesiosaurs were specialized for rapid manoeuvring by twisting and turning; a backing stroke with one limb coupled with a forward swimming stroke from the limb on the other side would have effected a sharp right-angled turn. The necks also became exaggeratedly long, culminating in the Upper Cretaceous *Elasmosaurus* which had more than 70 cervical vertebrae. With such long necks, the plesiosaurs were superbly adapted for life near the surface, feeding on fish by sometimes snaking their necks through the water in search of prey, and at other times swinging the neck and head out of the water to drop onto their unsuspecting victims.

For a long time it was thought that the plesiosaurs rowed themselves through the water. A study of the muscles of the limbs (reconstructed by analysis of preserved muscle scars) and a consideration of the hydrodynamics of swimming has resulted in a different evaluation. In a few specimens, skin impressions show that the limbs were hydrofoil-shaped with, in cross-section, a tapering trailing edge. This type of limb cannot be used effectively for rowing, but works like the forelimbs of sea lions or the wings of penguins, so that swimming becomes almost underwater flight. With the long-necked forms, this includes a backwards "flying" action of the forelimbs, similar to that of the humming bird, although in the plesiosaurs this would involve only the limbs on one side of the body while the other side executed a forward action to produce a sudden turn.

The short-necked plesiosaurs also showed a gradual change from their nothosaur ancestors. The neck became shorter, with only 20 cervical vertebrae, and the head was progressively enlarged until in the biggest forms – about 12 metres (40ft) in length – up to a quarter of this measurement was made up of the skull alone. The teeth were massive and concerned more with tackling cephalopods than fish; the presence of numerous chitinous hooks from cephalopod tentacles in the stomachs of some specimens is indicative of their diet.

The shoulder girdle was not extended much in

Plesiosaurs
Elasmosaurus, *from the Upper Cretaceous of North America, had a greatly elongated neck that made up a substantial part of its overall length of 10m (33ft).*

Pliocene

Their main food seems to have been cephalo-pods, which occurred in deep waters.

The success of both kinds of plesiosaur throughout the greater part of the Mesozoic was due to the fact that they occupied different niches in the ecology of the oceans, and hence did not compete directly with one another. L.B.H.

Pliocene

The penultimate geological period of the Cenozoic Era, beginning 5 million years ago and lasting for 3.2 million years. The name is of Greek derivation and means "more recent".

CONTINENTAL DRIFT had by this time brought the land masses close to their modern positions. North and South America were linked across the isthmus of Panama, resulting in the interchange of land faunas and the separation of marine faunas in the Pacific and Atlantic Oceans, The Alpine mountain chains continued to rise, accompanied in many areas by renewed volcanic activity. Ice caps developed in the Northern Hemisphere, and resulted in a cold current flowing along the Labrador coast, displacing the warm Gulf Stream to its present position. There was an overall cooling of oceanic and land temperatures.

In the seas numerous marine plankton died out, and the modern oceanic flora is a relict from the Pliocene. Most of the genera of Pliocene marine invertebrates are still living, although many of the individual species have become extinct. Toothed and baleen WHALES abounded, with many new genera, but squalodont and ziphid whales were largely replaced by sperm whales and dolphins; the cetotheres of the Miocene disappeared to be replaced by the balaenid and balaenopterid whales. In fresh water, a radiation and diversification of

Plesiosaurs
Peloneustes, *from the Upper Jurassic of England, was about 3m (10ft) long.*

front of the shoulder joint, which suggests that a backing stroke was not important in swimming. Furthermore, the propodial bones remained long so that the muscles moving the limbs were inserted farther away from the shoulder and hip joints. This meant that the pliosaurs could not make particularly rapid flicks with their paddles, but instead executed a powerful swimming stroke. The overall shape of the pliosaurs was highly compact and streamlined. They were built for power and sustained speed rather than the sudden sprints of their long-necked relatives.

Pliocene
Tetralophodon, *the characteristic Pliocene mastodon, occurred in the Old World and North America.*
Height: up to 2.5m (8ft)

Pollen analysis

molluscs and fishes is noteworthy, especially in the Rift Valley lakes of Africa, where the relatively rapid small-scale changes repeatedly produced new ecological niches and hence new speciation potential.

Pliocene land vegetation was similar to that of today at generic level. Conifer forests dominated the tundra regions and mountainous areas, with deciduous woodlands on the hills. In the mid-continental belts, steppe grasslands were replacing forests. This resulted in the loss of many browsing animals, and the uniformity of the steppe meant that the grazing mammals which adapted to it likewise became more uniform. The last of the browsing HORSES died out in the Plioene, and there was a severe reduction in browsing RHINOCEROSES, TAPIRS, Peccaries, CAMELS and proboscideans (ELEPHANTS).

The most striking characteristic of Pliocene mammal faunas is the rise to dominance of bovids (CATTLE, sheep, goats, antelopes, gazelles and their kin), which spread across the expanding continental steppes. Pliocene mammals are known from all continents except Antarctica, and localities with rich faunas occur in Argentina, Texas, Nebraska, the SIWALIKS, China, southern USSR, France, Kenya and South Africa. There was relatively little interchange between North America and Eurasia, the forests of Beringia acting as a barrier to migration of steppe faunas between central Asia and North America, and the open north Atlantic Ocean preventing migration between the New World and Europe.

In North America, the dominant groups were antilocaprids, equids, camels, deer, peccaries and gomphotheres, with the notable absence of bovids, which did not arrive from Asia until the Pleistocene. During the period, the last rhinoceroses in the Western Hemisphere and the last protoceratids became extinct, but carnivores included SABRE-TOOTHED CATS, WEASELS AND STOATS, and DOGS (including the bone-eating canid *Osteoborus*). RODENTS were also abundant, with many ground-squirrels, cricetids and beavers.

By the Pliocene, a land bridge had been re-established between North and South America, allowing ground-sloths, ARMADILLOS and opossums to migrate northwards into the southern USA; racoons, dogs, BEARS, peccaries, camels, horses and MASTODONS travelled in the opposite direction, radiating across South America and gradually replacing many of the native elements, although marsupial carnivores, EDENTATES, NOTOUNGULATES and caviomorph rodents continued to flourish during the Pliocene.

In Eurasia, a uniform fauna extended from Spain to China, and even invaded Africa. Bovids, especially antelopes, were diverse and abundant; along with them were DEER, GIRAFFES, horses, rhinoceroses, CHALICOTHERES and deinotheres.

Early elephants were replacing mastodons in Africa, where deer were absent but bovids became numerous and varied. Another important element in the African fauna was the rise of the higher PRIMATES, including early MAN.

Australopithecines are known from sites in South Africa, Tanzania, Kenya, Ethiopia and Chad, living in savanna woodlands and taking advantage of trees for shelter.

Australia remained isolated, enabling the marsupials to continue their domination of the area's fauna; the only invaders were rodents, probably carried on drifting vegetation rafts from south-eastern Asia.

See also the time chart.   R.J.G.S.

Pliocene
Deinotherium was a characteristic Pliocene animal but its range extended from the Lower Miocene to the Middle Pleistocene. These large proboscideans, with tusks projecting down and back from the lower jaw, are a specialized side branch of the elephant assemblage.
Height: about 3m (10ft) at the shoulder

Pollen analysis

The study of pollen grains from peat beds and sedimentary deposits. The term is also used to describe investigations of any wind-borne microspores that may be incorporated in sediments. All the higher plants produce microspores, pollen grains or spores which are released by various means into the atmosphere. They then settle, forming what is known as the pollen rain and, where conditions are suitable, become incorporated into peat bogs and sedimentary deposits.

The external wall of a pollen grain or spore is made up of one of the most resistant natural substances known, sporopollenin. The fundamental shape, ornamentation and size of the pollen grains vary among species, enabling almost all pollen and spores to be indentified with their genera; many are also identifiable as species. The pollen grains incorporated in sediments are recovered either by chemically breaking up and digesting the sediments, or by mechanical breaking and flotation methods.

Pre-Cambrian

Pollen analysis has been the major tool in investigations of the vegetation and climate of the past two million years. The deposit to be studied has its pollen grains extracted and identified, the numbers in each category being recorded. As a basis for interpretation, four basic assumptions are made: first, that the pollen grains become evenly distributed in the atmosphere so that the pollen rain produces a representative picture of the vegetation surrounding the deposit; second, that the amount of pollen per unit area is approximately equal for any given climate; third, that the abundance of the pollen of a species is proportional to the abundance of that species; and fourth, that in any deposit the older layers lie beneath the younger ones.

Using these assumptions as a framework, the pollen information is assembled as a pollen diagram. This is a composite graph with plant types and their abundance along the horizontal axis, and sampling points in sequence (time) on the vertical axis. From this diagram the pollen analyst can build up a picture of the vegetation at each point and make deductions about the climatic and ecological conditions.   J.W.F.

Pre-Cambrian

The time from the formation of the Earth to the beginning of the CAMBRIAN Period, comprising an older (Archaean) and a younger (Proterozoic) sub-division. The Earth is believed to have been formed about 4,600 million years ago, and the Cambrian (although an exact horizon for its base has yet to be decided) started about 570 million years ago. The Pre-Cambrian therefore accounts for about 87 per cent of the history of the Earth, ie it is about eight times as long as the interval since the beginning of the Cambrian to the present day (the Phanerozoic).

Although rocks on the Moon (which is thought to be of similar age to the Earth) have been dated by radioisotope methods at more than 4,000 million years and there are few younger than 3,200 million years, the oldest Earth rocks for which a reliable age date has been determined are about 3,800 million years old. These ancient granitic rocks in south-western Greenland were intruded into sediments that are now metamorphosed. The sedimentary sequence has, among other rock types, conglomerates containing pebbles of even older rocks, but it is not known how much older than the dated granites the sediments and conglomerate pebbles are.

The rocks of the Pre-Cambrian are of all types. Most are metamorphosed, but some predominantly sedimentary sequences have been found which, because of their structural position on cratons that have remained stable and undeformed, are relatively unchanged. Some of these sedimentary sequences are exceedingly thick, and a minor proportion of the rocks in them have yielded fossils, TRACE FOSSILS and chemical fossils.

The oldest direct evidence of life comes from microscopic fossils in the Fig Tree Series, which occurs near Barberton, South Africa. From black, carbon-rich cherts at this locality (forming part of a sequence that also contains grey and green cherts, ironstones, siltstones and shales), various cylindrical, bacterium-like forms and spheroidal strands of alga-like organisms have been obtained. The rod-shaped structures (which have been named *Eobacterium isolatum*) are up to 0.7 micrometres $(2.3 \times 10^{-6}\text{ft})$ long and have the dimensions of bacteria; the spheroidal strands (*Archaeosphaeroides barbertonensis*) are up to 20 micrometres $(65.6 \times 10^{-6}\text{ft})$ in diameter, and resemble modern blue-green algae. The fossils are considered to be about 3,200 million years old, because the cherts from which they were obtained lie in a sequence with rocks below dated at 3,360 million years and overlying rocks aged 3,100 million years.

On the shores of Lake Superior in western Ontario, the Gunflint Iron Formation, 1,900 million years old, crops out over a distance of more than 150km (93 miles). Near its base, black cherts 8–25cm (3–10in) thick yield a variety of microfossils, including filaments (some septate) up to 1.5 micrometres $(5 \times 10^{-6}\text{ft})$ across and a few hundred micrometres long (similar to Recent blue-green algae), spheroids up to 16 micrometres $(52 \times 10^{-6}\text{ft})$ in diameter, star-shaped filamentous structures, and mushroom-shaped bodies.

In the Northern Territory of Australia, black cherts occur along with limestone, dolomite and sandstones in the Bitter Springs Formation, which is generally regarded as about 1,000 million years old. About 30 species of fossils have been described from this rock. They are all small and consist of blue-green alga-like filaments, colonial bacteria, possible fungal filaments, and spheres that resemble Recent green algae. A series of fossils from this locality demonstrates in a serial way that cells with nuclei were dividing mitotically.

The Ediacara fauna occurs in South Australia, in quartzites lying well below rocks of proven Cambrian age. As the definition of the base of the Cambrian has not been decided, it is conceivable that the Ediacara fossils (about 700 million years old) may eventually be referred to the basal part of the Cambrian. Nevertheless, the fauna is unlike any that postdates it, and may conveniently be regarded as Pre-Cambrian. This same fauna, or elements of it, is also known from rocks of similar type and age in South Africa, Siberia and Great Britain (at Charnwood Forest and in south Wales). Although the fossils are undoubtedly animals, they are all difficult to fit into modern phyla. Medusoids and pennatulids occur, as do presumed annelids (perhaps including an arthropod ancestor), and a strange discoid animal exhibiting three-fold symmetry. These four major occurrences of Pre-Cambrian organisms correlate well with a theoretical scheme for the origin and early evolution of life.

The Fig Tree Chert forms show that the first major step in the history of life had been taken at least 3,200 million years ago: the transition from simple organic compounds to self-reproducing organic compounds.

Protozoans

The Gunflint Chert, 1,900 million years old, includes blue-green algae and the chemical fossils pristane and phytane (which may be the breakdown products of chlorophyll). Diversification of form was occurring in these life-forms that were presumably adapted to various ecological niches (or chemical conditions).

The Bitter Springs organisms show that by 1,000 million years ago the eucaryotic (nucleus-bearing) cell had appeared. The evolution of such a cell, with its specialized nucleus in which the genetic material is concentrated, was a necessity before life could advance from the earliest phases. Only with cell division and the possibility of recombinations of genetic material is potential genetic diversity created.

The Ediacara fauna shows that the cells had become organized into tissues, and that 700 million years ago metazoans had evolved. P.D.L.

Primates

An order of mammals that includes MAN, APES, MONKEYS and prosimians (LEMURS, TARSIERS). The primates originated nearly 70 million years ago from a small mammal (about the size of a rat) which probably resembled the modern tree shrew. The fossil record contains evidence of several adaptive radiations, none of which includes the ancestors of living primates.

Although the early primates were arboreal, they and their descendants, nevertheless remained remarkably unspecialized.

There are, however, some specific characteristics found in most primates. They all have five fingers, and the hands and often the feet can be used for holding, with the claws replaced by nails which help to protect the sensitive finger pads. The adoption of an arboreal way of life meant that there was less need for an acute sense of smell, and the nose and olfactory centres of the brain became smaller, leading to a reduction in the size of the snout. Major changes also occurred in the position and size of the eyes, because of a diminished need for all-round vision to detect predators and the increasing use of the hands to hold objects, especially food, close to the face. The eyes have consequently moved forwards in the skull to give binocular vision, and this in turn has led to increased development of the optic centre of the brain, with the cerebral cortex undergoing extensive enlargement.

The teeth include incisors, canines, premolars and molars (with a simple cusp pattern). Gestation periods are relatively long, ranging from four to nine months, and even after birth the infants are dependent on their mothers for food and for protection. This longer infant dependency time has probably brought about an increase in learning ability because the infants are able to learn from their parents. The same factor was, in all likelihood, responsible for the development of the complex family and social groups that are characteristic of primates.

The first group of primates for which there is any fossil evidence dates from 60 million years ago (eg the Palaeocene *Plesiadapis*) and seems to be half-way between the ancestral mammals and the modern prosimians.

Fossil primates ranging in age from 35 million to 50 million years are, in many respects, comparable to modern prosimians. The Adapidae, for example, resemble the living lorises, pottos and bush babies. Another fossil group was apparently akin to the tarsier, which today has become restricted to the East Indies. Although prosimians now have a limited distribution, the early fossil prosimians lived throughout the Old and New World continents. D.T.

Proboscideans

See ELEPHANTS, MAMMOTHS, MASTODONS.

Protozoans

The unicellular members of the animal kingdom (Protozoa). They consist essentially of liquid-like cytoplasm normally containing only one nucleus. An external test or shell is sometimes developed, but many otherwise important groups lack "hard parts" and are therefore unknown as fossils. Protozoans are typically solitary, although occasionally they form loosely aggregated colonies. They vary in size from less than 5 micrometres (16×10^{-6}ft) in diameter to several centimetres, with alternating sexually and asexually produced generations resulting in marked shell dimorphism.

Protozoans represent the most primitive form of eucaryote life, from which all multicellular organisms are assumed to have evolved. A long geological history is therefore implied. The earliest acceptable fossil evidence for the origin of the eucaryote cell dates from about 1,300 million years ago, and geochemical evidence suggests that conditions favourable for this far-reaching step in evolution could have occurred as early as 2,000 million years ago.

Modern protozoans populate practically every type of environment, living in marine, brackish and fresh water, and even as parasites on man. They are found at all depths of the sea from shallow to abyssal, and in warm and cold water. Some are planktonic, whereas other benthic forms are sessile or vagrant. Some deep-ocean deposits are composed almost entirely of protozoan shells (radiolarian and *Globigerina* oozes), slowly accumulating from the "fall-out" originating at the planktonic zone above.

The protozoan fossil record (more than 20,000 species) is overwhelmingly dominated by the calcareous-shelled marine to brackish-water FORAMINIFERANS (order Foraminiferida), which range from the Cambrian to the Recent. Of the other fossil groups, only the siliceous, lattice-like shelled RADIOLARIANS (Cambrian–Recent) are noteworthy. The widespread occurrence and rapid evolution of the planktonic foraminiferans in geological time have led to their extensive use as biostratigraphic tools for the zonation and correlation of post-Jurassic strata. Larger foraminiferans 5–20mm (0.2–0.8in) or more in diameter are evidence of warm shallow water carbonate sedimentation and have been important rock formers, particularly in the Permian, Cretaceous and Eocene (eg the nummulitic limestones of the Tethyan. J.E.P.W.

Pseudosuchians

Pseudosuchians

A suborder of the extinct THECODONTIANS from which all later ARCHOSAURS are probably derived. Pseudosuchians are difficult to define on any specific characteristics, but they comprise all thecodontians which cannot be placed either in the more primitive Proterosuchia or in the more specialized Phytosauria (*see* PHYTOSAURS) and Aëtosauria. It is therefore probable that the pseudosuchians do not form a natural grouping, but represent an artificial assemblage of families and genera that have evolved independently from older groups. They range in age from the Lower Triassic to the end of the period and are the only group of archosaurs that were important in the Middle Triassic.

Like their proterosuchian forebears, the pseudosuchians were exclusively carnivorous.

Their teeth were conical and flattened from side to side, with serrated edges and pointed tips curved slighly backwards. Some pseudosuchians could run on their hindlegs in bipedal fashion, and the group was extremely variable in size, ranging from the primitive *Euparkeria* about 65cm (2ft) in length, to the massive *Prestosuchus*, measuring up to 5 metres (16.4ft).

Most of them, like the related aëtosaurs and phytosaurs, are characterized by the "semi-improved" stance and gait and, in particular, by the complex crurotarsal ankle-joint with its ball-and-socket articulation and backwardly directed calcaneal tuber.

It is generally believed that the Pseudosuchia gave direct origin to the Aëtosauria, the Phytosauria, and to all the archosaurian daughter-orders (CROCODILES, SAURISCHIANS, ORNITHISCHIANS and PTEROSAURS). Conventionally, although perhaps mistakenly, the birds too are included in the list of their direct descendants.

Like the Pseudosuchia, the Saurischia may represent two or more distinct evolutionary lines of independent origin. Some authorities claim to have identified transitional forms between pseudosuchians and crocodilians, and also between pseudosuchians and some saurischians, but the precise origins of all the other archosaur groups and the birds are still obscure. Some workers even deny that the origin of the dinosaurs lay anywhere within the Pseudosuchia, basing this conclusion on the complexity of the pseudosuchian ankle-joint and the comparative simplicity of the mesotarsal type of joint found in dinosaurs; they prefer to postulate the existence of another group of early archosaurs, as yet unknown, from which the dinosaurs have arisen.

The division of the Pseudosuchia into families is highly variable, but three groups are well established. The small lightly built Euparkeriidae (late Lower Triassic) are generally regarded as the starting point of the archosaur radiation. The much bigger Prestosuchidae (sometimes called Rauisuchidae), mostly Middle Triassic, were ecologically important because these spectacularly successful predators were probably a major factor in producing the intense selection pressure that resulted in a great explosion of tetrapod evolution during the second half of the Triassic Period. The Middle to Upper Triassic Ornithosuchidae include some advanced forms which have occasionally been classified with the earliest carnivorous dinosaurs.   A.J.C.

Pteraspids

Psilophytes

An ancient and presumably primitive group of plants whose name is derived from a fossil of Devonian age that occurs in the Gaspé Peninsula of Canada. This plant, called *Psilophyton*, had ridged stems with a central strand of conducting tissue and bore small leaves. *Psilophyton* is not such a primitive plant as was once supposed. The branching of the stem was not always equal, as had originally been asserted, and its vascular system was well developed and complex.

The family Psilophytales was established to contain all similar extinct and primitive plants, but this assemblage incorporates two distinct groups. One of these had leafless stems with dichotomous branching and terminal spore-bearing organs (sporangia), typical examples being *Rhynia* (from the Rhynie Chert of Scotland) and *Horneophyton*. The other group, which includes the well known *Zosterophyllum*, is distinguished by stems clothed with appendages (leaves) and bearing the sporangia. In a sub-division of this group, the dichotomous branching becomes unequal, enabling more complex structures to develop.

The Psilophytales are no longer accepted as a useful group within the psilophytes, which are now classified in three families: the Rhyniales (for *Rhynia*), the Zosterophyllales (eg *Zosterophyllum*), and the Trimerophytales (*Psilophyton* itself).

The excellent preservation of *Rhynia* and the associated plants of the Rhynie Chert has enabled botanists to study the internal anatomy of such plants in great detail. For this reason *Rhynia* is illustrated as the archetypal early land plant and has assumed an importance which cannot really be justified.　J.W.F.

Pteraspids

Extinct jawless fishes (OSTRACODERMS) comprising the order Heterostraci of the class Agnatha.

Pteraspids are the first vertebrates to appear in the fossil record, fragments attributable to them occurring in the Cambrian of Wyoming. Some more complete Early Ordovician material has been described from Australia, and they are relatively common in the Silurian and Devonian of Europe.

These most primitive of all known vertebrates were covered by a bony armour, and the different patterns of plates covering the head and front of the trunk are used as the basis of classifying the pteraspids into different groups. The rear of the trunk and the tail were covered by bony scales, and the tail had its lower lobe more developed than the upper. The effect of a side-to-side movement by such a tail was to lower it and simultaneously lift the front part of the animal. The ventral surface of the carapace was convex, so that any forward movement would automatically have lifted the front of the animal off the substrate, and the breadth of the carapace gave a small degree of stability in the water by counteracting any tendency to roll from side to side. No lateral fins were developed, so there was little control over direction; these

fishes could not have been very manoeuvrable.

Like all the other ostracoderms, the pteraspids obtained their nutrients by either scooping or sucking up mud from which they extracted organic matter. *Pteraspis* itself had a series of oral plates which were extended to form a scoop. This genus developed lateral extensions of the armour (cornual plates) and a large dorsal spine which acted as stabilizers.

In some specimens of pteraspids there are impressions of the underlying soft parts preserved on the inner surface of major dermal plates. For example, along the mid-line of the ventral carapace was an elongated structure which must have been the endostyle, an organ that in primitive chordates was concerned with producing mucus as part of the feeding mechanism. In the higher vertebrates this organ becomes transformed into the thyroid gland. On the inner dorsal surface there are impressions of the front and rear semicircular canals of the ear (there is no sign of the third semicircular canal which is aligned in a horizontal plane and hence could not have made any impression vertically). In the mid-line there is the impression of the rain which consisted of the spinal cord developed into three major swellings: the olfactory lobes, a pineal organ with the mid-brain, and finally the hindbrain. The front of the carapace showed impressions of paired nasal sacs and in this regard the pteraspids resemble the later jawed vertebrates rather than the other jawless forms which had only a single nasal organ. Also preserved on the inner surface of the carapace were impressions of the muscle somites including some of the preotic somites, which in later vertebrates migrated to the orbit to make up the extrinsic eye muscles. The pteraspids are at a stage of evolution where this development had not yet taken place.

In one group of pteraspids, the amphiaspids from Siberia, the first or hyoidean GILL had been transformed into a spiracle which was the first step towards the evolution of JAWS. It is now generally believed that all the jawed vertebrates must ultimately have been derived from pteraspids.　L.B.H.

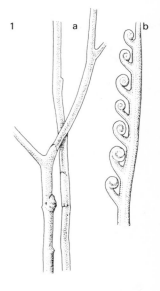

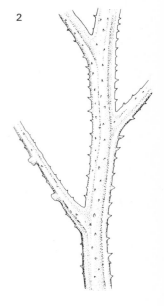

Psilophytes
Two Lower Devonian psilophytes from Wales:
(1) Zosterophyllum, showing (a) axes and (b) sporangia (approx. natural size);
(2) the stem of Psilophyton (approx. natural size).

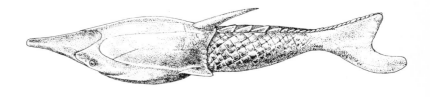

Pteraspids
Pteraspis *lived in the Lower Devonian.*
Length: about 23cm (9in)

Pteridosperms

Pteridosperms

A large and varied group of gymnospermous plants which ranged from the Devonian through the Mesozoic and has no modern representatives. They were woody plants with slender rather than massive stems and large fern-like leaves, usually pinnately divided as in a typical fern frond. The seeds were borne either on the leafy fronds or on modified versions of them.

There was an abundance of fern-like leaves in the Carboniferous, some of which are attributable to true ferns whereas some are pteridospermous. The various fronds were classified into form-genera according to their shapes. These artificial categories often contain a mixture of types, but the use of form-genera is necessary when dealing with fragmented fossils such as the pteridosperms. For example, in the family Lyginopteridaceae there are at least eight stem genera (including *Lyginopteris* and *Heterangium*), several frond genera (of which *Sphenopteris* is the most important) and about 14 seed genera, among them *Eosperma* and *Lagenostoma* and several pollen-bearing organs (notably *Telangium* and *Crossotheca*). Any attempt to reconstruct a typical pteridosperm is at best speculative, although the stems and fronds were of a fairly uniform type.

Lyginopteris is perhaps the best genus from which to build up a picture of a Palaeozoic pteridosperm. The stems of *Lyginopteris oldhamia* are extremely common in Yorkshire coal ball material. Often 4cm (1.6in) in diameter and (in all but the smallest examples) of woody construction, they bore leaves in a spiral pattern. The fronds of this plant, *Sphenopteris hoeninghausi*, have an identical internal anatomical structure to the *Lyginopteris oldhamia* stems; spines of a distinctive nature also occur on both organs, and serve to confirm

that the seeds are those described as *Lagenostoma lomaxii*. The nature of the pollen-bearing organs is less certain, although they were probably of the *Crossotheca* type.

In the Mesozoic the pteridosperm line culminated in the Caytoniales. At the time of their discovery these were thought to be the much sought-after link with the FLOWERING PLANTS but they are now regarded as pteridospermous gymnosperms.   J.W.F.

Pterosaurs

An order (Pterosauria) of ARCHOSAUR reptiles that became the first true flying vertebrates. The oldest known pterosaur, *Eudimorphodon*, occurred in the Triassic of Italy, and the group continued to the end of the Cretaceous. The wing was made of a membrane of skin carried on an enormously elongated fourth finger and attached to the ankles. The origin of the pterosaurs is indicated by the small archosaur *Podopteryx* from the Triassic of Soviet Kirgizstan, north of the Himalaya Mountains. This reptile was a tree-living parachutist, with a large membrane of skin joining the ankle to part-way down the tail, and a second, smaller, membrane that joined the elbows to the knees. The extension of this front membrane along the trailing edge of the forelimb eventually produced the real wing.

The membrane between the hindfeet was important in the flight of pterosaurs. Its function was probably the same as the similar membrane in modern bats. The main flying action was effected by the wing, but the hindlimbs controlled the curvature or camber of the wing. During the recovery or upstroke, it was important for the minimum surface area to be presented to the air and this was, to a large extent, controlled by the hindlimbs. At the front

1

2

Pteridosperms
(1) Frond of Rhodea, *from the Lower Carboniferous of Wales (approx. twice natural size).*
(2) Incomplete frond of Rhacopteris *from the Lower Carboniferous of Wales (approx. natural size).*

Pterosaurs
Dimorphodon, *a primitive Lower Jurassic pterosaur from southern England, had a wing span of about 1.5m (5ft).*

of the wing, the pteroid membrane filled the angle between the wrist and shoulder. The pteroid bone, which articulated with a ball-and-socket joint at the wrist, acted like a leading-edge flap, and had the same effect as a front slot such as the alula ("bastard wing") of a bird's wing. This prevents stalling by reducing turbulence so that there is a smooth flow of air over the wing.

Lift and propulsion are provided by the wings, and it is therefore essential to strengthen the shoulder. In pterosaurs, the vertebrae in this region are fused together to form a solid structure (the notarium) and the scapulae, instead of being joined by a muscular sling to the backbone, have a strong fibrous joint which gives greatly increased strength. One of the necessary features of a flying animal is the need to reduce weight, and in the pterosaurs the bones are invaded by air sacs that are extensions of the lungs. This pneumatic bone structure is also characteristic of birds, in which it evolved independently.

All the early pterosaurs bore teeth in their jaws and had long, bony tails, as did the first bird ARCHAEOPTERYX. The teeth were inherited from their carnivorous archosaur ancestors, but because teeth are heavy and dense, they were eventually lost in both these flying groups in order to reduce weight. The long, bony tail also involved extra weight but served as an automatic stabilizer, correcting any tendency for the front of the animal to pitch forwards when it was in flight. The disadvantage of such a stabilizer was that the stalling speed, at which the animal could no longer remain airborne, remained high and the degree of manoeuvrability was impaired because it is difficult to twist and turn in the air with a stiff projection at the rear. Loss of the bony tail reduced weight, but the animal became unstable. The answer was to correct the tendency to pitch by making conscious muscular adjustments. With the loss of the tail there is an accompanying development of a larger brain providing enhanced muscular co-ordination and balance, as well as a substantial increase in the size of the eyes.

One of the most essential attributes of an active flying vertebrate is the need to have a high metabolic rate and hence a high degree of endothermy (see WARM-BLOODED ANIMALS). The size of a flying animal is severely restricted and this means that there is a large surface to volume

Pterosaurs
Rhamphorhynchus, *from the Upper Jurassic of Europe and eastern Africa, was slenderly proportioned and had a wing span of about 1.8m (6ft).*

ratio, necessitating some kind of insulating covering. In birds, this takes the form of feathers whereas in at least some pterosaurs it was apparently provided by hair. A small pterosaur from the Upper Jurassic of Kazakhstan was evidently covered in fur and has been named *Sordes pilosus* ("hairy devil").

The pterosaurs ranged from small, sparrow-sized forms to the giant, ocean-soaring *Pteranodon* with a wing span of more than 8 metres (26ft), and the vulture-like *Quetzalcoatlus* spanning 10 metres (33ft). *Pteranodon* is known from complete skeletons, and from a computerized analysis of its flight characteristics it is evident that this animal was an exceedingly slow glider; its optimum flying speed was between 5.7 and 7.7 metres per second (18.7 and 25 feet per second). One of the more surprising results to emerge from this study was

Pterosaurs
Pteranodon, *from the Upper Cretaceous, was toothless and tailless.*
Wing span: about 8m (26ft)

Quaternary

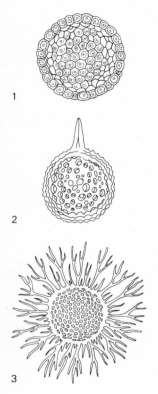

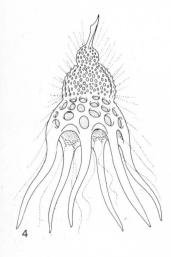

Radiolarians
(1) A colony of Sphaerozoum, *a genus that occurs from the Ordovician to the Recent (approx. 12 times natural size).*
(2) Dorysphaera *ranges from the Ordovician to the Miocene (approx. 125 times natural size).*
(3) Heliocladus *occurs from the Eocene to the Recent (approx. 100 times natural size).*
(4) Cryptoprora *is present from the Eocene to the Recent (approx. 150 times natural size).*

that in a *Pteranodon* with an 8.2 metres (26.9ft) wing span, the minimum turning circle had a radius of only 5.2 metres (17ft), which is remarkably tight when it is realized that a pigeon with a wing span of 0.67 metres (2.2ft) has a turning circle of 3.4 metres (11ft). The centripetal force on a pigeon in such a turn is about $4g$ whereas with *Pteranodon*, it would have been a mere $1.45g$.

Study of the biomechanics of *Pteranodon* has established details of its feeding habits. If *Pteranodon* caught fish using its feet, the centre of gravity would have shifted backwards to such an extent that the stalling speed would have been markedly affected, and the animal would have ceased to be airborne. With fish caught in the beak and carried in a throat sac, however, the displacement of the centre of gravity would have been minimal. In contrast, the long-necked *Quetzalcoatlus* inhabited open plains exploiting thermals and feeding on carrion.

In spite of the fact that the pterosaurs dominated the skies throughout most of the Mesozoic, they were eventually replaced by the birds, which had two fundamental advantages. First, when grounded, birds can tuck their wings into their body and move agilely about, in contrast to the clumsy shuffling of the pterosaurs attested by fossil FOOTPRINTS. Second, a bird's wing is composed of feathers which can part and close over again, whereas a simple tear of the pterosaur wing membrane would probably have proved fatal.   L.B.H.

Quaternary
A division of geological time that includes the PLEISTOCENE Period and the HOLOCENE (Recent). It therefore extends from about 1.8 million years ago to the Recent, and usually distinguishes that part of the CENOZOIC in which the remains and artefacts of human beings occur. The pre-human periods of the age of mammals are included in the TERTIARY.

Rabbits and hares
Members of the small mammalian order Lagomorpha. Although rodent-like in many ways, lagomorphs are not related to rodents. Lagomorphs always have two pairs of incisor teeth in each jaw, and the enamel band is continuous around each tooth. A diastema separates the incisors from the cheek teeth, which are high-crowned and transversely ridged. All the teeth are open rooted, and therefore continue to grow thoughout the animal's life – a necessity to prevent them wearing out rapidly when cutting and chewing tough vegetation.

The earliest known fossil lagomorphs occur in the Mongolian Palaeocene. From these evolved two families: the leporids (rabbits and hares) and the ochotonids (pikas). By the Eocene, lagomorphs had spread into North America, reaching Europe in the Oligocene, Africa in the Miocene, and finally invading South America during the Pleistocene. Early forms were small, scampering animals, and from these there later evolved running and leaping types.   R.J.G.S.

Radiolarians
Microscopic, entirely marine PROTOZOANS, each consisting of a shell surrounded in life by a frothy mass of cytoplasm. The shell (or test), normally composed of opaline silica, is arranged in an intricate, lattice-like fashion.

In general, the colder and deeper-water individuals tend to have larger, less diversified and more massively constructed tests than those of warmer and near-surface waters. Modern radiolarians are planktonic, occurring in all seas and at all latitudes and depths. Most are near-surface dwellers, susceptible to current, wind and wave dispersal. Species diversity is highest in warm waters; swarms of individuals, but few species, are characteristic of the colder water, higher latitude belts.

Radiolarian oozes, formed largely from the gradual accumulation of their shells, are well-documented features of abyssal zones in modern oceans. Radiolarian-rich horizons in the stratigraphic record do not, however, necessarily imply sedimentation at depth. These deposits can also signify shallow, silica-rich water (eg near volcanic activity), as possibly occurs with many radiolarian cherts.

In spite of their worldwide distribution and long geological history (Cambrian–Recent), radiolarians pose taxonomic problems because of their diversity and abundance, and many are too small to be studied with an ordinary binocular microscope: they require a scanning electron microscope. The use of radiolarians as biostratigraphical tools is consequently still limited, and most detailed studies relate to post-Palaeozoic (especially Cenozoic) strata. Notable occurrences include the classic Tertiary marls of Barbados; the Oligocene of New Zealand, Cuba and Trinidad; and the extensive areas of Jurassic radiolarian-bearing rocks in California. The earliest well-preserved faunas come from the Lower Ordovician of Spitzbergen.   J.E.P.W.

Rancho La Brea
The site of asphalt pits near Los Angeles where thousands of animals and birds died trapped in tar pools during the Late Pleistocene.

The underlying Pliocene strata contains oil that is forced to the surface by gas pressure and forms pools of tar which eventually become transformed into asphalt by oxidation and the evaporation of volatile constituents. At one stage of this process the tar is exceedingly sticky, and animals seeking water lying on the surface or wandering carelessly too far out on the hardened asphalt around the perimeter of the pool become trapped in the viscous tar.

The herbivorous mammals whose remains occur in greatest abundance at Rancho La Brea include a HORSE (*Equus occidentalis*), a CAMEL (*Camelops hesternus*), and an extinct bison (*Bison antiquus*).

SABRE-TOOTHED CATS (*Smilodon californicus*) and dire wolves (*Canis dirus*) arrived to attack the trapped plant-eaters and were themselves frequently caught by the tar, although most of the carnivores that died in the asphalt were either young animals or aged individuals (often

Ratites

diseased or injured), which presumably had difficulty in capturing more active prey.

Animals that occur less frequently at Rancho La Brea include the La Brea "lion" (*Felis atrox*), a coyote (*Canis orcutti*), the extinct short-faced bear (*Tremarctotherium simum*), a grizzly bear (*Ursus horribilis*), a black bear (*Ursus optimus*), skunks, weasels, badgers, pumas (including two extinct species), a lynx, rats, mice, ground squirrels, rabbits and hares, the desert shrew (*Notiosorex*), deer, an antilocaprid antelope (*Breameryx minor*), the American mastodon, the imperial mammoth, grazing ground SLOTHS (*Glossotherium*), and browsing ground sloths (*Nothrotherium*). Birds include a giant, condor-like vulture (*Teratornis*), hawks, bald and golden eagles, true condors, geese, ducks, herons, storks (*Ciconia maltha*), owls, pigeons, cranes, turkeys, ravens, fowls, and many representatives of sparrow-like Passeriformes.

When the tar pools were extensive, the area supported pines, cypress trees, the coast live oak, elderberries and hackberries, with small ponds and streams set amid grassland. The climate was similar to that prevailing in the Los Angeles region today, with perhaps slightly more rainfall and lower summer humidity, but higher temperatures. It was essentially an interior climate, less under the influence of coastal weather than at present.

Oil still exudes into pools at La Brea, but in nowhere near such copious quantities as during the Pleistocene. The area is now within a residential area of Los Angeles, and has a museum devoted to the extinct life of the tar pits.

See also LOS ANGELES COUNTY MUSEUM.   R.S.

Ratites

Flightless ground birds, usually of large size, that include the ostriches (Struthioniformes), rheas (Rheiformes), cassowaries (Casuariiformes), kiwis (Apterygiformes) and tinamous (Tinamiformes) among the living avifauna, as well as the extinct moas (Dinornithiformes) and elephant birds (Aepyornithiformes). They are all placed within the superorder Palaeognathae because of the palaeognathous condition of the palate (the bones of the palate and upper jaw are much more firmly united than is customary in birds); other common features include reduction of the forelimb skeleton, an unkeeled sternum, powerfully developed hindlimbs, and (usually) the absence of a pygostyle (tail bone, the "parson's nose"). It is doubtful whether they really form a natural group or are simply an assemblage of unrelated forms that have followed parallel lines of evolution. It has been suggested that the ratites are related through a common ancestor in South America, which migrated via Antarctica to the areas of subsequent ratite development before CONTINENTAL DRIFT fragmented the continents and moved them to their present positions. The geological record has so far failed to produce any evidence in support of this hypothesis.

The earliest examples of ratite-type birds appear to be the ostrich-like *Eleutherornis*,

known from the Eocene deposits of Switzerland, and two elephant birds (*Eremopezus* and *Stromeria*) which were found, respectively, in the Eocene and Oligocene sediments of northern Africa. The material is so fragmentary, however, that there must be some doubt as to the correctness of these assignments. If these early records are disregarded, the geological history of the ratites is short: there are no subsequent records before the Pliocene, although all the orders except the kiwis (which appear to be a recent development) occur in the Pleistocene.

The most spectacular forms of this group are found among the extinct moas of New Zealand

Rancho La Brea
The remains of Smilodon, *a powerful sabre-toothed cat, occur in immense abundance at Rancho La Brea.*
Height: about 1m (3.3ft) at the shoulder

Ratites
The huge flightless bird Diatryma *flourished in Europe and North America from the Upper Palaeocene to the Middle Eocene.*
Height: 2m (6.6ft)

Ray-fin fishes

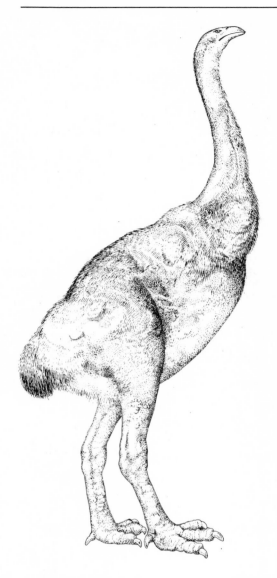

Ratites
The New Zealand moa Dinornis
was about 3.5m (11.5ft) tall.

Ray-fin fishes

Members of the class Osteichthyes, which includes the Chondrostei (primitive Palaeozoic and early Mesozoic types with a few specialized or degenerate survivors), the Holostei (abundant in the Mesozoic but now likewise only sparsely represented) and the Teleostei (the advanced ray-fins that are the most abundant group of living aquatic vertebrates).

The earliest ray-fins were the PALAEONISCIDS, which represent the basic structural grade of the chondrosteans. The TAIL FIN is primitively heterocercal, and the SCALES are thick and heavy, with a basal bony layer, a middle stratum of dentine or cosmine and a thick outer covering of enameloid or ganoine. The major bone of the upper jaw, the maxilla, was expanded rearwards and made contact with the opercular bones, covering the gills.

Several advanced palaeoniscids showed the beginnings of the higher holostean grade of organization. In *Redfieldia*, for example, the fleshy lobe of the tail was shortened, leaving the rays to make up the symmetrical outline of the fin – an abbreviated heterocercal configuration.

The change towards a symmetrical tail, in which the entire fin is made up of rays, is associated with the change in function of the primitive lungs to form an air bladder, thus making the tail less important for generating lift. This significant step in the evolution of ray-fin fishes was brought about by their return to the sea, where an accessory breathing organ was of little consequence and the lungs were transformed into an air bladder – a buoyancy organ positioned above the alimentary canal.

The other important change that occurred at this time was in the jaw apparatus. Among sub-holosteans (the most advanced chondrosteans) the maxilla was reduced so that it no longer made direct contact with the opercular bones, and the jaw was simultaneously shortened.

In true holosteans further advances occurred. The abbreviation of the heterocercal tail continued, although the posterior end of the vertebral column was still upturned as clear evidence of the original heterocercal condition. The jaw became much shorter and in many instances articulated forward of the eye sockets. The maxilla was separated from the opercular bone by several cheek bones, and had also been loosened from its anterior connection with the bones in front of the orbit. The breakdown of the cheek bones meant that the force of the lower jaw's action was now taken by the hyomandibular and the quadrate, an arrangement that gave the shorter jaw increased strength. The teeth were usually rounded and it seems that several holosteans had taken to crushing shellfish with their newly developed powerful jaws. Furthermore, the freeing of the maxilla allowed the actual hinge of the jaw to be swung forwards, and this allowed the gape to be increased.

The other change that occurred at the holostean level was in the structure of the scales. The dentine layer disappeared so that the scales were made up simply of basal bony layers surmounted by a varying thickness of enameloid or

and the elephant birds of Madagascar. The largest moa, *Dinornis maximus*, reached a height of 3.5 metres (11.5ft), but not all species were as large; *Anomalopteryx parva* probably did not exceed 90cm (3ft). The elephant birds also produced a large species, *Aepyornis maximus*, which is known to have attained a height of 3 metres (9.9ft), and probably inspired some historical legends, such as the Rukh (or Roc) of Sinbad the Sailor and Marco Polo. Eggs attributable to *Aepyornis* are commonly found in sand dunes, where they were laid many thousands of years ago, and are exceptionally large – one such example had a liquid capacity of more than 9 litres (2 gallons), which is enormous even for a bird the size of *Aepyornis*.

Why these two highly successful groups became extinct is not fully understood, although the moas appear to have suffered from man's arrival in New Zealand and the resulting moa-hunter culture that developed. Many of the larger species, however, were probably already declining before man's involvement, possibly due to changing habitats caused by the changes in temperature during the Pleistocene.   C.W.

Ray-fins (cont'd)

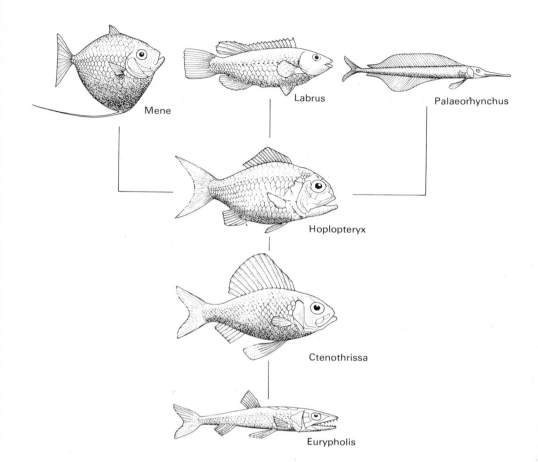

Mene

Labrus

Palaeorhynchus

Hoplopteryx

Ctenothrissa

Eurypholis

Ray-fin fishes
Stages in the evolution of teleosts: the Cretaceous salmoniform Eurypholis, *a deep-sea fish, 14cm (5.5in) long;* Ctenothrissa *from the Cretaceous, 32cm (12.6in) long; the beryciform* Hoplopteryx, *a primitive spiny-rayed fish from the Upper Cretaceous, 26cm (10in) long; the deep-bodied percomorph* Mene *from the Eocene, 27cm (10.6in) long;* Labrus, *a typical living member of the perch group, about 45cm (18in) long;* Palaeorhynchus, *a slender, surface-dwelling scombroid of the mackerel group that was present in the Eocene, 45cm (18in) long.*

ganoine. The holosteans, like the palaeoniscids, are known as ganoid fishes. There are still two holostean survivors, confined to the fresh waters of North America; these are the garpike *Lepidosteus*, which still retains an abbreviated heterocercal tail, and the bow-fin *Amia*.

During the Triassic and Early Jurassic, the holosteans underwent the same type of adaptive radiation as the palaeoniscids that preceded them, with the appearance of long, thin predaceous forms, as well as deep-bodied types.

The final structural stage of the ray-fin fishes, represented by the teleosts, was achieved during the Jurassic, when the herring-like *Leptolepis* appeared. The teleosts are characterized by a homocercal tail in which the symmetrical fin is made up simply of rays – the only vestige of the ancestral heterocercal condition is seen in the last few vertebrae, which are upturned; the hypural bones are expanded from the haemal arches to ensure that the internal skeleton gives symmetry to the tail.

Further development of the air bladder and increased speed of swimming also led to a reduction in the scales. The heavy mineralized enameloid is lost and the scales are composed only of thin laminae of bone or isopedin. In the jaw apparatus, the premaxilla is lengthened and the maxilla ceases to form part of the edge of the jaws; it no longer bears teeth and instead constitutes a strut of bone connecting the premaxilla and the hinge of the jaw, serving to help

the articulation of the jaw to swing far forwards. The effect of this is to enlarge enormously the gape and the volume of the mouth cavity. When the mouth is opened a vacuum is created which is filled by a sudden inrush of water – one of the most effective methods of capturing prey that has ever been evolved. Even in herring, which feed by sifting small planktonic organisms with their gill rakers, the ability to protrude the jaws gives them a potentially enormous volume of intake.

With the ability to dart rapidly through the water, the pectoral fins became especially significant in rapid manoeuvring, whereas the posteriorly positioned pelvics declined in importance. In some of the more advanced teleosts the pelvic fins migrated forwards until they came to lie in front of the pectorals, thus concentrating control of manoeuvring in the region where it is most effective.

The principal evolutionary lineages of the teleosts were already established in the Cretaceous, but not until the beginning of the Cenozoic did the major adaptive radiation of the group get properly under way, with many forms re-invading fresh water. The ostariophysians developed a set of ossicles linking the air bladder to the ear regions which transmit sound vibrations. These Weberian ossicles parallel, in some respects, the sound amplification system of the mammalian middle ear, but are in fact derived from modified vertebrae. L.B.H.

Rays

Ray-fin fishes
Evolutionary stages of ray-fins leading up from the ancestral palaeoniscids:
Redfieldia *from the Triassic, 14cm (5.5in) long;*
Lepidotes *from the Jurassic, 30.5cm (1ft) long;*
Hypsocormus *from the Jurassic, 1.4m (4.6ft) long;*
Pholidophorus *from the Jurassic, 23cm (9in) long;*
Leptolepis *from the Jurassic, 23cm (9in) long.*

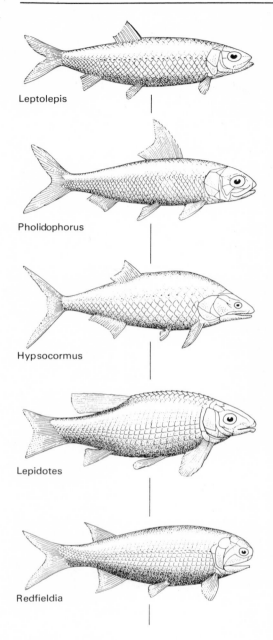

Leptolepis

Pholidophorus

Hypsocormus

Lepidotes

Redfieldia

Rays
Myliobatis, the living eagle ray, has a fossil history extending back to the Upper Cretaceous. Its length is about 4.5m (15ft), including the tail.

Rays

Cartilaginous fishes (Chondrichthyes) belonging to the order Batoidea.

The skates and rays are classified with the SHARKS as elasmobranchs. They have become specialized for a benthic mode of life, with the first gill transformed into a spiracle through which water is drawn from the dorsal surface to pass over the gills, leaving them via openings on the ventral surface. The anal fin is lost and the tail has diminished to a whip-like organ sometimes bearing a poisonous spine. The dorsal fins are either absent or reduced to the merest vestiges. Pelvic fins tend to be well developed, but the pectorals are enormously expanded into wide triangular lateral extensions that run from the head to the rear of the body. These fishes swim by making wave-like undulations pass along their pectoral fins.

All the skates and rays are bottom-dwelling forms feeding on molluscs and crustaceans, which they crush with batteries of flattened teeth that form wide, flat pavements and act like a crushing mill. The rays closely resemble some of the PLACODERMS (eg the rhenanid *Gemuendina*), but these similarities are due to convergent evolution of different groups becoming adapted to the same benthic mode of life.

The history of the sharks and the existence of such forms as *Squatina* suggest that the modern rays and skates were evolved from the normal hybodont shark stock during the Jurassic. *Squatina*, which appeared during this period, indicates the way in which the skates and rays could have arisen. The pectoral fins were greatly developed but not connected to the head, and the body was still rounded in cross-section rather than flattened as in the rays.

In the Palaeocene one of the more highly specialized of the rays, *Eotorpedo*, made its appearance. In this genus part of the musculature was transformed into a powerful electric organ.

L.B.H.

Reefs

A wide range of organic constructions including large, tropical shallow-water coral-algal growths such as the Great Barrier Reef of Australia. Barrier reefs, fringing reefs and atolls, in which lime-secreting organisms have formed a framework in the surf zone that separates a forereef slope from a protected backreef lagoon, extend almost as far back in time as the record of animals with calcareous skeletons, although the earliest well-documented reef comparable with the Great Barrier Reef is of Devonian age (and is similarly situated in Australia). Scleractinian CORALS, usually encrusted on the reef rim by calcareous ALGAE, are the principal constructors of Recent reefs, but the Devonian Canning Basin reef is built by a combination of stromatoporoids (an extinct group of calcareous SPONGES), rugose and tabulate corals, and stromatolites (masses of finely laminated limestone whose deposition was controlled by algal mats). The stromatoporoids formed the major part of the reef edge.

Coral-algal reefs are prominent in the Recent and the Cenozoic, as well as being present in the Mesozoic. Stromatoporoid reefs are a feature of the Silurian and, particularly, the Devonian. At other times, stromatolitic algae formed reefs on their own account, particularly in the Permian.

Significant organic build-ups, not necessarily in shallow water, of mat-like or mound-like form (respectively biostromes and bioherms) occur throughout the post-Archaean geological record and were constructed by different lime-secreting organisms – eg stromatolitic algae from the Proterozoic onwards, ARCHAEOCYATHINES in the Lower and Middle Cambrian, various corals from the Ordovician onwards and rudist BIVALVES in the Cretaceous. These structures may vary enormously in size and complexity, from tens of square kilometres down to about 1 metre (3ft) across, but all tend to be referred to generally as reefs.

Rhinoceroses

High organic productivity is usually a feature of reefs. This is particularly true of Cenozoic and Recent coral-algal reefs, which are more diverse in numbers of different associated organisms than any other community. C.T.S.

Reptiles

The first VERTEBRATE group to become entirely independent of water. Reptiles evolved an amniote egg, embodying a yolk sac to nourish an embryo lying in a liquid-filled amnion. Waste products formed by the developing embryo are stored in the allantois. The tough outer shell prevents desiccation but remains porous enough to allow the entry of oxygen and the outward passage of carbon dioxide. The chorion lining the shell and the allantois act as a lung for gaseous exchange.

This reproductive advance makes it unnecessary for reptiles to return to lakes or rivers to breed, as AMPHIBIANS have to, and enabled them to become the dominant terrestrial vertebrates of the Mesozoic with some groups assuming secondarily aquatic habits to colonize the seas and others developing flight.

The most primitive reptiles are the COTYLOSAURS, which first appeared in the Early Pennsylvanian after arising from amphibian ancestors. These early forms have no temporal openings in the skull (the anapsid condition) and in this respect resemble the living TURTLES AND TORTOISES.

Subsequently the reptilian skull developed variously orientated openings (fenestrae) to accommodate the temporal muscles, anapsids being regarded as the basic primitive type.

The Synapsida (PELYCOSAURS, MAMMAL-LIKE REPTILES) appeared in the Pennsylvanian, and have a single opening low down in the cheek region bounded above by the postorbital and squamosal bones. This subclass eventually yielded the MAMMALS.

A single cheek opening is also found in NOTHOSAURS and their descendants, the PLESIOSAURS, but in this instance the postorbital and squamosal bones constitute the lower margin of the opening (the parapsid condition). These forms, together with the placodonts and some primitive terrestrial genera from the Permian and Triassic (*Protorosaurus*, *Trilophosaurus*, *Araeoscelis*, *Tanystropheus*), constitute the Euryapsida.

ICHTHYOSAURS are another group with a single temporal opening on each side, but they are located high in the skull and demarcated laterally by the postfrontal and supratemporal bones. These fully aquatic marine reptiles are consequently assigned to a separate subclass, the Ichthyopterygia.

The most prolific group of reptiles are the diapsids, in which the skull has two openings in each temporal region, separated by the postorbital and squamosal. These forms include the subclasses Lepidosauria (LIZARDS and SNAKES) and Archosauria (the ARCHOSAURS). Although living reptiles are COLD-BLOODED, there is evidence that both the mammal-like reptiles and the archosaurs may have been WARM-BLOODED. R.S.

Rhinoceroses

A large and complex group of PERISSODACTYL mammals comprising about 60 genera, of which four are still extant (two in Africa, one in greater India and one in Sumatra). Although they are extremely rare today, rhinoceroses were varied and abundant during most of the Cenozoic and included the largest land mammals that ever lived. They have their origins in TAPIR stocks, and can be traced back to the Eocene.

Three families are recognized: hyracodontids, amynodontids and rhinocerotids. They all have in common the characteristic rhinocerotoid molar tooth patterns, with a Π on the upper molars and two crescents on the lower molars. They differ in the details of these patterns, on the degree of reduction or specialization of the incisor and canine teeth, on the presence or absence of horns (which are composed of matted hair), and in their modes of living.

Hyracodontids flourished during the Eocene and Oligocene in North America and Asia, the pony-sized *Hyracodon* being a typical example of the family. They paralleled the HORSES in many ways, and remained relatively small, hornless running types. Their incisor teeth were of uniform size and spatulate, the canines attained only moderate proportions, and the rear premolars were molarized. The limbs became elongated, with three hoofed toes on the front and the hindfeet.

Contemporaneous with the hyracodontids were the amynodontids, which occur in both North America and Europe. These rhinoceroses paralleled the hippopotamuses of the later Cenozoic: they were hornless, short-legged and amphibious, with three-toed feet, small pointed incisors, and canines enlarged into tusks. The premolars were reduced and the molars much enlarged. These families died out about the end of the Oligocene without leaving any descendants.

Rhinocerotids (or true rhinoceroses) constitute the third, largest and most successful family of the group, and include all living and post-Oligocene rhinoceroses, distributed among seven subfamilies. Their ancestry can be traced back into the Eocene, and fossil remains are recorded from North America, Eurasia and Africa.

The caenopines are the central stock, trace-

Rhinoceros
With three toes only on each foot, Hyracodon, an Oligocene running rhinoceros, was adapted for a cursorial existence on the open plains.
Length: about 1.5m (5ft)

181

Rhynchocephalians

Rhinoceros
The largest known land mammals were the giant hornless rhinoceroses that lived in the Oligocene and Lower Miocene of southern Asia. Indricotherium stood 5.5m (18ft) at the shoulder.

able back to tapiroid ancestry and surviving into the Pliocene. The Oligocene genus *Caenopus* had short, stout limbs, four-toed forefeet, a last upper premolar that was molarizing and low-crowned molar teeth.

The aceratherines were a small subfamily that was abundant in Eurasia and Africa in the Oligocene and the Miocene. *Aceratherium* was a medium-sized hornless rhinoceros, lacking tusks but with high-crowned teeth that could have coped with the grasses which, in the Miocene, had begun to spread extensively.

The indricotheres are usually included here, although sometimes placed among the hyracodontids. Indricotheres are essentially confined to the Oligocene of Asia, and are best known from the southern USSR and the Indian sub-continent. They grew to gargantuan size, standing 5.5 metres (18ft) at the shoulder – the largest elephants reach about 4 metres (13ft), and a giraffe's head can top only 5 metres (16.4ft).

Teleoceratines occur mainly in the Miocene of North America, Europe and Africa; they had short legs and were hippopotamus-like. Rhinoceratines are one-horned and confined to Asia, with a species in India and another in Java. The Indian rhinoceros is the largest living species and inhabits tall grass and reed beds in swamps.

The elasmotherines were another mainly Asiatic group that lived during the Plio-Pleistocene. *Elasmotherium* was a giant rhinoceros with a frontal horn, and cheek teeth that had evolved complex enamel patterns.

The two-horned dicerorhinines comprise the Sumatran rhinoceros and both the African rhinoceroses, together with the woolly rhinoceros (*see* PLEISTOCENE) of the ice age. Although living species are confined to the Old World tropical zones, the woolly rhinoceros was well adapted to live close to the ice. / R.J.G.S.

Rhynchocephalians

One of the four surviving orders of REPTILES, although it includes only one living representative, the tuatara (*Sphenodon punctatus*).

Like the Squamata (LIZARDS and SNAKES), the Rhynchocephalia are classified as lepidosaurs. As in the lizards, the skull is typically diapsid, but all the bony arcades surrounding the two temporal openings are still complete and, again as in some lizards, the teeth are acrodont (fused to the edges of the jaws). The only characteristic specialization of the Rhynchocephalia is the overhanging beak formed by the upper jaw.

The two most important families conventionally assigned to the Rhynchocephalia are the Rhynchosauridae (which may in fact have originated separately from early diapsid ancestors) and the Sphenodontidae, the group that includes *Sphenodon* itself.

The earliest known occurrences of the Sphenodontidae are in the Lower Triassic of South Africa and the USSR. It seems likely that sphenodontids and lizards shared a common origin from among the eosuchians (early diapsids). Sphenodontids are the "typical" rhynchocephalians – small animals in which the beak was not strongly developed. Several genera are known from the Triassic and Jurassic, such as *Homoeosaurus* from the Upper Jurassic of Bavaria, but after the end of the Jurassic there is no certain record of any rhynchocephalian apart from the living *Sphenodon*.

The tuatara is a superficially lizard-like reptile, about 65–70cm (25.6–27.6in) long, which survives only on a few islets off the coast of the North Island of New Zealand, where it is a protected species. It formerly ranged throughout New Zealand but was hunted to near extinction by man.

The earliest known occurrence of the Rhynchosauridae is also in the Lower Triassic of South Africa, where *Noteosuchus* occurs in the *Lystrosaurus* zone of the KARROO SYSTEM, and *Mesosuchus* and *Howesia* are small forms from the overlying *Cynognathus* zone. In the Middle and Late Triassic, the rhynchosaurs evolved rapidly, but died out at the end of the period. There were not many genera, and they were mostly much alike, but they seem to have been extremely abundant as individuals – for example, *Stenaulorhynchus* the common rhynchosaur from the Middle Triassic Manda Formation of Tanzania. They were much larger than sphenodontids and heavily built; the skull alone sometimes reached a length of more than 30cm (11.8in). They were apparently herbivorous, with a prominent, toothless beak and batteries of small, close-set teeth farther back on the jaws as well as on the palate, but the teeth differ from those of typical rhynchocephalians – they are implanted in deep sockets and arranged in multiple rows. The specializations of the postcranial skeleton suggest a separate origin from the Eosuchia much earlier than the common origin postulated for the sphenodontids and the lizards. It has also been tentatively suggested that *Noteosuchus* may be related to the early ARCHOSAUR *Proterosuchus*, a THECODONTIAN.

Other families assigned to the Rhynchoce-

Royal Ontario Museum

phalia with varying degrees of confidence are the Claraziidae of the Middle Triassic and the Sapheosauridae and Pleurosauridae of the Upper Jurassic, all from Europe. A.J.C.

Rodents

An order (Rodentia) that includes about half of all the living species of mammals, comprising about 350 modern genera and more than 400 extinct genera. In terms of individual numbers, rodents are more numerous than any other mammals and they occur abundantly on all continents except Antarctica.

The most striking feature of rodents is the single pair of incisor teeth in each jaw modified to chisel through nuts, wood and even bone. On these teeth, enamel is restricted to the front side, and the softer dentine behind wears more rapidly, thus producing a chisel edge; the teeth are also open rooted, which enables continual growth to counter the rapid wear. A gap behind the incisor teeth and a sliding jaw articulation allows the cheek teeth to grind food without the incisor teeth occluding.

Most rodents are small, scampering animals, but their numbers include many specialized for jumping, climbing and burrowing, as well as a few gliding and swimming kinds. The harvest mice are among the smallest mammals, with head and body length of about 5cm (2in) and weight of 5 grammes (0.2oz), whereas the largest living rodent is the capybara of South America, which reaches more than 1 metre (3.3ft) in length and about 50kg (110lb) in weight. Some extinct rodents from South America were twice as large as the capybara.

The classification of rodents is usually based on the patterns of jaw muscles and cheek teeth. There are about 45 families, which can be grouped into three major stocks, with a fourth stock to accommodate miscellaneous families.

The first major group are the sciuromorph rodents, typified by squirrels, with ground-dwelling, arboreal and gliding forms. Their cheek teeth are typically and distinctively multi-cusped. Included with them are the paramyids, the most primitive known rodents, from the Palaeocene of North America and Europe, together with the highly specialized extinct mylagaulids (eg *Epigaulus*) that had a bony horn on the forehead.

The myomorphs are the largest stock, with rats, mice, lemmings, voles, jerboas, mole rats and many other small rodents. Some have highly specialized cheek teeth with transverse ridges and open roots that allow continual growth, as in the incisors. The specifically diagnostic teeth of myomorph rodents are abundant in many deposits, and the rapid evolution of the group allows them to be used to correlate continental sediments over wide areas with more precision than is possible using any other mammals.

The caviomorphs are well known in South America from the Oligocene onwards. They have cheek teeth with wide transverse ridges and open roots, and include chinchillas, agoutis, guinea pigs, coypus and the capybara. Some fossil forms are as large as a wild boar, and have

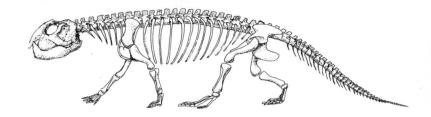

skulls of more than 50cm (19.7in) in length.

The miscellaneous families which cannot be grouped with any of the three main stocks include beavers, known from the Oligocene onwards in Europe and North America, the porcupines of Africa, and several extinct families, of which the theridomyids abound in European early Cenozoic deposits. R.J.G.S.

Rhynchocephalians
Rhynchosaurs such as Scaphonyx *were exceedingly abundant in Gondwanaland during the Middle Triassic.*
Length: about 1m (3.3ft)

Romer, Alfred Sherwood (1894–1973)

American palaeontologist and author of a highly regarded series of textbooks: *Vertebrate Paleontology* (1933), *Man and the Vertebrates* (1933), *The Vertebrate Body* (1949) and *The Osteology of the Reptiles* (1956). Romer was a graduate of Amherst College, and undertook his post-graduate studies at Columbia University. In 1923 he was appointed an associate professor at the University of Chicago. He was director (1946–61) of the MUSEUM OF COMPARATIVE ZOOLOGY.

Apart from his textbook writing, Romer did original research, often based on specimens he had himself collected. His contributions added to the understanding of the evolution of fishes, reptiles and amphibians and particularly to the origins of the major vertebrate classes. A.P.H.

Royal Ontario Museum

Founded in 1912 in Toronto as the museum of the University, although suggestions for a "Lyceum of Natural History and Fine Arts" can be traced back to 1833. The current title was adopted in 1968, with the change in administration away from the University. A close relationship still exists, however, between the two organizations.

The Royal Ontario Museum is the largest public museum in Canada, as well as being a major research institute with extensive collections of fossils, which are particularly rich in North American vertebrates. A.P.H.

Rodents
Epigaulus, a horned gopher from the Lower Pliocene of the USA, was about 26cm (10in) long.

Sabre-toothed cats

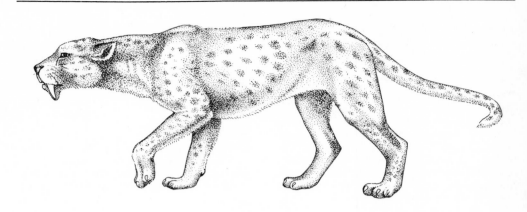

Sabre-toothed cats
Hoplophoneus, *a North American machairodont, occurred from the Lower Oligocene to the Lower Miocene. The species in this genus ranged in size from animals no bigger than a bobcat to a large puma.*

Sabre-toothed cats

Extinct members of the Felidae (CATS) distinguished by the development of greatly enlarged upper canine teeth. These cats were the most formidable mammalian predators for the greater part of the Cenozoic. The enormous upper canine teeth were used as sabre-like stabbing weapons to kill prey – probably consisting primarily of large, tough-skinned herbivorous mammals (eg MASTODONS, ELEPHANTS, BRONTOTHERES and RHINOCEROSES). The jaw articulation was carried low down by a descending process so that the lower jaw could open wide enough to clear the points of the huge upper canines. Some sabre-tooths developed flanges on the lower jaw that sheathed the upper canines when the mouth was closed. The sabre-tooths had powerful forequarters, apparently for clinging to their prey, but the hindlimbs were relatively weak.

The origin of the sabre-tooths (Machairodontinae) is unknown, but they apparently arose during the Eocene, *Dinictis* was a primitive North American Oligocene genus that is probably close to the common origin of not only machairodonts but also the true cats (Felinae) and the "false sabre-tooths" (Nimravinae, with only moderately elongated upper canines). This elongated cat, about the size of a puma, had short, slender limbs and partly retractile claws. The "sabres" were only

marginally longer than normal, and the lower canines were still large.

In the powerfully built *Hoplophoneus*, a contemporary of *Dinictis* in the North American Oligocene, the upper canines had acquired the typical sabre-like proportions, with lower jaw flanges to protect them, and the lower canines were greatly reduced. Even more specialized was *Eusmilus*, which appeared in Eurasia during the Late Eocene and spread to North America during the Oligocene. This big carnivore had enormous sabres protected by deep lower jaw shields, but the lower canines were so reduced that they resembled incisor teeth.

During the Miocene, sabre-tooths became rare in North America, but in the Old World they remained common (*Metailurus*) and proliferated into the Pliocene as *Machairodus*, which attained the size of a lion and had lower jaw flanges to shield the long "sabres".

In the European Lower Pleistocene, *Megantereon* (about the size of a small panther) was the common sabre-tooth in the Mediterranean region, extending its range into Africa and Asia during the mid-Pleistocene, and possibly reaching North America via the Bering region to evolve into the powerful *Smilodon*.

Accompanying *Megantereon* in the Villafranchian was *Homotherium*, the "sword-toothed cat", with laterally compressed, razor-sharp canines of only moderate length and cheek teeth transformed into thin, slicing blades. *Homotherium* was present in China during the mid-Pleistocene and was well established in North America by the Upper Pleistocene. It had disproportionately long forelimbs and probably preyed on young elephants (the bones of juvenile mammoths have been found in its dens).

By the Upper Pleistocene, the short-tailed *Smilodon* (*see* RANCHO LA BREA) had appeared in North America and eventually reached the pampas. In this final member of the group the lower jaw flanges were absent, despite the presence of huge upper canines. The widespread dying out of large herbivorous mammals towards the end of the Pleistocene would have deprived the sabre-tooths of their main food supply and thus brought about their extinction.

"False sabre-tooths" (Nimravinae) were slim-limbed, swift-running felids that appeared during the Eocene and became common in the Oligocene of North America (*Nimravus*,

Sabre-toothed cats
Eusmilus, *an early sabre-toothed cat, first appeared in the Upper Eocene of the Old World and spread to North America in the Oligocene. The animal was about the size of a leopard.*

Sauropods

Archaelurus, Dinaelurus) and Europe (*Aelurogale*). The characteristic Old World nimravine of the Miocene and Pliocene was *Pseudaelurus*, which eventually reached North America, where it occurred with *Nimravides*.

The "false sabre-tooths" did not survive into the Pleistocene, but they might have been the ancestors of the true cats if their moderately enlarged upper canines had undergone secondary reduction.   R.S.

Sahni, Birbal (1891–1949)

Indian palaeontologist and founder of palaeobotany in India. He was born at Bhera, India, and received his graduate education in his home country and at Cambridge University, where he came under the influence of Sir Albert SEWARD.

In 1919 he was head of the Botany Department of Lucknow University, India, and later became its first professor. In 1946 he founded the Birbal Sahni Institute of Palaeobotany, the only institute of its kind in the world.

He was interested in geology and botany, and was an expert on the living plants of India. His palaeobotanical studies were wide-ranging, including work on the Saline Series of the Punjab Salt Range and the GLOSSOPTERIS FLORA.   A.P.H.

Salamanders

One of the three groups of living AMPHIBIANS. Contemporary practice is to separate the FROGS AND TOADS, salamanders and caecilians from the extinct LABYRINTHODONTS and LEPOSPONDYLS as Lissamphibia. No probable common ancestor of the three lissamphibian groups is known and a few authorities would trace the separate ancestry of frogs and salamanders back to the fish level.

Salamanders are distinguished by having a well-developed tail, four limbs of similar size (although these may be reduced in some species), and a tadpole which, apart from external gills and incompletely developed legs, looks similar to the adult (in contrast to frogs). They appear more primitive than frogs, but have a skeleton in which much of the bone is replaced by cartilage.

Salamanders are first known from the Late Jurassic of Wyoming at the famous dinosaur locality of Como Bluff; the species *Comonecturoides marshi* is probably related to the living cave-dwelling form *Proteus*. Several fossil Salamanders have been found in Israel, *Hylaeobatrachys* (a proteid) occurs in Wyoming, and several sirenids (relations of the living *Siren* of North America) were present in the USA. Members of other salamander families, including the giant salamander, *Andrias*, occur in Cenozoic deposits.

In 1972 a single diagnostic caecilian vertebra (*Apodops*) was described from the Palaeocene of Brazil. Caecilians have no limbs, virtually no tail, degenerate eyes and no tadpole stage. Their relationship to the Anura and Urodela is doubtful, and it has been suggested that their ancestry is from microsaur lepospondyls.   A.L.P.

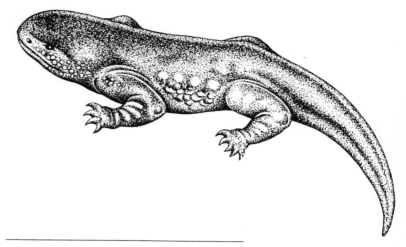

Salamanders
The giant salamander Andrias *(also known as* Megalobatrachus*) first appeared in the Oligocene; about 1m (3.3ft) long.*

Saurischians

An extinct order of ARCHOSAURS, one of the two groups of Mesozoic reptiles that are commonly described as DINOSAURS.

The Saurischia ("lizard-hipped") have a triradiate pelvis that is typically reptilian. Two principal lines of evolution are present within the order: the Theropoda ("beast-footed"), including the bipedal COELUROSAURS, DEINONYCHIDS and CARNOSAURS, and the Sauropodomorpha ("lizard-footed"), which comprises the prosauropods of the Triassic and the quadrupedal SAUROPODS of the Jurassic and Cretaceous.

It seems probable that the Saurischia includes more than one line of descent from PSEUDOSUCHIAN ancestors. The coelurosaurs represent the central stem of the Theropoda, but it is not certain that the carnosaurs are directly derived from them. It is also difficult to conceive that the massively built prosauropods and their successors, the sauropods, originated from a common primitive theropod stock.   R.S.

Sauropods

The long-necked saurischian DINOSAURS which are the largest known terrestrial animals. They had a small head, a short trunk supported by graviportal limbs, and a long tail terminating in a "whip lash" that might have had some defensive function. The sauropods were probably plant eaters. They are conventionally regarded as semi-aquatic reptiles that sought refuge from predators in lakes and rivers, using their long necks to keep the head above the surface for breathing while wading in deep water.

Although fossil sauropod trackways that lack a tail-drag mark indicate that they did wade through water deep enough to float their tails clear of the bottom, there is some doubt about the ability of any vertebrate to breathe if its body is more than a few metres below the surface: the pressure of the water on the chest cavity would make it almost impossible to expand the lungs. An alternative explanation for the long neck is that it would have enabled these reptiles to browse the tops of high trees, indicating a more fully terrestrial existence.

The earliest members of the suborder

Sauropods (cont'd)

Sauropodomorpha are the Prosauropoda, which appeared in the Middle Triassic. A fairly generalized family in this group is the Anchisauridae, which may have retained some bipedal capability inherited from their PSEUDOSUCHIAN forebears. They attained a length of 2–3 metres (6.6–9.8ft) and were still lightly built, with short forelimbs, long necks and tails, and a large skull; the jaws contained small, equal-sized teeth of spatulate form.

Anchisaurids occur in southern Africa, South America, North America, Europe and Asia, but only a few genera are represented by reasonably comprehensive skeletons (eg *Efraasia*, *Gyposaurus* and *Yaleosaurus*).

Some of the larger, more heavily built prosauropods are assigned to the Plateosauridae, which reached 8 metres (26ft) in length and must have been largely quadrupedal, although the forelimbs remained short. *Plateosaurus* (*see* TRIASSIC) was common in the European Upper Triassic, with *Lufengosaurus* present in China.

The direct ancestors of the sauropods themselves are probably to be found among the inadequately known Melanorosauridae, which occur in the Middle and Upper Triassic. These large prosauropods seem to have become almost totally quadrupedal, the forelimbs being nearly as long as the hindlimbs. They occur in southern Africa, Europe and Asia, but apparently failed to survive into the Lower Jurassic.

The more conservative of the two sauropod families, the Camarasauridae, had short-faced skulls with the external nasal opening in front of the eye sockets and spatulate teeth extending well back along the jaw margins. The neural spines of the neck vertebrae were poorly developed, and the tail vertebrae had amphiplatyan centra.

Cetiosaurus represents an early, primitive subfamily, present throughout the Jurassic, in which the neck was only moderately elongated. *Brachiosaurus* and its allies in the Brachiosaurinae are the most massive of all known sauropods (estimated weight 80 to 100 tonnes) and had forelimbs longer than the hindlimbs – an exceptional feature among sauropods. Various poorly known forms that lived in eastern Asia from the Late Jurassic to the Late Cretaceous are grouped as the Euhelopodinae, and the Camarasaurinae includes only the well-known North American *Camarasaurus* (*see* MORRISON FORMATION), a heavily built genus about 10 metres (33ft) long.

Advanced sauropods constitute the Atlantosauridae, in which the nostrils had moved to the top of the skull, the teeth were weak and concentrated at the front of the jaws, and the centra of the vertebrae at the beginning of the tail were concave anteriorly and convex posteriorly (procoelous).

Sauropods
The massive Upper Jurassic Brachiosaurus, *from North America, Portugal, the Sahara and eastern Africa, was about 25m (80ft) long. A shoulder blade and other bones discovered at Dry Mesa, Colorado, which are probably attributable to a sauropod of this type, indicate an animal weighing 100 tonnes.*

Scales

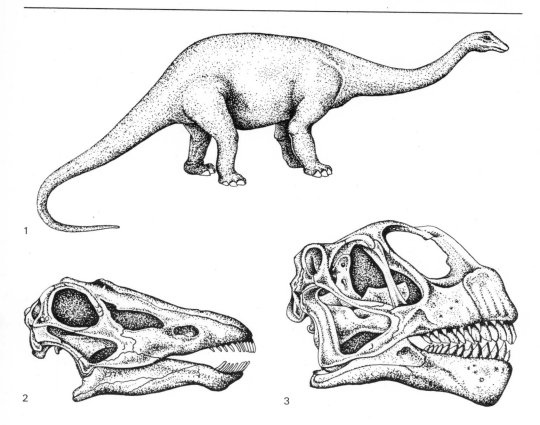

1

2

3

Sauropods
*(1) Diplodocus, a titanosaurid
from the Upper Jurassic of North
America and the longest
dinosaur known, was more than
25m (80ft) long.
(2) Diplodocus had external nostrils
at the top of the skull and weak,
peg-like teeth at the front of the
jaws; skull length about 60cm (2ft).
(3) Camarasaurus, the Upper
Jurassic brachiosaurid, was a
relatively conservative genus with
the external nostrils at the front of
the face and long rows of strong
teeth; skull length about
30cm (12in).*

The Titanosaurinae contain various genera based on fragmentary material that extend from the Upper Jurassic (*Tornieria*) to the end of the Mesozoic. Among them is *Antarcto-saurus*, with a femur 2.3 metres (7.6ft) long.

The familiar *Atlantosaurus* (known also as *Apatosaurus* and *Brontosaurus*) is accorded a subfamily of its own, and the slender *Diplo-docus*, which measured up to 25 metres (82ft), is grouped with *Barosaurus*, *Amphicoelias* and *Uintasaurus* in the Diplodocinae. *Dicraeosaurus* (TENDAGURU) and *Nemegtosaurus* (Mongolia) are assigned to the Dicraeosaurinae.   R.S.

Scales

The characteristic covering of fishes. Scales originated as a means of excreting calcium salts, later acted as a phosphate store, and eventually became a bony armour that served a protective function. The simple placoid scales of the SHARKS and their allies are sharp, pointed and tooth-like. They have a shiny, enameloid outer layer and are composed largely of dentine with a complex pulp cavity. In spite of its apparent simplicity, the placoid scale evolved from the gradual fusion of numerous minute, tooth-like structures (known as lepidomoria), which formed complex scales by gradually aggregating around a central

unit or primordium. Eventually these elements fused to produce the placoid scale.

The scales of the bony fishes were originally similar to those of the earliest sharks, with numerous small units of dentine covered by layers of enameloid. In the bony fishes the enameloid is often termed ganoine and such fishes are frequently known as ganoid fishes. The basal part of the scales is composed of thin layers of bone. The most primitive of the RAY-FIN FISHES, the PALAEONISCIDS, have three layers in their scales: a thick outer enameloid layer, a thin layer of dentine frequently termed cosmine, and a basal layer of bone (isopedin). The more advanced ray-fins, the holosteans, have lost the cosmine and their heavy scales were made up of only an outer enameloid covering and an inner bony layer. These fishes are still known as ganoids because of the ganoine outer layer, but the most advanced ray-fins, the teleosts, have thin scales composed simply of isopedin.

In LOBE-FIN FISHES and LUNGFISHES the inner part of the scale is still made of bone and there is a thin enameloid layer on the outside, but the main part is composed of dentine or cosmine. Minute pores on the surface give the scale a matt finish, unlike ganoid scales which are glassy. In the living lungfish the outer layers have been lost, leaving scales of bone.   L.B.H.

Scales
*Sectional views show:
(1) the dermal armour of a
placoderm in which outer
denticles surmount a layer of
spongy bone and basal lamellar
bone;
(2) a cosmoid scale characteristic
of early lobe-fin fishes with a thin
coating of enamel immediately
above a cosmine layer that is
supported by spongy bone and
deep lamellar bone;
(3) the ganoid scale of early ray-
fin fishes with multiple outer
layers of ganoine above the
cosmine layer and the basal
lamellar bone – later ray-fins
tended to lose the ganoine and
cosmine layers altogether;
(4) the placoid dermal denticle of
a shark with a central pulp cavity,
dentine permeated by a system of
nutrient canals, and an enamel
outer covering.*

1
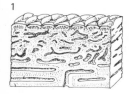

2
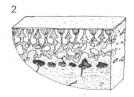

3
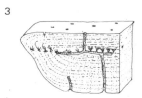

4

Scheuchzer

Scheuchzer, Johann Jakob (1672–1733)
Swiss palaeontologist, born in Zurich, who is often credited as the founder of Swiss palaeontology. He was the author of *Herbarium Diluvianum* (1709), one of the first books to illustrate fossil plants, and was a supporter of the work of John WOODWARD; he translated Woodward's work into Latin.

As a professor of the University of Zurich, he travelled extensively and stimulated interest in the study of fossils. Late in life Scheuchzer described in his *Physica Sacra* (1731) a specimen he had discovered at Oeningen (Germany) which he considered to be "the bony skeleton of one of those infamous men whose sins brought upon the world the dire misfortune of the deluge". To this he gave the name *Homo diluvii testis*, leaving Georges CUVIER to show that it was in fact the skeleton of a salamander.   A.P.H.

Schlotheim, Ernst von (1764–1832)
Pioneer German palaeontologist (born in Almenhausen), who promoted the use of fossils in determining the relative ages of strata. He was a Privy Councillor and President of the Chamber of the Court of Gotha. He amassed a considerable collection of fossils and wrote *Beschreibung merkwürdiger Kräuter-Abdrücke und Pflanzen-Versteinerungen* (1804), which described plant fossils from the Carboniferous. This work is noted for its excellent illustrations and the comparative nature of the research; it stimulated the development of palaeobotany. A catalogue of his collection *Die Petrefaktenkunde* (1820–23) was the first German palaeontological work to use binomial nomenclature.   A.P.H.

Scorpions, *see* SPIDERS AND SCORPIONS.

Sea cows, *see* DUGONGS.

Sea scorpions
Extinct members of the ARTHROPOD class Merostomata, assigned to the order Eurypterida. Sea scorpions had an elongated body composed of a prosoma, an opisthosoma and a telson. The body was covered with a chitinous external skeleton that was periodically

Sea scorpions
The massive sea scorpion Pterygotus *flourished in Silurian seas.*
Length: 2.3m (7.5ft)

moulted. The prosoma incorporated large, faceted lateral eyes and a pair of median ocelli. It bore six pairs of legs: the foremost pair was chelate (grasping), the next four pairs were for walking, and the last pair usually formed large, broad swimming paddles. The opisthosoma was composed of twelve segments, the first six being broader and formed from dorsal and ventral half-rings, with gills present on the underside. The six narrower, posterior segments were complete rings which did not carry any appendages. The last segment was usually a large spine (the telson), but sometimes became modified into a tail fin (as in the Pterygotidae) or into cercal blades (as in *Megalograptus*). The sexes were separate, distinguished by the shape of the middle appendage of the operculum: the male possessed a clasping organ into which the extension of the female appendage fitted.

Eurypterids may be found in marine or freshwater deposits, but generally the animals seem to have preferred an estuarine or brackish-water environment. Although sea scorpions are known for their enormous size – *Pterygotus anglicus* reached 2.3 metres (7.5ft) – many species are small and measure only 5–10cm (2–4in) long. The feeding habits of sea scorpions are largely unknown, although COPROLITES probably originating from the Ordovician *Megalograptus* contain eurypterid fragments, suggesting post-mating cannibalism as in some Recent SPIDERS AND SCORPIONS. The large teeth of the coxae and strong chelicerae suggest that hard-shelled animals were part of their diet.

The earliest merostome, *Paleomerus* from the Lower Cambrian of Sweden, incorporates characteristics of primitive HORSESHOE CRABS and eurypterids. An Upper Ordovician eurypterid from Wales, *Brachyopterus*, has the body and short walking legs of an early horseshoe crab combined with the prosoma of a eurypterid. It may have been intermediate between *Paleomerus* and the more specialized eurypterids with modified prosomal appendages and a telson.

The most obvious development is the changing of the last prosomal walking leg into a swimming leg, although among the stylonurids this occurs in only a few genera. Among all groups of sea scorpions there is a tendency to increase in size, with elaboration of the ornamentation.

The first true sea scorpions occur in the Lower Ordovician rocks of the USA. Remains of eurypterids may subsequently be found in all periods from the Ordovician to the Permian, but most finds come from brackish-water to freshwater deposits such as the OLD RED SANDSTONE of Scotland. The extinction of the eurypterids was probably due to increased competition from fishes.   S.F.M.

Sea urchins
A group of ECHINODERMS that occurs from the Ordovician onwards. Sea urchins are of two main types: regular and irregular.

A representative regular echinoid is *Stereocidaris* from the CHALK. This consists of a rigid, bun-shaped shell or test to which large, moveable spines are attached. The anus is at the top of the test in a circular piece of flexible skin known as the periproct, and the mouth is at the bottom of the test in a similar circular piece of skin called the peristome. Around the periproct is a ring (the apical disc) made of five ocular plates and five genital plates. Each genital plate is penetrated by a large pore through which, in life, sperm and eggs were released from the sex glands beneath. In addition, one of the genital plates is perforated by several smaller pores, and this sieve-like plate is the madreporite of the water-vascular system.

Extending down from the five ocular plates are sinuous double rows (ambulacra) of small plates (ambulacral plates). A pair of pores penetrates each of these plates and represents the attachment point of a single tube-foot. The mid-line of each double row overlays a radial water vessel living inside the test.

Between the ambulacra are double rows (interambulacra) of large plates, each having a prominent spine attached to its centre by a ball-and-socket articulation; the ball is represented by a smooth hemisphere (mamelon) in the centre of the interambulacral plate. The spines were used for walking, and round the mamelon is a smooth circular region where, in life, the muscles of the spine base were attached. The five massive jaws ("Aristotle's lantern") each carry a gouge-like tooth that grew continuously downwards.

A representative irregular echinoid is *Micraster*, also from the Chalk. Regular sea urchins live on the sea bed, but irregular sea urchins either plough, half-buried, through the top layer of the sea bottom or burrow in it. For this reason their original five-rayed symmetry has partly given way to a bilateral symmetry which helps them force their way through mud. *Micraster* was a truly burrowing form and is heart-shaped. The notch of the heart corresponds to one of the ambulacra which has sunk into a groove (the front groove) that was foremost when the animal was burrowing. The apical disc was a small group of plates near the centre of the upper surface but, unlike *Stereocidaris*, this no longer contained the anus, which had moved out of the disc onto the rear surface of the test.

Micraster had lost its jaws and teeth, and fed by picking food particles out of the mud as it extended its burrow forwards, using a special concentration of tube-feet round the mouth. The tube-feet moved forwards to a position just behind the front groove, so they in life would have been near the front end of the burrow. Ambulacra and interambulacra still extended as double rows of plates from the apical disc to the mouth, but were not so distinct as in *Stereocidaris*. Both types of plate were covered with many tubercles to which were attached small, flattened spines that could be stroked backwards but not forwards and were used to dig the burrow, some being flattened at the end like spades.

The ambulacra of *Micraster* were most obvious near the apical disc where they showed as five small elliptical petals. *Micraster* ("little star") gets its name from these petals, which

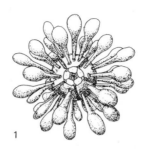 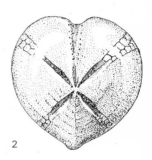

represent the places where great numbers of flattened respiratory tube-feet were attached. The animal dug out, above itself, a vertical respiratory tunnel for these tube-feet, so that it could breathe when buried.   R.P.S.J.

Sea urchins
(1) The cidarid Tylocidaris *occurred from the Upper Cretaceous to the Lower Eocene (approx. 1/2 natural size). (2) The heart-urchin* Micraster *occurred from the Upper Cretaceous to the Palaeocene (approx. 2/3 natural size).*

Senckenberg Natural History Museum
See Natur-Museum und Forschungsinstitut.

Seward, Sir Albert Charles (1863–1941)
British palaeobotanist, who taught botany at Cambridge University. He was born in Lancaster, England, and attended Cambridge University, where he was appointed lecturer in botany (1890) and professor (1906). He was interested in botany and geology and, early in his career, received guidance from the palaeobotanist W. C. Williamson (1816–95). His earliest researches were on plants of Permo-Carboniferous age from greater India, although he later specialized in the Mesozoic flora.

Altogether, Seward published about 160 contributions to the scientific literature, including the catalogue of Mesozoic plants in the British Museum (Natural History) and two standard textbooks: *Fossil Plants* (1898–1919, in four volumes) and *Plant Life through the Ages* (1931). He received many honours from the scientific community and was knighted in 1936.   A.P.H.

Sharks
Members of the class Chondrichthyes, which comprises fishes that have retained an internal skeleton of cartilage. Rays and chimaeras also belong to this assemblage.

Sharks originated from placoderms, which had a bony armour but gradually lost it as they evolved into sharks; all that remains is the covering of placoid scales. Most sharks are exclusively marine and so never developed many of the features that occur among bony fishes. For example, no accessory breathing organs evolved, and hence there are no hydrostatic buoyancy structures. Sharks therefore retained the primitive heterocercal tail, but they and their allies

Silurian

evolved special copulatory organs (the claspers of the males) which are concerned with internal fertilization. Such structures are also found in some placoderms and confirm the close relationship between the two groups. The Chondrichthyes fall into two major divisions: the Elasmobranchii (sharks and rays) and the Holocephali (chimaeras and the mollusc-eating bradyodonts of the Palaeozoic).

The most primitive sharks are the clado-selachians, in which the jaws were fused to the braincase and supported by the hyomandibular (the amphistylic condition). The primitive triangular fins had a broad base and the tail appeared symmetrical (although in fact the main lobe was the dorsal one). There was no anal fin, but a pair of horizontal stabilizers were present at the base of the tail.

From this type of generalized shark there developed two main lines. One of these, the Carboniferous pleuracanths (also known as Xenacanths) was the only major group of sharks to colonize fresh water, but the main evolutionary line passed upwards through the hybodonts. The principal advance was in the structure of the fins. They narrowed at the base to three basal elements, beyond which the fine radials spread out – a basic pattern that remains characteristic of all sharks to the present day. A small anal fin also developed, and the teeth at the rear became blunter, frequently forming a pavement of crushing teeth. During the Jurassic the first modern sharks originated from the hybodonts. In these advanced forms the jaws were sus-pended from the skull only by the hyomandi-bular (hyostylic jaw suspension).

The modern flesh-eating sharks belong to the suborder Galeoidea and have serrated, blade-like teeth *Carcharodon*, the great white shark, is a member of this assemblage, and extinct species of the genus grew to a length of about 27 metres (90ft).

A second major group of modern sharks is the suborder Squaloidea, characterized by a bony spine in front of each dorsal fin. These bottom-dwelling forms possess a large spiracle but have lost their anal fin.   I.B.H.

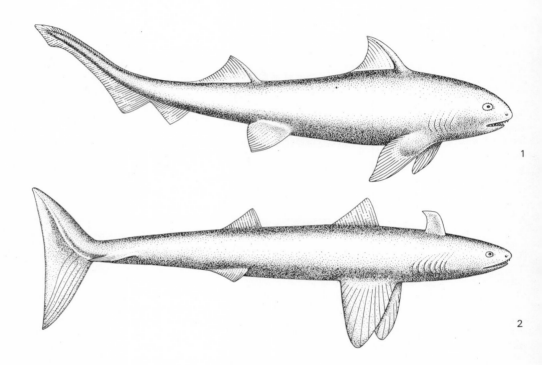

1

2

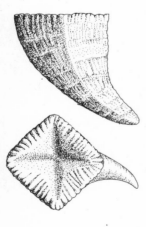

Silurian

The last of the three geological periods that constitute the Lower PALAEOZOIC. The Silurian began about 435 million years ago and lasted for 40 million years. It takes its name from the Silures, a Celtic tribe which, at the time of the Roman occupation of Britain, inhabited the Welsh Borderland where rocks of the period were first studied. The Silurian system comprises (in order of decreasing age) the Llandovery, Wenlock, Ludlow and Pridoli series.

Silurian rocks are widely distributed and occur on all the modern continents except Antarctica. Non-marine sequences appear to be uncommon, although the geography of the period differed little from that of the succeeding DEVONIAN, except for a narrow seaway close to the line of the present Atlantic Ocean separating North America, Greenland and north-western Scotland from the rest of north-western Europe plus south-eastern Newfoundland and Nova Scotia.

Siwalik series

In many respects life in the Silurian continued evolutionary patterns established in the ORDOVICIAN, and no new major group of invertebrates appeared. Among the VERTEBRATES and plants, however, significant developments occurred. The agnathans (jawless "fishes") diversified considerably in the Middle and Late Silurian, colonizing brackish-water and fresh-water habitats, and the first true fishes also appeared although they remained spase and undifferentiated until the Devonian. The earliest authenticated land plants occur in the Silurian, although Ordovician and even Cambrian records have been claimed, but again it was not until the Devonian that they show significant evolutionary diversification.

The shallow sea floors of the period supported rich benthic (bottom-dwelling) faunas of BRACHIOPODS, CORALS, BRYOZOANS, TRILOBITES, MOLLUSCS, and ECHINODERMS (particularly CRINOIDS). Among pelagic organisms, the GRAPTOLITES were of great importance and the soft-bodied organism, of which the tooth-shaped CONODONT microfossils apparently formed a part, is also thought to have been pelagic. Other microfossils, benthic and pelagic, that were present in Silurian deposits include FORAMINIFERANS, OSTRACODS, chitinozoans and acritarchs.

The graptolites and the conodonts are important as international ZONE FOSSILS for correlating Silurian rocks. The graptolites of the period include the distinctive monograptids, with a single, uniserial stipe; more than 30 graptolite zones, almost all based on monograptids, are recognized in the Silurian.

More locally, brachiopods and trilobites are used for the relative dating of Silurian rocks. The brachiopods were an actively evolving group at this time, the pentamerids being particularly distinctive, but the trilobites were declining although still reasonably diverse and characterized by, among others, calymenids, cheirurids, phacopids and illaenids.

Another group of ARTHROPODS, the eurypterids (SEA SCORPIONS), reached their peak in the Silurian and Devonian. These brackish-water to freshwater predators grew to 2 metres (6.6ft) or more in length and probably preyed on early fishes. Among the corals, which are too sensitive to environmental factors to be of much use in correlation, the Rugosa diversified considerably whereas the tabulate corals, although abundant in carbonate environments, began a gradual decline. Bryozoans were widespread but small, and therefore less obvious as fossils. Cephalopods were the most prominent, if temporarily declining, of the molluscs, but BIVALVES and GASTROPODS were evolving slowly and relatively unspectacularly. The crinoids underwent a great diversification during the period and their ossicles are often common in carbonate sediments.

Faunal provinces were not strongly marked in the Silurian. Most groups were cosmopolitan, with only minor local differences, suggesting the lack of major barriers to migration. Only ostracods, most of which have a benthic larval stage, show provincialism in circum-equatorial areas, but restricted faunas characteristic of high latitudes are known in southern South America, southern and western Africa (the Malvinokaffric province) and in southern Siberia (the Tuvaella province, named after an orthid brachiopod).

See also the time chart.   C.T.S.

Siwalik series

The Middle Miocene–Upper Pleistocene rocks of the Indian sub-continent that are exposed on the Potwar Plateau, an elevated area of about 20,000sq km (7,720sq miles). The plateau is bounded to the north by the Kala Chitta and Margala Hills, to the south by the Salt Range, to the east by the Jhelum River and to the west by the Indus River.

The Siwalik deposits are rich in fossil mammals and were apparently laid down by a fast-flowing, multi-channelled river. Evidence of alternating sandstones, silts and clays indicate numerous wet cycles. During the NEOGENE the whole area consisted of subsiding basins on the southern flanks of the rising Himalaya Mountains.

The lowest beds of the Siwalik sequence are the Middle Miocene Kamlial deposits, but the first important mammalian fauna is from the Upper Miocene Chinji Formation. The environment appears to have been essentially subtropical forest. The fauna included the PRIMATES *Sivapithecus* and *Ramapithecus*, at least one late-surviving CREODONT (*Dissopsalis*), HYAENAS (*Percrocuta, Miohyaena*), small carnivores (*Martes, Vishnuonyx, Amphicyon, Sivaelurus, Vishnucyon*), a CHALICOTHERE, swine (*Listriodon, Conohyus, Lophochoerus*), an ANTHRACOTHERE (*Merycopotamus*), giraffids (*Giraffokeryx*), bovids (*Protragocerus, Miotragocerus, Kubanotragus* and *Sivoreas*), small SABRE-TOOTHED CATS (*Sivasmilus, Sansanosmilus, Paramachaerodus*), early felines (*Vishnufelis, Vinayakia*), and cricetid RODENTS similar to those found in deposits of comparable age in Europe. The three-toed HORSE *Hipparion*, a common Old World Pliocene form, seems to be absent.

Pliocene Nagri Formation, and during these two stages there seems to have been a gradual transition to a woodland or bush habitat, with open patches of grassland. Large mammals are rare, grazing species are relatively few in number, and arboreal forms occur only infrequently.

The Nagri fauna still includes *Sivapithecus* and *Ramapithecus*, as well as *Merycopotamus* and *Miotragocerus*, but the creodonts, chalicotheres and giraffes seem to have dwindled. *Hipparion* is now present, however, along with the roboscidean *Deinotherium*, various swine (*Schizochoerus, Propotamochoerus, Hippopotamodon, Conohyus* and possibly (*Tetraconodon*), tragulids (*Dorcabune, Dorcatherium*), bovids (*Selenopartax*), and numerous rodents. Carnivores comprise sabre-toothed cats (*Megantereon*), felines (*Vinayakia*), hyaenas (*Percrocuta, Palhyaena, Miohyaena*), and mustelids.

In the Dhok Pathan Formation of Upper Pliocene age, *Miotragocerus* and various other

Silurian
Goniophyllum *was a characteristic Lower and Middle Silurian coral.*
Approx. natural size.

395 million years ago

Upper	Salopian	Ludlovian	Cayugan
Middle		Wenlockian	Niagaran
Lower	Llandoverian (Valentian)		Albian (Medinian)

435 million years ago
The Silurian succession

191

Skates

bovids apparently became extinct but reedbucks make their appearance, together with a *Prostrepsiceros*-like form and some cervids. Sabre-toothed cats (*Propontosmilus*, *Paramachaerodus*), felines (*Mellivorodon*) and a species of *Sus* are also present, together with the suid genera *Sivachoerus*, *Hippohyus* and *Sivahyus*. The rodents of the Dhok Pathan are clearly distinguished from their Nagri predecessors, and the oldest Siwalik cercopithecoid primate, *Presbytis sivalensis*, is a Dhok Pathan species. Crocodiles include the gavial and the extinct *Crocodylus palaeindicus*.

The closing stages of the Siwalik series are the Villafranchian (Lower Pleistocene) Tatrot Formation and the Upper Pleistocene Pinjor beds, containing the large feline *Sivapanthera* (possibly a cheetah) as well as *Felis cristata*, which equalled a tiger in size. R.S.

Skates, *see* RAYS.

Skeleton

In VERTEBRATES, the skeleton has a dual origin. The first bony material was formed in the skin of the earliest vertebrates as an exoskeleton, the internal skeleton being composed of gristle or cartilage. The living SHARKS are derived from armoured PLACODERMS, their placoid scales being the remains of a formerly extensive bony covering. The sharks have retained the primitive internal skeleton of cartilage, but during the embryonic development of the higher vertebrates the internal skeleton is only initially formed of cartilage: subsequently it is replaced by bone. Cartilage is retained only in the young individual because no other hard tissue is capable of growth by internal expansion. This ensures that the relationships of the skeletal elements to the associated muscles, nerves and blood vessels are not disrupted during growth. The beginning of this change is seen in the jawless CEPHALASPIDS, in which the interior of the head region is at first composed of connective tissue, which is only later replaced by bone derived from the inner layers of the outer armour.

The internal skeleton comprises two major elements: a protective covering for the brain (the cranium) which is the diagnostic feature of the vertebrates, and the vertebral column or BACKBONE. In fishes this acts as a compression member along the length of the body against which the segmental swimming muscles act. The development of paired fins with their own internal skeletal supports led to the development of the shoulder and hip girdles, which became attached to the vertebral column, the former via a sling musculature, the latter directly.

When the vertebrates emerged on to dry land,

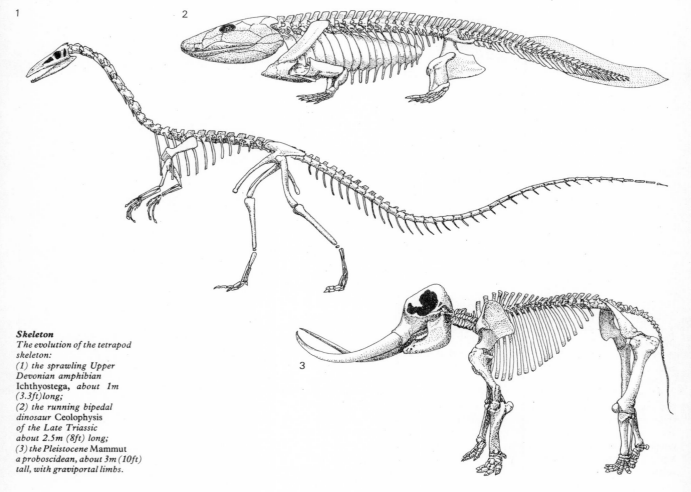

1

2

3

Skeleton
The evolution of the tetrapod skeleton:
(1) the sprawling Upper Devonian amphibian Ichthyostega, *about 1m (3.3ft) long;*
(2) the running bipedal dinosaur Ceolophysis *of the Late Triassic about 2.5m (8ft) long;*
(3) the Pleistocene Mammut *a proboscidean, about 3m (10ft) tall, with graviportal limbs.*

Skull

important changes occurred in the skeleton. Instead of the animal floating in the medium in which it lived, the body had to be supported at only four specific points: the four limbs. At the same time, the vertebral column developed articulations which prevented the backbone sagging under the animal's weight. At this evolutionary stage all forward movement was still achieved by throwing the body into sinuous waves that would swing the limbs forwards, but during the further development of the higher vertebrates, the backbone became a more rigid structure and the limbs were held vertically beneath the trunk instead of projecting laterally in a sprawling position.

This improvement enabled animals to take longer strides at greater speed. In forms with a large discrepancy in the length of forelimbs and hindlimbs there developed a tendency towards bipedalism, for example, in carnivorous DINOSAURS. Bipedalism also occurred when tree-living animals began to swing from the forelimbs through the branches so that the body hung upright. These animals developed an upright stance and when on the ground walked on their hindlimbs, as in man. Among the larger vertebrates such as elephants and SAUROPOD dinosaurs, the limbs formed massive, pillar-like columns to support the vast weight (graviportal limbs). At the other extreme, flying vertebrates developed exceptionally light skeletons: the bone in giant PTEROSAURS, for example, was less than 1mm (0.04in) thick.

The ability to produce an internal bony skeleton is such that bone can be laid down in a large variety of sites. Some CATTLE, for example, develop large bones in the heart, and many mammals (eg CARNIVORA, WHALES, RODENTS and bats) have penis bones. Perhaps the most dramatic example of the evolution of bone is found in the extinct South American glyptodonts, which developed a thick bony carapace that formed a virtually impenetrable armour. This was a completely new feature among the mammals, and had arisen independently of the bony armour that was found in many groups of early reptiles. L.B.H.

Skull

The cranium or skeletal protection for the BRAIN; the fundamental feature that distinguishes the VERTEBRATES from other members of the phylum Chordata. The term "craniate" is often preferred to the more familiar "vertebrate".

Primitively the braincase was composed of cartilage, and plates of dermal armour were positioned on the outer part of the head. The skull of the higher vertebrates is derived from elements of the original internal cartilaginous chondrocranium and the external dermal bones of the head. During evolution, changes in the skull have reflected changes in the mode of life of the animals concerned. Fishes, which breathe through their gills and possess a lateral-line system, have the rear part of the skull more developed than the front; the senses of hearing and balance are among their key senses and, together with the gills, are located towards the

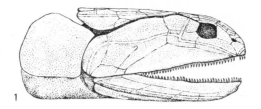

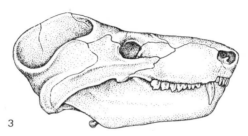

Skull
Evolution of the vertebrate skull:
(1) the primitive lobe-fin fish
Osteolepis *occurred in the Middle and Upper Devonian;*
(2) the anthracosaurian amphibian Seymouria *from the Lower Permian of North America;*
(3) the mammal-like reptile Cynognathus *present in the Lower and Middle Triassic of southern Africa.*

back of the head. The sense of smell is less important.

With the transition to land life, the relative importance of the sense organs changed significantly. The gills were completely replaced by lungs and disappeared, while the acoustico-lateralis system became defunct. The sense of smell was now, however, of prime importance and had to be highly developed in order to detect the more dilute constituent aromas in air. These changes were reflected in the different proportions of the skull: the posterior part was reduced and the snouth became elongated.

When the conquest of the land was fully accomplished by reptiles, a further major change occurred in the construction of the skull. The dentition no longer acted merely to prevent prey such as fishes from slipping out of the mouth, but now had to be capable of despatching large struggling reptiles. The entire apparatus was strengthened and this involved increasing the musculature. The jaw muscles were situated in the confined space between the brainbox and the skull roofing bones, and the only way for the muscles to expand was to open up the bones covering the temporal or cheek region. In this part of the skull there were two points where three bones met, and temporal openings developed in just these places. In TURTLES and their allies no such openings formed but the rear and lower margins of the skull roofing bones were emarginated to accommodate the increase in the muscles of the jaw and neck. In the marine ICHTHYOSAURS and PLESIOSAURS the upper opening alone developed, whereas in the paramammals (MAMMAL-LIKE REPTILES) only the lower opening appeared. The group from which the LIZARDS and ARCHOSAURS evolved developed both openings, but the later

Sloths

lizards and the SNAKES continued the trend of opening up the roofing bones so that in the advanced snakes both the lower and upper temporal bars are lost, and even the rear margin of the orbit has disappeared. The living reptiles are customarily classified according to the type of temporal openings that are present.

The mammals modified the skull further as a consequence of the enormous increase in the size of the brain. The human skull embodies a proportionately huge braincase together with relatively weak jaws, grasping hands having been evolved to accomplish manipulatory functions for which other mammals use the mouth.   L.B.H.

Sloths

Members of the mammalian infraorder Pilosa, a group of EDENTATES that includes numerous extinct ground sloths as well as two genera of living tree sloths. The history of the modern sloths is unknown because fossils are lacking, but anatomically they have much in common with some Miocene ground sloths.

The first ground sloths appeared in the Oligocene, and by the Miocene a large variety had evolved. *Hapalops*, one of the earlier representatives of the group, was a slender animal about 1 metre (3.3ft) long that occurred in the Lower and Middle Miocene of South America. It had clawed toes on all its feet and walked on the knuckles of the hands and the outer sides of the hindfeet. The skull was moderately elongated, with small premaxillae, a spout-like mandibular symphysis, and five upper teeth in each jaw opposed by four lower teeth in each mandibular ramus.

One evolutionary line that is readily traceable to *Hapalops* or its relatives culminated in the megatheres, typically large, massively proportioned animals reaching a length of about 6 metres (19.7ft). During the long history of this group several poorly known genera evolved, apparently radiating from the area of Argentina and Uruguay. The teeth became huge, bilophodont with twin transverse ridges and deeply open-rooted. The sturdy tail enabled the animals to rear up to feed on leaves and twigs with the

aid of their claws and well-developed tongue – a food preference that is confirmed by analysis of excrement (*see* COPROLITES) from North and South America. The culmination of the megatheriid line is seen in *Megatherium* itself, which is common in the Late Pleistocene of southern and eastern South America.

Eremotherium, an equally large but more conservatively evolved megathere, spread throughout the remainder of South America, Central America, and across coastal south-eastern North America as far north as New Jersey. It reached the weight of perhaps three oxen, and is known to have evolved into several species in North and South America.

The family Megalonychidae is obviously derived from the South American *Hapalops* stock, but its early history is not well known. Megalonychids probably reached North America in the Pliocene, having migrated via the islands then constituting Central America and the West Indies, where dwarfed fossil forms have been found. *Megalonyx* itself became the most widespread sloth in North America, reaching all parts except the far north-east. It was apparently a hardy animal, occurring in numerous inland sites at high·altitudes and latitudes.

About the size of a cow, *Megalonyx* showed variable morphology, so that many generic and specific names are used to describe it. These can probably be reduced to the single genus, with only a few species, showing a trend towards increased size during the span of the Pleistocene. *Megalonyx* has an unusually short snout and a massive lower jaw, reflecting the fact that the large, truncated canine teeth are located at the extreme front of the skull. The cheek teeth are sub-triangular in section, the occlusal surfaces showing valleys and ridges.

The family Mylodontidae apparently had a long independent evolutionary history, having separated from other sloths at least as early as the Oligocene. Mylodontids became prominent in numbers and variety only in the Pliocene and Pleistocene, when they were evolving along several phyletic lines, but they eventually occurred from the tip of South America to the northern USA.

Sloths
Mylodon *was a ground sloth from the Pleistocene of South America. Length: about 4.5m (15ft)*

Sowerby

Only one group of mylodonts, characterized by the genus *Glossotherium*, reached North America, where it spread across the entire USA. First described as *Mylodon* and then as *Paramylodon*, *Glossotherium harlani* is the most common sloth at RANCHO LA BREA. It was about ox-size and stockily built, with relatively short, robust legs. South American mylodonts, such as *Mylodon* itself and *Lestodon*, were similar in general appearance.

Another mylodon line, best exemplified by *Scelidotherium*, was more lightly built and ranged widely over the southern and western parts of South America. The skull was exceedingly long and cylindrical, with weak teeth.

Reasons for the extinction of the ground sloths are speculative. Competition from immigrant North American herbivores and carnivores has been suggested, but many types of South American sloths persisted along with the immigrants until after the last glacial period. Furthermore, those species that emigrated to North America flourished during the Pleistocene and died out only at the same time as their South American relatives. *Nothrotheriops*, for example, a common ground sloth in western North America, is known from mummified remains complete with bones, skin, tendons, hair and faeces preserved in dry caves. A.G.E.

Smith, William (1769–1839)
British geologist, born in Churchill, Oxfordshire, who is considered the father of English geology. He was the son of a blacksmith and, at the age of 18, became an apprentice surveyor. During his early years in the profession he worked in the coal mines and canals of Somerset, where he was concerned mainly with drainage, and became well acquainted with the different strata. He travelled about 100,000 miles throughout England on horseback, investigating rocks and fossils.

His significant contribution to geology was in recognizing that sedimentary rock can be identified by its fossil content. He produced the first geological column and the first geological map of any part of Britain. He compiled the first geological map of England and Wales in 1815. A.P.H.

Snakes
Members of the reptilian suborder Ophidia, a sub-division of the Lacertilia.

Snakes were the last major group of reptiles to appear in the fossil record, the earliest known forms being from the Late Cretaceous. Essentially, the skull of the Ophidia is derived from that of LIZARDS by loss of the postorbital-squamosal bar separating the upper and lower temporal openings. In addition, the entire skull and lower jaw are highly specialized, consisting of several freely movable sections.

Other characteristic ophidian specializations include the loss of the limbs and girdles (except, occasionally, for traces of the pelvic girdle and hindlimbs), and extreme elongation of the trunk and tail by the addition of extra segments.

Snakes are uncommon as fossils. Their lightly constructed skulls are generally too fragile to be preserved, and the vertebrae by themselves are not always recognizable as ophidian. It seems probable that the snakes evolved originally from lizards as burrowers, although most modern forms have returned to life above ground. It also seems likely that their ancestry is related to the varanoid (monitor) lizards which, like snakes, have flexible jaws. The Upper Cretaceous *Simoliophis* and the Eocene *Palaeophis*, with monitor-like vertebrae but long snake-like bodies, may represent a transitional group.

Sub-division of the snakes is generally into three superfamilies, all of which survive today. The Typhlopoidea, first recorded in the Eocene, are small, worm-like tropical burrowers. The Booidea, comprising the boas and pythons and many smaller forms, also date from the Eocene but doubtfully include some Late Cretaceous fossils such as *Dinilysia*. The Colubroidea, including all the more specialized snakes, have not been recorded with certainty before the Miocene. A.J.C.

South African Museum
Founded in 1855 in Cape Town, although it dates back to proposals made for the establishment of a museum in 1825.

The first KARROO specimens were collected with the aid of a government grant in 1883 from the Fraserburg-Beaufort West area, and the Museum now has one of the finest collections of Karroo reptiles in the world. The extensive vertebrate collections also include an extinct buffalo with a horn span of 3 metres (10ft).

Although slow to develop, the invertebrate collections now form the basis for several research projects. A Palaeontology Hall was opened in 1970 to provide a survey of South Africa's prehistoric past, particularly the Karroo plants and animals and the Quaternary fossils of Cape Province. A.P.H.

Sowerby
A British family of naturalists who achieved distinction during the 19th century.

James Sowerby (1757–1822) was the first of the family to write, illustrate and publish natural history books – among them the *Mineral Conchology* (1812–46) which, largely because of its fine illustrations, is still prized in palaeontological research. This book was continued by James de Carle Sowerby (1787–1871), James Sowerby's eldest son. James Sowerby's other contribution to palaeontology was mainly the preparation of illustrations for other workers in studies on invertebrates, palaeobotany and micropalaeontology.

The other members of the family contributed little to palaeontological publication, with the exception of George Brettingham Sowerby (1812–84). John William Salter (1820–69), who was apprenticed to J. de Carle Sowerby and later married his daughter, joined the then Geological Survey of Great Britain, and became their palaeontologist in 1854. A.P.H.

Spiders and scorpions

Spiders and scorpions

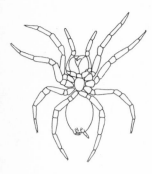

Spiders and scorpions
The fossil spider Eodiplurina *lived in the Oligocene of Colorado (approx. 6 times natural size).*

Members of the ARTHROPOD class Arachnida that are characterized as air-breathing chelicerates, with a body divided into cephalothorax and abdomen. The cephalothorax carries six pairs of legs, the first pair being chelate (grasping), with the number of leg joints increasing posteriorly; there are usually four pairs of walking legs. The abdomen is composed of a maximum of twelve segments, but during arachnid evolution segments may have been either fused or lost. Scorpions always retain at least the last five abdominal segments as a tail, but the most advanced spiders have only completely fused segments in the adult, although evidence of segmentation persists in the young.

The earliest scorpion, *Palaeophonus* from the Lower Silurian of Sweden, Scotland and the USA was aquatic, but later arachnids became totally terrestrial, with some forms eventually returning to the water as secondarily aquatic animals.

The large size attained by some of the early scorpions required the support of water. The largest known, *Brontoscorpio anglicus* from England, has a calculated length of about 80cm (31.5in). Two genera have been described from the Devonian Rhynie Chert of Scotland. In the Coal Measures of Europe, spiders with segmented abdomina are relatively abundant in nodules. Post-Palaeozoic beds yield a negligible record of arachnids. There are only two known Mesozoic arachnids, and although there are more occurrences in the Cenozoic they are found only in a few insect-bearing beds. The small number of finds is not so surprising in spiders because they have a thin cuticle, but scorpions are more robustly constructed and their absence is difficult to explain.   S.F.M.

Sponges

Simple aquatic multi-celled animals comparable in some respects to colonial protozoans, from which they are thought to have evolved in the Pre-Cambrian. By the Middle Cambrian, sponges were represented by many genera, including *Protospongia* from Britain and *Chancelloria* and *Vauxia* from North America. They continued to flourish, attaining a maximum abundance in the Cretaceous. More than 1,000 fossil genera have been established, fewer than 20 of which are represented in the 1,400 Recent genera.

Basically, sponges consist of germ cells and somatic cells that perform specialized functions, choanocytes (collar cells), and amoebocytes (amoeboid cells). In the simplest form of sponge structure (ascon), a sac-like body opening (osculum) at the top is composed of two layers of cells, and perforated by numerous pores. A skeleton composed of mineral spicules or horny spongin fibres in the outer layer supports the body wall, and incorporated in the layer lining the central cavity (vent) are choanocytes, each with a whip-like flagellum. By rapid movement of the flagellum, water containing food particles and oxygen is drawn through the pores into the vent, and expelled with waste products through the osculum. The sponge has no digestive tract and therefore the food is absorbed by the choanocytes. The amoebocytes form the outer parts of the body, and secrete the spicular skeletons. In the more complex forms the wall is folded in such a manner that sycon sponges consist of a group of ascon chambers around a vent and in those with leucon structure several sycon units are aggregated. Most sponges are leucon, the grade with the most efficient water circulation.

Sponges may be solitary or colonial and vary widely in shape and size. They are commonly vase-shaped (eg *Ventriculites*), pear-shaped (*Siphonia*), leaf-shaped (*Elasmostoma, Verruculina*), branching (*Peronidella, Thamnospongia*), irregular, or encrusting. In some sponges the diameter is less than 1cm (0.4in), and in others it is more than 1 metre (3.3ft).

Sponge classification is based primarily on the composition of the skeleton. In the Calcarea, such as *Corynella* and *Amblysiphonella*, the spicules are composed of calcium carbonate, whereas they are of colloidal silica in the Hexactinellida and Demospongea. Hexactinellids, typified by the Devonian glass sponge *Hydnoceras*, have six-rayed spicules (hexacts). Most fossil Demospongea (such as *Jerea, Astylospongia*) belong to the Lithistida, characterized by lumpy spicules (desmas) interlocked in a rigid, box-like framework.

Sponges are predominantly marine and one family only, the Spongillidae, is adapted to freshwater conditions. Anchored to the sea bed by root-tufts, stems or by the under surface, they range from the inter-tidal zone to abyssal depths. Most Calcarea live in the warm, shallow water above the 200 metres (656ft) mark; the Hexactinellida and Demospongea live in the cooler, less turbulent water of the continental slope and abyssal region, mainly between 200 and 600 metres (656 and 1,968ft) below the surface. They range from tropical water, where they are most abundant in species and numbers, to polar regions, and have a worldwide distribu-

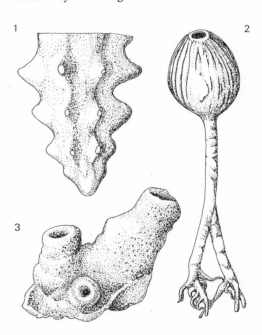

Sponges
(1) The glass sponge Hydnoceras *ranges from the Upper Devonian to the Carboniferous (approx. 1/4 natural size).*
(2) Corynella *occurred from the Triassic to the Cretaceous (approx. 3/4 natural size).*
(3) The lithistid sponge Siphonia *was present from the Middle Cretaceous through the Cenozoic (approx. 1/2 natural size).*

Stratigraphy

tion. Fossil sponges have little stratigraphical value but they have proved useful in interpreting the palaeoecology of rocks bearing their remains.

Two poorly known groups that may be included with the sponges are the Stromatoporata (exclusively colonial hydrozoans that are sheet-like or dendroid in form and have a calcareous coenosteum of a basically trabecular (nature) and the Chaetetida, which have a massive coralla composed of extremely slender aseptate corallites with imperforated walls and complete abulae.   S.W.

Starfishes

A group of ECHINODERMS that, together with the brittle stars (ophiuroids), forms the Asterozoa. These animals are relatively infrequent as fossils but range in known age from Ordovician to Recent. Starfishes (asteroids) have broad, inflexible arms and move by walking on the tube-feet, whereas ophiuroids have long, slender mobile arms which they use as "legs" in locomotion. The fossil somasteroids seem to represent primitive asterozoans, which are neither asteroids nor ophiuroids but the evolutionary source of both.   R.P.S.J.

Stegosaurs, *see* PLATED DINOSAURS.

Sternberg, Kasper von (1761–1838)

Czechoslovak palaeobotanist who integrated the classification of fossil plants with that used for the Recent forms. He was born in Serowitz, Czechoslovakia, and was a student of theology.

Sternberg was initially interested in living plants, but then turned to describing the fossil plants of the Carboniferous found on his estate. One of Sternberg's major contributions was *Versuch einer geognostisch-botanischen Darstellung der Flora der Vorwelt* (1820–32, in seven volumes). He achieved the integration of the fossil species with the classification of Recent forms.   A.P.H.

Stigmaria

A fossil plant form-genus used to identify the roots of large lycopods. Stigmaria were massive roots that branched dichotomously. Smaller roots or rootlets were borne spirally on the main axes but usually became detached, leaving a pattern of circular scars on the surface. The internal anatomy of these rootlets closely resembles that of the modern *Isoetes*, an aquatic lycopod.   J.W.F.

Stoats, *see* WEASELS AND STOATS.

Stone age

A cultural sub-division of the PLEISTOCENE which spans the time between the Oldowan culture of 1.75 million years ago and the adoption of agriculture in about 7000BC. During this

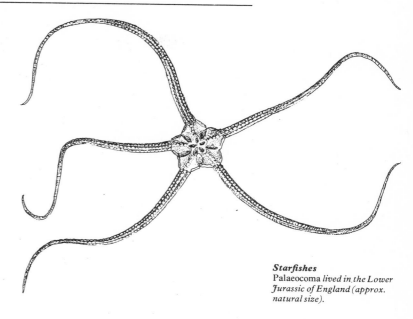

Starfishes
Palaeocoma *lived in the Lower Jurassic of England (approx. natural size).*

interval the main tools and weapons of MAN were made of stone, and man himself underwent the final stages of his physical evolution.

All through this period man and his ancestors were hunter-gatherers, that is, they hunted animals for meat and collected seeds, berries and fruits. It was a time of great climatic change, with the previous equable climate being replaced by the ICE AGE glaciations. The alterations in climate brought about changes in the fauna and flora, and it was probably the need for adapting to meet this environmental challenge that helped man to evolve so rapidly.

The climatic changes had important consequences for man's hunting, because with the approach of the glaciers the forests were replaced by open grasslands and tundra with a subsequent alteration in the animal species, the reverse occurring when the ice sheets retreated during milder, interglacial phases. These ecological disturbances were even felt towards the equator by movements of the arid zones and subsequent expansion and contraction of the equatorial rain forests. Man was forced not only to adapt his way of obtaining food, but also to manufacture clothes and find shelter as a protection against the cold.

Water became locked up in glaciers and ice caps, and the level of the seas fell, creating landbridges that afforded man access to areas hitherto excluded from him by water. Such landbridges allowed man to colonize the Americas and Australasia. Man would also have followed the movements of game caused by glaciation and in this way he spread across much of the Earth's surface until the ice retreated for the last time and he followed the herds of animals northwards into northern Europe and Asia.   D.T.

Stratigraphy

The study of stratified rocks, and their use in determining geological history. Rocks of sedimentary origin are generally laid down in layers (or strata), the oldest at the base overlain by

Submerged forests

successively younger units. Igneous rocks may contribute to this layered sequence as extruded lava-flows, as the pyroclastic products of volcanic eruptions, or as intrusions – for example, dykes. The geological cartographer, in the first instance, records the distribution of the rocks of an area and interprets the succession. The units employed are based on the characteristics of the rocks and can be readily observed in the field (lithostratigraphic units). The basic unit is the formation that is identified and distinguished from strata above and below throughout its extent by characteristic properties. Formations may include distinctive thinner units, members or beds, which can also be mapped individually.

One of the main problems facing the geologist is the correlation of the rocks in one local area with those laid down simultaneously elsewhere. Here an approach based on lithological units has limitations, because strata tend to vary in thickness and change in character laterally. The type of sediment deposited depends largely on the environment of deposition: it is impossible to correlate on purely lithological grounds, for example, the shales laid down in a deep marine basin with the limestones formed at the same time in the shallow water of the continental shelf. As well as varying in character laterally (lateral facies change), formations tend to be diachronous, ie the entire extent of the unit may not be deposited simultaneously. A shallow-water deposit migrates laterally through time, for example during a marine transgression.

In the early 19th century William Smith used fossils to identify the formations he mapped, but only in the sense that he used other properties of sedimentary rocks – as distinctive clasts. Soon it was realized that fossils could be used in a much more fundamental way to establish a chronology independent of any local considerations, lithological or palaeontological (biostratigraphy). The basic unit of the biostratigrapher is the biozone. A biozone is defined by the occurrence of a particular fossil group or assemblage of groups (zone fossils) and is bounded above and below by other biozones containing different characteristic fossils, the zonal scheme ideally based on rapidly evolving lineages. The British Silurian, for example, is divided into more than 30 biozones based on graptolites, each lasting about 1 million years. Thus superimposed on the lithostratigraphic units, recognized during primary field studies, are the zones of the biostratigrapher which allow reliable correlation with adjacent areas. The biostratigrapher deals with divisions of a standard column delimited by fossils regardless of lithology and the thickness of strata.

The rock record is usually incomplete (due to non-deposition or erosion, for example) and it can therefore never be ascertained that the strata or succession of faunas represent all the time available for their deposition. Accordingly, there is a hierarchy of time-stratigraphical (chronostratigraphical) units which apply to all the rocks formed in a given time interval, regardless of the presence or absence of diagnostic fossils. For example, the strata of the Llandovery series occur at the base of the Silurian system, the series being divided into four stages. The International Commission on Stratigraphy is involved in designating boundary stratotypes for the major chrono-stratigraphical divisions in well-exposed successions containing ample fossils suitable for correlation. The first major boundary treated in this way was that between the Silurian and Devonian systems, defined in 1972 by a hypothetical "golden spike" in a section near Klonk in Czechoslovakia. This has become the reference point from which the boundary must be identified elsewhere in the world by correlation.

A different approach to the delimitation and correlation of stratigraphic units is required in regions of Pre-Cambrian strata, where fossils are essentially absent. Here divisions are necessarily larger in scale and must be based on criteria such as periods and styles of folding and metamorphism, and on igneous activity. Radioisotope dating may be used to provide an indication of the absolute ages of metamorphic events and igneous rocks. Palaeoclimatological evidence has also proved useful in correlating Pre-Cambrian rocks: late Pre-Cambrian glacial deposits, tillites, for example, occur in western Ireland, the Scottish Highlands, Scandinavia and elsewhere in Europe (see CLIMATES OF THE PAST). Palaeoclimatology is most widely used, however, by Quaternary geologists, who subdivide the Pleistocene on the basis of climatic fluctuations which are reflected in the fossil content (especially pollen) of the sediments deposited (see POLLEN ANALYSIS).

Stratigraphy also provides evidence for the distribution of land and sea (palaeogeography; see GEOGRAPHY OF THE PAST) through time, and for the configuration of the continents.   D.E.G.B.

Submerged forests

The remains of forests that grew immediately after the last ICE AGE on the flat areas of the continental shelf. They are always associated with peat beds.

There are about a hundred recorded submerged forest localities around the coasts of the British Isles. At low tide they can be seen as beds of dark brown peat showing through the sand with the projecting upright stumps of birch and pine. In addition to the submerged forests visible at low tide, there are further forests known from peat and pieces of wood (moorlog) dredged up by trawlers from the floor of the North Sea.

POLLEN ANALYSIS has disclosed that these forests are 9,000 years old, which places them in that part of the Late Quaternary period known as the Boreal. At that time the areas in which the remains occur had a warm, dry continental climate, and the woodland vegetation was dominated by birch and pine. In the west particularly, there were spectacular stands of hazel which produced such vast amounts of pollen that it has to be excluded from the totals on which calculations are made, so that significant variations in the abundance of the other species can be seen.

With the melting of the ice sheets, more water

was released to the oceans and sea-levels around the coasts rose, progressively submerging more of the continental shelf and the vegetation growing on it. This sequence of events was probably repeated more than once during the Pleistocene.   J.W.F.

Tail fin

The major organ of propulsion in aquatic VERTEBRATES. Among the most primitive vertebrates, the PTERASPIDS (or heterostracans), there were no paired fins to control movement and the lower lobe of the tail was extended – a condition known as hypocercal or reversed heterocercal. Lateral movement of such a tail depresses it and has the further effect of raising the front part of the animal. As well as driving the animal forwards, this arrangement ensures that the animal does not become ensnared in the mud on the sea or river bed. The more active-swimming ANASPIDS also had a markedly hypocercal tail, but this was in addition to lateral fin folds. Again the effect of this type of tail fin was to lift the front part of the body.

The other jawless vertebrates, the CEPHALASPIDS, had a true heterocercal tail in which the upper lobe carrying the main axis of the body was turned upwards. The effect of lateral movements by this type of tail is to raise the hind part of the body while depressing the front. This tends to keep the animal closely pressed to the substrate. A heterocercal tail develops only in conjunction with movable paired pectoral fins, which can counteract the tendency to depress the head by altering the angle of attack. Cephalaspids were usual in possessing a pair of horizontal tail flaps at the ventral margin of the tail fin. These prevented the lower lobe of the tail from sinking into the sediments, thus protecting the vulnerable leading edge from undue wear.

All the early jawed fishes (SHARKS, PLACODERMS, early RAY-FIN FISHES, and LOBE-FIN FISHES) possessed heterocercal tails which, with the pectoral fins, enabled them to control their movement through the water. The sharks and primitive ray-fins such as the sturgeon have retained this type of tail.

With the development of LUNGS, later developed into hydrostatic organs in ray-fins, the tail fin was no longer required to help to provide lift and it merely generated forward thrust. The advanced lobe-fin fishes and the COELACANTHS developed a diphycercal tail in which the fleshy axis of the body ran to the tip of the tail and even extended beyond the equally developed upper and lower lobes. In the ray-fins the fleshy axis was eventually shortened and a wide, symmetrical homocercal fin developed which was made up simply of fin rays.   L.B.H.

Tapirs

The most primitive living PERISSODACTYLS, now confined to south-eastern Asia and Central and South America. They have a short proboscis, browse on forest vegetation, and live from sea-level to heights of about 4,500 metres (14,760ft).

Their limbs are short and stubby, with the ulna failing to fuse with the radius and the fibula remaining distinct from the tibia. Tapirs have three toes on the hindfeet and four on the forefeet, each toe possessing a hoof and a pad. The upper canine tooth is reduced and an incisor tooth has become caniniform to occlude with the lower canine. A diastema is present and the posterior premolars have become partly molarized. The characteristic tooth pattern of the upper and lower molars is two transverse lophs or ridges.

Protapirus from the Oligocene of Europe and North America is the earliest known true tapir. The group is not common in the fossil record, but tapirs have been recorded from middle and late Cenozoic deposits in the Northern Hemisphere, and from the Pleistocene in Central and South America.

In the Eocene there were many tapir-like and tapir-related stocks, for example, *Homogalax* in North America and *Lophiodon* in Europe. *Hyrachyus* from the North American Eocene was close to the ancestor of the RHINOCEROSES. R.J.G.S.

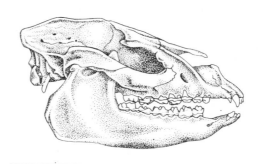

Tarsiers

Small, primitive PRIMATES which are now restricted to the East Indies. Tarsiers move only at night and have enormous eyes with full stereoscopic vision which they use in capturing insects; they also have large ears, but their olfactory sense is reduced.

Tarsiers live in trees, hopping from branch to branch. Hopping normally involves elongation of the hindlimbs, in particular the metatarsal bones, to provide an extra joint and so substantially improve the mechanics of jumping. The hindlimbs are used in one plane only (for to-and-fro movements) and therefore the tibia and fibula tend to fuse. By contrast, arboreal locomotion requires limbs that can be twisted, with an opposable digit to grasp the branches.

In tarsiers the tibia and fibula are fused but, instead of the metatarsals becoming elongated, two bones of the ankle (the calcaneum and navicular) are extended to establish the extra joint, thus ensuring that the animal can still use its opposable first digit to grasp branches. To retain such a facility the elongation had to be sited proximal to the digits, and the tarsier owes its name to this characteristic feature of the tarsal joint.

Specializations in tarsioids can be traced back to the Eocene of North America and Europe. *Tetonius*, for example, had large eyes, short

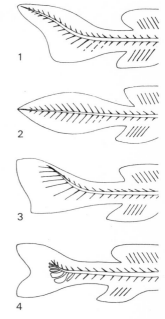

Taxonomy

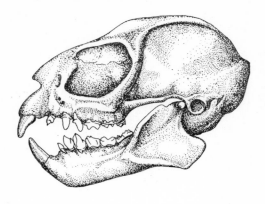

jaws, big canines, primitive molars and a relatively large brain.

The classification of tarsiers is uncertain. Some authorities place them with LEMURS and lorises as the most advanced prosimians; others place tarsiers with the MONKEYS and APES as the most primitive anthropoids, and yet others leave them in a lineage of their own.   R.J.G.S.

Taxonomy

The theory and practice of classifying organisms. Classification is the process by which individuals are grouped into a hierarchy of categories (or taxa), which are then assigned names within a system of nomenclature. The practical importance of taxonomy is to facilitate identification of specimens, communication concerning them, and the organization of data.

A classification could be entirely arbitrary because the taxonomist may, in principle, select any characteristics he wishes. In practice, taxonomists attempt to relate taxonomic boundaries to natural discontinuities between different kinds of living things. Discontinuities between different kinds of plants and animals exist because there are discontinuities in the environment: in order to survive, organisms must become variously adapted to living under particular conditions. Much taxonomic work concerns the description of taxa not previously known and rearrangement of taxa into higher categories in the light of new information.

It suffices for everyday usage to label plants and animals with informal names in the local language. For scientific purposes, however, names need to be unique, stable and internationally accepted. Nomenclature is governed by the international codes of botanic and zoological nomenclature.

Organisms are named according to a system first consistently used by Carolus Linnaeus (1708–78). Under this scheme every named organism has a species (or trivial) name and a generic name (the genus), the two together constituting a unique specific name. These names consist of latinized words, and the name of the author who originally described the species should follow. For example, the lion is *Felis leo* Linnaeus (genus *Felis*, species *leo*, first described by Linnaeus). Genera usually include more than one species: the tiger, for instance, is *Felis tigris* and belongs to the same genus as the lion. Above the generic level several successively more inclusive groupings are available as is illustrated below for the lion. (A similar hierarchy exists for the plant kingdom.

Category	Nomenclature
Kingdom	Animalia (animals)
Phylum	Chordata (animals with a notochord)
Class	Mammalia (mammals)
Order	Carnivora (carnivorous mammals)
Family	Felidae (cats)
Genus	*Felis*
Species	*Felis leo*
Individuals	

Flexibility is introduced by the use of subordinate categories (subphylum, superfamily, etc) between the main ones.

The standard of reference for the application of a name is the type. The type of a species or subspecies is a specimen, that of a genus a type species, that of a family or subfamily a type genus. Higher taxa than these do not have types. Type specimens are housed in a museum or other institution where they are secure and available for study. Their type status should be clearly marked and accompanying labels give data concerning locality, bibliographical details, and other relevant information.

Three philosophies of classification are in general use: phenetics, cladistics and phyletics. Phenetics is concerned with phenotypic similarity between taxa. The procedure involves the quantification of numerous characteristics which are assigned equal weighting and statistical techniques are then used to sort the data. Cladistics is a taxonomy of monophyletic groupings, membership of which is determined by the possession of shared characteristics derived from a common ancestor. Taxa are defined in terms of a series of nodal (or branching) points on a kinship table (cladogram), kinship being defined in terms of recency of common origin. Phyletic (or evolutionary) classification attempt to recognize the natural groupings that evolution has produced. The phyleticist considers some characteristics to have greater value for determining relationship than others, and commonly emphasizes stratigraphical relationships.   A.T.T.

Teeth

The biting or crushing structures, sometimes modified as weapons, that line the jaws (and occasionally the palate) of VERTEBRATES. As soon as jaws were evolved by vertebrates, teeth were developed. The basic vertebrate tooth is a conical structure composed principally of dentine, with a hard outer surface of enamel and an inner pulp cavity containing blood vessels and nerves. It may simply be fused to the jaw bones (acrodont, as in *Sphenodon* and teleost fishes), attached to the jaw by one of its sides (pleurodont, as in lizards and snakes), or implanted in a socket (thecodont), with (in mammals) one or more deep roots. Enamel originates from the same tissue that forms the skin (ectoderm), and wherever ectoderm occurs in the mouth region, teeth have appeared. Many bony fishes, amphibians and reptiles have teeth in the roof of the mouth and on the inner surface of the lower jaw.

The oldest fishes (the jawless OSTRACODERMS) had bony plates protecting the body, which frequently bore tubercles that structurally resemble both primitive teeth and the denticles present in a shark's skin. When jaws developed in PLACODERMS, tubercles on the bony plates lining the mouth became true teeth. In sharks, the protective plates were gradually dispensed with, although the denticles remained.

Advanced reptiles (ie DINOSAURS and CROCODILES) have thecodont marginal teeth, and in Mesozoic birds (*Archaeopteryx*) there were still teeth along the edges of the jaws. MAMMAL-LIKE REPTILES had begun to evolve differentiated teeth, with chisel-shaped incisors at the front, followed by canines and finally a series of grinding teeth. Mammals have a fully differentiated dentition. The primitive placentals possess in each half of each jaw three incisors, one canine, four premolars and three molars, although many groups eventually lost some of these teeth or modified their structure. Replacement of old teeth continues throughout the life of lower vertebrates, but in placental mammals there is only a single set of permanent teeth; the incisors, canines and premolars are preceded by deciduous milk teeth.

The molar teeth of placental mammals develop characteristic crown patterns. In the most primitive placentals, the upper molars bear three principal cusps, forming a triangle (hence they are called tritubercular molars) with its base at the outside edge of the tooth. The point of the triangle is marked by the protocone, which was once thought to represent the crown of a simple reptilian tooth; at the front corner of the triangle is the paracone, and at the back corner the metacone. An intermediate cusp (the protoconule) may appear on a ridge linking the protocone and the paracone, a similar ridge between the protocone and the metacone incorporating the metaconule.

There is also a triangle of cusps (trigonid) on the lower molars, but its base is on the inside of the tooth. The outside cusp at the point of the triangle is the protoconulid, the front cusp at the base of the triangle is the paraconid, and the posterior cusp is the metaconid. There are primitively two further cusps on the talonid, the inner one being the entoconid and the outer one the hypoconid, with an intermediate hypoconulid also frequently present. When the jaws are closed the lower teeth each fit in front of the corresponding upper tooth to give a shearing action, except that the talonid receives the protocone of the upper molar.

The protoconulid of the lower molars probably represents the original reptilian crown, but in the upper series the paracone is the first cusp to appear during the development of a tooth, and when the jaws are closed it is the paracone and metacone that align themselves with the protoconulid. The paracone therefore seems to be the principal cusp in the upper teeth, and the protocone is misnamed.

The cusps may remain low and rounded (bunodont) as they do in a mixed feeder such as man, or they may become crescentic in shape (selenodont). In the upper molars, a ridge (the ectoloph) may link the outer cusps, with similar ridges joining the anterior row of cusps (the protoloph) or the hypocone-metaconule-metacone series (the metaloph). On the lower molars, the cusps of the trigonid may be united by a metalophid and those of the talonid by a hypolophid.

R.S.

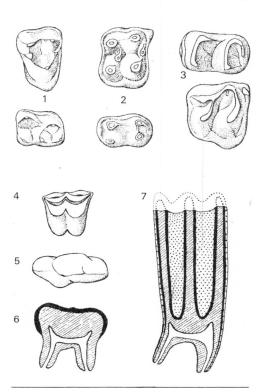

Teeth
(1) A right upper molar (above) and a left lower molar (below) of a primitive placental mammal with a simple tritubercular crown pattern (the Eocene tarsioid (Omomys);
(2) a right upper molar (above) and a left lower molar (below) of the oldest known horse, Hyracotherium, in which the cusp pattern has been squared off by the acquisition of a hypocone in the upper molar and loss of the paraconid in the lower molar (with the talonid built up to the level of the front of the crown);
(3) a right upper molar (above) and a left lower molar (below) of a fossil rhinoceros, showing how lophs (grinding ridges) join up the cusps in advanced herbivorous mammals;
(4) a selenodont crown pattern on the upper molar of an ox (dorsal view);
(5) the crown of the fourth upper premolar in the sabre-toothed cat Smilodon, an example of a slicing carnassial (dorsal view);
(6) longitudinal section of a low-crowned tooth (a human molar);
(7) longitudinal section of a high-crowned tooth (the grinding tooth of a modern horse).

Teleosts
The most highly evolved RAY-FIN FISHES.

Tendaguru
A village 56km (35 miles) inland from the East African coastal town of Lindi, where a rich deposit of Upper Jurassic DINOSAUR bones was discovered in 1907 by W. B. Sattler, a German engineer.

Tendaguru is now in Tanzania which, before the first world war, constituted part of German East Africa. In 1909 Werner Janensch (1878–1969), a fossil reptile expert at the Berlin Museum, conducted an expedition to the newly discovered dinosaur locality. The bones were weathering out of the ground over a substantial area around Tendaguru Hill, and an extensive series of pits were dug among the dense cover of scrubby trees to unearth the almost complete skeletons that lay just beneath the surface. Using cheaply obtained local native labour, the Germans excavated an immense quantity of dinosaur bones in the years 1909–12. A British expedition continued the work at Tendaguru from 1924 to 1929, making further collections.

Tertiary

Tendaguru
*The plated dinosaur
Kentrosaurus is characteristic of
the Tendaguru fauna.
Length: about 5m (16ft)*

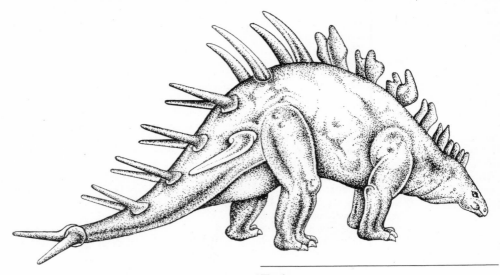

The Tendaguru fauna is of similar age to that of the MORRISON FORMATION, and resembles it closely. The remains of SAUROPODS are more numerous than those of any other dinosaurs at Tendaguru and bones of *Brachiosaurus* are common. This gigantic genus also occurs in the Sahara Desert and in Portugal, as well as in the North American Morrison Formation, indicating that there was a common dinosaur fauna extending across this region at the end of the Jurassic, separation of the Eastern and Western Hemispheres by CONTINENTAL DRIFT having barely begun. *Dicraeosaurus* is a sauropod exclusive to Tendaguru, but *Barosaurus* (a relative of *Diplodocus*) is also present and occurs additionally in the Morrison Formation.

PLATED DINOSAURS are represented by *Kentrosaurus*, COELUROSAURS by *Elaphrosaurus*, and cursorial ORNITHOPODS by the bipedal *Dysalotosaurus*, which ranged in size from the dimensions of a cat to those of a large dog. There was also the PTEROSAUR *Rhamphorhynchus* (present also in the European Upper Jurassic) and a huge CARNOSAUR (*Megalosaurus ingens*) represented in the collections only by teeth that are 14.5cm (5.7in) long, which indicate a reptile equal in size to the Late Cretaceous *Tyrannosaurus*.

The bones of the Tendaguru dinosaurs occur in freshwater deposits, and these reptiles probably lived along the banks of a river which had a sandbar at its mouth. There are, however, alternating marine sediments separating the dinosaur beds, so periodic incursions of the sea obviously occurred. R.S.

Tertiary

A division of geological time that comprises the PALAEOCENE, EOCENE, OLIGOCENE, MIOCENE and PLIOCENE Periods. In 1760 G. Arduino (1714–95) divided the geological strata into Primary (equalling PALAEOZOIC), Secondary (corresponding to MESOZOIC) and Tertiary.

Unlike the CENOZOIC, the Tertiary excludes PLEISTOCENE, which is designated the QUATERNARY.

See also the time chart.

Tethys

An ancient sea that extended between PANGAEA and its southern component, GONDWANALAND. The crust and sediments of this old sea were thrust up and folded during the late Mesozoic and Cenozoic to form the Alpine mountain chains extending from the Atlas Mountains of northern Africa through the Alps, the Carpathians, Turkey and the Middle East to the Himalayas. Reconstructions of Pangaea which assume an Earth of constant modern dimensions, the Tethys is shown as an oceanic region widening progressively from the western Mediterranean eastward towards the Pacific Ocean. Reconstructions assuming global expansion show the Tethys to fill the site of a major shear zone between Gondwanaland and the northern portion of Pangaea (Laurasia).

Whatever reconstruction is used, the Tethys acted as a major barrier to the migration of land faunas and, conversely, an important migration path for marine faunas. It is known, however, that other seaways occupying tectonic belts formed important migration routes within Europe, particularly in the Palaeozoic. Furthermore, the Tethys was not a barrier in the Triassic to the migration of land-living dicynodont reptiles (characteristic of Gondwanaland) into China, and at times in the Late Jurassic and Lower Cretaceous the northern part of the Tethyan zone formed a definite barrier to the migration of marine ammonite faunas. H.G.O.

Thecodontians

An extinct order (Thecodontia) of diapsid reptiles that constitute the basal stock of the ARCHOSAURS. The teeth of thecodontians are characteristically implanted in sockets, a feature from which the group derives its name.

The earliest thecodontian, *Archosaurus*, is from the uppermost Permian, but all other members of the group are of Triassic age. They were mostly large, heavy reptiles, including some Early and Middle Triassic forms that were the biggest animals of their time. Most were wholly quadrupedal, and few are connected with dinosaur or bird origins.

The typical archosaurian limb disparity is fully

Toothed birds

developed in the Thecodontia, with the hindlimbs much longer than the forelimbs. The diapsid skull has not only two temporal fenestrae on either side, but also an antorbital opening in front of the eye. There are usually 25 presacral vertebrae (seven or eight of them in the neck) and only two sacrals. The acetabulum (hip-socket) forms a complete bony basin, without the wide central hole which is generally the characteristic that distinguishes both DINOSAUR groups (the SAURISCHIANS and the ORNITHISCHIANS) from their thecodontian amcestors. There is no proper inturned head to the femur, which is usually longer than the tibia-fibula, with the humerus likewise longer than the radius-ulna. The "hand" and foot retain all five digits, but the outer toes and "fingers" may be reduced.

The Thecodontia are usually classified into four suborders, of which the Proterosuchia (Upper Permian and Lower Triassic) are the earliest and most primitive. The Pseudosuchians made their first appearance in the late Lower Triassic, presumably evolving from proterosuchians, and continued to prosper until the end of the period. It seems likely, however, that they do not form a natural group and have become a convenient taxonomic receptacle in which are placed all thecodontians not clearly assignable elsewhere. Nevertheless, the later archosaur orders probably evolved from various unspecified pseudosuchians, as did the other two thecodontian stocks, the Aëtosauria (sometimes regarded only as a family within the Pseudosuchia) and the PHYTOSAURS. The heavily armoured aëtosaurs seem to have been terrestrial herbivores (the only plant-eating thecodontians), and after arising in the late Middle Triassic they proliferated extensively during the later stages of the period, representatives of the group occurring in North America (*Desmatosuchus, Typothorax*), Europe (*Stagonolepis, Aëtosaurus*) and South America (*Aëtosauroides, Argentinosuchus*).

The most important evolutionary trend within the Archosauria (the Thecodontia and their descendants) was concerned with the way they used their LIMBS, especially their hindlimbs, in locomotion. The Proterosuchia retained the sprawling posture found in most earlier reptiles, and also in modern reptiles such as tortoises and lizards, in which the upper arm and thigh project sideways from the body. The other sub-orders are characterized by the "semi-improved" stance and gait found in modern crocodilians, with the elbow and knee drawn downwards and inwards to raise the body off the ground for faster locomotion. A continuation of this trend results in the "fully improved" stance and gait found among dinosaurs (and advanced mammals) in which the upper arm and thigh swing in a vertical plane beneath the body.

Many of the anatomical features of these "semi-improved" thecodontians, for example the imperforated hip-socket, are functionally connected with their posture and mode of locomotion. Especially characteristic is the complex "crurotarsal" ankle joint (a crocodile-like feature), in which the calcaneum (locked to the foot) has a backwardly directed tuber ("heel")

Thecodontians
Kuehneosaurus *was a highly specialized primitive lizard from the Upper Triassic of Great Britain. Its ribs projected sideways and presumably supported a gliding membrane. Length: about 57cm (22in)*

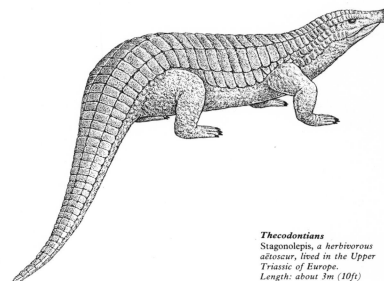

Thecodontians
Stagonolepis, *a herbivorous aëtoscur, lived in the Upper Triassic of Europe. Length: about 3m (10ft)*

and moves by means of a ball-and-socket articulation against the astragalus, which is locked to the lower leg.   A.J.C.

Time, geological
See individual periods and eras. *See also* the time chart.

Toads, *see* FROGS AND TOADS.

Toothed birds
Primitive birds, restricted to the Mesozoic Era, which still retained teeth as a legacy from their reptilian forebears. They became extinct before the beginning of the Cenozoic, and apparently left no living descendants.

ARCHAEOPTERYX, from the Upper Jurassic, is customarily assigned to a special subclass of its own. The Cretaceous toothed birds comprise another subclass, the Odontoholcae, in which two lines of evolution can be observed: the flightless families Hesperornithidae, Baptornithidae and, probably, Enaliornithidae constitute the order Hesperornithiformes, and the flying birds of the families Ichthyornithidae and Apator-

Tortoises

Toothed birds
Hesperornis, a flightless diving bird, lived in the Upper Cretaceous.
Length: about 1m (3.3ft)

nithidae constitute the order Ichthyornithiformes.

The best known example of the flightless group is *Hesperornis* (commonly referred to as the Dawn Bird), whose remains have been collected from the Upper Cretaceous marine sediments of North America. From various skeletons, it can be postulated that the largest species would have exceeded 1.8 metres (6ft) in length, with a body shape resembling that of the modern divers (loons). *Hesperornis* was well adapted for an aquatic life. The trunk was apparently cigar-shaped and the short, powerful legs, although virtually useless for walking on land, were placed well back on the body where they would have had optimum efficiency for swimming. Evidently the Hesperornithiformes caught their prey under water, but they differed from modern divers in possessing a poorly developed forelimb skeleton which was even more degenerate than that found in living flightless water birds, such as penguins. The breastbone, for example, was smooth and lacked the keel which is necessary for the attachment of flight muscles. The hesperornithiform skull also possessed several non-avian features. In addition to having teeth in the jaws there were six bones in each lower jaw ramus (which thus resembled the mandible of CARNOSAURS) and a jaw articulation similar to that of MOSASAURS.

The Enaliornithidae are now thought to be the earliest group of the Hesperornithiformes, having been found in the Lower Cretaceous rocks of England. Like the North American Baptornithidae, they were once believed to be the ancestors of modern grebes, but are now regarded as members of the toothed-bird group, although no skull material has yet been discovered.

The Ichthyornithiformes occur in the same Upper Cretaceous deposits as the Hesperornithiformes but demonstrate a completely different line of evolution, with a well-developed keel on the sternum that indicates considerable powers of flight. *Ichthyornis*, commonly referred to as the Fish-bird, stood only about 20cm (8in) tall, and probably resembled the living terns in appearance and in its mode of life. C.A.W.

Tortoises, *see* TURTLES AND TORTOISES.

Trace fossils

Structures in sediments that have been left by animal activities such as crawling, swimming, running, eating and dwelling. Fossil tracks, trails, burrows, borings and allied features are all traces of formerly living organisms.

Trace fossils (ichnofossils) are known mainly from marine sediments and are especially well represented in the alternating coarse and fine lithologies of flysch deposits. They also occur in most other sedimentary facies, including continental deposits, but generally in less abundance and with less diversity. Reflecting the appearance of some of the earliest life forms, trace fossils range from the Pre-Cambrian (eg the crawling trail *Bunyerichnus* from South Australia) to the Recent. Many are invisible to the eye and are revealed only by the application of modern techniques such as X-ray photography.

Essentially, traces are either exogenic (on the surface, eg tracks) or endogenic (within layers of sediment, eg burrows). Surface trails in shallow marine water stood least chance of survival, because they were subjected to wave and current action. Quiet, deeper-water environments tended, however, to be more favourable to the preservation of what are often exceedingly fine trace structures.

The origin of trace fossils and the usual lack of knowledge of the "parent" organism combine to pose special problems of classification and nomenclature. Binary Linnaean nomenclature (*see* TAXONOMY) is extensively employed, but some palaeontologists prefer to adopt other terms or ecologically based names. Classification also varies: systems have been based on morphology, animal behaviour, position of occurrence, and preservational aspects of trace fossils.

The study of trace fossils (palaeoichnology) provides an indication of the former existence and composition of benthic (bottom-dwelling) life. Studies of trace fossils across the Late Pre-Cambrian to Cambrian boundary have helped in the understanding of early metazoan evolution. Sometimes trace fossils can be of local value as guide fossils or even as aids in dating rocks; the burrow *Arenicolites franconicus*, for example, is a virtual index fossil for a 4cm (1.6in) layer of the Muschelkalk throughout wide areas of southern Germany. Forms of *Cruziana*, believed to have been formed by the movements of trilobites and allied arthropods, can be used to distinguish parts of the Cambrian and Ordovician of Wales. Careful study of bioturbation structures often help to clarify problems of sedimentation associated with depositional history, and trace fossil associations as a whole are potentially significant tools in palaeoenvironmental and palaeogeographical research.

See also FOOTPRINTS. J.E.W.

Tree-ferns

Members of the fern family Cyathaceae. Most modern tree-ferns belong to either *Cyathea* or *Dicksonia*, which are distinguished by the posi-

Triassic

tion of the spore-bearing organs (sori) on the pinnules.

The earliest recorded *Dicksonia* type of tree-fern is from the Jurassic rocks of the Yorkshire coast. The fossil is known as *Coniopteris* and was a tree-fern with a highly compound frond, the sori being borne on the margins of the pinnules. Tree-ferns of the *Cyathea* type are also recorded from rocks of Jurassic age, the first fossil representative being *Alsophilites*.

The largest tree-ferns may grow to about 20 metres (65ft), but many are much smaller. Although the diameter of the trunk may often appear to be large, it is usually composed principally of adventitious roots and leaf bases surrounding a relatively slender stem.　　J.W.F.

Tree ferns
The Carboniferous tree ferns Psaronius *grew to a height of about 15m (50ft).*

Triassic

The first geological period of the MESOZOIC Era, named after the threefold sequence in which rocks of this age occur in southern Germany (Bunter, Muschelkalk and Rhaetic). The Triassic lasted for 35 million years (from 230 million to 195 million years ago) and ushered in the so-called age of reptiles; it also marked the end of several ancient Palaeozoic lineages, notably labyrinthodont amphibians, cotylosaurs and most of the mammal-like reptiles.

During the Triassic the Palaeozoic super-continent of PANGAEA was still in existence, but later in the period the anti-clockwise rotation of GONDWANALAND led to the opening up of the Tethys Sea.

Climatic conditions were warm but predominantly dry, with extensive deserts, shifting sand dunes, and scree-covered mountains. Here and there temporary lakes and salt pools existed, with occasionally even coal-forming swamps, but the extensive deposition of red-coloured sandstones and marls is indicative of an essentially arid environment. There is no evidence of ice caps and, with relatively large land areas of generally low relief, exceedingly stable weather conditions probably prevailed. The seas also appear to have been warm with an abundance of reef-forming CORALS and calcareous seaweeds. In a shallow arm of the Tethys that stretched across Germany and part of France, the shelly limestone of the Muschelkalk was laid down in the mid-Triassic, and elsewhere there was extensive deposition of dolomitic limestone (carbonates of calcium and magnesium).

In the seas INVERTEBRATE marine life had begun to take on a more modern look with the end of the Palaeozoic Era, all of the principal living groups of ECHINODERMS having appeared, and hexacorals (represented today by anemones and stony corals) made their first appearance. Some older types of BRACHIOPOD were still present, but early terebratulids and rhynchonelids had begun to establish themselves; BELEMNITES were increasingly numerous and AMMONITES included genera with marginally frilled partitions (eg *Ceratites*). In shallower waters, BIVALVES (eg *Myophoria*) and marine snails occurred in abundance.

Some relatively primitive PALAEONISCID fishes were still to be found, but as the period progressed the subholosteans became the dominant RAY-FIN FISHES, characteristic genera including the deep-bodied *Cleithrolepis*, the long-jawed predaceous *Saurichthys*, and such conservative forms as *Parasemionotus* and *Perleidus*. Towards the end of the Triassic, however, true holosteans started to appear (eg *Semionotus* and *Furo*) and the older types declined rapidly. SHARKS seem to have become rare, with hybodonts present in the seas and a few pleuracanths lingering in fresh water. COELACANTHS still enjoyed considerable success, and in the shrinking pools of the arid continents LUNGFISHES were numerous (eg *Ceratodus*, a close relative of the living Australian lungfish).

195 million years ago

Upper	Rhaetic	
	Norian	Keuper
	Carnian	
Middle	Ladinian	Muschelkalk
	Anisian	
Lower	Scythian	Bunter

230 million years ago
The Triassic succession

Triassic
The prosauropod Plateosaurus *was a characteristic dinosaur of the European Upper Triassic. Length: about 8m (26ft)*

Trilobites

Triassic
Ornithosuchus was a powerful pseudosuchian from the Upper Triassic of Scotland.
Length: about 3.7m (12ft)

On land, there were FERNS, CYCADS, CYCADE-OIDS and CONIFERS growing on the northern continents; flourishing more especially during the latter part of the period, whereas Gondwanaland had a distinctive flora of seed-ferns. LABYRINTH-ODONTS were still numerous, despite the dry conditions, with various late surviving neo-rhachitomes among them (eg *Rhinesuchus*) as well as fully evolved stereospondyls. These included the *Capitosaurus* group, the short-skulled brachyopoids, *Metoposaurus* and its allies with eye sockets at the front of their long skulls, and the remarkable rematosaurs – the only amphibians that ever successfully colonized salt water.

The future, however, belonged to the reptiles. Among the ancient Palaeozoic groups which still persisted there were procolophonid COTYLOSAURS and an abundance of MAMMAL-LIKE REPTILES: cynodonts and bauriamorphs were purely carnivorous forms, gomphodonts were a cynodont off-shoot that had begun to acquire herbivorous habits (with grinding-type cheek teeth), and the small, highly specialized tritylodonts were a feature of the Upper Triassic (*Oligokyphus*, *Bienotherium*). Dicynodonts were declining but still had an extensive distribution and some attained a considerable size – *Kannemeyeria* was 2 metres (6.6ft) long. By the end of the period, however, the first indisputable mammals had evolved (*Eozostrodon*, *Sinoconodon*), probably from either cynodonts or ictidosaurs.

The most dynamic reptiles of the Triassic were unquestionably the ARCHOSAURS. The basic THECODONTIAN stock was represented in the early part of the period by both the quadrupedal proterosuchians (*Chasmatosaurus*, *Erythrosuchus*) and the first bipedal pseudosuchians (*Euparkeria*). During the Middle and Upper Triassic, the pseudosuchians proliferated widely

and were joined in the latter part of the period by two other groups of thecodontians. These were the heavily armoured quadrupedal aëtosaurs, some of which measured up to 3 metres (10ft) long, and the crocodile-like PHYTOSAURS, which were almost exclusive to the Northern Hemisphere, although *Mystriosuchus* has been reported from Madagascar.

Early DINOSAURS had already arisen from pseudosuchian forebears by the Middle Triassic, with SAURISCHIANS represented by prosauropods and COELUROSAURS, while ORNITHISCHIAN evolution was being initiated by the first ORNITHOPODS (*Heterodontosaurus* and its allies, and *Fabrosaurus*). Judging by the abundance of fossilized three-toed dinosaurian FOOTPRINTS in some localities (notably the Connecticut Valley), coelurosaurs and some of the more lightly built prosauropods must have been exceedingly numerous, and the massive, semi-quadrupedal plateosaurs probably ranged in herds across the Rhaetic deserts of Europe.

Other reptilian groups that were just beginning their rise to eminence during the Triassic include the CROCODILES (*Protosuchus*, from Arizona), the PTEROSAURS (*Eudimorphodon*, from Italy), the PLESIOSAURS (represented by NOTHOSAURS), and the ICHTHYOSAURS (*Mixosaurus* and *Shastasaurus*, with imperfectly developed tail fins and short-faced skulls).

Conspicuous types that failed to survive beyond the end of the period include the mollusc-eating PLACODONTS (euryapsids related to the plesiosaurs), the protorosaurs (lizard-like forms that were primitive early members of the euryapsid assemblage, among them the extraordinary, long-necked *Tanystrophaeus*), and the beak-snouted rhynchosaurs.

Early lepidosaurs included, in addition to the unspecialized *Prolacerta*, a "flying" form – *Kuehneosaurus*, with spreading ribs that presumably supported a gliding membrane in life. Primitive TURTLES are represented by *Proganochelys*, which was 1 metre (3.3ft) long.

There is evidence, based largely on pollen and spore analysis, that some rocks generally regarded as being of Upper Triassic age may in fact be Lower Jurassic. In North America this hypothesis applies to part of the Newark series and to the Glen Canyon group, and the upper Stormberg rocks of southern Africa are also possibly post-Triassic. Such a revision would automatically extend the geological range of some fossil groups, with prosauropod dinosaurs, for example, persisting into the Jurassic.

See also the time chart. R.S.

Trilobites

The dominant animals of Lower PALAEOZOIC seas, which survived in declining numbers until the Middle Permian. The reason for their extinction is not clear, but it was presumably the result of competition from fishes and the spread of MOLLUSCS. Only the least specialized group of trilobites, the Proetacea, survived from the Carboniferous into the Permian, and the long-spined Late Devonian forms (eg *Ceratarges armatus*) did not survive for long.

Triassic
Protosuchus was a crocodile that lived in the Upper Triassic of Arizona.
Length: about 1m (3.3ft)

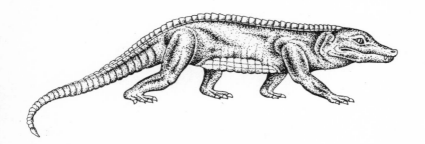

Turkana

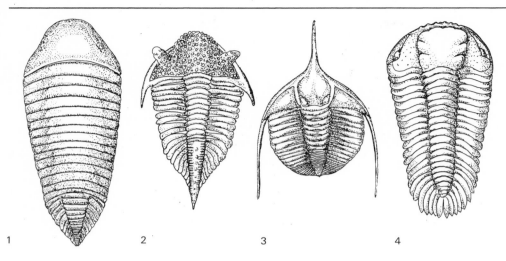

1 2 3 4

The name "trilobite" refers to the three lobes into which the animal's exoskeleton is longitudinally divided – the median ridge and two flatter areas on each side. On the head shield (cephalon) the median part is represented by a swollen area, the glabella, and the flattened lateral areas are the cheeks. Each cheek is divided into a fixed cheek fused to the glabella and a free cheek weakly joined by a suture to the fixed cheek. The facial suture is present as an aid to moulting, especially freeing the eyes (which are on the cheeks), and its shape and direction is a major distinguishing feature within the group. The underside of the head shield is composed of plates usually connected by lines of weakness (sutures) surrounded probably by a soft integument. The most prominent plate is the hypostome, which is either in front of the mouth or covers it.

The thorax consists of various articulated segments (the number is fixed within each species) which allow flexion and in some forms even permitted the animal to roll up on itself for protection. Each segment of the thoracic exoskeleton is divided into three parts, the two flatter lateral pleurae and the central raised axis or rhachis. Along the front and rear margins of the segments are articulating bosses and sockets, which allow the movement of the segments.

The tail or pygidium consists again of a variable number of segments decreasing in size from front to rear, but fused into a rigid shield. During development the thoracic segments are budded off from the front of the pygidium. The thoracic and pygidial pleurae may be extended into spines, and in addition the terminal end of the pygidium may bear a tail-spine or mucro.

Each segment of the animal carries a pair of limbs, but the pair in front of the mouth are specialized as sensory antennae. The other limbs are jointed walking organs incorporating a feathery breathing and swimming organ and a masticating organ which picks up food particles and passes them along the body to the mouth. Filling most of the swollen glabella are the liver and the stomach, with an intestine passing down the length of the axis to the last pygidial segment.

The exoskeleton may be ornamented by ridges, granules and tubercles, and because some of the tubercles are perforated they may have been the site of a sensory hair.

The eyes are sophisticated, based on correctly oriented calcite crystals. They may be of the compound or holochroal type, such as a fly has, or aggregate (schizochroal) eyes in which all the lenses are separated. Trilobites may be secondarily blind or have a tendency to eye reduction, for example, the Olenidae and the Shumardiidae. Other trilobites such as the Cyclopygidae developed enormous eyes which cover the sides and front of the head: these were probably planktonic forms, in which the ability to see all around was of paramount importance.

Trilobites are virtually universal in Lower Palaeozoic lithologies representing continental marginal seas, and planktonic forms may occasionally be found in rocks laid down in deeper water. Trilobite genera are often restricted by temperature, water depth, oxygen content and sea-floor type. The illaenid-cheirurid community is typical of shallow-water limestones (especially near reefs), whereas olenid trilobites are found in fine-grained muds with a low oxygen content that were deposited in deep water. Traditionally trilobites have been regarded as relatives of HORSESHOE CRABS because of broad morphological similarities, especially in the appendages, and because horseshoe crabs have a "trilobite" stage during their larval development. Cephalocarid crustaceans are even more similar to trilobites, and a crustacean relationship seems still more likely since the discovery of a possible early larval stage of a trilobite which is comparable to the crustacean nauplius larva.

Trilobite remains are usually disarticulated skeletons which have been dismembered by current action, exceptions being specimens from the Cambrian BURGESS SHALE. Where the water was quiet, complete specimens may be found, as in the Wenlock limestone of Dudley, England. The hard exoskeleton provides only limited information about these animals, but the study of tracks, grazing trails and burrowing trails discloses some of their walking and feeding habits.   S.F.M.

Turkana, Lake, *see* LAKE RUDOLF.

Trilobites
(1) Trimerus, *a burrowing trilobite, occurred from the Middle Silurian to the Middle Devonian (approx. 1/4 natural size).*
(2) Encrinurus, *a bottom-dweller with a heavy head and eyes on stalks, occurred from the Middle Ordovician to the Silurian (approx. 1.5 times natural size).*
(3) Ampyx *was a lightly built, swimming trilobite from the Lower and Middle Ordovician (approx. natural size).*
(4) Pliomera *lived in the Middle Ordovician. In this genus the row of denticles at the front of the head meshed with the free extremity of the pygidium when the animal rolled up (slightly reduced).*

Turtles and tortoises

Turtles and tortoises

An order of reptiles (the Chelonia) characterized principally by the development of a massive protective carapace. The skulls of later types are frequently emarginated or reduced, but never develop temporal openings and are therefore of the anapsid type (*see* REPTILES). For this reason, chelonians are grouped in the Anapsida along with the COTYLOSAURS, but no intermediate forms are known, although a small reptile from the Middle Permian of South Africa with widely expanded ribs (*Eunotosaurus*) has sometimes been proposed as a chelonian ancestor. It is now considered that this genus is a captorhinomorph cotylosaur with no specific chelonian affinities.

The first turtles appeared in the Upper Triassic of Germany (*Proganochelys*) and already had a fully developed shell in which the elements that make up the carapace of living chelonians are identifiable. These early forms were probably unable to withdraw the head or limbs into the shell and still retained small teeth on the palate and along the jaw margins.

From the Proganochelydia there evolved the Amphichelydia, the typical primitive Mesozoic turtles, with the Pleurosteroidea of the Jurassic and Cretaceous encompassing a notably conservative group. This included the massive Thalassemyidae (with their probable ancestors, the Plesiochelyidae, and a possible highly specialized off-shoot, the Apertotemporalididae), and the common water turtles of the mid-Mesozoic (Pleurosternidae). The Baenoidea were progressive proganochelyds that survived into the Cenozoic. *Baena* itself and *Chisternon* occurred in the North American Eocene, and the massive *Meiolania*, with an extraordinary, horned skull 60cm (2ft) across, persisted as late as the Pleistocene in Australia. The Late Cretaceous *Eubaena* appears to be ancestral to the toothless cryptodires – the dominant modern chelonians, in which the neck has an S-shaped curvature to pull the head back under the carapace.

The most primitive living cryptodire is *Dermatemys*, the "tabasco turtle" from Central America, which has several close fossil relatives that may be assigned to the same family (the Dermatemydidae) within the Testudinoidea, a superfamily which also embraces the Chelydridae and the Testudinidae. The Chelydridae includes

snapping turtles, known from the Eocene onwards, together with the diminutive *Kinosternon* of New World marshes and its ancestors (represented by *Staurotypus*, the three-keeled Central American mud turtle). The Testudinidae first appeared in the Upper Jurassic (*Scutemys*) and proliferated widely in the Cenozoic to evolve the living terrestrial tortoises (*Testudo*) as well as the pond tortoises (*Emys*), terrapins (*Clemmys*) and box-turtles (*Terrapene*).

The Chelonioidea are marine turtles, and presumably arose from the basal cryptodire stock near the chelydrid's point of origin. Conservative Late Cretaceous and Eocene forms in which there is little reduction of the shell are assigned to the Toxochelyidae, but the massive Upper Cretaceous *Archelon* and its allies (the Protostegidae) have only a weakly ossified carapace and may be ancestral to the living leathery turtle (*Dermochelys*). The green turtle (*Chelonia*) and the loggerhead turtle (*Caretta*) trace back to the Upper Cretaceous, and togethe with the other living marine turtle (the hawksbill, *Eretmochelys*, which has no fossil record) these genera are assigned to the Cheloniidae, which also includes various extinct late Mesozoic and early Cenozoic forms.

Carettochelys, the pitted-shell turtle, is an aberrant, living New Guinea cryptodire, with several fossil relatives occurring from the Upper Cretaceous to the Oligocene, *Carettochelys* itself having appeared in the Miocene. The "soft-shelled" river and lake turtles (eg *Trionyx*) have lost the outer horny scutes of the carapace. They originated in the Late Jurassic, became common in the Cenozoic and appear to be an off-shoot from near the base of the central cryptodire stock.

Less successful than the cryptodires are the pleurodires, in which the neck is withdrawn sideways under the shell. Now exclusively Southern Hemisphere river-dwellers, they were much more widely distributed in the Cretaceous: the living *Podocnemis* (greaved tortoise) was present in the Cretaceous of North America and Europe. The more conservative pleurodires such as *Podocnemis* are assigned to the Pelomedusidae, which have a well-documented geological history, but the aberrant Chelidae are rare as fossils, although the long-necked terrapin (*Chelodina*) occurs in the Oligocene of Australia. R.S.

Vertebral column, *see* BACKBONE.

Vertebrates

Members of the phylum Chordata, which includes bilaterally symmetrical animals that, at some stage in their life history, possess gill slits in the pharynx, a notochord that lies longitudinally down the body and constitutes an axial stengthening structure, and a dorsal nerve cord. Primitive chordates (eg *Amphioxus*) have a notochord extending all the way along the body from the nose to the tail, but in the subphylum Vertebrata a SKULL is developed (hence the alternative name Craniata often used for this group), together with a BACKBONE composed of individual vertebrae.

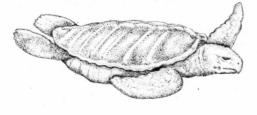

Turtles and tortoises
Above: the Cretaceous marine turtle Archelon *attained a length of nearly 4m (13ft).*
Below: Proganochelys, *from the Triassic of Europe, was an early chelonian measuring about 1m (3.3ft) in length.*

Warm-blooded animals

The spine of vertebrates serves partly to provide a protective channel for the passage of nerves down the trunk and partly as a framework to which the pectoral and pelvic girdles are articulated, together with the ribs that enclose the thoracic cavity.

The first vertebrates were the jawless fishes of the early Palaeozoic, the class Agnatha (OSTRACODERMS). By the Silurian the class Placodermi (PLACODERMS, primitive jawed fishes) had appeared, followed in the Middle Devonian by the class Chondrichthyes (fishes that had a cartilaginous rather than bony skeleton, eg the SHARKS and the later CHIMAERAS and (RAYS).

Bony fishes comprise the class Osteichthyes, divided into RAY-FIN FISHES (Actinopterygii) and LOBE-FIN FISHES (Choanichthyes).

AMPHIBIANS (class Amphibia) arose during the Devonian from lobe-fin fishes, and in turn yielded the REPTILES (class Reptilia) sometime during the Carboniferous. BIRDS (class Aves) were a Jurassic development from reptilian ancestors, the first MAMMALS (class Mammalia) having already appeared during the Late Triassic after evolving from more MAMMAL-LIKE REPTILES.

The ancestors of the vertebrates as a whole are unknown. There are, however, three groups of apparently degenerate water-dwelling chordates. First, *Amphioxus* and its relatives (subphylum Cephalochorda), which have a notochord extending to the front of the head; second, the tunicates or sea squirts (subphylum Urochorda), sessile animals found clinging to rocks in shallow water but possessing an active larval form with a nerve cord and a notochord; and third, the acorn worms (subphylum Hemichorda), which have gill slits and a free-swimming larva closely resembling the larvae of some ECHINODERMS. The colonial pterobranches are also apparently chordates, and seem also to be distant relatives of GRAPTOLITES.

It is probable that the chordates are more closely related to the echinoderms than to any other invertebrate group, because in both of these phyla the embryonic mesodermal tissue arises from outpocketings of the primitive endoderm (in other invertebrates, the mesoderm usually originates from two special "primitive mesoderm cells"). Subsequently, in chordates and echinoderms, the coelom (body cavity) is formed from hollow mesodermal pouches. Fossil evidence for an echinoid vertebrate origin is to be found in the calcichordates. The chordate ancestor might have been a sessile form with a free-swimming larval stage that had a tendency to remain technically immature. The larva may have continued as a motile juvenile (with a notochord, nerve cord and swimming tail) throughout its life and reproduced similar active, natatory offspring instead of eventually anchoring itself permanently to a rock and maturing into an immobile adult. R.S.

Vienna Natural History Museum
See NATURHISTORISCHES MUSEUM.

Vinci, Leonardo da
See LEONARDO DA VINCI.

von Koenigswald, Gustav
See KOENIGSWALD, GUSTAV VON.

von Schlotheim, Ernst
See SCHLOTHEIM, ERNST VON.

von Waldheim, Fischer
See FISCHER VON WALDHEIM.

von Zittel, Karl Alfred
See ZITTEL, KARL ALFRED VON.

Walcott, Charles (1850–1927)
American palaeontologist and scientific administrator, born in New York Mills, He did not attend university but joined, in 1879, the newly founded United States Geological Survey and became its third director in 1894.

His earliest fossil collecting was in the Trenton Falls area of New York State where he collected trilobites. He found the first specimens with appendages preserved and, through his researches, the value and importance of the group was established.

He was a most able administrator and transferred in 1907 from the United States Geological Survey to the Smithsonian Institution where he was appointed Secretary. A.P.H.

Waldheim, *see* FISCHER VON WALDHEIM.

Warm-blooded animals
Birds and mammals which can maintain their body temperature within narrow limits. They use the heat generated in muscles and internal organs through the energy-producing breakdown (oxidation) of carbohydrates and fats.

Living reptiles are COLD-BLOODED (ectothermic), but there is evidence that the MAMMAL-LIKE REPTILES and the extinct ARCHOSAURS were warm-blooded (endothermic).

The bipedal structure of CARNOSAURS, COELUROSAURS and DEINONYCHIDS indicates adaptation for a high level of activity, and the brain of deinonychids and ornithomimids is comparable in many respects to that of birds, with well-developed cerebral hemispheres and expanded optic lobes.

A reptile with ectothermic physiology has only a limited capacity for sustained rapid movement, but the carnivorous bipedal DINOSAURS had hindlimbs with the long shank and proportionately short thigh that provides the mechanically most efficient combination for an essentially cursorial animal.

It is perhaps significant that the only surviving archosaurs, the CROCODILES, have a partly four-chambered heart, whereas other reptiles have an unpartitioned ventricle. The crocodilian system represents an advance towards the arrangement found in birds and mammals, in which the ventricle is fully divided and de-oxygenated venous blood is pumped to the lungs only.

Wealden series

Some of the dinosaurs that walked on all-fours could probably also move as rapidly as their warm-blooded mammalian successors. SAUROPODS have graviportal limbs articulated to form vertical pillars for carrying the animal's immense weight, in the same way that an elephant's legs function. HORNED DINOSAURS could probably charge as fast as a rhinoceros, some of the small bipedal ORNITHOPODS could evidently run at considerable speed, and even the large DUCK-BILLED DINOSAURS were apparently rapid movers.

PTEROSAURS had to generate sufficient energy to maintain flight, and to keep themselves warm as the cooling airflow blew along their bodies. At least one of them, *Sordes pilosus* from the Upper Jurassic of Kazakhstan, appears to have had a furry body covering.

Histological studies indicate that the mammal-like reptiles may also have been warm-blooded, their limb bones being generously supplied with blood vessels and Haversian canals, although their body temperatures may have been maintained at a lower level than that of mammals.   R.S.

Wealden series

The oldest Lower Cretaceous sediments laid down in south-eastern England and the adjacent area of continental Europe. The Wealden series consists of a depth of about 750 metres (2,460ft) of sands and clays deposited in fresh and brackish water. The name is derived from the Weald of Surrey, Sussex and Kent – an area, once densely forested, which lies between the parallel CHALK hills of the English North and South Downs. The strata was uplifted into an elongated dome, its longest axis running roughly east-west, before the chalk covering the top of the dome was eroded away to reveal the Lower Cretaceous beds underneath. The outcrops are essentially horseshoe-shaped, each surrounded by the outcrop of the next, younger, formation and open on the south-east.

The primary division of the Wealden Series is into the Hastings beds below and the Weald clay above; the Hastings beds are sub-divided into (from below upwards) the Fairlight clays, the Ashdown sand, the Wadhurst clay and the Tunbridge Wells sand. Correlation with marine beds elsewhere is uncertain, but it is generally supposed that the Hastings beds are approximately equivalent to the Valanginian and Hauterivian stages and that the Weald clay is Barremian.

It has been variously claimed that the Wealden beds were laid down in a lake, in a delta, or in a subsiding graben-basin, open to the sea spasmodically and surrounded by active horsts; increased river flow produced sandy braidplains and coalescent alluvial fans where herbaceous pteridophytes grew abundantly. The climate was warm, with marked seasonal (and perhaps diurnal) rhythms of precipitation.

Commonly found as fossils in the Wealden are freshwater MOLLUSCS, OSTRACODS, INSECTS, FISHES, TURTLES, CROCODILES, DINOSAURS of various kinds (especially *Iguanodon*), PTEROSAURS and, occasionally, MESOZOIC MAMMALS. The fossil plants include FERNS, TREE-FINS, HORSETAILS, CONIFERS and early FLOWERING PLANTS. Also noteworthy are the dinosaur FOOTPRINTS which, together with sun-cracks, rain-pitting and ripple marks, seem to have been made on ancient sand flats.

The Weald is famed for its connections with Gideon MANTELL who, in 1825, named and first described *Iguanodon* from Wealden remains found in Sussex. This genus is also represented by numerous complete skeletons found at Bernissart, in Belgium, in 1877–78, where Wealden deposits that apparently accumulated in a Lower Cretaceous ravine occur in a coal mine.   A.J.C.

Weasels and stoats

The smallest mammalian carnivores, forming the family Mustelidae which occupies a phylogenetic position at the base of the arctoid stock (DOGS and BEARS). The group includes mink, polecats and ferrets, and characteristically comprises animals with long, thin bodies and short legs.

Mustelids are widely distributed in the Northern Hemisphere as the dominant small carnivores, feeding primarily on rodents and birds, their place being taken in the tropics by the CIVETS. One-third of all the genera in the CARNIVORA are mustelids.

The earliest members of the family are found in the Oligocene, and they subsequently developed into five main stocks. *Gulo*, the wolverine, is an exceptionally large musteline that can bring down a moose, whereas the melines (badgers) specialize in burrowing, using strong forelimbs, and have an omnivorous diet which includes much insect and plant material. The mellivorines (or honey badgers) fill a similar role in Africa and some parts of Asia. The mephitines (skunks) are now limited to the Americas but have Cenozoic ancestors in Eurasia: mostly small, their speciality is to spray their foes with a stinking fluid from anal glands.

The most widespread mustelid stock are the lutrines or otters. There are no serious competitors to them as medium-sized aquatic carnivores and they have occupied this niche since *Potamotherium* appeared in the Early Miocene. Their swimming adaptations include waterproof fur, short legs, webbed feet and a strong tail. They have a poor sense of smell, but their vibrissae (whiskers) are used to detect the movements of fish. Most otters are lake- or river-dwellers, and they occur on all continents except Australia and Antarctica. *Enhydra*, the sea otter, lives in the Pacific Ocean and feeds not on fishes but on molluscs.   R.J.G.S.

Whales

Mammals belonging to the order Cetacea, which includes the largest animals that have ever lived. The modern blue whale reaches a length of 30 metres (100ft) and weighs more than 100 tonnes. Most whales live in the oceans, but a few dolphin species inhabit rivers in South America, greater India and China. All whales are totally aquatic, never coming ashore and even giving birth in the water. They are efficient swimmers, using their powerful tails; hindlimbs are lacking and the forelimbs are modified as paddles. Their thick

Worms

blubber protects them from the cold and their specialized physiology enables them to dive to great depths. Although their sight is poor and sense of smell is lost, their hearing is extremely good and they have evolved a system of echo-location. The brains of whales are extremely complex, and they rival primates in intelligence. Three cetacean stocks are recognized: the extinct archaeocetes, the toothed or odontocete whales, and the baleen or mysticete whales.

The origins of whales are unknown; the earliest known whales (from the Eocene) are already fully aquatic with many of the specializations seen in modern whales. Because of the structures of the base of the skull, whales are thought to have evolved from mesonychid CONDYLARTHS. All the early Cenozoic whales are archaeocetes and occur in areas as far apart as Britain, Egypt, western Africa, the eastern USA and New Zealand. Some, such as *Basilosaurus*, were more than 15 metres (50ft) long and all had distinctive, saw-edged cheek teeth. From the archaeocetes, the other two stocks evolved.

The odontocetes or toothed whales, which include the killer whales, dolphins and porpoises, first appeared in the Eocene and are characterized by having in each jaw a long row of simple, single-cusped teeth. They are carnivorous, feeding on fishes, sea birds, seals and even other whales. A few have invaded fresh water, and there is a record of one in a lake deposit of Miocene age in Kenya.

The mysticetes or baleen whales appeared in the Oligocene and grew to enormous size (they include the blue whale). All the normal teeth have been lost and replaced by plates of baleen, a chitinous material. They feed on krill, minute sea plankton which is sieved through the baleen plates; the baleen does not fossilize, and so fossil jaws look toothless.

Whales are rarely abundant in the fossil record and are almost always found in near-shore sediments. Their characteristic ribs, vertebrae, ear bones and jaws make them readily recognizable, however, and they occur in all parts of the world. R.J.G.S.

Wolves

The most powerful living members of the Canidae (DOGS), represented today by *Canis lupus* (the Eurasiatic wolf and the North American timber wolf).

In the Pleistocene, the dire wolf (*Canis dirus*) ranged from Mexico north through Florida and the Mississippi valley to California. R.S.

Woodward, Arthur Smith (1864–1944)

British vertebrate palaeontologist and museum administrator. He was born in Macclesfield, England, and was educated at Manchester University. He joined the British Museum (Natural History) in 1882 and became Keeper of Geology in 1901.

His first appointment was in the vertebrate palaeontology section of the Museum, where he compiled (1887–1901) his extensive catalogue of fossil fishes. It was particularly noteworthy for the changes in fossil fish classification which were adopted.

Woodward made more than 600 contributions to the scientific literature – mainly, although not exclusively, devoted to fossil fishes. His research gave him an opportunity for worldwide travel; he described the fossil fishes of South Africa, Brazil, Greenland and Spitzbergen.

He received many honours from the scientific community, and contributed also to the discussion on the PILTDOWN MAN finds. A.P.H.

Woodward, John (1665–1728)

British palaeontologist who produced one of the earliest classifications of fossils. The early part of his life is obscure, but his initial medical training was under Peter Barwick, physician to Charles II. During this period he began to study fossils and was introduced to Edward LHWYD. Woodward was created Professor of Physick at Gresham College, London, and promoted interest in the earth sciences. He is best remembered for his *Essay towards a natural history of the Earth* (1695) and *An attempt towards a natural history of the fossils of England* (1729).

Although a believer in the theory of the universal deluge, Woodward did believe that fossil represent once-living creatures, a view to which he converted the Swiss palaeontologist Johann SCHEUCHZER. Through a bequest in his will, Woodward established a lectureship at Cambridge University which later became the Woodwardian Chair in Geology. A.P.H.

Worms

A group of invertebrate animals (Vermes) which includes a great diversity of forms varying widely in structure and habitat. The two main categories are the Annelida with segmented bodies – comprising the Polychaeta (bristle-worms), the Oligochaeta (earthworms) and the leeches – and unsegmented worms including flat-worms and ribbon-worms.

Predominantly marine, most worms live in shallow water to a depth of 40 metres (130ft), some in tubes (*Serpula*) attached to objects on the sea bed or buried in marine mud; free swimming species range to a depth of 5,500 metres (18,000ft). Non-marine worms include some that burrow in soils and sands, freshwater and brackish-water species, and those that live as parasites in other animals.

Whales
Basilosaurus, *an early member of the Cetacea, was common in the Upper Eocene seas of the Northern Hemisphere.*
Length: more than 15m (50ft)

Zittel

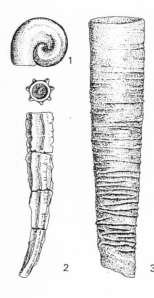

Worms
Fossil remains of polychaete worms.
(1) Spirorbis first appeared in the Ordovician (approx. 7 times natural size).
(2) Tube and capping operculum of Sclerostyla, from the Eocene (approx. natural size).
(3) Keilorites from the Ordovician and Silurian (approx. natural size).

Fossil evidence of soft-bodied unsegmented worms is confined to specimens that occur as flattened impressions in fine sediments, such as the BURGESS SHALE of Middle Cambrian age in British Columbia (*Amiskwia*) and the Jurassic Solnhofen limestone (*see* LITHOGRAPHIC STONE) of Germany (*Hirudella*).

Annelids are bilaterally symmetrical animals composed of a distinct head, a body of many ringed segments, and a pygidium. Internally, they are highly developed with digestive, circulatory, respiratory, nervous and reproductive systems. Their segmented structure and nervous system are similar to that of the ARTHROPODS to which they are believed to be ancestral. They vary in length from a few millimetres to 3 metres (10ft) and may attain a diameter of 25mm (1in).

Most fossil annelids belong to the Polychaeta. Their remains consist primarily of the notched chitinous jaws (scolecodonts) of free-living Errantida, and the tubes, operculae and burrows of sedentary worms (Sedentaria). The tubes of most genera are calcareous (*Ditrupa, Rotularia, Pomatoceros*), whereas in *Terebella* the tube is composed of shell, sand or rock fragments cemented together.

Apart from trails, the earliest recorded worms are *Spriggina* and *Dickinsonites* from the Late Pre-Cambrian of Ediacara in South Australia. By the Middle Cambrian the fauna of the Burgess Shale included many genera such as *Miskoia, Canadia* and *Ottoia*, indicating an increased diversity. Scolecodonts are common in Ordovician to Triassic strata, whereas Sedentaria are represented in the Palaeozoic mainly by *Spirorbis* and are abundant only from the Jurassic onwards. Vertical tubes (or infillings) in Ordovician sandstones were made by *Scolithus*, a sand-dwelling organism resembling the modern *Phoronis*. Evidence of fossil Oligochaeta is confined to a few dubious records, notably *Protoscolex* from the Ordovican and Silurian Periods.

Although worms are represented in every geological period, they have limited stratigraphical value.   S.W.

Zittel, Karl Alfred von (1839–1904)
German palaeontological encyclopaedist and historian of palaeontology. Zittel was born in Bahlingen, Germany, and attended the universities of Heidelberg and Paris. After a period in Vienna he became professor at the University of Munich and helped to enhance the collections and to make the university an important centre for palaeontological research. During his early years at the University of Munich he began to collect information for his book, *Handbuch der Paläontologie* (1876–93, in four volumes). This work, together with the *Grundzüge der Paläontologie* (1895), earned Zittel the title of the "Linnaeus of Palaeontology".

For many years he also edited the only palaeontological journal, *Palaeontographica*, which had begun publication in 1851. He also wrote the classic history of palaeontology, *Geschichte der Geologie und Paläontologie* (1899, English translation 1901).   A.P.H.

Zone fossils
Fossil genera or species that occur at one specific geological horizon, and are used to correlate deposits of the same age in different localities.

INVERTEBRATES occur in greater abundance than VERTEBRATES in the fossil record. Many zone fossils are therefore from invertebrate groups, especially in Palaeozoic rocks. Some of these characteristic organisms demonstrate a progressive change in structure as they evolve through successive series of geological strata. GRAPTOLITES are a good example, the Lower Ordovician representatives of this group beginning with 32-branched forms (*Clonograptus*) and then becoming 16-branched (*Loganograptus*), 8-branched (*Dichograptus*), 4-branched (*Tetragraptus*), 2-branched (*Didymograptus*) and, finally, single-branched (*Monograptus*).

Such an evolutionary pattern can be correlated with the occurrences of each genus in the geological series at a given location, and this information may then be used to identify similar strata at distant outcrops.

The richly fossiliferous KARROO SYSTEM of southern Africa contains abundant reptile remains and the Permian-Triassic sequence of this area is identified by a succession of MAMMAL-LIKE REPTILES.

The Mesozoic Era witnessed a huge proliferation of AMMONITES. These cephalopods are extensively used as zone fossils, particularly in the Early Jurassic (Lias) and in the Cretaceous (Neocomian, Aptian, Albian). Brachiopods (eg rhynchonellids and terebratulids) are valuable in the later Cretaceous (Middle Chalk), and foraminiferans become significant zone fossils once again at the end of the Mesozoic, with nummulites forming an evolutionary series that extends from the Cretaceous through the Eocene and Oligocene to the Miocene.

In North America, the well-documented Cenozoic land faunas can be zoned by reference to certain genera of mammals that became particularly numerous at specific stages. The Lower Oligocene is delineated by the presence of BRONTOTHERES, with OREODONTS becoming the dominant Middle Oligocene forms, and the traguloid genus *Protoceras* typifying the early Upper Oligocene.

The astonishingly abundant oreodonts are still valuable zone fossils in the Lower Miocene (*Promerycochoerus, Merycochoerus*) and Middle Miocene (*Ticholeptus*), but species of the equid genus *Merychippus* mark the later Middle Miocene and the Upper Miocene.

Hipparion, the three-toed Pliocene horse, is a familiar fossil in the Pontian (Lower Pliocene) of Eurasia, the "Hipparion fauna" (abundantly represented in the BONE BEDS of PIKERMI) extending from Spain to China.

The South American Cenozoic is also zoned by reference to its mammal faunas, with the primitive NOTOUNGULATE *Notostylops* characterizing the Lower Eocene, and *Astraponotus* the typical Middle Eocene genus. The remarkable *Pyrotherium* distinguishes the Lower Oligocene, and the toxodon *Colpodon* becomes the most characteristic South American mammal of the Upper Oligocene.   R.S.

Bibliography

There are two major guides to palaeontological literature and both are contained within volumes devoted to the earth sciences in general:
SARJEANT, W.A.S. & HARVEY, A.P. Palaeontology. In D.N. Wood (Editor) *The use of earth sciences literature* (1973). London; Butterworths; pp.254–289.
WARD, D.C. & WHEELER, M.W. *Geologic reference sources* (1972). Metuchen, N.J.; Scarecrow Press; 453pp. Palaeontology, pp.132–151.

The naming of animal and plant fossils is controlled by international regulations in the form of: *International Code of Zoological Nomenclature* (1964) and the *International Code of Botanical Nomenclature* (1978). The use of these codes is explained by C. JEFFREY *Biological nomenclature* (1973). London; Arnold; 78pp.

Identification guides to fossils are produced by many countries. The earliest guides were those of the Palaeontographical Society (United Kingdom) under the general title *Monographs* (1847—).

A list of palaeontologists and the institutions in which they work is:
GERRY, E. *Directory of palaeontologists of the world* (1976). International Palaeontological Association; 305pp.

BIRDS
HEILMANN, G. *The origin of birds* (1926). London; Witherby; illustrated; 208pp.
LAMBRECHT, K. *Handbuch der paläornithologie* (1933, reprinted 1964). Berlin; Borntraeger; illustrated; 1033pp.
SWINTON, W.E. *Fossil birds* (3rd edition). London; British Museum (Natural History); illustrated; 86pp.

CONTINENTAL DRIFT
CONTINENTS ADRIFT. READINGS FROM THE SCIENTIFIC AMERICAN (1970). San Francisco; W.H. Freeman. illustrated; 172pp.
MARVIN, U.B. *Continental drift. The evolution of a concept* (1974). Washington, D.C; Smithsonian Institution Press; illustrated; 247pp.
TARLING, D.H. & M.P. *Continental drift* (1971). London; Bell; illustrated; 112pp.

EVOLUTION
DE BEER, G.R. *Atlas of evolution* (1964). London; Nelson; illustrated; 202pp.
HUTCHINSON, P. *Evolution explained* (1974). Newton Abbot; David and Charles; illustrated; 238pp.
HUXLEY, J. *Evolution* (1947, 3rd edition by J.R. BAKER). London; George Allen and Unwin; illustrated; 783pp.
STANSFIELD, W.D. *The science of evolution* (1977). New York; Macmillan; illustrated; 622pp.

FISHES
SCHULTZE, H.–P. *Handbook of paleoichthyology* (1978—, 10 volumes planned). Stuttgart; Fischer.

GENERAL PALAEONTOLOGY
ATTENBOROUGH, D. *Life on earth. A natural history* (1979). London; Collins and the British Broadcasting Corporation; illustrated; 319pp.
KIRKALDY, J.F. *Fossils in colour* (1967). Poole, Dorset; Blandford; illustrated; 223pp.
McALESTER, A.L. *The history of life* (1968). Englewood Cliffs, N.J.; Prentice Hall; illustrated; 159pp.
MULLER, A.H. *Lehrbuch der paläozoologie* (1957–70). Stuttgart; Fischer; 7 volumes.
RAUP, D.M. & STANLEY, S.M. *Principles of paleontology* (1978, 2nd edition). San Francisco; W.H. Freeman; illustrated; 491pp.

ROMER, A.S. *The procession of life* (1968). London; Weidenfeld and Nicholson; 379pp.
SPINAR, Z.V. & BURIAN, Z. *Life before man* (1972). London; Thames and Hudson; illustrated; 228pp.
SWINNERTON, H.H. *Fossils* (1960). London; Collins; illustrated; 288pp.
MAJOR JOURNALS:
Journal of Paleontology (1927—, bimonthly). Tulsa, Okla; Society of Economic Paleontologists and Mineralogists and the Paleontological Society.
Lethaia (1968—, quarterly). Oslo; Universitetsforlaget.
Palaeontology (1957—, quarterly). London; Palaeontological Association.
Paleobiology (1973—, quarterly). Lancaster, Pa; The Paleontological Society.

GEOGRAPHY, CLIMATE AND ECOLOGY
HALLAM, A. (Editor). *Atlas of palaeobiogeography* (1973). Amsterdam; Elsevier; illustrated; 543pp.
McKERROW, W.S. (Editor). *The ecology of fossils: an illustrated guide* (1978). London; Duckworth; illustrated; 384pp.
NAIRN, A.E.M. (Editor). *Descriptive palaeoclimatology* (1961). New York; Interscience; illustrated; 391pp.
SCHWARZBACH, M. *Climates of the past. An introduction to paleoclimatology* (1963). London; Van Nostrand; illustrated; 340pp.
JOURNAL:
Palaeogeography, palaeoclimatology, palaeoecology (1965—, monthly). Amsterdam; Elsevier.

INVERTEBRATES
MACFALL, R.P. & Wollin, J. *Fossils for amateurs. A guide to collecting and preparing invertebrate fossils* (1972). New York; Van Nostrand; illustrated; 350pp.
MOORE. R.C. and others. *Invertebrate fossils* (1952). New York; McGraw-Hill; illustrated; 779pp.
PINNA, G. *The dawn of life* (1972). London; Orbis; illustrated; 128pp.

MAMMALS
CLARK, W.E. Le G. *History of the primates. An introduction to the study of fossil man* (1970, 10th edition). London; British Museum (Natural History); illustrated; 127pp.
DAY, M.H. *Guide to fossil man: a handbook of human palaeontology* (1977, 3rd edition). London; Cassell; illustrated; 346pp.
HALSTEAD, L.B. *The evolution of the mammals* (1978). London; Lowe; illustrated; 116pp.
KURTEN, B. *The age of mammals* (1971). London; Weidenfeld and Nicholson; illustrated; 350pp.
LEAKEY, R.E. & LEWIN, R. *Origins. What new discoveries reveal about the emergence of our species and its possible future* (1977). London; Macdonald and Jane's; illustrated; 264pp.
SCOTT, W.B. *A history of the land mammals in the western hemisphere* (1937, 2nd edition). New York; Macmillan; illustrated; 800pp.
MAJOR JOURNALS:
American Journal of Physical Anthropology (1918—, 8 issues per annum). Philadelphia, Pa.; American Association of Physical Anthropologists.
Journal of human evolution (1972—, 8 issues per annum). London; Academic Press.

MICROPALAEONTOLOGY
FOKORNY, V. *Principles of zoological micropalaeontology* (1963–65). Translated from the Russian. Oxford; Pergamon Press; 2 volumes; illustrated.
JOURNALS:
Micropaleontology (1955—, quarterly). New York; Micropaleontology Press (American Museum of Natural History).
Revista Espanola di Micropaleontologia (1969—, quarterly). Madrid.
Revue de Micropaleontologie (1958—, quarterly). Paris; Universite Paris VI.
ABSTRACTING SERVICE:
Bibliography and index of micropaleontology (1972—, monthly). New York; American Museum of Natural History.

PALYNOLOGY
TSCHUDY, R.H. & SCOTT, R.A. (Editors). *Aspects of palynology* (1969). New York; Interscience; illustrated; 517pp.
MAJOR BIBLIOGRAPHIES:
HULSHOF, O.K. & MANTEN, A.A. Bibliography of actuopalynology 1671–1966. *Review of Palaeobotany and Palynology* (1971). 243pp.
MANTEN, A.A. Bibliography of palaeopalynology 1836–1966. *Review of Palaeobotany and Palynology* 1969. 570pp.

PLANTS
DARRAH, W.C. *Textbook of paleobotany* (1960, 2nd edition). New York; illustrated; 302pp.
TIDWELL, W.D. *Common fossil plants of western North America* (1975). Provo, Utah; Brigham Young University Press; illustrated; 197pp.
MAJOR JOURNALS:
Palaeobotanist (1952—, irregular). Lucknow; Birbal Sahni Institute of Palaeobotany.
Review of Palaeobotany and Palynology (1967—, 2 issues per annum). Amsterdam; Elsevier.

REPTILES AND AMPHIBIANS
COLBERT, E.H. *Men and dinosaurs* (1968). New York; Dutton; illustrated; 301pp.
DESMOND, A.J. *The hot-blooded dinosaurs* (1973). London; Blond and Briggs; illustrated; 238pp.
KUHN, O. *Handbuch der paläoherpetologie. Encyclopedia of Paleoherpetology* (1969—). Stuttgart; Fischer. To be completed in 19 volumes.
MOODY, R. *A natural history of dinosaurs* (1977). London; Hamlyn; illustrated; 124pp.
ROMER, A.S. *Osteology of the reptiles* (1956). Chicago University Press; illustrated; 793pp.
RUSSELL, D.A. *A vanished world: the dinosaurs of western Canada* (1977). Ottawa; National Museums of Canada; illustrated; 142pp.
SWINTON, W.E. *Dinosaurs* (1974, 5th edition). London; illustrated; 55pp.
SWINTON, W.E. *Fossil amphibians and reptiles* (1973, 5th edition). London; British Museum (Natural History); 142pp.

STRATIGRAPHY AND TIME
BERRY, W.B.N. *Growth of a prehistoric time-scale based on organic evolution* (1968). San Francisco; W.H. Freeman; 158pp.
NEAVERSON, E. *Stratigraphical palaeontology* (1955, 2nd edition). Oxford; Clarendon Press; 336pp.

VERTEBRATES
COLBERT, E.H. *Evolution of the vertebrates. A history of the backboned animals through time* (1969, 2nd edition). New York; Wiley; illustrated; 551pp.
HALSTEAD, L.B. *The pattern of vertebrate evolution* (1969). Edinburgh; Oliver and Boyd; illustrated; 222pp.
ROMER, A.S. *Vertebrate paleontology* (1966, 3rd edition). University of Chicago Press; 478pp.
STAHL, B.J. *Vertebrate history: problems in evolution* (1974). New York; McGraw-Hill; illustrated; 603pp.

Glossary

Acetabulum The socket in the hip for the head of the femur.

Acousticolateralis system A sensory system present in fishes, including the lateral line grooves which contain organs sensitive to water currents and pressure. The internal ear of higher vertebrates may be a modified remnant of this system.

Adaptive radiation The adaptation of organisms belonging to a single evolutionary line so that they occupy a range of ecological niches.

Adductors Muscles that draw a structure towards the mid-line, eg the adductor muscles that hold together the two shells of bivalve molluscs.

Amphiplatyan vertebra A vertebra in which the ends of the centrum are flat.

Anthozoans Polypoid coelenterates of the sea anemone and coral type.

Araeoscelidians Primitive terrestrial euryapsid reptiles, including nothosaurs, placodonts and plesiosaurs; they are restricted to the Permian and Triassic.

Aragonite An orthorhombic crystal (ie, with three unequal axes at right angles) of calcium carbonate.

Argillaceous A geological deposit containing clay.

Articular In lower vertebrates, a bone of the lower jaw that forms the articulation with the skull. In mammals, it has become the malleus ("hammer") of the middle ear.

Auditory bulla In mammals, the bony protection for the middle ear cavity.

Bedding The layering of rock strata.

Biomass The weight or volume of living matter in a given unit area or unit volume of habitat.

Bioturbation The churning or stirring of a sediment by living organisms.

Braid plain Level area formed by a large, slow-moving river that has deposited mud, sand and shingle in its bed, thus splitting its stream into a series of interlaced channels.

Buccal cavity The inside of the mouth or cheek.

Bulla See AUDITORY BULLA in this glossary.

Bunodont Low-crowned mammalian cheek teeth.

Calcaneal tuber The heel bone of tetrapods.

Calcaneum A tarsal bone on the inside of the vertebrate ankle joint that primitively articulates with the fibula. In amphibians the calcaneum is known as the fibulare; in birds it fuses with the tibia and in mammals it has lost most or all of its contact with the epipodial bones.

Cannon bone The elongated metapodial bone of advanced ungulates; it is a single element where it occurs in perissodactyls but forms from the fusion of the two middle metapodials in artiodactyls.

Carnassials Specialized shearing teeth developed by meat-eating mammals from certain members of the premolar and molar series.

Carpals The bones of the vertebrate wrist, lying between the metacarpals and the radius and ulna.

Cement Spongy, bone-like material that secures a vertebrate tooth in its socket. In advanced ungulates cement is present on the hypsodont tooth crowns to buttress the high crests and fill the intervening valleys; being softer than the enamel of the crests, cement wears away more quickly than the enamel to leave a sharp grinding ridge.

Centrum The principal lower component of the vertebra in most vertebrate groups; it is apparently derived from the pleurocentrum, but in some fishes and amphibians the intercentrum is important to the structure of the vertebrae.

Cephalothorax The fused head and thorax of some arthropods.

Cercal blade Blade-like appendage of sea scorpions arising from the last abdominal segment of the body.

Cerebral hemispheres Paired outgrowths of the forward part of the vertebrate brain that are concerned with the higher mental faculties.

Charophytes Algae of the stonewort group.

Cheek teeth The premolar and molar teeth of a mammal; sometimes applied to the rear (grinding) teeth of reptiles.

Chelicera The most anterior pair of appendages in some arthropods (the chelicerates, including spiders, scorpions, horseshoe crabs, mites, ticks etc).

Chitin A colourless, horny polysaccharide occurring in the exoskeleton of arthropods and some other animals; hence chitinous.

Choanoflagellates Sedentary single-celled animals with a funnel-like extension of the protoplasm around the base of the flagellum at the free end of the body; they resemble the collar-cells of sponges and may be a link between that group and the protozoans.

Chondrocranium A cartilaginous skull, such as is found in sharks.

Clast A rock composed of fragments of other rocks that have been weathered, eroded and re-deposited.

Cnidarians A phylum of coelenterates that includes animals with stinging thread-cells for catching prey.

Coal measures The coal deposits laid down in the British Isles during the Upper Carboniferous.

Cochlea Coiled structure within the inner ear of mammals (present also in simpler form in birds and some reptiles) that houses the organ of Corti and is responsible for differentiating sounds of varying pitch, enabling the animal to distinguish tones.

Coenosteum The calcareous skeleton of some colonial hydrozoans.

Commisure A group of connective nerve fibres uniting paired structures on each side of the brain or spinal cord.

Conchoidal With shell-shaped depressions.

Conchostracan A branchiopod (a small crustacean of the brine-shrimp group) with a translucent bivalve shell and a claw-like furca (forked appendage) at the posterior end.

Continental shelf The locally submerged edge of a continental mass over which the depth of sea water does not exceed 200 metres (660 ft).

Coralla A combination of numerous corallites forming a colonial coral or chaetetid.

Corallite A single polyp, often forming part of the coralla in a colonial organism such as Chaetetids.

Cosmine A substance similar to the dentine of vertebrate teeth that formed around the pulp cavities. In fishes, it underlies the enamel of the cosmoid scales and the enameloid of the ganoid scales.

Craton A part of the Earth's crust which has attained stability and been subjected to only minor deformation for a prolonged period. It now occurs in continental areas only, eg the continental shields composed of Pre-Cambrian rocks.

Cruro-tarsal joint The articulation between the vertebrate lower leg bones (crus) and the tarsal bones of the foot.

Dentary The principal (and in mammals the only) bone of the vertebrate lower jaw.

Dentine The substance that forms most of the inside of a vertebrate tooth; chemically similar to bone, it is permeated by fine tubules which contain processes from the cell bodies lying in the pulp cavity.

Dermal bones Bones laid down in the skin by the mesenchyme cells of the dermis.

Diagenetic process The chemical, physical and biological changes, modifications and transformations to which a sediment is subjected after its deposition.

Digitgrade Walking on the toes.

Diphycercal tail The tail of a fish in which the spinal column extends straight backwards to the end of the body with the fin developed symmetrically above and below.

Diplopod A member of the millipede group, a section of the Myriapoda.

Dolerite A coarse, crystalline basalt (dense, fine-grained igneous rock of high density and dark colour) containing feldspar (crystalline rock-forming material consisting of silicates of aluminium with potassium, sodium or calcium) and augite (dark-coloured aluminous rock-making pyroxene); alternatively, any dark, greenish igneous rock not readily identified by visual examination.

Ecosystem A community of animals and plants considered in association with the non-living components of the environment.

Endostyle A ciliated groove in the floor of the pharynx of *Amphioxus* and tunicates along which food particles strained out by the gills are passed back to the intestine. In advanced vertebrates, this structure becomes the thyroid gland.

Entoconid A cusp on mammalian cheek teeth in the lower jaw, occurring on the inside of the tooth's extended heel (talonid) into which the opposing upper tooth bites.

Epicontinental sea A sea that has encroached on a continental land mass, or which covers the continental shelf.

Epipodial The outer segment of a vertebrate limb. It is formed by the radius and ulna (forearm) or the tibia and fibula (lower leg).

Eucaryotic cell A living cell possessing a visibly evident nucleus.

Eutheria Placental mammals – those with a placenta to attach the foetus to the wall of the uterus and facilitate foetal nourishment, respiration and excretion.

Euxinic shale A black, graphitic shale, usually laid down in stagnant de-oxygenated water.

Evaporites Sedimentary rock composed of minerals precipitated from a saline solution as a result of evaporation; usually indicative of a formerly arid climate.

Facies A geological deposit with a readily observable structural or faunal characteristic.

Flagellate A single-celled organism moving by means of a flagellum – a long, whip-like cytoplasmic process capable of vibration that projects from a cell.

Fluviatile Pertaining to, or formed by, a river.

Flysch A thick or extensive sandstone deposit formed in a geosyncline (downward flexure of the Earth's crust) adjacent to a rising mountain belt.

Fold belt A belt of rock strata crumpled by compressive forces in the Earth's crust.

Foliated Having leaves, or leaf-shaped.

Fossorial Burrowing into the ground.

Frontal bone Paired dermal bones of the vertebrate skull positioned between the eye sockets.

Gallery forest In the tropics, trees fringing the banks of a river.

Ganoine Also known as enameloid; a shiny, enamel-like material in layers on the outer surface of the scales of acanthodians and primitive ray-fin fishes.

Girdle, limb The pectoral (shoulder) and pelvic bones of vertebrates through which the limbs articulate with the body.

Graben basin Valley-like depression caused by subsidence of a series of blocks of the Earth's crust.

Haemal arch In vertebrates, extensions of the intercentra in the tail vertebrae that form an arch through which the major blood vessels of the tail pass. They are also known as chevron bones because of their shape.

Hallux The first toe of the hindfoot.

Heterocercal tail A primitive type of tail fin, commonly found in early fishes, in which the upper lobe is dominant.

Holarctic The zoogeographic realm that includes the Palaearctic and Nearctic realms; it encompasses North Africa, Europe, Asia (except the southern part), and boreal North America (the northern mountainous part).

Horizon A specific position in a series of strata, usually a bed or beds characterized by a distinctive fauna and flora.

Horst A block, usually with level summit, sharply defined by geological faults and left standing either by the sinking of the crust on each side of two series of faults, or by the raising of a mass between these fault series.

Hyponome The swimming funnel of a cephalopod mollusc.

Hyoid The second gill arch in fishes, which first became modified to act as a jaw support through the hyomandibular bone; in tetrapods the lower part of the arch eventually contributes to the hyoid apparatus at or near the base of the tongue.

Hyolithids Slender, conical mollusc shells, generally less than 5cm (2in) long, that are exceedingly common in the Cambrian. The group became extinct at the end of the Palaeozoic.

Hyomandibular The upper bone of the second (hyoid) gill arch in fishes, which first becomes modified to brace the jaw articulation against the brain case and eventually (in tetrapods) becomes the stapes (a sound-conducting bone inside the ear).

Hypocercal tail A tail fin structure of fishes in which the posterior end of the body turns downwards into the lower lobe of the tail fin.

Hyposodont High-crowned teeth like those of advanced ungulates that graze abrasive grasses.

Hypural bones Enlarged haemal spines supporting the homocercal tail fin of advanced bony fishes beneath the up-turned end of the backbone.

Igneous rocks Rocks consolidated from molten magma (larva).

Intercentrum The dominant lower element in the vertebrae of lobe-fin fishes and labyrinthodont amphibians; it is reduced or greatly modified in advanced reptiles, small or vestigial in mammals.

Ironstone Any mineral or rock containing iron.

Ischium The posterior of the two paired ventral bones in the vertebrate pelvis.

Isopedin The basal layer of bone underlying the structure of fish scales.

Lamella A thin, leaf-like layer of tissue.

Land bridge A land connection between continents that emerges when sea levels fall or land rises.

Lateral line system A system of small nerve organs in fishes that extends from the head along the length of the body.

Mandibular ramus One side of the lower jaw of vertebrates.

Mandibular symphysis See SYMPHYSIS, MANIBULAR in this glossary.

Manus The vertebrate forefoot.

Marginal teeth Teeth set along the edges of a vertebrate's jaw (as distinct from palatal teeth).

Marl A type of rock that includes various sorts of calcareous clays and argillaceous limestones; commonly laid down in freshwater lakes.

Matrix The material in which a fossil is embedded.

Maxilla Part of the jaw apparatus in arthropods; the principal bone of the upper jaw in vertebrates.

Megafauna Animals large enough to be seen with the naked eye; alternatively a large or widespread group of animals.

Mesotarsal joint An ankle joint found in bipedal reptiles and in which the articulation between the lower leg and foot is located in the middle of the tarsal bones.
Metacarpals A row of bones in the vertebrate forefeet.
Metamorphosis In insects, the marked structural change or transformation that occurs during development, eg from larva to adult. In geology, change in the structure of rocks caused by heat or pressure.
Metapodials The metacarpal bones of the forelimb and the metatarsal bones of the hindlimb.
Metatarsals A row of bones in the vertebrate hindfeet.
Metazoans Multicellular animals with differentiated body cells – ie all animals except protozoans.
Microbiota The microscopic fauna and flora of a region.
Micropyle In plants, the aperture in the coats of the ovule through which the pollen tube penetrates.
Mitosis Cell division in which chromosomes appear to become doubled longitudinally, the halves of each one passing into separate daughter cells. The term is sometimes applied simply to nuclear division.
Monocotyledons Flowering plants in which the embryo bears only one cotyledon (seed leaf); they include palms, orchids, lilies and grasses.
Monophyletic Evolved from a single ancestral type.
Mudstone A clay that has lost its plasticity through drying and compression.
Muschelkalk A European Middle Triassic limestone deposit about 330 metres (1,000ft) thick.
Mycelia The vegetative portions (thallus) of a fungus, consisting of thread-like tubes (hyphae).
Nasal bone A paired dermal bone of the vertebrate skull forming the upper surface of the snout.
Navicular Name applied variously to: the scaphoid (also known as the radiale) of the mammalian wrist; the centrale (scaphoid) of the mammalian ankle; and a sesamoid (accessory) bone formed in the feet of horses behind the junction of the second and third phalanges under the flexor tendons.
Nektonic Swimming at the surface of the sea.
Nemertines Ribbon-worms, most of which are marine, living among seaweeds and corals.
Neopallium Primitively a small area of superficial grey matter appearing for the first time in the brains of some reptiles; in mammals it expands to form most of the cerebral hemispheres.
Neoteny A sexually mature larval state in which metamorphosis into adult does not occur.
Neotropical The zoogeographical region that includes Central and South America and the adjacent islands.
Neural arch The upper part of a vertebra, through which the spinal cord passes.
Neural spine The process projecting upwards at the top of a vertebra that provides an attachment point for the muscles and tendons extending along the top of the trunk.
Occipital crest A ridge for muscle attachments running transversely across the back of the skull.
Occlusion The closing together of the upper and lower teeth of a vertebrate.
Ocelli Eyes of a simple type found in many invertebrates, notably in insects.
Olfactory bulbs A pair of enlargements at the extreme forward end of the vertebrate brain that are concerned with the sense of smell.
Operculum In fishes, the structure covering the gills, composed originally of a large opercular bone with a suboperculum below. In arthropods it is an exoskeletal plate; it is also the lid of a worm-tube.
Opisthosoma The abdomen of an arthropod.
Orbit The eye socket.
Orogeny A period during which mountains were being pushed up by folding of the earth's crust.
Otic notch A notch in the skull high up in the back margin of the temporal region that occurs in early tetrapods and is presumed to have been the location of the eardrum. It developed after the loss of the operculum from the slit which, in fishes, had become the spiracle. The otic notch was a primitive feature quickly eliminated from early reptile stocks.
Palatine A paired bone forming the roof of the mouth in vertebrates.
Pallial sinus In molluscs, canals formed in the mesenteric membranes occurring in the mantle (the thin, fleshy lining of the shell or shells).
Pedicle or peduncle In brachiopods, a stalk which emerges from an aperture in the beak of the dorsal valve (or shell) to anchor the animal to the substrate.
Perianth The combined calyx (outer part of a flower, composed of sepals which are usually green and leaf-like but may be coloured and petaloid) and corolla (true petals) of a flower when these components are indistinguishable from each other.
Permafrost The permanent freezing of soil.
Pes The tetrapod hindfoot.
Phosphatic nodules Nodular masses of phosphate of lime occurring in sedimentary deposits. Sometimes formed from the fossilized excreta of animals, but often simply calcareous mud that has been turned into phosphate.
Phyletic Pertaining to a specific group (not necessarily a phylum).
Phyllopods An alternative name for branchiopods.
Phytoplankton Aquatic plants, mostly microscopic, that float or drift in the water.
Pineal organ A structure occurring on the roof of the vertebrate brain that is phylogenetically associated with a median eye.
Plantigrade Walking on the flat of the foot.
Planuloid larva The ciliated, free-swimming larva of coelenterates.
Pleurocentrum The dominant lower element in the vertebrae of anthracosaur amphibians, having originated in lobe-fin fishes as small paired plates of bone located just below the neural arch on each side; in higher tetrapods it becomes the true centrum.
Polyp A coelenterate, in the form of an elongated cylinder anchored to the sea floor at its base with the mouth and tentacles at the free (oral) end.
Postfrontal A paired dermal bone of vertebrates forming the dorsal or postero-dorsal margin of the eye socket; it has been lost in mammals.
Postorbital A paired dermal bone of the vertebrate skull, forming the posterior margin of the eye socket; it has been lost in mammals.
Premaxilla A paired dermal bone of the vertebrate skull forming the end of the snout; in mammals it contains the incisor teeth.
Premolars The first four pairs of cheek teeth primitively present in the jaws of a mammal. Always preceded by milk teeth.
Procoelous vertebra A vertebra in which the front of the centrum is concave and the back of the centrum is convex.
Prosimians Primitive primates below the level of monkeys, ie the lemurs and tarsiers.
Prosoma The front of the arthropod body.
Proteolytic enzymes Enzymes that promote hydrolysis of proteins or peptides with the formation of simpler, soluble products.
Province, faunal An area, smaller than a faunal region, possessing its own distinctive animals.
Pterobranch Minute colonial marine animals believed to be related to chordates; *Rhabdopleura* is the characteristic genus.
Pteroid A bone developed by pterosaurs that projects from the inner (radial) side of the carpus (wrist) and is believed to have supported an extension of the flying membrane that extended inwards to the neck.
Pubis The anterior of the two paired ventral bones in the vertebrate pelvis.
Pygidium The terminal or posterior segment of an invertebrate, sometimes forming a caudal (tail) shield.
Pyrites A metallic, pale yellow, opaque isometric disulphide of iron.
Pyroclastic Rocks that are formed from or consist of the fragmentary or cominuted ejecta of volcanic or igneous eruptions.
Quadrate The skull bone on which the lower jaw articulates in the lower vertebrates; in mammals it has become the incus (anvil) of the middle ear.
Quadratojugal A bone contributing to the lower edge of the cheek region in amphibians and reptiles; a corresponding bone is sometimes seen in fishes, but it has been lost in mammals.
Racemization Changing an optically active compound into an optically inactive one.
Radiation, phylogenetic Evolutionary dispersal of a group of organisms from a common ancestry to fill a variety of ecological niches.
Radius The inner bone (on the thumb side) of the tetrapod forearm.
Red beds Sedimentary rocks formed in a highly oxidizing environment that contain iron in the form of red ferric sulphide. Usually occurs in an arid, continental environment.
Rhaetic The uppermost part of the European Triassic Series.
Riparian Occurring or growing on the banks of a river or pond.
Rugosity Uneven projection or rough-textured nodule in the skin.
Sacral Pertaining to the hip region of the back.
Sagittal crest A crest extending along the mid-line of the skull roof for the attachment of temporal muscles that act on the lower jaw.
Sandstone Rock consisting chiefly of quartz sand cemented with silica.
Saprophyte An organism that lives on dead or decaying organic matter, eg some fungi and various bacteria.
Scapula The vertebrate shoulder blade.
Sclerotic bones A ring of protective bones occurring in the outer sheath (the scleroid coat) of the vertebrate eye.
Secondary palate An airway in the skull from the external nostrils to the back of the mouth formed by inward-growing extensions of the premaxillae, maxillae and palatines below the surface of the original palate. This arrangement enables breathing to continue while prey is held in the jaws or during the chewing of food.
Sedimentary rocks Rocks formed by the deposition of sediment.
Selenodont Mammalian cheek teeth with a crescentic pattern on the crown.
Shear zone An area (such as at a fault or thrust plane) in which cracking or breaking of rock is being caused by compression or tension.
Sicula The skeleton of the first individual in a graptolite colony.
Siltstone Rock composed chiefly of indurated silt.
Siphuncle The gas-filled canal passing through the chambers of an ammonite shell.
Somites, muscle The segments of muscles that are arranged in vertical series along the body of an animal that is metameric, ie made up of a succession of homologous parts.
Spiracle In cartilaginous fishes and ostracoderms, the modified first gill slit; in insects, the external opening of one of the respiratory tracheae.
Splenial A bone (primitively two bones) of the lower jaw occurring in lobe-fin fishes, amphibians and reptiles. It has been lost in advanced ray-fin fishes and in mammals.
Splint bone A rudimentary metacarpal or metatarsal bone which is all that remains of a side digit lost during evolution; it occurs frequently in ungulates.
Squamosal The principal bone in the cheek of amphibians and reptiles, in which it articulates with the quadrate and braces the jaw articulation; a corresponding bone may be present in fishes. In mammals the squamosal articulates directly with the lower jaw.
Stolon In graptolites, the slender chitinous thread from which thecae (chitinous tubes or cups containing individual zooids) appear to originate.
Styliform Shaped like a stylus (ie a sharp-pointed writing instrument).
Styliolinids Conical shells belonging to extinct marine animals of uncertain relationship that are assigned to the class Cricoconarids, provisionally within the phylum Mollusca.
Supratemporal Paired dermal bones of the vertebrate skull located in the temple region. They are present in fishes and amphibians, but were reduced and eventually lost in reptiles.
Suture In a vertebrate, the line of union between adjacent interlocking bones; in ammonites, the junction between adjacent shell chambers.
Symphysis, mandibular The front junction of the left and right halves of the vertebrate lower jaw.
Synonym An invalid scientific name applied to an animal or plant that has already been satisfactorily designated by a Latin indentification.
Systematics The classification of biological organisms.
Tabulae Partitions extending across the corallite of a coral or a member of the Chaetetida.
Telson The terminal extension of the last abdominal appendage of an arthropod.
Terriginous Geological deposits derived from the land (eg sediments laid down in a marine environment after being washed into the sea from the land).
Test The rigid outer covering of an invertebrate.
Therian mammals Metatheria (marsupials) and Eutheria (placentals) – as opposed to the Prototheria (monotremes).
Thoracic Pertaining to the chest region.
Thrust plane Plane of movement in a reversed fault (where older beds on one side of a fault plane are thrust over younger beds on the other side) over which the upper beds of rock thrust, usually at a small angle of inclination.
Tibia The large inner bone of the tetrapod hindleg.
Trabecular Pertaining to a trabecula (a structure in an animal or plant resembling a small beam or crossbar spanning a cavity).
Tube feet Tubular organs of locomotion occurring in the ambulacral grooves of echinoderms.
Univalve A shellfish with only one shell, eg a gastropod.
Wrench fault An almost vertical fracture, along which the separated segments have slid in a horizontal direction.
Zooplankton Aquatic animals, mostly microscopic, that drift or float in the water.
Zygomatic arch In the mammalian skull, the remnants of the lower margin of the lateral temporal fenestra; formed from the jugal and the squamosal.